KB033369

KYOHAKSA'S

# FIRST

ENGLISH-ENGLISH-KOREAN
DICTIONARY

(주) 교 학 사

# 머 리 말

'영영한(英英韓) 사전'은 글자 그대로 영어 단어를 영어로 풀이해 주는 한편, 말뜻의 완전 이해를 돕기 위해 우리말 풀이를 곁들인 사전이다. 영어가 초등학교의 정규 과목이 된 이 마당에 중학생 여러분이 여전히 일반 영한 사전에만 매달려 공부하는 것이 안스러워서 이번에 교학사가 처음으로 개발한 것이 이 FIRST 영영한 사전이다. "중학생이 무슨 수로 영영 사전을 본담!"하고 겁먹던 학생도 한번 이 사전의 내용을 펼쳐 보면 "이런 수가 있었구나!"하고 반할 것이다. 다행히 여러분이 이번에 이 사전과 친숙해질 수 있는 계기를 만든다면 앞으로 영어는 여러분의 것이 될 것이다.

## 이 사전의 짜임새와 특색들

1. **영영 사전과 영한 사전의 완전 분리** : 제 1 편은 영영 사전, 제 2 편은 영한 사전으로 완전 분리 구성되어 있다.

2. **표제어 2,400** : 중학교와 고교 초급의 필수 기본어 약 2,400 단어를 표제어로 삼았다.

3. **쉬운 영어 풀이** : 영어 풀이는 중 2 학년이면 충분히 이해할 수 있는 쉬운 영어 단어와 문장 구성으로 하였다.

4. **표제어마다 모범 예문 제시** : 표제어마다 살아 있는 영어 표현으로 된 모범 예문이 제시되어 있다. 학습 암기용 표준 문형들이다.

5. **단어 활용력의 자동 향상** : 표제어의 영어 풀이를 익혀 가는 가운데 단어와 단어의 연관 관계, 단어의 실제 활용법을 저절로 익힌다.

6. **생동감 있는 원색 삽화** : 영영 사전에는 물론, 영한 사전에도 생동감 넘치는 원색 사진 또는 그림을 넣어 흥미를 돋우고 단어의 이미지를 머리에 깊이 새기게 했다.

7. **영한 사전** : 영한 사전은 가급적 덮어 두고 영영 사전만으로는 잘 이해할 수 없는 부분만 펼치어보는 것이 좋다. 한 가지 알아둘 것은 영한 사전은 곧 영영 사전의 직역이 아니라는 점이다. 즉 영한 사전은 우리말의 특성을 살려 우리말답게 다듬어 놓은 것이다.

Think in English. (영어로 생각하라) 영어로 생각하는 습관을 어

려서부터 들이는 것이 높고 험한 영어 고지를 먼저 차지하는 지름
길임을 잊지 말아야 한다.

　이 사전은 중학생뿐 아니라 고교생도 함께 이용할 수 있도록 꾸
민 것이므로 고교생은 속독용(速讀用), 실력 확인용, 입시 준비용
으로 널리 활용해 주었으면 좋겠다.

　부디 이 알뜰하고 공들인 국내 최초의 중학 영영한 사전이 21 세
기의 주역이 될 여러분의 생활과 성공의 필수 도구가 될 영어를 정
복하는 데 크게 이바지해 주었으면 한다.

1997 년 2 월

**교학사 사서부**

# 미리 보는 영영 사전

## theater | theatre
A **theater** is a place where you can go to see a movie or a play. My family enjoys seeing new plays at the **theater**.

표제어
※ 일러두기 표제어 참조

## igloo, iglu
An **igloo** is a kind of house. It is made of blocks of snow. People who live in cold places where there are no trees sometimes build **igloos**.

표제어의 뜻풀이는 간단하고 이해하기 쉽도록 하였다

## neighbo(u)r
A **neighbor** is someone who lives near you. Our **neighbor** cared for Sinbad, our dog, when we went on vacation.

예문은 표제어가 어떻게 쓰이는 가를 보여주었다

## calf[1]
A **calf** is a baby cow. A baby seal, elephant, or whale is also called a **calf**.

동형이의어
(표제어의 철자가 같아도 어원이 다르면 별개의 표제어로 처리하였다)

## calf[2]
The **calf** is a part of the leg. The **calf** is at the back of the leg, a little below the knee.

## catsup, ketchup
**Catsup** is a thick liquid made from tomatoes. It is eaten on other foods. Another way to spell **catsup** is ketchup.

표제어의 철자를 다르게 쓰는 경우

## south

South is a direction. When you look at a map, the bottom part is **south**. If you face the sun when it goes down in the evening, **south** is on your left. The opposite of south is north.

반의어
(표제어와 반대의 뜻을 갖고 있는 단어를 가리킨다)

## taxi

A **taxi** is a car you pay to ride in. We took a **taxi** to the airport. Another word for taxi is cab.

동의어
(표제어와 같은 뜻을 갖고 있는 단어를 가리킨다)

## telephone

A **telephone** is used to talk to someone who is far away. It has electric wires that carry the sound of your voice. I like to talk to my friends on the **telephone**. Phone is a short word for telephone.

단축형
(표제어를 간단하게 줄여서 쓰는 단어다)

## plan

1. Plan means to think out a way to do something before you do it. The team **planned** how they were going to win the game.
2. A plan is the way you think of doing something. We are making **plans** for our summer vacation.

표제어에 두 가지 이상의 어의가 있는 경우에는 가장 보편적인 것부터 표기하였다

## feed

Feed means to give food to an animal or a person. Todd **feeds** his pet rabbit carrots. Hannah **fed** her baby brother. A container used for feeding is called a feeder. In the winter we put seeds in the feeder for the birds.

파생어와 그 예문
(관련어를 수록하여 어휘의 폭을 넓혔다)

# 일 러 두 기

## 1. 표제어

1) 고딕체며 배열은 알파벳 순으로 하였다.
2) 동일한 단어지만 두 가지 이상의 철자법이 있을 때는, 다음의 원칙에 따라 표시하였다.

    a) 미국과 영국에 따라 철자가 다른 경우에는, 미국식 철자를 우선하고 다음에 영국식 철자를 썼으며 이를 종선(|)으로 구별하였다.

        **theater | theatre**

    b) 미국식 철자와 영국식 철자가 같은 경우에는 콤마(,)로 구별하였다.

        **igloo, iglu**

    c) 생략할 수 있는 철자는 ( )안에 표시하였다.

        **neighbo(u)r**

    d) 철자가 같은 어휘라도 어원이 다를 경우에는 별개의 표제어로 내세웠으며, 그 표제어 오른쪽 어깨에 번호를 붙여서 구별하였다.

        **calf**[1] (송아지)

        **calf**[2] (종아리)

## 2. 발음

1) 영한 사전의 발음은 국제 음성 기호로서, 표제어 바로 다음의 [ ]속에 표기하였다.
2) 악센트는 해당 모음의 바로 위에 표시하되, [ ´ ]로 제 1 악센트를, [ ` ]로 제 2 악센트를 표시하였다.

        **activity** [æktívity]

3) 미국식 발음과 영국식 발음이 다른 경우에는, 미국식 발음을 우선하고 다음에 영국식 발음을 썼으며 이를 종선(|)으로 구별하였다.

        **block** [blák | blɔ́k]

4) 같은 단어에 두 가지 이상의 발음이 있을 경우에는, 콤마(,)로 구별하고 공통 부분은 하이픈(-)을 써서 생략하였다.

**interest** [íntrəst, -tərèst]

5) 발음이 같고 악센트만 다른 경우에는, 각 음절을 짧은 대시 (－)로 표시하고 악센트의 위치가 다름을 표시하였다.

**loudspeaker** [làudspíːkər, ⸋⸋－]

6) 사람이나 경우에 따라서 발음되지 않는 음은 이탤릭체를 써서 표시하였다.

**number** [nʌ́mbər]

7) 같은 단어에 강음과 약음의 두 가지 발음이 있을 경우에는, 약음을 우선하고 다음에 강음을 표시하였다.

**he** [《약》hi, i, 《강》híː]

8) 같은 단어일지라도 품사에 따라 발음이 다른 단어는 다음과 같이 표시하였다.

**close** [klóuz] 1 타자 **닫다**, 닫히다 ; 끝내다, 끝나다

2 [klóus] 형부 **가까운**, 접근한 ; 가깝게, 곁에

## 3. 품사

1) 영한 사전의 품사는 발음 기호 다음에 약어로 표시하였다.
2) 한 표제어에 둘 이상의 품사가 있을 경우에는 **1**, **2** …로 구별하였다.
3) 품사의 약어 표시는 다음과 같다.

| 명 …… 명사 | 동 …… 동사 | 자 …… 자동사 |
|---|---|---|
| 타 …… 타동사 | 부 …… 부사 | 형 …… 형용사 |
| 관 …… 관사 | 전 …… 전치사 | 접 …… 접속사 |
| 조 …… 조동사 | 감 …… 감탄사 | 대 …… 대명사 |

## 4. 뜻풀이

1) 영한 사전의 표제어 뜻풀이는 비슷한 뜻일 때는 콤마(,)를, 그 뜻이 약간 바뀔 때는 세미콜론( ; )을 사용하였으며, 뜻이 크게 바뀔 때는 ①, ② …로 표시하였다.
2) 표제어의 중요한 뜻이나 예문과 연관이 있는 뜻은 고딕체로 표시하였다.
3) 영영 사전에서 명사형인 표제어의 예문을 번역한 경우에는, 원어의 개념을 문맥과 함께 쉽게 이해할 수 있도록 표제어 원어를 그대로 사용하였다. 그러나 원어를 사용한 번역 문맥이 아주 어색할 때는 우리말로 풀어서 번역을 하였다.

**magician**

A magician is a person who uses magic to do tricks. The magician pulled a rabbit out of the hat.

**magician** [mədʒíʃən] 명

**마법사**, 마술사, 요술쟁이 magician은 마술을 써서 묘기를 부리는 사람이다 : magician이 모자에서 토끼를 꺼냈다.

## 5. 괄호의 용도

1) 영한 사전에서 표제어의 뜻풀이를 보충 설명할 때는 《 》를 사용하였다.

   **푸딩**《밀가루에 과일·우유·계란 등을 넣고 단맛이 나게 구운 디저트용 과자》

2) 문법과 어법을 설명할 때는 [ ]를 사용하였다.

   [be의 1인칭 단수 현재형], [복수로]

3) 복합어의 풀이나 생략 가능한 어구 혹은 간단한 보충 설명은 ( )로 표시하였다.

   **dairy farm** (낙농장), **대추야자나무**(의 열매), (…의 특징을) **말하다**

4) 바로 앞의 말과 바꿔 쓸 수 있는 경우에는 〔 〕를 사용하였다.

   **…과 같이**〔처럼, 대로, 만큼〕

5) 영영 사전의 표제어 정의를 서술형으로 풀어 쓰기 곤란한 경우에는 「 」를 사용하였다.

   **actually**는 「정말로」의 뜻이다.

## a

A means one. Red is a color. Our friends will stay with us for **a** day or two.

## able

When you are **able** to do something, you know how to do it or have the power to do it. Michael is **able** to count up to 10. Penguins are not able to fly.

## about

1. Mary has a book that shows pictures of dogs and tells how to take care of them. Mary's book is **about** dogs.

2. **About** also means almost. You use **about** when you are not really sure of something. There

are **about** 20 children in the second grade.

# above

Above means over or in a higher place than something. The birds flew above the tops of the trees. There is a light **above** my bed.

# absent

Absent means not here. Two students were **absent** because they were sick.

# accident

An accident is something you did not want or expect to happen. I broke my glasses by **accident**.

# accomplish

When you **accomplish** something, you finish it. It took us a long time to **accomplish** everything on our list, but we did it.

# ache

Ache means to hurt. Dad's back **aches** because he

A

moved furniture all after-noon. Susan's arm **ached** after she pitched in the baseball game.

## acorn

An acorn is the nut that grows on an oak tree. The squirrel carried an **acorn** in its mouth.

## across

**Across** means from one side to the other. A bridge was built across the river.

## act

To **act** means to behave in some way. Sometimes Tom **acts** like a clown.

## activity

An **activity** is something that you do. My favorite activity is swimming.

## actually

**Actually** means really. Maria didn't think she would like the party, but when she got there, she

**actually** had fun.

# add

1. To add means to put together. Billy drew a picture of his brother. Then he **added** a funny nose and glasses.

2. To **add** also means to put numbers together. When you **add** three and one, you get four.

## address

An **address** is the name of a place. You put an **address** on a letter to tell the post office where to send it.

## adopt

When you **adopt** a child, that child becomes part of your family. Mr. and Mrs. Brown were very happy when they **adopted** the new baby. My best friend was **adopted** when he was 2 years old.

## adult

An adult is a person who is

a grown-up. Your parents are **adults**.

# adventure

An **adventure** is a special thing to do. Adventures are new and different and are maybe a little frightening. I like to read books about **adventures** in space.

# advertisement

An **advertisement** tells you about something to buy or something to go to. It can be words or pictures. I see **advertisements** for cereal on television. A short word for **advertisement** is **ad**.

# afford

Afford means to have the money to pay for something. Claire counted her money to see if she could **afford** the red sweater.

# afraid

To be **afraid** means to think something bad will happen to you. Some people are afraid of the dark.

# after

After means following. **After** the ball game, we went home. Al ran fast when his brother came **after** him.

# afternoon

Afternoon is the part of the day between noon and sunset. **Afternoons** are short in winter and long in summer.

# again

When you do something **again**, you do it one more time. Albert liked the dinosaurs so much that he wanted to go to the museum **again**. We're going to stay at the lake **again** next summer.

# against

1. **Against** means not on the same side. Our school played a baseball game against another school. Only three people voted **against** Diana for class

president.

2. **Against** also means toward or touching something. Tom threw the ball **against** the wall. Hannah left her bicycle against the tree.

# age

**Age** is how old a person or thing is. What **age** are you? My brother learned to play the piano when he was my age.

# ago

**Ago** means before now. Our kittens were born two days **ago**.

# agree

When you **agree** with someone, you think or feel the same way that person does. We **agreed** to name our cat Tabby.

# ahead

**Ahead** means in front of something or someone. Arthur was ahead of the

others in the race. Four people were **ahead** of us in line.

## air

**Air** is a gas that people breathe. **Air** is all around us. We cannot see it, but we can feel it when the wind blows.

## air conditioner

An **air** conditioner is a machine that makes air cool and clean. **Air conditioners** are used in cars and in offices, homes, and other buildings. The **air conditioner** in our car has not been working very well.

## airplane

An airplane is a machine with wings that flies in the air. **Airplanes** carry people from one place to another.

## airport

An airport is a place where airplanes take off and land. It has buildings where peo-

ple can wait and where airplanes can be checked and
fixed. The **airport** was really
busy the night we waited
for Helen's plane to arrive.

# alarm

An alarm is a bell or some
other thing that makes a
loud noise. We use the
**alarm** on our clock to wake
us up in the morning. When
the fire **alarm** rang, everyone left the building quickly.

# alike

Alike means the same.
Twins look alike.

# alive

When a person or thing is
**alive**, it is living. When there
is no rain, we water the
garden to keep the flowers
**alive**.

# all

All means with nothing left
out. **All** horses have four
legs. Margaret ate **all** of her

breakfast.

# alligator

An alligator is a very large reptile. It has short legs, a long tail, and strong jaws with sharp teeth. **Alligators** live in rivers and swamps where the weather is warm.

# allow

**Allow** means to let someone do something. Todd and Tom's parents sometimes **allow** them to stay up later on Saturday nights.

# allowance

An **allowance** is an amount of money that is given to someone. Margaret gets an **allowance** once a week. George earns his allowance by setting the table and helping with the dishes.

# all right

When something is **all right**, it is good enough. His work is **all right** but he could be faster.  When you are **all** right, you feel fine. Marie fell off her bicycle, but she is **all right**.

## almost

**Almost** means close to. Lewis is **almost** as tall as his father. It is **almost** 2 o'clock.

## alone

**Alone** means by yourself. Mary likes to be alone in her room.

## along

1. **Along** means in a line with. It is nice to walk along the beach.
2. **Along** also means together. Susan went to the store and her brother went **along** with her.

## aloud

**Aloud** means loud enough so that others can hear you. The children took turns reading the story **aloud**.

# alphabet

An **alphabet** is the letters that people write with. The English alphabet is A, B, C, D, E, F, G, H, I, J, K, L, M, N, O, P, Q, R, S, T, U, V, W, X, Y, Z.

# alphabetize

When you **alphabetize** things, you put them in order by the letters of the alphabet. The words ant, baby, cat, door, drum, kite, machine, monkey, and paint are **alphabetized**.

# already

**Already** means before this. Al missed the bus today. When he got to the bus stop, it had already gone.

# also

**Also** shows something added. Claire plays the piano. She can **also** play a trombone.

# always

**Always** means all the time

or every time. Leopards always have spots. Our dog **always** barks when she sees me.

**A**

## am

**Am** is a form of **be**. It is used with **I**. "Are you six years old?" "No, I **am** seven."

## amaze

When something **amazes** you, it surprises you very much. It will **amaze** me if I win the race. The magician's tricks **amazed** us all.

## ambulance

An ambulance is a special kind of car that is used to carry people who are sick or hurt to a hospital.

## American

**1.** A person who lives in the United States is called an American. A person who lives in North America or South America is also called an **American**.

**2.** If something is **American**, it comes from or is about the United States. **American** also means something that comes from or is about North America or South America.

## among

**1. Among** means with or in the middle of things or people. Barry sat among his friends.
**2. Among** also means that there is some for each. Bob divided the paper and pencils **among** the children.

## amount

An **amount** is how much of something you have. We brought a large amount of food to the picnic. He paid the full **amount** of the expenses.

## amuse

**Amuse** means to make someone smile or laugh. We **amused** the baby by making funny sounds.

A

## an

**An** is a form of **a**. It is used before words that begin with A, E, I, O, or U. A new pen writes better than **an** old one.

## anchor

An **anchor** is a heavy object that helps a ship stay in one place. Anchors come in many different shapes.

## and

**And** joins two things together. Three **and** two are five. Diana **and** Hannah are best friends.

## angry

To be angry means to feel very upset with someone. Bill's dad was **angry** at him because he broke a window.

## animal

An animal is anything alive that is not a plant. Dogs, cats, fish, birds, and insects are all **animals**.

## anniversary

An anniversary is the day of the year when something important happened in an earlier year. March 9th is my parents' wedding **anni-versary**.

## annoy

**Annoy** means to bother someone. Loud noises can **annoy** me.

## another

**Another** means a second one. Helen ate a carrot. She liked it so much she ate **another** one.

## answer

An **answer** is what you give when someone asks a question. The teacher asked a question. Tom knew the right **answer**.

## ant

An ant is an insect. **Ants** live in large groups in trees or in tunnels in the ground.

## any

1. **Any** means that it does not matter which one. Take **any** seat you like.

2. **Any** also means some. Do you want **any** of my sandwich? Do you have **any** money?

## anybody

**Anybody** means any person. Blake didn't know **anybody** at the party. I did not meet **anybody**.

## anyone

**Anyone** means **anybody**. Invite anyone you like for dinner.

## anything

**Anything** means any thing. My brother will eat **anything**.

## anyway

**Anyway** means that something doesn't matter. Michael's foot hurt, but he tried to walk anyway.

A

# anywhere

Anywhere means in any place. Did you go **anywhere** yesterday?

# apart

1. **Apart** means away from each other. A chicken's toes are far **apart**.
2. **Apart** also means in pieces. Billy likes to take things **apart** to see how they work.

# apartment

An apartment is a room or a group of rooms that people live in. There are 20 **apartments** in that building.

# ape

An ape is a large animal that can walk and stand almost as straight as a person can. **Apes** are like monkeys, but they do not have a tail.

# apologize

**Apologize** means to say you are sorry for something you

said or did. I **apologized** to my brother for breaking his toy.

## appear

**Appear** means to be seen. The sun is just beginning to appear over the mountains. A herd of deer **appeared** at the edge of the woods this morning.

## appetite

When you have an **appetite**, you want to eat. Billy has a big **appetite** after he plays football.

## apple

An apple is a round fruit with red, yellow, or green skin. **Apples** grow on trees.

## April

**April** is a month of the year. It has thirty days. **April** comes after March and before May.

## aquarium

An aquarium is a glass box

or bowl that is filled with water. People who have fish at home keep them in **aquariums**.

## are

Are is a form of **be**. It is used with **you**, **we**, and **they**. "Where can my shoes be?" "They **are** in the closet."

## area

An **area** is a space. The kitchen is an area where we cook food. An ocean covers a large **area**.

## aren't

Aren't is a short way to say **are not**. Bananas aren't blue. They are yellow.

## argue

Argue means to fight with words. When people **argue**, they sometimes talk in aloud, angry way. The children **argued** about who would pitch for their baseball team.

**A**

## arm

An arm is a part of the body. It is between the shoulder and the hand. Charlie used both **arms** to carry wood for the fireplace. The baby monkey put its **arms** around its mother and went to sleep.

## armor | armour

Armor is a heavy suit that is made of metal. People wore **armor** long ago to protect themselves during battles. We saw many suits of **armor** at the museum.

## army

An army is a large group of people who fight for their country in a war. After three days, the **armies** stopped fighting.

## around

**Around** means on all sides. David built a fence **around** his yard. Margaret looked **around** the room for her shoes.

## arrive

Arrive means to come to a place. The train **arrived** 10 minutes late. We will be **arriving** in town at 9 o'clock.

## arrow

**1.** An arrow is a thin stick that has a point at one end and feathers at the other. **Arrows** are shot from bows.
**2.** An **arrow** is often shown on a sign to point the way to something. The **arrow** on the sign shows the way to the beach.

## art

Art is something made to be beautiful. Pictures, poems, and music are kinds of **art**.

## artist

An **artist** is a person who makes art. You can see the work of many **artists** in a museum.

## as

As means the same

amount. Tom and Geoffrey are the same height. Tom is **as** tall **as** Geoffrey.

# ash

Ash is what is left after something burns. It is a soft gray powder. Ray watched his father clean the **ashes** out of the fireplace.

# ashamed

Ashamed means feeling bad because of something you did. Sue felt **ashamed** because she lied to her sister.

# ask

1. To **ask** means to say a question. The teacher asks, "Who knows the answer?"
2. To **ask** for something means to say that you want it. Oliver **asked** for more soup because he was hungry.

# asleep

Asleep means sleeping. Margaret was **asleep** until a

loud noise woke her up.

## astronaut

An astronaut is a person who goes into space. **Astronauts** travel in space-ships. Some **astronauts** have walked on the moon.

## at

1. **At** tells where a person or a thing is. Maria went to school this morning. She is **at** school now.
2. **At** tells when something happens. School begins **at** nine o'clock.
3. **At** also means toward. Susan looked **at** the sky to watch for falling stars.

## ate

Ate is a form of **eat**. Harry eats three meals every day. Last night he **ate** pizza for supper.

## attach

**Attach** means to join one thing to another. Joe used tape to **attach** the sign to the wall. Claire **attached** a yellow straw basket to her bicycle.

# attention

When you pay attention, you watch and listen carefully. The children paid **attention** to what the teacher was saying.

# attic

An attic is the space or room below the roof of a house. **Attics** are sometimes used as places to keep old clothes or furniture.

# audience

An audience is a group of people gathered to hear and see something. My family was in the **audience** for my school play.

# August

**August** is a month of the year. It has 31 days. **August** comes after July and before September.

## aunt

Your **aunt** is your father's sister or your mother's sister. Your uncle's wife is also your **aunt**.

## author

An **author** is someone who writes a story, a play, or a poem. Many **authors** write books for children.

## automobile

Automobile is a another word for car. People drive **automobiles** on roads.

## autumn

**Autumn** is a season of the year. **Autumn** comes after summer and before winter. During the autumn, in some places the leaves turn red, yellow, and orange before they fall from the trees. Another word for **autumn** is fall.

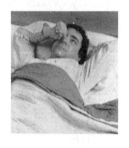

## awake

Awake means not asleep. David tried to stay **awake**

all night.

# award

An award is something that is given to a person who has done something special. Joe and Mark got **awards** for writing the best stories.

# away

1. **Away** shows distance. The ocean is three miles **away** from here.
2. **Away** also shows direction. Joseph walked **away** from the house and toward the street.
3. To give something **away** means to give it to someone else. Marie gave her bicycle to her cousin. She gave it away because she got a new one.

# awful

**Awful** means terrible or very bad. An awful fire caused that store to close. The medicine I had to take tasted **awful**.

## ax | axe

An ax is a tool. It has a flat, sharp metal head and a long handle. **Axes** are used to cut wood.

# baby

A baby is a very young child. **Babies** eat and sleep a lot.

# baby-sitter

A **baby-sitter** is a person who takes care of children when their parents are not at home. Our **baby-sitter** reads stories to us.

# back

1. The back is a part of the body. We like to lie on our **backs** and look up at the sky.

2. **Back** is the opposite of **front**. The caboose is at the **back** of the train.

3. To go **back** means to return. Students go **back** to school every fall.

## backpack

A backpack is a soft bag that is worn on the back. It fits over the shoulders and is used to carry things. Students use **backpacks** to carry books and other small things. Campers use **backpacks** to carry food, clothes, and other things.

## backward

1. **Backward** means in the opposite order. Bat spelled backward is tab.
2. **Backward** also means toward the back. Jack looked **backward** to see if his brother was behind him.

## backyard

A **backyard** is the yard behind a house. Mike planted a vegetable garden in the **backyard**. Marry has a swing in her backyard.

## bad

1. **Bad** means not good.

We couldn't eat the fruit because it was **bad**.

**2. Bad** also means not nice. Margaret is angry. She is shouting at everybody. Margaret is in a **bad** mood.

**3. Bad** can mean able to hurt. Too much candy is **bad** for your teeth.

**4. Bad** can also mean serious. Mary had a **bad** cold, so she stayed in bed.

B

# bag

A bag is used to hold things. It can be made of paper, plastic, cloth, or leather. George brings his lunch to school in a paper **bag**.

# bake

Bake means to cook food in an oven. We **baked** a birthday cake for Mom last night.

# bakery

A bakery is a store that bakes and sells breads, cakes, and cookies. Our

**bakery** sells carrot cake.

# balance

**Balance** means to keep something in a place so it does not fall off or roll away. The seal at the circus can **balance** a ball on its nose.

# bald

When people are **bald**, they have little or no hair on their heads. Jack was **bald** when he was born.

# ball

A **ball** is a round object. Balls of many sizes are used in games and sports.

# ballet

A ballet is a kind of dance. People who dance in **ballets** must learn special steps and ways of holding their bodies as they move to the music.

# balloon

A balloon is a kind of bag

filled with gas. Some **bal-loons** are huge and can carry people high into the sky. A **balloon** went high up in the sky.

# banana

A banana is a kind of fruit. It has a long curved shape and a yellow skin.

# band

A band is a group of peo-ple who play music together. Everyone in the parade marched to the music of the **band**.

# bandage

A **bandage** is a piece of cloth that is put over a cut to keep it clean and protect it.

# bang

A **bang** is a loud, sudden noise. When it is windy, the door shuts with a **bang**.

# bank

A **bank** is a place to keep

money. Sometimes people borrow money from **banks**. My aunt works in a **bank**. Bob put a nickel in his toy **bank**.

## bar

A **bar** is something that is longer than it is wide. You can wash your hands with the bar of soap in the bathroom. The bird cage had metal **bars**.

## barbecue

When people barbecue, they cook food outdoors over a fire. Last night we **barbecued** chicken and corn.

## barber

A barber is a person who cuts hair. Mom took me to the **barber** because my hair was too long.

## bare

Bare means not covered with anything. Peter did not have any socks or shoes on. He was walking around with **bare** feet.

# barefoot

When your feet are bare, we say you are barefoot. Peter likes to take off his shoes and socks and walk **barefoot** on the grass.

# bargain

When something costs less than usual, it is called a **bargain**. This shirt is a **bargain** for 9 dollars.

# barge

A barge is a boat with a flat bottom. **Barges** are used to carry things like logs and sand on rivers.

# bark<sup>1</sup>

Bark is the outside cover of a tree. The **bark** on most trees is thick and rough.

# bark<sup>2</sup>

**Bark** means to make the sound that a dog makes. Our dog **barks** when it is

hungry or frightened.

## barn

A **barn** is a building on a farm. Cows and horses are kept in the **barn**. We went to feed the horses in the **barn**.

## barrel

A barrel is used to hold things. It is made of wood or metal. The top and the bottom of **barrels** are flat circles. Some **barrels** have curved sides.

## base

1. A **base** is the bottom part of something. It is the part that something stands on. The base of the statue is made of marble.

2. A **base** is also one of the four corners of a baseball field. I hit the ball so far I was able to run all the way to second **base**.

## baseball

1. Baseball is a sport. It is

played by two teams with a bat and a ball.
2. A baseball is the hard white ball used in a game of baseball.

## basement

The **basement** is the bottom floor of a building. **Basements** are usually below the ground. Dad made a room in the **basement** where we can play games and have parties.

## basket

A basket is used to hold things. It can be made of strips of wood or grass. **Baskets** are often shaped like bowls and have handles.

## basketball

1. Basketball is a sport. It is played by two teams with a large ball and two baskets.
2. A **basketball** is the large rubber ball used in a game of basketball.

# bat¹

A **bat** is a strong stick that is made of wood. It is used in playing baseball and other games.

# bat²

A bat is also a small animal that looks like a mouse with wings. **Bats** sleep during the day and fly around at night.

# bath

When you take a **bath**, you wash yourself with soap and water. Mom gave the baby a **bath**.

# bathing suit

A bathing suit is something you wear when you swim. After Billy and Helen went swimming, they hung their **bathing suits** outside to dry.

# bathrobe

A **bathrobe** is a loose coat you wear before and after you take a bath or when you relax.

B

## bathroom

A bathroom is a room with a sink, a toilet, and often a bathtub or a shower. Mike brushes his teeth in the bathroom.

## bathtub

A **bathtub** is a very big container that you fill with water and sit in to take a bath.

## battery

A **battery** is something that makes electricity. Smoke alarms, flashlights, and some radios run on **batteries**.

## battle

A **battle** is a fight between two persons or groups. Weapons are often used in a battle. The two armies fought a **battle**.

## bay

A bay is a part of an ocean or lake that stretches out

into the land.

# be

1. To **be** means to live or fill space. A person cannot **be** in two places at the same time. Elizabeth wants to **be** a doctor when she grows up.

2. To **be** tells what something is like. Tomorrow will **be** sunny.

# beach

A beach is land that is close to a lake or an ocean. Most **beaches** are covered with sand.

# bead

A **bead** is a small, round piece of plastic, glass, or wood with a hole in it. We made necklaces with **beads**.

# beak

A beak is the hard part of a bird's mouth. Some birds have long, sharp **beaks**.

# bean

A **bean** is a seed that is eaten as a vegetable. There were green **beans** and yellow **beans** in the salad.

# bear

A bear is a large animal. It has thick fur and strong claws. Many **bears** sleep all winter.

# beard

A beard is the hair that grows on a man's face. My grandfather has a short, white **beard**.

# beast

A beast is any animal with four legs. Lions, tigers, and dogs are all **beasts**.

# beat

1. **Beat** means to hit something again and again. The rain **beat** against the window.
2. **Beat** also means that a person does something better than someone else.

Diana **beat** Maria in the race.

## beaten

**Beaten** is a form of **beat**. Jack's father asked Jack to beat the eggs, but Jack said he had **beaten** them already.

## beautiful

When something is **beautiful**, it is very pretty to look at or listen to. Mary drew a **beautiful** picture of a horse. The chorus sang a **beautiful** song. The sunset last night was beautiful.

## beaver

A beaver is a kind of amimal. It has a flat tail and large, strong front teeth. **Beavers** build dams across streams. They live in these dams.

## became

**Became** is a form of **become**. George wants to become a pilot one day.

His father **became** a pilot many years ago.

## because

We use **because** to tell why something is happening. I am closing the door **because** it is cold in here. The players are happy **because** they won the game.

## become

**Become** means to grow to be something different. The seed I planted will become a flower.

## bed

A **bed** is a place to sleep. She was in **bed** by 8 o'clock. The dog's **bed** is in my room.

## bedroom

A bedroom is a room that people use for sleeping. Our apartment has two **bedrooms**. When I woke up this morning, the sun was coming in through my **bed-**

room window.

# bee
A bee is an insect. It can fly. Some **bees** make honey.

# beef
Beef is a kind of meat. It comes from cattle. Hamburger is made from beef.

# been
**Been** comes from the word **be**. Susan and Albert have **been** playing in the yard. I have never **been** to a rodeo.

# beetle
A beetle is a flying insect. **Beetles** have hard, shiny wing cases to protect the soft parts of their bodies.

# before
1. **Before** means first. Marie washes her hands first and then she eats supper. Marie washes her hands **before** she eats.

**2. Before** also means in the past. Alice rode in a plane for the first time last week. She had never been on a plane before.

B

# beg

Beg means to ask for money or other help. The poor woman **begged** for food.

# began

Began is a form of **begin**. The grass began to grow after it rained.

# begin

To begin means to start. Grass **begins** to grow in the spring. It stops growing in the fall.

# beginning

Beginning means the first part or the time something begins. The **beginning** of the story was better than the end. Tomorrow is the **beginning** of winter vacation.

# begun

**Begun** is a form of **begin**. Dictionaries have always **begun** with the word a.

# behave

1. **Behave** means to act in a good way. Our teacher told us to **behave** in the classroom.
2. **Behave** also means to act in any one way. How did the baby **behave** at the doctor's office?

# behind

Behind means at the back of. David sits **behind** Wendy in school. The baby ducks walked **behind** their mother. Harry hid **behind** the tree.

# being

1. **Being** comes from the word **be**. The children were having a good time **being** silly.
2. A **being** is a person or animal. People are human beings.

## believe

When you **believe** something, it means that you think it is true or real. Aunt Claire could not **believe** that she won a thousand dollars.

## bell

When it is struck, a bell makes a sound that rings. The sheep all wore little **bells** around their necks. We heard the school **bell** ring and knew we were late.

## belong

1. To **belong** means to feel good in a place. Fish belong in the water.
2. To **belong** also means to be owned by somebody. That shirt **belongs** to Mark. It is his shirt.

## below

Below means in a lower place. Terry hung the picture he drew **below** mine.

# belt

A belt is something you wear to keep your pants or skirt up. I need to wear a **belt** with these pants because they are too big for me.

# bench

A bench is a long seat. Grandmother and I sat on a **bench** in the park and fed the birds.

# bend

To **bend** means to make a curve. Hannah **bends** over to put water in her pail.

# beneath

When something is **beneath** something else, it is below it or under it. We keep our brooms in the closet **beneath** the stairs. The dog's bed is **beneath** the table.

# bent

Bent is a form of **bend**. I **bent** my knees and jumped. Susan's glasses were **bent**

after she sat on them.

# beret

A beret is a soft, round, flat cap. My grandfather wears a plaid scarf and a **beret** on chilly days.

# berry

A **berry** is a small fruit that we can eat. A **berry** has many seeds. We went to Mr. John's farm to pick **berries**.

# beside

Beside means next to a person or thing. Richard and Margaret are **beside** each other in the photo-graph.

# best

Best means better than all the others. Of all the ani-mals at the zoo, I like the monkeys best. Billy won the race because he was the **best** runner.

B

## better

**Better** means very good, but not the best. Richard swims **better** than Mark. Bill likes warm days better than cold ones.

## between

**Between** means in the middle of two other things. In the alphabet, s comes **between** r and t. The dog sat **between** us in the truck. Mom told us not to eat any cookies **between** meals.

## beyond

**Beyond** means on the other side of something. Maria climbed over a fence and into the field. She went **beyond** the fence.

## bicycle

A bicycle is something to ride on. It has two wheels with one in front of the other. You use your feet to make the wheels turn. **Bike** is a short word for **bicycle**.

B

## big

Big means large in size or amount. The box was too **big** for Richard to pick up. We live in a **big** city.

## bill

A bill is a bird's beak. Ducks have big **bills**.

## biography

A **biography** is a true story of someone's life written by another person.

## bird

A bird is an animal with wings. **Birds** are covered with feathers and have two legs. Most **birds** can fly. **Birds** lay eggs. Chickens and penguins are **birds**.

## birth

Birth is the moment when a person is born. Most **births** happen in hospitals.

## birthday

Your **birthday** is the day of

your birth. Maria was born on November 8. November 8 is her **birthday**.

# bit

1. **Bit** is a form of **bite**. Anne bit into an apple.
2. **Bit** also means a small amount. David put a **bit** of pepper into his soup.

# bite

1. To **bite** means to cut with your teeth. Wendy is hungry. She **bites** her sandwich. Then she chews and swallows.
2. A **bite** is a small amount you can cut off with your teeth. Wendy took a **bite** of her sandwich. She will eat the rest later.

# bitten

**Bitten** is a form of **bite**. My brother was **bitten** by a dog.

# bitter

bitter means having a sharp taste. George tasted the

medicine and made a face.
It was very **bitter**.

# black

Black is a very dark color.
These letters are **black**. The
opposite of **black** is **white**.

# blacksmith

A **blacksmith** is a person
who makes things out of
iron. Blacksmiths make
horseshoes.

# blame

**Blame** means to say that a
person has done some-
thing wrong or bad. Mother
**blamed** me for letting the
bird out of its cage.

# blanket

A blanket is a large soft
cloth. People cover them-
selves with **blankets** to
keep warm.

# bleed

**Bleed** means to lose blood
from the body. Tom **bled**
when he fell and cut his

chin.

# blew

Blew comes from the word blow. The wind **blew** the door shut.

# blind

Blind means not able to see. Anybody who cannot see is **blind**.

# block

1. A block is hard and has flat sides. Elizabeth built a house with her toy **blocks**.
2. A **block** is an area with four streets around it. A **block** is also the part between two streets. Bob lives on my **block**.

# blood

Blood is a red liquid.
**Blood** is inside our bodies. Nobody can live without **blood**.

# bloom

Bloom means to have flowers. Cherry trees **bloom**

in the spring.

# blossom

A **blossom** is a flower. The **blossoms** on apple trees are white or pink.

# blouse

A blouse is a piece of clothing worn on the top part of the body.

# blow

1. Blow means to put air into something. Will you help us **blow** up these balloons?
2. **Blow** also means to move with air. Hold on to your umbrella or the wind will **blow** it away.

# blown

**Blown** is a form of **blow**. The leaves were **blown** off the tree by the wind.

# blue

Blue is a color. The sky is **blue** when no clouds cover it.

## board

A board is a long, flat piece of wood. **Boards** are used to build houses. The floor was made of **boards**.

## boat

A boat is something that is used to travel on water. Some **boats** are moved by the wind blowing on sails. Other **boats** are moved by motors. I crossed the river in a **boat**.

## body

A **body** is all of a person or an animal. An elephant has a huge, heavy body. Snakes have long, thin **bodies**.

## boil

1. **Boil** means to make water very hot. When water **boils**, little bubbles come to the top.
2. **Boil** also means to cook something in water that is boiling. John **boiled** an egg for breakfast.

## bone

A bone is the hard part of a person's body under the skin and muscles. People have big, long **bones** in their legs and many tiny bones in their feet. Susan broke a **bone** in her arm when she fell on the ice.

## book

A **book** is made up of pieces of paper that are sewed or pasted together at one edge. The pages of a **book** have words and pictures on them for people to read and look at. This dictionary is a book. There are many **books** in our school library.

## boom

A **boom** is a deep, hollow sound. During the storm we heard **booms** of thunder.

## boost

Boost means to push up. George **boosted** his friend into the tree so that he could reach the apple.

# boot

A boot is a large shoe. **Boots** are made of rubber or leather. Most people wear **boots** in the rain or snow.

# border

A border is an edge. It is a line where one area ends and another begins. We made a **border** of stones around the garden.

# borrow

Borrow means to take something to use for a while. Albert let me **borrow** his roller skates. Elizabeth **borrowed** a book from me.

# both

Both means two people or two things. **Both** children won a prize. I like **both** apples and bananas.

# bother

Bother means to give trouble to or annoy someone. Alice's little sister **bothers** her when she is on the phone.

## bottle

A bottle is something that is used to hold liquids. **Bottles** may be made of glass or plastic.

## bottom

The **bottom** is the lowest part of something. The rock sank to the **bottom** of the pool.

## bought

Bought comes from the word **buy.** We **bought** food for the picnic.

## bounce

**Bounce** means to move back after hitting something. Paul threw the ball and it **bounced** off the sidewalk.

## bow[1]

1. A bow is a special kind of

knot. It is made with a ribbon or string. Helen tied a
big red **bow** on the gift.
**2.** A bow is also a thin
piece of wood with a string
tied from one end to the
other. It is used for shoot-
ing arrows.

# bow²

To **bow** means to bend the
body forward. In the story
the knight meets a king. He
**bows** to the king with re-
spect.

# bowl

A **bowl** is used to hold
things. Bowls are round
and hollow. People eat
soup and cereal out of
them.

# bowling

Bowling is a sport. **Bowling**
is played with a heavy ball
and pieces of wood
shaped like bottles.

# box

A **box** is used to hold

things. Boxes are often made of wood or heavy paper.

# boy

A boy is a child who will grow up to be a man. **Boys** are male children.

# brace

**1.** A **brace** is something that holds parts together or keeps a thing from shaking. Terry wore a metal **brace** on his weak leg to help him walk.

**2. Braces** are also metal wires that are put on teeth to help them grow straight.

# bracelet

A bracelet is a chain or a large ring that is worn around your arm as jewelry.

# braid

**1.** When you **braid** your hair, you divide it into three parts and then put one part over the other until you get a long strip.

**2.** A long strip of hair that is **braided** is called a **braid**.

# brain

The **brain** is a part of the body that is inside the head of people and animals. It lets us think, learn, and remember.

# brainstorm

**1.** Brainstorm means to get together in a group and collect ideas from each person to try to find an answer to a problem. We **brainstormed** for a long time and finally thought of a good name for our team.
**2.** A **brainstorm** is a sudden, clever idea.

# brake

A **brake** is something that makes a bicycle, a car, or a train go slower or stop. You make some brakes work with your hands, like those on many bicycles. Other **brakes** work with the feet. Mom put her foot on the **brake** to make the car stop.

# branch

A branch is the part of a tree or bush that grows out from the trunk. Leaves grow on **branches**.

# brave

If you are **brave,** it means that you have courage. The **brave** child climbed the tree to get the kitten.

# bread

Bread is a kind of food. It is made with flour and water and other things mixed together. **Bread** is baked in an oven.

# break

1. When something **breaks,** it divides into pieces. If you drop that mirror, it will **break**.

2. When something **breaks,** it stops working. Our oven is **broken** and doesn't get hot. George **broke** his toy

truck when he threw it.

# breakfast

Breakfast is the first meal of the day. We eat break-fast in the morning. I like cereal and a banana for breakfast.

# breath

Breath is the air you take in and let out when you breathe. When it is very cold, you can see your breath.

# breathe

When you breathe, you take air into your body and let it out again. You breathe through your nose and mouth.

# breeze

A breeze is a soft, gentle wind. The ocean breeze made us feel cool.

# brick

A brick is a block of clay that has been baked in an

oven or in the sun. Our chimney is made of **bricks**.

# bridge

A bridge is used to cross from one side to the other. **Bridges** are often built over water.

# bright

When something is **bright**, it gives out light or is filled with light. The sun made the room bright.

# bring

Bring means to take someone or something with you. Hannah asked if she could **bring** her friend Mary to the party. Will you please **bring** me the newspaper?

# broke

Broke is a form of **break**. It is easy for glass to break. Yesterday I dropped a glass. It **broke** into pieces.

# broken

Broken is a form of **break**.

That window has **broken** into five pieces of glass.

# broom

A **broom** is a brush with a long handle. It is used to sweep the floor or ground. Mr. Kelly uses a wide broom to sweep the leaves from his sidewalk.

# brother

Your brother is a boy who has the same mother and father as you do.

# brought

**Brought** comes from the word **bring**. Everyone at the party **brought** a birthday present for Harry.

# brown

**Brown** is the color of the earth. Some people have **brown** hair and **brown** eyes.

# brush

1. A brush is something used for cleaning or paint-

B

ing. **Brushes** have hairs or wires that are usually attached to a handle. A toothbrush is a special kind of **brush**.

2. **Brush** also means to clean or make something neat. Wendy likes to **brush** and braid her sister's long hair. Paul **brushed** his dog at least once a week.

# bubble

A **bubble** is a round drop of something filled with air. Mike and Sarah blew soap bubbles.

# bucket

A **bucket** is used to carry things. It can be made of wood, metal, or plastic. It has a flat round bottom and a handle. **Buckets** are often used to carry water.

# bug

A bug is an insect. Ants, bees, and mosquitoes are kinds of **bugs**.

B

# build

**Build** means to make something. We are going to **build** a castle out of sand. Paul **built** a large cage for his rabbit.

# building

A **building** is something built to live, work, or do things in. Houses, schools, churches, offices, and stores are buildings.

# built

**Built** is a form of **build**. The carpenters **built** that house in one summer.

# bulb

1. A **bulb** is the part of a plant that grows under-ground. Tulips grow from **bulbs.** Onions are bulbs you can eat.

2. A **bulb** can also be any-thing that has a part that is round. A **bulb** that is used in a lamp is called a light **bulb**.

# bull

A bull is a large animal. It lives on a farm. **Bulls** have horns and eat grass.

# bulldozer

A bulldozer is a machine that is used to move rocks and dirt. **Bulldozers** get the land ready before roads and buildings are built.

# bully

A **bully** is a person who likes to frighten people or be mean to them.

# bump

**1.** To **bump** means to hit against something. Duncan **bumped** his head on the table by accident.
**2.** A **bump** is a round place that sticks out. The road had a lot of **bumps** in it.

# bumper

A bumper is a heavy bar across the front or back of a car or truck that protects it when it hits something.

# bunch

A **bunch** is a group of things that are together. Mom picked a bunch of flowers from the garden. Mary bought two **bunches** of carrots and one **bunch** of bananas.

# bunny

A bunny is a small animal with long ears, a small tail, and soft fur. Another word for **bunny** is rabbit.

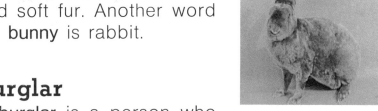

# burglar

A **burglar** is a person who gets into a house, store, or other place and steals things. **Burglars** stole jewelry from the hotel room.

# burn

1. **Burn** means to be on fire. We burn wood in the fireplace to keep us warm on a cold day.

2. **Burn** also means to hurt yourself by touching something hot. Billy **burned**

his hand on the stove.

# bury
**Bury** means to put in the earth or the sea. Tom's dog is **burying** its bone in our backyard.

# bus
A bus is a machine. It has four wheels, an engine, and many seats and windows. **Buses** carry many people from one place to another.

# bush
A bush is a plant. It has many branches and leaves. **Bushes** are not as big as trees. Some flowers grow on **bushes**.

# business
1. Business is the work that a person does to earn money. My father's **business** is selling jewelry.
2. A **business** is also a factory, a store, a farm, or any other place where people work to earn money.

# busy

**Busy** means doing many things. Mary has a lot of work to do. She is very busy today. I am **busy** with my homework.

# but

**1.** We use **but** when we talk about how things are different. Dick is tall, **but** his brother is taller. I want to play, **but** I have to work.
**2.** We also use **but** to mean except. Everyone **but** Sarah liked the movie.

# butter

Butter is a soft, yellow food that is made from cream or milk. People put **butter** on bread or use it to cook with. I spread **butter** on bread.

# butterfly

A butterfly is an insect that has four large wings with bright colors. A **butterfly**'s body is very thin.

# button

A **button** is a small round piece of wood or plastic. **Buttons** are sewn on clothes to keep them closed.

# buy

To **buy** means to give money for something. You can buy all kinds of food at a supermarket.

# by

1. **By** means near something. My dog stands **by** the door when she wants to go out. We drove **by** my friend's house.

2. **By** also means not later than. We have to be at school **by** 8 o'clock.

## cab

A **cab** is a car that people pay to ride in. Aunt Joe took a **cab** to the airport. Another word for **cab** is taxi.

## cabin

A cabin is a small house built of rough boards or logs. There are **cabins** all around the lake.

## caboose

A caboose is the last car on a train. The people who work on the train eat and sleep in the **caboose**.

## cactus

A **cactus** is a plant that grows in the desert. Cactuses have sharp needles instead of leaves.

Cactuses grow in many shapes, and some have large, bright flowers.

## cafeteria

A cafeteria is a kind of restaurant. In **cafeterias**, you choose your food at a counter and carry it to a table. Joyce eats soup and a sandwich for lunch in the school **cafeteria**.

## cage

A cage is a kind of box. The sides are made of metal or wood poles. Birds and other animals are sometimes kept in **cages**.

## cake

A cake is a sweet food that is baked in an oven. It is often made with flour, butter, eggs, and sugar.

## calendar

A **calendar** is something that shows all the days,

weeks, and months of the year. Jack marked the day of the party on the **calendar** so that he wouldn't forget.

## calf[1]

A **calf** is a baby cow. A baby seal, elephant, or whale is also called a **calf**.

## calf[2]

The calf is a part of the leg. The **calf** is at the back of the leg, a little below the knee.

## call

1. To **call** means to say in a loud voice. I heard the teacher **call** my name.
2. To call means to use the telephone. Leon **calls** his friends on the telephone almost every day.

3. To **call** means to give a name to. Anne **calls** her doll Emily.
4. A **call** is a loud sound made by a person. The police heard someone's **call** for help.

## calm

1. **Calm** means quiet and not moving. The wind is **calm** today.

2. **Calm** means quiet and not bothered. Tom is very **calm** about his first day at school.

## came

**Came** is a form of **come**. Bill **came** into the kitchen.

## camel

A camel is a large animal. It has long legs and a long neck. It also has one or two humps on its back. **Camels** can carry people and things across the desert.

## camera

A camera is a small machine that makes pictures. People often take **cameras** along on their vacations.

## camouflage

Camouflage is a way of

hiding something by making it look like the things around it. The skin or fur of some animals is a **camouflage**. The fox's white fur was a good **camouflage** because it could not be seen in the snow.

## camp

1. A camp is a place where people live outside. They sleep in tents or huts and cook over a fire. Many children go to a **camp** in the summer.
2. To **camp** means to live in a camp. Claire and her family **camped** near the lake.

## can[1]

Can means to be able to. Kelly **can** run fast. Murray **can** speak two languages.

## can[2]

A can is a container made of metal. **Cans** are used to hold food and other things. Let's play "Kick the **Can**."

Mom bought two **cans** of white paint.

# candle

A candle is a stick of wax with a piece of string in it. **Candles** make light when they burn.

C

# candy

Candy is a kind of food. It is made of sugar and is very sweet. **Candy** can be made with chocolate, nuts, or fruit.

# cannot

**Cannot** means is not able to. A dog can run, but it **cannot** fly.

# canoe

A canoe is a kind of small boat. It is long, narrow, and light. **Canoes** go through the water very quietly.

# can't

Can't is a short way to say **cannot**. Fish can swim, but they **can't** talk.

## cap

A cap is a kind of hat. People who play baseball wear **caps**.

## capital

**1.** A **capital** is a city where people in the government of a country or state meet to make laws and to work. Washington, D.C. is the capital of the United States.
**2.** A **capital** is also a large letter of the alphabet. E and M are the **capitals** for the letters e and m. When we write a name or a sentence, we start with a **capital**.

## car

**1.** A car is a machine. It has four wheels, an engine, seats, and windows. People travel over roads in **cars**.
**2.** A **car** is also one part of a train. It is like a big room on wheels. Most trains have several **cars**.

## card

**1.** A **card** is a small piece of

thick paper. It is shaped like a rectangle. **Cards** have numbers and pictures on them. People play games with **cards**.

2. A card is also a small folded piece of paper. It has a message on it. You send **cards** to people in the mail.

## care

When you **care** about something, you have a good feeling about it. Tony **cares** about his cat and feeds it and fills its water bowl twice every day.

## careful

If you are **careful**, it means that you are thinking about what you are doing. Diana is very careful not to spill the paint. She works carefully.

## careless

**Careless** means that you are not thinking about what

you are doing. Al and Barry were **careless** and spilled the paint. They worked carelessly.

## carnival

A carnival is a kind of fair that has food, games, and many things to amuse people.

## carpenter

A carpenter is a person who builds and fixes houses and other things made of wood. The **carpenter** built shelves and a seat under the window in my room.

## carriage

A **carriage** is a kind of wagon on four wheels for carrying people.

## carrot

A carrot is a kind of vegetable. It is long and orange. **Carrots** grow under the ground.

## carry

To **carry** means to hold something and take it somewhere. Hannah **carries** her lunch in a bag.

## cart

A **cart** is a kind of wagon. Most **carts** have two wheels and are pulled. Carts at the supermarket have four wheels and are pushed.

## carton

A carton is a box made of very heavy paper. Anne bought a **carton** of milk.

## cartoon

A **cartoon** is a picture that makes people laugh. There are **cartoons** in newspapers and magazines, in movies, and on television.

## carve

1. Carve means to cut out a shape. The artist **carved** animals from wood.
2. **Carve** also means to cut meat into pieces. It is

almost time to **carve** the turkey.

## case

A **case** holds or covers a thing. My glasses fit into a narrow **case**.

## castle

A castle is a very big building with high walls and towers. A long time ago, kings and queens lived in **castles**. She saw the King in the **castle**.

## cat

1. A cat is a small animal that has soft fur and a long tail. Mary has a pet **cat**. I have two **cats**.
2. Some kinds of **cats** are large and wild. Tigers and leopards are large, wild **cats**.

## catch

**Catch** means to take hold of something that is moving. Blake ran to **catch** the ball.

### catcher
A **catcher** is a person or thing that catches. The catcher in a baseball game is behind the person who is ready to hit the ball.

### caterpillar
A **caterpillar** is an insect. It looks like a worm covered with fur. **Caterpillars** change into butterflies or moths.

### catsup, ketchup
Catsup is a thick liquid made from tomatoes. It is eaten on other foods. Another way to spell **catsup** is ketchup.

### cattle
Cattle are large animals. They have four legs and two horns. They are raised for milk and meat. Cows and bulls are **cattle**.

### caught
**Caught** is a form of **catch**. Bob threw the ball, and Helen **caught** it.

## cause

**1. Cause** means to make something happen. If you don't hurry, you will **cause** us to be late for school.

**2.** A **cause** is a person or thing that makes something happen. A car going too fast was the **cause** of the accident. What was the **cause** of the fire?

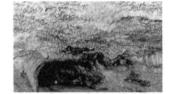

## cave

A cave is a hollow place that goes deep under the ground. **Caves** are very dark inside.

## cavity

A **cavity** is a hole in a tooth. After my dentist showed me how to brush my teeth, I got fewer **cavities**.

## ceiling

A ceiling is the top side of a room. You look up at the **ceiling**.

## celebrate

When you **celebrate** something, you show that it is important in a special way. Our town **celebrated** the Fourth of July with a parade and fireworks.

## cellar
A **cellar** is a room under a house.

## cent
A cent is an amount of money. A nickel is five **cents**, and a dollar is 100 **cents**.

## center | -tre
The **center** is the middle of something. Tom's doughnut had jelly in the center

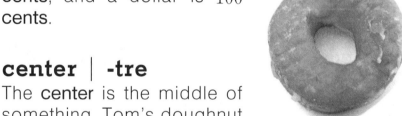

## cereal
Cereal is a food often made from wheat, corn, or rice. We like **cereal** for breakfast.

## certain
Certain means that you are very sure about something.

Are you **certain** that you closed the door?

# chain

A **chain** is a row of rings that are joined together. Margaret wore a heart on a chain around her neck.

# chair

A chair is a kind of furniture. It has four legs and a seat. People sit on **chairs**.

# chalk

**Chalk** is a small stick that is used for writing or drawing. Our new teacher wrote her name on the chalkboard with yellow **chalk**.

# chalkboard

A chalkboard is a hard, smooth board made of a special material that can be written on and erased. **Chalkboards** may be black or green.

# chance

1. **Chance** means luck. I

found three dollars by **chance**.

2. **Chance** means that something may happen. There is a **chance** it will rain today. **Chances** are it will rain all day.

# change

1. To **change** means to become different. In the fall, leaves change color from green to red, orange, and yellow.

2. To **change** means to put on other clothes. After school Arthur and Pablo **change** before they go out to play.

3. **Change** means coins. Joyce has a dollar and some **change**.

# channel

A television has many channels. Each **channel** can carry a different program. One **channel** has science programs for children. Billy changed the **channel** on the television so that we could

watch cartoons.

## chant

A **chant** is a singing or shouting of words again and again. Each team yelled a chant before the football game began.

## chapter

A **chapter** is a main part of a book. Albert's book has 10 **chapters**.

## character

A character is a person in a book, play, story, or movie.

## charge

1. **Charge** means to ask an amount of money as a price for something. How much did the store **charge** for fixing the radio?
2. **Charge** also means to buy something and pay for it later.

## chase

**Chase** means to run after something and try to catch

it. My dog **chased** the car down the road.

## cheap

**Cheap** means that something costs very little. These cars are the **cheapest** toys in the store.

## check

**1.** A **check** is a mark. You make a **check** next to something to show that it is right. A **check** looks like this : ✓.
**2.** To **check** also means to look for something. Mary can't find her shoes. Her mother tells her to **check** under her bed.
**3.** A check is also a square. Lucy's shirt has big red and white **checks** all over it.

## checkers

Checkers is a game for two people played on a board, with 12 pieces for each person. George and his friends like to play **checkers**.

c

# checkup

A checkup means a careful look to see if somebody or something is all right. Jane went to the doctor for a **checkup** last week.

# cheek

Your **cheek** is the part of your face that is under your eyes. Terry's **cheeks** became red when he played in the snow.

# cheerful

When you are **cheerful**, it means that you feel happy. The **cheerful** boy whistled while waiting for the bus.

# cheese

Cheese is a kind of food. It is made from milk. **Cheese** can be hard or soft. Many **cheeses** are yellow or white.

# cherry

A cherry is a kind of fruit. It is small, round, and red. **Cherries** grow on cherry trees.

## chess

Chess is a game for two people played on a board, with 16 pieces for each person. Mom showed me how different **chess** pieces move in different ways.

## chest

1. Your chest is the front part of your body just below the shoulders. Your heart is in your **chest**.
2. A **chest** is also a big box that holds things. Grandma keeps her blankets in a wood **chest**. Bill put the hammer back in the tool **chest**.

## chew

To **chew** means to break something into small pieces with the teeth. Our puppy **chewed** an old shoe.

## chicken

A chicken is a bird. **Chickens** lay eggs that

people eat. People also eat meat from **chickens**.

## chief

A **chief** is a person who is the leader of a group. Each year the **chief** of police gives medals to the bravest police officers.

## child

A **child** is a young girl or boy. Twelve **children** played in the school band.

## children

Children means more than one child. **Children** grow up to be men and women.

## chill

A **chill** is a feeling of cold. There was a **chill** in the air this morning.

## chimney

A chimney is something that carries smoke away from a fireplace or a furnace to the outdoors.

# chin

The **chin** is the part of your face between your mouth and your neck. My Dad's beard covers his chin.

C

# chocolate

Chocolate is a kind of food. It is usually brown and very sweet. Candy and cake are often made with **chocolate**.

# choose

**Choose** means to pick out something you want to have. Billy **chose** a red balloon with his name on it.

# chorus

A **chorus** is a group of people who sing or dance together. Mark and Anne sing in the **chorus** at school.

# chose

**Chose** is a form of **choose**. Peter and Ray chose to play soccer.

## chosen
**Chosen** is a form of **choose**. Anne has **chosen** a peanut butter sandwich.

## Christmas
Christmas is a Christian holiday celebrated on December 25. Many people go to church and give presents on **Christmas**.

## church
A church is a building where Christian people go to pray and sing.

## circle
A **circle** is a round shape. It is made by a line that turns until the two ends touch. **Circles** do not have any corners or straight parts.

## circus
A circus is a kind of show. **Circuses** usually happen in a big tent. You can see clowns, magicians, and animals at the **circus**.

## city

A city is a place where a lot of people live and work. **Cities** have many tall buildings. A **city** is bigger than a town.

## class

A **class** is a group of students who learn together. Our **class** went on a trip to the museum.

## classroom

A classroom is a room where a class works with a teacher.

## claw

A **claw** is a part of the foot of an animal or a bird. It is sharp and curved. Birds hold on to branches with their **claws**.

## clay

Clay is a kind of earth. Wet **clay** can be made into many different shapes. When **clay** is dried or

baked, it becomes hard.

# clean

**1. Clean** means without any dirt. Blake keeps his dog **clean**. He gives him a bath every Saturday.

**2.** To clean is to take away dirt. Margaret **cleaned** her face with soap and water.

# clear

Clear means easy to see through. The water in the lake was so **clear** we could see the bottom.

# clever

When people are **clever**, they can think quickly. The **clever** child learned how to do the puzzle in a very short time.

# climb

Climb means to move up something. People use their hands or feet when they **climb**. Mom had to **climb** a ladder to get the kite out of the tree. Tony **climbed** into

bed and went right to sleep.

# clock

We read the numbers on a clock to know what time it is. Some **clocks** have hands that move around. Other **clocks** show numbers that change as the time changes.

# close

1. **Close** means near. The child stayed **close** to its mother.
2. To **close** something means to keep the inside in and the outside out. Maria **closed** the door after she came into the room.
3. To **close** is to become shut. The store **closes** at the same time every night.

# closet

A closet is a small room used for storing clothes and other things. A **closet** usually has a door.

# cloth

**Cloth** is material that is used to make clothes, blankets, and other things. Cotton **cloth** is made from plants, and wool **cloth** is made from the hair of animals.

# clothes

People wear **clothes** to cover their bodies. Coats, dresses, pants, and jackets are kinds of **clothes**. Another word for **clothes** is clothing. We put on warm clothing to play outdoors in the winter.

# cloud

A **cloud** is made of tiny drops of water that float high in the sky. There were dark clouds in the sky before the storm.

# clown

A clown is a person who dresses in funny clothes and does tricks to make people laugh. The **clowns**

at the circus wore paint on their faces.

# club

A **club** is a group of people who meet together for fun or some special purpose. Our book **club** meets on Friday.

# clue

A **clue** is something that helps us find the answer to a problem or mystery. The footprints were the **clue** that helped us catch the burglar.

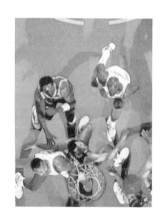

# coach

A **coach** is a person who trains people who play sports. The coach made the basketball team practice every afternoon until the big game.

# coast

A coast is the land next to the sea. Al and Tom walked along the **coast** looking at all the sea birds.

## coat

A  coat is something that covers your body. **Coats** are usually made from thick cloth. They keep you warm when the weather is cold.

## cocoon

A **cocoon** is a small, soft case that a caterpillar makes around itself. A caterpillar lives in a **cocoon** until it changes into a butterfly.

## coin

A coin is a kind of money. **Coins** are usually round. They are made of metal. Pennies, nickels, dimes, and quarters are all **coins**.

## cold

1. To be **cold** means to have a low temperature. Snow and ice are **cold**.
2. When you have a **cold** you are sick. Your head may hurt. You may sneeze a lot. People with **colds** often rest in bed.

# collar

1. A collar is the part of a shirt or dress that fits around the neck.
2. A **collar** is also a short belt worn around an animal's neck. My dog's **collar** has my address on it.

C

# collect

Collect means to gather things together. I like to **collect** different kinds of rocks as a hobby.

# color | colour

Red, blue, and yellow are the main **colors**. All other **colors** have some red, blue, or yellow in them. If we mix blue and yellow together, we get the **color** green. Orange is my favorite color.

# comb

A comb is a piece of plastic or metal with teeth in it. You use a **comb** in your hair to make it smooth.

## come

Come means to move toward a person or place. My cat **comes** to me when I call her. I hope you can **come** with me.

## comfortable

If something is comfortable, it feels nice. The chair is so **comfortable** that Dad falls asleep in it.

## comic

1. **Comic** means funny. A mouse chasing a cat is a **comic** thing to see.
2. **Comic** is a magazine that contains stories told in pictures.

## company

Company is a person or a group of people who visit you. We had company for dinner on Thanksgiving.

## compare

Compare means to look at people or things to see

how they are alike or different. If you **compare** your book with mine, you will see that yours is much thicker.

## complete

1. When something is **complete**, it has all its parts. Our school library has a complete set of books by my favorite author.
2. **Complete** also means finished. Andrew can't go out until his homework is **complete**.

## computer

A computer is a machine that can do many kinds of work very fast. People use **computers** to work with numbers or words or even to draw pictures.

## concert

A concert is a show of music. The new school orchestra is going to give three **concerts** this year.

# cone

**1.** A cone is a shape that has a round, flat bottom and a top that comes to a point.

**2.** A cone is also anything that has the shape of a cone. For Halloween, I made a witch's hat in the shape of a **cone**.

# confuse

**1.** To **confuse** means to mix things up in your mind. I can't understand my sister. She **confuses** me when she talks.

**2.** To **confuse** also means to think one thing is another. My teachers sometimes **confuse** me with my brother.

# consonant

A consonant is a kind of letter. B, c, d, f, g, h, j, k, l, m, n, p, q, r, s, t, v, w, x, and z are **consonants**. **Consonants** and vowels make the letters of the alphabet.

## container

A container is something that is used to hold things. Boxes and jars are **containers**.

## contest

A contest is a game or a race that people try to win. Maria won the swimming **contest**.

## continue

To **continue** means to start again. We played baseball all morning. Then we **continued** the game after lunch.

## control

To **control** something means to make it do what you want it to do. David **controls** his kite with a long string.

## cook

**1.** To cook is to heat food to make it ready to eat. We **cooked** the turkey in the oven for six hours.

2. A cook is a person who makes meals. **Cooks** work in kitchens.

## cookie, cookey

A cookie is a small, flat, sweet food. Some **cookies** have chocolate in them.

## cool

**Cool** means not very cold. The weather was **cool** this morning, but it got warm this afternoon.

## copper

**Copper** is a kind of metal. Pennies and wire are made from copper.

## copy

1. **Copy** means to make or do something that is like something else. Lewis **copied** a picture of a lion to show me.

2. A **copy** is a thing that is just like something else. I'd like two **copies** of each photograph, please.

## corn

Corn is a kind of vegetable. It grows on a tall green plant. **Corn** can be yellow or white.

## corner

A corner is a place where two lines or sides come together. Paul bumped his knee on the **corner** of the table.

## correct

1. **Correct** means without mistakes. Jack's answer was **correct**.
2. To **correct** means to check for mistakes in something. The teacher **corrects** all our tests.

## cost

1. Cost is how much money you have to pay to buy something. What is the **cost** of that bicycle?
2. **Cost** also means that you can buy something for a certain amount of money.

My new shoes **cost** 20 dollars.

## costume

A costume is clothing you
wear to look like someone
or something else. Marie
wore a **costume** in the
school play.

## cotton

Cotton is a kind of cloth
that is made from the cotton plant. It is used to make
clothes and other things.

## couch

A **couch** is a soft piece of
furniture that more than
one person can sit on.

## cough

Cough means to make a
noise by making air come
out of the throat.

## could

Could is a form of **can**[1]. Tom
can whistle. He **could** whistle when he was five years

old.

## couldn't

Couldn't means could not.
The baby lamb couldn't
walk well.

## count

1. Count means to find out
how many of something
there are. Let's count how
many apples we picked.
2. Count also means to say
numbers in order. Can you
count to 10?

## counter

A counter is a long table.
Things are sold at counters
in stores. In some restaurants people can eat at a
counter.

## country

1. Country means the land
outside of cities and towns
where there are woods and
farms.
2. A country is an area of
land and the people who
live there. A country has its

own government.

## courage

When you do something even though you are afraid, you show **courage**. Fire-fighters have a lot of courage.

## cousin

A **cousin** is the child of an aunt or uncle. My **cousin** and I have the same grand-father.

## cover

1. To **cover** means to put something on top of some-thing else. Wendy **covered** herself with thick blankets to keep warm.

2. A **cover** goes on the top or outside of something. Books have **covers**. Pots and pans also have covers.

## cow

A cow is a large animal that lives on a farm. **Cows** give milk.

# cowboy

A **cowboy** is a man who takes care of cattle on a ranch. Cowboys ride horses and sometimes do tricks in shows that are called rodeos. **Cowboys** work on big farms.

# cowgirl

A **cowgirl** is a woman who takes care of cattle on a ranch. **Cowgirls** ride horses and sometimes do tricks in shows that are called rodeos.

# crack

A **crack** is a narrow open space. When something has a **crack** it is broken but it does not fall into pieces. There was a **crack** in the mirror after I dropped it. There is a **crack** in the wall.

# cracker

A cracker is a small, hard, flat food that is baked. **Crackers** are like cookies, but they are not sweet.

## crane

A crane is a large machine with a long arm that can be moved up and down and in a circle. **Cranes** are used for lifting and moving heavy things.

## crash

1. To **crash** means to hit something and break with a lot of noise. We saw two cars **crash** into each other. 2. A **crash** is a loud noise. We heard a **crash** in the next room.

## crawl

To **crawl** is to move on your hands and knees. Babies crawl until they learn to walk.

## crayon

A **crayon** is a wax stick that is used for writing and drawing. **Crayons** come in many colors.

## cream

Cream is a kind of food. It

is part of the milk that comes from a cow. Butter is made from **cream**.

## creep
When something creeps, it moves slowly and quietly along the ground. A spider **crept** across the floor.

## cried
Cried comes from the word **cry**. Mike **cried** when he fell down and hurt his knee.

## crime
A **crime** is anything that is against the law. To steal something is a **crime**.

## crocodile
A crocodile is a large animal that lives in the water. It has short legs and a long tail. It also has sharp teeth.

## crooked
Crooked means not straight. Lightning looks like a crooked line in the sky.

## cross

1. A **cross** is a shape. It is made by two lines that touch in the middle. It looks like this : + .
2. To **cross** means to go to the other side. The bridge crosses the river.

## crow

A **crow** is a large bird with black feathers. **Crows** can make a loud noise.

## crowd

A crowd is a large group of people in one place. The **crowd** waited for the game to start.

## crown

A crown is a special kind of hat that is worn by kings and queens. **Crowns** are often made of gold or silver and have beautiful stones in them.

## cruel

If people are **cruel**, it means that they are ready to hurt others. It is **cruel** of him to beat the dog like that.

## crutch

A **crutch** helps a person with weak legs to walk. A **crutch** is a pole with a soft top that fits under the arm.

## cry

To **cry** is to have tears fall from your eyes. People sometimes **cry** when they are sad.

## cub

A cub is a very young bear, wolf, lion, or tiger.

## cube

A cube is a solid shape like a block. It has six equal, square sides.

## cup

A cup is used to hold liquid. It has a handle on the side. **Cups** are usually round. You can drink milk, water, or juice from a **cup**.

### curious

A **curious** person wants to know or learn something. My brother and I were **curious** about our new neighbors. Murray was **curious** about how birds fly.

### curl

A **curl** is a piece of hair that has the shape of a little circle. Mary has curls all over her head.

### curly

Curly means twisting around in small circles. Billy's hair is **curly**, but Peter's is straight.

### curve

1. A **curve** is a round line. The bottom of a U is a **curve**.
2. To **curve** means to follow a round line. This road curves to the left.

### customer

A customer is a person who buys something.

There were many **customers** at the grocery store.

## cut

**1.** Cut means to divide something into pieces by using a knife, scissors, or other sharp thing. Paul **cut** the pizza into eight pieces.

**2. Cut** also means to make something shorter by taking away a part. The barber **cut** my hair last week.

**3. Cut** also means to hurt yourself on something sharp. Susan **cut** her foot on a rock.

## dad

Dad is a name for your father. Some children also call their father Daddy.

## dairy

A **dairy** is a place where milk is put into bottles or cartons. It is also a place where butter, cheese, and other foods are made from milk. A farm where cows are raised for their milk is sometimes called a **dairy** farm.

## daisy

A daisy is a flower with a round yellow center and white petals.

## dam

A dam is a wall that is built across a river to hold back

water. When the water is held back, it makes a lake. Beavers build **dams** in rivers with sticks and mud.

D

# damp

When something is **damp**, it is a little wet. Michael used a **damp** napkin to wipe up the milk that spilled.

# dance

1. **Dance** means to move your body to music. At the party, we played music and danced. A person who **dances** is called a **dancer**.
2. A **dance** is the way you move your body to music. My friend showed me how to do a **dance** that she learned in another country.

# dandelion

A dandelion is a kind of flower. **Dandelions** are round and yellow.

# danger

Danger is something that

can hurt you. Tornadoes can put people in **danger**.

# dangerous

When something can hurt you, it is **dangerous**. It is **dangerous** to cross the street without looking both ways. Riding a bicycle at night without lights is **dangerous**.

# dark

**Dark** means without light. At night it is dark outside.

# dash

Dash means to move fast. The chicken **dashed** for cover when it started to rain.

# date¹

A date is any one day. July 7 is a **date**. November 20 is also a **date**. Every day has a **date**.

# date²

A **date** is a dark, sweet fruit that grows on trees.

# daughter

A daughter is a person's female child. Wendy parents have two **daughters**. One is Wendy and the other is Maria.

# day

1. **Day** is the time when it is light outside. On our vacation, we played and swam during the **day** and slept in a tent at night.

2. A **day** is also part of a week. There are seven **days** in one week. Tuesday is the third **day** of the week.

# dead

Dead means not alive. Plants and flowers die without water. They become **dead**.

# deaf

**Deaf** means not able to hear.

# dear

Something **dear** is something you love. People also

use **dear** to begin a letter. Susan's letter to her aunt began with "**Dear** Aunt Claire." He said good-bye to his **dear** friends.

# December

December is the last month of the year. It has 31 days. **December** comes after November and before January.

# decide

When you **decide** to do something, you choose to do one thing instead of another. For breakfast Bob **decided** to have cereal instead of eggs. Our town **decided** to put a traffic light in front of the school. We **decided** to go at once.

# deck

1. A **deck** is a set of cards that people use in playing games. Most **decks** have 52 cards, and they are all different.
2. A deck is also the floor

on a ship or a boat. A **deck** may have a roof or cover over it or be all open. There may be many **decks** on a large ship.

# deep
**Deep** means very far down. The dog dug a **deep** hole in the ground to hide its bone.

# deer
A deer is an animal with four legs, a small tail, and brown fur. Some **deer** have big horns. A **deer** runs very fast and lives in the woods.

# define
When you **define** something, you give the meaning of it. A dictionary **defines** words.

# delicious
Delicious means very good to taste. We enjoyed a **delicious** lunch.

# den
A **den** is a place where wild

animals rest or sleep. The bear used a cave as a **den** during the winter.

# dentist

A dentist is a doctor who takes care of people's teeth. The **dentist** showed the children how to brush their teeth.

# describe

**Describe** means to give a picture of something in words. Grandma asked Jack to **describe** the fish he caught. Jack **described** it as 6 inches long, with thin stripes on its body from head to tail.

# desert

A desert is a hot place with very little water and a lot of sand.

# design

A design is a group of different shapes and colors that is drawn or painted. The cards had pretty

designs on one side.

# desk

A **desk** is a kind of table for writing or doing work. Some desks have drawers.

# dessert

Dessert is food that is eaten after lunch or dinner. Today we had fruit salad for **dessert**.

# detective

A **detective** is someone who tries to find out things. The **detective's** job was to find out who stole the jewelry.

# dial

1. A dial is the front part of an instrument. A **dial** has numbers or letters on it and a kind of arrow that points to them. Many clocks have **dials** that show the time.

2. A **dial** is also the disk on a radio or television that is used to choose a program.

# diamond

**1.** A diamond is a hard, clear, shiny stone. Some rings have **diamonds** in them.

**2.** A **diamond** is also a shape. It has four sides and four corners and looks like this ◆. A baseball field is shaped like a **diamond**.

# dictionary

A **dictionary** is a book that shows how words are spelled and what they mean. This book is a dictionary.

# did

**Did** comes from the word **do. Did** you go to the supermarket? Yes, I **did**. She **did** her homework after supper.

# didn't

**Didn't** means **did not**. The footprints on the floor show that Billy **didn't** wipe his feet before going into the house.

# die

To **die** means to become dead. The cold weather made all the flowers **die**.

# different

**Different** means not alike. Birds and fish are very **different** kinds of animals. A dog's tail is **different** from a cat's tail.

**D**

# dig

**Dig** means to make a hole in something. Carlos likes to **dig** in the sand at the beach.

# dime

A **dime** is a coin. One **dime** is the same as ten pennies or two nickels. A dollar is ten **dimes**.

# dining room

A **dining room** is a room to eat in. The hotel has a **dining room** where all the guests can eat. At camp, everyone ate their meals in a large **dining room**.

# dinner

Dinner is a meal. It is the big meal of the day. Some people eat **dinner** at noon. Some people eat **dinner** at night.

# dinosaur

A dinosaur was an animal that lived millions of years ago. Some **dinosaurs** were huge. There are no **dinosaurs** alive today.

# dip

To **dip** means to put something in liquid and then take it out quickly. Susan **dips** her cookies in milk before she eats them.

# direction

1. A **direction** is the way you go to get to another place. If we keep walking in this **direction**, we will get to the park.
2. A direction is also the way that something points. That sign points in the **direction** of the zoo.

# dirt

Dirt means earth. The ground is made of **dirt** and rocks. Mark gets **dirt** on his clothes when he plays outside.

# dirty

**Dirty** means covered with dirt. Our dog gets **dirty** when he swims in the swamp.

# disappear

To disappear means to stop being seen. The sun **disappeared** behind a cloud.

# disappoint

When something **disappoints** you, you are unhappy because it did not happen. Susan and Todd were **disappointed** when it rained and they could not ride their new bikes.

# discover

Discover means to find

something or learn something for the first time. You will **discover** how to make orange paint if you mix red and yellow paints together.

## disguise

1. **Disguise** means to hide something by making it look like something else. The children wore masks and costumes to **disguise** themselves on Halloween.

2. A disguise is something that hides or changes the way you look. Tom wore a funny nose and glasses as a **disguise**.

## dish

A **dish** is something to put food in. Dishes are usually round. Mike washed all the **dishes** after supper.

## disk, disc

1. A disk is something that is flat, thin, and round. Coins and plates and records are **disks**.

2. A **disk** is also a flat, thin

piece of plastic or metal that is used to store information for a computer.

## distance

**Distance** means the space between two things. The distance between my bed and my sister's bed is about 3 feet. Paul lives a long **distance** from his grandmother and flies on an airplane to visit her.

D

## dive

Dive means to go into the water with your head first. When Maria and Albert took swimming lessons, they learned how to **dive**.
A person who **dives** is called a **diver**. The **divers** took pictures of animals that live in the ocean.

## divide

**Divide** means to break something into parts. The children divided into two teams for the game. We **divided** the fruit among us.

A fence **divides** the yard into two parts. Mary **divided** the apple into two halves.

# divorce

**Divorce** means to end a marriage by law. Mrs. John **divorced** her husband.

# dizzy

When you are dizzy, you have the feeling of spinning and being about to fall. The children ran in circles until they were **dizzy**.

# do

To **do** means to make something happen. Hannah always **does** a good job cleaning her room. She has always **done** it without being asked. Hannah and Elizabeth **did** some work together.

# dock

A dock is a place to tie up a boat. Richard ties a rope to his boat when it is at the **dock**.

## doctor

A doctor is a person who helps sick people get well. Many **doctors** work in hospitals.

## does

**Does** is a form of **do**. Joe **does** his homework every night. Sue **does** hers, too.

**D**

## doesn't

**Doesn't** means **does not**. George's dog loves the water, but Albert's dog **doesn't** like it at all.

## dog

A dog is an animal that has four legs and barks. A young **dog** has soft fur and is called a **puppy**. Some **dogs** can be trained to help people.

## doll

A doll is a toy that looks like a baby, a child, or a grown-up. Wendy pretends that her **doll** is her baby.

## dollar

A dollar is an amount of money. A **dollar** is usually made of a piece of green paper shaped like a rectangle. One **dollar** is the same as 100 pennies.

## done

1. **Done** comes from the word **do**. What have you **done** with the book I gave you?
2. **Done** also means finished. George is **done** with his homework.

## donkey

A donkey is an animal. It looks like a small horse with long ears. **Donkeys** can carry heavy loads.

## don't

Don't means **do not**. I **don't** know when the game starts, but I'll ask.

## door

1. A **door** is something that closes off a space. A **door**

opens and shuts so that people can go in and out. The elevator **door** closed after everyone was inside.
2. Sometimes a ceiling or wall or floor has a small door in it. This kind of **door** is often called a **trapdoor**.

# dot

A dot is a small round spot. The letter i has a **dot** over it.

# double

1. **Double** means to make twice as much of something. I hope I can **double** the amount I save this year.
2. Double also means two of the same thing or twice as much. The children formed a **double** line to go into school.

# doubt

1. **Doubt** means to not be certain. We **doubted** that our team would win the trophy.
2. A **doubt** is a feeling of

not believing or of not being certain. When you're in **doubt**, look up the word in your dictionary.

## doughnut

A doughnut is a small round cake. Many **doughnuts** have a hole in the center. Some have jelly in the center. People like to eat **doughnuts** for breakfast.

## dove

**Dove** comes from the word **dive**. The dog **dove** into the water to get the stick I threw.

## down

Down means to move from a higher place to a lower place. The cat jumped **down** from the tree. You can put your books **down** on the table.

## dozen

Dozen means twelve of anything. Marie bought a **dozen** eggs at the store.

# Dr.

Dr. is a short way to write **doctor**. People use **Dr.** with a doctor's name. Our family doctor is **Dr.** Smith.

# drag

Drag means to pull something slowly along the floor or the ground. The dog came in **dragging** its leash behind it.

# dragon

A dragon is a make-believe animal that is big and scary. Some **dragons** have wings and long tails, and some breathe fire.

# drain

1. **Drain** means to take water or another liquid away from something. We **drained** the can of peas.

2. A **drain** is a kind of pipe that is used to take water or another liquid away from something. Sue took a bath and then let the water go down the **drain**.

**D**

# drank

Drank comes from the word **drink**. Sarah **drank** all of her milk.

# draw

Draw means to make a picture of something with a pencil or crayon. I **drew** a picture of my cat.

# drawbridge

A drawbridge is a kind of bridge that can be moved or opened, so that tall ships can pass under it.
I saw the boats go by when the **drawbridge** was raised.

# drawer

A drawer is a box inside a piece of furniture. A **drawer** can be pulled out or pushed in. My sweaters are in the bottom **drawer**.

# drawing

A **drawing** is a picture that someone has made using a pencil or crayon. Yesterday

I made a large **drawing** of an elephant and a giraffe.

# drawn

**Drawn** is a form of **draw**. Marie has **drawn** a picture of Dick. Now Dick will draw one of Marie.

# dream

**1.** A **dream** is a picture in your mind that you have when you are asleep. Last night Alice had a **dream** that she could fly.
**2.** To **dream** means to have thoughts and pictures going through your mind while you are asleep. Albert **dreamed** that he rode a dinosaur.

# dress

A dress looks like a blouse and a skirt that are made in one piece. Girls and women wear **dresses**.

# dresser

A dresser is a piece of furniture that has drawers.

People usually put their clothes in **dressers**. My jewelry and mirror are on top of my **dresser**.

# drew

Drew is a form of **draw**. Terry used a red crayon to draw a circle on the paper. Then he **drew** some squares with a blue crayon.

# dried

**Dried** comes from the word **dry**. The hot sun **dried** the puddles on the sidewalk.

# drill

1. **Drill** means to cut a hole in wood, plastic, and other hard materials. Tyler and Peter measured the wood carefully before **drilling** any holes.

2. The word drill can also mean a tool used for drilling.

3. A **drill** is also a way of training people by having them do something over and over again. In a fire

**drill**, people learn what to do if there is a fire.

# drink

**Drink** means to put a liquid into your mouth and swallow it. Milk and juice are foods that we drink. Bob **drank** all of his milk at breakfast. Sue has **drunk** only half of her juice, but all of her milk.

# drip

**Drip** means to fall in drops. The painter tried not to **drip** paint on the rug.

# drive

To drive is to make a car, a truck, or a train go. My sister is old enough to **drive** a car. Yesterday she **drove** us to the beach.

# driven

**Driven** is a form of **drive**. Engineers drive trains. Al's uncle is an engineer. He has **driven** trains for most of his life.

# drop

**1. Drop** means to let something fall. Walter cried when he **dropped** his ice-cream cone.

**2.** A drop is a tiny amount of liquid. There were **drops** of rain on the flowers.

# drove

**Drove** is a form of **drive**. When Susan missed the bus, her father **drove** her to school.

# drown

**Drown** means to die by staying under water and not getting air to breathe. Someone at the beach swam out too far and almost **drowned**.

# drug

**1.** A **drug** is a medicine that can help make a sick person feel better. Drugs can be pills or liquids.

**2.** There is another kind of **drug** that is not a medicine.

It can hurt a person's body and make that person sick.

# drugstore

A drugstore is a store where people can buy medicine. **Drugstores** also sell newspapers and other things.

# drum

A drum is a musical instrument that makes a sound when it is hit. A person who plays the **drum** is called a **drummer**.

# drunk

Drunk comes from the word **drink**. The baby has **drunk** all of her juice.

# dry

1. **Dry** means without water. It didn't rain for three weeks, and the garden got very **dry**.
2. **Dry** also means to make something dry. We left our beach towels out in the sun to **dry**.

# duck

A duck is a bird that lives in the water. There is a family of **ducks** in the pond at the park.

# dug

**Dug** comes from the word **dig**. The workers have dug a large hole in the ground where the new store is to be built.

# dull

1. When something is **dull**, it is not sharp. The knife is so dull that I can't cut the meat.

2. **Dull** means not interesting. The program was so **dull** that I didn't want to watch the end of it.

# dump

**Dump** means to drop things in a pile. The truck is going to **dump** the dirt on the side of the road.

# during

**During** means the whole

time. It is light outside **during** the day. We stayed inside **during** the storm.

## dust

Dust is tiny pieces of dirt. **Dust** can make you sneeze. Wind blows **dust** around on dirt roads.

## dying

Dying comes from the word **die**. The plant in our classroom is **dying** because we forgot to water it before vacation.

D

## each

1. **Each** means every one of a group of people, animals, or things. **Each** student has a pencil and paper. Each pupil takes a lunch to school.
2. **Each** also means for one. These pencils cost 10 cents **each**.

## each other

**Each other** means one and the other. Bob and Mary like **each other**. Mike and Sue saw **each other** at the fair.

## eagle

An eagle is a large bird with long wings and strong claws. When **eagles** hunt for food, they can see things very far away.

## ear

An ear is the part of the body that you hear with. There is one **ear** on each side of your head. We hear with our **ears**. Rabbits have very long **ears**.

## early

1. **Early** means near the time when something begins. Wendy wakes up **early** in the morning. Her father wakes up **earlier** to get ready for work. Wendy's baby brother wakes up **earliest** of all.
2. **Early** also means before the usual time. We had dinner **early** because we were going to a puppet show.

## earn

**Earn** means to get money or something else for work that you do. Susan earns a dollar when she cuts the lawn. Mark **earns** seven dollars a day. Billy **earned** high marks in school by working hard.

# earth

**1.** The earth is the planet we live on. The **earth** moves around the sun, and the moon moves around the **earth**. It takes one year for the **earth** to go around the sun.

**2. Earth** also means dirt. The farmer dug up the earth to make it loose enough to plant seeds for a garden.

# earthquake

An earthquake happens when a part of the earth moves suddenly. The ground shakes and sometimes buildings fall down during an **earthquake**.

# easily

Easily means in an easy way. When something can be done **easily**, it can be done without hard work. Now that Anthony knows the alphabet, he is able to find words in the dictionary **easily**.

## east

**East** is a direction. The sun rises in the east **East** is the opposite of **west**.

## Easter

**Easter** is a Christian holiday that is celebrated on a Sunday either in late March or in early April. Sometimes children paint eggs bright colors for Easter

## easy

**Easy** means not hard to do. Bob thinks it is **easy** to ride a bicycle.

## eat

Eat means to put food into your mouth and to chew it and swallow it. The giraffe **ate** leaves from the tree.

## echo

An **echo** is a sound that comes back again. If you shout at a mountain, you may hear **echoes** of your voice.

## edge

An **edge** is the line or place where something ends. The dime rolled off the **edge** of the table. I live near the edge of a lake.

## egg

An egg is a smooth round shell with a baby animal inside of it. Birds grow inside **eggs** until they are ready to hatch. Many people eat **eggs** from chickens for breakfast.

## eight

**Eight** is a number. **Eight** is one more than seven. **Eight** is written **8**. $7+1=8$.

## either

1. **Either** means one or the other. For her birthday Wendy wants either a puppy or a pony. She would be happy to get **either** of them.
2. **Either** means not also. Tom did not want to play soccer. He did not want to

play basketball **either**.

# elbow

The elbow is the part of the body where the arm bends. Susan sat with her elbows on the table.

# election

When people vote in an **election**, they are choosing someone to do something. In the United States there is an **election** for president every four years.

E

# electricity

Electricity is a kind of energy. It makes lamps light up. **Electricity** also makes refrigerators, computers, and many other things work.

# elephant

An elephant is the biggest and strongest animal that lives on land. It has thick gray skin and a long nose called a trunk.

## elevator

An elevator is a small room or cage that goes up and down in a building. Sometimes an **elevator** is on the outside of a building. **Elevators** are used to carry people or things from one floor to another.

## else

**1. Else** means other or different. What **else** would you like to play instead of baseball?

**2. Else** also means if not. Eat your breakfast or **else** you will be hungry before lunch.

## emerald

An emerald is a kind of jewel. **Emeralds** are green.

## emergency

Sometimes something important or dangerous happens very fast, and we must act immediately. This is called an emergency Police officers, doctors,

and firefighters help people with **emergencies**.

## empty

Empty means with nothing inside. Ray drank all his juice. He left his **empty** glass on the table.

## end

1. The **end** is the last part of something. The principal's office is at the **end** of the hall.
2. **End** also means to stop. The teacher **ended** the lesson just before lunch.

E

## enemy

1. An **enemy** is a person who hates someone else. The cruel ruler had many **enemies**.
2. An **enemy** is also a country that is at war with another country. The two countries that were **enemies** are now friends.

## energy

Energy makes things move

and makes machines work. Light, heat, and electricity are kinds of **energy**. When you run and jump, you use your own **energy**.

## engine

1. An engine is a machine that uses energy to make other machines work. The **engine** of a car makes it move.
2. An engine is also the first car of a train that pulls the other cars. An engineer drives the **engine** of a train.

## engineer

1. An **engineer** is a person who drives a train. **Engineers** work the engines in the front of trains.
2. An engineer is also someone who tells people how to make engines, machines, or buildings.

## English

**English** is the name of the language that is spoken in the United States and many

other countries.

# enjoy

To **enjoy** something means to like it. We all **enjoyed** our vacation this year. We especially enjoy vacations in the country.

# enough

**Enough** means that there is as much of something as you need. There was **enough** food for everyone at the picnic. I have saved **enough** money for a new bat.

# enter

Enter means to go into a place. You **enter** a room through a door. We **entered** the garden through a gate.

# envelope

An **envelope** is a folded piece of paper for holding things. People mail letters and cards in envelopes. I wrote address on the **envelope**.

## environment

The environment is the air, the water, the earth, and all the other things around us.

## equal

**Equal** means the same in amount or size. One dime is **equal** to ten pennies.

## erase

When you wipe off marks that were made with pencil or chalk, you **erase** them. Mark **erased** everything on the chalkboard.

## eraser

An **eraser** is something we use to make marks disappear. I need some pencils with **erasers** on them. You can take chalk marks off the chalkboard with an **eraser**.

## escalator

An escalator is a set of stairs that move up or down. Tom and his mother took an **escalator** to the third floor of the store.

## escape

**Escape** means to get away from something. The parrot **escaped** from its cage. People knew that a hurricane was coming and were able to **escape** without getting hurt.

## especially

**Especially** means more than anything else. Sarah likes to do a lot of things. She especially likes to act in plays.

## even

**1.** When something is **even**, it is flat or straight. The floor of the room is **even**. Let me see if your skirt is **even** all the way around.

**2. Even** can also mean the same height. The snow is so high that it is even with the top of the car.

**3.** An **even** number is a number that can be divided by two. The numbers 2, 4,

6, 8, and 10 are **even** numbers.

# evening
Evening is the time of day when it starts to get dark. **Evening** is between afternoon and night. We eat dinner at 6 o'clock in the **evening**.

# ever
**Ever** means at any time. Have you ever seen an elephant?

# every
**Every** means all or each one of a group. **Every** goat was eating grass. **Every** person in our class went on the trip.

# everybody
**Everybody** means every person. Everybody in my family likes to fish.

# everyone
**Everyone** means **everybody**. **Everyone** at the party had a

good time.

## everything
Everything means every thing. After the storm the snow covered everything.

## everywhere
Everywhere means in all places. Elizabeth looked everywhere in the house for her shoes.

E

## evil
To be evil is to try to hurt people. In the story an evil wizard used magic to turn the prince and princess into donkeys.

## excellent
Excellent means very, very good. Billy had an excellent idea.

## except
Except means that something or someone has been left out. Everyone except Joe liked the movie. I put everything in my backpack

**except** my lunch money and my keys.

# excited

When you are excited, you are very happy about something. It's hard for you to think about anything else. Sue was **excited** when she saw her new kitten. Billy was too **excited** about Christmas to go to sleep.

# exciting

To be exciting is to make people feel a lot of energy. We read an **exciting** story. Peter felt a little afraid of the fireworks, but he thought they were **exciting**, too.

# excuse

1. **Excuse** means to allow someone not to do something. The teacher **excused** Jill from the class to see the school nurse. I was **excused** from gym class because I hurt my knee.

2. **Excuse** also means to forgive. Please **excuse** me for leaving early.

3. An **excuse** tells why someone did or did not do something. Albert's cold and sore throat were his **excuse** for not being in school on Monday.

## exercise

1. **Exercise** is something done to help the body stay healthy and strong. Swimming is good exercise.

2. When people **exercise**, they use their muscles.

## exit

An exit is the way out of a room or a building. Our classroom has two **exits**.

## expand

To **expand** is to get bigger. A balloon **expands** when you blow air into it.

## expect

**Expect** means to look forward to something or to

think that something will happen. We are **expecting** 50 people to come to the family picnic on Sunday.

## expensive

Expensive means that something costs a lot of money. I bought the blue pen because it was less **expensive** than the red one.

## explain

To explain means to tell about something so that other people can under-stand it. Paul **explained** the rules of the game so we could all play it.

## explode

Explode means to break open suddenly and with a loud noise. When the fire-works exploded, there were bright and beautiful lights in the sky.

## explore

To **explore** means to go into a place you have never

been before to see what is there. Some people like to **explore** caves and jungles. People also **explore** under-water and other places.

## explorer

An explorer is a person who travels to places that are far away to discover new things. **Explorers** look on land, under water, and in space.

## explosion

When something explodes, it is called an explosion. An **explosion** of gas broke the windows in our building.

## extra

**Extra** means more than you need. I keep **extra** batteries for my radio.

## eye

An eye is the part of the body that you see with. People have two **eyes**. Most animals also have two **eyes**. The baby closed his **eyes** and went to sleep.

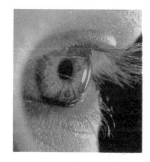

## face

1. The face is the front part of your head. Your eyes, nose, and mouth are on your **face**.
2. Face also means to turn your face toward something. When you **faced** the sun early this morning, you were **facing** east.

## fact

A **fact** is something that is true. It is a **fact** that there are 50 states in the United States.

## factory

A factory is a building where a lot of people work together to make something. Cars are made in factories.

# fair[1]

To be **fair** means to treat everyone the same. Breaking the rules is not **fair**.

# fair[2]

A **fair** is a place where people go to have fun. Some people show things there that they have grown or made. At most fairs there are machines to ride on and games to play.

# fairy

A **fairy** is a tiny, make-believe person who can make magical things happen. **Fairies** can fly. Carmen likes to read stories about fairies.

# fall

1. **Fall** means to come down from a place. Snow was falling from the sky.
2. When something or someone comes down suddenly to the floor or ground, it is called a **fall**.

Henry had a bad **fall** from his bicycle.

3. Fall is also a season of the year. **Fall** comes after summer and before winter. Many people call this season **fall** because it is the time when leaves **fall** from the trees. Another word for **fall** is autumn.

## fallen

**Fallen** is a form of **fall**. The temperature has **fallen**.

## false

When something is **false**, it is not true or correct. The idea that plants do not need light is **false**.

## family

1. A family is usually a mother, a father, and their children. Some **families** are made up of children and one of their parents. Grandparents, aunts, uncles, and cousins are also part of a **family**.

2. Animals, plants, or any

group of things that are alike in some way may also belong to **family**.

# famous

When people or things are **famous**, many people know about them. Thomas Edison became **famous** when he invented the electric light. New York City is **famous** for its skyscrapers. The Statue of Liberty is a famous statue.

# fancy

Fancy means prettier or better than usual. Claire wore a **fancy** new dress to the party.

# fantasy, phan-

**Fantasy** is anything that is not real. Books about people who live on other planets are **fantasies**. **Fantasy** is the opposite of **reality**.

# far

Far means at a distance.

The moon is **far** away from here. It takes a long time to get there.

# farm

A farm is a place where people raise animals and plants. Much of the food we eat comes from **farms**.

# farmer

A farmer is someone who works on a farm. **Farmers** start to work early in the morning.

# farther

**Farther** comes from the word **far**. Ray's paper airplane flew **farther** than Terry's did.

# fast

**Fast** means to go quickly. The children could not catch the bunny because it ran **faster** than they did.

# fat

Fat means big and round. Pigs and hippopotamuses

are **fat**.

# father

A father is a man who has at least one child. **Fathers** and mothers take care of their children.

# faucet

A faucet is something you use to turn water on and off. A sink and a bathtub both have **faucets**.

# fault

When you have done something wrong, it means that it is your **fault**. It was my **fault** that the baseball broke the window because I threw the ball.

# favor | favour

**1.** A **favor** is something kind that you do for someone else. I did Jane a **favor** by taking her books back to the library.
**2.** A **favor** is also something given to everyone at a party. All the children got

balloons    as    **favors**    at Leon's party.

# favorite

**Favorite** means to be liked best. Tony always wears his favorite cap.

# fear

1. **Fear** is what you feel when you are afraid. Many people have a **fear** of water, high places, or very small rooms.
2. To **fear** is to be afraid. Charlie **fears** the water because he doesn't know how to swim yet.

# feast

A **feast** is a large, special meal that is usually made for many guests. The table was piled high with food for the holiday **feast**.

# feather

A feather is something that grows from a bird's skin. Most birds are covered with them. **Feathers** are

light and soft.

# February

**February** is the second month of the year. It has 28 or 29 days. **February** comes after January and before March.

# fed

**Fed** is a form of **feed**. Diana **fed** her rabbit some lettuce this morning.

# feed

Feed means to give food to an animal or a person. Todd **feeds** his pet rabbit carrots. Hannah **fed** her baby brother. A container used for **feeding** is called a **feeder**. In the winter we put seeds in the **feeder** for the birds.

# feel

1. **Feel** means to learn about something because you touch it or it touches you. I can **feel** the rain on my face. I felt the kitten's

soft fur.
**2. Feel** also means to know how you are. Do you **feel** sick? Jimmy is **feeling** happy today because he is going to the circus.
**3. Feel** also means the way that something seems when you touch it. Albert likes the **feel** of cotton.

## feeling

A **feeling** is a way of knowing how you are. Feelings tell you when you are afraid, happy, excited, sad, tired, or angry. Sometimes my **feelings** get hurt when someone yells at me.

## feet

Feet means more than one foot. People have two **feet**. Dogs and cats have four **feet**. Arthur is over four **feet** tall.

## fell

Fell comes from the word **fall**. The streets are very wet because a lot of rain

fell last night.

## felt
Felt is a form of **feel**. Yesterday Barry **felt** too sick to go out. The cat's fur **felt** soft when I touched it.

## female
A female is a girl or a woman. Mothers and aunts are females. An animal may be a **female**, too. Our cat Matilda is a **female**.

## fence
A fence is made to keep two places apart. **Fences** can be made of wood, metal, or stone.

## fern
A **fern** is a plant with many thin leaves and no flowers. There are **ferns** growing in the forest.

## ferry
A ferry is a boat that carries people and cars across water. We took a **ferry** to

the island.

# festival

A festival is a special time to celebrate. Most **festivals** take place once a year and may last for one or more days. **Festivals** often have feasts, dances, and parades.

# fever

When you have a fever, your temperature is high and your body feels hot. If you have a **fever**, you are sick.

# few

Few means not many of something. I have a **few** pages left to read. We went on a trip for a **few** days.

# fiction

Fiction means stories that are written about people and things that are not real. The characters in **fiction** are make-believe and imagined by an author.

# field

1. A field is an area of land that has no trees. It is used for growing grass or food. We planted corn in this **field**.
2. A field is also an area of land where some games are played. Football is played on a football **field**.

# fierce

When something is fierce, it is wild and dangerous. A hungry lion is **fierce**. This storm is the **fiercest** storm I've ever seen.

# fight

1. To fight is to get mad at someone when you cannot agree. People who **fight** yell at each other and sometimes hit one another. Elizabeth was punished when she **fought** with other children at school.
2. When people are angry and yell at each other, we call that a **fight**. I had a **fight**

with my sister today.

## fill

Fill means to make something full. Blake **filled** his pail with sand.

## fin

A fin is one of the thin, flat parts of a fish. A fish has **fins** on both sides of its body. It uses its **fins** to swim and balance itself in water.

## finally

Finally means at the end. After riding for 3 hours in a bus, we **finally** reached our camp in the mountains.

## find

To **find** is to see where something is. Bob looks around his room for his shoes. He **finds** them under the bed. Yesterday he **found** three socks there.

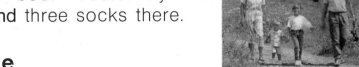

## fine

Fine means very good.

Today is a **fine** day for a walk. Helen was sick last week, but she feels fine now.

# finger

A finger is a part of your hand. You have five **fingers** on each hand. One of these **fingers** is your thumb. A fingernail is the hard part on the end of each **finger**.

# finish

**Finish** means to get to the end of something. I am almost **finished** with the letter I am writing.

# fire

A fire is the flame, heat, and light made by something that is burning. A **fire** burned down the old factory.

# fire engine

A fire engine is a truck that carries a ladder and other things to help firefighters put out a fire. Firefighters

ride to fires in **fire engines**.

## firefighter

A firefighter is a person whose job it is to put out fires. **Firefighters** help people escape from burning buildings. They use very long ladders to put out fires in tall buildings.

## firefly

A **firefly** is a small bug that gives off light. At night, **fireflies** look like very tiny lights going on and off.

## fireplace

A fireplace is an open place that is used for building fires indoors. A **fireplace** has a chimney to carry away the smoke. When we come home from skiing, my family and I like to build a fire in the **fireplace** to make ourselves warm.

## fireworks

Fireworks make loud noises

and bright shows of light. **Fireworks** are used at special times. Our town exploded **fireworks** at night to celebrate the Fourth of July.

# first

First means before all the others. The letter A is the **first** letter in the alphabet.

# first aid

Sometimes a person has an accident or gets sick suddenly. **First aid** is the help we give this person before the doctor comes.

# fish

1. A fish is an animal that lives in the water.
2. Fish also means to catch fish. The children like to **fish** close to shore. People who **fish** are called **fishermen**. Some **fishermen** catch fish and then sell them.

# fist

A fist is a hand that is

closed tight. Tom and Billy knocked on the door with their **fists**.

## fit

1. To **fit** means to be the right size. Carmen's favorite shirt **fitted** him last year, but now he is too big for it.
2. To **fit** is to put something into a small space. Charlie could not fit all of his toys into one box.

## five

Five is one more than four. Five is written **5**. $4+1=5$.

## fix

To fix is to make something work again when it is broken. The wheel of Paul's bicycle was bent, but he **fixed** it as good as new.

## flag

A flag is a piece of cloth with different colors on it. Some **flags** have pictures on them. Every country has its own **flag**. The **flag** of the

United States is red, white, and blue.

# flame

A flame is the bright, moving part of a fire. Flames are very hot.

# flash

To flash is to show a bright light for a short moment. A lighthouse **flashes** in the night and the fog so that sailors can find their way.

# flashlight

A flashlight is a small lamp that you can carry in your hand. People carry **flashlights** when they go out at night.

# flat

If something is **flat**, it has no bumps or holes. Walls and floors are **flat**.

# flavor | -vour

Flavor is the taste of food or drink. This dessert has an orange **flavor**.

# flew

Flew comes from the word fly². The birds **flew** away from the barking dog.

# float

1. Float means to stay on top of the water. Ray has a toy boat that **floats**. We went to the lake to **float** the sailboat.

2. **Float** also means to move slowly in the air. The baby let the balloon go, and it **floated** high above the house.

# flock

A flock is a group of sheep. Some dogs know how to keep the **flock** together.

# flood

A flood is what happens when water comes up over the edges of a river. **Floods** usually come after there is a lot of rain. Sometimes they happen in the spring when the snow melts.

# floor

1. A floor is the part of a room that you walk on or stand on. There is a blue rug on the **floor** of our bedroom.
2. A **floor** is also a part of a building. Tall buildings have many **floors**. Mom's office is on the second **floor**.

# flour

Flour comes from wheat. **Flour** is used to bake foods like bread and cake. We bought milk, eggs, margarine, and **flour** at the supermarket.

# flower

A flower is the part of a plant that makes seeds. **Flowers** grow in many different colors. Most **flowers** bloom when the weather is warm. Some flowers are nice to smell.

# flown

Flown comes from the word **fly**$^2$. The parrot has

**flown** out of its cage.

# flu

When someone has the **flu**, that person has a fever and feels sick. When Charlie had the **flu**, his head and stomach hurt, and he ached all over.

# fly[1]

A fly is an insect with two very thin wings. The **fly** we often see is called a **house-fly**.

# fly[2]

1. Fly means to move through the air with wings. Dale **flew** in an airplane to visit his grandmother. Butterflies were **flying** around the flowers.
2. **Fly** also means to float in the air. We like to **fly** our kites in the park on a windy day.

# fog

Fog is a cloud that is close to the ground. We couldn't

see the road because of the **fog**.

# fold

**Fold** means to bend. David showed me how to **fold** my tent and put it into a bag. Geoffrey and Robert **folded** the blanket and put it in the closet.

# follow

**1.** To follow is to go behind. Jane likes to **follow** her brother around. She **follows** him everywhere he goes.
**2.** To **follow** also means to come later. March **follows** February every year.

# food

Food is what we eat. Everything that lives needs **food** to grow and to stay alive. Bread, milk, and vegetables are important **foods**.

# foot

A foot is the part of the body at the end of a leg. George wears special shoes on his **feet** to play soccer.

# football

1. Football is a game played by two teams on a large field. Each team has 11 players. The players on one team throw the ball and run with it toward the other team's goal. The other team tries to stop them.

2. **Football** is also the name of the ball used in this game.

# footprint

A footprint is a mark made by a foot or shoe. The children made **footprints** on the floor with their dirty boots. Did you see the **footprints** the deer left in the snow?

# for

1. **For** tells why something is there. A carpenter has a box **for** his tools. I bought this book **for** you.
2. **For** also means toward. People can reach **for** the

sky, but they can't touch it. **3. For** tells how long something continues. We played baseball **for** two hours. I learn English **for** an hour every day.

# forest
A forest is a place with many trees. Many kinds of animals live in **forests**, but few people live there.

# forever
**Forever** means that something will never end. The boy and girl in the fairy tale wanted to stay young **forever**.

# forgave
Forgave comes from the word **forgive**. Henry **forgave** his brother for taking his bike without asking.

# forget
**Forget** means to not remember something. Jane was afraid she would **forget** my address, so she wrote it

down.

# forgive

**Forgive** means to stop being angry at someone. Anne's brother Jack tore her sweater and asked her to **forgive** him. Anne **forgave** her brother.

# forgot

**Forgot** is a form of **forget**. Margaret **forgot** to put her bicycle in the garage, so it got wet in the rain.

# forgotten

Forgotten is a form of **forget**. Joe forgets to bring his lunch to school with him sometimes. He has **forgotten** it twice this week.

# fork

A fork is a tool that we use for eating food. **Forks** have a handle at one end and two or more points at the other end. I eat meat and vegetables with a **fork**.

# form

1. The **form** of something is its shape or what it is like. Clouds have many different forms.

2. To **form** something is to give it a shape. Maria **forms** a piece of clay into a dog. She **formed** another piece of clay into a giraffe.
3. A **form** is also a kind of something. Ice is another **form** of water.

F

# forward

**Forward** means toward the front. Stuart stepped **forward** when his name was called.

# fossil

A fossil is what is left of an animal or plant that lived a long time ago. **Fossils** are found in rocks, earth, or clay. The bones and footprints of dinosaurs are **fossils**.

# fought

Fought comes from the

word **fight**. Dad said I should not have **fought** with my sister.

## found

**Found** is a form of **find**. Dick always finds something under his bed. Last night he **found** a baseball bat there.

## fountain

A fountain is a stream of water that shoots up into the air. Some **fountains** are pretty to look at. Other **fountains** are used for drinking.

## four

**Four** is one more than three. **Four** is written **4**. $3+1=4$.

## Fourth of July

The Fourth of July is an American holiday that celebrates the birthday of the United States. It is also called **Independence Day**.

# fox

A fox is a wild animal. Most **foxes** look like small, thin dogs, but they have thick fur and a big tail. They also have large ears that are pointed and a long nose.

# free

1. **Free** means that a person does not have to pay any money for something. The magic show in the park is free.
2. **Free** also means not held back or kept in. The cat was free to walk around.

# freeze

Freeze means to become solid when it is very cold. When water **freezes**, it changes into ice. We skated on the pond after it froze.

# fresh

1. When something is fresh, it has just been made, done, or gathered. We ate **fresh** tomatoes from

Johnny's garden. Our supermarket sells **fresh** fish. This bread was baked this morning and is very **fresh**.
2. **Fresh** also means not having salt. Water in rivers, lakes, and ponds is **fresh** water. Water in the ocean is salt water.

## Friday

**Friday** is a day of the week. **Friday** comes after Thursday and before Saturday.

## fried

**Fried** is a form of **fry**. Many people like to eat fried chicken.

## friend

A friend is someone you like very much and enjoy being with. Joyce and Kendrew are good **friends** and often play together. I made **friends** with my new neighbors.

## friendly

When people or animals

are **friendly**, they are nice to you. When I went traveling, I met **friendly** people in every place. Leon's dog is **friendlier** than mine.

# frighten

**Frighten** means to make a person or an animal afraid. I hope my Halloween costume will **frighten** the other children. The cat **frightened** the birds away.

# frog

A **frog** is a small animal. It has smooth skin, large eyes, and strong back legs. **Frogs** live near water and eat flies.

# from

**1. From** means where something started or when it began. Our family moved **from** the city to the country. Lewis is in school **from** 8 o'clock until 3 o'clock.

**2. From** also means having a person, place, or thing as a beginning. I got a letter

**from** my friend at camp.
3. **From** also means a distance away. Marie's school is 2 miles **from** her house.

# front

The front is the part that faces forward or comes first. Your chest is on the **front** of your body. There is an apple tree in **front** of Mark's house.

# frost

**Frost** is water on the ground that freezes into ice. You can see **frost** on windows on cold days.

# frown

1. A **frown** is the opposite of a **smile**. It can tell people that you are not happy, or that you are thinking.
2. To **frown** means to make a frown. Mike frowned because he did not know what to do.

# froze

**Froze** is a form of **freeze**.

Last night it was so cold that the lake **froze** solid.

## frozen

**Frozen** is a form of **freeze**. Ice is water that has frozen.

## fruit

A fruit is a part of a plant that holds the seeds. Apples, peaches, and oranges are kinds of **fruit**. We cut up **fruit** and made a salad.

F

## fry

To **fry** is to cook in very hot oil. On Thursdays Jim's father **fries** chicken for the family's supper.

## full

Full means that something cannot hold any more. Tom poured juice into his glass until it was **full**, and then he stopped.

## fun

Fun is something you like to do. Paul and his friends

sang songs and played games at his birthday party. Everybody had a lot of **fun**.

# funeral

A funeral is a time when people get together after someone dies. **Funerals** give people a chance to show how sad they feel and to share their feelings with friends and family.

# funny

1. To be **funny** means to make people laugh. Joe's uncle tells **funny** jokes.
2. **Funny** also means strange. Mary smelled a **funny** smell in the back yard.

# fur

Fur is soft, thick hair. Cats, dogs, squirrels, bears, and other animals are covered with **fur**. It keeps them warm in cold weather.

# furnace

A furnace is like a big

stove. **Furnaces** are used to heat houses and buildings. Our **furnace** keeps us warm in the winter.

## furniture

Tables and chairs and beds are different kinds of furniture. When we moved, all of our **furniture** was put into a truck.

## future

1. **Future** means the time that is to come. At the fair we saw a model of the car of the **future**.

2. **Future** also means happening in the time that is to come. My **future** plan is to become a writer.

## gallon

A **gallon** is an amount of a liquid. It is the same as four quarts. Milk and gasoline are sold by the **gallon**.

## gallop

Gallop means to run fast. When horses run as fast as they can, they are galloping.

## game

A **game** is a way to play or have fun. Some **games** are played with cards.
Others are played with a ball. Every **game** has rules or directions.

## garage

A garage is a building where cars and trucks are kept. Many houses have

garages. A big **garage** in the city can hold hundreds of cars.

# garbage

Food and other things that are thrown away are called garbage. After the picnic, we put our **garbage** in the **garbage** can.

# garden

A garden is a place where people grow flowers or vegetables. When our cousins visit, they always bring us fresh tomatoes from their **garden**.

# gas

1. A **gas** is something that is neither solid nor liquid and can expand to fill any container completely. Air and steam are **gases**.

2. Gas also means a group of gases that are mixed together to use for cooking or keeping houses warm. Our house has a **gas** stove and **gas** heat.

**3. Gas** is also a short way to say **gasoline**.

## gasoline, -lene

**Gasoline** is a kind of liquid that can burn. It is burned in cars and trucks to make them go.

## gate

A gate is a door in a fence. Some **gates** swing in, and others swing out. Enter the school only through the main **gate**.

## gather

To **gather** means to come together or put together. People often gather to listen to music. Peter **gathered** up all his toys and put them in one box.

## gave

**Gave** comes from the word **give**. Claire **gave** her grandfather a big hug. Mother **gave** Oliver vegetable soup and a peanut butter sandwich for lunch.

## geese

Geese means more than one goose. In the fall you can watch geese flying south for the winter.

## genius

A **genius** is a person who is extremely intelligent. That scientist was a **genius**.

## gentle

When you are **gentle**, you are very careful not to hurt someone or something.

## geography

When you study geography, you learn about different parts of the earth. **Geography** tells you where places are and what they are like.

## germ

A **germ** is a very tiny living thing that can make you sick. Germs are so small that you cannot see them without a microscope. I cover my mouth and nose when I sneeze so I won't

get **germs** on anyone.

## get

1. To **get** means to have something come to you. Diana **gets** a pair of socks from her grandmother every year.

2. To get also means to go and take. Helen was hungry, so she went and **got** an apple from the refrigerator.
3. To **get** can mean to become. Terry **gets** tired from running all the way home.
4. To **get** means to arrive. The day the bus broke down, everyone **got** to school late.
5. To **get** up means to stand up. Sometimes Todd falls down, but he always **gets** up again.

## ghost

A ghost is a kind of make-believe person. Some people believe that a dead person may come back as a **ghost**. The children dressed up as **ghosts** for Halloween.

# giant

**1. Giant** means much bigger than usual. A mouse as big as a horse would be a **giant** mouse.

**2.** A **giant** is a very tall person. Many children's stories have **giants** in them.

# gift

A gift is something special that one person gives to another person. These books were birthday **gifts** from my cousins. Another word for **gift** is present.

# gigantic

**Gigantic** means as big as a giant. We saw gigantic rocks when we got to the top of the mountain.

# giggle

**1.** When people **giggle**, they laugh in a silly way. We **giggled** when my little brother put his socks on his ears.

2. **Giggle** also means a short, silly laugh. When the clown slipped and fell, there were lots of **giggles** from the children in the audience.

# ginger

Ginger is the root of a plant. It is made into a powder and used in some foods. It is also made into candy and gingerbread.

# gingerbread

Gingerbread is a kind of cake. Part of its flavor comes from ginger.

# giraffe

A giraffe is a large animal. It has long legs and a very long neck. **Giraffes** are covered with brown spots. Their necks are long so that they can eat leaves from the tops of trees.

# girl

A girl is a female child. **Girls** grow up to be women.

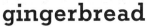

# give

To give is to let someone else have something. Albert **gives** his sister a present every year on her birthday.

# given

Given is a form of **give**. Tom has **given** away some of his toys.

# glad

Glad means happy. We went to a ball game yesterday. We were **glad** because the weather was good.

# glass

1. **Glass** is a hard material that you can see through. Windows are made of **glass**. **Glass** is easy to break if you are not careful.
2. A glass is a container that is used for drinking. It is usually made of glass or plastic. The baby is learning to drink from a **glass**. There are six **glasses** and six plates on the table.

**3.** Some people wear **glasses** in front of their eyes to help them see better. Dad wears his glasses to read the newspaper.

## globe

A globe is a ball with a map of the world on it. For our geography lesson we studied where the United States and other countries are on the **globe**.

## glove

**1.** A glove fits over your hand to protect it. It is made of cloth, wool, leather, or plastic. People usually wear **gloves** to keep their hands warm in cold weather.

**2.** Baseball players wear a special kind of **glove** to help them catch the ball. There are many kinds of baseball **gloves**.

## glue

**Glue** is a thick liquid. After it dries, **glue** holds things so they do not come apart.

## go

**1.** To go is to move from one place to another. Tom **goes** to school in the morning. He **went** to school late yesterday because the weather was bad.

**2.** To **go** also means to leave a place. It is very late, so we have to **go**.

**3.** To **go** can mean to lead somewhere. The road **goes** through the forest. It **goes** all the way to the city.

**4.** To **go** to sleep means to begin sleeping. Harry closed his eyes, but he could not **go** to sleep.

## goal

**1.** A **goal** is something that a person wants to have or tries to become. Tony's **goal** is to own a store. My **goal** is to be an actor.

**2.** A goal is a place in some games where the players try to put the ball.

## goat

A goat is an animal. Most goats have horns, and many goats have beards. Some goats are raised on farms for their milk. Others are wild animals and live in the mountains. A goat is a gentle animal.

## goggles

Goggles are a kind of glasses that are worn over the eyes to protect them. Some people wear goggles at work to protect their eyes from dust and flying dirt. Some people wear goggles under the water to look at the fish and the rocks.

## gold

1. Gold is a yellow metal that is found in the ground or in streams. People make jewelry and coins from gold. He wore a gold watch.
2. Gold is also the color of the metal. In fall, the leaves turn red and gold.

# goldfish

A goldfish is a kind of fish. **Goldfish** are usually small and orange. Many people keep **goldfish** in a bowl at home.

# gone

**Gone** comes from the word **go**. Stuart got to the playground so late that all his friends had already **gone** home.

# good

When something is **good**, it pleases you or other people. This peach tastes **good**. Richard is reading a **good** book about whales. My dog is **good** and doesn't jump on the furniture.

# good-bye

good-bye is what you say when you are going away. After school, I said **good-bye** to my teacher.

# gooey

To be **gooey** means to

stick to everything. Honey sticks to your peanut butter sandwich. It sticks to the spoon you use to get it out of the jar. It sticks to your fingers. Honey is very **gooey**.

## goose

A **goose** is a bird that can fly and swim. A goose is like a duck, but is much larger.

## gorilla

A gorilla is a large, very strong animal. It is a kind of ape with short legs and long arms. **Gorillas** are shy animals that eat fruits and vegetables.

## got

Got comes from the word **get**. The band got a new drummer. My mother **got** home from work at 6 o'clock.

## gotten

Gotten is a form of **get**.

Elizabeth has **gotten** more socks than she knows what to do with. I offered to get a banana for my sister, but she had already **gotten** one. Albert has never **gotten** too tired to play. Barry had already **gotten** up by seven o'clock.

## government

The **government** is a group of people who rule a country, state, or city. The **government** makes laws and makes sure that everyone obeys the laws. In the United States, the leader of the government is called the president.

## grab

Grab means to take hold of suddenly. The baby **grabbed** my hair.

## grade

1. A **grade** is a year of work in school. Most children in the same **grade** are almost the same age. What **grade**

are you in?

2. A **grade** is also a mark showing the quality of a student's work. Arthur got a **grade** of 90 on his test.

# grain

1. A grain is a seed of wheat, rice, or corn. Flour and cereal are made from many kinds of **grain**.

2. A **grain** also means a very tiny piece. **Grains** of sand are very, very small.

## gram, gramme

A **gram** is a small amount of weight. A penny weighs almost three **grams**.

# grandchild

Grandchild is a son or daughter's child. A **grand-child** is either a grand-daughter or grandson.

# grandfather

Your grandfather is your father's father or your mother's father. Sometimes a **grandfather** is called

grandpa.

# grandmother

Your **grandmother** is your father's mother or your mother's mother. Sometimes a **grandmother** is called grandma or nana. My **grandmother** was knitting my sweater out of wool.

# grandparent

Your grandparents are the parents of your mother and the parents of your father. Your grandfather and grandmother are your **grandparents**.

G

# grape

A grape is a kind of fruit. It is small and round. **Grapes** are usually larger than berries. **Grapes** are purple or green.

# grapefruit

A **grapefruit** is a round, yellow fruit. It is larger than an orange. Some **grapefruits** are pink inside.

### grass

Grass is a green plant that grows in lawns and fields. Many animals eat grass.

## grasshopper

A grasshopper is an insect. A grasshopper has long back legs that it uses for jumping. Grasshoppers also have wings, but most cannot fly.

## gray | grey

Gray is the color we get when we mix black and white. Some people have gray eyes or gray hair. Storm clouds are usually gray. She saw a big gray cat.

### great

1. Great means large or a lot. A great number of people voted in the election. He bought a great house.
2. Great also means excellent or very important. My sister wants to be a great singer when she grows up.

G

## green

Green is the color of growing grass and of leaves in the spring and summer. **Green** vegetables are good to eat. You can make the color **green** by mixing blue and yellow together. Pine trees stay **green** all year long.

## greenhouse

A greenhouse is a special building to grow plants in. **Greenhouses** usually have glass roofs. The air inside is always warm.

## grew

**Grew** comes from the word **grow**. The small plant **grew** quickly after I put it in the sun.

## grin

A **grin** is a big smile. Bob cut a grin on his pumpkin for Halloween. He likes to cut crooked **grins** because they look funny.

## grocery

1. A grocery is a store that sells food and other things. We bought eggs, milk, bread, and soap at the **grocery** store.

2. **Groceries** are the foods and other things that can be bought in a grocery store. We bought three bags of **groceries** on Saturday morning.

## ground

The **ground** is the earth. John fell on the **ground** and hurt his knee. Plants grow out of the ground.

## group

A **group** is three or more people or things that are together. A group of children played ball at the park on Saturday.

## grow

1. To **grow** is to get bigger. Animals and plants **grow** as they get older.
2. To **grow** up means to

become a woman or a man. When you **grow** up, you may be taller than your father.

## growl

**Growl** means to make a deep, angry sound in the throat. The dogs growled when someone knocked on the door.

## grown

**Grown** is a form of **grow**. That tree has **grown** so big that it covers the house.

## grown-up

A grown-up is a person who has finished growing. Your parents are **grown-ups**. Another word for **grown-up** is adult.

## guard

1. Guard means to keep safe from danger or to watch something closely. Our dog **guards** the house when we go away on vacation.

2. A **guard** is also a person who **guards** someone or something. The museum **guard** told us not to touch the paintings.

## guess
**Guess** means to try to think of an answer. Ellen tried to **guess** who was behind her.

## guest
A guest is someone who comes to visit. Mom's friend, Ms. Long, stayed for dinner yesterday. Ms. Long was our **guest**.

## guitar
A guitar is a musical instrument with six or more strings. A person plays the **guitar** by hitting or pulling the strings.

## gun
A gun is a weapon that is used to shoot something. I ran into my house and got a **gun**.

# gym

A **gym** is a big room or a building where people play games or do exercises. We play basketball in the gym.

G

# habit

A **habit** is something you do often. George has a **habit** of drinking a glass of water every night before he goes to bed. People can have good **habits** or bad **habits**.

# habitat

A **habitat** is the place where an animal or plant lives and grows. The desert is the habitat of the camel.

# had

Had comes from the word **have**. We use **had** when we talk about something that has already happened or that already belongs to you. Helen had an exercise class yesterday.

# hadn't

Hadn't is a short way to say had not. James wanted to watch television, but he hadn't done his homework yet.

# hair

Hair is what grows on your head. You also have tiny hairs on your arms and legs. Mark is having his hair cut for the first time.

# haircut

A haircut is when or how your hair is cut. Mary gets a haircut every month.

# half

A half is one of two pieces that are the same size. Al cut his sandwich in half. Both halves were the same.

# hall

A hall is a place inside a building. It leads from one room to another room or rooms. Some halls are

short and some are long
and narrow.

## Halloween

Halloween is a holiday. It
comes on the last day of
October. People wear cos-
tumes on **Halloween**. Then
they may go out to collect
candy in their neighbor-
hood.

## halves

Halves is the plural of **half**.
David will eat both **halves**
of the potato. A basketball
game is divided into two
halves.

## ham

Ham is a kind of meat. It
comes from pigs. You can
buy **hams** at the supermarket.

## hamburger

1. **Hamburger** is a kind of
beef. It has been cut up in
very small pieces so you
can make it into different
shapes.

**2.** A hamburger is a sandwich. It is made from hamburger and is flat and round. Albert likes to eat **hamburgers** on a roll with onions and ketchup.

# hammer

**1.** A hammer is a tool that is used for hitting nails. It has a heavy piece of metal at the top of a long handle. A **hammer** is also used to pull nails out of things. Please put the **hammer** back in the tool chest when you are finished with it.

**2. Hammer** also means to hit something with a hammer. The carpenter put two boards together and **hammered** a nail into each corner.

# hamster

A hamster is an animal that looks like a mouse. **Hamsters** have fat bodies and short tails. They are often kept as pets. We keep our **hamster** in a cage.

# hand

**1.** Your hand is the part of your arm from the wrist down. We use our **hands** to pick up things and hold them. What do you have in your **hand**?

**2.** A **hand** is also an arrow that points to a number on a clock, meter, or dial. The **hands** of the clock pointed to 1 o'clock.

**3.** When you **hand** something to someone, you give it to that person. Please **hand** me the margarine.

# handkerchief

A handkerchief is a piece of cloth. You put it over your nose when you sneeze. Many **handkerchiefs** are white.

# handle

A handle is the part of something that you hold when you lift that thing. George picked up the suitcase by the **handle**.

# hang

Hang means to be attached from above. Martin **hung** his new calendar on the wall.

# hanger

You hang clothes on a hanger. **Hangers** are often made of plastic or wood. There are a few empty **hangers** in my closet.

# Hanukkah

Hanukkah is a Jewish holiday celebrated in December. It lasts for eight days. People light a candle each night of **Hanukkah** until all the candles are lit. **Hanukkah** is sometimes spelled Chanukah.

# happen

Happen means to take place. If you listen to the story, you will hear what **happens** next. What **happened** in school today? A car accident **happened** in front of my house yesterday.

# happy

To be happy means to feel good. Susan smiled and laughed at the party because she was **happy**.

# harbor | harbour

A harbor is a safe place for boats near the shore. **Harbors** are on lakes, rivers, or oceans. We watched the fishing boats come into the harbor.

# hard

1. **Hard** means not soft. Rocks are **hard** and pillows are soft.
2. When something is **hard**, it needs a lot of work. This puzzle is very **hard** to do.

# hardly

**Hardly** means almost not at all. There were so many clouds that we **hardly** saw the sun all day.

# harvest

1. The time of the year when corn, wheat, fruits, and

other plants are picked and gathered is called **harvest**. Many people work during the **harvest**.

**2.** Harvest means to pick and gather corn, wheat, fruits, and other plants. The farmers used special machines to **harvest** the corn.

## has

**Has** is a form of **have**. Paul **has** two dollars. Billy **has** two dollars, too. Together they have four dollars.

## hat

A hat is something you wear on your head. **Hats** come in many different shapes and sizes.

## hatch

Hatch means to come from an egg. A hen **hatches** chickens.

## hate

**Hate** means to have very strong feelings against

someone or something. Harry **hates** scary movies.

# have

To **have** something means that it is with you. Tom **has** a book in his hand. Cats have soft fur.

# haven't

**Haven't** is a short way to say **have not**. Margaret and Elizabeth **haven't** seen their new baby brother yet.

# hawk

A hawk is a bird. It has a short, curved beak and strong claws. **Hawks** fly high in the sky and catch small animals on the ground.

# hay

Hay is a kind of tall grass that has been cut and dried. Horses and cows eat hay.

# he

1. **He** is a work for a boy or

a man or a male animal. Thomas said that he wants to go for a ride.

**2. He'd** means **he had** or **he would**. **He'd** never been to the circus before. **He'd** do it if **he** could.

**3. He'll** means **he will**. Richard says that **he'll** come to the picnic.

**4. He's** means **he is** or **he has**. Blake lives near me. **He's** my neighbor. **He's** been my friend for two months.

# head

**1.** The head is the part of the body above the neck. Eyes, ears, nose, and mouth are all parts of the **head**. The brain is inside the **head**. Richard is a **head** taller than Billy.

**2. Head** also means the front part of something. Margaret is at the **head** of the line.

# heal

Heal means to become well

again. When a cut or a broken bone gets better, it
**heals**. The cut on my arm
**healed** quickly.

## healthy

Healthy means not sick.
Sue eats good food so that
she will stay **healthy**.

## hear

To **hear** is to take in sounds
with your ears. Rabbits hear
well because of their large
ears.

## heard

Heard is a form of **hear**.
Dick **heard** a loud noise in
the other room.

## hearing aid

A **hearing aid** is something
worn in the ear to help
someone hear better. I
think my **hearing aid** needs
a new battery.

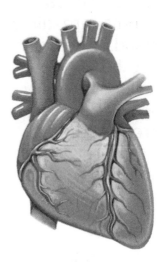

## heart

1. The heart is a part of the
body. It is in the chest and

sends blood to all parts of the body.

**2.** A heart is also a shape that looks like this : ♥. **Hearts** are often red, and sometimes they mean "I love you."

# heat

**1. Heat** means being warm or hot. The **heat** in an oven will bake bread.

**2.** When you **heat** something, it becomes warm or hot. Mary **heated** the milk before giving it to the baby.

# heavy

**1.** When something is heavy, it is hard to lift. The bag of groceries was too **heavy** for Bob to lift. This large suitcase is **heavier** than that small one.

**2. Heavy** also means thick. The children used **heavy** paper to make covers for their books.

# heel

**1.** The heel is a part of the

body. It is the back part of the foot. When you put your feet into shoes, your **heels** go in last.

**2.** The heel is a part of a shoe. It holds up the back of your foot. Some shoes have high **heels**.

# height

**Height** is how far something is from the ground. Tom's **height** is 3 feet.

# held

**Held** comes from the word **hold**. Dad **held** the twins until they were asleep.

# helicopter

A helicopter is a machine that can fly in the air. **Helicopters** can fly straight up and down and land in very small spaces.

# hello

We say hello when we see someone we know or when we answer the telephone.

# helmet

A helmet is a hard hat that is worn to protect the head. Soldiers, astronauts, and football players wear **helmets**.

# help

**Help** means to do something for someone else. We **helped** Dad clean the garage. A person or thing that does something for someone else is called a helper. My teacher asked for a **helper** to hold the cups while she poured the juice.

# hen

A hen is a female chicken. A **hen** can lay eggs.

# her

Her is a word for a girl or a woman. Sue's friend came to visit **her. Her** also means belonging to a girl or a woman. Sue left **her** umbrella in the hall.

## herd

A **herd** is a group of animals that live or travel together. **Herds** of cattle ate the grass until the ground was almost bare.

## here

**Here** means where you are right now. Please bring the cup **here**. I'm **here** in the kitchen.

## hero

A **hero** is someone we think of as special because of the good or brave things that person has done.

## heroine

A **heroine** is a woman or girl we think of as special because of the good or brave things she has done.

## hers

**Hers** means belonging to her. Billy has his own room, and his sister has **hers**. Everything in her room is **hers**.

# herself

**Herself** means her and nobody else. Helen looked at herself in the mirror. Then she put on her shoes. Nobody helped her. She put them on by **herself**.

# hid

**Hid** is a form of **hide**. Bob told his sister to hide so that he could look for her. She **hid** behind the house.

# hidden

**Hidden** is a form of **hide**. I found my shoe **hidden** behind the bed.

H

# hide

To hide something is to put it where nobody will see it. Sometimes Dick likes to **hide** himself, then jump out and surprise people.

# high

1. **High** means far up from the ground. That fish can jump **high** out of the water.

The eagle flew higher and higher into the clouds. That is one of the **highest** mountains in the United States.
**2. High** also means a large amount. I don't want to pay such a **high** price for a new car.

# hill

A hill is a high area of land. A **hill** is not as high as a mountain. We walked our bicycles up the **hill**.

# him

**Him** is a word for a boy or a man. Mr. John asked me to help **him** train his dog.

# himself

**Himself** means him and nobody else. Mark had a mask on his face. When he looked at **himself** in the mirror, he scared **himself**.

# hippopotamus

A hippopotamus is a huge animal with a very large mouth. It has short legs and thick skin with no hair on it. **Hippopotamuses** spend a lot of time in the water. **Hippo** is a short word for **hippopotamus**.

# his

**His** means belonging to a boy or a man. This is my piece of pizza and that one is **his**. I know his father well. Jack's baseball glove has **his** name written on it.

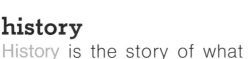

# history

History is the story of what has happened in the past. This year in school we are studying the **history** of our city. That old house has an interesting **history**.

# hit

To hit is to touch something very hard. Baseball players try to **hit** the ball with a bat. An apple fell from the tree and **hit** the ground. I **hit** my head against the door.

H

## hive

A **hive** is a box or house for bees to live in.

## hobby

A **hobby** is something that people do just for fun. The Smiths' hobbies are collecting stamps, fishing, and swimming. Peter's **hobby** is doing puzzles.

## hockey

1. Hockey is a game played on ice. There are two teams, and each team has six players. The players wear ice skates and use long sticks to try to get a small rubber disk into the other team's goal.
2. Another kind of **hockey** is played on a large field. For this game, each team has 11 players. The players use shorter sticks and a ball instead of a rubber disk.

## hog

A **hog** is a grown pig. **Hogs**

are raised for their meat. **Hogs** have short legs but can run as fast as most people.

# hold

**1. Hold** means to take something in your hands or arms. Scott asked Mike to **hold** his package while he opened the door. Sue **held** her mother's hand when crossing the street.

**2. Hold** also means to have space for something. The school bus holds 50 people. This suitcase is much too small to **hold** all of your toys and all of your clothes.

H

# hole

A **hole** is an empty or open place in something. Last fall the squirrels dug **holes** in the ground and put nuts in them.

# holiday

A holiday is a special day when we remember an important thing or a famous person. Thanks-giving, Christmas, and Hanukkah are **holidays**.

## hollow

**Hollow** means with an empty space inside. Basketballs are **hollow**. Some animals live in **hollow** trees.

## home

A home is a place where people or animals live. Most people have **homes** in houses or apartments.

## homework

Homework is work that a teacher asks students to do at home. Our teacher asked us to write a story for **homework**.

## honest

When you are **honest**, you tell the truth. **Honest** people do not tell lies or take things that do not belong to them.

# honey

Honey is a sweet liquid that is made by bees. It is yellow and thick. Joe likes to eat **honey** on toast.

# hook

A **hook** is a curved piece of metal. Some hooks have points on the end and are used to catch fish. Other **hooks** are used to hang up clothes.

# hop

**Hop** means to make a short jump on one foot. You can also **hop** on both feet. Elizabeth can **hop** for a long time.

# hope

**Hope** means to want something very much. We **hope** that tomorrow is a sunny day so that we can go to the beach.

# horn

**1.** A horn is part of an animal's body. Bulls and goats

have two **horns** on their heads.

2. A horn is also an instrument. Alice blows into her **horn** to make music.

3. A **horn** can be something that makes a loud noise in the air. We heard the truck's **horn** blow two times.

# horse

A horse is a large animal with four legs and a long tail. Before there were cars, people rode **horses** to get from one place to another. Now people ride **horses** for fun.

# horseshoe

A horseshoe is a piece of iron that is shaped like a U. Horses wear **horseshoes** to protect their feet.

# hose

A hose is a tube made of rubber or cloth. Firefighters use **hoses** to put water on fires.

# hospital

A **hospital** is a place where people who are sick or hurt go to get better. Doctors and nurses work in **hospitals**. Many babies are born in hospitals.

# hot

**Hot** means very, very warm. When something is **hot**, it can burn you when you touch or taste it. Dick burned his hand when he touched the **hot** stove.

# hot dog

A hot dog is meat that is rolled into a long, thin shape and cooked. There were **hot dogs** for sale at the baseball game.

# hotel

A hotel is a big building with many rooms. People who are away from home stay in them. Big cities have many **hotels**, because many people visit the city.

# hour

An **hour** is an amount of time. There are 24 **hours** in one day. One **hour** has 60 minutes in it.

# house

A house is a building where people live. Usually only one or two families live in a **house**. There are many **houses** on our street.

# how

1. **How** is a word that you use to ask a question. **How** cold is it outside?
2. We also use **how** when we talk about the way to do something. I don't know **how** to drive a car.

# huddle

**Huddle** means to get close together into a small group. The baby chickens **huddled** under their mother's wing.

# hug

To hug is to put your arms

around something and hold it tight. Many people **hug** each other to show that they are glad to see each other.

# huge

**Huge** means very, very big. An elephant is a huge animal.

# hum

When you **hum**, you make a sound with your lips closed and do not say words. When I don't know the words to a song, I **hum** the part I don't know.

# human

**Human** means about people. A **human** body is the body of a person. Girls and boys and men and women are **human**.

# hump

A **hump** is a round bump. Some camels have two humps on their backs and some have one.

# hundred

A hundred is a number. It is written **100**. It takes ten tens to make one **hundred**. One **hundred** is ten times ten.

# hung

**Hung** comes from the word **hang**. The monkey **hung** by its tail.

# hungry

To be **hungry** is to want to eat. Marie has not eaten yet. Her stomach is empty. Marie is very **hungry**.

# hunt

**Hunt** means to chase something and try to catch it. Many animals **hunt** for food at night. Some people **hunt** also. A person who **hunts** is called a hunter.

# hurricane

A **hurricane** is a storm with very strong winds and a large amount of rain. **Hurricanes** can cause huge waves in the ocean that flood the land. Some **hurricanes** are strong enough to make trees fall.

## hurry

To **hurry** is to try to go quickly. When you are late, you have to **hurry**.

## hurt

When people hurt, they feel pain. My stomach **hurts**. Andrew fell on the floor and **hurt** his arm.

## husband

A husband is a married man. He is the **husband** of the woman he married. **Husbands** and wives are married to each other.

## hut

A **hut** is a very simple, small house. **Huts** are usually built in places where the weather is warm. Some huts are made of grass.

# I

I is a word you use when you speak about yourself. This coat belongs to me. I wear it during the winter to keep me warm.

## ice

Ice is water that has frozen. It is hard and cold. Margaret skates on the **ice** that covers the pond. Bill put ice in his drink to keep it cold.

## iceberg

An **iceberg** is a huge piece of ice that floats in the ocean.

## ice cream

Ice cream is a sweet food that is frozen. It is made

from cream and sugar.

## ice skate

**1.** An **ice skate** is a kind of boot with a long, sharp piece of metal on the bottom.

**2.** When people ice-skate, they wear ice skates and move on ice. Al **ice-skates** backward.

## idea

An **idea** is something that you think of. We all had different **ideas** about what to name our pet turtle.

## if

**If** asks what might happen. Jack may decide to go to the store, or he may not. **If** he goes, he will buy some bread. **If** it rains today, we will need to use our umbrellas.

## igloo, iglu

An igloo is a kind of house. It is made of blocks of snow. People who live in

cold places where there are no trees sometimes build **igloos**.

# ill

Ill means sick. Richard is too **ill** to go outside today.

# I'll

I'll is a short way to say I **will**. After I finish this book, I'll be glad to let you borrow it.

# I'm

I'm is a short way to say I **am**. I'm almost as tall as my brother.

# imagine

When you **imagine** something, you have a picture of it in your mind. When the snow is falling outside her window, Sarah likes to **imagine** that it is summer. She imagines herself at the beach in the warm sun.

# imitate

Imitate means to do the

same thing that someone else is doing. When Albert touched his nose, his baby sister Anne **imitated** him by touching her nose.

# immediately

**Immediately** means now. If we leave **immediately**, we can get to the airport before our plane leaves.

# important

When something is **important**, it means that you should pay attention to it. It is important for you to look both ways before you cross the street.

# impossible

**Impossible** means that something cannot be. It is **impossible** for the sun to come up in the west.

# in

1. **In** means toward the middle. I put the bird **in** its cage. The hippopotamus is standing in the water.

2. **In** can also mean during a time. The leaves change colors **in** the fall. I'll finish my homework **in** an hour.

# inch

An **inch** is an amount of length. There are twelve **inches** in one foot. He is five feet four **inches** tall.

# incubator

An **incubator** is a special kind of box. It has heat and air to keep new babies warm. We saw the baby chickens hatch in the **incubator** at the farm.

# independence

**Independence** means not to be ruled by another country. The United States celebrates its **independence** on the Fourth of July.

# indoor

**Indoor** means inside a building. Our school has an **indoor** pool. Ping-pong is an **indoor** game.

## indoors

When you go into a build-ing, you are **indoors**. The children went **indoors** when it began to rain.

## information

Information is a group of facts that help you learn something. A dictionary gives you **information** on how words are spelled and what they mean.

## injure

To **injure** means to hurt. Two people were **injured** in the accident.

## ink

Ink is a liquid that people write with. When you write with a pen, **ink** comes out onto the paper. Many pens have blue or black **ink**, but **ink** can also be other colors.

## insect

An insect is a very small animal that has six legs.

Most **insects** have wings. Flies, grasshoppers, and ants are **insects**.

# inside

1. Inside means the side of something that is in. The **inside** of our car is green.
2. **Inside** can also mean in or indoors. There is nothing **inside**.

# instant

An **instant** is a very short amount of time. **Instants** are almost too short to notice. Lightning only flashes for an instant.

# instead

**Instead** means that something is done in place of something else. I think I'll wear my red sneakers today **instead** of my brown shoes.

# instrument

1. An instrument is a tool that helps you do something. Pens are **instruments**

for writing. Forks are **instruments** for eating.

**2.** Another kind of instrument can make music. A piano and a violin are musical **instruments**.

## interest

An **interest** is something you like to learn more about. Anne has a great **interest** in drawing. She has many other **interests**, too.

## interested

To be **interested** in something means to be curious about it. Barry is very interested in music.

## interesting

If something is **interesting** to you, you like to do it or pay attention to it. We thought the science museum was very **interesting**.

## into

**1. Into** tells where something goes. My father drives

the car **into** the garage.

**2. Into** also tells what something becomes when it changes. Caterpillars change into moths and butterflies.

## invent

To **invent** means to make something that nobody has ever made before. My uncle has **invented** many useful machines.

## invention

An **invention** is something that is made or thought of for the first time. One of the earliest inventions was the wheel.

## invisible

If something is **invisible**, it cannot be seen. In the story, nobody could see the good fairy because she was **invisible**.

## invitation

When you ask people to go somewhere, you are giving

them an **invitation**. Invitations are often written on cards.

## invite

To **invite** is to ask someone to come and visit you. Mary **invited** three of her friends for dinner.

## iron

1. Iron is a hard, strong metal. The bars of the fence were made of **iron**.

2. An iron is something you use to make your clothes smooth. It is flat on the bottom and gets hot.

## is

Is comes from the word **be**. Bill's coat **is** blue and Susan's **is** red. **Is** it going to rain?

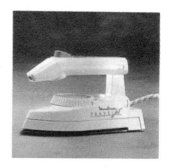

## island

An island is land that has water all around it. Some **islands** are tiny. Other **islands** are big enough to have people living on them.

The state of Hawaii is made up of **islands**.

## isn't

Isn't is a short way to say **is not**. "Is Helen home?" "No, she **isn't**."

## it

**It** is a word for what you are talking about. My friend threw the ball and I caught it.

## itch

When you itch, you feel that your skin is being tickled or stung and you want to scratch it. The mosquito bite on my arm **itches** a lot.

## its

**Its** means that something belongs to the animal or thing you are talking about. The cat licked **its** paws.

## it's

1. **It's** means **it is**. It's very hot in here.
2. **It's** also means **it has**.

It's been three days since my baby sister came home.

## itself

Itself means it and nothing else. The story **itself** isn't interesting at all.

## I've

I've is a short way to say **I have**. I would like to go to the circus. I've never been to one before.

## jacket

A jacket is a short, light coat. **Jackets** are good for spring and fall when the weather is cool.

## jail, gaol

A **jail** is a place where people who do not obey laws have to stay. The police officer took the burglar to **jail**.

## jam

Jam is a kind of food. It is made from fruit and sugar boiled together. **Jams** are thick and sweet.

## January

**January** is the first month of the year. It has 31 days. **January** comes after

December and before February.

## jar

A **jar** is used to hold things. **Jars** are often made out of glass and have covers that fit tight. The teacher keeps our paints in **jars**.

## jaw

A jaw is a part of the body. It is a bone at the bottom of your face. When you speak, your **jaw** moves.

## jealous

When you feel **jealous**, you are unhappy because someone has something that you do not have. Ray was **jealous** because his friend Charlie had a new baseball glove.

## jeans

Jeans are pants made from a stong cotton cloth. When the children paint or play with clay, they wear old **jeans**.

# jelly

Jelly is a kind of food. It is made from fruit juice and sugar boiled together. Jellies can be made from many kinds of fruit.

# jellyfish

A jellyfish is an animal. It has a soft body and floats in the ocean. Jellyfish can hurt you if they touch you.

# jet

A jet is a kind of airplane. Its engines do not use propellers. Jets fly faster than other planes.

# jewel

A jewel is a kind of stone. Light can pass through it. Diamonds, emeralds, and rubies are jewels. People often pay a lot of money for jewels.

# jewelry | -ellery

Rings, bracelets, and necklaces are kinds of jewelry.

# job

1. A **job** is something that needs to be done. Peter's **job** is to wash the dog. Tom has the **job** of setting the table for dinner.

2. A **job** is also something a person does to earn money. Mom's job is teaching.

# jog

To jog is to run. People who **jog** do not try to run fast. They jog for exercise, to make themselves healthy.

# join

1. **Join** means to put things together. I **joined** my toy railroad cars to make a train.

2. **Join** also means to become a part of something. Diana wants to join the swimming club.

# joke

1. A **joke** is a story that

makes people laugh. When my sister broke her leg, I told her **jokes** to make her feel more cheerful.

2. A **joke** is also a trick that you play on someone. We hid Dad's slippers as a **joke**.

# jolly

To be jolly means to laugh and smile a lot. Helen's father was very **jolly** at his birthday party.

# journal

A journal is a book that you write in about things you have done or thought.

# journey

A journey is a long trip. Carlos was very excited about his **journey** across the ocean.

# joy

When you feel **joy**, you are very happy. Mary felt **joy** when she took her new puppy home from the pet

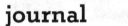

store.

# judge

1. A **judge** is a person who decides things. When people cannot agree, they sometimes go to a **judge** who helps to decide who is right.

2. To **judge** is to decide. Betty and Ray asked their father to **judge** who drew the better picture.

# juggle

Juggle means to throw two or more things into the air one after the other and catch them very quickly. When you **juggle**, you are throwing and catching things at the same time. I can **juggle** three balls at once without dropping any.

# juice

Juice is a liquid that you get from fruits or vegetables. Claire likes tomato **juice**. Mike's favorite fruit **juice** is apple **juice**.

# July

**July** is a month of the year. It has 31 days. **July** comes after June and before August.

# jump

Jump means to go up into the air using your foot and leg muscles. Scott had to **jump** to catch the ball. The deer **jumped** over the fence and ran into the woods. Billy **jumped** over the rope while the other children turned it.

# June

**June** is a month of the year. It has 30 days. **June** comes after May and before July.

# jungle

A jungle is a place where many trees and plants grow. It is hot and rains a lot in a **jungle**. Monkeys, snakes, parrots, and mosquitoes live in the **jungle**.

J

# junk

Junk is something that people do not want. Old cars and broken furniture are junk.

# just

1. **Just** means only. Wendy thought she heard a monster outside the window, but it was **just** a squirrel.

2. **Just** also means a little before. Walter's birthday was yesterday. He has **just** turned seven.

3. **Just** can also mean the right amount. The kite George wanted cost two dollars. He had two dollars in his pocket. George had **just** enough to buy the kite.

J

## kangaroo

A kangaroo is a large animal. **Kangaroos** move very fast when they jump on their strong back legs. **Kangaroo** mothers carry their babies in a pocket in front of their stomachs.

## keep

1. **Keep** means to have something. Wilbur's mother let him keep the puppy he found.

K

2. **Keep** also means to stay the same way. Mr. Terry asked the children to **keep** quiet during the movie.

## kept

kept is a form of **keep**. Al **kept** the book for three

weeks.

## ketchup

**Ketchup** is a kind of food. It is a thick, red liquid that is made from tomatoes.

## kettle

A kettle is a metal pot for boiling water. You can pour the water from a **kettle** without taking off the cover. Our **kettle** whistles when the water begins to boil.

## key

1. A key is something that is used to open or close a lock. Each lock has a special **key** that fits into it. This **key** opens the front door.
2. A **key** is also the part of a machine or musical instrument that is pressed down to make it work. A computer has **keys** for letters and numbers. A piano has black and white **keys**.

## keyboard

A **keyboard** is a set or row of keys. Pianos and computers have keyboards.

## keyhole

A **keyhole** is the hole in a lock. You put the key into the **keyhole** and turn it to open the lock.

## kick

Kick means to hit something with your foot. Mike **kicked** the can.

## kid

1. A **kid** is a baby goat.
2. A kid is also a child. Uncle Kelly asked, "Do you **kids** want to play baseball?"

## kill

Kill means to make something die. The cat **killed** the mouse.

## kilometer | -tre

A **kilometer** is an amount of

length. One **kilometer** is a thousand meters. A **kilometer** is a little more than half a mile.

# kind¹

Kind means a form of something. Lettuce is one **kind** of vegetable. Carrots and potatoes are other **kinds**.

# kind²

To be kind is to try to help others. Sarah tries to be **kind** to people who have no home.

# kindergarten

Kindergarten is a grade in school. It comes before the first grade. In **kindergarten** we play games, build with blocks, use clay and paints, and listen to stories. We also sing and play instruments, care for pets, look at picture books, and make our own books.

# king

A **king** is a man who rules a country. I like the story about a **king** and a queen who live in a castle.

# kingdom

A kingdom is a country that is ruled by a king or a queen. Mrs. Brown read the class a fairy tale about a magical **kingdom**.

# kiss

Kiss means to touch with your lips. We **kiss** people to show we love them. Claire and Tony always **kiss** their parents before going to sleep each night.

**K**

# kit

A **kit** is a set of things that you have to put together. Model cars and airplanes often come in **kits**.

# kitchen

A kitchen is a room where

people cook food and make meals. We have a stove, a refrigerator, a sink, and a table and chairs in our **kitchen**. Betty and Martin's family eats in the **kitchen**.

# kite

A kite is a toy that you fly in the air at the end of a long string. **Kites** are made of sticks that are covered with paper or plastic or cloth. They sometimes have pictures on them.

# kitten

A kitten is a young cat. Most people like **kittens**.

# knee

The **knee** is the part of the body where the leg bends. Your **knee** is in the middle of your leg.

# kneel

Kneel means to get down on your knees. You can also **kneel** on one knee. Mr.

MacMillan **kneels** when he works in the garden.

## knew

**Knew** is a form of **know**. Anne **knew** how to write her name when she was four years old.

## knife

A knife is a kind of tool. It has a handle and a piece of metal with a sharp edge. Paul used a **knife** to cut an apple.

## knight

Long ago, a knight was a soldier for a king or queen. **Knights** were brave and honest and protected people who needed help. They wore armor and rode horses.

## knit

When you **knit**, you use long needles and wool to make scarves, sweaters, other clothes, and cloth. Maria **knitted** a red wool sweater for her doll.

## knives

**Knives** means more than one knife. **Knives** come in many different sizes and shapes.

## knob

A knob is a round handle for opening a door or a drawer. When Sue tried to open the drawer, the **knob** came off in her hand. A **knob** is also used on a radio, television, or other machine. If you turn that **knob** to the right, the radio will get louder.

## knock

1. Knock means to hit something. When you **knock** on a door, you hit it with your fist to make a sound. On Halloween, we **knocked** on the doors of our neighbors to ask for treats. The branch of the tree was **knocking** against the window during the

**K**

storm.

**2. Knock** also means to push and make something fall. The puppy **knocked** the lamp off the table.

# knot

A knot is a place where two things are tied together. People make **knots** in string, rope, and ribbon.

# know

When you know something, it means that you are very sure about it. Dick **knows** everyone who lives on his street. By the end of the summer, all the children at camp **knew** how to swim.

# known

**Known** is a form of **know**. Al and Wendy have **known** each other for two years.

## ladder

A ladder is used to climb up and down. It is made of wood, metal, or rope. Firefighters use **ladders** to work in tall buildings.

## lady

A lady is a woman. There is a **lady** on the telephone who wants to speak with Mom.

## laid

**Laid** comes from the word lay[1]. The turtle **laid** its eggs in the sand.

## lain

**Lain** is a form lie[2]. Oliver likes to lie on his bed. When he has **lain** there for a few minutes, he usually falls asleep.

## lake

A lake is water that has land all around it. The water in most **lakes** has no salt. We swim in the **lake** during the summer.

## lamb

A lamb is a young sheep. Wool from **lambs** is very soft.

## lamp

A **lamp** is used to make dark places light. Most **lamps** use electricity to make light.

## land

1. Land is the part of the world that is not water. People live on **land**.
2. A **land** is a country. You can collect stamps from many different **lands**.
3. The **land** is the earth or ground that someone uses. The farmers planted potatoes on their **land**.

L

**4.** To land is to come down to the ground. Blake saw the airplane when it **landed** in a field.

# language

Language is what people use when they speak or write to each other. Some people can speak several **languages**.

# lap

Your lap is the top of your legs when you are sitting down. When you stand up, your **lap** disappears. Our cat likes to sit in my **lap**.

# large

Large means big. Things that are **large** take up a lot of space. Elephants and whales are large animals.

# last[1]

**1.** When something is **last**, it is at the end. What is the **last** word in this dictionary? Saturday is the **last** day of the week.

2. **Last** also means a time before the time now. I learned to ski last winter. **Last** night, Billy saw a movie.

## last[2]

**Last** means to stay the way it is. The milk will **last** in the refrigerator for a few days. Snow on the mountain lasted until spring.

## late

When you come **late**, you come after the time you were supposed to come. Albert was **late** for school today. Bob was **later** than Albert. Carlos came last. He was **latest** of all.

## later

Later means after more time. We can't come now, but we will see you **later**.

## laugh

To laugh is to make a sound that shows that something is funny. Barry always **laughs** when he hears a good joke.

# launch

**Launch** means to start something and send it forward.

# laundry

**Laundry** is dirty clothes that are ready to be washed. Laundry is also clean clothes that have just been washed.

# law

A **law** is a rule made by the government of a city, state, or country. **Laws** help to keep people safe.

# lawn

A lawn is an area of grass around a house or building. Charlie cuts the **lawn** every other Saturday.

# lay[1]

1. **Lay** means to put something down. Please **lay** that book on the table.

2. Lay also means to make an egg. The hen **laid** two eggs.

# lay²
Lay comes from the word lie². We **lay** on the grass watching the clouds.

# lazy
To be **lazy** is to want to do nothing. Yesterday was so nice that Jack did not want to cut the grass. He felt too **lazy** to work.

# lead¹
When **lead** sounds like seed, **lead** means to show the way or to go first. Joe is **leading** in the race. The band led the parade.

# lead²
When **lead** sounds like bed, lead means the black part of a pencil that makes a mark.

# leader
A **leader** shows people the

way or goes first. The **leader** of the United States is called the president.

# leaf

A leaf is part of a plant. Many trees and flowers have green **leaves**. In the fall some **leaves** turn different colors.

# leak

When something **leaks**, what is inside comes out slowly through a small hole or a crack. The air has been **leaking** out of the tire.

# learn

To learn is to get to know something. Both young people and old people can always **learn** new things.

# leash

A leash is a kind of rope or chain that you tie to a dog's collar. Tony tied the **leash** to a tree so that his dog wouldn't run away.

L

# least

**Least** means less than any other. A car makes some noise. A bicycle makes less noise. Walking makes the **least** noise of all.

# leather

Leather is a material made from the skins of animals. It is used to make shoes, gloves, and other things. Ray's sneakers are made of **leather**.

# leave

1. To leave is to go away. We have to **leave** at five o'clock.
2. To **leave** also means to put something somewhere and then go away. You can **leave** your books on the chair until after dinner.

# leaves

**Leaves** comes from the word **leaf**.    The leaves of the tree turned bright red in the fall.

# led

Led is a form of **lead**[1]. Anne **led** her sister by the hand.

# left[1]

Your body has a **left** side and a right side. When you look at the face of a clock, the 9 is on the **left** side. When you read, you start at the **left** side of the page. My sister writes with her **left** hand.

# left[2]

**Left** comes from the word **leave**. We **left** our cat with a friend when our family went on vacation.

# leg

1. A leg is a part of the body. Animals and people walk on their **legs**.
2. A leg is also a piece that holds something up. Most furniture has **legs**.

# lemon

A lemon is a kind of fruit. It

is yellow. **Lemons** have a sour taste.

# length

The **length** of something is how long it is from one end to the other. The length of the swimming pool is 50 feet. The **length** of my bed is 6 feet.

# leopard

A leopard is a large, wild animal. It is a kind of cat with dark yellow fur and black spots.

# less

**Less** means not as much as something else. You have 7 cents, and I have 9 cents. You have **less** money than I do. If we take the bus, it will take **less** time than if we walk. This shirt is **less** expensive than that one.

# lesson

A lesson is something you are supposed to learn. Sue takes dancing **lessons**.

# let

If you **let** someone do something, you say that the person can do it. Dad **let** us stay up later last night.

# let's

**Let's** means **let us**. We say **let's** when we want someone to do something with us. **Let's** go to the zoo tomorrow.

# letter

1. A **letter** is one of the symbols people use to write words. The **letters** of the English alphabet are A, B, C, D, E, F, G, H, I, J, K, L, M, N, O, P, Q, R, S, T, U, V, W, X, Y, and Z.

2. A letter is also a message you write on paper. Dick writes **letters** to all his friends.

# lettuce

Lettuce is a vegetable that has large, green leaves. It is used in salads and sandwiches.

# liar
A **liar** is a person who does not tell the truth.

# librarian
A **librarian** is a person who works in a library. The **librarian** in our school helps us find the books we need.

# library
A library is a place where many books are kept. People borrow books from the **library** to take home and read.

# lick
Lick means to touch something with your tongue. The cat **licked** itself.  Elizabeth **licked** her ice-cream cone.

# lie¹
1. To **lie** is to say something that is not true. When Maria broke a window, she did not want to get into trouble. So she **lied** and said she

had not done it.
**2.** A **lie** is something you say that is not true. Carlos told his mother a **lie**, but later he decided to tell the truth.

# lie²

Lie means to be stretched out flat. When you **lie**, you are not sitting or standing. The dog likes to **lie** by the gate while the baby plays in the yard.

# life

**1. Life** is what animals and plants have when they are alive.
**2.** A **life** is the time something is alive. Insects have short **lives**.   Some trees have very long lives.

# lift

Lift means to pick something up. It was hard for Mike to lift the heavy bag. Jane **lifted** her arm and waved good-bye.

# light¹

1. **Light** is energy that comes from the sun. When there is **light**, we are able to see things.

2. Something that gives light is called a **light**. Lamps and candles are **lights**. Margaret turned on the light in her bedroom to read her book.

3. When you **light** something, you make it burn or give off **light**.  Be careful when you **light** the candles. We are **lighting** our Christmas tree tonight.

4. **Light** is also a way to describe color. Pink is a **light** color.

# light²

When something is **light**, it is not heavy. The empty suitcase was **light**.

# lighthouse

A lighthouse is a tower with a bright light on top. **Lighthouses** are built near dangerous places in the water to help ships pass safely. We saw the **lighthouse** from our boat and passed the rocks safely.

# lightning

Lightning is a big flash of light in the sky. It is a form of electricity. **Lightning** can come from the sky to the ground during storms. I saw a flash of **lightning** in the dark sky.

# like[1]

To **like** something means that it makes you feel good. Jack and his friends **like** pizza.

# like[2]

**Like** means the same. Tom and Tony are twin brothers. They look just **like** each other.

# lime

A lime is a kind of fruit. It is green and looks like a small lemon. **Limes** have a sour taste.

# line

1. A **line** is a long, thin mark. Susan used a pencil to draw a **line** across the paper.
2. A **line** is also things in a row. We stood in **line** for the bus.

# lion

A lion is a large wild animal. It is like a big cat. **Lions** hunt other animals for food. Male **lions** have long, thick hair around their heads.

# lioness

A **lioness** is a female lion. **Lionesses** are smaller than male lions. They do not have long hair around their heads.

# lip

A lip is the part of your face around your mouth. People have two **lips**.

# liquid

A liquid is something that is

wet when you touch it. A **liquid** can be poured. Water and milk are **liquids**.

## list

A **list** is a number of things that are written down. Hannah made a **list** of the people she wanted at her party.

## listen

Listen means to try to hear in a careful way. The children **listened** to the story. George likes to **listen** to music. I like **listening** to the sound of rain falling on the roof.

## lit

Lit comes from the word **light**. We **lit** a candle to find our way down the dark hall. Uncle David lit the logs in the fireplace.

## liter | -tre

A **liter** is an amount of a liquid. A **liter** is a little more than a quart.

# little

**1.** When something is **little**, it is small. My little sister can't walk yet. An ant is **little**.    That is the **littlest** puppy that I have ever seen.

**2.** Little also means not very much. Jack drank only a **little** juice because he wasn't thirsty. Mary used a **little** red in her painting. We only spent a **little** time picking apples because it started to rain.

# live

**1. Live** means to be alive. No dinosaurs live on earth now.

**2. Live** also means to have a home. Billy and Johnny **live** next door to us.

# lives

**Lives** comes from the word **life**. The **lives** of the early explorers were filled with danger. Leon likes to read stories about the **lives** of heroes and heroines.

# lizard

A lizard is an animal with four legs and a long tail. Most **lizards** like to eat insects. **Lizards**, snakes, turtles, and alligators are all reptiles.

# load

1. A **load** is something to be carried. Mark brought two **loads** of wood into the house.

2. To **load** is to put something in a place where it can be carried away. Liz and her brother **loaded** boxes onto the truck. They **loaded** the coal in the ship.

# loaf

1. A loaf is bread that is baked in one long piece. We bought two **loaves** of bread at the bakery.

2. A **loaf** can also be another kind of food that is shaped like a bread. Joe's favorite dinner is meat **loaf** and salad.

## loan

To **loan** is to let someone borrow. Peter forgot to bring a pencil, so Helen **loaned** him one of hers.

## loaves

**Loaves** means more than one loaf. **Loaves** of bread in the store often come already cut in pieces.

## lobster

A lobster is an animal. It lives on the bottom of the ocean. **Lobsters** have hard shells and big claws and tails.

## lock

1. A **lock** is an object used to keep something shut. You can open the **lock** only if you have a key.
2. To **lock** means to put the key in the lock and turn it. All the door are **locked** from outside.

## log

A log is a large, round

piece of wood. **Logs** are cut from trees. Some **logs** are used in fireplaces. Other **logs** are cut up into boards.

## lonely

When you feel lonely, you feel unhappy about being alone. Murray is **lonely** because all his friends are away for the summer.

## long

**1.** Long means that one end of something is far away from the other end. There is a **long** hall between the first grade and second grade classrooms.

**2.** **Long** also means taking a lot of time. Mike was tired and took a **long** nap after lunch. An hour is **longer** than a minute. It is a **long** drive from where I live to the ocean.

## look

**1.** When you look, you use your eyes to see.

Harry let me **look** at his new book. We **looked** out of the window at the deer. Terry and Stuart **looked** carefully before they crossed the street.

2. **Look** also means how people see you. Sue looked happy when she found her lost dog.

## loose

Loose is the opposite of **tight**. Mary tried to walk in her mother's shoes, but they were so big that they fell off her feet. The shoes were too **loose** for her.

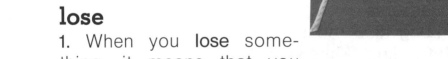

## lose

1. When you **lose** something, it means that you cannot find it. Don't **lose** your new gloves. Jenny **lost** her pencil in the play-ground.

2. **Lose** also means not being able to keep some-thing. Many trees **lost** their branches during the hurri-cane. Elizabeth **lost** her bal-

ance and slipped on the ice.

3. **Lose** also means to not win. Did Joe lose the race?

# loss

1. A **loss** is the act or fact of losing something. The accident victim suffered a **loss** of memory. The team had two wins and three **losses**.

2. A **loss** is the pain or hardship caused by losing something or someone. We all felt the **loss** of our dog.

# lost

When something is **lost**, it is hard to find. We found the **lost** sock behind the dresser.

# lot

A **lot** means that something takes a long time to count or measure. There are a **lot** of things to do in the summer. A hippopotamus eats a lot of food.

# loud

To be **loud** means to make a lot of noise. Thunder in a storm is heard for many miles. Thunder is a loud noise.

# loudspeaker

A **loudspeaker** is something that makes sound louder. Radios have **loudspeakers**. Some telephones have **loudspeakers** too.

# love

To **love** means to like something very much. Linda **loves** to swim. Henry **loves** to eat sandwiches.

# low

**Low** means close to the floor or ground. The fence was low enough to jump over without touching it.

# luck

**Luck** is something that happens to you by chance, without being planned. If you have good **luck**, you may find a quarter on the ground. If your luck is bad, your bicycle may get a flat tire.

# lucky

Lucky means that you have good things happen to you. Mark was **lucky** to find two quarters and a nickel lying in the middle of the side-walk.

# lullaby

A **lullaby** is a song sung to a baby to help the baby go to sleep.

# lumber

Lumber means boards that have been cut from logs. Dad brought home some **lumber** to build me a new desk.

# lunch

Lunch is the meal we eat in the middle of the day. Tyler has lunch at school every day.

# lunch box

A lunch box is a metal or plastic container with a handle. Some people carry their lunches to school or work in a **lunch box**.

# lung

A **lung** is a part of the body. You have two **lungs** inside your chest. Air goes in and out of your **lungs** when you breathe.

L

## macaroni, macca-

Macaroni is a kind of food. It is made from flour and comes in the shape of little hollow tubes.

## machine

A **machine** is an object that does work for people. It may be large or small and may have many parts. Airplanes, computers, and windmills are all machines.

## mad

When someone is **mad**, it means that the person is angry about something. Jill was **mad** because we had to stop the game just when she was winning.

## made

Made comes from the word

make. The clown **made** us laugh. The wall was made of stone. Mother **made** a doll for me.

## magazine

A magazine has stories to read and pictures to look at. It has paper covers. Some **magazines** are published every week. Some are published once a month. Ray likes a **magazine** with jokes and word games.

## magic

Magic is a special power to make unusual things happen. **Magic** seems to be real, but it is not. The tricks Albert did at the party seemed to be done by **magic**. We wondered at his display of **magic**.

## magician

A **magician** is a person who uses magic to do tricks. The magician pulled a rabbit out of the hat.

## magnet

A magnet is a piece of metal that sticks to other metals. Oliver used his **magnet** to pick up the nails that spilled.

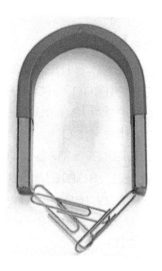

## magnifying glass

A magnifying glass is a piece of glass that makes things look bigger than they are. When we looked at the shell through the **magnifying glass**, we could see its pattern of lines.

## mail

1. The **mail** is the way we send letters and packages from one place to another.
2. To mail something is to send it through the mail. Blake's parents **mailed** him a package at camp last week.

## main

Main means most important. The bank is on the **main** street in town. Dinner is the **main** meal in our

M

house.

## make

1. **Make** means to put something together. We helped Dad make a house for the dog.
2. **Make** also means to cause something to happen. When you tell funny stories, it always **makes** me laugh.

## make-believe

When something is **make-believe**, it means that it is not real. Fairies are **make-believe**.

## male

A **male** is a boy or a man. Fathers and uncles are male people.

## man

A man is a grown-up male person. My uncle is a tall **man**.

## manners

When you have good **man-**

**map** 309

ners, you act in a polite way toward people. You show good **manners** when you say "please" and "thank you." You show bad **manners** when you chew with your mouth open.

## mansion
A mansion is a very large house with many rooms. She lives in a **mansion**.

## many
**Many** means a large number of things. There are very **many** grains of sand on the beach.

## map
A map is a drawing that shows where different places are. There are many kinds of **maps**. **Maps** can show countries, weather, oceans and rivers, mountains, and other things. Can you find your town on a **map**? When we study geography, we look at **maps**.

M

# maple

A **maple** is a kind of tree. Maple trees turn beautiful colors in the fall.

# marble

1. **Marble** is a kind of hard, smooth stone. Artists carve statues from **marble**. **Marble** is often used on the walls and floors of buildings.

2. A marble is also a small, hard ball of glass used in games. Bob drew a big circle on the ground for a game of **marbles**.

# march

To **march** with someone means to take the same size steps at the same time. Our band **marched** in the parade. The soldiers marched along the street.

# March

March is the third month of the year. It has 31 days. **March** comes after February and before April.

# margarine

Margarine is a soft, yellow food that is usually made from vegetable oils. Many people use **margarine** instead of butter.

# mark

1. **Mark** means to make a line or spot on something. Your dirty shoes **marked** the clean floor.
2. A **mark** is a scratch or spot on a surface. The baby made **marks** on the wall with a crayon.
3. A **mark** is also a letter or number that shows how good a person's work is. Roberto got better **marks** in art than in science.

# marry

Marry means to join with someone as husband or wife. My aunt and uncle have been **married** for five years.

M

# marsh

A marsh is an area of land

that is soft and wet. Frogs, water birds, and mosquitoes live in **marshes**.

# marshmallow

Marshmallow is a kind of candy. It is soft and white.

# mask

A **mask** is something you wear over your face to hide or protect it. Firefighters wear masks to protect them from smoke.

# match[1]

To **match** is to be the same. Susan's shirt and shoes are the same color. She bought the shoes because they **matched** the shirt.

# match[2]

A match is a short, thin piece of wood or paper. When the tip is rubbed against something, it makes a flame. **Matches** are used to light a fire.

# material

Material is what something is made of. Alice's winter coat is made of wool **material**. Wood, stone, and glass are **materials** that are used to make houses.

# mathematics

When you study **mathematics**, you learn about numbers, amounts, shapes, and measurements. When you add and subtract, you are using **mathematics**.

# mattress

A **mattress** is the thick, soft part of a bed. Claire put a new cover on the **mattress**.

# may

1. You say **may** when you ask for something. **May** I have some juice?

2. If you aren't sure something will happen but there is a chance that it will, you say it **may** happen. Since there are dark clouds in the sky, it may rain this after-

M

noon.

# May

May is a month of the year. It has 31 days. **May** comes after April and before June.

# maybe

**Maybe** means that something might be. I can't see who is knocking at the door. **Maybe** it is John.

# maze

A **maze** has many paths that are alike. It is hard to find your way through a **maze**. Tony got lost in the **maze** of halls in his new school.

# me

**Me** is a word you use when you speak about yourself. The bus takes me to school.

# meadow

A meadow is an area of land that is covered with long grass. Mice, rabbits, and butterflies live in **meadows**.

## meal

A meal is the food you eat at one time. We eat three **meals** every day. They are called breakfast, lunch, and dinner.

## mean[1]

1. **Mean** is a word you use to show that two things are the same. Huge means very big.

2. **Mean** is also a word you use to show what you are thinking. When Diana said "early," she **meant** "before breakfast."

## mean[2]

If you are **mean** to someone, you are not nice or friendly. It was **mean** of the children to hide the new student's books in the closet.

## meant

Meant is a form of **mean**[1].

Did you understand what I **meant**? Going to the movies **meant** a lot to Al.

## measure

Measure means to find out the size or amount of something. Maria helped her father **measure** the length of the new fence.

## measurement

The size or amount that is found by measuring something is called its **measurement**. The carpenter used a ruler to get the **measurements** of the shelf.

## meat

Meat is a kind of food. It comes from animals. Chicken, beef, and ham are all **meats**.

## medal

A medal is a piece of metal in the shape of a coin. **Medals** often hang from a ribbon or a chain. A **medal** is sometimes given as a

**M**

reward to someone who has done something brave or important. Dale was given a **medal** for helping to save the boy who fell in the water.

# medicine

Medicine is something we take when we are sick to help us get well. When Jane had the flu, her mother gave her **medicine** twice a day.

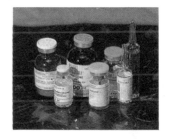

# meet

**1.** To meet is to get to know someone. You **meet** many new people on the first day of school.
**2.** To **meet** also means to be at the same place at the same time. Tom and Bill **met** at the corner at three o'clock.

# melt

To **melt** is to change from something solid into a liquid. When the weather gets warm, ice **melts** and becomes water.

## memory

1. **Memory** is being able to remember things. Aunt Mimi has a good **memory** for dates and never forgets anyone's birthday.

2. A **memory** is also a person or thing that is remembered. My summer in camp is one of my happiest memories.

## men

**Men** means more than one man. Boys grow up to be **men**.

## mess

Something is a mess when a lot of things are not where they belong. The kitchen was a **mess** after we made a cake.

## message

A message is a group of words that is sent from one person to another. Many people send **messages**

through the mail.

## met

Met is a form of **meet**. David **met** six new friends at the school picnic. Harry and Richard met to have lunch at a restaurant.

## metal

Metal is a shiny material that is found in the earth. Gold is a kind of **metal**. A dime, a ring, and a car are all made of **metal**.

## meter | metre

A **meter** is an amount of length. One **meter** is a little more than a yard. There are 1,000 **meters** in a kilometer.

## mice

Mice means more than one mouse. The **mice** ate all the cheese. Kendrew, Albert, and George dressed up as three **mice** for the Halloween party.

M

## microscope

A microscope is used to see things that are too small to see with our eyes alone. **Microscopes** can make tiny things look big.

## middle

The **middle** is the part in the center between the ends. Noon is in the **middle** of the day. We swam to the raft in the **middle** of the lake.

## midnight

**Midnight** is 12 o'clock at night. Everyone in our house is asleep at midnight.

## might

**Might** comes from the word **may**. Blake said we **might** be late if we don't hurry.

## mile

A mile is an amount of distance. There are 5,280 feet in a **mile**. It takes a man or woman about 20 minutes to walk a mile.

M

# milk

Milk is a white liquid that we drink. **Milk** comes from cows and goats. I like **milk** on my cereal. Cheese is made from **milk**.

# million

A **million** is a number. It is written 1,000,000. There are a thousand thousands in a **million**. The sun is **millions** of miles away from the earth.

# mind

The **mind** is the part of a person that thinks, feels, learns, remembers, wishes, and imagines. Without **minds** humans would not be humans.

# mine

**Mine** means belonging to me. After I bought the book, it was mine.

**M**

# minus

**Minus** means taken away. If you take two away from six,

you have four. Six **minus** two is four. Six **minus** two can also be written $6-2$.

## minute

A minute is an amount of time. One **minute** has 60 seconds in it. There are 60 **minutes** in one hour.

## mirror

A mirror is a smooth piece of glass that we can see ourselves in. Some **mirrors** hang on the wall and some can be held in your hand. The dentist uses a tiny **mirror** to see into the back of my mouth.

## miss

1. **Miss** means not to do something that you plan to do. If we don't hurry, we will **miss** the beginning of the movie. Jack swung the bat at the ball, but he missed it.

2. **Miss** also means to be sorry that you don't have something, or that some-

M

one you like isn't with you. I **miss** my sister when she goes to camp in the summer.

**3. Miss** also means to be without something. My old jacket is **missing** a button. Your blue and green crayons are **missing**.

# Miss

Miss is a word people use with a woman's name if she is not married. Our music teacher's name is **Miss Brown**.

# mistake

A **mistake** is something that is wrong. I made only one **mistake** on the spelling test. It was a **mistake** to wear a heavy sweater on such a warm day.

# mitten

A mitten is something you wear on your hand to keep it warm. A glove has parts for each finger, but a **mitten** doesn't. I lost my **mittens** at school.

# mix

Mix means to put different things together. My friends and I are **mixing** lemon juice, water, and sugar to make lemonade. We **mixed** red paint and white paint to make pink.

# model

A **model** is a small copy of something. Paul is painting his airplane **model** to make the wood look like metal.

# mom

Mom is a name for your mother. Some children also call their mother **mommy**.

# moment

A moment is a very small amount of time. If you will wait just a **moment**, I will help you as soon as I can.

# Monday

Monday is a day of the week. **Monday** comes after

M

Sunday and before Tuesday.

## money

Money is what people use to buy things. When people work, they are paid **money** for what they do. Pennies, nickels, dimes, quarters, and dollars are all kinds of **money**.

## monkey

A monkey is an animal with long arms and legs, fur all over its body, and a long tail. Some **monkeys** live in trees and some live on the ground.

## monster

A **monster** is a big, scary animal that is not real. I read a story about a red **monster** with two heads and six legs.

M

## month

A **month** is part of a year. There are 12 **months** in a year. The **months** are January, February, March, April, May, June, July, August, September, October, November, and December.

## mood

A **mood** is the way you feel. When the weather is bad, Jack is in a bad **mood**.

## moon

The **moon** moves around the earth. At night the moon shines in the sky. Sometimes you can see all of the **moon**, and sometimes you can see only a part of it. It takes one month for the **moon** to move around the earth.

## more

More means a larger number or a larger amount. Four is **more** than three. There is **more** juice in my glass than in yours.

## morning

Morning is the part of the day before noon.  I like to

wake up early in the **morn-ing** when the sun shines through my window.

## mosquito

A mosquito is a small insect that flies. When a **mosquito** bites me, it makes me want to scratch.

## most

**Most** means the largest number or part of something. **Most** of the children got to school on time. Lewis spelled **most** of the words right.

## moth

A **moth** is a kind of insect. Moths look a lot like butter-flies. A caterpillar changes into a **moth** inside a cocoon.

## mother

A mother is a woman who has one or more children. **Mothers** and fathers are parents.

M

## motor

A **motor** is a machine that makes other machines work. This clock has an electric **motor** to move the hands. The motor of a car makes the car go. An electric **motor** runs the washing machine.

## motorcycle

A **motorcycle** is a machine. It is like a big, heavy bicycle with an engine. Some motorcycles can go as fast as cars.

## mountain

A **mountain** is a very high area of land. **Mountains** are much higher than hills. Some people go skiing in the mountains for a vacation.

## mouse

A **mouse** is a very small animal. It has a long tail, short fur, and sharp teeth. **Mice** live in fields, forests, or houses.

## mouth

You use your mouth to speak and eat. You also use your **mouth** to smile or frown. Your teeth and tongue are in your **mouth**. The children wiped their **mouths** with their napkins after they finished eating. The dentist said, "Open your **mouth** wide."

## move

**Move** means to go from one place to another. Billy **moved** the box from the floor to the table. Helen and her family **moved** to the country last year.

## movie

A movie is a story made with pictures that move. People watch **movies** in theaters or on television.

## Mr., Mr

Mr. is used before a man's name. Mr. Walker is my teacher this year.

M

## Mrs., Mrs

Mrs. is often used before a married woman's name. Mrs. Kelly is Richard's mother.

## Ms., Ms

Ms. is often used before a woman's name. Ms. Marie, I'd like you to meet my brother and sister.

## much

Much means a lot of something. Dad had so much work that he had to stay late at the office.

## mud

Mud is wet dirt. Many animals like to roll in the mud.

## muffin

A muffin is a food like bread in the shape of a cup. When our friends came to our house for breakfast, we had muffins, fruit, and milk.

M

## mug

A mug is a large cup with a handle. You can drink milk or eat soup from a **mug**. My friend gave me a clay **mug** that she made in art class.

## multiply

To **multiply** is to add a number to itself several times. The symbol for **multiply** is ×. 2×4 is the same as 2+2+2+2.

## muscle

**Muscle** is the part of your body that gives you strength to move and to lift things. A dancer has strong leg **muscles**.

## museum

A museum is a place that collects and keeps things for people to see and learn about. Some **museums** show art. Some show things from long ago. My class visited a science **museum** that had dinosaur

M

bones and old rocks.

# mushroom

A mushroom is a fungus that is shaped like a small umbrella. **Mushrooms** do not have flowers or leaves, and they grow very quickly. Some **mushrooms** can be eaten, but many are dangerous to eat.

# music

Music is sounds that people make with instruments and their voices. There are many kinds of **music** all over the world.

# musician

A musician is someone who plays a musical instrument or sings. A group of **musicians** played music at Uncle Peter's wedding.

# must

1. **Must** means that you have to do something. You **must** put a string on your kite, or it will fly away.

2. **must** also means probably. That book **must** be around here somewhere.

## mustache, mous-

A mustache is the hair that grows above a man's lip. My daddy's **mustache** tickles me when I kiss him.

## mustard

Mustard is a thick, yellow liquid that you put on food to add flavor. It is made from the seeds of a plant. Mom likes to put **mustard** on her hamburger, but my brother and I like ketchup better.

## my

My means that something belongs to me. This is my book.

## myself

Myself means me and nobody else. When I look in a mirror, I see **myself**. I dressed **myself** in a hurry.

M

## mysterious

When something is **mysteri-ous**, it is very hard to explain or understand. We heard some **mysterious** sounds coming from the empty house.

## mystery

A **mystery** is something that you do not understand. Margaret does not understand why plants grow. It is a mystery to her. Nature is full of **mysteries**.

M

## nail

**1.** A nail is the hard part on the ends of your fingers and toes.

**2.** A **nail** is also a thin piece of metal that has a point at one end and a flat part at the other end. You hammer a **nail** into two things to keep them together.

**3. Nail** means to attach something with a nail. We **nailed** a picture to the wall.

## name

A **name** is a word that people use to call something by. Everything has a **name**. People have **names**, too.

## nap

When you sleep for a short time, you take a nap. We take a **nap** after lunch every

day. Our new baby takes lots of **naps**.

# napkin

A napkin is a piece of cloth or paper that you use to cover your lap while you are eating. You also use a **napkin** to wipe your mouth and hands. We took paper **napkins** to the picnic. I put a **napkin** by my plate.

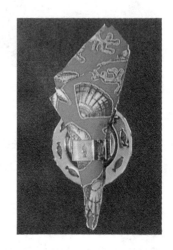

## narrow

Something that is **narrow** is not wide. The deer jumped across the **narrow** stream. We walked in a line along the **narrow** path. There are many **narrow** streets in this city.

## nature

Nature is everything that is not made by people. Mountains, trees, rivers, and stars are all part of **nature**. People and animals are part of **nature**, too. Buildings and telephones are not part of **nature**.

## near

**Near** means close to or not far from someone or something. The **nearest** grocery store is four blocks from here.

## neat

When something is **neat**, it looks clean and everything is in its place. My brother's room is neat, but mine is a mess.

## neck

1. Your **neck** is the part of your body just below your head. I pull my jacket zipper up to my **neck** when it is cold outside. A giraffe has a long, thin neck. Sue wears a scarf around her **neck**.

2. A **neck** is also a narrow part that is like a neck in shape. The **neck** of a violin is made of a special kind of wood.

## necklace

A necklace is jewelry that is

worn around the neck. We gave Mom a silver **neck-lace** for her birthday.

## need

To **need** means that you must have something. Plants cannot live without water. They need water to live.

## needle

1. A needle is a thin piece of metal that you use when you sew or knit. A sewing **needle** has a hole at one end for thread and a point at the other end. The leaves of some plants are called **needles** because of their shape.

2. Another kind of needle holds the medicine a doctor or a nurse gives you. Doctor Blake used a **needle** to give me medicine for the flu.

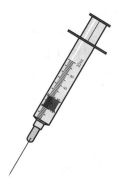

## neighbo(u)r

A **neighbor** is someone who lives near you. Our **neighbor** cared for Sinbad, our dog, when we went on vacation.

# neighbo (u) rhood

A neighborhood is an area of a city or town where people live. Most of the children in my **neighbor-hood** go to the same school.

# neither

**Neither** means not one and not the other. **Neither** one of the two children wanted to go into the water. **Neither** George nor David won the race. **Neither** team played very well today.

# nest

A **nest** is a bird's home. Birds build their **nests** with leaves, sticks, mud, and other things. Most birds lay their eggs in nests.

# net

A **net** is a kind of material that has holes in it. **Nets** are often made of string or rope. We need a new basketball **net** because the one we have now is torn in four places. One of the acrobats fell from the swing, but he landed in the **net** below. Some fishermen go out into the ocean and put large nets into the water to catch fish.

## never

You say **never** when you mean not at any time. We were surprised when Mike said he had **never** been to the circus. I have never seen a flower as beautiful as this one.

## new

**1.** Something that is **new** has never been used before. We bought a new television after our old one broke. Terry's skateboard is **newer** than mine, but Harry's is the **newest** of all. **2.** We also say that something is **new** if it is just starting or beginning. We

started a **new** game.

## news

News is the story of something that has just happened. We hear **news** on the radio and on television. We read **news** in newspapers and magazines. Did you read the **news** about the fire at the factory?

## newspaper

A newspaper tells you the news about your neighborhood and other places. **Newspapers** are printed on paper. You can read about sports and books in a **newspaper**. Many **newspapers** have advertisements in them, and some have comics.

## next

1. **Next** means coming after someone or something. Bill is the **next** person in line to pay for groceries.
2. **Next** also means beside

or near something. The baby deer stayed next to its mother.

# nice

To be **nice** is to make people feel good. Yesterday the weather was so nice that Dana played outside. Our neighbors are **nice**, friendly people.

# nickel

A nickel is a kind of coin. One **nickel** is the same as five pennies. Five **nickels** are the same as a quarter.

# nickname

A **nickname** is a name that you use instead of a real name. Bob is a **nickname** for Robert. Rob's **nickname** is Red because of the color of his hair.

# night

Night is the part of the day when it is dark outside. **Night** begins at sunset. You can see the moon and stars

at **night**. There are some animals that hunt at **night**. He works by day and reads by **night**.

# nightmare

A nightmare is a very bad dream. A **nightmare** can scare the person who dreams it. Last night I had a **nightmare** about being lost in a dark forest.

# nine

**Nine** is a number. **Nine** is written 9. $8+1=9$.

# no

**1.** No means that you do not agree. Margaret asked if she could have another dessert. Her mother said, "**No**."

**2. No** also means not any. There is **no** snow during the summer. Peter was sick yesterday, and he is still sick today. He feels **no** better today than he did yesterday.

## nobody

**Nobody** means no person. **Nobody** can fly like a bird.

## nod

To **nod** is to move your head up and down. People often **nod** to show that they agree.

## noise

A **noise** is a sound, often a loud sound. At the airport there is always a lot of noise

## none

**None** means not one or not any. David wanted an apple, but there was **none** left in the basket. **None** of us can jump as high as Bill can.

## nonfiction

Nonfiction means anything that is written about real people and real things. **Nonfiction** is the opposite of **fiction**. A story in the newspaper is one kind of nonfiction. The story of a person's life is also **nonfiction**.

# noodle

A noodle is food in the shape of a long, flat strip. **Noodles** are made of flour, water, and eggs. **Noodles** and hamburgers are my favorite foods. Peter wanted **noodles** in his soup instead of rice.

# noon

**Noon** is 12 o'clock in the day. We eat our lunch at noon.

# nor

**Nor** is a word we use with **neither**. Neither Sarah **nor** Paul likes to play football.

# north

When you look at a map, the direction toward the top is **north**. If you look toward the sun when it comes up in the morning, **north** is on your left. The opposite of **north** is **south**.

## nose

Your nose is in the center of your face. You breathe and smell things through your **nose**.

## not

You use **not** to make a word or group of words negative. Marie is **not** home.

## note

1. A note is one sound in music. Music is made of many **notes**. The **notes** can be written down so that other people can read them and play the same music.
2. A note is also a short message that you write down.

## nothing

**Nothing** means no thing. The dinner was so good, there was nothing left on anyone's plate. The oppo-

site of **nothing** is **something**.

## notice

To notice is to see or hear something. Bill **noticed** that his brother had on two socks that did not match. He **noticed** me and began to wave.

## November

**November** is a month of the year. It has 30 days. **November** comes after October and before December.

## now

**Now** means at this minute. Do you really have to leave **now**? It is snowing now.

## number

1. A **number** tells you how many there are of something. Both 2 and 50 are **numbers**.
2. A **number** is also used to tell one thing from another. Do you know your telephone **number**?

## nurse

A nurse is a person who takes care of sick people. Some **nurses** work in hospitals, and others visit people in their homes.

## nut

A nut grows on a tree. **Nuts** usually have hard shells. Most **nuts** can be eaten.

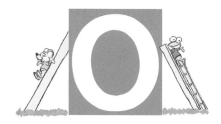

## oak

An oak is a tree that has acorns. The wood from **oak** trees is very strong and is used in making furniture and boats. Mom and Dad bought a kitchen table made of **oak**.

## obey

When you obey someone, you do what that person tells you to do. Elizabeth **obeys** her parents and gets home from school by 4 o'clock. When Andy told his dog to sit, it **obeyed** him immediately.

## object

An object is anything that people can see or touch that is not alive. Buildings, tables, chairs, books, scis-

sors, pens, and pencils are all **objects**.

## ocean

The ocean is made of salt water and covers large areas of the earth. Fish and whales live in the **ocean**. Ships sail on the **ocean**.

## o'clock

We use the word **o'clock** when we say what time it is. We go to school at 8 o'clock in the morning.

## October

**October** is a month of the year. It has 31 days. **October** comes after September and before November.

## octopus

An octopus is an animal that lives in the ocean. It has a soft body and eight arms. The **octopus** uses its arms to move and to catch food.

# odd

**1. Odd** means strange or different. Our car is making an **odd** noise and needs to be fixed.

**2.** Some numbers are odd numbers, and some are even numbers. The numbers 1, 3, 5, 7, and 9 are **odd** numbers. The numbers 2, 4, 6, 8, and 10 are even numbers.

# of

**1. Of** means from. Most tables are made of wood.

**2. Of** also tells what something has in it. Paul was carrying a pail of water.

**3.** When you tell time, **of** means before. The time is ten minutes **of** four.

# off

**1. Off** is the opposite of **on**. Our house is dark when the lights are **off**.

**2. Off** also means away from. Please take your books **off** the table before supper.

## offer

To **offer** is to say you will give or do something. Maria **offered** to help her father rake the leaves.

## office

An office is a place where people work. Some buildings have many **offices** in them. The principal's **office** is at the end of the hall.

## officer

1. An **officer** is a person in an army who leads others and tells them what to do.
2. An officer is also a man or woman who works for the police. The police **officer** helped the lost child find her mother and father.

## often

**Often** means many times. It **often** rains in April.

## oil

1. Oil is a liquid that comes from vegetables and animals. It is used in cooking.

We got out the pan and corn **oil** to make popcorn.
2. Another kind of oil comes from the ground. This **oil** is burned for heat and to make machines run. Our furnace burned a lot of **oil** last week because it was so cold outside.

O

## okay, okey

**Okay** means that something is fine. Mary thought the radio was broken, but it was **okay**. This word is also spelled **OK**. Is it **OK** if I borrow your skateboard?

## old

1. To be old means to have been alive a long time. Grandfather is **old**, but Toni is young.
2. Things are called **old** when they have been used for a long time. We gave away our **old** clothes to people who needed them.
3. We also use the word **old** when we talk about someone's age. I am 7

years **old**. Are you **older** than I am?

## on

1. **On** is the opposite of **off**. The room is bright when the light is on.
2. **On** tells where something is. The dishes are on the table.
3. **On** means about. Richard has a book **on** dinosaurs.
4. **On** also tells what day something happens. We play ball **on** Sundays.

## once

1. If you do something **once**, you do it only one time. We buy groceries once a week.
2. **Once** also means as soon as. **Once** it stops raining, we can go outside.

## one

1. **One** is a number. **One** is written **1**. **One** is the first number when you count.
2. **One** is used for something you have already

talked about. Sarah likes green grapes, but she doesn't like purple **ones**.

## onion

An onion is a kind of vege-table. It is round and has a strong smell and taste. **Onions** grow in the ground.

## only

**Only** means one and no more. There is only one moon in our sky.

## open

1. **Open** means not shut or closed. If a jar is **open**, there is no cover on it. The door was **open**, so I walked in.

2. **Open** also means to make something open. Please **open** the window.
3. **Open** also means to begin. The new play **opened** last Saturday night.

## opening

An **opening** is an empty space. The rabbit pushed

o

through an **opening** in the fence.

## opossum

An opossum is a small animal with gray fur. **Opossums** carry their babies in a pocket on their stomachs as kangaroos do.

## opposite

1. **Opposite** means different in every way. Up is the **opposite** of down.
2. To be **opposite** also means to be at either end of a line. East and west are **opposite** directions.

## or

The word **or** helps us when we are talking about two different things **or** people. Which do you like better, apples **or** pears? When I get home from school, I'll either play baseball **or** read.

## orange

1. An orange is a small, round fruit. Would you like

an **orange** with your breakfast?

2. Orange is also a color.
Pumpkins are **orange**. I
have an **orange** scarf.

## orchestra

An orchestra is a large
group of people who play
instruments together. **Or-
chestras** can have more
than a hundred people.

## order

When things are in **order**,
they are in the right place.
Billy can say the letters of
the alphabet in **order** from
A to Z. Arthur knows num-
bers in **order** from 1 to 25.

## ostrich

An ostrich is a very large
bird. It has long legs and a
long neck. **Ostriches** cannot
fly.

## other

1. **Other** means one of two.
One of Dale's socks has a
hole in it. The **other** one has

no holes.

2. **Other** also means different. Susan has no time to play today. She will have time some **other** day.

## ounce

An **ounce** is an amount of weight. There are 16 **ounces** in one pound.

## our

**Our** means that something belongs to us. **Our** house is near the school.

## ours

**Ours** means belonging to us. Those are your books. These are ours.

## ourselves

**Ourselves** means us and nobody else. When Mark and I looked in a mirror, we saw ourselves there.

## out

1. **Out** means away from the inside. Tom took the toy train **out** of the box.

2. **Out** also means out-doors. Let's go **out** and play in the backyard.

3. **Out** can also mean through. We looked **out** the window to see if it was raining.

# outdoor

**Outdoor** means outside a building instead of inside. We went to an outdoor con-cert.

# outdoors

When you are **outdoors**, you are out under the sky. On warm evenings, we like to have our dinner outdoors.

# outer space

Outer space is far away from the earth. The moon, the planets, and the stars are in **outer space**. Astro-nauts explore **outer space** in a spaceship.

# outgrow

When you **outgrow** some-thing, you get too big for it.

The baby **outgrows** his clothes every few months. Anne **outgrew** her sneakers and had to buy some new ones.

## outside

1. Outside means the part of something that is out. The **outside** of our house is painted white.
2. **Outside** also means out-doors or not inside. I was **outside** of the school when I heard the bell. The boys went outside to play in the yard.

## oval

When something is **oval**, it is shaped like an egg. The turkey is on a big **oval** plate.

## oven

An oven is the inside of a stove where you put things to heat or cook. Claire and her sister baked some bread in the **oven**. We watched the man put our

pizza in the **oven** to cook. A microwave oven is a special kind of **oven** that can cook food very fast.

## over

1. Over means above. A helicopter flew **over** our house.

2. **Over** also means on top of. Helen wore a sweater **over** her shirt.
3. **Over** can also mean more than. Andrew's father is **over** six feet tall.
4. **Over** can also mean down. Albert knocked **over** a glass of milk.
5. **Over** also means again. The band played a song. Then they played it over because everyone liked it.

6. **Over** can mean finished. After the movie was **over**, we went home.

## owe

To **owe** means that you must give someone something. Todd **owes** the store a quarter for his apple.

# owl

An owl is a bird with a large head and big, round eyes. **Owls** usually hunt for food at night.

# own

To **own** means to have and keep something. Jane **owns** a lot of books and toys.

o

## pack

To **pack** is to put some-thing in a suitcase or a box to take with you. Walter **packed** his clothes and some books to go on vaca-tion.

## package

A package is something you tie up and send through the mail. People bring **packages** to the post office to mail.

## pad

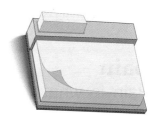

A pad is made up of pieces of paper that are glued together at one edge. The pages of a **pad** are empty so that you can write or draw on them. We leave a **pad** and pencil near the phone to write messages. Sarah drew pictures on the pages of her **pad**.

## page

A page is one side of a piece of paper in a book, magazine, or newspaper. Wendy wrote her name on the first **page** of her book. Please don't tear any **pages** out of the magazine.

## paid

**Paid** is a form of **pay**. Bill paid four dollars for a movie ticket.

## pail

A **pail** is used to hold things. It is made of metal or plastic and has a flat, round bottom. **Pails** are the same thing as buckets.

## pain

**Pain** is what you feel when you are hurt. If you eat too fast you might get pains in your stomach.

# paint

1. **Paint** is a liquid with color in it. People put **paint** on things to make them look good. Artists make pictures with **paints**.

2. To **paint** is to cover with paint. Betty and her mother **painted** one room yellow and one room blue.

# painting

A painting is a picture that you paint. My **painting** of a dinosaur is in the art show.

# pair

A pair is two things that match each other. Shoes, socks, and gloves come in **pairs**.

# pajamas | pyjamas

Pajamas are a kind of clothes that people wear when they sleep. Most **pajamas** are warm and soft.

# palace

A palace is a very large and beautiful house where a

king, queen, or other ruler lives. The **palace** has many gardens around it. Maria and Dale visited a **palace** with 50 rooms and marble floors.

## palm

The **palm** is the inside part of the hand. There are many lines on the **palms** of our hands.

## pan

A pan is a flat metal dish used for cooking. Many **pans** have long handles. We cooked the fish in a large **pan**.

## pancake

A pancake is a kind of food. It is a thin, flat cake. **Pancakes** are made of flour, eggs, and milk that you mix together and cook in a hot pan.

## pants

**Pants** are a kind of clothes. People wear **pants** over

their legs. Most **pants** have pockets in the sides.

## paper

**Paper** is something people use to write on. It is made from wood. Books and newspapers are made of paper.

## parachute

A parachute is used to drop people or things slowly and safely from an airplane. **Parachutes** look like big umbrellas.

## parade

A parade is a group of people who march together down the street. Most **parades** have bands that play music as they march. **Parades** often happen on holidays.

## parakeet

A **parakeet** is a small bird with a long, pointed tail. **Parakeets** have blue, green, and yellow feathers.

## parent

A parent is a mother or a father. Jane's **parents** took us skating.

## park

1. A park is an area of land where people can play or rest. Most **parks** have trees and grass and benches.

2. **Park** also means to put something in a place where it can stay for a while. Bob **parked** the car in the garage.

## parking lot

A parking lot is a place where people can leave their cars for a short time. We left the car in the **parking lot** when we went shopping.

## parrot

A parrot is a kind of bird. It has a large beak and feathers in bright colors. Some **parrots** can learn to say a few words.

## part

A part is a piece of some-thing. Your head is a **part** of your body. A television has many **parts**.

## party

A party is a time when peo-ple get together to have fun. Many people have a **party** on their birthday.

## pass

1. Pass means to go by. We **pass** your house on the way to school.
2. **Pass** also means to move something from one person to another. Please **pass** the cereal to me.
3. **Pass** also means to know something well enough so that you do not have to learn it again. I hope I **pass** the spelling test tomorrow.

# Passover

**Passover** is a Jewish holi-day celebrated in the

spring. Families and friends gather together for a special meal on **Passover** and tell the story of the holiday.

## past

1. The **past** is the part of time that has already happened. Yesterday is in the **past**.

2. To go past means to go beside. A big river goes past many towns and cities.

## paste

1. **Paste** is something you use to make things stick together. Remember to put the top back on the **paste** jar, or the **paste** will dry up.

2. Paste also means to stick things together with paste. Charlie **pasted** the photographs on all of the pages of his book.

## pat

Pat means to touch gently with your hand. My horse likes it when I **pat** him on the head.

## patch

1. A **patch** is a small piece of cloth. People sew **patches** on clothes to cover up holes.
2. A **patch** also means an area of ground. The farmer grew pumpkins in his pumpkin **patch**.

## path

A path is a place where you can walk through a field or a forest. David and his friends followed a **path** to the lake.

## pattern

A pattern is how colors or lines or marks are placed and look on something. There is a **pattern** of pink flowers on Alice's shirt. This butterfly's wing has a **pattern** of green and black dots on it.

## paw

A paw is the foot of some animals. Dogs, cats, bears,

and rabbits all have four **paws**.

## pay
Pay means to give money for something. I'll **pay** for the popcorn. Dad **paid** the person who fixed our car.

## pea
A pea is a small, round green vegetable. Dad made **pea** soup last night.

## peace
Peace means a time when there is no fighting. When the world is at **peace**, there are no wars. Our country is at **peace**.

## peach
A peach is a round, sweet fruit. It has a yellow and red skin. We had **peaches** for dessert.

## peak
A peak is the point at the top of a mountain. We took a picture of the **peaks** cov-

ered with snow.

# peanut

A peanut is something to eat. **Peanuts** have brown shells and grow under the ground. We always get a bag of **peanuts** at the baseball game.

# peanut butter

**Peanut butter** is a soft food that is made from peanuts. Michael likes to eat **peanut butter** on crackers.

# pear

A pear is a sweet fruit. It has a yellow, brown, or red skin. **Pears** are bigger around the bottom than they are around the top. We had **pears** and cheese for dessert.

# pebble

A pebble is a small stone. There wasn't much sand at the beach, but there were lots of **pebbles**. I found a **pebble** in my shoe.

## peek

Peek means to look at something quickly or without anyone knowing. The squirrel **peeked** out from behind the tree.

## peel

Peel means to take off the skin or outside part of some fruits and vegetables. Jane **peeled** the orange for her younger sister.

## pen[1]

A pen is a tool to write with. **Pens** are usually made of plastic or metal. He wrote his name with a blue **pen**.

## pen[2]

A **pen** is an area with a fence to keep animals in. The pigs live in a **pen**.

## pencil

A pencil is a tool to write with. It is often a long stick of wood with lead in it. Most **pencils** have an

eraser on one end. Sue broke the point on her **pencil**.

# penguin

A penguin is a kind of bird. It lives near the ocean in places where it is very cold. **Penguins** cannot fly, but they can use their wings to swim in the water.

# penny

A penny is a coin. It is the smallest amount of money. One **penny** is one cent. There are 25 **pennies** in a quarter and 100 **pennies** in one dollar.

# people

People means more than one person. No two **people** are the same.

# pepper

1. Pepper is something we use on food to make it spicy. **Pepper** is usually black, but sometimes it is red or white.

2. A **pepper** is also a vegetable. Peppers can be red, green, or yellow. They are eaten raw or cooked.

# perfect
When something is **perfect**, it means that nothing is wrong with it. Jane's math test was **perfect**. She made no mistakes.

# perhaps
**Perhaps** means that something may happen. It is supposed to rain this afternoon, but **perhaps** the sun will shine instead.

# period
1. A **period** is the small dot at the end of a sentence. A sentence ends with a **period**.
2. A **period** is also an amount of time. They were on vacation for a period of six weeks.

# permit
**Permit** means to allow

someone to do something. My parents will not **permit** my sister and me to play outside after it is dark.

## person

A **person** is a man, woman, or child. Fifty people can ride on the bus, but only one **person** can drive it.

## pet

A pet is an animal that people care for in their homes. Dogs and cats are **pets**. Helen has two parakeets as **pets**.

## petal

A petal is a part of a flower. The **petals** of a daisy are narrow and white or yellow.

## pharmacy

A pharmacy is a store where drugs and medicines are sold. Another name for **pharmacy** is drugstore.

## phone

1. Phone is a short word for

telephone. The Kellys have three **phones** in their house. 2. **Phone** means to use a telephone. We **phoned** my aunt tonight to sing "Happy Birthday" to her.

# photograph

A photograph is a picture that you take with a camera. Elizabeth took a **photograph** of our class.

# piano

A piano is an instrument. It has 88 white and black keys. We push down on the keys with our fingers to make music.

# pick

1. Pick means to take something in your hand. We're going to **pick** some flowers for Dad's birthday. The children **picked** up their toys and put them away.

2. **Pick** also means to choose something. Mom helped me **pick** a dress to wear to the party.

## picnic

When you go on a picnic, you take food with you to eat outdoors. We brought sandwiches and fruit for a **picnic**.

## picture

A **picture** is something that you draw or paint. You can also take pictures with a camera. I have a **picture** of a boat on my wall.

## pie

A pie is something to eat. **Pies** are usually round. **Pies** can be filled with fruit, meat, eggs, or other things. Have you ever eaten an apple **pie**?

## piece

1. A **piece** is one part of a whole thing. We each had a **piece** of pumpkin pie after lunch.
2. A **piece** is also one out of many things. Please put all the **pieces** of the puzzle in this box.

## pig

A pig is an animal with a fat body, short legs, and a short, curly tail.

## pile

1. A pile is a lot of things lying on top of each other. We put all our old newspapers in a **pile** by the door.

2. When we put things on top of each other, we **pile** them. Dad **piled** the logs next to the garage.

## pill

A **pill** is a small, hard kind of medicine that people take when they are sick. The nurse gave me a **pill** to take with a glass of water.

## pillow

You use a pillow under your head when you rest or sleep. **Pillows** are usually soft. Most **pillows** are made of feathers or a kind of rubber.

## pilot

A pilot is someone who flies an airplane. The pilot told us to wear our seatbelts.

## pin

A **pin** is a short, thin piece of metal with a sharp point. **Pins** are used to hold clothes together while they are being sewn.

## pine

A pine is a tree that has leaves that look like needles and stay on the tree all year. The wood of the **pine** is used to make furniture.

## pink

Pink is a light red color. When we mix white and red, we get **pink**. Our cheeks were **pink** when we were outside in the cold.

## pint

A **pint** is an amount of liquid. Two **pints** are the same as one quart.

# pipe

A pipe is a long piece of metal or plastic that liquids or gases can go through. The water in your house or apartment gets to your sink through **pipes**.

# pirate

A pirate is a person on a ship who steals from other ships at sea. The **pirates** buried the treasure on an island.

# pitch

When you pitch a ball in a game, you throw it to a player who tries to hit it with a bat. Bob **pitched** for our baseball team. The person who is **pitching** is called the **pitcher**. Gail was the **pitcher** for the other team.

# pizza

Pizza is a food that is usually flat and round. The bottom is made of a kind of

bread. **Pizzas** have cheese and tomatoes on top. Sometimes **pizza** also has vegetables or meat on top of it.

# place

1. A **place** is where something is. A **place** is also where something happens. We had to look for **places** to hang our coats. Our town is a nice place to live. 2. A **place** is also a space or seat for a person. There weren't enough **places** for everyone at the table.

# plaid

A plaid is a kind of pattern that has lines of different colors going across each other. Helen wore a **plaid** skirt with a red sweater.

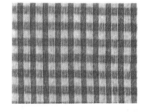

# plain

When something is **plain**, it is easy to see, hear, or understand. As the airplane started to land, the people and houses on the ground were in **plain** sight. My friends made it **plain** that they did not agree with me.

# plan

1. **Plan** means to think out a way to do something before you do it. The team **planned** how they were going to win the game.

2. A **plan** is an idea about how to do something. We are making **plans** for our summer vacation.

# plane

Plane is a short word for **airplane**. Maria likes to make model **planes**.

# planet

A **planet** moves around the sun. There are nine **planets** that travel around the sun. The earth is one of the planets.

# plant

1. A plant is anything alive that is not a person or an animal. Most **plants** grow in

the ground. Flowers, trees, and vegetables are all **plants**.

2. To **plant** means to put seeds or small plants in the ground. The seeds Jane **planted** in the spring grew into big pumpkins by fall.

## plastic

Plastic is a material that many things are made from. It can be hard or soft. Some bottles are made of **plastic**.

## plate

A plate is a dish. It is usually round and flat, and you put food on it. Johnny put the **plates** on the table for dinner.

## play

1. **Play** means to do something for fun. We're going to **play** a game of baseball.

2. Play also means to make music. Joe **played** the piano at school yesterday.

3. **Play** can also mean to

act in a play, movie, or other show. The actor who **played** the pirate was funny. 4. A **play** is a story that you act out. Our class is putting on a **play**.

# player

A player is a person who plays sports, games, musical instruments, or other things. Marie is a **player** on our hockey team.

# playground

A playground is a place where you can play outdoors.

# please

**Please** is a word that we use when we ask for something in a polite way. **Please** pass the peanuts.

# plenty

Plenty means that there is more than enough of something. There was **plenty** of corn for everybody at the picnic.

# plow | plough

A plow is a large tool that farmers use to dig up the earth. **Plows** are usually pulled by tractors or animals.

# plural

**Plural** means more than one. We use the **plural** when we want to say more than one person or thing. The **plural** of **child** is **children**. The **plural** of **book** is **books**.

# plus

**Plus** means added. If you add two and three, you get five. Two **plus** three is five. Two **plus** three can also be written $2+3$.

# pocket

A pocket is a place that holds things. Sue put her gloves in one **pocket** and her keys in another **pocket**. He was walking with his hands in his **pockets**.

## poem

A **poem** is a special kind of writing. Some **poems** have words that rhyme. Another word for **poems** is poetry.

## poet

A **poet** is a person who writes poems.

## point

1. A point is a sharp end. Pins, needles, and arrows have **points**.
2. To point is to show where something is. When Mark's brother asked where the moon was, Mark **pointed** to it in the sky with his finger.

## pole

A **pole** is a long piece of wood or metal. Telephone **poles** hold wires up in the air.

## police

The police are people whose job is to protect other people. But if people

break the law, the **police** can put them in jail.

# polite

**Polite** people are kind and think of others. People who are **polite** have good manners.

# polka dot

A polka dot is one of many round dots that make a pattern on cloth or other material. Johnny's grandma bought her a scarf with red **polka dots** on it.

# pollute

Pollute means to make something in nature dirty.

# pollution

**Pollution** means that something in nature has been made dirty. **Pollution** in the river is killing the fish. **Pollution** in the air can make it hard to breathe.

# pond

A pond is a large amount

of water that is all in one place. Some **ponds** are big enough to swim in. A **pond** is smaller than a lake.

## pony

A pony is a small kind of horse. I rode a **pony** at the fair.

## pool

A pool is filled with water to swim in. Our school has an indoor **pool**. We go swimming in the **pool** at the park during the summer.

## poor

When people are **poor**, they have very little money. The money from the concert will be used to help **poor** people.

## pop

Pop means to make a short, loud noise. When a balloon breaks, we say that it **pops**. Ray is sad because his balloon **popped**.

# popcorn

Popcorn is a kind of food. Pieces of **popcorn** get big and soft when they are cooked. They make a loud sound when they cook.

# porch

A porch is a part of a house that is outdoors. Sometimes a **porch** has a roof. We sit on our **porch** in the summer because it is cool there.

# possible

Possible means that something can happen. It is **possible** to teach some birds to talk. It is not **possible** to teach fish to write. Mastering English is **possible** for everyone.

# post office

A post office is a place where you mail letters and packages. You also buy stamps there. Some people pick up their mail at the **post office**.

## pot

A pot is a deep, round container used for cooking. We make stew in a big **pot**.

## potato

A potato is a vegetable that grows under the ground. We baked **potatoes** for dinner.

## pound

A **pound** is an amount of weight. One **pound** is 16 ounces.

## pour

To pour is to make liquid go from one place to another. Diana **poured** juice from a bottle into her glass.

## powder

Powder is something made of many very small, dry pieces. When my feet itched, Mom put some **powder** on them.

## power

1. Power is being able to

do work. A bulldozer has enough power to move big piles of dirt.

2. To have **power** means to be able to decide things. In the past, kings and queens had a lot of **power**.

3. **Power** means electricity. Our neighborhood had no **power** after the big storm.

# practice, -tise

To **practice** is to do something many times so that you can do it well. People who play music have to take a lot of time to practice.

# pray

When you **pray**, you speak to God.

# prepare

To **prepare** is to get ready. Bill **prepared** to go to camp by packing his clothes in a suitcase.

# present[1]

A present is something you

give for a special reason. Each of the children brought a **present** to the party. Another word for **present** is gift.

# present²

The present is the part of time that is here now. This minute is part of the present.

# president

A **president** is the leader of a group of people. The election to choose a **president** for the United States is held every four years in November. George Washington and Abraham Lincoln were famous presidents. We are going to have an election to choose the **president** of our class next week.

# press

1. **Press** means to push something. Murray **pressed** the button and the elevator came.

**2.** Press also means to use an iron. I **pressed** my favorite shirt so that I could wear it to the party.

## pretend

Pretend means to make believe. James and Marie **pretended** to be robots. David played a trick on me by **pretending** to be asleep.

## pretty

Pretty means nice to look at. Everyone likes **pretty** flowers.

## pretzel

A pretzel is a food baked in the shape of a knot or stick. It has salt on the outside. Joe and Wendy like to share a bag of **pretzels** after school.

## price

A **price** is how much money you have to pay for something. The **price** of a movie ticket is six dollars.

# prince

A **prince** is the son of a king or queen.

# princess

A **princess** is the daughter of a king or queen.

# principal

A principal is the leader of a school. Our **principal** is Mrs. Brown.

# print

1. **Print** means to write using letters like the letters in a book. The teacher **printed** his name on the chalkboard.

2. **Print** also means to use machines to make letters and pictures on paper. On our class trip, we saw machines **printing** books.

# printer

A printer is a machine that is used with a computer. A **printer** takes the words stored in the computer and prints them on paper.

# prison

A prison is a place where someone who has not obeyed the law has to stay. **Prison** is another word for jail.

# privacy

When people want to be alone, we say that they want privacy. Johnny went to his room because he wanted **privacy** to think.

# prize

A prize is something that you win. **Prizes** can be cups, ribbons, money, or many other things.

# probably

**Probably** means that you are almost sure something is true. Stevens comes to my house every Saturday. He will **probably** come this Saturday, too.

# problem

1. A **problem** is a question

that has not been an-
swered. There are 10
**problems** on our mathematics test today.
2. A **problem** is also something that you have to think
about. We had a **problem**
finding Anthony's house
because we had lost his
address.

## program | -gramme

A program is a show that
you watch on television or
hear on the radio. My
favorite **program** comes on
at 6 o'clock.

## promise

1. To **promise** is to say you
will do something. When
Ray borrowed Jane's base-
ball glove, he **promised** to
return it the next day.
2. A **promise** is something
that you say you will do.
People should always keep
their **promises**.

## propeller

A propeller is a part of a

machine. It is made of wood or metal. **Propellers** make planes and boats move by pushing against the air or water.

# protect

**Protect** means to keep from danger. The mother bear protected her cubs from the other animals. Seatbelts help to **protect** people in automobile accidents.

# proud

To be **proud** is to be glad to have people see what you have or what you have done. Betty was **proud** of the cake she made.

# prove

**Prove** means to show that something is true. I can **prove** that this book is mine because it has my name on it.

# public

If something is public, it means that it is for all people. Most of the children in our town go to **public** school. Our **public** library is open every day except Sunday.

## publish

Publish means to print a newspaper, magazine, book, or other written thing and try to sell it. My grandmother wrote a book of poems that was **published** a long time ago. Margaret's uncle **publishes** a magazine about horses.

## pudding

Pudding is a soft, sweet dessert. Sue's favorite dessert is chocolate **pudding**.

## puddle

A puddle is a small area of water that is made when it rains or when snow melts. I like to step in **puddles** and make the water splash. There were **puddles** in the road after the rain.

# pull

To **pull** is to make something follow you. Charlie **pulled** a big box out of the garage and took everything out of it.

# pumpkin

A pumpkin is a big, round, orange fruit that grows on the ground. We cut a face in a **pumpkin** for Halloween.

# punch

Punch means to hit something hard with your fist. Al **punched** Bob on the arm when they had a fight.

# punish

**Punish** means to cause someone to suffer for a crime, fault, or misbehavior. To **punish** me my parents took away my allowance.

# pupil

A pupil is someone who goes to school. There are 25 **pupils** in our class. Another word for **pupil** is

student.

## puppet

A puppet is a doll that you put over your hand and move with your fingers. Another kind of **puppet** has strings that you pull to make it move. In school, we put on a show using **puppets**.

## puppy

A puppy is a baby dog. The **puppies** slept close to their mother.

## purchase

Purchase means to get something by paying money. We **purchased** our train tickets at the railroad station. He **purchased** a new car.

## pure

When something is **pure**, it is not mixed with anything else. My scarf is made of pure wool. We want **pure** air.

## purple

Purple is a color. When we mix red and blue, we get purple.

## purpose

When you do something on **purpose**, it means that you have a reason for what you do. Margaret dropped the books on **purpose** to make a loud noise and scare us.

## purr

**Purr** means to make a soft, quiet sound. Cats **purr** when they are happy. My cat always **purrs** when I scratch her back.

## purse

A purse is a bag for carrying money and other small things. **Purses** are made of cloth, plastic, or other soft material. Elizabeth put her keys in her **purse**.

## push

To push is to make something go ahead of you.

George **pushed** the shopping cart for her mother.

## put

To **put** is to find a place for something and leave it there. Diana **put** a sandwich in her lunch box to take to school.

## puzzle

1. A puzzle is a game. Some **puzzles** are pieces of paper or wood that you have to put together to make pictures. Other **puzzles** are hard questions that you work out in your head or with a pencil and paper. 2. A **puzzle** is also something that is hard to understand. It was a **puzzle** to Jane how her sister got home before she did.

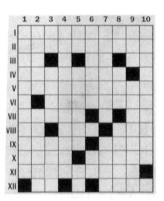

## quart

A **quart** is an amount of liquid. There are four **quarts** in one gallon. A **quart** is a little smaller than a liter.

## quarter

1. A quarter is a kind of coin. One **quarter** is the same as five nickels. Four **quarters** is the same as one dollar.

2. A quarter is one of four pieces that are the same size. You can cut a pie into **quarters**.

## queen

A queen is a woman who rules a country. The **queen** waved to the people as she rode in the carriage.

## question

A **question** is a group of words that ask something that you want to know. Sometimes the teacher asks **questions** that nobody can answer.

## question mark

A question mark comes at the end of a sentence that is a question. Does this sentence end with a **question mark** or a period?

## quick

When something is quick, it means that it moves fast or happens in a short time. We ate a **quick** lunch.

## quickly

When you do something fast, you do it **quickly**. When the traffic light changed to green, Irving **quickly** crossed the street.

## quiet

To be quiet means to make very little sound. Our neighborhood is very **quiet** at night.

## quilt

A quilt is like a blanket. It is made of two pieces of cloth that are filled with soft material. I sleep under a soft, warm **quilt** during the winter.

## quite

**Quite** means very or a lot. It is **quite** warm today. There was quite a crowd of people at the new store when it opened.

## quiz

A **quiz** is a short test. We had a spelling **quiz** today on the new words we learned yesterday.

# rabbit

A rabbit is a small animal with long ears, soft fur, and a short tail. **Rabbits** have strong legs in the back and can hop very fast.

# raccoon

A raccoon is a small, furry animal. It has black marks on its face that look like a mask and black rings on its tail. We saw two **raccoons** in the woods yesterday.

# race

A race is a contest to find who is fastest. People have **races** on foot, in cars, on horses, and in many other ways.

# radar

Radar is an instrument used

R

to find and follow things like airplanes, automobiles, and storms. **Radar** helps pilots land their airplanes safely.

# radio

A radio is a machine that you can turn on to listen to music, news, or other programs. Some evenings we listen to music on our **radio**. Turn off the **radio** please.

# raft

A **raft** is a kind of flat boat made of logs or boards that have been joined together. Some **rafts** are made of rubber or plastic and are filled with air. Floating on a **raft** in the middle of a lake is a perfect way to spend a hot afternoon.

# rag

A **rag** is a small piece of cloth. It is usually made of torn material. Arthur and Billy used rags to wash the car.

# railing

A railing is a fence that protects you from falling over or into something. We put a **railing** around our pool.

# railroad

A railroad is the metal path that trains ride on. **Railroads** can go across bridges, through tunnels, and over mountains.

# rain

1. **Rain** is water that falls in drops from clouds. Plants need **rain** to grow.
2. To **rain** means to fall as drops of water. When it **rains**, everything gets wet.

# rainbow

The colors that you some-times see in the sky after it rains are called a rainbow. **Rainbows** have the shape of a curve. They happen when light from the sun

shines through tiny drops of water in the air.

## raincoat

A **raincoat** is a coat that you wear to keep dry in the rain. We put on our **raincoats**, boots, and hats to go outside when it was raining.

## raise

**1.** When you **raise** something, you lift it up. Jack and Alice helped the teacher **raise** the flag to the top of the flagpole. Mary raised her hand because she knew the answer to the teacher's question.

**2. Raise** also means to help something to grow. One farmer in our town is **raising** corn, and another is **raising** chickens.

## rake

**1.** A rake is a tool for gathering leaves or other things together. A **rake** has teeth like a comb and a

long handle.

**2. Rake** can also mean to gather things together with a rake. Richard and Jim **raked** all the leaves into a big pile.

## ramp

A **ramp** is a kind of road or sidewalk that goes up from one place to another. A **ramp** does not have steps. There are **ramps** at our school for people who can't use the stairs.

## ran

**Ran** comes from the word **run**. The fox ran back into the woods when it saw us coming toward it.

## ranch

A ranch is a kind of farm that has cattle, sheep, or horses on it. My aunt and uncle live on a **ranch** and raise cattle.

## rang

Rang comes from the word

ring². Charlie **rang** the bell, and Mr. Brown opened the door. When the fire alarm **rang**, we rushed out of the building.

## ranger

A **ranger** is a person whose work is to protect forests, parks, and other areas. The **ranger** showed us where the picnic area was.

## rat

A rat is an animal. It has a long tail, short fur, and sharp teeth. **Rats** are bigger than mice.

## raw

Raw means not cooked. Mark likes to eat a salad made of **raw** carrots, tomatoes, and lettuce.

## reach

1. When you **reach** for something, you put out your hand to touch it. Joe can't **reach** the top shelf

unless he stands on his toes.

2. **Reach** also means to get to a place. When the bus **reached** our street, we asked the driver to stop.

# read

To read means to look at words and know what they mean. Ray is learning to **read**. He often **reads** stories with his mother or father.

# ready

If you are **ready**, it means that when there is something to do, you can do it. Once I pack my clothes, I will be **ready** to go on the trip. Everyone is ready to start the race.

# real

When something is **real**, you know it is true. Is that a **real** bug, or is it made of plastic? The giant in the fairy tale was not **real**. It was make-believe.

## reality

**Reality** means something that is real. The things that happen every day are **reality**. When you write about the things you do, you are writing about **reality**. The opposite of **reality** is **fantasy**.

## really

1. **Really** comes from the word **real**. We use **really** when we are very sure about something. I **really** want to be a doctor.

2. **Really** also means very. We had really good time at the carnival.

## reason

A **reason** tells you why something happened. The reason Anne gave for being late for the concert was that there was a lot of traffic.

## recess

A recess is a short time

R

when you stop working. We played outside the school during **recess**.

# recipe

A recipe tells you how to make something to eat or drink. Read the **recipe** before you start to make the soup.

# record

A record is a round, flat disk made of plastic. It has music or other sounds on it. At the party, we listened to **records** and sang along.

# rectangle

A **rectangle** is a shape with four sides and four corners. The cover of this book is in the shape of a rectangle.

# recycle

When we **recycle** something, we make it so that it can be used again. Our town **recycles** cans, bottles, and newspapers.

## red

Red is the color of blood. Most fire engines are painted red.

## reflection

A reflection is what you see when you look in a mirror or in still water. I see my reflection in the pond.

## refrigerator

A refrigerator is a large machine that keeps food cold. We put milk in the refrigerator to keep it fresh.

## relative

A relative is someone who is part of your family. Your parents, sisters and brothers, and grandparents are your relatives. So are your aunts, uncles, and cousins.

## relax

Relax means to rest and feel comfortable. Reading, watching television, or taking a walk are some ways

to **relax**. Hannah likes to **relax** by reading mystery stories.

## remember

When we **remember** something, we think of it again, or we do not forget it. Joe remembered to close the door when he went outdoors.

## remind

**Remind** means to make someone remember. My sister **reminded** me to feed the cat before I left for school.

## rent

**Rent** is money that you pay to use something. My parents pay **rent** every month for our apartment.

## repeat

If you repeat something, you do it or say it again. The teacher asked me to **repeat** my answer because he could not hear me.

## reptile

A reptile is a kind of animal that crawls on its stomach or walks on very short legs. Snakes, turtles, and lizards are all **reptiles**. Most **reptiles** lay eggs. An alligator is a kind of **reptile**.

## responsibility

When you have a **respon-sibility**, you have a job or something that you are supposed to do. Jane has the responsibility of caring for her pet.

## rest$^1$

1. When you rest, you stop what you are doing for a while because you are tired. The children need to **rest** after lunch before they go out to play again.
2. A **rest** is the time you are resting. After the long hike, we all took a **rest**.

## rest$^2$

The **rest** of something is

what is left. Tom ate half of his sandwich for lunch. He saved the **rest** for after school.

## restaurant

A restaurant is a place where people go to eat meals. Most **restaurants** make many different kinds of food. We had dinner at a **restaurant**.

## return

1. To **return** is to come back. Birds that have gone south in the winter return every spring.   He has just **returned** home.
2. To **return** also means to bring back. Peter **returned** the books to the library after he read them.

## reward

If you lose something important, you may give a **reward** to someone for finding it. Mrs. Brown gave Bob a **$5 reward** for finding her lost dog.

# rhinoceros

A rhinoceros is an animal with one or two big horns on its nose. **Rhinoceroses** have very thick, heavy skin and short legs.

# rhyme, rime

To **rhyme** means to end with the same sound. Cook **rhymes** with book. Group **rhymes** with soup. Tall **rhymes** with small. Many poems use words that **rhyme**.

# ribbon

A **ribbon** is a long, thin piece of cloth or paper. **Ribbons** come in many colors. Presents are often wrapped in paper and tied with a ribbon.

# rice

**Rice** is a kind of food. Grains of **rice** are soft when they are cooked. Rice is the seeds of a kind of grass that grows in warm places.

# rich

To be rich means to have a lot of money. **Rich** people often live in big houses and have fancy cars and other things.

# ridden

**Ridden** is a form of **ride**. Margaret likes to ride her bicycle. She has ridden it every day this week. Have you ever **ridden** on a horse?

# riddle

A **riddle** is a question or problem that is hard to answer or understand. Here is a **riddle** : What has two hands but no fingers? Answer : A clock.

# ride

1. To **ride** is to sit in or on something that moves. Cowboys **ride** horses. Children ride to school on a bus.

2. A **ride** is a time when you ride in something. Every Sunday our family goes for

a **ride** in the country.

# right

**1. Right** is the opposite of **left**. In the United States, people drive cars on the right side of the road.

**2. Right** also means not having a mistake. Nancy knew the **right** answers to all the questions on the test.

**3. Right** also means immediately. Let's leave **right** after lunch.

# ring¹

A ring is a circle that has an empty center. Some people wear **rings** of gold and silver on their fingers.

# ring²

**Ring** means to make a sound with a bell. At camp, they **ring** a bell when dinner is ready.

# rink

A rink is a place where people ice-skate or roller-skate.

## rip
Rip means to tear some-thing like paper or cloth. Don't let the baby **rip** the pages out of the book.

## ripe
When something is ripe, it has finished growing and is ready to be eaten. When bananas turn yellow, they are **ripe**.

## rise
To **rise** is to go up. The sun rises in the east every morning. The temperature outside **rises** on hot days.

## risen
Risen is a form of **rise**. Mike wanted to watch the sun rise, but he slept too late. It had already **risen** when he woke up.

## river
A river is a wide path of water that has land on both

sides. Some **rivers** are hundreds of miles long.

# road

A road is a wide path that cars travel on. Before there were cars, horses and wagons traveled on **roads**. Yesterday we watched the workers fill the hole in the **road**.

# roar

**Roar** means to make a loud, deep sound. Bears, lions, and tigers can **roar**. When the airplane was landing, we could hear the engine roar.

# roast

Roast means to cook in an oven or over a fire. Grandma **roasted** a chicken for dinner tonight.

# rob

To **rob** means to take something away from someone. Three people **robbed** the bank on Tues-

R

day. They took all the
money.

# robin

A robin is a kind of bird.
**Robins** are red in front.

# robot

A **robot** is a machine. It can
do some of the same work
that people do. Some
**robots** do work that is dangerous for people to do.

# rock[1]

A rock is a big stone. Bill
and Kendrew climbed over
the **rocks** at the park.

# rock[2]

When you **rock**, you gently
move backward and for-
ward or from side to side. I
**rocked** the baby in my
arms.

# rocket

A rocket is a machine that
can fly up into the air very
quickly. People travel into
outer space in very large

rockets.

# rocking chair

A rocking chair is a chair that rests on two long pieces of wood in the shape of a curve. When you sit in a **rocking chair** and lean forward and backward, the chair rocks.

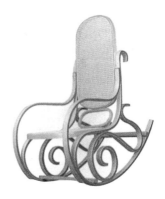

# rode

Rode comes from the word **ride**. We **rode** horses on the beach.

# rodeo

A rodeo is a show with contests in which cowboys and cowgirls ride horses and do tricks.

# roll

1. **Roll** means to move by turning over and over. **Roll** the ball to me and I will kick it back to you.

2. **Roll** also means to move on wheels. Diana and her friends **rolled** down the street on their skateboards.

## roller skate

1. A **roller skate** is a skate with wheels on the bottom.
2. When you roller-skate, you move on roller skates. We went to the park on Saturday morning to **roller-skate**.

## roof

A roof is the top part of a building. In the city, many houses have flat **roofs**. There is a chimney on top of our **roof**. Don't climb on to the **roof**.

## room

1. A room is a part of a house or other building. The **room** you sleep in is your bedroom. Whose **room** is this?
2. **Room** can also mean space. There is plenty of **room** in the car for six people. I ate so much dinner that I had no **room** for dessert.

## rooster

A rooster is a male chicken. Roosters make a loud noise early in the morning when the sun comes up.

## root

A root is a part of a plant. It usually grows under the ground. Plants get food from the ground through their roots.

R

## rope

A rope is a very strong, thick string for pulling, lifting, or hanging things. Rope is also used to hold something in place. We used rope to tie all the boxes together.

## rose¹

A rose is a flower that grows on a bush. Roses are red, white, yellow, or other colors. Mary has a garden of roses.

## rose²

Rose is a form of rise. The

sun **rose** this morning at six o'clock.

# rough

**1.** Something that feels **rough** is full of bumps. The bark of a tree feels rough.
**2. Rough** also means not gentle. The children were too **rough** playing football, and Lewis hurt his hand.

# round

When something is round, it has the shape of a ball or a globe. A circle is **round**. The earth is **round**.

# row

A **row** is a line of people or things. My desk is in the last row in our classroom. Susan planted a **row** of flowers along the wall.

# rub

To **rub** means to press something down and move it back and forth. Geoffrey **rubbed** the window with a cloth to clean the dirt off.

# rubber

Rubber is a material that you can pull and it won't break. Tires are made of rubber. **Rubber** also keeps out water. Some boots are made of **rubber**. Harry wears **rubber** boots when it rains.

# ruby

A ruby is a kind of jewel. **Rubies** are red.

# rude

When you are **rude**, you are not being polite to someone. It was **rude** of Elizabeth to yell at Tom when he asked to borrow her book.

# rug

A rug is made of very strong cloth and is used to cover a floor. I have a **rug** in my bedroom.

# rule

1. A rule tells you what you can do and what you can-

not do. One of the **rules** at school is that you cannot run in the halls.

2. **Rule** also means to lead. The queen **ruled** her country well.

## ruler

1. A ruler is a tool for measuring how long something is. **Rulers** are long and straight. You can also use a **ruler** to draw a straight line. I measured my drawing with a **ruler**.

2. A **ruler** is also someone who is the leader of a country. The king and queen were fair **rulers**.

## rumble

**Rumble** means to make a deep sound. David heard thunder rumbling just after he saw the lightning. The old truck **rumbled** over the bumps in the road.

## run

1. Run means to move with your legs as fast as you

can. Tony had to **run** to catch the bus. My parents exercise by **running** every day.

**2. Run** also means to work without any problems. When our car was broken, it wouldn't **run**. After we got it fixed, it **ran** again.

## rung

**Rung** comes from the word ring[2]. When the bell is **rung**, we can go out to the playground for recess.

## rush

**Rush** means to move, go, or come quickly. We have to **rush** or we'll be late for school. The police **rushed** the sick person to the hospital.

## sad

When you are sad, you feel very unhappy. Sometimes you cry when you are **sad**. She was **sad** to hear the news.

## safe

To be **safe** means to be in no danger. There was a terrible storm outside, but inside the house everyone was **safe**.

## said

Said comes from the word **say**. He **said**, "I know where your baseball glove is."

## sail

1. A sail is a large piece of cloth on a boat. When the wind blows on the **sail**, it

makes the boat move for-
ward.

**2.** Sail also means to move
over water. The children
**sailed** their toy boats on the
pond.

# sailboat

A **sailboat** is a boat that
uses a sail to make it move
on the water.

# sailor

A sailor is someone who
sails a boat. **Sailors** know a
lot about wind and water.

# salad

A salad is a cold food that
is made with different vegetables, fruits, or meats.
Some **salads** are made with
lettuce and tomatoes.
Some **salads** have chicken
or fish or noodles in them.

# sale

When there is a **sale**, things
are sold for less than they
usually cost. The store is
having a **sale** on jeans.

## salt

Salt is found in the ocean and in the ground. Some people put **salt** in their food to make it taste better. It is white.

## same

To be the same means to agree in every way. Betty and Sarah both have blue eyes. Their eyes are the **same** color.

## sand

Sand is a kind of earth that is made of tiny pieces of rock. There is sand on beaches and in deserts.

# sandwich

A sandwich is a kind of food. It is made of meat, cheese, peanut butter, or other things between two pieces of bread. Many people eat **sandwiches** for lunch.

## sang

Sang is a form of **sing**.

Diana learned a new song yesterday. She **sang** it all day long.

## sank

**Sank** comes from the word **sink**. My feet **sank** into the sand.

## sat

Sat comes from the word **sit**. The bird **sat** on the fence.

# Saturday

**Saturday** is a day of the week. **Saturday** comes after Friday and before Sunday.

## saucer

A saucer is a small dish that isn't very deep. It usually fits under a cup. People sometimes put milk into **saucers** for cats to drink.

## save

1. **Save** means to keep someone or something safe. The firefighters **saved**

the family from the burning building.

**2. Save** also means to keep something to have or use later. Mom and Dad **saved** all my baby pictures. I am going to **save** my money to buy a game.

# saw[1]

A **saw** is a tool that has a blade with sharp, metal teeth. **Saws** are used to cut wood, metal, and plastic.

# saw[2]

**Saw** comes from the word **see**. We **saw** elephants at the zoo.

# say

To **say** means to speak words. When Dick answers the telephone, he says, "Hello!"

# scale

**1.** A scale is a machine that tells how heavy something is. There are different kinds of **scales** for weighing people, vegetables, and trucks. We put two more tomatoes on the **scale**.

2. Scales are also hard little pieces of skin that cover fish, snakes, and some other kinds of animals.

## scare

If something **scares** you, it makes you feel afraid. Loud noises always **scare** the puppy.

## scarecrow

A **scarecrow** is put in a field to keep the birds away. A **scarecrow** looks like a person who is dressed in old clothes.

## scarf

A scarf is a piece of cloth that you wear around your head or your neck.

## school

A school is a place where you go to learn. At **school** your teacher teaches you important things such as

how to read, write, and count.

## science

Science is something you study in school. **Science** can teach you about animals and plants. You can also learn about the earth and the stars from **science**.

## scientist

A scientist is a person who works in a special part of science. Some **scientists** study the weather.

## scissors

Scissors are a tool with two sharp blades. You use **scissors** to cut things.

## scratch

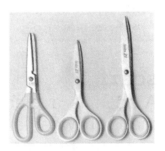

To **scratch** means to make marks on something. A rock can **scratch** a piece of glass. Cats can **scratch** with their claws.

## scream

Scream means to shout or

call in a loud voice. People **scream** when they are frightened or angry or excited.

## screen

You put a **screen** over a window to keep the bugs out and to let the air in.

## scrub

**Scrub** means to wash or clean by rubbing. After we played with clay, we had to **scrub** our hands to get them clean.

## sea

Sea is another word for ocean. Many years ago pirates sailed the **seas** looking for treasure.

## seal[1]

A seal is an animal that lives in the ocean most of the time and swims very well. **Seals** have thick, smooth fur and a long body. They make a sound like a dog barking.

## seal²

Seal means to close something so that it cannot come open. Before we mailed our valentines, we checked to be sure that we had sealed all the envelopes.

## season

A season is a time of year. There are four seasons in a year. They are spring, summer, fall, and winter. What's your favorite season?

## seat

A seat is anywhere you can sit. Bob took a seat in the back of the room. Go back to your seat.

## seatbelt

A seatbelt is a kind of belt that goes around you when you ride in a car or an airplane. A seatbelt keeps you from falling out of your seat if there is a bump or an accident.

## second¹

Second is next after first. The **second** letter of the alphabet is B.

## second²

A **second** is part of a minute. There are 60 **seconds** in a minute.

## secret

A **secret** is something that not many people know. Sometimes only one person knows a **secret**. The present I'm giving Mother for her birthday is my **secret**.

## secretary

A secretary is a person who writes letters and does work for another person or a group. Joe won the election for **secretary** of the stamp club.

## see

1. **See** means to look at something with your eyes. I could **see** Peter's kite up in

the sky.

**2. See** also means to find out. Let's **see** if there is any more juice.

# seed

A seed is a part of a plant. New plants grow from **seeds**. The **seeds** we plant-ed in our vegetable garden grew into tomatoes and green peppers. We also planted some pumpkin **seeds**.

# seem

To **seem** means to look like. This **seems** like a good place to have a picnic.

# seen

**Seen** comes from the word **see**. Have you ever **seen** an elephant?

# seesaw

A seesaw is a long board that two people sit on to make it go up and down. When one end of the **see-saw** is down, the other end is up.

## select

Select means to pick out. Mom said we could **select** the tape our family would watch tonight. Have you **selected** the baseball bat you want?

## selfish

If a person is **selfish**, that person does not like to share things. Smith was **selfish** when he wouldn't let his cousin Joe play with any of his toys.

## sell

When you sell something you give it to someone who gives you money for it. The furniture store **sells** tables, chairs, and beds. I **sold** my old bicycle and bought a new one.

## send

To send means to make someone or something go somewhere. Susan likes to

**send** letters to her friends. Frank's mother **sent** him to the store to buy some bread.

## sent

Sent is a form of **send**. Diana's grandfather sent her a present on her birthday.

## sentence

A **sentence** is a group of words that makes a whole thought. The first word in a **sentence** begins with a capital letter. This is a very long **sentence**.

## September

September is a month of the year. It has 30 days. **September** comes after August and before October.

## serious

Serious means not funny. When Bart is in a **serious** mood, he does not feel like laughing at jokes.

## serve

Serve means to bring food to the place where someone is going to eat it. We **served** lunch in the kitchen.

## set

1. **Set** means to put one thing on another. Anne **set** her books on the table. I set the table for dinner.
2. A **set** is a group of things that go together.

## seven

Seven is one more than six. **Seven** is witten **7**. $6+1=7$.

## several

Several means more than three or four. Maria has **several** new books. **Several** people left the room.

## sew

Sew means to put together with a needle and thread. I **sewed** a button on my shirt. Mom is **sewing** a patch over the hole in my jeans.

# shade

1. **Shade** is a place that is protected from the sun. It was a hot day, so we sat in the **shade**. Some children are playing under the **shade** of a tree.

2. A **shade** is also something that keeps light out or makes light less bright. There is a shade on the window in my bedroom.

# shadow

A shadow is a dark area that is sometimes made when light shines on a person or thing. The **shadow** is the same shape as the person or thing. Mom can make a **shadow** with her hands that looks like a talking rabbit.

# shake

Shake means to move up and down or from side to side. **Shake** the bottle of juice before you open it. Our dog **shook** water off its fur.

# shaken

**shaken** is a form of **shake**. When our dog gets wet, we make sure he has **shaken** all the water off before he comes in the house.

# shall

**Shall** means will. I **shall** be happy when school starts.

# shape

1. A **shape** is the outline or form of an object. Baseballs and basketballs have a round shape. Boxes have a square **shape**.
2. To shape is to give a shape to something. Dale's uncle **shaped** a piece of clay into a ball.

# share

1. **Share** means to give some of what you have to someone else. Richard said he would **share** his cookies with us.
2. **share** also means to use something together. I **share**

my toys with my sister and brother.

## shark

A shark is a fish that lives in the ocean. It has a large mouth with sharp teeth. **Sharks** eat other fish.

## sharp

To be **sharp** is to have a point or a thin edge that cuts. Some knives have sharp edges.

## she

1. **She** is a word for a girl or a woman or a female animal. My mother told me that **she** would return soon.
2. **She'd** means **she had** or **she would**. **She'd** always wanted to ride in a helicopter.
3. **She'll** means **she will**. **She'll** be late if she doesn't hurry.
4. **She's** means **she is**. **She's** going to the library with me.

# sheep

A sheep is an animal with curly hair. Wool is made from the hair of **sheep**. Baby **sheep** are called lambs.

# shelf

A shelf is a place to put things. It can be made of wood, metal, or plastic. In my room, I have **shelves** on the wall to hold my books and toys.

# shell

A shell is a hard part that covers something. Eggs and nuts have **shells**. Some animals, like turtles, have **shells**. The **shells** that you find at the beach used to have animals living in them.

# shine

1. **Shine** means to give out light or to be bright. The sun **shines** during the day.
2. **Shine** also means to make something bright. Uncle Mark **shined** his

shoes before he left for work this morning.

# ship

1. A ship is a big boat that travels in the ocean or on big lakes or rivers. It carries people and things over the water. **Ships** use sails and engines to make them run. There are **ships** in the harbor.

2. **Ship** also means to send something to another place. When we move to a new town, we will **ship** our furniture there on a truck.

# shirt

A shirt is a kind of clothes. People wear **shirts** on the top part of their bodies. Many **shirts** have buttons.

# shoe

A shoe is something that covers a foot. It may be made of leather, cloth, or plastic. People usually wear **shoes** over socks.

# shoelace

A shoelace is a string that helps a shoe stay on your foot. Mike knows how to tie his **shoelaces**.

# shone

Shone comes from the word **shine**. The moon **shone** in my window.

# shook

Shook is a form of **shake**. Bill **shook** the jar until the juice was all mixed up. When he asked Sue if she wanted any, she **shook** her head to say no.

# shoot

1. To **shoot** is to go up or out quickly. Rockets shoot up into the air.
2. To **shoot** also means to make go toward something. Tony **shoots** a basketball at the basket.

# shop

1. A shop is a place where you can buy things. Alice

went to the pet **shop** to buy food for her fish. Anne bought three apples at that **shop**.

2. **Shop** also means to buy things. We went shopping for groceries on Saturday morning.

## shore

The shore is the land along the edge of an ocean, a lake, or a river. We found pretty shells as we walked along the **shore**. It is important to keep the **shore** clean.

## short

**Short** means not far from one end to another. If something is **short**, it is not long or tall. My dog has **short** legs. Maria has **short**, red hair. Terry took a **short** nap after lunch.

## shot

**Shot** is a form of **shoot**. They shot a rocket into outer space.

## should

**Should** means that it is important to do something. You **should** eat breakfast.

## shoulder

A shoulder is a part of the body. It is between your neck and your arm.

## shouldn't

**Shouldn't** means **should not**. You **shouldn't** run into the street.

## shout

To **shout** means to speak in a very loud voice. Sometimes we shout when we are excited or angry.

## shovel

1. A shovel is a tool with a long handle. It is used for digging.
2. **Shovel** also means to use a shovel. Let's **shovel** the snow.

## show

1. **Show** means to let some-

one see something or to explain something. I want to **show** my friends my new bicycle. Sarah **showed** me how to use the new computer program. Will you **show** me the way to the station?

2. A **show** is also something that you see on television or in a theater. We are going to a puppet show today.

## shower

1. When you take a shower, you wash yourself in water that is coming down on you. Marie took a **shower** instead of a bath.

2. A shower is also a short period of rain. We brought our umbrellas because we expected **showers** today.

## shut

**Shut** means to close something. Please shut the window. When Barry **shut** his eyes, his friends ran and hid.

## shy

When you are **shy**, you feel a little scared when there are people around. The **shy** little boy hid behind his mother when the guests came.

## sick

To be **sick** is to have something wrong with you. Sometimes when you are **sick**, your head or your stomach hurts. Doctors and nurses take care of **sick** people.

## side

A side is a flat part of the outside of something. A piece of paper has two **sides**. A square has four **sides**.

## sidewalk

A sidewalk is a place to walk that is next to the street. I like to roller-skate on the **sidewalk** in front of our house.

# sight

1. **Sight** is the ability to see. George's **sight** got better when he started wearing glasses.
2. **Sight** is also the distance you can see. The plane flew out of **sight**.

# sign

1. A **sign** is a symbol. The **signs** for plus and minus are + and −.
2. A **sign** is also a flat piece of metal or wood with a message printed on it. Road signs give people directions. The room has the **sign** of "No Smoking".

# signal

A signal is a way of showing people what to do. **Signals** are used instead of words. A **signal** may be a light, a sign, a flag, a moving hand, or a sound. The red lights are a **signal** that a train will be coming very soon. He raised his hand as a **signal**.

### silence

**Silence** means that there are no sounds. When there is **silence**, it is very, very quiet. Our teacher asked for silence during the spelling test.

### silent

To be **silent** is to make no sound at all. Dick tried to stay **silent** so his sister would not find him hiding behind the door.

### silly

To be **silly** means to act funny. Scott and his friends were giggling and running around the room. They were acting **silly**.

### silver

Silver is a shiny white metal that can be made into many shapes. It is used to make coins, jewelry, bowls, forks, and other things.

### simple

Simple means not fancy.

Helen can make a **simple** drawing of a person with only four lines and a circle.

## since

1. **Since** means from that time until now. Bill has been sick **since** Monday. We have lived in this house **since** I was a baby.

2. **Since** also means because. **Since** it's Sunday, we don't have to go to school.

## sing

Sing means to make music with your voice. Let's **sing** the song together. The birds **sang** in the trees. A person who **sings** is called a **singer**.

## sink

1. A sink is something that you wash things in. **Sinks** have special parts to let water in and out. We washed the vegetables in the kitchen **sink**.

2. **Sink** also means to go

down into water. I threw a rock into the pond and watched it **sink** to the bottom. The divers looked for treasure in the ship that had **sunk**.

## sip

When you **sip** something, you drink only a tiny amount at a time. The soup is hot, so please **sip** it slowly.

## sister

Your sister is a girl who has the same mother and father as you do. My **sister** and I both have blue eyes.

## sit

Sit means to rest the bottom part of your body on something. Harry **sat** on his dad's lap. My dog and I will **sit** on the floor.

## six

Six is one more than five. Six is written **6**. $5+1=6$.

## size

The **size** of something is how big or little it is. Can you guess the **size** of that tree? All of my shoes are the same **size**. What **size** do you want? This book is the same size at that.

## skate

1. You put **skates** on your feet when you roller-skate or ice-skate. Some **skates** fit over your shoes, and other **skates** are like shoes. My father bought me a pair of **skates**.

2. Skate also means to move on skates. We **skate** on the lake when it freezes. She **skated** to the music very well. A person who **skates** is called a **skater**.

## skateboard

A skateboard is a low, flat board with wheels on the bottom. You ride a **skateboard** by standing on it and pushing off with one foot.

# ski

1. A **ski** is a long, narrow piece of wood, metal, or plastic. People wear **skis** on their feet to go fast on snow.

2. To ski means to move over the snow on skis. Alice **skied** down a mountain.

# skin

Skin covers the outside of something. My **skin** gets little bumps all over it when I am cold.

# skip

Skip means to move by hopping first on one foot and then on the other. Mary **skipped** down the street.

# skirt

A skirt is a piece of clothing worn by a girl or woman, that hangs down from the waist.

# skunk

A skunk is an animal. It is

about as big as a cat. **Skunks** have big tails and white stripes on their backs. They can make a very strong smell to make other animals go away.

## sky

The sky is what you see above you when you are outdoors. You can see the moon and the stars in the **sky** at night.

## skyscraper

A skyscraper is a very tall building. New York City and Chicago are famous for their **skyscrapers**.

## sled

A sled is a toy. People ride on **sleds** over the snow. **Sleds** are made of wood, metal, or plastic.

## sleep

When you **sleep**, you rest with your eyes closed. My cat likes to **sleep** in the sun.

I **slept** for 8 hours last night.

# slept

Slept is a form of **sleep**. Wendy **slept** at her friend's house last night.

# slide

1. **Slide** means to move easily on something. She **slid** the book across the table to me.
2. A slide is something that you play on by climbing up and then sliding down.

# slip

Slip means to slide and fall down. Be careful not to **slip** on the wet floor. The dish **slipped** out of my hand and broke on the floor.

# slipper

A slipper is a soft, comfortable, loose shoe worn indoors.

# slippery

When something is **slippery**, it means that you might slip or slide on it. Roads get **slippery** when they have water or ice on them.

# slow

To be **slow** means to take a long time. Turtles are very slow.

# small

**Small** means not big. A mouse is a small animal. It is much **smaller** than a cat.

# smell

**1.** To **smell** is to take in something through your nose. Maria **smelled** the smoke in the kitchen when the food burned in the oven.

**2.** Something that **smells** is something you notice by smelling it. The bread baking in the kitchen **smells** wonderful.

**3.** A **smell** is what something has that lets you smell it. Skunks can give off a very strong **smell**.

# smile

**1.** When you **smile**, the corners of your mouth turn up. You **smile** when you are happy. Everyone smiled when we had our picture taken.

**2.** When you **smile**, you have a smile on your face. The winning team had **smiles** on their faces.

# smoke

Smoke is a dark cloud that comes from something that is burning. We saw **smoke** coming from the chimney.

# smooth

If something is **smooth**, you do not feel any bumps on it when you touch it. The skin of an apple is **smoother** than the skin of an orange.

# snake

A snake is a reptile. It has a long, narrow body and no arms or legs. Most **snakes** are small, but some can be very long.

## snap

Snap means to make a quick, sudden noise. The dry twigs **snapped** when we stepped on them.

## sneak

Sneak means to move or act in a secret way. The guests **sneaked** into Joe's house for his surprise party.

## sneaker

A sneaker is a soft, comfortable shoe with rubber on the bottom and cloth or other material on top. I put my **sneakers** on before I go out to play.

## sneeze

When you **sneeze**, you blow air out of your mouth and nose in a loud way. I always **sneeze** a lot when I have a cold.

## snow

1. Snow is rain that freezes

in the sky. We had some heavy **snow** last night.

2. **Snow** also means to fall as snow. We like to take out our sleds when it **snows**. It **snowed** all day yesterday, and it is still **snowing** today.

## snowman

Snow that has been made into the shape of a person is called a snowman. We made a **snowman** by putting three large balls of snow on top of each other.

## so

1. **So** means very. It was so cold last night that the lake froze.

2. **So** also means too. I am going to the football game and **so** is David.

## soap

Soap helps take dirt off things when it is mixed with water. Johnny uses **soap** and water to wash her hands.

## soccer

Soccer is a game played by two teams on a long, wide field. Each team has 11 people. The players try to move a round ball into a goal by kicking it or hitting it with any part of the body except their hands or arms.

## sock

A sock is a soft cover for your foot. **Socks** are worn inside shoes.

## soft

1. When something is **soft**, it feels smooth. My kitten has **soft** fur.
2. When something is **soft**, it is also not hard. Richard likes to sleep with a soft pillow.

## soil

Soil is the top part of the ground. Most plants grow in **soil**.

## sold

Sold is a form of **sell**. Mark

father sells cars. Last week he **sold** four cars.

# soldier

A soldier is a person who is a member of an army.

# solid

Solid means hard. Things made of wood and steel are solid.

# some

Some means a part of a thing or group of things. I'd like **some** of that sandwich. Some of the puppies were black and white, and **some** were all black.

# somebody

Somebody means any person. We do not know who won the race. But **somebody** must have won it.

# someone

Someone is another word for somebody. **Someone** turned on the radio in my room while I was outside.

## somersault

When you do a somersault, you roll your body so that your feet go over your head. First the acrobat did a forward **somersault**, and then he did a backward one.

## something

**Something** means a thing, but you don't know what it is. Please give me **something** to eat. When something was wrong with our new radio, we took it back to the store.

## sometimes

**Sometimes** means once in a while but not always. **Sometimes** my older sister lets me wear her clothes.

## somewhere

**Somewhere** means some place, but you do not know where. I forgot my jacket at school or **somewhere** else.

## son

A son is the male child of a mother and a father. A **son** can be a boy or a man. Your father is the **son** of your grandparents.

## song

A **song** is music that has words you sing. Susan played the piano, and we sang a song.

## soon

**Soon** means in a very short time. We'll **soon** know if we passed the test.

## sore

If you feel **sore**, it means that a part of your body hurts. After I fell down the stairs, my back felt **sore**.

## sorry

If you are **sorry**, it means that you feel sad about something. Paul was **sorry** that he broke the glass. I'm **sorry** that you can't visit me today.

## sort

Sort means to put things into groups. Arthur **sorted** his socks by putting the brown ones in one pile and the blue ones in another pile.

## sound

1. A **sound** is something that you hear. Thunder makes a loud sound. I like the **sound** of the birds singing outside my window. A piano, a trumpet, and a drum are all musical instruments that make different **sounds**.

2. A **sound** is also the noise you make when you speak. The words "bat" and "cat" begin with different **sounds**, but they end with the same **sound**.

## soup

Soup is a kind of food that you eat with a spoon. **Soup** is a liquid and is usually hot. Do you like tomato

soup or chicken **soup** better?

## sour
**Sour** is a kind of taste.
Lemon juice tastes **sour**.

## south
South is a direction. When
you look at a map, the bottom part is **south**. If you
face the sun when it goes
down in the evening, **south**
is on your left. The opposite of **south** is **north**.

## space
**1. Space** is a place that has
nothing in it. Mom found a
**space** to park the car in.
Write your name in the
**space** at the top of the
paper.
**2.** Space is also the place
where all of the planets and
stars are. The earth, moon,
and sun are in **space**.

## spaceship
A spaceship carries astronauts and their tools into

outer space. The **spaceship** took the astronauts to the moon. A camera in the **spaceship** took pictures during the trip. Another word for **spaceship** is spacecraft.

## spaghetti

Spaghetti is a long, thin noodle that looks like string. I like to eat **spaghetti** with tomatoes and cheese on it.

## speak

Speak means to say words. Jane is going to **speak** to her Aunt Nancy on the telephone.

## special

When something is **special**, it is important and not like anything else. Your birthday is a special day. Andy is a **special** friend of mine.

## spell

Spell means to put letters together so that they make

a word. Can you **spell** your name? Anne **spelled** nine words right and one word wrong.

## spelling

**Spelling** is the way words are spelled. Ketchup and catsup are two **spellings** of the same word. We study **spelling** in school every afternoon.

## spend

To spend means to give money to buy things. Mike often **spends** his money on books. This morning he **spent** six dollars and bought three new books.

## spent

**Spent** is a form of **spend**. Joe **spent** most of his money on toys.

## spice

Spices come from the seeds or other parts of certain plants and are used to add flavor to food. Pepper is a **spice**.

# spider

A spider is a very small animal with eight legs. **Spiders** are not insects. But they catch insects in the webs they make.

# spill

When you **spill** something, it falls out of what it was in. I dropped the box of crayons, and most of them **spilled** all over the floor.

# spin

**Spin** means to go around in a circle. The boy is **spinning** his top.

# splash

Splash means to throw water or some other liquid around. Stand back or the car will **splash** mud on you. The seal **splashed** into the cold ocean water.

# spoke

Spoke comes from the

word **speak**. I **spoke** to Billy
on the phone.

## spoken

Spoken comes from the
word **speak**. Terry has
**spoken** with a lot of
people today.

## spoon

A spoon is a tool to eat
with. It looks like a tiny
bowl with a handle. People
eat soup and ice cream
with **spoons**.

## sport

A sport is a kind of game.
Baseball, football, hockey,
tennis, basketball, and soccer are all different **sports**.

## spot

1. A **spot** is a small mark
that is a different color
from the area around it.
Some animals are covered
with spots.

2. A **spot** is also a place.
Henry found a very nice
**spot** to sit down.

## spring

Spring is a season. It comes after winter and before summer. The weather gets warmer and flowers begin to grow in the spring.

## spun

Spun comes from the word spin. The wheels of the car spun in the mud.

## square

A square is a shape. All four sides of a square are the same length.

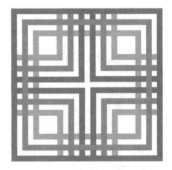

## squeeze

Squeeze means that you push hard on the sides of something. Mary squeezed juice from the oranges.

## squirrel

A squirrel is a small animal with a big tail. It lives in trees.

## stable

A stable is a building on a

farm where horses and other animals are kept.

## stage

A stage is a place where people act, dance, or sing while an audience watches them. The orchestra played a concert on the school **stage**.

## stairs

Stairs are a set of steps. You use **stairs** to go up or down. We walked up the **stairs** to the second floor.

## stamp

A stamp is a small piece of paper that is put on a letter to mail it. You buy **stamps** at the post office. Sometimes people collect **stamps**.

## stand

To **stand** is to keep your body straight and rest all your weight on your feet. Objects can **stand** on their legs or bases. Kate's desk **stands** by the door.

## star

1. A **star** is a small, bright light that can be seen in the sky at night. **Stars** are very, very far away. Some groups of stars make shapes in the sky.

2. A **star** is also a shape that has five or more points. The American flag has 50 stars on it. My jacket has small **stars** on each pocket.

## stare

To **stare** is to look long and hard at something. Jack and Tom **stared** at a man who was wearing a funny hat.

## start

1. **Start** means to begin to do something. Linda's piano lesson will **start** at 4 o'clock.

2. Start also means to make something happen or go.

Lewis got in the boat and **started** the engine.

## state

A **state** is one part of a country. There are 50 **states** in the United **States**. Most of the **states** in the United **States** are near other **states**. Alaska and Hawaii are **states** that are far away from the other **states**.

## station

A **station** is a special place or building. A train **station** is a place where trains stop. A gas station is where people buy gasoline for their cars. Television shows come from television **stations**. The police can be found at a police **station**.

## statue

A statue is a kind of art. **Statues** usually look like people or animals. **Statues** are made from stone, clay, wood, or metal and can be small or large.

## stay

To **stay** means to be in a place and not go away. Bob and Albert **stayed** at school in the afternoon to play baseball with some other children.

## steady

**Steady** means not shaking. Ray held the ladder **steady** while Dale climbed up to the tree house.

## steak

A steak is a kind of food. Most **steaks** are made of beef. They are cooked over a fire outside or in the oven.

## steal

**Steal** means to take something that does not belong to you. Someone tried to **steal** money from the bank.

## steam

When water is boiled, it changes into steam. **Steam**

is often used to heat buildings and to run engines.
We turned off the stove
when **steam** came out of
the kettle.

## steel

Steel is a metal. It is made
from iron that has been
melted. **Steel** is very hard
and strong. It is used to
make bridges, buildings,
and many other things.

## stem

A stem is the part of a plant
that holds the leaves and
the flowers. Food and
water travel up the **stem**
from the ground to all parts
of the plant.

## step

1. **Step** means to raise your
foot from one place and
put it down somewhere
else. Be careful not to **step**
in the puddle.
2. Step also means a place
to put your foot when you
are going up or down. He

ran up the **steps**. We sat on the front **steps** of our house.

# stethoscope

A stethoscope is an instrument that a doctor or a nurse uses to listen to your heart.

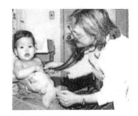

# stew

Stew is meat or fish and vegetables cooked together in one pot.

# stick[1]

A **stick** is a long, thin piece of wood. I threw a **stick**, and my dog ran after it.

# stick[2]

1. **Stick** means to push something that is sharp into something else. If you **stick** a pin into a balloon, it will pop.
2. **Stick** also means to make something stay on something else. George **stuck** a stamp on the envelope.

# still

1. **Still** means that something has not stopped. My
sister was mad at me yes-
terday. She is **still** mad at
me today.
2. Still also means not moving. When there is no wind,
the water is very **still**.

# sting

A  **sting** is a tiny cut made
by an insect. The bee **sting**
on my foot hurts.

# stir

Stir means to mix some-
thing by moving it around
with a spoon or a stick. **Stir**
the paint before you use it.
I **stirred** milk into the soup.

# stole

Stole comes from the word
**steal**. The cat **stole** a piece
of fish from the counter.

# stolen

Stolen comes from the
word **steal**. Some books

were **stolen** from the library last year.

## stomach

The **stomach** is a part of the body. The food we eat goes into our **stomachs**.

## stone

A stone is a small piece of rock. Smooth **stones** are found on the shores of oceans, lakes, and rivers.

## stood

Stood comes from the word **stand**. Everyone **stood** when the President walked into the room.

## stool

A **stool** is a kind of seat. It does not have a place for your back or arms. That piano player is sitting on a **stool** instead of a bench.

## stop

To **stop** means not to move. Buses stop at different places to let people get on and off.

# stoplight

Stoplight is another word for traffic light.

# store

1. A **store** is a place where you buy things. We went to the shoe **store**, and I got a new pair of shoes.
2. **Store** also means to put something away so that you can use it later. The squirrels **stored** food in autumn to eat during winter.

S

# storm

A storm is a strong wind. **Storms** usually bring rain or snow. Many also have thunder and lightning.

# story

A **story** is a group of words that tell what happened to people and places. **Stories** can be real or they can be made up.

## stove

A stove is something that is used to cook food on. Stoves use electricity, gas, or wood to make them hot.

## straight

If something is **straight**, it does not bend or turn to one side. Dad made sure that the picture on the wall was hung straight. Please try to sit up **straight** at your desk. Go **straight** along this road.

## strange

Strange means very different from what you expect. The kitchen had a **strange** smell. Joseph drew a picture of a **strange** animal with red ears.

## stranger

A **stranger** is someone you do not know. He is a perfect **stranger** to me.

## straw

1. A straw is a thin tube

used for drinking things. It is made of paper or plastic. Tom drinks his milk through a **straw**.

2. **Straw** is also the dry stems of some plants. Our pony sleeps on **straw** in the barn. Some brooms are made of **straw**.

## strawberry

A strawberry is a small, red fruit with little seeds on it. I like to eat **strawberry** jelly on my toast.

## stream

A stream is a narrow path of water. It moves in one direction. **Streams** are not as big as rivers.

## street

A street is a road in a city or a town. Large cities have many **streets**.

## stretch

To **stretch** is to change the shape of something by pulling it. Rubber and some kinds of plastic are easy to **stretch**.

## strike

**Strike** means to hit something. My toy plane **struck** a tree trunk, but it did not break.

## string

**String** is used to tie things. It is made from long, strong plants or from a special kind of plastic. **String** comes in many different sizes and colors. Rope is made of many strings twisted together.

## string bean

A string bean is a kind of vegetable. **String beans** are long and green. They grow on bushes.

## strip

A **strip** is a long, narrow piece of something. They tore the paper into **strips** of different lengths.

# stripe

A **stripe** is a long line that is a different color from what is next to it. Tigers and zebras have stripes.

# strong

**1.** To be **strong** is to have a lot of power. Oliver is so **strong** that he can lift two full suitcases.
**2. Strong** also means hard to break. Things made from steel are very **strong**.

# struck

**Struck** comes from the word **strike**. Lightning **struck** the tree and hurt it.

# stuck

**Stuck** comes from the word **stick**[2]. Our car got **stuck** in the mud.

# student

A student is someone who goes to school to learn. **Students** learn from teachers in class.

# study

When you study, you try hard to learn about something. Maria **studies** ballet. Harry **studied** a book about whales, and then he wrote a story about them. Our class is **studying** the planets.

# stuff

**Stuff** means to pack something very full. We **stuffed** all our clothes into one suitcase. Jenny **stuffed** her books and jacket into her backpack.

# stung

**Stung** comes from the word **sting**. My arm hurt when the bee **stung** me. A bee has **stung** the pony.

# submarine

A submarine is a ship that can travel under water.

# subtract

To **subtract** is to take away one number from another

number. When you **subtrack** four from nine, you get five. The symbol for **subtract** is $-$. $9-4=5$.

# subway

A subway is a railroad in a city that goes under the ground. Many people ride to work on the **subway**.

# such

Such means very much. We had **such** a nice time at the party!

# sudden

To be **sudden** is to happen quickly without anyone expecting it. The **sudden** storm was a surprise to us.

# suddenly

Suddenly means very quickly. We were having a good time at the picnic, when **suddenly** it began to rain.

# suds

Suds are many tiny bubbles

made by soap and water. Tony likes to have a lot of **suds** when he washes the car.

## sugar

**Sugar** is something that is put in food to make it sweet. **Sugar** can be white or brown. There is a lot of **sugar** in candy.

## suit

A suit is a set of clothes that match. A jacket and pants or a jacket and a skirt made from the same cloth are a **suit**. Many men and women wear **suits** to work.

## suitcase

A suitcase is a kind of box to carry clothes in when you travel. All **suitcases** have handles, and many have small wheels.

## sum

The **sum** is the number you

get when you add two numbers together. The **sum** of $2$ and $3$ is $5$. Another way of writing this is $2+3= 5$.

## summer

Summer is a season. It comes after spring and before fall. The weather is often hot during the **summer**. Many schools are closed in **summer**.

## sun

The sun is a star. We see it in the sky during the day. The **sun** gives us light and keeps us warm.

## sunburn

You have a sunburn when the light from the sun makes your skin hurt and become red. Sue played in the shade so she wouldn't get a **sunburn**.

## Sunday

Sunday is a day of the week. **Sunday** comes after

Saturday and before Monday.

## sung

Sung comes from the word sing. The school chorus has sung many times at the music festival.

## sunk

Sunk comes from the word sink. The old ship sunk during the hurricane.

## sunlight

Sunlight is light from the sun. Sunlight is good for plants and animals.

## sunrise

Sunrise is when the sun comes up. There is a sunrise every morning, but we can't see it if there are too many clouds.

## sunset

Sunset is when the sun goes down. Many people like to go out to watch a beautiful sunset.

# supermarket

A supermarket is a large store that sells food and other things like soap and paper towels.

# supper

Supper is a meal. People eat supper in the evening.

# suppose

To suppose means to think when you do not know for sure. When five students were late, we supposed it was because the school bus broke down.

# sure

When you are sure about something, you know that what you are thinking is true. I am sure you can find information on reptiles in our school library.

# surface

A surface is the outside or top part of something. Boats sail on the surface of the ocean. The surface of a mirror is smooth.

## surprise

1. A **surprise** is something you did not expect. We thought today would be sunny. It was a **surprise** to us when it started to rain.
2. To **surprise** someone is to do something they did not expect. Joe's friends **surprised** him with a party on his birthday.

## swallow

To **swallow** is to make food go from your mouth to your stomach. Bart's mother tells him to chew his food before he **swallows** it.

## swam

Swam comes from the word **swim**. We **swam** in the pool all morning.

## swamp

A swamp is an area of land that is soft and wet. Frogs, mosquitoes, snakes, and

alligators live in **swamps**.

## swan

A swan is a large bird that lives in the water. **Swans** have long necks. Many **swans** have white feathers.

## sweater

A sweater is a kind of clothes. People wear **sweaters** over their shirts. **Sweaters** are often made of wool or cotton.

## sweep

Sweep means to clean with a broom or brush. Mrs. Brown **sweeps** the sidewalk in front of her store every day.

## sweet

Sweet is a kind of taste. Sugar, candy, cake, and cookies are **sweet**.

## swept

Swept comes from the word **sweep**. My brother **swept** the kitchen floor.

## swim

Swim means to move in the water. People **swim** by using their arms and legs. We will **swim** in the lake this summer. The ducks **swam** in the pond.

## swing

1. To **swing** something is to move it from one side to the other while holding it at one end. Tina swings her bat to hit the ball.
2. A **swing** is a seat held up by ropes or chains. Children play on **swings** in parks or playgrounds or in their yards.

## swum

Swum is a form of **swim**. Peter has been swimming all morning. He must have **swum** about a mile.

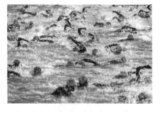

## swung

Swung is a form of **swing**. Richard **swung** his bat and hit the ball.

## symbol

A **symbol** is a mark or a sign that means something. Letters of the alphabet are **symbols** for sounds.

## synagogue

A **synagogue** is a building where Jewish people go to pray, sing, and learn.

## syrup

Syrup is a thick, sweet liquid. It is made from sugar or the juice from some plants.

S

## table

A **table** is a kind of furniture. It has a flat top and four legs. People sit at tables to eat.

## tadpole

A tadpole is a young frog. **Tadpoles** hatch from eggs. They are tiny and have tails. Some are black and some are clear.

## tag

**Tag** is a game in which one of the players is "it." The person who is "it" chases the other players until he or she touches someone. Then the person who is touched becomes "it."

## tail

A tail is the part of an animal's body at the end of the back. Cats and dogs and fish have **tails**.

# take

1. **Take** means to bring or carry with you. Dad will **take** us to the movies this afternoon. We are **taking** cheese sandwiches on the picnic. **Take** your umbrella with you.

2. **Take** also means to get hold of something. **Take** the book off the desk.
3. Take also means to get or use something. We **take** the bus to school.
4. **Take** also means to do or study something. Anne **took** a photograph of her friends at camp. Maria is taking computer lessons.

# taken

**Taken** is a form of **take**. When Diana had **taken** two pictures of her brother, he said "Please take one more!"

### tale

A tale is a story. Joe likes to hear **tales** of life at sea.

### talk

To talk is to speak with someone. Carlos and Tom **talked** about the picnic.

### tall

To be **tall** is to stand high above the ground. Large cities have many tall buildings.

### tame

To be tame is to do as people want. **Tame** animals make good pets.

### tap

**Tap** means to hit something gently. The teacher **tapped** on the desk to get our attention.

### tape

1. **Tape** is a long, thin piece of plastic, cloth, or metal. Some **tape** has glue on it

and is used to make things stick together. Jane used **tape** to fix the torn page in her book.

2. Tape is also a strip of plastic that has music or pictures on it. You listen to or watch this kind of **tape** on a machine.

## taste

1. **Taste** tells you the flavor of food when you put it in your mouth. Lemons have a sour **taste**. Sugar has a sweet **taste**.

2. Taste also means to put food in your mouth to see what it is like. May I **taste** your soup?  Susan is **tasting** the pudding to see if it is ready. Barry **tasted** the fish that he and his father cooked.

## taught

**Taught** comes from the word **teach**. My uncle Frank **taught** my cousin and me how to swim last summer.

## taxi

A taxi is a car you pay to ride in. We took a **taxi** to the airport. Another word for **taxi** is cab.

## teach

**Teach** means to help someone learn something. Our neighbor is going to **teach** me how to use my new camera. I am **teaching** our dog a new trick.

## teacher

A teacher is someone who helps people learn things. Ms. Green is a second grade **teacher**.

## team

A **team** is a group of people who work or play together. **Teams** can have different numbers of people. In many sports two teams play against each other.

## tear[1]

Tear means to pull something apart. **Tear** sounds like hair. The art teacher told us to **tear** the piece of paper in half. Harry was careless and **tore** his pants on a nail.

# tear²

A tear is a drop of water that comes out of your eye when you cry. **Tear** sounds like hear. Ray wiped the **tears** from the baby's face. Mary laughed so much that **tears** came to her eyes.

## tease

When you **tease** people, you bother them or make fun of them. The players on the other team **teased** Claire when she missed the ball. It was mean of them to **tease** her.

# teddy bear

A teddy bear is a kind of toy. It is soft and brown. **Teddy bears** can be large or small.

## teeth

Teeth comes from the word **tooth**. The baby has two new **teeth**. Billy is going to have braces put on his **teeth**.

## telephone

A telephone is used to talk to someone who is far away. It has electric wires that carry the sound of your voice. I like to talk to my friends on the **telephone**. **Phone** is a short word for telephone.

## telescope

A telescope is an instrument that makes things that are far away seem larger and nearer. When we looked through the **telescope**, we could see stars and planets that we couldn't see before.

## television

A television shows pictures with sound. People watch

the news and other programs on **television**. **TV** is a short word for **television**.

# tell

**1.** To tell is to talk about something. After Bob does a magic trick, he **tells** his friends how he did it.

**2.** To **tell** also means to know. Susan can **tell** that winter is coming because the days are getting shorter.

# temperature

The **temperature** of something tells you how hot or cold it is. The temperature outside was so cold that the puddles changed into ice. The doctor used a thermometer to take my **temperature** to see if I had a fever.

# temple

A temple is any building where people go to sing and pray.

## ten

Ten is one more than nine. Ten is written **10**. $9+1=10$.

## tennis

Tennis is a game played by two or four people. When people play **tennis**, they hit a ball to each other over a net. My sister plays on the **tennis** team at school. We played **tennis** after work.

## tent

A tent is a place to sleep when you camp. It is made of cloth. The circus was in a big **tent**.

## tepee, tee-

A tepee is a tent that has a shape like a cone. **Tepees** are made from animal skins that have been stretched over poles. A long time ago, American Indians lived in **tepees**.

## terrible

1. When something is **terrible**, it means that it makes

you feel afraid. The thunder made a **terrible** noise.

**2. Terrible** also means very bad. We had terrible weather on our vacation. It rained every day. The food at that new restaurant was **terrible**.

# test

A test shows how much a person knows about something. A **test** has questions to answer and problems to do. I spelled two words wrong on the spelling **test** today.

# than

We use **than** when we tell how things are different. The mother cat is bigger **than** her kittens. An hour is much longer **than** a minute. I am 2 inches taller **than** my brother.

# thank

To **thank** means to tell someone you are glad they did something for you or gave something to you. Alice **thanked** her friends for the birthday presents they gave her.

## Thanksgiving

Thanksgiving is a holiday celebrated on the fourth Thursday in November. Many people eat turkey for dinner on **Thanksgiving** and give thanks for what they have.

## that

1. **That** means something not near you. I can see two cars on the street. One car is near me. This car is blue. The other car is far away. **That** car is red.

2. **That** is used to put two parts of a sentence together. Margaret told her mother **that** she wanted a new dress.

## the

We use the when we talk about one special person, thing, or group. **The** woman

wearing a red dress is my mother. Please close **the** door. **The** sun is very bright.

## theater | theatre

A theater is a place where you can go to see a movie or a play. My family enjoys seeing new plays at the **theater**.

## their

**Their** means that something belongs to other people. Their dog is white, and ours is brown. Our car is outside, and **theirs** is in the garage.

## theirs

**Theirs** means belonging to them. The students all bought some fish for an aquarium. The fish are **theirs**.

## them

**Them** means more than one. There are some birds in Nancy's yard. She feeds

**them** seeds and bread.

# themselves

Themselves means them and nobody else. Babies have to be dressed because they cannot dress **themselves**.

# then

1. **Then** means at that time. It is cold now. But it was not cold last summer. The weather was warm **then**.

2. **Then** also means next. Paul pulled his sled up the hill. Then he rode back down again.

# there

1. **There** means at that place. "Where should I put these logs?" Dale asked his father. He pointed to the fireplace. "Put them down there," he said.

2. **There** is or **there** are mean that something can be found. "**There** is a chicken in the back yard!" Steve shouted.

# thermometer

A thermometer is a tool that is used to measure temperature. Some **thermometers** show how hot or cold it is outside. Others are used to show the temperatures of people who are sick.

# these

**These** comes from the word **this**. **These** cars are mine, and those cars are yours. These flowers are pretty.

# they

1. We use **they** when we talk about more than one person or thing. Tom and Mike were late for school because **they** missed the bus.

2. **They'd** means **they had** or **they would**. Sue and Bob said **they'd** seen the play before. I wish **they'd** come with us.

3. **They'll** means **they will**. **They'll** be here in a few minutes.

4. **They're** means **they are**. **They're** building a new house on our street.
5. **They've** means **they have**. They've gone to the party already.

# thick

1. When something is **thick**, there is much space from one side to the other. This is a thick book.
2. When a liquid is **thick**, it is hard to pour. It took a long time for Tony to pour the **thick** glue into the jar.

## thief

A **thief** is a person who steals. **Thieves** stole televisions from the store.

## thin

1. When something is **thin**, there is not much space between one side of it and the other. I would like a **thin** piece of cheese on my sandwich. The paper was so **thin** that we could see through it.

**T**

2. **Thin** also means not fat. A horse has a long, thin face.

# thing

1. A **thing** is an object, animal, or plant. You can see many interesting things in a museum.

2. A **thing** can also be what someone does. Hannah gave Lewis some of her lunch. That was a nice **thing** for her to do.

# think

1. To **think** means to use your mind to form ideas and make decisions. David **thinks** about what he will do on Saturday.

2. To **think** also means to believe. I **think** the storm is over.

# third

Third means next after the second one. My sister is in the **third** grade. March is the **third** month of the year.

# thirsty

When you are thirsty, you want something to drink. We were so **thirsty** that we each drank two large glasses of water.

# this

1. We use **this** when we talk about something that is closer than something else. **This** coat is mine, and that one is yours.

2. We also use **this** when we talk about something that is here. **This** morning it is sunny. This book is a dictionary. **This** is my cousin Andrew.

# those

**Those** comes from the word **that**. These gloves are mine and **those** are Andy's. I baked **those** cookies. I do not know who those people are.

# though

I was late for school, **though** I got up early. The

movie was funny, **though** it was not as funny as the one I saw last week. I enjoyed it, **though**.

## thought

1. **Thought** comes from the word **think**. We took our umbrellas because we **thought** it might rain.
2. A **thought** is an idea. Helen wrote down her **thoughts** about the book she read.

## thousand

A **thousand** is a number. **Thousand** is written **1,000**. There are ten hundreds in a **thousand**. Thousands of people went to watch the football game.

## thread

Thread is very thin string. It comes in many different colors. People sew clothes with a needle and **thread**.

## three

Three is one more than

two. **Three** is written **3**.
$2+1=3$.

## threw

**Threw** comes from the word **throw**. Robert caught the ball and threw it back to Jane.

## throat

The **throat** is the part of your body that is at the front of your neck. When I was sick, my **throat** felt sore.

## through

**Through** means from one side to the other. Geoffrey walked **through** a field to get to school. A bird flew into our house **through** an open window.

## throw

1. **Throw** means to send something through the air. **Throw** the ball to the dog, and she will bring it back to you.

2. When you **throw** something away, you don't want it any longer. If the milk smells bad, you should **throw** it away. Mark **threw** away some broken toys.

# thumb

The **thumb** is the short, thick finger at the side of your hand. Your thumb makes it easier to pick things up.

# thunder

Thunder is a loud sound in the sky that comes after lightning. We hear **thunder** during a storm.

# Thursday

**Thursday** is a day of the week. **Thursday** comes after Wednesday and before Friday.

# ticket

A ticket is a piece of paper that shows you have paid for something. You need a **ticket** to ride on a train. We

gave our **tickets** to the man at the door of the theater.

## tickle

When you **tickle** people, you touch them gently in a way that makes them laugh.

## tie

1. To **tie** is to hold something together with string or rope. George keeps his boat tied to the dock.
2. A tie is a kind of clothes. It is a narrow piece of cloth that people wear around their necks. **Ties** come in many different colors.

## tiger

A tiger is a large wild animal. It looks like a very big cat. **Tigers** have fur with black stripes.

## tight

To be **tight** means to be hard to take off or apart. Dick's shoes felt **tight** because they were too small for him.

# time

**1. Time** is when something happens. A clock or a watch tells us what time it is. It is almost **time** for my favorite TV program.

**2. Time** is also how long something takes. We don't have much **time** to finish the test.

**3. Time** can also be something you have done. We had a good time at the beach today.

# times

When a number is multiplied by a number, we use the word **times**: 2 **times** 2 is 4. Another way of writing 2 **times** 2 is $2 \times 2$.

# tin

Tin is a kind of metal. It is used to make cans, toys, and other things.

# tiny

If something is **tiny**, it is very small. An ant is a tiny insect.

## tire | tyre

A tire is a round piece of rubber that fits around a wheel. Cars, buses, bicycles, and trucks all have **tires**. Most **tires** are filled with air. I changed the **tire** because it was flat.

## tired

To bo **tired** is to feel weak and need rest. People get **tired** when they work or play a lot. We were **tired** when we finished cleaning the garage.

## to

1. **To** tells where something goes. Astronauts have flown to the moon.
2. **To** also means until. The store opens at nine o'clock. It closes at six o'clock. It is open from nine **to** six.
3. **To** also tells how something changes. Michael painted the yellow walls white. He changed the walls from yellow **to** white.

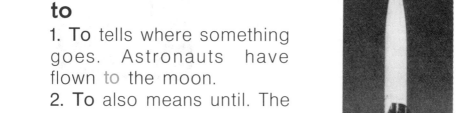

# toad

A toad is an animal that is like a frog. **Toads** have dry, rough skin, and they can jump very far. **Toads** like to live on dry land instead of in the water like frogs.

# toast

Toast is bread that has been made brown by heat. A **toaster** is a machine for making **toast**. I had **toast** with cheese for lunch.

# today

Today is the day that it is now. **Today** is Murray's birthday. Do you want to go to the park **today**?

# toe

A **toe** is a part of your foot. Each foot has five **toes**. My **toes** were cold, so I put on a pair of socks.

# together

When people or things are in the same place, they are together. Maria and Jane

ride the bus to school **together**. Dad mixed the milk and eggs **together**. All the cows stood **together** in the middle of the field.

## toilet

A toilet is where you go to get rid of the waste in your body.

## told

**Told** is a form of **tell**. Mary **told** us about her trip yesterday.

## tomato

A tomato is a fruit. It is round and red. Ketchup is made from **tomatoes**.

## tomorrow

**Tomorrow** is the day after today. **Tomorrow** is in the future. If today is Monday, then **tomorrow** will be Tuesday.

## tongue

The tongue is a part of your mouth. It is long and you

can push it out of your mouth. Your **tongue** helps you to taste and swallow food and to speak.

## tonight

**Tonight** is the night between today and tomorrow. We are going to the museum this morning, and tonight we're going to a hockey game.

## too

**1.** We use **too** to mean also. George and Arthur like to play baseball, and their little brother does too.

**2.** We also use **too** when we mean that something is more than enough. There were too many toys in the box, and it wouldn't close. It's **too** cold to swim in the ocean.

## took

**Took** comes from the word **take**. Jim **took** his new book to school to show his friends.

## tool

A tool is something you use to do a job. A hammer, a rake, and a ruler are different kinds of **tools**.

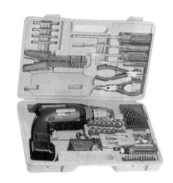

## tooth

1. A **tooth** is one of the hard, white parts in your mouth. **Teeth** are used for biting and chewing food. The dentist told me to brush my **teeth** twice a day.
2. A **tooth** may also be one of a row of points that are on a comb or rake. My comb is missing two **teeth**.

## toothbrush

A toothbrush is a small brush with a long handle. It is used to clean the teeth.

## top¹

1. The **top** of something is the highest part. Claire climbed to the **top** of the slide.
2. The top of something is also a part that covers it.

Please put the **top** back on the box.

# top²

A **top** is a toy in the shape of a cone. A **top** spins on the end that has a point.

# tore

Tore comes from the word **tear**¹. Elizabeth **tore** her shirt on the fence.

# torn

Torn comes from the word **tear**¹. Her shirt was **torn** in two places.

# tornado

A tornado is a very strong wind. It is shaped like a cone that twists in the air. **Tornadoes** can knock down houses and pull trees out of the ground.

# toss

Toss means to throw gently. Please **toss** me a pair of socks.

# touch

**Touch** means to put your hand on something. If you touch the kitten's fur, you will feel how soft it is.

# tow

**Tow** means to pull or drag something behind you. When our car broke down, a truck **towed** it to the gas station. Yesterday I saw a truck **towing** a bus.

# toward

**Toward** is used when we talk about going in the direction of something. All the puppies ran **toward** their mother. Another way to spell **toward** is **towards**. I started walking **towards** the playground to meet my friends.

# towel

A towel is a piece of paper or cloth that is used for wiping or drying something. Tom wrapped himself in a **towel** after he took a

shower.

## tower

A tower is a tall, narrow part on top of a building. The church on our street has a **tower** with bells in it.

## town

A **town** is a place where people live and work. A town has houses and other buildings in it. It is smaller than a city. Our **town** has a post office, a bank, a gas station, a theater, and a restaurant on the main street.

## tow truck

A **tow truck** is able to pull a car that cannot be driven. **Tow trucks** are used to move cars that have broken down or are stuck in mud or snow. A **tow truck** pulled our car to the garage after the accident.

## toy

A **toy** is a thing to play with.

People and animals play with **toys**. Dolls, kites, and balls are **toys**. Our cat likes to play with a **toy** mouse.

## trace

When you **trace** a picture, you put a thin piece of paper over it. Then you follow the lines of the picture with your pencil. When you finish, you have a copy of the picture on your paper. Tony **traced** a picture of a dinosaur.

## track

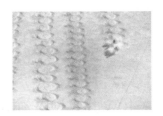

1. A track is one of the long metal pieces that the wheels of a train go on.
2. A track is also the mark left by the foot of an animal. We saw deer **tracks** in the woods.

## tractor

A tractor is a machine with a strong engine and heavy tires. **Tractors** are used to pull heavy things over rough ground.

## trade

**Trade** means to give a person something of yours for something of his or hers. My friends and I like to **trade** toy cars.

## traffic

**Traffic** is cars, trucks, and buses moving along a road at the same time. There is not much **traffic** on the road where I live.

## traffic light

A traffic light is a big light at a street corner. **Traffic lights** change color to show cars and people what to do. A green light means to go, a yellow light means to be careful, and a red light means to stop. Even though the **traffic light** was green, we stopped to let a fire engine pass.

## trail

1. A trail is a path through an area that is not lived in.

The campers followed the **trail** through the woods.

2. A **trail** is also a mark, smell, or path made by a person or animal. The rabbit left a **trail** of footprints in the snow.

## trailer

A trailer is something that is pulled by a car or truck. A **trailer** has wheels, but it does not have a motor. Some **trailers** are used to carry things, and some are made for people to live in.

## train

1. A train is a line of railroad cars that are joined together. **Trains** are used to carry people or things from one place to another. We took a **train** when we went to visit my grandfather.

2. **Train** also means to teach a person or animal how to do something. My mother **trains** people to use computers. We **trained** our dog to bring back the ball

when we throw it.

## trap

1. A trap is a way to catch wild animals. Some **traps** are made of steel. Other **traps** are holes in the ground.
2. To **trap** is to catch an animal or a person in a trap. Spiders **trap** insects in their webs.

## trash

Trash is stuff that you throw away. Most of our **trash** is paper, boxes, and old food.

## travel

Travel means to go from one place to another. We traveled by car on our vacation.

## treasure

A treasure is money, jewelry, or other things that are important. The king and queen hid their **treasure** in a special room.

## treat

A **treat** is a nice, special thing. Going to the circus was a treat for us.

## tree

A tree is a kind of plant. It has branches and leaves. **Trees** can grow to be very tall. Wood comes from trees.

## triangle

1. A **triangle** is a shape that has three straight sides.
2. A triangle is also a musical instrument with three sides. It is made of metal and rings when you hit it with a metal stick.

## trick

1. A **trick** is something that seems impossible. Jack saw a magician make a rabbit disappear. He knew it was a **trick** because nobody can make something really disappear.
2. To **trick** is to get someone to do something he or

she does not want to do. When Chris's dog was sick, it did not want to take its medicine. Chris's mother **tricked** the dog by putting the medicine in its food.

## tricycle

A tricycle has two wheels in the back and one wheel in the front. **Tricycles** are like bicycles, but they are easier to ride. Anne likes to ride her **tricycle** on a path through the park.

## tried

**Tried** comes from the word **try**. Maria **tried** to lift the big suitcase, but it was too heavy for her.

## trip

When you go on a **trip**, you go from one place to another. We took a trip to the mountains.

## trombone

A trombone is an instrument. It is a kind of horn. **Trombones** are made of long metal tubes that fit together.

## troop

A **troop** is a group of people. Many troops of boys and girls went to camp last summer.

## trophy

A trophy is a small statue or other prize. A **trophy** is given to someone who wins a contest or game or does something special. My brother won a **trophy** for being the best player on his school basketball team.

## trouble

1. **Trouble** is something that makes it hard to know what to do. Dick does not add or subtract very well. He has **trouble** with numbers.
2. To be in **trouble** means that someone is angry with you. Henry tore his new

shirt playing football. He knew he would be in **trouble** when he got home.

## trousers

Trousers are a kind of clothes. People wear **trousers** over their legs. Most **trousers** have pockets in them.

## truck

A truck is like a large automobile. People use **trucks** to carry big, heavy things. We used a **truck** to move our furniture to our new house.

## true

True means correct and not wrong. Is it **true** that Joe will be going to our school next year? It is **true** that an elephant has four legs.

## trumpet

A trumpet is a musical instrument that is made of metal. You blow into one end of a **trumpet**, and the

sound comes out the other end.

## trunk

**1.** A trunk is the thick middle part of a tree. The **trunk** of a tree grows up from the ground. Branches grow out of it.
**2.** A **trunk** is also part of an elephant. It is like a very long nose. Elephants can pick up things with their **trunks**.
**3.** A trunk can also be a large box. People often pack clothes and other things in **trunks** when they travel.

## trust

If you **trust** a person, you believe the person is honest. I told Bill my secret because I know I can **trust** him.

## truth

The **truth** is what is true. If people do not tell the **truth**, you cannot trust them.

## try

When you **try** to do something, you find out if you can do it. I **tried** to run up the hill, but I got too tired.

## tub

1. A tub is a large open container that you use for taking a bath. She washes clothes in a **tub**. Another word for **tub** is bathtub.

2. A **tub** also is a round container that is used to hold butter, honey, or other foods.

## tube

A tube is a hollow piece of glass, rubber, plastic, or metal. It sometimes has the shape of a pipe. **Tubes** are used to carry or hold liquids and gases.

## Tuesday

**Tuesday** is a day of the week. **Tuesday** comes after Monday and before Wednesday.

## tug

To **tug** is to pull hard at something. Small children sometimes **tug** at their parents' coats to get their attention.

## tugboat

A **tugboat** is a boat with a very strong engine. **Tugboats** push and pull large ships when there is not much room for them to move.

## tulip

A tulip is a flower that has the shape of a cup. **Tulips** grow from bulbs.

## tunnel

A tunnel is a long hole under the ground. Some **tunnels** go through mountains so that people can travel from one place to another.

## turkey

1. A turkey is a kind of bird. It has a long neck. **Turkeys**

are raised for their meat. Some **turkeys** are wild.

2. **Turkey** is a kind of meat. It comes from a turkey.

# turn

1. To **turn** is to move in a circle. The wheels on a bicycle turn when the bicycle moves.

2. To **turn** your head is to move it from side to side. Tyler **turned** his head to see who had come into the room.

3. To take **turns** means that one goes, and then the other. Walter and Stuart shared a sandwich. First Walter took a bite of it, then Stuart did. They took **turns** until the sandwich was gone.

# turquoise, -quois

1. **Turquoise** is a color. You can make the color **turquoise** by mixing green and blue together.

2. Turquoise is also the name of a stone that is

used to make jewelry.

## turtle

A turtle is an animal with short legs and a hard shell covering its body. **Turtles** live on land and in water. When it is afraid, a **turtle** pulls its head and legs inside its shell.

## twice

**Twice** means two times. Alice liked the movie so much she saw it **twice**.

## twig

A twig is a tiny branch of a tree. We used dry **twigs** to start a fire when we went camping in the woods.

## twin

A **twin** is one of two children born at the same time to the same parents. Most twins look alike.

## twist

To twist is to turn around and around. Rope is made

of pieces of string that are **twisted** together.

## two

Two is the number that is one more than one. The number **two** is written **2**.

## tying

Tying comes from the word **tie**. Mitchell is **tying** the package with string.

T

## ugly

When something is **ugly**, it is not pretty. Richard made an **ugly** face to try and scare me, but it made me laugh instead.

## umbrella

An umbrella is something you use to protect yourself from rain or sun. It is shaped like an upside-down bowl with a long handle. The top part is made of cloth and metal.

## umpire

An umpire makes sure that the rules are followed in a baseball game. "Play ball!" the **umpire** shouted.

## uncle

Your **uncle** is your father's

brother or your mother's brother. Your aunt's husband is also your uncle.

## under

Under means in a place that is lower than something else. The dog was hiding **under** the bed. My missing paper was **under** the book. Jack is wearing a sweater under his jacket.

## underground

Underground means under the ground. Worms live **underground**.

## underline

To **underline** is to draw a line under something. Leon **underlines** his name on the page. People often **underline** things that are important.

## understand

When you understand something, you know what it means. English is the only language that Lewis **under-stands**. Andy **understands** both English and Spanish.

## understood
**Understood** is a form of **understand**. I did not understand how to play the game. Then Mark explained the rules to me and I **understood** it. Albert **understood** the teacher's question.

## underwater
**Underwater** means below the surface of the water. Nancy and George know how to swim **underwater**. One day they explored an underwater cave.

## underwear
Underwear is the clothing you wear under your clothes. I fold and put away my **underwear** when the laundry is done.

## undress
**Undress** means to take off

clothes. My little brother is learning how to **undress** himself. Hannah likes to dress and **undress** her dolls when she plays with them.

## uneasy

**Uneasy** means not feeling safe. Mary was a little bit afraid to go on an airplane for the first time. She was **uneasy** about it.

## uneven

Uneven means not smooth or straight. It was hard for us to walk in the field. The ground was very **uneven** there.

## unhappy

**Unhappy** means not happy. I was very **unhappy** when my sister broke my favorite toy truck.

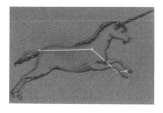

## unicorn

A unicorn is a make-believe animal that looks like a white horse with one long horn in the middle of its

head. I like to read fairy
tales about **unicorns**.

## uniform

A uniform is a special kind
of clothes. People wear
**uniforms** to show that they
belong to a group. Police,
nurses, and sports teams
wear **uniforms**.

## United States

The United States is a
country. It is also called the
**United States of America**.
The capital of the **United
States** is Washington, D.C.

## universe

The universe is everything
in our world and in space
put together. The earth, the
sun, the moon, and the
stars are all part of the **universe**.

## unless

You can't borrow my bicy-
cle **unless** you promise to
take care of it. The baseball
game will be played this

afternoon **unless** it rains. **Unless** we hurry, we will be late for the concert.

# unlucky

**Unlucky** means having bad luck. Jane wanted to have a picnic last Saturday, but it rained. She wanted to have a party on her birthday, but she got sick. Jane is very **unlucky**.

# untie

To untie something means to take the knots out of it. Mike **untied** his shoelaces by himself.

# until

**Until** means up to the time of. We can play outside until it gets dark.

# unusual

When something is **unusual**, it is not the way we expect it to be. Snow in July would be very **unusual** weather. It is **unusual** for her to get angry.

# up

1. **Up** means to go from a lower place to a higher place. Claire went up the steps and into the building. Susan looked **up** from her book when David came into the room.

2. Up also means out of bed. I didn't get **up** until 9 o'clock this morning. Joe and Billy aren't **up** yet.

# upon

**Upon** means on. The bird was sitting upon the branch.

# upset

To be **upset** is to feel angry, hurt, or unhappy. Anne was **upset** when her best friend did not come to her party.

# upside-down

**Upside-down** means with the top side down and the bottom side up. Margaret knocked her dessert off the table by accident. It landed

**upside-down** on the floor.

## us

We use the word **us** when we are talking about ourselves. Uncle Ben took us to the zoo yesterday.

## use

To **use** means to do work with something. A carpenter uses tools, wood, and nails to build a house.

## useful

Something is **useful** if it helps you do something. Tools are useful for fixing and building things.

U

## usual

When something is **usual**, it is expected. Hot weather is **usual** for July and August.

## usually

Usually means almost always. Bob usually rides his bicycle home from school.

## vacation

A **vacation** is a time when people do not work or go to school. Our family went on a vacation to the beach last summer.

## valentine

A valentine is a card that you send to someone you love on **Valentine's Day**. **Valentines** usually have hearts on them. **Valentine's Day** is February 14.

## valley

A valley is an area of low land between hills or mountains. **Valleys** often have rivers that go through them.

## van

A **van** is a truck or a car that looks like a small bus.

Large vans are used to move animals, furniture, or other big things. Small vans are used for carrying people or small things.

# vanilla

Vanilla is a flavor. It is made from a kind of seed. **Vanilla** is used in ice cream and other desserts.

# vegetable

A **vegetable** is a plant or a part of a plant that you can eat. Lettuce, onions, and peas are **vegetables**.

# very

**Very** means more than what is usual. Bears are big animals. Elephants are very big animals.

V

# veterinarian

A veterinarian is a doctor who takes care of animals. Eddie likes animals and wants to be a **veterinarian**. Nancy wants to be a **veterinarian** for a zoo and take

care of wild animals.

# village

A village is a small group of houses. It is usually in the country. **Villages** are not as big as towns.

# vine

A vine is a plant with a long, thin stem. **Vines** grow on the ground or up tree trunks and walls. Grapes and pumpkins grow on **vines**.

# violin

A violin is a wooden musical instrument with four strings. The **violin** body is held below the chin and played with a bow.

# visit

To **visit** is to stay somewhere or with somebody for a time. Our class visited the zoo last week.

# voice

Your **voice** is the sound you

make through your mouth. You are using your voice when you speak or sing.

# volcano

A volcano looks like a mountain with a big hole in the top. The rocks under a **volcano** are melted by heat in the earth. Sometimes the melted rocks shoot out of the **volcano**.

# volunteer

A **volunteer** is someone who does work without getting paid. In my town, all the firefighters are **volunteers**.

# vote

**Vote** means to say that you are for or against something. Our town **voted** to build a new playground.

# vowel

A **vowel** is a letter of the alphabet that is not a consonant. The **vowels** are a, e, i, o, u, and sometimes y.

## wagon

A wagon is used to carry people or things from one place to another. It has four wheels. Large **wagons** are sometimes pulled by horses.

## wait

**Wait** means to stay in a place until someone comes or something happens. Mary had to **wait** until it stopped raining before she could go outside to play. Please **wait** here in this room.

## wake

When you **wake**, you stop sleeping. What time do you wake up in the morning? We were noisy and **woke** the baby.

# walk

Walk means to move along by putting one foot in front of the other. My little sister is just learning to **walk**.

# wall

1. A wall is a side of a room. Most rooms have a ceiling, a floor, and four **walls**.

2. A wall is something that is built to keep one place apart from another. The farmer built a stone **wall** around his field.

# want

To **want** something means that you would like to have it. Peter **wants** a trumpet more than anything.

# war

A **war** is a fight between countries. Everyone was happy when the **war** ended.

# warm

Warm means not very hot. When it is cold outside, our

**W**

dog likes to stay in the house where it is **warm**.

## was

**Was** comes from the word **be**. The bird **was** building a nest. Who **was** at the door? Carmen **was** sick last week.

## wash

When you **wash** something, you clean it with soap and water. We **washed** our hands before dinner. We helped Lewis **wash** the car. Charlie and Fred take turns washing the dishes after dinner.

## wasn't

**Wasn't** is a short way to say **was not**. Albert went to Billy's house to see him, but he **wasn't** there.

## waste

When we **waste** something, we use more of it than we need. We waste water if we don't turn off the faucet.

# watch

1. **Watch** means to look at something carefully. The baby-sitter **watched** the children while they played.
2. A watch is also a small clock that you wear on your wrist. A **watch** shows you what time it is.

# water

**Water** is a kind of liquid. It is clear and it has no taste. People, plants, and animals need water to live.

# wave

1. **Wave** means to move something up and down or from side to side. People often wave a hand when they say hello or good-bye. The flag **waved** in the wind.
2. A **wave** is also the water as it moves up and down in the ocean. The boat bounced up and down in the waves.

# wax

**Wax** is a material that is

used to make things like candles and crayons. **Wax** is also used to shine furniture and cars.

## way

1. The **way** you do something is how you do it. I know two **ways** to play this game.

2. Way also means a road or a path that you take to go from one place to another. Arthur knows the **way** to the store.

## we

1. People use **we** when they are talking about themselves. We are good friends.

2. **We'd** means **we had** or **we would**. **We'd** slept about six hours before the day broke. **We'd** go with you if **we** could.

3. **We'll** means **we will**. I think **we'll** win the game tomorrow.

4. **We're** means **we are**. We're home.

**5. We've** means **we have**. **We've** visited that city twice.

## weak

**1.** When something is **weak**, it may break or fall. The legs of the table are **weak**.
**2. Weak** also means not strong. The sick pony was **weak**.

## weapon

When people fight, they use **weapons**. Guns and knives are weapons.

## wear

**Wear** means to have clothes or other things on your body. Mark **wears** a raincoat and boots when it rains. Alice is wearing her new necklace.

## weather

When we talk about rain or snow or how hot or cold it is, we are talking about the **weather**. The **weather** is sunny today.

# web

A web is made by a spider to catch food. **Webs** are made of thin threads. An insect got caught in the spider's **web**.

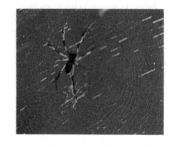

# wedding

A wedding is a special time when two people get married.

# Wednesday

**Wednesday** is a day of the week. **Wednesday** comes after Tuesday and before Thursday.

# week

There are seven days in a **week**. The days of the **week** are Sunday, Monday, Tuesday, Wednesday, Thursday, Friday, and Saturday.

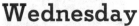

# weigh

To weigh means to measure how heavy something is. Many kinds of food are **weighed** before you buy

them.

# weight

**Weight** is how heavy something is. The doctor weighs James to see how much he has grown. She tells him his **weight** every time he visits her.

# welcome

To be **welcome** means that someone is glad to see you or to do something for you. We tried to make our new neighbors feel welcome. "Thank you for the beautiful gift," Jane said to Anne. "You're **welcome**," Anne said.

# well[1]

**1.** When you do something well, you do it in a good way. My uncle plays the piano **well**. Margaret writes **well**.

**2. Well** also means not sick. Emily was sick last week, but she's **well** now.

# well²

A well is a very deep hole in the ground. People dig wells to get water, oil, or other things that are in the earth.

# went

Went comes from the word **go**. My sister and I **went** to the dentist yesterday.

# were

Were comes from the word **be**. We were having such a good time in the park that we didn't want to go home. Bob and Tom **were** at the library all afternoon.

# weren't

Weren't means **were not**. We got to school on time. We **weren't** late.

# west

West is a direction. The sun sets in the west. **West** is the opposite of **east**.

# wet

If something is **wet**, it has water or another liquid on it. Hannah's shoes got **wet** when she stepped in the puddle.

# whale

A whale is a very large animal that lives in the ocean. **Whales** can swim, but they are not fish.

# what

**What** is used to ask questions about people and things. **What** book are you reading?

# whatever

**Whatever** means anything or everything. Blake eats whatever his father cooks for him.

# wheat

Wheat is a kind of grass. Its seeds are used to make flour and other foods. **Wheat** is an important food for people and animals.

# wheel

A wheel is a round piece of wood, metal, or rubber that helps things move easily. Cars, bicycles, wagons, and roller skates have **wheels**.

# wheelchair

A wheelchair is a chair on wheels. People who cannot walk use **wheelchairs** to get from one place to another. My school has a special ramp for children and teachers who use **wheel-chairs**.

# when

We use **when** to ask or tell what time something happens. **When** does the show start? Please tell me **when** I can visit you.

# where

We use **where** to ask a question or tell about a place. **Where** do you live? I can't remember **where** I left my book.

## which

**Which** is used to ask questions about one person or thing in a group. **Which** of these coats is yours? Which girl is your friend?

## while

1. **While** means a short time. Let's stop playing and rest for a **while**.
2. **While** also means during the time that something else is happening. Mom ate lunch **while** the baby took a nap.

## whisper

To whisper means to speak in a soft voice. People **whisper** in a library so they won't bother other people.

## whistle

1. When you **whistle**, you make a sound by pushing air out through your lips or teeth. My dog always comes when I **whistle**. The

kettle **whistled** when the water boiled.

2. A **whistle** is also something you blow into that makes a whistling sound. The police officer blew a **whistle** and all the cars stopped.

# white

**White** is the lightest color. Snow and salt are white.

# who

1. **Who** is used to ask questions about a person. **Who** knocked on the door?

2. **Who** tells which person. The man who works in the store is very friendly.

# whoever

**Whoever** means any person. Whoever runs the fastest will win the race. My parents said I could invite **whoever** I wanted to my party.

# whole

When something is **whole**, it

has no parts missing from it. Mike ate the **whole** orange by himself. We got a whole pizza, and everyone had a piece of it. Stuart read the **whole** book in just two days.

## whom

**Whom** is a form of **who**. Who did Peter see in the park? Anne is the girl **whom** he saw.

## who's

1. **Who's** is a short way to say **who is**. Who's in the kitchen?
2. **Who's** is also a short way to say **who has**. Who's been to the zoo?

## whose

We use **whose** when we talk about who the owner of something is. I don't know **whose** roller skates these are.

## why

**Why** is used to ask the

reason for something. I know **why** Maria can't come to the picnic with us. **Why** are you laughing?

## wide

**Wide** means very big from one side to the other. The chair was too **wide** to fit through the door. That bridge crosses the widest part of the river.

## width

**Width** is how wide something is. The **width** of Dale's paper is eight inches.

## wife

A wife is a woman who is married. She will make him a good **wife**.

## wild

Wild means not grown or cared for by people. The movie was about **wild** animals.

## will

We use **will** when we say

that we are going to do something. We **will** go to the park tomorrow. Peter **will** be 10 years old soon.

## win

Win means to be the best in a game or a contest. You will **win** the race because you can run faster than anyone else.

## wind

Wind is air that moves. Strong **winds** blew the tree down.

## windmill

A windmill is a machine. The power of the wind makes it work. Some **windmills** bring up water from the ground. Some help make electricity.

## window

A window is an open place in a wall that lets in air and light. **Windows** are made of glass. If you close the win-

**dow**, the cold air won't come in.

# wing

A **wing** is a part that is used for flying. Birds and insects have wings. Airplanes also have **wings**.

# winter

Winter is a season of the year. **Winter** comes after fall and before spring. I like to go ice-skating in the **winter**.

# wipe

**Wipe** means to clean or dry something by rubbing it. Please **wipe** your muddy shoes on the rug outside the door. Dad **wiped** up the milk that the baby spilled.

# wire

A wire is a piece of metal in the shape of a long string or thread that is easy to bend. Electricity moves through **wires**.

# wish

1. **Wish** means to want something very much. I **wish** it were summer now. Jack **wished** he could paint as well as his older brother. All the world **wishes** for peace.

2. A **wish** is something that you want very much. Susan made a **wish** for a new bicycle and then blew out the candles on the birthday cake.

# witch

A witch is a woman who has magic powers. We read about good and bad **witches** in stories.

# with

1. **With** means together. I went to the baseball game **with** my sister and brother.

2. **With** can be used to show that you use something. Anne dug the hole with a shovel.

3. **With** can also be used to show that someone has

W

something. The boy **with** the red jacket on is my brother. The girl with brown hair is my sister.

## without

**Without** means not having or not doing something. I love to walk on the sand without my shoes on. Helen was in such a hurry that she left **without** saying good-bye to us. Mom and Dad went to the movies **without** my brother and me.

## wives

**Wives** means more than one wife. Wives and hus-bands are married to each other.

## wizard

A **wizard** is a magician. The **wizard** in the movie had long white hair and a pointed hat.

## woke

**Woke** comes from the word **wake**. I **woke** up when I

heard the dog barking downstairs.

# woken

Woken comes from the word **wake**. It is nine o'clock, but Bob has not **woken** up yet.

# wolf

A wolf is a wild animal. It looks like a large dog. **Wolves** hunt for food in groups.

# wolves

Wolves means more than one wolf. **Wolves** have thick fur.

# woman

A **woman** is a grown female person. A girl grows up to be a **woman**.

# women

Women means more than one woman. How many women were there at the party?

W

## won

**Won** comes from the word **win**. Paul **won** the swimming race.

## wonder

To **wonder** means to think about something that you are curious about. I **wonder** what I will be when I grow up.

## wonderful

1. **Wonderful** means amazing or unusual. At the circus we all stared at the **wonderful** acrobats.
2. **Wonderful** also means very good. We saw a wonderful football game last Sunday.

## won't

**Won't** means **will not**. Jack said he **won't** be able to play with us today.

## wood

Wood is what trees are made of. **Wood** is used to build houses and other things. Mom put more **wood** on the fire.

## woods

An area with a lot of trees and other plants is called the woods. Animals live in the **woods**. We walked through the **woods**.

## wool

Wool is the hair that grows on sheep. **Wool** is used to make yarn and cloth for clothes and blankets. Many sweaters are made of **wool**.

## word

A **word** is sounds or letters that have a special meaning. We use **words** whenever we talk or write.

W

## word processor

A word processor is a kind of computer that writes, changes, stores, and prints words. Mom uses a **word processor** when she writes stories.

## wore

Wore comes from the word wear. Sarah wore a red ribbon in her hair.

## work

1. Work is the job that someone does. People usually do work to earn money. My mother does work in a bank.

2. Work also means to earn money. My father works in a bakery.

3. Work also means to use energy to do a job. The girls worked hard raking the leaves.

4. When a machine does a job, we say it works. The television is not working.

## worker

A worker is a person who works. Diana works in an office. She works hard at her job. She is a good worker.

## world

The world is where all people live. Another word for **world** is earth. There are many countries in the **world**. Maria's aunt took a trip around the **world**.

## worm

A worm is an animal that is long and has no legs. **Worms** move by crawling on the ground. David and George dug up some **worms** to use when they go fishing.

## worn

Worn comes from the word **wear**. Have you **worn** your new hat yet?

## worry

To worry means to feel that something bad may happen. My parents **worry** sometimes if I am late coming home.

## worse

Worse means less good. I am a bad skater, but my

friend is **worse**.

## worst

Worst means least good. This is the worst cold I've ever had.

## would

Would comes from the word **will**. We **would** like to go with you. **Would** you please hand me that book?

## wouldn't

Wouldn't is a short way to say **would not**. The cat **wouldn't** come down from the tree.

## wrap

To wrap means to cover something, as with paper or cloth. People usually **wrap** birthday presents and tie them with bows. Michael **wrapped** the puppy in a blanket.

## wren

A wren is a small bird. It

has brown feathers and a tail that sometimes sticks straight up. We heard the **wren** singing in the backyard.

## wrinkle

A **wrinkle** is a crease in the skin. This dog has **wrinkles**.

## wrist

Your **wrist** is the part of your body that is between your arm and your hand. You can bend your **wrist**. People wear bracelets and watches on their wrists.

## write

Write means to put words on paper or some other thing. You can **write** with a pencil, a pen, a crayon, or a piece of chalk. Susan **wrote** a letter to her grandfather.

W

## writer

A writer is someone who writes stories, poems, or

books to earn money. Henry's mother is a **writer** who writes about sports for our town's newspaper.

## written

Written is a form of **write** Kendrew has **written** many letters to his friend Johnny.

## wrong

**Wrong** means not correct. Claire gave the **wrong** answer to the teacher's question. The teacher told her the right answer.

## wrote

**Wrote** is form of **write**. Bill **wrote** the date at the top of the page.

## X ray

An **X ray** is a kind of energy. It can pass through objects. Doctors use X rays to take pictures of the inside of the body.

## xylophone

A xylophone is a musical instrument. A **xylophone** has a row of pieces of wood or metal. When you hit the pieces with a special hammer, they make sounds.

X

## yard[1]

A yard is an area of ground around a house or other building. We have a swing in our yard.

## yard[2]

A **yard** is an amount of length. One **yard** is the same as three feet. A **yard** is almost as long as a meter.

## yarn

Yarn is a kind of string. It is made from wool, cotton, or other threads that are twisted together. **Yarn** is used to make sweaters and socks.

## yawn

When you yawn, you open your mouth wide and take

a deep breath. The baby
**yawned** when she was tired.

## year

A **year** is a period of time
that is 12 months long. Carmen is 4 **years** old.

## yell

To **yell** means to shout. The
hockey game was very
exciting. We yelled for our
team.

## yellow

Yellow is the color of
bananas and butter and
lemons. I used my **yellow**
crayon to make a picture of
the sun.

## yes

Yes means that you agree.
Jane asked Susan to come
to her house after school.
Susan said, "**Yes**, I would
like to come."

## yesterday

Yesterday is the day before
today. If today is Monday,

then **yesterday** was Sunday. Mary started a letter to her Grandpa **yesterday** and finished it today.

## yet
**Yet** means up to this time. The movie has not started **yet**.

## you
1. **You** is a word that is used when one person speaks to another person. I like you. **You** look tired today.
2. **You'd** means **you had** or **you would**. I came late and **you'd** already left. **You'd** have enjoyed the program on astronauts.
3. **You'll** means **you will**. Let's play this new game. I think **you'll** like it.
4. **You're** means **you are**. You're a good swimmer.
5. **You've** means **you have**. You've got a nice smile.

## young
**Young** means not old. Anne

is the **younger** of my two sisters. I am the youngest of all.

## your

**Your** means that something belongs to you. Let's play at **your** house. **Your** coat is blue, and mine is red.

## yours

**Yours** means belonging to you. That cup is yours. This one is mine.

## yourself

**Yourself** means you and nobody else. Please be careful not to burn **yourself** on that hot iron.

## yo-yo

A **yo-yo** is a toy that rolls up and down on a string. Helen can do many tricks with her **yo-yo**.

Y

## zebra

A zebra is an animal that looks like a horse with black and white stripes on its body.

## zero

Zero means nothing. If you have **zero** pennies, it means that you don't have any pennies at all. **Zero** can also be written **0**. We won the game by nine to **zero**.

## zipper

A zipper holds clothes and other things together. **Zippers** can be made of metal or plastic. Does your jacket close with a **zipper** or with buttons? Clara finished packing and closed the **zipper** on her suitcase.

## ZOO

A **zoo** is a place where animals are kept so that you can look at them. Many animals in **zoos** live in cages, and some live outdoors in special areas. We saw the monkeys and the elephants at the zoo.

Z

# 영한사전

**a** [《약》ə, 《강》éi] 관 하나의 ; 한 사람의

a는 하나를 뜻한다 : 빨강은 색의 **일종**이다. 친구들이 **하루** 이틀 우리집에 묵을 것이다.

**able** [éibl] 형 할 수 있는

able은 무언가를 하는 방법을 알거나 할 능력이 있다는 뜻이다 : 마이클은 10까지 **셀 수 있다**. 펭귄은 **날 수 없다**.

**about** [əbáut] 1 전 …에 관하여 2 부 약, 거의

1 메리는 개의 사진들이 실리고, 그들을 돌보는 방법을 알려주는 책이 있다. 메리의 책은 개에 **관한** 것이다.

2 about은 또한 「대략」을 뜻한다. about은 무언가를 실제로 확신하지 못할 때에 사용한다 : 2학년에는 **약** 20명의 아이들이 있다.

**above** [əbʌ́v] 전 …보다 높이 ; …의 위에

above는 어떤 것보다 위나 더 높은 곳에 있음을 뜻한다 : 새들이 나무 꼭대기 **위를** 날아다녔다. 내 침대 **위에** 전등이 있다.

**absent** [ǽbsənt] 형 부재의, 결석의 ; …이 없는

absent는 여기에 없다는 뜻이다 : 두 명의 학생이 아파서 **결석했다**.

**accident** [ǽksidənt] 명 사고, 뜻밖의 사건

accident는 일어나지 않기를 원했거나 일어나리라고 예상하지 못한 일이다 : 나는 **우연히** 내 안경을 깼다.

**accomplish** [əkʌ́mpliʃ|əkʌ́m-] 타 이루다, 달성하다

accomplish는 무언가를 끝낸 다는 뜻이다 : 목록에 있는 것을 모두 **달성하는** 데에는 많은 시간이 걸렸지만, 우리는 그것을 모두 해냈다.

**ache** [éik] 재 **아프다**
ache는 아프다는 뜻이다 : 아버지는 오후 내내 가구를 날랐기 때문에 등이 **쑤셨다.** 수잔은 야구 경기에서 투수로 공을 던졌기 때문에 팔이 **아팠다.**

**acorn** [éikɔːrn] 명 **도토리**
acorn은 오크나무에 열리는 열매다 : 다람쥐는 입으로 acorn을 날랐다.

**across** [əkrɔ́ːs | əkrɔ́s] 전 **···을 가로질러, ···을 넘어**
across는 한 쪽에서 다른 쪽으로 가로지른다는 뜻이다 : 다리는 강을 **가로질러** 놓여 있었다.

**act** [ǽkt] 재 타 **행동하다**
act는 어떤 식으로 행동한다는 뜻이다 : 때때로 톰은 어릿광대처럼 행동한다.

**activity** [æktíviti] 명 **활동, 운동, 움직임**
activity는 행동하는 것을 말한다 : 내가 가장 좋아하는 activity는 수영이다.

**actually** [ǽktʃuəli] 부 **실제로, 참말로**
actually는 「정말로」의 뜻이다 : 마리아는 그 파티를 탐탁하게 생각하지 않았지만, 파티에 가서는 **실제로** 재미있게 놀았다.

**add** [ǽd] 타 재 **더하다, 보태다 ; 덧셈을 하다**
1 add는 합친다는 뜻이다 : 빌리는 자기 형을 그렸다. 그리고 나서 익살맞은 코가 달린 안경을 **더 그려넣었다.**
2 add는 또한 숫자를 더한다는 뜻이다 : 3과 1을 **더하면** 4다.

**address** [ǽdres, ədrés] 명 **(편지·소포 등의) 겉봉 ; 주소**
address는 장소의 이름이다. 편지 보낼 곳을 우체국에 알리기 위해서 편지에 address를 적는다.

**adopt** [ədápt | ədɔ́pt] 타 채용하다 ; 양자〔양녀〕로 삼다
adopt는 어떤 아이를 가족의 구성원이 되게 한다는 뜻이다 : 브라운 부부는 새 아기를 **입양했을** 때 매우 기뻤다. 나와 가장 친한 친구는 그가 두 살 때 **입양되었다.**

**adult** [ədʌ́əlt | ǽdʌ̀be] 명 어른
adult는 성숙한 사람이다. 부모님은 adults다.

**adventure** [ədvéntʃər] 명 모험
adventure는 특별하게 하는 일을 말한다. adventure는 새롭고 독특하며 어쩌면 약간은 두려운 일이다 : 나는 우주 adventure에 관한 책을 즐겨 읽는다.

**advertisement** [æ̀dvərtáizmənt, ədvə́ːrtis-, -tiz-] 명 광고
advertisement는 물품 구입이나 소용이 되는 것에 대해 알려준다. advertisement는 문구나 사진이 될 수도 있다 : 나는 텔레비전에서 시리얼 advertisement를 본다. advertisement를 줄여서 ad 라 한다.

**afford** [əfɔ́ːrd] 타 …할 여유〔돈〕가 있다 ; 주다
afford는 무언가를 살 수 있는 돈이 있다는 뜻이다 : 클레어는 빨간 스웨터를 **살 여유가 있는지** 알아보려고 돈을 세어 보았다.

**afraid** [əfréid] 형 두려워하는, 걱정하는
afraid는 나쁜 일이 일어나지 않을까 하고 생각한다는 뜻이다 : 어둠을 **무서워하는** 사람들도 있다.

**after** [ǽftər | áːf-] 1 부 뒤에 (서) 2 전 …의 뒤에 ; …을 뒤쫓아, …을 찾아
after 는 다음에 계속 이어지는 상황을 뜻한다 : 야구 시합이 **끝나자** 우리는 집에 갔다. 앨은 동생이 **뒤쫓아오자** 빨리 달렸다.

**afternoon** [æ̀ftərnúːn | àːf-] 명 오후
afternoon 은 하루 중 정오에서 일몰까지의 사이를 말한다. 겨울에는 afternoon이 짧고 여름에는 길다.

**again** [əgén, əgéin] 부 또, 다시
again 은 힌번 더 헤본디는 뜻
이다 : 앨버트는 공룡을 너무
좋아해서 박물관에 **다시** 가고
싶었다. 우리는 내년 여름을
**또** 그 호수에서 보내려 한다.

**against** [əgénst, əgéinst] 전 …
을 거슬러, …에 반대〔반항〕하
여, …에 기대어 ; **…을 향하여**
1 against는 같은 편이 아니라
는 뜻이다 : 우리 학교는 **다른**
학교와 야구 시합을 했다. 단
지 세 명만이 다이애나의 반장
선출에 **반대** 투표를 했다.
2 against는 또한 무언가를 향
하거나 접촉한다는 뜻이다 : 톰
은 벽을 **향해** 공을 던졌다. 한
나는 자전거를 나무에 **기대어**
놓았다.

**age** [éidʒ] 명 나이
age 는 사람의 나이나 물건의
오래된 정도를 말한다 : 너 몇
**살**이니? 나의 형은 내 age
때 피아노 치는 법을 배웠다.

**ago** [əgóu] 부 지금부터 …전에,
이전에
ago는 「…이전에」라는 뜻이
다 : 우리집 고양이 새끼들은
이틀 **전**에 태어났다.

**agree** [əgríː] 자 동 의〔찬 성〕하
다, 일치하다
agree는 다른 사람과 생각이
나 느낌이 같다는 뜻이다 : 우
리는 고양이 이름을 태비라고
짓는 데 **의견이 일치했다.**

**ahead** [əhéd] 부 앞에, 앞으로
ahead는 물건이나 사람 앞에
있다는 뜻이다 : 아서는 경주에
서 다른 사람들 보다 **앞서** 달
렸다. 네 사람이 우리들 **앞에**
줄서 있었다.

**air** [ɛər] 명 공기 ; 하늘
air 는 사람들이 숨쉬는 기체
다. air는 우리들 주위 어디에
나 있다. air는 볼 수 없지만,
바람이 불면 느낄 수 있다.

**air conditioner** [ɛər kəndìʃə-
nər] 명 에어 컨디셔너, **에어
컨**, 냉난방 장치
air conditioner는 공기를 시원
하고 청결하게 해주는 기계다.
자동차, 사무실, 가정 그리고

그 밖의 다른 건물에서 air conditioner를 쓴다 : 우리 차의 air conditioner는 작동이 잘 안된다.

**airplane** [ɛ́ərplèin] 몡 비행기
airplane은 하늘을 나는 날개가 달린 기계다. airplane은 사람들을 한 곳에서 다른 곳으로 실어 나른다.

**airport** [ɛ́ərpɔ̀ːrt] 몡 공항, 비행장
airport는 비행기들이 이·착륙하는 곳이다. airport에는 사람들이 기다릴 수 있는 곳과 비행기를 점검하고 수리하는 건물들이 있다 : 헬렌이 탄 비행기가 도착하기를 기다리던 그 날 밤, airport는 사람들로 매우 붐볐다.

**alarm** [əlɑ́ːrm] 몡 경보 ; 경보기, 경보 장치 ; **자명종**
alarm은 시끄러운 소리를 내는 종이나 다른 어떤 것이다 : 우리는 아침에 탁상 시계의 alarm소리를 듣고 일어난다. 화재 alarm이 울리자, 사람들은 모두 재빨리 건물을 빠져나왔다.

**alike** [əláik] 1 혱 서로 같은 2 븻 똑같이
alike 는 같다는 뜻이다 : 쌍둥이는 **똑같아** 보인다.

**alive** [əláiv] 혱 살아있는
alive는 살아 있다는 뜻이다 : 비가 안오면, 우리는 꽃이 **시들지 않게** 정원에 물을 준다.

**all** [ɔ́ːl] 1 혱 모든 2 떼 모두
all은 아무것도 빠진 것이 없다는 뜻이다 : **모든** 말은 다리가 네 개다. 마거릿은 아침을 **다** 먹었다.

**alligator** [ǽligèitər] 몡 악어
alligator는 대단히 큰 파충류다. alligator는 짧은 다리와 긴 꼬리 그리고 날카로운 이빨이 있는 강한 턱을 갖고 있다. alligator 는 기후가 따뜻한 강이나 늪에서 산다.

**allow** [əláu] 태 자 허락하다, 허용하다
allow는 무언가를 하게 둔다는 뜻이다 : 토드와 톰의 부모님은 토요일 밤에 간혹 그들이 늦게까지 안자도 **그냥 내버려 두신다.**

**allowance** [əláuəns] 명 용돈
allowance 는 누군가에게 주는 금액이다 : 마거릿은 일주일에 한 번 allowance를 받는다. 조지는 식탁을 차리고 음식을 나누어 주는 일을 해서 allowance를 번다.

**all right** [ɔ́:əl ráit] 부 ① 더할 나위 없이 ; 확실히 ② 안전하게, 무사히 ; **좋아, 알았어**
all right는 아주 좋다는 뜻이다 : 그가 일하는 것은 **만족스럽다.** 그러나 좀더 빨리 할 수도 있을 텐데. all right는 또한 몸 상태가 좋다는 말이다 : 마리는 자전거에서 떨어졌지만, **무사하다.**

**almost** [ɔ́:əlmoust, –⁻] 부 **거의**
almost는 「거의, 대략」이라는 뜻이다 : 루이스는 **거의** 아버지만큼 키가 크다. **조금 있으면** 2 시다.

**alone** [əlóun] 1 형 **혼자의, 고독한** 2 부 **홀로**
alone 은 「혼자서」의 뜻이다 : 메리는 자기 방에 **혼자** 있는 것을 좋아한다.

**along** [əlɔ́:ŋ | əlɔ́ŋ] 1 전 **…을 따라서** 2 부 **따라서 ; 함께**
1 along은 한 줄로 늘어서 있다는 뜻이다 : 해변을 **따라** 걸으면 기분이 좋다.

2 along은 또한 「함께」를 뜻한다 : 수잔이 가게를 가는 데, 동생이 그녀와 **함께** 갔다.

**aloud** [əláud] 부 **큰소리로**
aloud는 다른 사람들이 들을 수 있을 정도로 큰소리를 낸다는 뜻이다 : 아이들은 **큰소리로** 이야기책을 번갈아 읽었다.

**alphabet** [ǽlfəbèt] 명 **알파벳**
alphabet 은 사람들이 글로 쓰는 문자다. 영어 alphabet은 A, B, C, D, E, F, G, H, I, J, K, L, M, N, O, P, Q, R, S, T, U, V, W, X, Y, Z 다.

**alphabetize** [ǽlfəbetàiz] 타
알파벳순으로 하다〔맞추다〕
alphabetize는 알파벳 글자 순
서대로 배열한다는 뜻이다 : 단
어 ant, baby, cat, door,
drum, kite, machine, monkey
그리고 paint 는 **알파벳순으로**
**배열됐다.**

**already** [ɔːəlrédi] 부 이미, 벌
써 ; 예전에
already 는 「이전에」의 뜻이
다 : 앨은 오늘 버스를 놓쳤다.
그가 버스 정류장에 도착했을
때, 버스는 **이미** 떠나버렸다.

**also** [ɔ́ːəlsou] 부 또한, 역시
also는 무언가가 추가된 것을
나타낸다 : 클레어는 피아노를
친다. 그녀는 **또한** 트롬본도
불 줄 안다.

**always** [ɔ́ːəlweiz, -wəz] 부 늘,
언제나
always는 「언제나, 매번」이란
뜻이다 : 표범의 반점은 **영구적**
**인** 것이다. 우리집 개는 나를
보면 **항상** 짖는다.

**am** [《약》 əm, 《강》 ǽm] 동 be
의 1인칭 단수 현재형

am 은 be 의 한 형태로, I 와
같이 쓴다 : "너 여섯 살이
니 ? " "아니, 일곱 살이야. "

**amaze** [əméiz] 타 깜짝 놀라게
하다, 놀래다
amaze는 무언가가 몹시 놀라
게 한다는 뜻이다 : 내가 그 경
주에서 이긴다면 **놀라 까무러**
**칠 것이다.** 마술사의 묘기를
보고 모두 **깜짝 놀랐다.**

**ambulance** [ǽmbjuləns] 명 구
급차, 앰뷸런스
ambulance는 아프거나 다친
사람을 병원으로 옮기는 데 쓰
는 특수한 종류의 자동차다.

**American** [əmérikən] 1 형 아
메리카의, 미국 (사람)의 2 명
아메리카 사람, 미국 사람
1 미국에 사는 사람을 Amer-
ican 이라고 한다. 북미나 남
미에 사는 사람도 American
이라고 한다.

2 American은 미국에서 유래하거나 미국에 관한 것이다. American은 또한 북미나 남미에서 유래하거나 그곳에 관한 것을 뜻한다.

**among** [əmʌ́ŋ] 전 (여럿 있는) **가운데서 ; …사이에 각자**

1 among은 사물이나 사람들 가운데에 섞여 있다는 뜻이다 : 배리는 그의 친구들 **사이**에 앉았다.

2 among은 또한 각자에게 얼마 정도 돌아갈 몫이 있다는 뜻이다 : 보브는 아이들에게 종이와 연필을 나눠주었다.

**amount** [əmáunt] 명 **총계, 총액 ; 양**

amount는 소유량의 정도를 말한다 : 우리는 소풍에 많은 **양**의 음식을 가져 왔다. 그는 경비 전**액**을 지불했다.

**amuse** [əmjúːz] 타 **즐겁게 하다, 재미나게 하다, 웃기다**

amuse는 사람을 미소짓게 하거나 웃게 한다는 뜻이다 : 우리는 재미있는 소리를 내서 아기를 **즐겁게 해줬다.**

**an** [《약》 ən, 《강》 æn] 관 **하나의, 한…**

an은 a의 한 형태다. an은 A, E, I, O, U로 시작되는 단어 앞에 쓰인다 : 새 펜이 헌

펜 보다 더 잘 써진다.

**anchor** [ǽŋkər] 명 **닻**

anchor는 배를 한 곳에 머무르게 하는 무거운 물체다. anchor는 모양이 다양하다.

**and** [《약》 ənd, nd, 《강》 ǽnd] 전 **…와 …, 그리고**

and는 두 가지를 하나로 이어준다 : 3 **더하기** 2 는 5 다. 다이애나**와** 한나는 가장 친한 친구다.

**angry** [ǽŋgri] 형 **화가 난**

angry는 누군가에게 아주 노여운 감정이 든다는 뜻이다 : 빌의 아버지는 빌이 유리창을 깨서 그에게 **화**를 냈다.

**animal** [ǽniməl] 명 **동물, 짐승**

animal은 식물이 아닌 생명체를 말한다. 개, 고양이, 물고기, 새 그리고 곤충은 모두 다 animal이다.

**anniversary** [æ̀nivə́ːrsəri] 명
(매년의) **기념일**, 기념제
anniversary는 전해에 중요한
일이 있었던 바로 그 날이다 :
3월 9일은 부모님의 결혼 **기
념일**이다.

**annoy** [ənɔ́i] 타 **귀찮게 굴다,**
성가시게 하다, **괴롭히다**
annoy는 괴롭힌다는 뜻이다 :
시끄러운 소음 때문에 나는 **짜
증이 날 때가 있다.**

**another** [ənʌ́ðər] 1 형 **또하나
의, 또 한 사람의** ; 다른 2 대
또 다른 한 개 ; **다른 것**
another는 두 번째 것을 뜻한
다 : 헬렌은 당근을 먹었다. 그
녀는 그것을 너무 좋아해서 **하
나 더 먹었다.**

**answer** [ǽnsər | ɑ́ːn-] 1 타 자 **대
답하다** 2 명 **대답**
answer는 누군가가 질문을 할
때 자기 의견을 말하는 것이
다 : 선생님이 질문을 했을 때,

톰은 정확한 answer를 알고
있었다.

**ant** [ǽnt] 명 **개미**
ant는 곤충이다. ant는 나무나
땅 속 굴에서 큰 무리를 지어
산다.

**any** [《약》 əni, 《강》 éni] 1 형 **누
구나, 무엇이나** ; 조금은 ; 누군
가 ; 어떤 2 부 조금이라도 ;
조금도 3 대 무언가, 누군가,
**얼마쯤, 다소**
1 any는 어떤 것이든 문제되
지 않는다는 뜻이다 : 어디든
마음에 드는 자리에 앉아라.
2 any는 또한 「얼마쯤, 다소」
의 뜻이다 : 샌드위치 **좀** 먹을
래 ? 돈 **좀** 가진 것 있니 ?

**anybody** [énibàdi | -bɔ̀di] 대 **누
구도** ; 아무도 ; 누군가
anybody는 「누군가」의 뜻이
다 : 블레이크는 파티에 아는
사람이 **아무도** 없었다. 나는
**아무도** 만나지 않았다.

**anyone** [éniwʌ̀n] 대 **누구든지** ;
아무라도, 누군가

anyone은 anybody의 뜻이
다 : 저녁 식사에 내가 부르고
싶은 사람은 **누구든지** 초대해
라.

**anything** [éniθiŋ] 대 **무엇이든
지** ; 아무것도 ; 무엇인가
anything은 「어떤 것도」의 뜻
이다 : 내 남동생은 **무엇이든지**
먹으려고 한다.

**anyway** [éniwèi] 부 **어쨌든,**
어떻게든 ; 그럼에도 불구하고
anyway는 어떤 일이라도 문제
가 되지 않는다〔상관없다〕는
뜻이다 : 마이클은 발을 다쳤
지만, **어떻게든** 걸으려고 했다.

**anywhere** [énihwɛ̀ər] 부 **어딘
가에** ; 어디에(라)도 ; 아무데도
anywhere 는 「어딘가에」의 뜻
이다 : 너 어제 **어디** 갔었니?

**apart** [əpá:rt] 부 **떨어져서, 따
로 따로,** 개별적으로
1 apart는 서로 떨어져 있다는
뜻이다 : 닭의 발가락은 서로
**떨어져** 있다.
2 apart 는 또한 여러 조각이
나 있는 상태를 뜻한다 : 빌리
는 물체들이 어떻게 움직이는
지 살펴보려고 **분해해** 보는 것

을 좋아한다.

**apartment** [əpá:rtmənt] 명 **아
파트,** (공동 주택의) 한 세대
가 사는 방, 한 가족용의 거처
apartment는 사람들이 사는
하나로 된 방이나 여러 개의
방으로 된 공간을 말한다 : 저
건물에는 20 세대분의 apart-
ment가 있다.

**ape** [éip] 명 (꼬리 없는) **원숭이**
ape는 사람처럼 걷거나 거의
똑바로 설 수도 있는 큰 동물
이다. ape는 monkey와 닮았
지만 꼬리가 없다.

**apologize** [əpálədʒàiz | əpɔ́l-]
자 **사과하다,** 용서를 빌다
apologize는 한 말이나 행동에
대해 미안하다고 말한다는 뜻
이다 : 나는 남동생 장난감을
망가뜨려 동생에게 **사과했다.**

**appear** [əpíər] 자 **나타나다,**
나오다 ; …처럼 보이다
appear 는 보인다는 뜻이다 :
해가 산 위로 이제 막 **모습을**
드러내기 시작한다. 사슴 떼가
오늘 아침에 숲 언저리에 **나타**

났다.

**appetite** [ǽpətàit] 명 식욕, 시장함

appetite는 무언가를 먹고 싶어한다는 뜻이다 : 빌리는 (미식) 축구를 하고 난 뒤라서 appetite 가 왕성하다.

**apple** [ǽpl] 명 사과

apple은 껍질이 빨강, 노랑 혹은 녹색인 둥근 과일이다. apple은 나무에서 열린다.

**April** [éiprəl] 명 4 월

April은 한 해 가운데 한 달이다. April은 30 일이며, 3 월이 가고 5 월이 되기 전에 온다.

**aquarium** [əkwɛ́əriəm] 명 양어조 ; 수족관, 어항

aquarium은 물이 가득 차 있는 유리 상자나 유리 그릇이다. 집에서 물고기를 기르는 사람들은 물고기를 aquarium에 둔다.

**are** [《약》 ər, 《강》 á:r] 동 be의 2인칭 단수 현재형 ; be 의 1, 2, 3인칭 복수 현재형

are는 be의 한 형태로, you, we 그리고 they와 같이 쓴다 : "내 신발 어디 있니?" "벽장 안에 있어요."

**area** [ɛ́əriə] 명 면적 ; 지역 ; 범위 ; 지면

area는 공간이다. 부엌은 우리가 음식을 요리하는 area다. 많은 area가 바다로 덮여 있다.

**aren't** [á:rnt] are not 의 단축형

aren't는 are not을 줄여서 말하는 것이다 : 바나나는 파랗지 않고, 노랗다.

**argue** [á:rgju:] 자 타 의논하다, 논쟁하다 ; 주장하다

argue는 말로 다툰다는 뜻이다. 사람들은 논쟁을 할 때에 간혹 큰소리로 화를 내며 말한다 : 아이들은 그들의 야구팀에서 누가 투수를 할 것인가에 대해 논의했다.

**arm** [á:rm] 명 팔

arm은 몸의 한 부위로, 어깨와 손 사이에 있다 : 찰리는 두 arm으로 벽난로에 쓸 땔감을

날랐다. 새끼 원숭이는 두 arm으로 어미를 껴안고 잤다.

**armor | armour** [ɑ́:rmər] 몡 갑옷과 투구
armor는 금속으로 만든 두툼한 옷이다. 사람들은 오래전에 전투에서 자신들의 몸을 보호하기 위해 armor를 입었다 : 우리는 박물관에서 여러 종류의 armor를 보았다.

**army** [ɑ́:rmi] 몡 육군 ; 군대
army는 전쟁때 나라를 위해 싸우는 사람들이 모인 대규모 집단이다 : 3 일 뒤에야 army 들은 전투를 중지했다.

**around** [əráund] 1 몡 둘레에, 주위에 ; 여기저기에 2 젠 … 의 주위에 ; …경
around는 모든 방향을 뜻한다 : 데이비드는 마당 주위에 울타리를 쳤다. 마거릿은 신발을 찾으려고 방을 둘러 보았

다.

**arrive** [əráiv] 짜 닿다, 도착하다 ; 이르다, 도달하다
arrive는 어떤 곳에 닿는다는 뜻이다 : 기차가 10 분 늦게 도착했다. 우리는 9 시에 마을에 도착할 것이다.

**arrow** [ǽrou] 몡 화살 ; 화살표
1 한 쪽 끝이 뾰족하고 다른 쪽 끝에는 깃털이 있는 가는 막대다. arrow는 활에서 발사된다.

2 arrow는 어떤 곳으로 가는 길을 가리켜주는 표지판에서 종종 볼 수 있다 : 표지판의 arrow는 해변으로 가는 길을 가리켜준다.

**art** [ɑ́:rt] 몡 예술, 미술 ; 기술 ; 기교
art 는 아름답게 만들어진 것이다. 그림, 시, 음악은 art의 일종이다.

**artist** [ɑ́:rtist] 몡 예술가, 화가
artist는 예술을 창조하는 사람이다. 박물관에서 많은 artist 들의 작품을 볼 수 있다.

**as** [《약》 əz, 《강》 ǽz] 1 튀 …와 같이, …만큼 2 쩝 …와 같이 〔처럼, 대로, 만큼〕, …하고 있을 때, …이므로 3 때 …와 같은

as는 같은 양〔크기〕을 뜻한다 : 톰과 제프리는 키가 같다. 톰은 제프리 **만큼** 키가 크다.

**ash** [ǽʃ] 명 재

ash는 어떤 것이 타고 난 뒤에 남은 것이다. ash는 부드러운 회색 가루다 : 레이는 아버지가 벽난로의 ash를 치우는 것을 지켜보았다.

**ashamed** [əʃéimd] 형 부끄러워하는, …을 부끄럽게 생각하는

ashamed는 한 행동 때문에 미안한 생각이 든다는 뜻이다 : 수는 언니에게 거짓말을 한 것 때문에 **부끄럽게 생각했다.**

**ask** [ǽsk | áːsk] 타 자 물어보다, 묻다 ; 요구하다, 청하다

1 ask는 질문을 한다는 뜻이다 : 선생님은 "누가 답을 아느냐?"고 **물으셨다.**

2 ask는 무언가를 원한다고 말한다는 뜻이다 : 올리버는 배가 고파서 수프를 더 달라고 **부탁했다.**

**asleep** [əslíːp] 1 튀 잠들어 2 형 잠든

asleep은 자고 있다는 뜻이다 : 마거릿은 **자다가** 시끄러운 소리에 깼다.

**astronaut** [ǽstrənɔ̀ːt] 명 우주비행사, 우주인

astronaut는 우주 공간으로 들어가는 사람이다. astronaut는 우주선을 타고 여행한다. 달 위를 걸어 본 astronaut들도 있다.

**at** [《약》 ət, 《강》 ǽt] 전 ① [장소] …에서, …에 ② [때] …에 ③ [방향·목적] …을 향하여

1 at은 사람이나 물건이 어디 있는 지를 알려준다 : 마리아는 오늘 아침 학교에 갔다. 그녀는 지금 학교에 있다.

2 at은 일이 일어나는 때를

말해준다 : 학교 수업은 9시에 시작된다.

3 at은 또한 어떤 방향을 뜻한다 : 수잔은 유성을 관찰하기 위해서 하늘을 쳐다보았다.

**ate** [éit | ét] 통 eat(먹다)의 과거형

ate 는 eat 의 한 형태다 : 해리는 매일 세 끼를 먹는다. 어젯밤 그는 저녁 식사로 피자를 **먹었다.**

**attach** [ətǽtʃ] 타 자 붙이다 ; 달다, 부착하다

attach는 어떤 것을 다른 것과 결합시킨다는 뜻이다 : 조는 테이프로 벽에 게시문을 **붙였다.** 클레어는 자기 자전거에 노란 밀짚 바구니를 **달았다.**

**attention** [ətén∫ən] 명 주의

attention은 주의깊게 보고 듣는다는 뜻이다 : 아이들은 선생님 말씀에 attention을 기울였다.

**attic** [ǽtik] 명 **다락방**

attic은 집의 지붕 아래에 있는 공간이나 방이다. attic을 헌 옷이나 낡은 가구를 보관하는 장소로 이용하기도 한다.

**audience** [ɔ́:diəns] 명 **청중** ; 관중, 관객 ; 청취자, 시청자

audience는 무언가를 듣고 보기 위해서 모인 한 무리의 사람들이다 : 나의 가족은 학교 연극을 보러 온 audience속에 있었다.

**August** [ɔ́:gəst] 명 **8월**

August는 한 해 가운데 한 달이다. August는 31일이며, 7월이 지나고 9월이 되기 전에 온다.

**aunt** [ǽnt | ά:nt] 명 **아주머니,** 숙모, 백모, 고모, 이모

aunt는 아버지의 여자 형제나 어머니의 여자 형제를 말한다. 삼촌 부인도 aunt다.

**author** [ɔ́:θər] 명 **저자, 작가**

author 는 소설이나, 희곡 또는 시를 쓰는 사람이다 : 많은 author들이 아이들을 위한 책을 쓴다.

**automobile** [ɔ́:təmoubí:əl] 명 **자동차**

automobile은 자동차의 또다른 말이다. 사람들은 도로에서 automobile을 본다.

**autumn** [ɔ́:təm] 뗑 가을
autumn은 일 년중 한 계절이다. autumn은 여름이 가고 겨울이 되기 전에 온다. autumn에는 나무에서 잎이 떨어지기 전에 빨강, 노랑, 주황색으로 단풍이 드는 지역도 있다. autumn의 또 다른 말은 fall 이다.

**awake** [əwéik] 1 탄 재 (잠에서) 깨우다 ; 깨다 2 뗑 깨어서
awake는 자고 있지 않다는 뜻이다 : 데이비드는 뜬 눈으로 밤을 새우려고 했다.

**award** [əwɔ́:rd] 1 뗑 상, 상품 2 탄 주다, 수여하다
award는 특별한 일을 한 사람에게 주는 것이다 : 조와 마크는 이야기를 가장 잘 써서 award를 받았다.

**away** [əwéi] 뗑 떨어져서, 떠나서, 멀리로 (가서) ; 가 버려서, 없어져서 ; 집에 없어
1 away는 거리를 나타낸다 : 바다는 여기에서 3 마일 떨어져 있다.
2 away는 또한 방향을 나타낸다 : 조지프는 집에서 나와 거리를 향해 걸어갔다.
3 give away는 누군가에게 무언가를 준다는 뜻이다 : 마리는 그녀의 사촌에게 자기 자전거를 주었다. 그녀는 새 자전거를 샀기 때문에 주었다.

**awful** [ɔ́:fəl] 뗑 무서운 ; 지독한, 굉장한
awful은 무섭거나 아주 나쁘다는 뜻이다 : 큰 화재로 저 가게는 문을 닫았다. 내가 먹어야 했던 약은 지독하게 썼다.

**ax | axe** [æks] 뗑 (손)도끼, 큰 도끼
ax는 연장이다. ax는 금속으로 된 머리 부분이 납작하고 날카로우며, 자루는 길다. ax는 나무를 자르는 데 쓴다.

**baby** [béibi] 명 갓난아기, 어린 아이, 젖먹이
baby는 아주 어린 아이다. baby들은 많이 먹고 잠도 많이 잔다.

**baby-sitter** [béibisìtər] 명 집을 지키며 아이를 돌봐주는 사람
baby-sitter는 부모가 집에 없을 때 어린 아이들을 돌보아 주는 사람이다 : 우리집 baby-sitter 는 우리에게 이야기책을 읽어 준다.

**back** [bæk] 1 명 등, 등뼈 ; 뒤, 뒷면 2 부 뒤로
1 back은 신체의 일부다 : 우리는 back을 바닥에 대고 반듯이 누워, 하늘을 바라보기를 좋아한다.

2 back 은 front(앞)의 반대말이다 : (화물 열차의) 승무원칸은 그 열차의 back 부분에 있다.
3 go back 은 되돌아가다[오다]를 의미한다 : 학생들은 (방학이 끝나는) 매년 가을 학교로 되돌아간다.

**backpack** [bǽkpæk] 명 배낭, 등짐
backpack 은 등에 지는 부드러운 자루다. backpack 은 양 어깨에 메고 물건을 휴대하고 다니는 데 사용한다. 학생들은 backpack을 이용해 책과 다른 조그만 물건들을 가지고 다닌다. 야영하는 사람들은 식량과 의복, 기타 다른 물건들을 운반하기 위해 backpack을 이용한다.

**backward** [bǽkwərd] 1 형 반대의, **거꾸로의** ; 뒤쪽의 2 부 **거꾸로**, 역으로 ; 뒤로
1 backward는 순서가 정반대라는 의미다 : bat의 철자를 **거꾸로** 쓰면 tab이 된다.
2 backward는 또한 뒤로 향한다는 의미다 : 잭은 동생이 뒤에 있는지 확인하려고 **뒤돌아** 보았다.

**backyard** [bæ̀kjáːrd] 명 (집의) **뒤뜰**
backyard는 집 뒤에 있는 마당이다 : 마이크는 backyard에 채소밭을 가꾸었다. 메리의 backyard에는 그네가 있다.

**bad** [bǽd] 형 ① **나쁜** ② **불쾌한** ③ **해로운** ④ **심한**
1 bad는 좋지 않다는 의미다 : 우리는 과일이 **썩어서** 먹을 수가 없었다.
2 bad는 또한 기쁘지 않다는 의미다 : 마거릿은 화가 나서 아무에게나 소리를 치고 있다. 마거릿은 기분이 **좋지 않다.**
3 bad는 고통을 줄 수 있다는 의미다 : 사탕을 너무 많이 먹으면 치아가 **상한다.**
4 bad는 또한 (상태가) 심각하다는 의미도 될 수 있다 : 메리는 **지독한** 감기에 걸려서 누워있었다.

**bag** [bǽg] 명 자루, **가방**
bag은 물건을 담는 데 사용한다. bag은 종이, 플라스틱, 천 혹은 가죽으로 만든다 : 조지는 종이 bag에 점심을 담아 가지고 학교에 온다.

**bake** [béik] 타 자 (빵 · 과자를) **굽다**, (벽돌을) 구워 말리다 ; 익히다
bake는 오븐에 음식을 굽는다는 의미다 : 우리는 어젯밤에 엄마의 생일 케이크를 **구웠다.**

**bakery** [béikəri] 명 **빵집**
bakery는 빵, 케이크 그리고 쿠키를 구워서 파는 가게다 : 우리 bakery에서는 당근 케이크를 판다.

**balance** [bǽləns]  타  자  …의 균형〔평형〕을 유지하다
balance는 어떤 것이 떨어지거나 굴러가지 않도록 한 곳에 머물게 한다는 의미다 : 서커스의 물개는 공을 코 위에 얹고 **균형을 잡을 수 있다.**

**bald** [bɔ́:əld]  형  (머리 등이) 벗어진, 대머리의
bald는 머리카락이 거의 없거나 전혀 없다는 의미다 : 잭은 태어났을 때 **머리카락이 없었다.**

**ball** [bɔ́:əl]  명  공, (구기용) 볼
ball은 둥근 물체다. 여러 가지 크기의 ball이 놀이와 경기에 쓰인다.

**ballet** [bælléi, ‒‒]  명  발레
ballet는 무용의 일종이다 : ballet를 하는 사람들은 독특한 스텝과 음악에 맞추어 움직일 때 취해야 하는 몸동작을 배워야만 한다.

**balloon** [bəlú:n]  명  **기구,** 풍선
balloon은 가스를 채운 자루〔부대〕의 일종이다.  balloon 중에는 엄청나게 커서 사람들을 하늘 높이 실어 보낼 수 있는 것도 있다 : balloon 하나가 하늘 높이 날아가 버렸다.

**banana** [bənǽnə | -nά:nə]  명  바나나
banana는 과일의 일종이다. banana의 모양은 길게 휘어져 있으며 껍질은 노란색이다.

**band** [bǽnd]  명  ① 악대, 악단, 밴드 ② 그룹, 한 무리의 사람들 ③ 끈, 띠
band는 음악을 함께 연주하는 한 무리의 사람들이다 : 퍼레이드에 참가한 모든 사람들은 band 음악에 맞춰 행진했다.

**bandage** [bǽndidʒ]  명  붕대
bandage는 베인 상처를 깨끗이 하고, 보호하기 위해 상처 위에 대는 천조각이다.

**bang** [bǽŋ]  명  쿵(하는 소리) ; 강타(하는 소리)
bang은 갑자기 크게 나는 소리다 : 바람이 세게 불면, 문이 bang하고 닫힌다.

**bank** [bǽŋk] 명 은행 ; 저금통
bank는 돈을 맡아 주는 곳이
다. 사람들은 때때로 bank에
서 돈을 빌린다 : 나의 아주머
니는 bank에서 일하신다. 보
브는 자기의 장난감 bank(저
금통)에 5센트짜리 동전 하나
를 넣었다.

**bar** [bá:r] 명 ① (나무 또는 금
속의) 막대, 막대 모양의 덩어
리 ② 빗장, 가로대 ; (문·창
문의) 창살
bar는 폭보다 길이가 더 긴 것
이다 : 욕실에서 비누로 손을
씻을 수 있다. 새장에는 금속
bar가 있었다.

**barbecue** [bá:rbikjù:] 1 타
(돼지·소 등을) 통째로 굽다,
바비큐로 하다 2 명 (돼지·
소 등의) 통째로 굽기〔구운
것〕, 바비큐
barbecue는 야외에서 음식을
불에 굽는다는 의미다 : 우리
는 어젯밤 닭과 옥수수를
barbecue해 먹었다.

**barber** [bá:rbər] 명 이발사
barber는 머리털을 자르는 사
람이다 : 엄마는 내 머리가 너

무 길어서 나를 barber에게 데
리고 가셨다.

**bare** [bɛ́ər] 형 벌거벗은, 나체
의 ; 노출한
bare는 어떤 것으로도 덮여있
지 않다는 의미다 : 피터는 양
말이나 신발도 신지 않고, 맨
발로 걸어 다니고 있었다.

**barefoot** [bɛ́ərfùt] 1 형 맨발의
2 부 맨발로
발이 맨살로 드러났을 때
barefoot라고 말한다 : 피터는
신발과 양말을 벗고 잔디 위를
맨발로 걷는 것을 좋아한다.

**bargain** [bá:rgin] 명 값싸게
산 (좋은) 물건
어떤 것에 평상시보다 비용이
적게 들 때 bargain이라고 한
다 : 이 셔츠는 9달러를 주고
싸게 산 옷이다.

**barge** [bá:rdʒ] 명 밑이 평평한
짐배, 큰 거룻배 ; (2층으로
된) 유람선
barge는 밑바닥이 평평한 배
다. 강 위로 원목과 모래같은
물건을 나르는 데 barge 가 이
용된다.

**bark¹** [báːrk] 명 나무 껍질
bark는 나무의 껍질이다. 대부분의 bark는 두껍고 거칠거칠하다.

**bark²** [báːrk] 자 (개·여우 등이) **짖다**, 짖는 듯한 소리를 내다
bark는 개 짖는 소리를 낸다는 의미다 : 우리 개는 배가 고프거나 두려움을 느끼면 **짖는다.**

**barn** [báːrn] 명 (가축의) 우리, **외양간** ; (농가의) 헛간, 광
barn은 농장에 있는 건물이다. 젖소와 말들은 barn에서 사육한다 : 우리는 barn에 있는 말들에게 먹이를 주러 갔다.

**barrel** [bǽrəl] 명 (가운데가 불룩한) **통**
barrel은 물건을 보관하는 데 사용된다. barrel은 나무나 금속으로 만들며, 윗 부분과 밑바닥은 평평한 원형이다. 옆이 곡면인 barrel도 있다.

**base** [béis] 명 ① 바닥, **기초**, **토대**, 근거 ; (기둥, 비석 등의) 초석 ② (야구의) **베이스**, 누
1 base는 어떤 것의 밑부분으로 어떤 것 위에 세울 수 있는 부분이다 : 그 조각상의 base는 대리석으로 되어 있다.
2 base는 또한 야구장의 네 귀퉁이 중의 하나다 : 나는 공을 아주 멀리 쳐서 second base(2루)까지 내쳐 달릴 수 있었다.

**baseball** [béisbɔ̀ːl] 명 **야구** ; 야구공
1 baseball은 운동 경기다. baseball은 배트와 공을 가지고 두 팀이 하는 경기다.

2 baseball은 야구 경기에 사용하는 딱딱한 흰 공이다.

**basement** [béismənt] 명 (건물의) **지하층**, **지하실**, 최하부
basement는 건물의 최하층이다. basement는 대개 지면보다 낮다 : 아빠는 basement에다 우리가 게임을 하거나 파티를 열 수 있는 방을 하나 만드셨다.

**basket** [bǽskit | báːs-] 명 바구니, 광주리, **바스켓**
basket은 물건을 담는데 사용한다. basket은 길고 가느다란 나뭇조각이나 풀로 만들 수 있다. basket은 사발 같은 모양을 한 경우가 많으며 손잡이가 달려 있다.

**basketball** [bǽskitbɔ̀ːl | báːs-] 명 농구, 농구공
1 basketball은 운동 경기다 : basketball은 큰 공과 두 개의 바스켓으로 두 팀이 하는 경기다.

2 농구 경기에 사용하는 큰 고무공도 basketball이다.

**bat¹** [bǽt] 명 배트, 방망이
bat는 나무로 만든 딱딱한 막대기다. bat는 야구나 그 밖의 다른 경기를 하는데 사용된다.

**bat²** [bǽt] 명 박쥐
bat는 생쥐와 모양이 비슷한 날개가 있는 작은 동물이다.

bat는 낮에는 자고 밤에 날아다닌다.

**bath** [bǽθ | báːθ] 명 목욕
bath를 할 때는 비눗물로 씻는다 : 엄마가 갓난아기를 bath시켜 주셨다.

**bathing suit** [béiðiŋ sùːt] 명 수영복
bathing suit는 수영할 때 입는 것이다 : 빌리와 헬렌은 수영을 갔다온 후, bathing suit를 말리려고 밖에 내다 걸었다.

**bathrobe** [bǽθròub | báːθ-] 명 실내복, 화장옷
bathrobe는 목욕 전후나 편하게 쉴 때 입는 헐렁한 겉옷이다.

**bathroom** [bǽθrùːm, -rùm | báːθ-] 명 욕실, 화장실
bathroom은 세면대, 변기 때로는 욕조나 샤워기가 있는 방이다 : 마이크는 bathroom에서

B

이를 닦는다.

**bathtub** [bǽθtʌb|bάːθ-] 몡 목
욕통, (서양식) 욕조
bathtub 는 물을 채우고 들어
가 앉아서 목욕을 하는 상당히
큰 용기다.

**battery** [bǽtəri] 몡 전지, 배터
리
battery는 전기를 발생시키는
것이다 : 연기 탐지기, 손전등
그리고 몇몇 라디오는 battery
로 작동된다.

**battle** [bǽtl] 몡 전투, 싸움 ;
전쟁 ; 투쟁
battle은 두 사람이나 집단간
의 싸움이다. battle에는 보통
무기가 쓰인다 : 두 군대가
battle을 했다.

**bay** [béi] 몡 (작은) 만
bay는 바다나 호수가 육지 속
으로 쑥 들어간 부분이다.

**be** [《약》 bi, 《강》 bíː] 1 瓜 …
이다 ; 생존[존재]하다 2 조 ①
[동작] …되다 ② [상태] …되

고 있다
1 be는 살아가다 혹은 공간을
차지한다는 의미다 : 한 사람이
동시에 두 곳에 있을 수 없다.
엘리자베스는 커서 의사가 되
고 싶어한다.
2 be는 (상태가) 어떠한 가를
나타낸다 : 내일은 날씨가 맑을
것이다.

**beach** [bíːtʃ] 몡 해변, 물가, 바
닷가
beach는 호수나 바다에 접한
육지다. 대부분의 beach는 모
래로 덮여 있다.

**bead** [bíːd] 몡 구슬, 구멍이 뚫
린 작은 구슬 ; 염주알
bead는 구멍이 있는 작고 둥
근 모양의 플라스틱이나 유리
혹은  나뭇조각이다 : 우리는
bead로 목걸이를 만들었다.

**beak** [bíːk] 몡 부리, 부리 모양
의 것
beak는 딱딱한 새의 주둥이
다. 길고 날카로운 beak를 가
진 새도 있다.

**bean** [bíːn] 몡 콩
bean은 야채로 먹는 씨앗이

다 : 샐러드에는 녹색 bean과
노란색 bean이 들어 있었다.

**bear** [bέər] 몡 곰
　bear는 큰 동물이다. bear는
두꺼운 털가죽과 강한 발톱을
가지고 있다. 많은 bear들이
겨울 내내 잠을 잔다.

**beard** [bíərd] 몡 (턱) 수염
　beard는 남자 얼굴에 나는 털
이다 : 나의 할아버지는 짧고
흰 beard가 있다.

**beast** [bíːst] 몡 짐승, (특히) 네
**발 짐승, 동물**
　beast는 네 발 달린 동물이
다. 사자, 호랑이 그리고 개는
모두 beast다.

**beat** [bíːt] 탄 잰 연달아 **치다**,
두들기다 ; (상대·적을) **패배**

시키다, …을 능가하다 ; 휘젓
다
　1 beat는 어떤 것을 여러번 친
다는 의미다 : 비가 유리창을
**세차게 쳤다.**
　2 beat는 또한 어떤 일을 다
른 사람보다 더 잘한다는 뜻이
다 : 다이애나는 경주에서 마리
아를 **이겼다.**

**beaten** [bíːtən] 동 beat (치다,
휘젓다)의 과거분사형
　beaten은 beat의 한 형태다 :
잭의 아버지가 잭에게 달걀을
휘저어 달라고 부탁하자, 잭은
벌써 **저어 놓았다고** 말했다.

**beautiful** [bjúːtifəl] 혱 **아름다**
**운**, 예쁜, 멋있는 ; 훌륭한
　beautiful은 보거나 듣기에 아
주 좋다는 의미다 : 메리는 말
을 **멋있게** 그렸다. 합창단은
**아름다운** 노래를 불렀다. 어젯
밤 일몰은 **아름다웠다.**

**beaver** [bíːvər] 몡 비버, 해리
　beaver는 동물의 일종이다.
beaver는 꼬리가 납작하고 앞
니가 크고 강하다. beaver는
개울을 가로지르는 둑을 쌓으
며, 이 둑에서 산다.

**became** [bikéim] 图 become
(…이 되다)의 과거형
became은 become의 한 형태
다 : 조지는 언젠가 조종사가
되고 싶다. 그의 아버지는 여
러 해 전에 조종사가 **되었다.**

**because** [bikɔ́:z, -káz, -kʌ́z|
-kɔ́z] 젭 (왜냐하면) **…이므로**
〔**이니까**〕, (그 까닭은) …**때문
에**
어떤 일이 일어나고 있는 이유
를 말할 때 because를 쓴
다 : 이 곳이 **추워서** 문을 닫고
있다. 선수들이 시합에 **이겨서**
기뻐한다.

**become** [bikʌ́m] 区 …**이**〔**으로**〕
**되다**
become은 성장하여 다른 것
이 된다는 의미다 : 내가 심은
씨앗은 꽃이 **될 것이다.**

**bed** [béd] 명 **침대, 침상** ; (가축
의) **잠자리**
bed는 잠자는 곳이다 : 그녀는
8시까지 bed에서 자고 있었
다. 개의 bed는 내 방에 있
다.

**bedroom** [bédrù:m, -rùm] 명
**침실**
bedroom은 사람들이 잠을 자
기 위해 사용하는 방이다 : 우
리 아파트는 bedroom이 두 개
다. 오늘 아침 잠에서 깨어나
보니, 햇빛이 내 bedroom 창
문을 통해 들어와 방 안을 환
하게 비추고 있었다.

**bee** [bí:] 명 (특히) **꿀벌** ; 〔일반
적으로〕 **벌**
bee는 곤충이다. bee는 날 수
있으며, 꿀을 만드는 bee도
있다.

**beef** [bí:f] 명 **쇠고기**
beef는 일종의 고기다. beef
는 소에서 얻으며, 햄버거는
beef로 만든다.

**been** [bin|bí:n, bin] 图 be(…이
다)의 과거분사형
been은 단어 be에서 생긴 말
이다 : 수잔과 앨버트는 뜰에서
놀고 **있다.** 나는 로데오 경기
에 **가본 적이** 없다.

**beetle** [bíːtl] 명 딱정벌레
beetle은 날아 다니는 곤충이다. beetle에게는 자기 몸의 연약한 부위를 보호하는 단단하고 광택이 나는 겉날개가 있다.

**before** [bifɔ́ːr] 1 접 (… 하기에) 앞서서, **… 보다 먼저,** … 하기 전에 2 부 ① [위치] 앞에, 앞으로, 전방[전면]에 ② [때·시기] **이전에,** 일찍이 3 전 ① [위치] **…의 앞에** ② [때] …보다 먼저
1 before는 맨 먼저[첫째로]라는 의미다 : 마리는 먼저 손을 씻은 다음 저녁을 먹는다. 즉 마리는 식사를 하기 **전에** 손을 씻는다.
2 before는 또한 과거를 나타낸다 : 앨리스는 지난 주 처음으로 비행기를 탔다. 그녀는 **전에** 비행기를 타본 적이 없었다.

**beg** [bég] 타 자 (돈·음식 등을) **구걸하다,** 빌다 ; 부탁하다, 간청하다
beg는 돈이나 기타 다른 도움을 요청한다는 의미다 : 그 불쌍한 여자는 음식을 **구걸했다.**

**began** [bigǽn] 동 begin(시작하다)의 과거형
began은 begin의 한 형태다 : 비가 온 후 풀이 자라기 **시작했다.**

**begin** [bigín] 타 자 시작하다
begin은 시작한다는 의미다 : 풀은 봄에 자라기 **시작해서,** 가을에 성장을 멈춘다.

**beginning** [bigíniŋ] 명 ① 처음, 시작 ; 시초, 발단 ② [복수로] 초기, 첫 단계, 초창기
beginning은 어떤 것이 시작되는 첫 부분이나 그 시기를 의미한다 : 이야기의 beginning이 끝부분보다 좋았다. 내일부터 겨울 방학이 beginning된다.

**begun** [bigʌ́n] 동 begin(시작하다)의 과거분사형
begun은 begin의 한 형태다 : 사전은 항상 단어 a로 **시작된다.**

**behave** [bihéiv] 타 자 행동[처신]하다
1 behave는 좋게 행동한다는 의미다 : 선생님이 우리에게 교실에서 **예절 바르게 행동하라**고 말씀하셨다.
2 behave는 또한 어떤 방식으로 행동한다는 의미다 : 아기가 진료실에서 어떻게 **행동했습니까 ?**

**behind** [biháind] 1 전 ① [장소] …의 뒤에[로]  ② [때] … 보다 처져서, …보다 늦게
2 부 뒤로, 뒤에 ; 숨어서 ; (일 등이) 늦어서, 밀려서
behind는 「…의 뒤에」라는 의미다 : 데이비드는 학교에서 웬디 뒤에 앉는다. 새끼 오리들이 어미 오리 뒤를 따라갔다. 해리는 나무 뒤에 숨었다.

**being** [bíːiŋ] 1 동 be의 현재분사·동명사형  2 명 존재, 생존, 인생 ; 생물, 인간
1 being은 단어 be에서 생긴 말이다 : 아이들은 철부지 짓을 하며 즐겁게 지내고 있었다.
2 being은 사람이나 동물을 나타낸다 : 사람은 human being이다.

**believe** [bilíːv] 타 자 믿다 ; …라고 생각하다, 여기다
believe는 어떤 것이 사실이거나 진실이라고 생각한다는 의미다 : 클레어 아주머니는 자신이 1,000 달러의 상금을 받았다는 사실을 도저히 믿을 수가 없었다.

**bell** [bél] 명 종 ; 벨, 방울
bell은 두드리면, 울려 퍼지는 소리를 낸다 : 양들은 모두 목에 조그만 bell을 달고 있었다. 우리는 수업 시작 bell 소리를 듣고, 우리가 지각을 했다는 사실을 알았다.

**belong** [bilɔ́ːŋ | bilɔ́ŋ] 자 (…에) 속하다, (…의) 것이다 ; (있어야 할 곳에) 있다
1 belong은 어떤 장소에 있어야 안심이 된다는 의미다 : 물고기가 있어야 할 곳은 물이다.
2 belong은 또한 누군가가 소유하고 있다는 의미다 : 저 셔츠는 마크의 것이다. 즉 그의 셔츠다.

**below** [bilóu] 1 전 …보다 밑에 [아래로]  2 부 밑에 [으로, 을]
below는 더 낮은 곳을 의미한다 : 테리는 내 그림 밑에 자기가 그린 그림을 걸었다.

**belt** [bélt] 명 허리띠, 혁대, 벨트
belt는 바지나 스커트가 흘러 내리지 않도록 착용하는 것이다 : 이 바지는 내게 너무 커서 belt를 매지 않으면 안된다.

**bench** [béntʃ] 명 벤치
bench는 긴 의자다 : 할머니와 나는 공원 bench에 앉아서 새들에게 먹이를 주었다.

**bend** [bénd] 타 자 **구부리다,**
휘게 하다 ; (무릎을) 꿇다 ;
(머리를) 숙이다
bend는 휘어지게 한다는 의미다 : 한나는 몸을 **굽혀서** 양동이에 물을 담는다.

**beneath** [biníːθ] 1 전 **…의 바로 밑에, …보다 낮은** 2 부
**(바로) 아래에**
beneath는 다른 것보다 낮거나 밑에 있다는 말이다 : 우리는 계단 **밑에** 있는 수납장에 빗자루들을 보관한다. 그 개의 잠자리는 탁자 **밑이다.**

**bent** [bént] 동 bend(구부리다)의 과거·과거분사형
bent는 bend의 한 형태다 : 나

는 무릎을 **굽혔다가** 껑충 뛰었다. 수잔의 안경은 그녀가 안경 위에 앉아서 **휘어지고 말았다.**

**beret** [bəréi│bérei] 명 베레모
beret는 폭신하고 둥글 납작한 모자다 : 나의 할아버지께서는 쌀쌀한 날에는 격자 무늬의 스카프를 두르시고 beret를 쓰신다.

**berry** [béri] 명 ① 액과, 장과 ② [일반적으로] 딸기류
berry는 먹을 수 있는 작은 과일이다. berry에는 많은 씨가 있다 : 우리는 berry를 따러 존씨의 농장에 갔다.

**beside** [bisáid] 전 **…의 곁〔옆〕에, …와 나란히**
beside는 사람이나 사물의 바로 옆에 있다는 의미다 : 사진 속에 리처드와 마거릿은 서로 **나란히** 붙어 있다.

**best** [bést] [good, well의 최상급] 1 형 **가장 좋은, 최상의, 최선의** 2 부 **가장〔제일〕 좋게**

best는 다른 모든 것보다 좋다〔낫다〕는 의미다 : 동물원에 있는 모든 동물 중에, 나는 원숭이를 **가장** 좋아한다. 빌리가 **가장** 잘 달렸기 때문에 경주에서 이겼다.

**better** [bétər] [good, well의 비교급] 1 형 …보다 좋은, 더 나은〔우수한〕 2 부 …보다 더 좋게〔낫게〕
better는 매우 좋지만 최상은 아니라는 의미다 : 리처드는 마크보다 수영을 **더 잘한다**. 빌은 추운 날보다 따뜻한 날을 **더 좋아한다**.

**between** [bitwí:n] 1 전 (두개의) 사이에〔의, 를〕, …와 …와의 중간의 2 부 중간에〔으로〕
between은 서로 다른 두 사물의 중간에 있다는 의미다 : 알파벳에서, s는 r과 t **사이에** 온다. 개가 트럭안에서 우리 둘 **사이에** 앉았다. 엄마는 우리에게 **간식**으로 쿠키를 먹어서는 안된다고 말씀하셨다.

**beyond** [bijánd|-jɔ́nd] 1 전 …의 저쪽에, …을 넘어서 2 부 (저) 멀리에, 먼 저쪽에
beyond는 어떤 것의 맞은 편을 말한다 : 마리아는 울타리를 타고 올라가 밭으로 들어갔다. 즉, 그녀는 울타리를 **넘어** 갔다.

**bicycle** [báisikl] 명 자전거
bicycle은 타고 다니는 것이다. bicycle에는 나란히 달린 두 바퀴가 있는 데, 발을 사용해서 바퀴를 돌린다. bike는 bicycle의 줄임말이다.

**big** [bíg] 형 큰, 커진, 성장한
big은 크기나 양이 크다는 의미다 : 리처드가 들어 올리기에는 상자가 너무 **컸다**. 우리는 대도시에 살고 있다.

**bill** [bíəl] 명 부리
bill은 새의 부리다 : 오리에게는 큰 bill이 있다.

**biography** [baiágrəfi|-ɔ́g-] 명 전기, 일대기 ; 전기 문학
biography는 어떤 사람이 누군가의 생애를 사실대로 쓴 이야기다.

**bird** [bə́:rd] 명 새
bird는 날개가 있는 동물이다. bird의 몸은 깃털로 덮여 있고, 두 개의 다리가 있다. 대부분의 bird는 날 수 있으며, 알을 낳는다. 닭과 펭귄은 bird다.

**birth** [bə́:rθ] 명 출생, 탄생 ; 태생, 집안
birth는 사람이 태어난 순간을 말한다 : birth는 대부분 병원에서 이루어진다.

**birthday** [bə́:rθdèi] 명 (탄)생일 ; 창립 (기념)일
birthday는 태어난 날이다 : 마리아는 11월 8일에 태어났다. 즉, 그녀의 birthday는 11월 8일이다.

**bit** [bít] 1 동 bite(물다)의 과거·과거분사형 2 명 작은 조각, 작은 부분, (음식의) 한 입(거리) ; 조금, 소량
1 bit는 bite의 한 형태다 : 앤은 사과를 먹기 시작했다.
2 bit는 또한 소량을 의미한다 : 데이비드는 수프에 후추를 조금 뿌렸다.

**bite** [báit] 1 타 자 물다, 물어뜯다 2 명 (깨)물기 ; 한 입(의 분량) ; 소량(의 음식)
1 bite는 이로 자른다는 의미다 : 웬디는 배가 고파, 샌드위치를 한 입 베어 물고서 씹어 삼킨다.
2 bite는 이로 잘라낼 수 있는 작은 양을 말한다 : 웬디는 샌드위치를 한 입 베어 먹고, 나머지는 나중에 먹기로 했다.

**bitten** [bítən] 동 bite(물다)의 과거분사형
bitten은 bite의 한 형태다 : 내 동생이 개에게 물렸다.

**bitter** [bítər] 1 형 쓴 2 명 [the ~] 씀, 쓴맛
bitter는 자극적인 맛이 난다는 의미다 : 조지는 그 약을 맛보고는 얼굴을 찌푸렸다. 아주 쓰기 때문이었다.

**black** [blǽk] 1 형 검은, 검은색의, 어두운 2 명 검은색 ; 먹 ; 검은 옷 ; 암흑

black은 매우 어두운 색이
다 : 이 글자들은 **검정색이다.**
black의 반대말은 white(흰색)
다.

**blacksmith** [blǽksmiθ] 명 대
장장이
blacksmith는 철을 이용해 물
건을 만드는 사람이다. black-
smith는 편자를 만든다.

**blame** [bléim] 타 **나무라다, 비
난하다,** 책망하다 ; …의 죄를
…에게 씌우다
blame은 일을 잘못했다거나
틀리게 했다고 말한다는 의미
다 : 어머니는 내가 새장 속의
새를 놓아 주었다고 **나무라셨
다.**

**blanket** [blǽŋkit] 명 모포, 담
요
blanket은 크고 부드러운 천이
다. 사람들은 몸을 따뜻하게
하려고 blanket을 덮는다.

**bleed** [blíːd] 자 타 **피를 흘리
다,** 피를 빼다
bleed는 몸에서 피가 나온다
는 의미다 : 톰은 넘어져서 턱
이 까져 **피가 났다.**

**blew** [blúː] 동 blow(불다) 의
과거형
blew는 단어 blow에서 생긴
말이다 : 바람이 **불어** 문이 닫
혔다.

**blind** [bláind] 형 **눈이 먼,** 맹
인 (용) 의
blind는 볼 수 없다는 의미
다 : 볼 수 없는 사람은 **맹인이
다.**

**block** [blák|blɔ́k] 명 **덩어리,
토막** ; (시가의 도로로 둘러싸
인) **한 구획**
1 block은 단단하고 모든 면이
평평하다 : 엘리자베스는 장난
감 block으로 집을 지었다.

2 block은 네개의 도로로 둘
러싸인 지역이다. block은 또
한 두거리 사이에 위치한 구역
을 말한다 : 보브와 나는 같은
block에 살고 있다.

**blood** [blʌ́d] 명 **피, 혈액** ; 혈
통, 가문
blood는 붉은 액체며, 몸 속
에 있다. blood 없이 살 수
있는 사람은 아무도 없다.

**bloom** [blúːm] 1 명 (특히 관상
용 식물의) **꽃** 2 자 **꽃이 피다**
bloom은 꽃이 생긴다는 의미

다 : 벚나무는 봄에 **꽃이 핀다.**

**blossom** [blásəm|blɔ́s-] 명 (특히 과수의) 꽃
blossom은 꽃이다 : 사과나무에 열려 있는 blossom들은 흰색이거나 연분홍색이다.

**blouse** [bláus|bláuz] 명 (여성·어린이용의) 블라우스
blouse는 상체에 입는 의복이다.

**blow** [blóu] 자 타 (바람이) 불다, (바람에) 날려 휘날리다 ; 입김을 내뿜다
1 blow는 어떤 것에 공기를 넣는다는 뜻이다 : 이 풍선들을 **부풀리는** 것을 도와주겠니?
2 blow는 또한 공기와 함께 이동한다는 뜻이다 : 우산을 꼭 붙잡아라. 그렇지 않으면 바람에 우산이 **날아가** 버릴 것이다.

**blown** [blóun] 동 blow(불다)의 과거분사형
blown은 blow의 한 형태다 : 나뭇잎들이 바람에 떨어져 **날아갔다.**

**blue** [blú:] 1 형 푸른, 파란 2 명 파랑, 청색
blue는 색이다 : 구름 한 점 없는 날이면, 하늘은 **푸르다.**

**board** [bɔ́:rd] 명 판자, 널
board는 길고 평평한 나뭇조각이다. board는 집을 짓는 데 사용한다 : 마루는 board로 만들어졌다.

**boat** [bóut] 명 보트, 작은 배
boat는 물 위를 다니는데 쓰는 것이다. 돛에 바람을 받아 움직이는 boat도 있고, 모터로 움직이는 boat도 있다 : 나는 boat로 강을 건넜다.

**body** [bádi|bɔ́di] 명 몸, 신체 ; 육체 ; 몸통
body는 사람이나 동물의 몸 전체를 말한다 : 코끼리의 body는 크고 무거우며, 뱀의 body는 길고 가늘다.

**boil** [bɔ́iəl] 타 자 끓이다, 삶다
1 boil은 물을 아주 뜨겁게 한다는 의미다 : 물이 **끓으면**, 작은 거품들이 수면에 생긴다.
2 boil은 또한 끓는 물에 어떤 것을 삶는다는 의미다 : 존은 아침에 먹을 계란을 **삶았다**.

**bone** [bóun] 명 뼈
bone은 피부와 근육으로 싸여 있는 신체의 단단한 부분이다. 사람의 다리에는 크고 기다란 bone이 있으며, 발에는 작은 bone들이 많이 있다 : 수잔은 빙판에 넘어져 팔의 bone이 부러졌다.

**book** [búk] 명 책, 책자, 서적
book은 한쪽 가장자리를 꿰맸거나 풀로 붙인 종잇장들로 되어 있다. book의 페이지마다에는 사람들이 읽고 보는 글과 그림들이 있다 : 이 사전은 book 이다. 우리 학교 도서관에는 book이 많이 있다.

**boom** [búːm] 명 (대포·북·천둥·종의) 울리는 소리
boom은 굵직하고 낮게 울리는 소리를 말한다 : 폭풍이 치는 동안, 우리는 천둥이 **울리는 소리**를 들었다.

**boost** [búːst] 타 밀어 올리다
boost는 밀어 올린다는 의미다 : 조지는 친구가 사과를 딸 수 있도록 나무로 그를 **밀어 올렸다**.

**boot** [búːt] 명 장화, 부츠
boot는 큰 신발이다. boot는 고무나 가죽으로 만든다. 대부분의 사람들은 비나 눈이 올 때 boot를 신는다.

**border** [bɔ́ːrdər] 명 국경(선), 경계 ; 테두리, 가장자리
border는 가장자리를 말한다. border는 한 지역이 끝나면서 또 다른 지역이 시작되는 경계선이다 : 우리는 정원 주위에 돌로 border를 만들었다.

**borrow** [bárou, bɔ́ːr-|bɔ́r-] 타 자 빌리다, 꾸다, 차용하다
borrow는 잠시동안 사용하려

고 어떤 것을 가져 간다는 뜻이다 : 앨버트는 자기의 롤러스케이트를 내게 **빌려주었다.** 엘리자베스는 내게서 책을 **빌렸다.**

**both** [bóuθ] 1 형 양쪽의, 둘 다의 2 대 양쪽, 둘 다 3 부 …도 …도, 둘 다
both는 두 사람 혹은 두 개의 사물을 뜻한다 : 두 어린이가 상을 탔다. 나는 사과와 바나나를 **둘 다** 좋아한다.

**bother** [báðər | bɔ́ðə] 타 자 괴롭히다, 귀찮게 하다
bother는 누군가를 성가시게 하거나 괴롭힌다는 뜻이다 : 앨리스가 전화 중일 때면 여동생이 그녀를 **성가시게 한다.**

**bottle** [bátl | bɔ́tl] 명 병, 술병
bottle은 액체를 담아두는 데 쓴다 : bottle은 유리나 플라스틱으로 만들 수 있다.

**bottom** [bátəm | bɔ́t-] 명 밑바닥 ; 근본, 기초
bottom은 어떤 것의 가장 아래 부분을 말한다 : 바위가 물웅덩이 bottom에 가라앉았다.

**bought** [bɔ́:t] 동 buy(사다)의 과거·과거분사형
bought는 단어 buy에서 생긴 말이다 : 우리는 소풍가서 먹을 음식을 **샀다.**

**bounce** [báuns] 자 타 뛰어오르다, 되튀다, 바운드하다 ; 튀게 하다, 뛰어오르게 하다
bounce는 어떤 것에 부딪쳐 되튄다는 뜻이다 : 폴이 공을 던졌는 데, 공이 보도에 **부딪쳐 되튀어 왔다.**

**bow**¹ [bóu] 명 활, 활 모양의 것 ; (리본 등의) **나비 매듭,** 나비 모양의 리본〔넥타이〕
1 bow는 독특한 매듭의 일종이다. bow는 리본이나 끈으로 만든다 : 헬렌은 선물에 붉은 색의 큰 bow를 맸다.
2 bow는 또한 끈으로 양 끝을 묶은 가느다란 나뭇조각이다. bow는 화살을 쏘는 데 사용한다.

**bow**² [báu] 1 자 타 허리를 구부리다, 인사하다 2 명 인사, 절하기
bow는 몸을 앞으로 구부린다는 뜻이다 : 이야기 책에서는

기사가 왕을 만나자 왕에게 경의를 표하며 **허리를 굽힌다.**

**bowl** [bóuəl] 명 사발, 주발, 공기 ; 한 그릇
bowl은 물건을 담아두는 데 사용한다. bowl은 둥글고 속이 움푹 패어 있다. 사람들은 수프와 시리얼을 bowl에 담아 먹는다.

**bowling** [bóuliŋ] 명 볼링
bowling은 운동 경기다. bowling은 무거운 공과 병처럼 생긴 나무토막들로 경기를 한다.

**box** [báks|bɔ́ks] 명 상자
box는 물건을 담는데 사용한다. box는 대개 나무나 두꺼운 종이로 만든다.

**boy** [bɔ́i] 명 사내아이, 소년
boy는 커서 남자가 될 어린아이다. boy는 남자 아이다.

**brace** [bréis] 명 ① 버팀대, 버팀목, 지주 ② 고정기, **보조기** ; **치열 교정기**
1 brace는 부품을 결합시키거나 물건이 흔들리지 않게 하는 것이다 : 테리는 걷는 데 도움이 되도록 허약한 다리에 금속 brace를 찼다.
2 brace는 또한 치아가 고르게 자라도록 치아에 거는 금속 철사를 말한다.

**bracelet** [bréislət] 명 팔찌
bracelet은 장신구로 팔에 끼는 체인이나 커다란 고리다.

**braid** [bréid] 1 타 **머리를 땋다** [땋아 늘이다], 짜다, 꼬다 2 명 노끈, 꼰 끈, **땋은 머리**
1 braid는 머리카락을 세 가닥으로 나눈 다음, 길고 가느다란 한 가닥이 될 때까지 세 가닥을 서로 엇갈리게 짜 엮는 것이다.
2 길게 **땋여진** 한 가닥의 머리를 braid 라고 한다.

**brain** [bréin] 명 뇌
brain은 사람과 동물의 머리속에 있는 신체 기관이다. brain은 우리에게 생각하고 학습하며 기억을 할 수 있게 해준다.

**brainstorm** [bréinstɔ̀:rm] 1 자 브레인스토밍하다 2 명 (갑자

기 일어나는) **정신 착란 ; 영감, 갑자기 떠오른 묘안**
1 brainstorm은 문제의 해답을 찾아내기 위해, 단체로 모여서 각자의 생각을 모은다는 의미다 : 우리는 오랫동안 **브레인스토밍을 한** 결과, 마침내 우리 팀을 나타내는 좋은 이름을 생각해 냈다.
2 brainstorm은 갑자기 떠오른 좋은 생각이다.

**brake** [bréik] 圐 **브레이크, 제동기, 제동 장치**
brake는 자전거나 자동차 또는 기차를 천천히 가게 하거나 멈추게 하는 것이다. 많은 자전거에 부착된 brake처럼, 손으로 작동되는 brake도 있고, 발로 작동되는 brake도 있다 : 엄마는 자동차를 정지시키려고 brake에 발을 올려 놓으셨다 (brake를 밟으셨다).

**branch** [brǽntʃ | brάːntʃ] 圐 **나뭇가지, 가지처럼 갈라진 것**
branch는 줄기에서 뻗어 나온 나무나 관목의 일부다. 나뭇잎은 branch에서 싹튼다.

**brave** [bréiv] 圀 **용감한**
brave는 용기가 있다는 의미다 : 그 **용감한** 아이는 고양이 새끼를 잡으러 나무에 올라 갔다.

**bread** [bréd] 圐 **빵 ; 식량**
bread는 식품의 일종이다. bread는 밀가루와 물 그리고 다른 것들을 함께 섞어서 만든다. bread는 오븐에 굽는다.

**break** [bréik] 圙 圚 **깨뜨리다, 쪼개다 ; (기계 등을) 부수다, 고장내다**
1 break는 산산조각이 난다는 의미다 : 저 거울을 떨어뜨리면 **깨질 것이다.**
2 break는 작동을 멈춘다는 의미다 : 우리집 오븐은 **고장이 나서** 뜨거워지지 않는다. 조지는 자기의 장난감 트럭을 집어던져 **고장을 냈다.**

**breakfast** [brékfəst] 圐 **아침 식사, 조반**
breakfast는 하루 중 맨 먼저 하는 식사다 : 우리는 아침에 breakfast를 먹는다. 나는 breakfast로 시리얼과 바나나 한 개를 즐겨 먹는다.

**breath** [bréθ] 명 숨, 호흡
breath는 숨을 쉴 때 들이 마
시고 내뱉는 공기다. 날씨가
몹시 추우면 breath를 볼 수
있다.

**breathe** [bríːð]  자 타  호흡하
다 ; 살아있다 ; 한숨 돌리다
breathe는 몸 속으로 공기를
들여보냈다가 다시 밖으로 내
뱉는다는 뜻이다. 코와 입을
통해 **숨을 쉰다.**

**breeze** [bríːz] 명 산들 바람
breeze는 부드럽고 잔잔한 바
람이다 : 우리는 바다에서 불어
오는 breeze로 시원했다.

**brick** [brík] 명 벽돌
brick은 오븐에 구워 굳히거나
햇볕에 말린 흙덩어리다 : 우리
집 굴뚝은 brick 으로 되어 있
다.

**bridge** [brídʒ] 명 다리, 교량
bridge는 한 쪽에서 다른 쪽으
로 건너가는 데 이용한다.
bridge는 물위에 건설하는 경
우가 많다.

**bright** [bráit] 형 (햇빛 등이)
밝은, 밝게 빛나는 ; 화창한,
맑은 ; 투명한 ; 영리한
bright는 어떤 것이 빛을 내거
나 빛으로 꽉 차있다는 뜻이
다 : 햇빛이 방을 **환하게** 비추
었다.

**bring** [bríŋ] 타  가지고  오다,
데리고 오다, 함께 오다
bring은 사람이나 물건을 데리
고〔가지고〕온다는 뜻이다 : 한
나는 그녀의 친구 메리를 파티
에 **데리고 올** 수 있느냐고 물
었다. 신문 좀 **가져다 주시겠
습니까?**

**broke** [bróuk] 동 break(깨뜨리
다)의 과거형
broke는 break의 한 형태다 :
유리는 깨지기 쉽다. 나는 어
제 유리를 떨어뜨려 **산산 조각
냈다.**

**broken** [bróukən] 동 break(깨
뜨리다)의 과거분사형
broken은 break의 한 형태
다 : 저 창문은 유리가 다섯 조
각으로 **깨졌다.**

**broom** [brúːm] 명 비
broom은 긴 손잡이가 달린 솔
이다. broom은 바닥이나 지면
을 청소하기 위해 사용한다 :
켈리씨는 넓은 broom을 사용
해 보도에 있는 나뭇잎들을 쓸
어낸다.

**brother** [brʌ́ðər] 명 형제 ; 형,
동생
brother는 같은 부모를 둔 남
자를 말한다.

**brought** [brɔ́ːt] 통 bring (가지
고[데리고] 오다)의 과거 · 과
거분사형
brought는 단어 bring에서 생
긴 말이다 : 파티에 온 사람은
누구나 해리에게 줄 생일 선물
을 **가지고 왔다.**

**brown** [bráun] 1 형 **갈색의,** 밤
색의, 다갈색의 2 명 **갈색**
brown은 땅색깔이다 : 갈색 머
리털과 **갈색** 눈을 가진 사람도
있다.

**brush** [brʌ́ʃ] 1 명  **솔(질),**  붓
2 타 ···에 **솔질을 하다,** 닦
다 ; **머리를 빗다,** 이를 닦다
1 brush는 청소를 하거나 그림
을 그리는 데 쓰는 것이다.
brush는 대개 자루에 털이나
철사가 붙어 있다. 칫솔은 특
수한 종류의 brush다.
2 brush는 또한 청소를 하거
나 어떤 것을 깨끗하게 한다는
의미다 : 웬디는 여동생의 긴
머리를 **빗질해서** 땋아 주기를
좋아한다. 폴은 적어도 일주일
에 한번 개를 **솔질해 준다.**

**bubble** [bʌ́bl] 명 **거품,** 기포
bubble은 공기로 꽉찬 둥근
방울이다 : 마이크와   사라는
soap bubble(비눗방울)을 불
었다.

**bucket** [bʌ́kit] 명 **물통**
bucket은 물건을 나르는 데
사용한다.   bucket은 나무나
금속 혹은 플라스틱으로 만들
수 있다. bucket의 밑바닥은
평평한 원형이며, 손잡이가 달
려있다. bucket은 대개 물을
나르는 데 사용한다.

**bug** [bʌ́g] 명 **곤충** ; 벌레
bug는 곤충이다. 개미, 벌,

모기는 bug의 일종이다.

**build** [bíəld] 🔲 🔳 세우다, **건축〔건조〕하다**, 쌓다, 만들다, (새가 둥지를) 짓다
build는 어떤 것을 만든다는 의미다 : 우리는 모래로 성을 **쌓으려고** 한다. 폴은 토끼를 키울 큰 우리를 **만들었다.**

**building** [bíəldiŋ] 🔳 **건축물,** 빌딩 ; 건축술, 건축, 건조
building은 안에서 생활을 하거나 공부를 하기 위해, 혹은 일을 하기 위해 지은 것이다. 집, 학교, 교회, 사무실 그리고 가게는 모두 building이다.

**built** [bíəlt] 🔳 build(세우다)의 과거·과거분사형
built는 build의 한 형태다 : 목수들이 어느 해 여름에 저 집을 **지었다.**

**bulb** [bʌ́əlb] 🔳 ① **알뿌리,** 구경 ; 공 모양의 물건, 공 모양의 부분 ② **전구**
1 bulb는 땅 속에서 자라는 식물의 한 부분이다 : 튤립은 bulb에서 자란다. 양파는 먹을 수 있는 bulb다.

2 둥근 부분이 있는 것이면 어떤 것이든 bulb라고 할 수 있다 : 램프에 사용하는 bulb를 light bulb(백열 전구)라고 한다.

**bull** [búəl] 🔳 **황소** ; (코끼리·고래 등의) 수컷
bull은 커다란 동물이다. bull은 농장에서 살며, 뿔이 있고 풀을 먹는다.

**bulldozer** [búəldòuzər] 🔳 **불도저** ; 위협하는 사람, **협박자**
bulldozer는 바위나 흙을 옮기는 데 사용하는 기계다. 도로나 빌딩을 건설하기 전에 bulldozer가 땅을 고른다.

**bully** [búli] 🔳 **약한 자를 못살게 구는 사람** ; 깡패
bully는 사람들에게 겁을 주거나 비열한 짓을 하기를 좋아하는 사람이다.

**bump** [bʌ́mp] 1 🔲 🔳 (머리 등을) **부딪치다,** …와 충돌하다 2 🔳 충돌 ; 혹 ; 융기
1 bump는 어떤 것과 부딪친다는 의미다 : 덩컨은 우연히 탁자에 머리를 **부딪쳤다.**

2 bump는 동그랗게 튀어 나온 부분이다 : 그 도로에는 bump가 많았다(도로가 몹시 울퉁불퉁했다).

**bumper** [bʌ́mpər] 〔명〕 (자동차 앞뒤의) **완충기** ; 범퍼
bumper는 자동차나 트럭이 어떤 것에 부딪쳤을 때 차체를 보호하기 위해 앞이나 뒤에 대어진 육중한 가로대다.

**bunch** [bʌ́ntʃ] 〔명〕 **다발, 송이**
bunch는 물건들을 한데 모아 묶어 놓은 것이다 : 어머니는 정원에서 한 bunch의 꽃을 따셨다. 메리는 두 bunch의 당근과 한 bunch의 바나나를 샀다.

**bunny** [bʌ́ni] 〔명〕 **토끼**
bunny는 긴 귀와 짧은 꼬리 그리고 부드러운 털이 있는 작은 동물이다. bunny를 다른 말로 rabbit 이라고 한다.

**burglar** [bə́ːrglər] 〔명〕 (주거 침입) **강도, 빈집털이, 밤도둑**
burglar는 집이나 가게 혹은 다른 곳에 들어가 물건을 훔치는 사람이다 : burglar들이 호텔 방에서 보석을 훔쳤다.

**burn** [bə́ːrn] 〔타〕〔자〕 ① **불타다, 구워지다, 불태우다** ② (가스 등을) **점화하다, 켜다** ③ **…에게 화상을 입히다, 데다**
1 burn은 불타고 있다는 의미다 : 우리는 추운 날이면 몸을 따뜻하게 하려고 벽난로에 나무를 **땐다**.

2 burn은 또한 뜨거운 것을 만져 상처를 입는다는 의미다 : 빌리는 스토브에 손을 **데었다**.

**bury** [béri] 〔타〕 **묻다, 덮다** ; 매장하다
bury는 땅속이나 바닷속으로 집어 넣는다는 의미다 : 톰의 개가 우리집 뒷마당에 뼈다귀를 **파묻고 있다**.

**bus** [bʌ́s] 〔명〕 **버스**
bus는 기계〔자동차〕다. bus에는 바퀴 네 개와 엔진, 그리고 많은 좌석과 창문이 있다. bus는 많은 사람들을 한 곳에서 다른 곳으로 실어다 준다.

**bush** [búʃ] 뗑 관목 ; **수풀, 덤불**
bush는 식물이다. bush는 많은 가지와 잎들이 있지만, 나무 만큼 크지는 않다. bush에서 자라는 꽃들도 있다.

**business** [bíznəs] 뗑 ① **사무, 업무, 직업** ② **장사, 사업** ③ **상점, 회사** ④ **용무, 용건** ; 직무, 해야할 일, 본분
1 business는 사람이 돈을 벌기 위해 하는 일이다 : 나의 아버지는 보석을 판매하는 business를 하신다.
2 business는 또한 사람들이 돈을 벌기 위해 일하는 공장이나 상점 혹은 농장이나 그 외의 다른 장소를 말한다.

**busy** [bízi] 뗑 **바쁜,** 부지런히 일하는 ; 교통이 빈번한
busy는 많은 일을 한다는 의미다 : 메리는 할 일이 많다. 그녀는 오늘 몹시 **바쁘다.** 나는 숙제를 하느라고 **바쁘다.**

**but** [《약》bət, 《강》bʌ́t] 1 쩹 **그러나,** 그렇지만 ; …이외에는, …을 제외하고는 2 뛰 **다만,** 단지 3 쩐 **…을 제외하고**
1 사물이 서로 어떤 차이가 있는지를 말할 때 but을 사용한다 : 딕은 키가 크다. **그러나** 그의 형은 더 크다. 나는 놀고 싶**지만,** 일을 해야만 한다.
2 예외적인 의미를 나타낼 때도 but을 사용한다 : 사라를 **제외한** 모든 사람들이 그 영화를 좋아했다.

**butter** [bʌ́tər] 뗑 **버터** ; 버터 모양의 것
butter는 크림이나 우유로 만드는 노란색의 부드러운 식품이다. 사람들은 빵에 butter를 발라 먹거나, butter를 이용해 요리를 한다. 나는 빵에 butter를 발랐다.

**butterfly** [bʌ́tərflài] 뗑 **나비**
butterfly는 밝은 색깔의 커다란 날개가 네 개 있는 곤충이다. butterfly의 몸통은 매우 가늘다.

**button** [bʌ́tən] 뗑 (의복의) **단추** ; 단추 비슷한 것 ; (초인종의) 누름 단추
button은 나무나 플라스틱으로 된 작고 둥근 조각이다. 옷을 잠그기 위해 옷에 button을 꿰매어 단다.

**buy** [bái]  타  자  **사다**,  구입하
다 ; 손에 넣다, 획득하다
buy는 어떤 것을 얻기 위해
돈을 낸다는 의미다 : 슈퍼마켓
에서는 모든 종류의 식품을 **살**
수 있다.

**by** [bái] 1 전 ① [위치] …의 **곁**
**에** ② [통과] …을 지나서, 경
유하여 ③ [수단·방법] …으
로, …에 의하여 ④ [동작·상
태의 종료] …까지는 2 부 곁
을, **곁에** ; 곁을 지나서
1 by 는 무언가의 옆을 의미한
다 : 내 개는 자기가 나가고 싶
으면, 문 **옆**에 서 있다. 우
리는 내 친구집 **근처까지** 차를
몰고 갔다.
2 by는 또한 정해진 시간보다
늦지 않는다는 의미다 : 우리는
8 시**까지** 학교에 있어야 한다.

**cab** [kǽb] 명 택시

cab은 사람들이 요금을 내고
타는 자동차다 : 조 아주머니는
cab을 타고 공항에 갔다.
cab을 다른 말로 taxi라고
한다.

**cabin** [kǽbin] 명 오두막

cabin은 거칠은 판자나 통나
무로 지은 작은 집이다 : 호수
주변에 cabin들이 있다.

**caboose** [kəbúːs] 명 (화물열차
등의) **승무원 차〔칸〕**

caboose는 열차의 맨 끝 차
량이다. 열차에서 일하는 사람
들은 caboose에서 먹고 잔다.

**cactus** [kǽktəs] 명 선인장

cactus는 사막에서 자라는 식
물이다. cactus는 잎 대신에
날카로운 가시가 있다. cac-
tus는 다양한 형태로 자라며,
크고 밝은 색의 꽃이 피는 것
도 있다.

**cafeteria** [kæfətíəriə] 명 카페
테리아

cafeteria는 일종의 음식점이
다. cafeteria에서는 카운터에
서 먹을 음식을 골라 식탁으로
가지고 온다 : 조이스는 학교
cafeteria에서 점심으로 수프
와 샌드위치를 먹는다.

**cage** [kéidʒ] 명 새장 ; (짐승의)
우리

cage는 상자의 일종으로, 모
든 면이 금속이나 나무 막대기
로 되어 있다. 새와 그 밖의
동물을 때때로 cage 안에서
키운다.

**cake** [kéik] 명 케이크

cake는 오븐에 구운 단 음식
이다. cake는 흔히 밀가루,
버터, 달걀 그리고 설탕으로
만든다.

**calendar** [kǽləndər] 몡 달력
calendar는 한 해의 일(日),
주(週), 월(月)을 모두 기재해
놓은 것이다 : 잭은 파티 날짜
를 잊지 않기 위해 calendar에
표시해 두었다.

**calf**[1] [kǽf | ká:f] 몡 송아지 ; 새
끼 짐승
calf는 어린 소다. 물개, 코끼
리 또는 고래 새끼도 calf라고
한다.

**calf**[2] [kǽf | ká:f] 몡 종아리, 장
딴지
calf는 다리의 한 부분이다.
calf는 무릎 약간 아래쪽의 다
리 뒷부분이다.

**call** [kɔ́:l] 1 타 자 ① (소리쳐
서) **부르다** ② **초대하다** ; **방문
하다** ③ **…라고 이름짓다, 부
르다** ④ (…에게) **전화를 걸다**
2 몡 **부르는 소리, 외침** ; **초
대** ; **방문**
1 call은 큰소리로 말한다는
의미다 : 나는 선생님이 내 이

름을 **부르는** 소리를 들었다.
2 call은 전화를 쓴다는 의미
다 : 리언은 거의 날마다 친구
들에게 **전화를 건다.**

3 call은 이름을 지어 준다는
의미다 : 앤은 그녀의 인형을
에밀리라고 **부른다.**
4 call은 사람이 내는 큰소리
다 : 경찰은 누군가 도와 달라
고 **외치는** 소리를 들었다.

**calm** [ká:m] 1 혱 **고요한** ; **조용
한** ; (바람·파도가) **잔잔한** ;
**침착한, 냉정한** 2 몡 **고요함,
잔잔함** ; **평온**
1 calm은 조용하고 움직임이
없다는 의미다 : 오늘은 바람
**한 점 없다.**
2 calm은 얌전하고 귀찮게
굴지 않는다는 의미다 : 톰은
취학 첫날 치고는 아주 **침착하
다.**

**came** [kéim] 됭 come (오다) 의
과거형
came은 come의 한 형태
다 : 빌이 부엌에 **들어왔다.**

**camel** [kǽməl] 명 낙타
camel은 큰 동물이다. camel
은 다리와 목이 길다. camel
은 또한 등에 하나 내지 두 개
의 혹이 있다. camel은 사막
을 가로질러 사람과 물건을 나
를 수 있다.

**camera** [kǽmərə] 명 사진기,
카메라
camera는 사진을 찍는 작은
기계다. 흔히 휴가 때 camera
를 가지고 다닌다.

**camouflage** [kǽməflɑ̀ːʒ] 명 위
장, 변장 ; 속임수
camouflage는 주위에 있는
것들처럼 보이게 해서 무언가
를 감추는 방법이다. 몇몇 동
물의 가죽이나 털도 일종의
camouflage다 : 여우의 하얀
털은 눈 속에서 눈에 띄지 않
기 때문에 훌륭한 camouflage
가 되었다.

**camp** [kǽmp] 1 명 야영(지),
캠프장 ; 텐트 생활 2 자 천막
을 치다, **야영하다**
1 camp는 사람들이 야외에서
생활하는 곳이다. 사람들은 천
막이나 오두막에서 잠을 자고

모닥불에 요리를 한다 : 여름에
는 camp하러 가는 아이들이
많다.
2 camp는 캠프 생활을 한다
는 뜻이다 : 클레어와 그녀의
가족은 호수 근처에서 **야영했**
**다.**

**can**[1] [《약》 kən, 《강》 kǽn] 조 …
할 수 있다 ; …해도 좋다
can은 (어떤 것을) 할 수 있
다는 뜻이다 : 켈리는 빨리 달
릴 수 있다. 머리는 2개 국어
를 **할 줄 안다.**

**can**[2] [kǽn] 명 금속제 용기 ; 깡
통, 통조림통
can은 금속으로 만든 용기다.
can은 음식이나 다른 것을 보
관하는 데 사용된다 : 「can 차
기」를 하자. 어머니는 흰 색
페인트를 두 can(통) 사셨다.

**candle** [kǽndl] 명 초, 양초

candle은 속에 한 가닥의 실이 있는 밀랍 막대기다. candle은 타면서 빛을 낸다.

**candy** [kǽndi] 명 사탕 과자, 캔디
candy는 음식의 일종이다. candy는 설탕으로 만들어서 아주 달다. candy는 초콜릿, 견과 또는 과일로도 만들 수 있다.

**cannot** [kǽnɑt, kənát | kǽnɔt, -nət] can¹의 부정형
cannot은 (어떤 것을) 할 수 없다는 뜻이다 : 개는 달릴 수는 있지만, 날 수는 없다.

**canoe** [kənúː] 명 카누
canoe는 작은 배의 일종이다. canoe는 길고, 폭이 좁고, 가볍다. canoe는 강을 아주 조용하게 통과한다.

**can't** [kǽnt | kɑ́ːnt] cannot의 단축형
can't는 cannot을 줄여서 말한 것이다 : 물고기는 헤엄을 칠 수는 있지만, 말을 할 수는 없다.

**cap** [kǽp] 명 (테 없는) 모자
cap은 모자의 일종이다. 야구를 하는 사람들은 cap을 쓴다.

**capital** [kǽpitəl] 명 (나라의) 수도 ; 대문자, 머리글자
1 capital은 한 국가나 주의 행정부에 있는 사람들이 법률을 제정하고 일을 하기 위해 모이는 도시다 : 워싱턴 D.C.는 미국의 capital이다.
2 capital은 또한 알파벳의 대문자다. E와 M은 글자 e와 m의 capital이다. 이름이나 문장을 쓸 때 capital로 쓰기 시작한다.

**car** [kɑ́ːr] 명 자동차, 차 ; 철도 차량, 객차
1 car는 기계다. car에는 네 개의 바퀴, 엔진, 좌석 그리고 창문이 있다. 사람들은 car를 타고 도로를 달린다.
2 car는 또한 열차의 한 부분이다. car는 바퀴가 달린 큰

방과 같다. 대부분의 열차는 몇 개의 car로 되어 있다.

**card** [kɑ́ːrd] 몡 **카드** ; 두꺼운 종이 ; 트럼프 카드 ; **엽서, 초대장**

1 card는 조그마한 두꺼운 종잇장이다. card의 모양은 직사각형과 같고, 숫자와 그림이 그려져 있다. 사람들은 card로 게임을 한다.

2 card는 또한 조그맣게 접은 종이다. card에는 메시지가 담겨 있다. 사람들에게 우편으로 card를 보낸다.

**care** [kɛ́ər] 1 몡 근심, 걱정 ; 주의 ; 돌봄 2 짜 **걱정하다, 유의하다** ; 돌보다

care는 무언가에 좋은 감정을 갖고 있다는 의미다 : 토니는 그의 고양이를 **염려하여** 먹을 것도 주고 하루에 두 번 물그릇에 물을 채워 준다.

**careful** [kɛ́ərfəl] 혱 **주의 깊은, 조심하는** ; 신경을 쓰는

careful은 지금 하고 있는 일에 마음을 쓰고 있다는 의미다 : 다이애나는 페인트를 엎지르지 않으려고 매우 **조심하고** 있다. 그녀는 조심스럽게 일한다.

**careless** [kɛ́ərləs] 혱 **부주의한, 경솔한, 조심성 없는**

careless는 지금 하고 있는 일에 마음을 쓰고 있지 않다는 의미다 : 앨과 배리는 **조심성이 없어서** 페인트를 엎질렀다. 그들은 일을 소홀히 했다.

**carnival** [kɑ́ːrnivəl] 몡 **카니발, 사육제**

carnival은 사람들을 즐겁게 하려고 (정기적으로) 음식과 놀이 그리고 그밖의 여러가지 것들을 마련한 축제의 일종이다.

**carpenter** [kɑ́ːrpəntər] 몡 **목공, 목수**

carpenter는 나무로 된 집이나 그밖의 것들을 짓거나 수리하는 사람이다 : carpenter는 내 방 창문 아래에 선반과 의자를 만들어 주었다.

**carriage** [kǽridʒ] 몡 차, 탈

것 ; **마차**《주로 4 륜 자가용》 ;
《영》 (철도) 객차
carriage 는 사람을 실어 나르
는 바퀴가 네 개 달린 4 륜차
의 일종이다.

**carrot** [kǽrət] 명 당근
carrot 은 야채의 일종이다.
carrot 은 길고 주황색이다.
carrot 은 땅 속에서 자란다.

**carry** [kǽri] 타 **나르다, 가지
고 가다** ; …을 (몸에) 지니고
다니다
carry 는 무언가를 갖고 어디
론가 가져 간다는 의미다 : 한
나는 가방 안에 점심을 넣어
**가지고 다닌다.**

**cart** [káːrt] 명 짐마차《2 륜 또
는 4 륜》 ; (2 륜의) **짐수레, 운
반차** ; (한 필의 말이 끄는 2
륜의) 경마차
cart 는 일종의 짐수레다. 대
부분의 cart 는 바퀴가 두 개
고 끌고 다닌다. 슈퍼마켓의
cart 는 바퀴가 네 개고 밀고
다닌다.

**carton** [káːrtən] 명 **마분지 상
자**, 판지 ; (우유 등을 넣는)

납지 용기, 플라스틱 용기
carton 은 아주 두꺼운 종이로
만든 상자다 : 앤은 우유 한
carton을 샀다.

**cartoon** [kɑːrtúːn] 명 (시사)
만화 ; 만화 영화
cartoon 은 사람들을 웃게 만
드는 그림이다. cartoon 은 신
문, 잡지, 영화, 텔레비전에
나온다.

**carve** [káːrv] 타 **새기다, 조각
하다, 깎다** ; (식탁에서 고기
를) 썰어 분배하다
1 carve 는 잘라내서 모양을
만든다는 의미다 : 조각가가 나
무를 **깎아서** 여러 동물을 **만들
었다.**
2 carve 는 또한 고기를 조각
조각으로 자른다는 의미다 : 칠
면조 고기를 **썰어서 나눠줄** 시
간이 다 됐다.

**case** [kéis] 명 **상자**, 케이스
case 는 물건을 보관하거나 싸
준다 : 내 안경은 좁은 case 안
에 쏙 들어간다.

**castle** [kǽsl | káːsl] 명 성

castle 은 높은 담과 탑들이 있는 아주 큰 건축물이다. 옛날엔 왕과 여왕이 castle 에 살았다 : 그녀는 castle 에서 국왕을 보았다.

**cat** [kæt] 명 **고양이 ; 고양이과의 동물**
1 cat 은 부드러운 털과 긴 꼬리가 있는 작은 동물이다 : 메리는 애완용 cat 이 한 마리 있다. 나는 cat을 두 마리 기른다.
2 어떤 종류의 cat 은 크고 사납다. 호랑이와 표범은 크고 사나운 cat 이다.

**catch** [kætʃ] 타 **잡다, 붙잡다**
catch 는 움직이는 것을 붙잡는다는 의미다 : 블레이크는 공을 **잡으려고** 달려갔다.

**catcher** [kætʃər] 명 **잡는 사람〔물건〕 ; (야구의) 포수, 캐처**
catcher 는 잡는 사람이나 물건이다. 야구 경기에서 catcher 는 공을 치려고 하는 사람 뒤에 있다.

**caterpillar** [kǽtərpìlər] 명 **쐐기 벌레, 모충**
caterpillar 는 곤충이다. caterpillar 는 털로 덮인 벌레와 비슷하다. caterpillar 가 변해서 나비나 나방이 된다.

**catsup, ketchup** [kǽtsəp, kétʃ-] 명 **케첩**
catsup 은 토마토로 만든 걸쭉한 액체다. catsup 은 다른 음식 위에 쳐서 먹는다. catsup 의 또 다른 철자는 ketchup 이다.

**cattle** [kætl] 명 **소 ; 가축**
cattle 은 큰 동물들을 말한다. cattle 은 다리가 4 개고 뿔이 2 개며, 우유와 고기를 얻으려고 사육한다. 암소와 황소들을 모두 cattle 이라고 한다.

**caught** [kɑːt | kɔːt] 동 **catch (잡다)의 과거·과거분사형**
caught 는 catch 의 한 형태다 : 보브가 공을 던져서 헬렌이 **잡았다**.

**cause** [kɔːz] 1 명 **원인 ; 이유** 2 타 **…의 원인이 되다, …을 일으키다**

1 cause 는 어떤 일을 일으킨
다는 의미다 : 서둘지 않으면,
너 **때문에** 우리가 학교에 지각
하겠다.
2 cause 는 어떤 일을 일으키
는 사람이나 것이다 : 차를 과
속으로 몬 것이 사고의 cause
였다. 화재 cause 는 뭐냐?

**cave** [kéiv] 몡 동굴
cave 는 땅 속 깊이 움푹 패인
곳이다 : **동굴** 안은 매우 어둡
다.

**cavity** [kǽviti] 몡 움푹 패인
곳, **구멍** ; (이빨의) **구멍, 충
치**
cavity 는 이에 난 구멍이다 :
치과 의사가 내게 칫솔질하는
법을 가르쳐준 뒤로, cavity 가
점점 줄었다.

**ceiling** [síːliŋ] 몡 천장
ceiling 은 방의 위쪽이다. 사
람들은 ceiling을 올려다본다.

**celebrate** [séləbrèit] 타 (의
식·축전을) 거행하다 ; **식을 올
려 축하하다**
celebrate 는 특별히 무언가가
중요하다는 것을 보여준다는

의미다 : 우리 마을은 퍼레이드
와 불꽃놀이로 독립기념일을
**축하했다.**

**cellar** [sélər] 몡 지하실
cellar 는 집 밑에 만들어 놓은
방이다.

**cent** [sént] 몡 센트《미국·캐나다
등의 화폐 단위》
cent 는 금액이다. 1 니켈은 5
cent고, 1 달러는 100 cent 다.

**center|-tre** [séntər] 몡 중심 ;
중앙 ; 핵심 ; 중심지
center 는 어떤 것의 가운데
다 : 톰의 도넛에는 **가운데에**
젤리가 있었다.

**cereal** [síəriəl] 몡 곡식, 곡
물 ; (곡식으로 된) 아침
cereal 은 대개 밀이나 옥수수
혹은 쌀로 만든 음식이다 : 우
리는 아침 식사로 cereal 을
먹는 것을 좋아한다.

**certain** [sə́ːrtən] 혱 확신하는,
확실한 ; 반드시 …하는
certain 은 어떤 것을 아주 확

신한다는 의미다 : 문을 확실히
닫았니 ?

**chain** [tʃéin] 명 사슬 ; 연쇄, 연
속 ; 목걸이
chain 은 한데 이은 고리 줄이
다 : 마거릿은 목에 하트 모양
의 장식이 달린 chain을 했
다.

**chair** [tʃéər] 명 의자
chair 는 가구의 일종이다.
chair 에는 네 개의 다리와 앉
는 부분이 있다. 사람들은
chair 에 앉는다.

**chalk** [tʃɔ́ːk] 명 분필, 초크
chalk 는 글씨를 쓰거나 그리
는 데 쓰는 작은 토막이다 : 새
로 오신 우리 선생님은 칠판에
노란 chalk로 선생님의 이름
을 쓰셨다.

**chalkboard** [tʃɔ́ːkbɔ̀ːrd] 명 칠
판
chalkboard 는 글씨를 쓰거나
지울 수 있도록 특수한 재료로

만들어진 단단하고 매끄러운
판자다. chalkboard 는 검정색
이거나 녹색이다.

**chance** [tʃǽns | tʃɑ́ːns] 명 기회 ;
승산, **가능성** ; 우연, 운, 운수
1 chance 는 운을 뜻한다 : 나
는 우연히 3달러를 발견했다.
2 chance 는 어떤 일이 일어
날 수 있다는 뜻이다 : 오늘 비
올 chance 가 있는 데, 어쩌
면 하루 종일 올 것이다.

**change** [tʃéindʒ] 1 명 변화, 변
천 ; 거스름돈, 잔돈 2 자 타
바뀌다, 변화하다 ; 바꾸다 ; 옷
을 갈아입다 ; 돈을 바꾸다
1 change 는 다르게 된다는
뜻이다 : 가을에 나뭇잎은 녹색
에서 빨간색과 주황색 그리고
노란색으로 **변한다.**

2 change 는 다른 옷을 입는
다는 뜻이다 : 방과 후, 아서와

파블로는 **옷을 갈아입고** 나가
논다.
3 change 는 동전을 뜻한다 :
조이스는 1 달러와 change 몇
개가 있다.

**channel** [tʃǽnəl] 명 **해협** ; (라
디오・텔레비전의) **채널**
텔레비전에는 많은 channel이
있다. 각 channel 은 각각 다
른 프로그램을 전송한다. 어린
이들을 위한 과학 프로그램을
내보내는 channel 도 있다 : 빌
리는 우리가 만화 영화를 볼
수 있도록 텔레비전 channel
을 돌렸다.

**chant** [tʃǽnt | tʃɑ́ːnt] 명 **노래** ; 자
주 반복되는 구호
chant 는 노래나 반복해서 외
치는 말이다 : 각 팀은 축구 시
합을 시작하기 전에 chant 를
외쳤다.

**chapter** [tʃǽptər] 명 **장**
chapter 는 책의 내용을 나누
는 중요한 부분이다 : 앨버트

의 책은 열개의 chapter 로 되
어 있다.

**character** [kǽrəktər] 명 **특
징** ; **성격** ; (소설 등의) **등장
인물**
character 는 책, 연극, 소설
또는 영화 속에 나오는 사람이
다.

**charge** [tʃɑ́ːrdʒ] 자 타 **대가를
청구하다** ; **외상으로 사다**
1 charge 는 어떤 일에 대한
대가로 돈을 청구한다는 뜻이
다 : 그 가게는 라디오 수리비
를 얼마나 **내라고** 합니까 ?
2 charge 는 또한 물건을 사고
나중에 대금을 지불한다는 뜻
이다.

**chase** [tʃéis] 타 **쫓다**
chase 는 어떤 것의 뒤를 쫓
아 가서 붙잡으려고 한다는 뜻
이다 : 내 개는 자동차를 **쫓아**
서 도로를 내려갔다.

**cheap** [tʃíːp] 형 **값이 싼**, **싸구**

려의

cheap 는 비용이 아주 적게 든다는 뜻이다 : 이 차들은 그 가게에서 가장 **싼** 장난감이다.

**check** [tʃék] 1 타 자 ① **막다,** **저지하다** ② **대조하다, 체크하** **다, 점검하다** 2 명 ① **대조,** **점검 ; 대조 표시** ② **저지 ; 수** **표 ; 바둑판 무늬**

1 check 는 표시다. 무언가가 바르게 되어 있다는 것을 나타내기 위해 그 옆에 check 를 한다. check 는 √ 모양과 같다.

2 check 는 또한 어떤 것을 찾는다는 뜻이다 : 메리가 신을 못찾자, 그녀의 엄마는 침대 밑을 **확인해 보라고** 말했다.

3 check 는 또한 네모진 모양을 말한다 : 루시의 셔츠는 온통 빨갛고 흰 커다란 check로 되어 있다.

**checkers** [tʃékərz] 명 **체커**

checkers 는 체스판 위에서 두 사람이 각각 12개의 말을 이용해서 하는 놀이다 : 조지와 그의 친구들은 checkers 하는 것을 좋아한다.

**checkup** [tʃékʌp] 명 대조 ; 검

사 ; 건강진단

checkup 은 사람이나 물건의 상태가 괜찮은지 주의깊게 살펴본다는 뜻이다 : 제인은 지난 주에 checkup(건강진단)을 받으러 의사에게 갔다.

**cheek** [tʃíːk] 명 **뺨**

cheek 는 눈 아래에 있는 얼굴 부위다 : 눈 속에서 뛰어놀아서 테리의 cheek 는 발그레 상기되었다.

**cheerful** [tʃíərfəl] 형 **기분 좋** **은, 즐거운, 상쾌한 ; 명랑한**

cheerful 은 행복감에 젖어 있다는 뜻이다 : 그 **명랑한** 소년은 버스를 기다리면서 휘파람을 불었다.

**cheese** [tʃíːz] 명 **치즈**

cheese 는 음식의 일종으로, 우유로 만든다. 딱딱한 cheese 도 있고 부드러운 cheese 도 있다. cheese 는 노란색이나 흰색이 많다.

**cherry** [tʃéri] 명 **버찌**

cherry 는 과일의 일종이다. cherry 는 작고, 둥글고, 붉다. cherry 는 벚나무에서 열린다.

**chess** [tʃés] 몡 체스, 서양 장기
chess 는 판 위에서 두 사람이
각각 16 개의 말을 이용해서
하는 놀이다 : 어머니는 나에게
chess 말을 각각 다르게 움직
이는 방법을 가르쳐 주셨다.

**chest** [tʃést] 몡 가슴 ; 큰 상자
1 chest 는 몸의 앞 부분으로,
어깨 바로 밑에 있다. 심장은
chest 안에 있다.
2 chest 는 또한 물건을 보관
하는 큰 상자다 : 할머니는 담
요를 나무 chest 안에 넣어 두
신다. 빌은 망치를 연장
chest에 도로 갖다 넣었다.

**chew** [tʃúː] 퇸 퇸 씹다
chew 는 어떤 것을 이로 부수
어서 작게 조각낸다는 뜻이
다 : 우리집 강아지가 헌 신을
물어뜯었다.

**chicken** [tʃíkin] 몡 새끼 새 ;
병아리 ; 닭고기 ; 닭
chicken 은 새로, 사람들이 먹
는 달걀을 낳는다. 사람들은
chicken 고기를 먹기도 한다.

**chief** [tʃíːf] 몡 우두머리 ; (단체

의) 장 ; 두목, 보스
chief 는 한 집단의 지도자인
사람이다 : 매년 경찰서장은 가
장 용감한 경찰관들에게 훈장
을 수여한다.

**child** [tʃáiəld] 몡 아이, 어린이
child 는 어린 소녀나 소년을
말한다 : 12 명의 아이들이 학
교 취주악단에서 연주했다.

**children** [tʃíəldrən] 몡 child 의
복수형
children 은 두 명 이상의 아이
를 나타낸다. children 이 자라
서 성인 남녀가 된다.

**chill** [tʃíəl] 1 몡 차가움, 냉기 ;
한기 2 퇸 퇸 식히다 ; 추위를
느끼다
chill 은 추운 느낌이다 : 오늘
아침은 공기가 차가웠다.

**chimney** [tʃímni] 몡 굴뚝
chimney 는 벽난로나 용광로
에서 연기를 밖으로 내보내는
것이다.

**chin** [tʃín] 몡 턱
chin 은 입과 목 사이에 있는

얼굴 부위다 : 우리 아버지는 chin 에 수염이 나 있다.

**chocolate** [tʃɔ́ːklit, tʃák-|tʃɔ́k-] 몡 초콜릿
chocolate 은 음식의 일종으로 대개 갈색이며 아주 달콤하다. 흔히 캔디와 케이크는 choco-late 으로 만든다.

**choose** [tʃúːz] 탸 고르다, 선택하다 ; 결정하다, 정하다
choose 는 갖고 싶은 것을 선택한다는 뜻이다 : 빌리는 자기 이름이 써 있는 빨간 풍선을 **골랐다.**

**chorus** [kɔ́ːrəs] 몡 합창 ; 합창곡 ; 합창부, **합창단 ; 코러스**
chorus 는 사람들이 함께 노래를 하거나 춤을 추는 단체다 : 마크와 앤은 학교 chorus 에서 노래를 부른다.

**chose** [tʃóuz] 툉 choose (선택하다) 의 과거형
chose 는 choose 의 한 형태다 : 피터와 레이는 축구를 하**기로 했다.**

**chosen** [tʃóuzən] 툉 choose (선

택하다) 의 과거분사형
chosen 은 choose 의 한 형태다 : 앤은 땅콩 버터 샌드위치를 **골랐다.**

**Christmas** [krísməs] 몡 크리스마스, 성탄절
Christmas 는 12 월 25 일을 경축하는 기독교 축제일이다. Christmas 에는 교회에 가거나 선물을 하는 사람들이 많다.

**church** [tʃɔ́ːrtʃ] 몡 교회 ; (교회의) 예배
church 는 기독교인들이 기도하고, 찬송하러 가는 건물이다.

**circle** [sɔ́ːrkl] 몡 원 ; 둥근 것, 고리 ; 궤도 ; 집단, 사회 ; 주기, 순환
circle 은 둥근 모양으로, 한 선의 두 끝이 맞닿을 때까지 돌려서 만든다. circle 은 모나거나 곧은 부분이 없다.

**circus** [sɔ́ːrkəs] 몡 서커스, 곡마단 ; 곡예
circus 는 일종의 쇼다. circus 는 대개 대형 천막 안에서 공연한다. 사람들은 circus 에서

어릿광대, 마술사, 동물들을
볼 수 있다.

**city** [síti] 몡 시 ; 도시
city 는 많은 사람들이 살면서
일하는 곳이다. city 에는 높은
건물이 많이 있다. city는
town (읍)보다 크다.

**class** [klǽs|klɑ́:s] 몡 클래스,
학급, 반 ; 학습 시간, 수업
class 는 함께 배우는 학생들
의 집단이다 : 우리 class 는
박물관에 견학하러 갔다.

**classroom** [klǽsrù:m, -rùm|
klɑ́:s-] 몡 교실
classroom 은 한 학급이 선생
님과 함께 공부하는 방이다.

**claw** [klɔ́:] 몡 (고양이 · 매 등
의) 발톱 ; 발톱 모양의 것
claw 는 동물이나 새의 발의
일부다. claw 는 날카롭고 굽
어 있다. 새는 claw 로 나뭇가
지를 붙잡는다.

**clay** [kléi] 몡 점토 ; 흙, 진흙
clay 는 일종의 흙이다. 젖은
clay 로 여러 가지 다양한 모
양을 만들 수 있다. clay 는
마르거나 불에 구워지면 딱딱
해진다.

**clean** [klí:n] 1 혱 깨끗한 2 用
깨끗이 3 타 자 청결하게 하
다 ; 청소하다 ; 닦다
1 clean 은 더럽지 않다는 뜻
이다 : 블레이크는 개를 청결하
게 해준다. 그는 토요일마다
개를 목욕시킨다.
2 clean 은 더러움을 없앤다는
뜻이다 : 마거릿은 비눗물로 얼
굴을 씻었다.

**clear** [klíər] 혱 맑은
clear 는 쉽게 들여다 볼 수
있다는 뜻이다 : 호수의 물이
너무 맑아서 그 밑바닥까지 볼
수 있었다.

**clever** [klévər] 혱 영리한, 현
명한 ; 빈틈없는
clever 는 재빨리 생각해 낼
수 있다는 뜻이다 : 그 영리한
아이는 얼마 안되서 퍼즐 푸는
법을 알았다.

C

**climb** [kláim] 타 자 오르다, 기어오르다 ; 올라가다 ; (차에) 타다

climb 은 무언가로 올라간다는 뜻이다. 사람들은 **기어오를** 때 손발을 사용한다 : 어머니는 나무에서 연을 떼내기 위해 사닥다리를 **올라가야**만 했다. 토니는 침대에 **올라가자**(잠자리에 들자)마자 곧바로 잠이 들었다.

**clock** [klák | klɔ́k] 명 시계

시간을 알기 위해서 clock 의 숫자를 읽는다. 시계 바늘이 돌아가는 clock 도 있고, 시간이 바뀌면 숫자가 바뀌는 clock 도 있다.

**close** [klóuz] 1 타 자 **닫다**, 닫혀지다 ; 끝내다 ; 끝나다    2 [klóus] 형 **가까운**, 접근한 3 [klóus] 부 가깝게, 곁에

1 close 는 가깝다는 뜻이다 : 아이는 엄마 **곁에** 있었다.
2 close 는 안에 있는 것을 나가지 못하게 하거나 바깥에 있는 것을 안으로 들어오지 못하게 한다는 뜻이다 : 마리아는 방에 들어와서 문을 **닫았다**.
3 close 는 (문을) 닫는다는 뜻이다 : 그 가게는 매일밤 같은 시간에 문을 **닫는다**.

**closet** [klázət | klɔ́z-] 명 ① 개인 방, 작은 방 ② **벽장**, 다락, 찬장 ③ 변기

closet 은 옷이나 그밖의 다른 물건들을 보관하는 작은 방이다. closet 에는 대개 문이 있다.

**cloth** [klɔ́:θ | klɔ́θ] 명 **천**(조각), **옷감** ; 식탁보

cloth 는 옷이나 담요 혹은 그밖의 것들을 만드는 데 쓰이는 재료다. 면으로 된 cloth 는 식물로, 모로 된 cloth 는 동물의 털로 만든다.

**clothes** [klóuz, klóuðz] 명 **옷**, 의복

몸을 감싸기 위해 clothes 를 입는다. 코트, 드레스, 바지, 재킷은 모두 clothes 의 일종이다. clothes 를 다른 말로 clothing 이라 한다 : 우리는 겨울에 밖에서 놀기 위해 따뜻한 clothing을 입는다.

**cloud** [kláud] 몡 **구름**
cloud 는 하늘 높이 떠 있는 작은 물방울들로 되어 있다 : 폭풍우가 치기 전에 하늘에 dark cloud (먹구름)가 꼈다.

**clown** [kláun] 몡 **어릿광대**
clown 은 사람들을 웃기려고 우스꽝스런 옷을 입고 재주를 부리는 사람이다 : 서커스의 clown 은 얼굴에 물감을 칠했다.

**club** [kláb] 몡 **클럽**, 동호회, 사교회
club 은 오락이나 어떤 특별한 목적을 위해 함께 만나는 사람들의 모임이다 : 우리 독서 club 은 금요일에 모인다.

**clue** [klú:] 몡 **실마리, 단서**
clue 는 문제나 수수께끼의 해답을 찾는 데 도움이 되는 것이다 : 우리가 강도를 잡을 수 있었던 clue 는 발자국이었다.

**coach** [kóutʃ] 몡 ① **코치** ② **대형 4 륜 마차** ; 역마차
coach 는 운동 선수들을 훈련시키는 사람이다 : coach 는 큰 시합을 앞두고 매일 오후에 농구팀을 연습시켰다.

**coast** [kóust] 몡 **해안**, 연안
coast 는 바다에 인접한 땅이다 : 앨과 톰은 바닷새들을 보면서 coast 를 따라 걸었다.

**coat** [kóut] 몡 (양복의) **상의** ; (여성・어린이의) 긴 겉옷 ; 외투, 코트
coat 는 몸을 감싸는 것이다. coat 는 보통 두꺼운 천으로 만든다. coat 는 날씨가 추울 때 몸을 따뜻하게 해준다.

**cocoon** [kəkú:n] 몡 **누에고치, 고치**
cocoon 은 애벌레가 자기 몸을 둘러싸게 만든 작고, 부드러운 집이다. 애벌레는 나비가 될 때까지 cocoon 에서 산다.

**coin** [kóin] 몡 **동전**, 주화, 화폐 ; 경화 ; 금전

coin 은 돈의 일종이다. coin 은 대개 둥글며, 금속으로 만든다. 페니, 니켈, 다임 그리고 쿼터는 모두 coin 이다.

**cold** [kóuəld] 1 형 **추운, 찬, 차가운** ; 냉각된, 식은 ; 냉정한 2 명 추위 ; **감기**, 고뿔
1 cold 는 낮은 온도를 뜻한다 : 눈과 얼음은 **차갑다.**
2 cold 에 걸리면 병이 난 것으로, 머리가 아프거나 재채기를 많이 한다. cold 에 걸린 사람은 누워서 쉬는 경우가 많다.

**collar** [kálər|kɔ́lə] 명 **칼라, 옷깃** ; (개 등의) **목걸이** ; (말의) 목줄
1 collar 는 셔츠나 드레스의 목둘레에 닿는 부분이다.

2 collar 는 또한 동물의 목둘레에 채워진 짧은 줄이다 : 우리 개의 collar에는 우리집 주소가 적혀 있다.

**collect** [kəlékt] 타 자 **모으다** ; 수집하다 ; 모이다 ; 쌓이다
collect 는 물건을 한 데 모은다는 뜻이다 : 나는 취미로 다양한 종류의 돌을 **모으는** 것을

좋아한다.

**color | colour** [kʌ́lər] 명 **빛깔, 색채** ; 채색, 착색
빨강, 파랑, 노랑은 중요한 color다. 그밖의 모든 color 에도 빨간색이나 파란색 혹은 노란색이 들어 있다. 파란색에 노란색을 섞으면 녹색이 된다 : 오렌지색은 내가 가장 좋아하는 color 다.

**comb** [kóum] 명 **빗**
comb 은 플라스틱이나 금속으로 된 살이 있는 물건이다. 머리칼을 매만지기 위해 comb 으로 머리를 빗는다.

**come** [kʌ́m] 자 ① (말하는 사람 쪽으로) **오다** ; (상대방이 있는 곳으로·가는 곳으로) **가다** ② 도착하다 ; (…의 상태가) **되다**
come 은 어떤 사람이나 장소를 향해 움직인다는 뜻이다 : 내가 부르자 고양이가 내게로 **왔다.** 너와 같이 **가면** 좋겠다.

**comfortable** [kʌ́mfərtəbl] 형 **기분좋은** ; **편안한**
comfortable 은 기분좋게 느껴진다는 뜻이다 : 의자가 너무

편안해서 아버지는 그 의자에서 잠이 드셨다.

**comic** [kámik | kɔ́m-] 1 ⟨형⟩ 희극의 ; 우스운 2 ⟨명⟩ ① 희극 배우 ; **만화책** ② [복수로] (신문·잡지의) 만화란
1 comic 은 우습다는 뜻이다 : 생쥐가 고양이를 뒤쫓는다는 것은 생각만해도 **우스운** 일이다.
2 comic 은 그림에 스토리가 담긴 잡지다.

**company** [kʌ́mpəni] ⟨명⟩ ① 사귐, 교제 ; **친구들** ② 손님
company 는 찾아오는 사람이나 사람의 무리다 : 우리는 추수 감사절에 company (손님)에게 식사를 대접했다.

**compare** [kəmpέər] ⟨타⟩ ⟨자⟩ 비교하다, 대조하다 ; 비유하다
compare 는 사람이나 사물이 어떻게 같고 다른지를 알려고 살펴본다는 뜻이다 : 네 책과 내 책을 **비교해** 보면, 네 책이 더 두껍다는 것을 알게 될 것이다.

**complete** [kəmplí:t] 1 ⟨타⟩ 끝내다 ; 완성하다 2 ⟨형⟩ 전부의 ; **완전한** ; 완성한, 완비된
1 complete 는 전부 있다는 뜻이다 : 우리 학교 도서관에는 내가 좋아하는 작가의 **전집**이 있다.
2 complete 는 끝낸다는 뜻도 있다 : 앤드루는 숙제를 **끝내야** 외출할 수 있다.

**computer** [kəmpjú:tər] ⟨명⟩ 컴퓨터, 전자 계산기
computer 는 여러 가지 종류의 일을 매우 빠르게 처리할 수 있는 기계다. 사람들은 숫자를 계산하거나 글을 쓰거나 혹은 그림을 그리는 것조차도 computer 를 이용한다.

**concert** [kánsərt | kɔ́n-] ⟨명⟩ 음악회, 연주회, **콘서트**
concert 는 음악공연이다 : 새로 생긴 학교 관현악단은 금년에 concert 를 세 번 열 예정이다.

**cone** [kóun] ⟨명⟩ 원뿔체, **원뿔꼴** ; (아이스크림을 담는) 콘
1 cone 은 바닥이 둥글고 평평하며 위 끝이 뾰족한 형태다.
2 cone 은 또한 원뿔꼴 모양을 한 것이다 : 만성절 전야에

쓰려고, 나는 cone 모양의 마
녀 모자를 만들었다.

**confuse** [kənfjúːz]  **타**  혼동하
다 ; 혼란시키다 ; 당황하게  하
다
1 confuse 는 마음속의 생각들
이  혼란을  일으킨다는  뜻이
다 : 나는 내 여동생의 말을 알
아  들을  수가  없어서  그녀가
말을 하면 **당황한다.**
2 confuse 는  또한  어떤  것을
다른  것으로  생각한다는  뜻이
다 : 선생님들은  때때로  나와
내 동생을 **혼동하신다.**

**consonant** [kánsənənt | kɔ́n-]
**명**  자음 ; 자음자
consonant 는  글자의  일종이
다.  b, c, d, f, g, h, j, k, l, m,
n, p, q, r, s, t, v, w, x  그리
고  z 는 consonant 다.  conso-
nant와 모음은 알파벳을 구성
하는 글자다.

**container** [kəntéinər] **명** 그릇,
용기 ; 컨테이너《화물 수송용의
큰 금속 상자》
container 는  물건을  담는  데
쓰는 것이다. 상자와 항아리는
container 다.

**contest** [kántest | kɔ́n-]  **명**  경
쟁,  콘테스트 ; 경기,  경연
contest 는  사람들이  서로  이
기려고  하는  경기나  경주다 :
마리아는  수영   contest 에서
우승했다.

**continue** [kəntínju | -njuː]  **타**
**자**  계속하다,  지속하다,  연속
하다
continue 는  다시  시작한다는
뜻이다 : 우리는 오전 내내 야
구를 했다. 점심을 먹고 나서
도 경기를 **계속했다.**

**control** [kəntróuəl] 1 **명** 지배,
관리 ; 제어,  억제 ; 조종 장치
2 **타**  통제하다 ; **조종하다** ; 제
어하다
control 은  원하는  대로  되게
한다는 뜻이다 : 데이비드는 긴
실로 연을 **조종한다.**

**cook** [kúk] 1 **명** 요리사,  쿡 2
**타** 요리하다 ; 굽다
1 cook 은  먹을  수  있게  음식
에  열을  가한다는  뜻이다 : 우
리는 칠면조를 여섯 시간 동안
오븐에 **구웠다.**
2 cook 은  식사를  만드는  사
람이다 : cook 은  부엌에서  일
한다.

**cookie, cookey** [kúki] 명 **쿠키**
cookie 는 작고, 납작하고, 단
음식이다. 초콜릿이 든
cookie 도 있다.

**cool** [kúːəl] 형 **시원한, 서늘한**
cool 은 그다지 춥지 않다는
뜻이다 : 오늘 아침 날씨는 **서**
**늘했는데** 오후에는 따뜻했다.

**copper** [kápər|kɔ́pə] 명 **구**
**리 ; 동전**
copper 는 금속의 일종이다. 1
페니 짜리 청동화와 전선은
copper 로 만든다.

**copy** [kápi|kɔ́pi] 1 명 **사본,**
**복사** 2 타 자 **베끼다, 복사하**
**다, 복제하다**
1 copy 는 어떤 것과 똑같게
만들거나 한다는 뜻이다 : 루이
스는 사자 그림을 **복사해서** 나
에게 보여주었다.
2 copy 는 어떤 것과 똑같은
것이다 : 사진을 각각 두 장씩
**뽑아** 주세요.

**corn** [kɔ́ːrn] 명 **옥수수 ; 낟알 ;**
곡물, 곡식류
corn 은 야채의 일종이다.
corn 은 키가 큰 녹색 식물에
서 자란다. corn 은 노랗거나
하얗다.

**corner** [kɔ́ːrnər] 명 **귀퉁이 ;**
**모퉁이 ; 구석, 모서리**
corner 는 두 개의 선이나 면
이 서로 만나는 곳이다 : 폴은
식탁 corner 에 무릎을 부딪쳤
다.

**correct** [kərékt] 1 형 **올바른,**
**틀림없는, 정확한 ; 정당한** 2
타 (틀린 것을) **바로잡다,** 고
치다 ; 교정하다 ; …의 잘못을
지적하다
1 correct 는 틀림없다는 뜻이
다 : 잭의 답은 **정확했다.**
2 correct 는 잘못된 것을 점
검한다는 뜻이다 : 선생님은 시
험 답안이 틀린 곳을 전부 **고**
**쳐 주신다.**

**cost** [kɔ́ːst|kɔ́st] 1 명 **가격, 원**
**가 ; 비용** 2 타 (비용이 얼마)
**들다 ;** (시간 등이) 걸리다
1 cost 는 물건을 사기 위해
지불해야 하는 금액이다 : 저 자

전거는 cost 가 얼마입니까?
2 cost 는 또한 어떤 금액으로
물건을 살 수 있다는 뜻이다 :
새 신발을 사는 데 20 달러가
들었다.

**costume** [kástju:m|kɔ́s-] 명 복
장, 의상 ; (무대나 무도회에서
입는) 시대〔민속〕의상, **가장
복**
costume 은 다른 사람이나 다
른 사물처럼 보이게 하려고 입
는 옷이다 : 마리는 학교 연극
공연에서 costume 을 입었다.

**cotton** [kátən|kɔ́tən] 명 솜, 면
화 ; 무명, 면직물
cotton 은 목화로 만드는 옷감
의 일종이다. cotton 은 옷이
나 그밖의 것들을 만드는 데
쓰인다.

**couch** [káutʃ] 명 잠자는 의자,
소파 ; 잠자리
couch 는 한 사람 이상이 앉
을 수 있는 푹신푹신한 가구
다.

**cough** [kɔ́:f|kɔ́f] 1 자 기침하다
2 명 기침
cough 는 공기를 목구멍 밖으
로 나오게 하여 소리를 낸다는
뜻이다.

**could** [《약》 kəd, 《강》 kúd] 조
can¹ (…할 수 있다) 의 과거형
could 는 can¹ 의 한 형태다 :
톰은 휘파람을 불 줄 안다. 그
는 다섯 살 때부터 휘파람을
불 수 있었다.

**couldn't** [kúdənt] could not 의
단축형
couldn't 는 could not 의 뜻이
다 : 그 어린 양은 잘 걸을 수
가 없었다.

**count** [káunt] 타 자 세다, 계산
하다 ; 수를 세다
1 count 는 몇 개 있는지 알아
본다는 뜻이다 : 우리가 사과를
몇 개나 땄는지 한번 세어보
자.
2 count 는 또한 순서대로 숫
자를 말한다는 뜻이다 : 10 까
지 셀 수 있니 ?

**counter** [káuntər] 명 세는 사
람 ; (은행·상점의) **카운터**, 계
산대, 판매대 ; (식당의) 긴 대
counter 는 긴 탁자다. 가게에
서는 물건을 counter 에 놓고
판다. 사람들이 counter 에서
식사를 할 수 있는 음식점도

있다.

**country** [kʌ́ntri] 명 나라, 조
국 ; 시골, 지방
1 country 는 숲과 농장이 있
는 도시와 읍의 외곽 지역을
말한다.
2 country 는 영토와 그 곳에
사는 사람들을 말한다. coun-
try 에는 자체 정부가 있다.

**courage** [kə́:ridʒ | kʌ́r-] 명 용기
비록 두렵더라도 어떤 일을 할
때, courage를 보여주게 된
다 : 소방수들은 courage 가 많
다(대단히 용감하다).

**cousin** [kʌ́zən] 명 사촌
cousin 은 고모나 삼촌의 자식
이다. 내 cousin 과 나는 할아
버지가 같다.

**cover** [kʌ́vər] 1 타 덮다 ; 싸
다, 씌우다 ; 덮어 가리다 2
명 덮개, 커버 ; 뚜껑 ; 표지
1 cover 는 다른 것 위에 어떤
것을 놓는다는 뜻이다 : 웬디는
몸을 따뜻하게 하려고 두꺼운
담요를 **덮었다**.
2 cover 는 어떤 것 위나 겉에

놓인다. 책에는 cover 가 있
다. 항아리와 냄비에도 cover
가 있다.

**cow** [káu] 명 암소 ; 젖소
cow 는 농장에서 사는 큰 동
물이다. cow 에서 우유가 나
온다.

**cowboy** [káubɔ̀i] 명 목동 ; 카우
보이, 소몰이꾼
cowboy 는 목장에서 가축을
돌보는 남자다. cowboy 는 말
을 타고 다니며, 때때로 로데
오라고 불리는 쇼에서 묘기를
부린다. cowboy는 큰 농장에
서 일한다.

**cowgirl** [káugə̀:rəl] 명 목장에
서 일하는 여자
cowgirl 은 목장에서 가축을
돌보는 여자다. cowgirl 은 말
을 타고 다니며, 때때로 로데
오라고 불리는 쇼에서 묘기를
부린다.

**crack** [kræk] 명 째진 틈, 갈라
진 틈바구니 ; 흠, 금
crack 은 좁게 벌어진 공간이
다. crack 은 무언가가 깨졌지
만 산산조각 나지는 않았다는
뜻이다 : 내가 거울을 떨어뜨려

서 거울에 crack이 갔다. 벽
에 crack이 갔나.

**cracker** [krǽkər] 몡 크래커
cracker 는 구운 음식으로, 작
고 딱딱하며 납작하다.
cracker 는 쿠기와 비슷하지
만, 달지는 않다.

**crane** [kréin] 몡 기중기
crane 은 상하 및 원형으로 움
직일 수 있는 긴 팔이 달린 큰
기계다. crane 은 무거운 물건
을 들어 옮기는 데 사용된다.

**crash** [krǽʃ] 1 몡 (물건이 부서
지거나 충돌할 때의) **요란한
소리**; 꽝음; (비행기의) **추락**
2 짜 **와르르 무너지다**〔부서지
다〕; (요란한 소리를 내며) **충
돌하다**; 꽝음을 내다; (비행기
가) **추락하다**
1 crash 는 어떤 것과 부딪쳐
서 요란한 소리를 내며 부서진
다는 뜻이다 : 우리는 두 대의
자동차가 서로 **요란한 소리를
내면서 충돌하는** 것을 보았다.
2 crash 는 시끄러운 소리다 :
우리는 옆방에서 나는 crash
(요란한 소리)를 들었다.

**crawl** [krɔ́:əl] 짜 **기다**; 포복하
다
crawl 은 양 손과 무릎으로 움
직인다는 뜻이다 : 갓난아기들
은 걸을 수 있을 때까지 **기어
다닌다.**

**crayon** [kréiən|-ɔn, -ən] 몡 크
레용
crayon 은 글씨를 쓰거나 그림
을 그리는 데 쓰는 밀랍 막대
기다. crayon 에는 여러 가지
색깔이 있다.

**cream** [krí:m] 몡 크림; 아이스
크림; 화장용 크림
cream 은 음식의 일종이다.
cream 은 젖소에서 나는 우유
의 한 성분이다. 버터는
cream 으로 만든다.

**creep** [krí:p] 짜 **기다**; 살금살금
걷다
creep 는 천천히 그리고 소리
없이 지면을 따라 움직인다는
뜻이다 : 거미가 마루를 가로질
러 **기어갔다.**

**cried** [kráid] 통 cry(울다)의
과거·과거분사형
cried 는 단어 cry 에서 생긴

말이다 : 마이크는 넘어져서 무릎을 다치자 소리내어 **울었다.**

**crime** [kráim] 명 (법률상의) **죄, 범죄,** 범행
crime 은 무엇이든 법을 어기는 것〔행위〕이다. 물건을 훔치는 것은 crime 이다.

**crocodile** [krákədàiəl | krɔ́k-] 명 크로코다일《아프리카 · 아시아산의 악어》 ; 악어 가죽
crocodile 은 물에 사는 큰 동물로 다리가 짧고 꼬리가 길다. crocodile 은 또한 이빨도 날카롭다.

**crooked** [krúkid] 형 **구부러진,** 굴곡된, **비뚤어진**
crooked 는 똑바르지 않다는 뜻이다 : 번개는 하늘에 **비뚤어진** 줄이 그어진 것 같이 보인다.

**cross** [krɔ́ːs | krɔ́s] 1 명 **십자가** ; 십자형 2 타 자 ① **교차시키다** ; …에 십자를 긋다 ② **가로지르다** ③ **건너다** ; 넘다
1 cross 는 두 선이 가운데서 엇갈리는 모양이다. cross는 ＋모양과 같다.
2 cross 는 맞은 편으로 간다

는 뜻이다 : 강을 **가로질러** 다리가 놓여 있다.

**crow** [króu] 명 까마귀
crow 는 깃털이 검은 큰 새다.
crow 는 시끄럽게 운다.

**crowd** [kráud] 명 **군중** ; 붐빔 ; 다수
crowd 는 한 곳에 많이 모여 있는 사람의 무리다 : crowd 는 경기가 시작되기를 기다렸다.

**crown** [kráun] 명 **왕관,** 왕위
crown 은 왕이나 여왕이 쓰는 특별한 종류의 모자다. crown 은 보통 금이나 은으로 만들고 아름다운 보석이 박혀 있다.

**cruel** [krúːəl] 형 **잔인한,** 무자비한, 매정한 ; 참혹한
cruel 은 남에게 고통을 줄 수 있다는 뜻이다 : 그렇게 개를 때리다니 그는 **잔인하다.**

**crutch** [krʌ́tʃ] 명 **목발** ; 버팀, 의지 ; **버팀목,** 지주
crutch 는 다리가 약한 사람을 걸을 수 있게 해준다. crutch

는 겨드랑이에 끼게 되어 있는
윗부분이 부드러운 막대기〔지
팡이〕다.

**cry** [krái] **자타** ① 소리치다 ;
**외치다** ② (소리내어) **울다,
흐느끼다**
cry 는 눈물을 흘린다는 뜻이
다 : 사람들은 때때로 슬플 때
**흐느껴 운다.**

**cub** [kʌ́b] **명** (들짐승의) **새
끼** ; 고래〔상어〕의 새끼
cub 은 아주 어린 곰, 늑대,
사자 또는 호랑이다.

**cube** [kjúːb] **명 정육면체** ; (주
사위 등의) 입방형의 것 ; 세제
곱
cube 는 블록 같은 단단한 형
태다. cube 는 6 개의 똑같은
정사각형 면이 있다.

**cup** [kʌ́p] **명 손잡이가 달린 찻
잔, 컵** ; 우승컵
cup 은 액체를 담는 데 쓰인
다. cup은 옆에 손잡이가 달
려 있으며, 대개 둥글다. cup
으로 우유, 물 또는 주스를 마

실 수 있다.

**curious** [kjúəriəs] **형 알고 싶
어하는** ; 호기심이 강한
curious 는 어떤 것을 알거나
배우고 싶어한다는 뜻이다 : 내
동생과 나는 새로운 이웃에 대
해 **알고 싶어했다.** 머리는 새
가 어떻게 나는지 **궁금했다.**

**curl** [kə́ːrəl] **명 고수머리, 컬** ;
곱슬곱슬한 머리털
curl 은 작은 원 모양의 머리털
이다 : 메리의 머리털은 온통
**곱슬곱슬하다.**

**curly** [kə́ːrli] **형 곱슬머리의,**
퍼머넌트 머리의
curly 는 작은 원을 그리며 이
리저리 꼬여 있다는 뜻이다 :
빌리의 머리털은 **곱슬곱슬한데**
피터의 머리털은 곱슬곱슬하지
않다.

**curve** [kə́ːrv] 1 **명 곡선** ; 굴
곡, 만곡부 ; (야구의) 커브 2
**타자 구부리다, 구부러지다** ;
커브시키다
1 curve 는 둥근 선이다. U 자
의 밑부분은 curve다.
2 curve 는 둥근 선 모양을 따

른다는 뜻이다 : 이 길은 왼쪽
으로 **굽어 있다.**

**customer** [kʌ́stəmər] 명 (가게
의) **손님,** 단골
customer 는 물건을 사는 사람
이다 : 식품점에는 customer 가
많이 있었다.

**cut** [kʌt] 1 타 ① (칼 등으로)
베다, 상처내다 ; **자르다** ②
(풀·머리를) **깎다** ; 새기다 ③
**짧게 하다,** 줄이다 2 명 절
단 ; 벤 상처 ; 삭제
1 cut 은 칼, 가위 또는 다른
날카로운 것으로 조각조각 나
눈다는 뜻이다 : 폴은 피자를
여덟 조각으로 **잘랐다.**
2 cut 은 또한 한 부분을 없애
서 더 짧게 한다는 뜻이다 : 지
난 주에 이발사에게 머리를 **깎**
**았다.**
3 cut 은 또한 날카로운 것에
다친다는 뜻이다 : 수잔은 돌에
부딪쳐 발에 **상처가 났다.**

**dad** [dæd] 몡 아빠, **아버지**
　dad 는 아버지를 나타내는 호
　칭이다. 자기 아버지를
　Daddy 라고 부르는 아이들도
　있다.

**dairy** [dɛ́əri] 몡 (농장 내의) **젖**
　**짜는 곳**, 버터 제조장 ; 우유
　〔버터〕 판매점 ; **낙농장**
　dairy 는 우유를 병이나 납지
　용기에 넣는 곳이다. dairy 는
　또한 우유로 버터와 치즈, 그
　외의 다른 식품들을 만드는 곳
　이다. 우유를 얻기 위해 젖소
　를 기르는 농장을 때로 dairy
　farm (낙농장)이라고도 한다.

**daisy** [déizi] 몡 데이지 ; 프랑스
　국화
　daisy는 가운데가 둥글고 노란
　색이며 흰 꽃잎들이 달린 꽃이
　다.

**dam** [dæm] 몡 **댐, 둑** ; 둑으로
　막은 물
　dam 은 물을 막아 두기 위해
　강을 가로질러 쌓은 벽이다.
　강물이 흐르지 못하고 막혀 있
　게 되면, dam 은 호수가 된
　다 : 비버는 나뭇가지와 진흙으

로 강에 dam 을 쌓는다.

**damp** [dæmp] 혱 **축축한,** 습기
　가 있는
　damp 는 물기가 약간 있다는
　말이다 : 마이클은 **축축한** 냅킨
　으로 엎질러진 우유를 닦았다.

**dance** [dæns | dɑ́:ns] 1 몡 탸 춤
　을 **추다,** 춤추게 하다 2 몡
　**춤,** 댄스, 무용 ; 춤곡 ; 무도회
　1 dance 는 음악에 맞춰 몸을
　움직인다는 뜻이다 : 우리는 파
　티에서 음악을 연주하며 **춤을**
　**추었다.** **춤을 추는** 사람을
　dancer 라고 한다.
　2 dance 는 음악에 맞춰 몸을
　움직이는 방법을 말한다 : 내
　친구는 자기가 다른 나라에서
　배운 dance 를 어떻게 추는지
　내게 가르쳐 주었다.

**dandelion** [dǽndəlàiən] 몡 민

들레
dandelion은 꽃의 일종이다.
dandelion은 둥글고 노랗다.

**danger** [déindʒər] 몡 위험 ; 위
험물 ; (신호의) 위험 표시
danger는 사람을 다치게 할
수 있는 것이다 : 회오리바람은
사람들을 danger에 빠뜨릴 수
있다.

**dangerous** [déindʒərəs] 혱 위
험한, 위태로운
dangerous는 무언가에 다칠
수 있다는 뜻이다 : 양쪽 길을
살피지 않고 도로를 횡단하는
것은 **위험하다.** 불빛이 없는
밤에 자전거를 타는 것은 **위험
하다.**

**dark** [dá:rk] 혱 어두운 ; 거무스
름한 ; 검은
dark는 빛이 없다는 뜻이다 :
밤에는 밖이 **어둡다.**

**dash** [dǽʃ] 쟈 탸 돌진하다
dash는 빠르게 움직인다는 뜻
이다 : 비가 내리기 시작하자

닭은 비를 피할 수 있는 곳으
로 **급히 내달았다.**

**date**[1] [déit] 몡 날짜, 연월일
date는 어느 특정한 한 날을
말한다 : 7월 7일은 date다.
11월 20일도 date다. 모든
날에는 date가 있다.

**date**[2] [déit] 몡 대추야자나무 (의
열매)
date는 나무에서 자라는 검은
빛깔이 나는 달콤한 과일이다.

**daughter** [dɔ́:tər] 몡 딸
daughter는 사람에게서 태어
난 여자 아이를 말한다 : 웬디
의 부모님에게는 daughter가
둘 있는데, 그 중 한 명이 웬
디고 다른 한 명은 마리아다.

**day** [déi] 몡 낮 ; 하루, 날
1 day는 밝이 환한 때를 말한
다 : 우리는 휴가 때 day에는
놀거나 수영을 했고, 밤에는
텐트에서 잤다.
2 day는 또한 일주일 중의 하
루다. 일주일은 7 days다. 화
요일은 일주일 중 세번째 day
다.

**dead** [déd] 형 죽은, 죽어 있는 ; 시든 ; 그친 ; (식물이) **말라 죽은**

dead 는 살아 있지 않다는 의미다. 식물과 꽃들은 물이 없으면 시들어 버려, **말라 죽게** 된다.

**deaf** [déf] 형 귀머거리의, (가는) 귀먹은

deaf 는 소리를 들을 수 없다는 의미다.

**dear** [díər] 형 **사랑스러운**, 귀여운, 친애하는

dear 는 사랑한다는 의미다. 사람들은 또한 **사랑하는**(친애하는)이라는 말로 편지를 쓰기 시작한다 : 수잔이 그녀의 이모에게 보낸 편지는 "**사랑하는** 클레어 이모에게"로 시작되었다. 그는 그의 **소중한** 친구들에게 작별을 고했다.

**December** [disémbər] 명 **12 월**

December 는 한 해의 마지막 달이다. December 는 31 일이며, 11 월이 지나고 1 월이 되기 전에 온다.

**decide** [disáid] 타 자 **결심하다**, 결정하다

decide 는 (여러가지 중에) 다른 것을 하지 않고 어느 한가지를 하기로 결심한다는 의미다 : 보브는 아침 식사로 계란 대신 시리얼을 먹기로 **결심했다.** 우리 마을은 학교 앞에 교통 신호등을 설치하기로 **결정했다.** 우리는 곧 가기로 **결정했다.**

**deck** [dék] 명 **갑판** ; 갑판 모양의 것 ; **카드 한 벌**

1 deck 은 사람들이 게임을 하는 데 쓰는 한 벌의 카드를 말한다. 대부분의 deck 은 52 장의 카드로 되어 있는 데, 한장 한장이 모두 다르다.

2 deck 은 또한 배나 보트의 평평한 바닥을 말한다. 지붕이나 덮개로 덮인 deck 도 있고, 전체가 개방된 deck 도 있다. 큰 배에는 deck 이 많이 있을 수 있다.

**deep** [díːp] 형 **깊은**, 깊이[길이]가 있는 ; 깊이 …의

deep 은 아래까지의 거리가 상당히 멀다는 뜻이다 : 그 개는 뼈다귀를 숨기려고 땅에 **깊은 구덩이를** 팠다.

**deer** [díər] 명 사슴
deer 는 네 다리와 작은 꼬리, 그리고 갈색 털이 있는 동물이다. 큰 뿔이 있는 deer 도 있다. deer 는 아주 빨리 달리며 숲에서 산다.

**define** [difáin] 타 (말의) **정의를 내리다,** (뜻을) **밝히다**
define 은 어떤 것의 의미를 밝힌다는 뜻이다 : 사전에는 단어의 **뜻이 밝혀져** 있다.

**delicious** [dilíʃəs] 형 **맛있는, 맛좋은**
delicious 는 맛이 아주 좋다는 뜻이다 : 우리는 점심을 **맛있게** 먹었다.

**den** [dén] 명 (야생 동물의) **보금자리, 소굴 ; 굴, 동굴 ; 구멍**

den 은 야생 동물이 쉬거나 잠을 자는 곳이다 : 곰은 겨울 동안에 동굴을 den 으로 사용했다.

**dentist** [déntist] 명 **치과 의사**
dentist 는 사람들의 치아를 보살펴 주는 의사다 : dentist 가 아이들에게 칫솔질하는 법을 가르쳐 주었다.

**describe** [diskráib] 타 (… 의 특징을) **말하다,** 묘사하다
describe 는 어떤 것을 말로 묘사한다는 뜻이다 : 할머니가 잭에게 그가 잡은 물고기에 대해 **말해 달라고** 하자, 잭은 길이는 6 인치고 몸에는 가는 줄무늬가 머리에서 꼬리까지 나 있다고 **말해주었다.**

**desert** [dézərt] 명 **사막**
desert 는 물이 거의 없고 모래가 많은 (기후가) 더운 곳이다.

**design** [dizáin] 명 **디자인 ; 도안 ; 무늬 ; 설계 ; 계획**
design 은 각기 다른 모양과

색깔로 그림을 그리거나 색칠을 한 것들을 한 데 모아 놓은 것이다 : 그 카드들의 한면에는 예쁜 design 이 그려져 있었다.

**desk** [désk] 명 (공부·사무용의) **책상** ; (신문사의) **편집부**, 데스크
desk 는 글씨를 쓰거나 공부를 하는 데 필요한 탁자의 일종이다. 서랍이 달린 desk 도 있다.

**dessert** [dizə́ːrt] 명 **디저트**
dessert 는 점심이나 저녁 식사 후에 먹는 음식이다 : 우리는 오늘 dessert 로 과일 샐러드를 먹었다.

**detective** [ditéktiv] 명 **탐정**, 형사
detective 는 물건[사람]을 찾아내려고 애쓰는 사람이다 : 보석을 훔친 사람을 찾아내는 것이 그 detective 가 해야 할 일이었다.

**dial** [dáiəl] 명 (시계·나침반 등의) **지침면**, 문자반 ; (라디오 등의) **회전 눈금판, 다이얼** ; 숫자판

1 dial 은 기계의 앞 부분이다. dial 에는 숫자나 문자가 있으며 그것들을 가리키는 화살 모양의 지침이 있다. 많은 시계에는 시간을 나타내는 dial 이 있다.
2 dial 은 또한 라디오나 텔레비전에서 프로그램을 선택하는 디스크를 말한다.

**diamond** [dáiəmənd] 명 **다이아몬드, 금강석** ; **다이아몬드 모양, 마름모꼴** ; (야구의) **내야**, 야구장
1 diamond 는 단단하고 투명하며 광채가 나는 돌이다. 반지 중에는 diamond 를 박은 반지도 있다.
2 diamond 는 또한 생김새다. diamond 에는 네 변과 네 모서리가 있고, ◆ 처럼 생겼다. 야구장은 diamond 모양과 비슷하다.

**dictionary** [díkʃənèri|-ʃənəri] 명 **사전**
dictionary 는 단어의 철자를 어떻게 쓰고 그 뜻이 무엇인지를 보여주는 책이다 : 이 책은 dictionary 다.

**did** [díd] 통 조 do (하다) 의 과거형
did 는 단어 do 에서 생긴 말이다 : 슈퍼마켓에 **갔었습니까**? 예, **갔었습니다**. 그녀는 저녁 식사 후에 숙제를 **했다**.

**didn't** [dídnt] did not 의 단축형

didn't 는 did not의 의미다 : 마루에 난 발자국으로 보아 빌리가 발을 닦지 **않고** 집에 들어 왔다는 사실을 알 수 있다.

**die** [dái] 짜 죽다 ; (식물·꽃이) 시들다

die 는 죽게 된다는 의미다 : 날씨가 추워서 꽃이 모두 **죽었다.**

**different** [dífərənt] 형 **다른,** 틀린

different 는 서로 같지 않다는 의미다 : 새와 물고기는 전혀 **다른** 종류의 동물이다. 개의 꼬리는 고양이 꼬리와 **다르다.**

**dig** [díg] 타 짜 (땅을) 파헤치다 ; (구멍·우물·무덤 등을) **파다,** 파서 만들다

dig 는 구멍을 낸다는 의미다 : 카를로스는 바닷가에서 모래를 **파헤치는** 걸 좋아한다.

**dime** [dáim] 명 10 센트 은화

dime 은 주화다. 1 dime은 10 페니 혹은 5 센트짜리 백동화 두 개와 같다. 1 달러는 10 dime 이다.

**dining room** [dáiniŋ rùːm] 명 식당

dining room 은 식사를 하는 방이다 : 그 호텔에는 모든 손님들이 식사를 할 수 있는 dinning room 이 하나 있다. 야영에 참가한 사람은 누구나 큰 dining room 에서 식사를 했다.

**dinner** [dínər] 명 **정찬** ; 저녁 식사 ; 정식

dinner 는 식사를 말하는 데 하루 중 가장 중요한 식사다. 사람들 중에는 정오에 dinner 를 먹는 사람도 있고, 밤중에 dinner 를 먹는 사람도 있다.

**dinosaur** [dáinəsɔ̀ːr] 명 **공룡**

dinosaur 는 수 백 만년 전에 살았던 동물이다. 몸십이 엄청나게 큰 dinosaur 도 있었다. 오늘날 살아 남아 있는 dinosaur 는 없다.

**dip** [díp] 타 자 (살짝) **적시다**
〔담그다〕
dip 은 어떤 것을 액체에 넣었
다가 재빨리 꺼낸다는 의미
다 : 수잔은 쿠키를 우유에 **살
짝 적셔서** 먹는다.

**direction** [dirékʃən, dái-] 명 **방
향, 방면 ; 지시, 명령**
1 direction 은 다른 곳에 닿기
위해서 가야하는 방향이다 : 이
direction 으로 계속 걸어가면,
우리는 공원에 닿을 것이다.
2 direction 은 또한 어떤 것이
가리키는 길이다 : 저 표지는
동물원 direction 을 가리키고
있다.

**dirt** [də́ːrt] 명 **흙 ; 먼지 ; 오물**
dirt 는 흙을 의미한다. 땅은
dirt 와 바위로 되어 있다 : 마
크는 밖에 나가서 놀면 옷에
dirt 를 묻힌다.

**dirty** [də́ːrti] 형 **더러운 ; 흙투성
이의 ; 야비한 ; 불쾌한**
dirty 는 흙으로 뒤덮여 있다는
의미다 : 우리집 개는 늪에서
헤엄을 쳐서 **더럽다.**

**disappear** [dìsəpíər] 자 **사라지**

다, 없어지다
disappear 는 보이지 않게 된
다는 의미다 : 태양이 구름 뒤
로 **사라졌다.**

**disappoint** [dìsəpɔ́int] 타 **실망
시키다**
disappoint 는 어떤 일이 생기
지 않아서 기분이 나쁘다는 의
미다 : 수잔과 토드는 비가 와
서 새 자전거를 탈 수 없게 되
자 **실망했다.**

**discover** [diskʌ́vər] 타 **발견하
다, 깨닫다**
discover 는 처음으로 어떤 것
을 찾아내거나 배운다는 의미
다 : 빨간색과 노란색 그림물감
을 섞어 보면, 주황색 그림물
감을 어떻게 만드는지 **알게 될
것이다.**

**disguise** [disgáiz] 1 타 **변장하
다 ; 속이다, 숨기다** 2 명 **변
장, 가장 ; 변장〔위장〕수단**
1 disguise 는 어떤 것을 전혀

다른 것 처럼 보이게 해서 숨긴다는 의미다 : 만성절 전날 밤 아이들은 가면과 축제 의상으로 **변장했다**.
2 disguise 는 모습을 숨기거나 변화시키는 것이다 : 톰은 disguise 로 익살맞게 생긴 코가 달린 안경을 썼다.

**dish** [díʃ] 명 주발 ; 접시
dish 는 음식을 담아 놓는 것이다. dish 는 보통 둥근 모양이다 : 마이크는 저녁 식사후 dish 를 모두 닦았다(설겆이를 했다).

**disk, disc** [dísk] 명 평원반 (모양의 것), 디스크 ; (컴퓨터의) **디스크**
1 disk 는 납작하고 얇으며 둥근 모양을 한 것이다. 주화나 접시 그리고 음반들은 모두 disk 다.
2 disk 는 또한 컴퓨터용으로 정보를 저장하기 위해 사용하는, 납작하고 얇은 플라스틱 조각이나 금속 조각을 말한다.

**distance** [dístəns] 명 거리, 간격 ; 원거리, 먼곳
distance 는 두 물체 사이의 공간[거리]을 의미한다 : 내 침대와 언니 침대 사이의 distance 는 약 3피트다. 폴은 할머니와 먼 distance 를 떨어져 살고 있어서, 그녀를 방문하려면 비행기를 타고 가야 한다.

**dive** [dáiv] 자 (물 속에 머리부터) 뛰어들다, **다이빙하다**
dive 는 머리가 먼저 물 속에 들어 간다는 의미다 : 마리아와 앨버트는 수영 강습을 받을 때 **다이빙하는** 법을 배웠다. **다이빙하는** 사람을 diver라고 한다. diver 들이 바닷속에 사는 동물들의 사진을 찍었다.

**divide** [diváid] 타 자 **나누다**, 쪼개다 ; 분할하다 ; 분류하다
divide 는 여러 조각으로 쪼갠다는 의미다 : 아이들은 게임을 하려고 두 팀으로 **나눴다**. 우리는 그 과일을 우리들끼리 **나눴다**. 울타리 때문에 마당이 둘로 **갈라져 있다**. 메리는 사과를 반으로 **쪼갰다**.

**divorce** [divɔ́:rs] 타 자 이혼시키다, **이혼하다**
divorce 는 법률적으로 결혼 생

활을 끝낸다는 의미다. 존 부
인은 남편과 **이혼했다.**

**dizzy** [dízi] 형 현기증이 나는,
머리가 어찔어찔하는
dizzy 는 어지러워서 쓰러질
것만 같다는 의미다 : 아이들은
**현기증이 날** 때까지 원을 그리
며 뛰었다.

**do** [《약》 də,　d, 《강》 dú:] 타 자
조 하다, 수행하다 ; 행동하다,
**일하다**
do 는 어떤 일이 일어나게 한
다는 의미다 : 한나는 항상 자
기 방을 잘 청소**한다.** 그녀는
누가 시키지 않아도 항상 청소
를 **해 왔다.** 한나와 엘리자베
스는 함께 일을 **했다.**

**dock** [dák | dɔ́k] 명 독 ; 방파제,
선창, 부두
dock 은 배를 묶어 두는 곳이
다 : 리처드는 자기 배를 dock
에 둘 때면, 배에 로프를 묶어
놓는다.

**doctor** [dáktər | dɔ́k-] 명 의
사 ; 박사, 박사 학위
doctor 는 아픈 사람들이 낫도
록 도와주는 사람이다 : 많은
doctor 들이 병원에서 일한다.

**does** [《약》 dəz, dz, 《강》 dʌ́z]
동 조 do의 3인칭 단수직설법
현재형
does 는 do 의 한 형태다 : 조
는 매일 밤 숙제를 **한다.** 수
또한 숙제를 **한다.**

**doesn't** [dʌ́znt] does not 의 단
축형
doesn't 는 does not 의 의미
다 : 조지의 개는 물을 좋아하
지만, 앨버트의 개는 물을 전
혀 좋아하지 **않는다.**

**dog** [dɔ́:g | dɔ́g] 명 개
dog 은 발이 네 개고 짖는 동
물이다. 강아지는 부드러운 털
이 있으며 puppy 라고 한다.
사람들을 돕도록 훈련시킬 수
있는 dog 도 있다.

**doll** [dáəl | dɔ́əl] 명 인형
doll 은 갓난아기나 어린이 혹
은 어른의 모습을 닮은 장난감

이다 : 웬디는 doll 을 자기의 아기인 것처럼 다룬다.

**dollar** [dálər | dɔ́lə] 몡 달러《미국·캐나다의 화폐 단위》
dollar 는 금액을 말한다. dollar 는 보통 직사각형 모양의 녹색 종이로 되어 있다. 1 dollar 는 100 페니와 같다.

**done** [dʌ́n] 동 조 do (하다) 의 과거분사형
1 done 은 단어 do 에서 생긴 말이다 : 내가 너에게 준 책을 얼마나 읽었느냐 ?
2 done 은 또한 끝냈다는 의미다 : 조지는 숙제를 끝냈다.

**donkey** [dáŋki | dɔ́ŋ-] 몡 당나귀
donkey 는 동물이다. donkey 는 긴 귀가 있는 작은 말과 비슷해 보인다. donkey 는 무거운 짐을 나를 수 있다.

**don't** [dóunt] do not 의 단축형
don't 는 do not 의 의미다 : 나는 경기가 언제 시작되는지 몰라서 물어 보려고 한다.

**door** [dɔ́ːr] 몡 문

1 door 는 공간을 막아서 고립시키는 것을 말한다. door 는 사람들이 드나들 수 있도록 열리고 닫힌다 : 사람들이 모두 타자 엘리베이터 door 가 닫혔다.
2 때때로 천장이나 벽 혹은 마루에 조그만 door 가 있다. 이런 종류의 door를 보통 trapdoor (들창, 뚜껑문) 라고 부른다.

**dot** [dát | dɔ́t] 몡 점, 얼룩, 반점
dot 는 작고 둥근 점이다 : 글자 i 위에 dot 가 있다.

**double** [dʌ́bl] 1 타 자 두 배로 하다 2 혱 두 배의, 이중의
1 double 은 어떤 것을 두 배로 늘린다는 의미다 : 올해는 저축을 두배로 할 수 있었으면 좋겠다.
2 double 은 또한 같은 것이 두개 있다거나 두배라는 의미다 : 아이들은 두 줄을 지어 등교했다.

**doubt** [dáut] 1 타 자 의심하다,

…을 미심쩍게 여기다 2 명 의심, 의혹

1 doubt 는 확실하지 않다는 의미다 : 우리는 우리 팀이 과연 우승할 수 있을 지 의심스러웠다.

2 doubt 는 믿어지지 않거나 확실하지 않은 느낌을 말한다 : doubt가 나면 사전에서 단어를 찾아보아라.

**doughnut** [dóunʌ̀t] 명 도넛

doughnut 은 작고 둥근 케이크다. 중앙에 구멍이 있는 doughnut 이 많지만, 가운데에 젤리가 들어 있는 doughnut 도 있다 : 사람들은 아침식사로 doughnut 을 즐겨 먹는다.

**dove** [dóuv] 동 dive(다이빙하다)의 과거형

dove 는 단어 dive 에서 생긴 말이다 : 개는 내가 던진 막대기를 잡으려고 물에 뛰어 들었다.

**down** [dáun] 1 부 아래로, 아래쪽으로 2 전 …을 내려가, …의 아래쪽으로

down 은 높은 곳에서 낮은 곳으로 움직인다는 의미다 : 고양이가 나무에서 뛰어 내렸다. 당신 책을 탁자 위에 내려 놓아도 괜찮습니다.

**dozen** [dʌ́zən] 명 열두개, 다스

dozen 은 어떤 것이 열두 개라는 의미다 : 마리는 가게에서 달걀 한 dozen 을 샀다.

**Dr.** [dɑ́ktər | dɔ́k-] doctor 의 단축형

doctor 를 줄여서 쓸 때 Dr. 라고 쓴다. 사람들은 의사 이름에 Dr.를 붙여 쓴다 : 우리 가족 주치의는 Dr. 스미스다.

**drag** [dræg] 타 자 (무거운 짐을) 끌다 ; (발·꼬리를) 질질 끌다

drag 는 마룻바닥이나 지면을 따라 어떤 것을 천천히 끌어 당긴다는 의미다 : 개는 목에 매인 쇠사슬을 뒤로 질질 끌며 들어 왔다.

**dragon** [drǽgən] 명 용

dragon 은 크고 무시무시한 상상 속의 동물이다. 날개와 긴 꼬리가 있는 dragon 도 있고, 불을 내뿜는 dragon 도 있다.

**drain** [dréin] 1 타 자 (물을) 빼내다, (물기를) 빼다〔없애다〕 2 명 하수도, 하수구
1 drain 은 어떤 것에서 물이나 다른 종류의 액체를 빼낸다는 의미다 : 우리는 완두콩 통조림에서 물기를 **빼냈다**.
2 drain 은 또한 어떤 것에서 물이나 다른 종류의 액체를 빼내는 데 사용하는 일종의 파이프다 : 수는 목욕 후 목욕물을 drain으로 흘러 내보냈다.

**drank** [drǽŋk] 동 drink (마시다) 의 과거형
drank 는 단어 drink 에서 생긴 말이다 : 사라는 우유를 다 **마셨다**.

**draw** [drɔ́:] 타 자 ① **끌다**, 당기다 ; 잡아 빼다, (잡아) 뽑다 ② (선·그림 등을) 긋다, **그리다**
draw 는 연필이나 크레용으로 무언가를 그린다는 의미다 : 나는 우리집 고양이를 **그렸다**.

**drawbridge** [drɔ́:brìdʒ] 명 도개교, 들어올리는 다리
drawbridge 는 키 큰 배들이 그 밑을 통과할 수 있도록 움직이게 하거나 들려서 열릴 수 있게 만든 다리의 일종이다 : 나는 drawbridge 가 들어 올려지자 보트들이 지나가는 것을 보았다.

**drawer** [drɔ́:r] 명 draw 하는 사람, (특히) 제도사 ; **서랍**
drawer 는 가구 안에 있는 상자를 말한다. drawer 는 빼내거나 밀어넣을 수 있다 : 내 스웨터들은 맨 밑 drawer 에 들어있다.

**drawing** [drɔ́:iŋ] 명 (연필·펜·크레용·목탄 등으로 그린) **그림** ; 제도, 도면
drawing 은 연필이나 크레용으로 그린 그림이다 : 어제 나는 코끼리와 기린 drawing 을 커다랗게 그렸다.

**drawn** [drɔ́:n] 동 draw (끌다, 그리다) 의 과거분사형
drawn 은 draw의 한 형태다 : 마리가 딕의 그림을 **그렸는**

데, 이제는 딕이 마리의 그림을 ㄱ리려 한다.

**dream** [dríːm] 1 **명** 꿈 2 **자** **타** **꿈꾸다**, **꿈에 보다**

1 dream 은 잠을 잘 때 마음 속에 일어나는 영상이다 : 어젯 밤 앨리스는 자기가 날아다니는 dream을 꾸었다.

2 dream 은 잠을 자는 동안 생각이나 영상이 마음속을 스쳐 지나간다는 의미다 : 앨버트는 공룡을 타고 다니는 **꿈을 꾸었다.**

**dress** [drés] **명** **의복** ; 정장 ; (원피스로 된) 여성복, **드레스** dress 는 블라우스와 스커트를 하나로 붙여 놓은 것 처럼 보이는 옷이다. 여자 아이와 성인 여성들이 dress 를 입는다.

**dresser** [drésər] **명** **화장대**, 경 대 ; 조리대, 찬장 dresser 는 서랍이 달린 가구 를 말한다. 사람들은 대개 옷을 dresser 에 넣어 둔다 : 내 보석과 거울이 dresser 위에 있다.

**drew** [drúː] **동** draw(끌다, 그 리다) 의 과거형 drew 는 draw 의 한 형태다 : 테리는 종이 위에 빨간 크레용으로 원을 하나 그린 다음, 파란 크레용으로 정사각형을 몇개 더 **그렸다.**

**dried** [dráid] **동** dry(말리다) 의 과거 · 과거분사형 dried 는 단어 dry 에서 생긴 말이다 : 뜨거운 태양으로 보도에 있는 물웅덩이들이 **바싹 말라 버렸다.**

**drill** [dríəl] 1 **명** **드릴**, **송곳**, **착암기** ; (엄격한) **훈련**, 반복 연습 2 **타** **자** …에 **구멍을 뚫다** ; **훈련하다**

1 drill 은 나무, 플라스틱, 그리고 그 밖의 단단한 재료에 구멍을 낸다는 의미다 : 타일러와 피터는 구멍을 **뚫기** 전에 나무의 치수를 꼼꼼하게 쟀다.

2 drill 은 또한 구멍을 뚫기 위해 사용하는 도구를 말한다.

3 drill 은 어떤 일을 계속 반복하게 해서, 사람을 훈련시키는 방법을 말하기도 한다 : fire drill(소방 연습)을 통해, 사람들은 화재가 발생하면 어떻게 행동해야 하는가를 배운다.

**drink** [dríŋk] 타 자 **마시다,** (잔을) 다 비우다

drink 는 입 속에 액체를 넣어서 삼킨다는 의미다. 우유와 주스는 우리가 **마시는** 식품이다 : 보브는 아침 식사 때 우유를 다 **마셔 버렸다.** 수는 주스는 반밖에 **마시지** 않았지만, 우유는 다 **마셨다.**

**drip** [dríp] 자 타 (액체가) 방울지다, **뚝뚝 떨어지다,** 물방울이 떨어지다

drip 은 방울져 떨어진다는 의미다 : 화가는 양탄자에 그림물감을 **떨어뜨리지** 않으려고 애썼다.

**drive** [dráiv] 타 자 (자동차·마차 등을) 몰다, **운전하다,** 조종하다 ; **자동차로 가다,** 드라이브하다

drive 는 자동차, 트럭 혹은 열차를 가게 한다는 의미다 : 언니는 차를 **운전해도** 될만한 나이다. 어제 그녀가 우리를 해변까지 **차로 태워다 주었다.**

**driven** [drívən] 동 drive(운전하다) 의 과거분사형

driven 은 drive 의 한 형태다 : 기관사들은 열차를 운전한다. 앨의 삼촌은 기관사인 데, 인생의 대부분을 열차를 **운전하는** 데 바쳤다.

**drop** [dráp | drɔ́p] 1 자 타 방울지다, 물방울이 떨어지다, (물건이) **떨어지다** 2 명 물방울, (액체의) 소량

1 drop 은 어떤 것을 떨어지게 한다는 의미다 : 월터는 자기의 아이스크림 콘을 **떨어뜨리자** 울고 말았다.

2 drop 은 적은 양의 액체를 말한다 : 꽃에 비의 drop(빗방울)들이 맺혀 있었다.

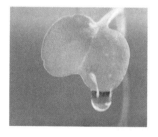

**drove** [dróuv] 동 drive(운전하다) 의 과거형

drove 는 drive 의 한 형태다 : 수잔이 버스를 놓치자, 그녀의 아버지가 그녀를 학교까지 **차로 데려다 주었다.**

**drown** [dráun] 타 자 물에 빠뜨리다, **익사시키다**

drown 은 물 속에서 숨을 쉴

수가 없게 되어서 죽는다는 의미다 : 해변에 누군가가 너무 먼 곳까지 헤엄쳐 나가서 거의 **익사할** 뻔했다.

**drug** [drʌ́g] 명 **약, 약품, 약제 ; 마약**
1 drug 는 아픈 사람을 낫게 하는 약이다. drug 는 알약도 있고 물약도 있다.
2 약이 아닌 또 다른 종류의 drug 도 있다. 그런 종류의 drug 는 사람 몸을 상하게 하고 병들게 할 수 있다.

**drugstore** [drʌ́gstɔ̀ːr] 명 **약국**
drugstore 는 사람들이 약을 살 수 있는 가게다. drugstore 에서는 신문과 다른 물건들도 판다.

**drum** [drʌ́m] 명 **북, 드럼 ; 북소리**
drum 은 두드리면 소리가 나는 악기다. drum을 연주하는 사람을 drummer 라고 한다.

**drunk** [drʌ́ŋk] 동 drink (마시다) 의 과거분사형
drunk 는 단어 drink 에서 생긴 말이다 : 갓난아기는 주스를 다 마셨다.

**dry** [drái] 1 형 **마른, 건조한, 비가 안오는** 2 타 자 **말리다, 건조시키다 ; (물이) 바싹 마르다**
1 dry 는 물이 없다는 의미다 : 3주 동안 비가 오지 않아서 정원이 바싹 **말랐다.**
2 dry 는 또한 어떤 것을 건조시킨다는 의미다 : 우리는 비치 타월들을 **말리려고** 햇볕에 내다 놓았다.

**duck** [dʌ́k] 명 **오리**
duck 은 물에서 사는 새다 : 그 공원 연못에는 duck 가족이 있다.

**dug** [dʌ́g] 동 dig (파다) 의 과거 · 과거분사형
dug 는 단어 dig 에서 생긴 말이다 : 일꾼들은 새 가게가 들어 설 땅에 커다란 구덩이를 **팠다.**

**dull** [dʌ́əl] 형 **(날이) 무딘, 잘 들지 않는 ; 재미없는, 지루한 ; 우둔한**
1 dull 은 날카롭지 않다는 의

미다 : 칼이 너무 **무디어서** 고기를 자를 수가 없다.

2 dull 은 재미있지 않다는 의미다 : 나는 프로그램이 너무나 **재미없어서** 끝까지 보고 싶지 않았다.

**dump** [dʌ́mp] 타 자 (내버리는 곳에) **털썩 떨어뜨리다** ; (쓰레기를) **내버리다**

dump 는 물건을 무더기로 털썩 떨어뜨린다는 의미다 : 트럭이 길가에 흙을 **쏟아 부으려고** 한다.

**during** [djúəriŋ] 전 …동안(내내), …사이에

during은 전(全)기간을 의미한다 : 낮**에는** 밤이 환하다. 우리는 폭풍이 치는 **동안** 집안에

머물러 있었다.

**dust** [dʌ́st] 명 **먼지**, 티끌

dust는 흙의 잔 부스러기다.
dust 는 재채기를 일으킬 수 있다 : 바람이 불어 비포장도로에 dust가 날린다.

**dying** [dáiiŋ] 형 **죽어가는**

dying 은 단어 die 에서 생긴 말이다 : 방학하기 전에 물 주는 것을 잊어버려서, 교실에 있는 식물이 **죽어가고** 있다.

**each** [íːtʃ] 1 형 제각기의, **각각의**, 각자의 2 부 한 사람〔한 개〕에 대해
1 each는 집단에 속해 있는 사람이나 동물 혹은 사물의 개체 하나 하나를 전부 의미한다 : 학생마다 **각자** 연필과 종이를 갖고 있다. 학생은 **각자** 학교에 도시락을 가지고 간다.

2 each는 또한 한 개를 의미한다 : 이 연필들은 **한 개에** 10 센트다.

**each other** [íːtʃ ʌðəɾ] 서로
each other 는 두 사람 모두를 의미한다 : 보브와 메리는 **서로** 좋아한다. 마이크와 수는 박람회에서 **서로** 만났다.

**eagle** [íːgl] 명 독수리
eagle은 긴 날개와 힘센 발톱이 있는 커다란 새다. eagle이 먹이를 사냥할 때는 아주 멀리 있는 물체도 볼 수 있다.

**ear** [íəɾ] 명 귀 ; 청각
ear는 소리를 들을 수 있는 신체 기관이다. 머리 양쪽에 ear가 하나씩 있다. 우리는 ear로 소리를 듣는다 : 토끼의 ear는 매우 길다.

**early** [ə́ːɾli] 1 부 일찍이 2 형 이른, 빠른 ; 초기의, 처음의
1 early 는 무언가가 시작될 무렵이라는 의미다 : 웬디는 아침 **일찍** 일어난다. 그녀의 아버지는 출근 준비를 하려고 **더 일찍** 일어나신다. 웬디의 젖먹이 남동생은 가족 중에서 **가장 일찍** 일어난다.
2 early는 또한 보통 때보다 이르다는 의미다 : 우리는 인형

극을 구경가려고 **일찍** 저녁을
먹었다.

**earn** [ə́ːrn] 타 벌 어 서〔일 하 여〕
**얻다**, 벌다 ; (명성 · 비판 등
을) 얻다, 받다
earn은 일한 대가로 돈이나
그 밖의 무언가를 받는다는 의
미다 : 수잔은 잔디를 깎아주고
1달러를 **받는다.** 마크는 하루
에 7달러를 **번다.** 빌리는 열
심히 공부해서 학교에서 높은
점수를 **받았다.**

**earth** [ə́ːrθ] 명 **지구** ; 흙, 땅
1 earth 는 우리가 살고 있는
행성이다. earth는 태양 주위
를 돌고, 달은 earth 주위를
돈다. earth 가 태양 주위를
도는 데 1년이 걸린다.

2 earth 는 또한 흙이란 의미
다 : 농부는 정원에 씨를 심을
수 있게 earth를 갈아엎었다.

**earthquake** [ə́ːrθkwèik] 명 **지
진** ; 대변동
earthquake는 지구의 일부분
이 갑자기 움직일 때 일어난
다. earthquake가 일어나면,

땅이 흔들리고 때때로 건물도
무너진다.

**easily** [íːzili] 부 **쉽게** ; 편하게
easily는 「쉬운 방식으로」라는
의미다. 무언가를 **쉽게** 할 수
있을 때는, 힘들이지 않고 일
을 끝낼 수 있다 : 이제 앤터니
는 알파벳을 알게 되어서, 단
어를 사전에서 **쉽게** 찾을 수
있다.

**east** [íːst] 명 **동쪽**
east는 방향이다. 태양은 east
에서 뜬다. east 는 west(서
쪽)의 반대말이다.

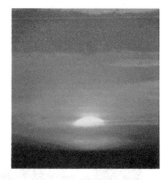

**Easter** [íːstər] 명 **부활절**
Easter는 3월 말이나 4월 초
중에 오는 일요일에 의식을 거
행하는 기독교의 축제일이다 :
때때로 아이들은 Easter를 축
하하기 위해 달걀을 밝은 색깔
로 칠한다.

**easy** [íːzi] 1 형 **쉬운**, 편안한
2 부 **쉽게**, 마음 편하게
easy는 일하기가 힘들지 않다

는 의미다 : 보브는 자전거를 타는게 **쉽다고** 생각한다.

**eat** [íːt] 타 자  **먹다**, 식사하다
eat는 입속에 음식을 넣고 씹어 삼킨다는 의미다 : 기린은 나뭇잎을 뜯어 **먹었다**.

**echo** [ékou] 명 메아리, 울림, 반향
echo는 되돌아오는 소리다. 산에서 큰 소리를 지르면, 목소리가 echo되는(메아리치는) 소리를 들을 수 있다.

**edge** [édʒ] 명 테두리, **가장자리**, 변두리, 모서리 ; (칼 등의) 날
edge는 어떤 것이 끝나는 선이나 장소다 : 10센트짜리 은화가 테이블 edge에서 굴러 떨어졌다. 나는 호수의 edge(호숫가) 근처에 살고 있다.

**egg** [ég] 명 (새의) **알** ; 달걀
egg는 그 안에 동물의 새끼가 있는 매끄러운 원형의 껍질이다. 새들은 부화하기 전까지 egg 속에서 자란다. 많은 사람들이 아침 식사로 닭이 난 egg(달걀)를 먹는다.

**eight** [éit] 1 명 8, 여덟 개
2 형 8의, 여덟 개의
eight는 숫자다. eight는 7보다 하나 더 크다. eight를 **8**이라고 쓴다. 7+1=**8**.

**either** [íːðər | áiðə] 1 형 **어느 한쪽의**, 어느 쪽이든 2 대 (둘 중) **어느 한쪽**, 어느 쪽이든 3 부 [부정문에서 not ... either의 형태로] **…도 또한 아니다** 4 접 [either ... or의 형태로] **…(이)든가 또는 …(이)든가**
1 either는 (두 개중) 어느 한쪽이라는 뜻이다 : 웬디는 생일 선물로 강아지나 조랑말을 받고 싶어 하는 데, 둘 중 **어느 것을 받아도** 기뻐할 것이다.
2 either는 「…도 또한 아니다」라는 뜻이다 : 톰은 축구를 하고 싶지 않았다. 그는 **또한** 농구**도** 하고 싶은 마음이 **없었다**.

**elbow** [élbou] 명 **팔꿈치** ; 팔꿈치 모양의 굴곡
elbow는 팔이 굽혀지는 신체 부위다 : 수잔은 탁자 위에 두 elbow를 얹고 앉았다.

**election** [ilékʃən] 명 **선거** ; 선

택, 선정 ; 선임
election에서 투표를 한다는
것은 어떤 일을 하도록 일할
사람을 선택한다는 것이다 : 미
국은 4년마다 대통령 election
을 한다.

**electricity** [ilèktrísiti, ì:lek-]
명 전기
electricity는 에너지의 일종이
다. electricity는 등불을 밝혀
주고, 또한 냉장고, 컴퓨터,
그밖의 많은 것을 작동시킨다.

**elephant** [éləfənt] 명 코끼리
elephant는 육지에 사는 가장
크고, 가장 힘이 센 동물이다.
elephant의 가죽은 두꺼운 회
색이며, 트렁크라고 하는 긴
코가 있다.

**elevator** [éləvèitər] 명 엘리베
이터, 승강기 ; 물건을 올리는
장치 [사람]
elevator는 건물을 올라갔다
내려갔다하는 작은 공간이나
칸이다. 간혹 elevator가 건물
밖에 있는 경우도 있다.
elevator는 사람이나 물건들을
한 층에서 다른 층으로 실어나

르는 데 이용된다.

**else** [éls] 부 ① 그밖에, 달리 ;
다른 누구의 것이라도 ; …이
아니면 ② [보통 or 뒤에서]
그렇지 않으면
1 else는 다르거나 상이하다는
뜻이다 : 야구말고 그밖에 어떤
경기를 하고 싶으냐 ?
2 else는 또한 「만일 …이 아
니라고 한다면」의 뜻이다 : 아
침을 먹어라, 그렇지 않으면
점심 시간전에 배가 고플 것이
다.

**emerald** [émərəld] 명 에메랄
드, 취옥 ; 에메랄드 빛깔
emerald는 보석의 일종이다.
emerald는 초록색이다.

**emergency** [imə́:rdʒənsi] 명
비상 사태, 위급한 경우, 긴
급, 응급
때때로 중요하거나 위태로운
일이 아주 급하게 발생하면,
우리는 즉시 (어떠한) 행동을
취해야만 하는 데, 이러한 상
황을 emergency라고 한다.
경찰관, 의사, 소방수들은
emergency에 처한 사람들을
돕는다.

**empty** [émpti] 형 빈, 비어 있
는 ; 없는 ; 공허한
empty는 속에 아무것도 없다
는 뜻이다 : 레이는 주스를 다
마시고, 빈 유리컵을 식탁 위

에 놓았다.

**end** [énd] 1 몡 **끝** ; 가장자리 ;
한계 ; 목적 ; 결국 ; 종국 ; 최후
2 탸쟈 **끝내다**, 중지하다
1 end는 어떤 것의 마지막 부
분이다 : 교장실은 복도 end
(맨 끝)에 있다.
2 end는 또한 중지한다는 뜻
이다 : 선생님은 수업을 점심
시간 바로 전에 **끝내셨다.**

**enemy** [énəmi] 몡 **적**, 원수 ;
적군, **적국**
1 enemy는 누군가 딴 사람을
미워하는 사람이다 : 그 잔인한
통치자에게는 많은 enemy 가
있었다.
2 enemy는 또한 다른 나라와
전쟁 중인 나라를 말한다 : 과
거에 enemy였던 두 나라가
이제는 우방이 되었다.

**energy** [énərdʒi] 몡 **에너지** ;
힘, 세력 ; 정력, 끈기 ; 활동
력, 행동력
energy는 사물을 움직이게 하
거나 기계를 작동시켜 준다.
빛, 열 그리고 전기는 energy
의 일종이다. 달리거나 뛰어오
를 때, 자신의 energy를 사용

한다.

**engine** [éndʒin] 몡 **엔진**, 기
관 ; 발동기 ; **기관차**
1 engine은 에너지를 이용해
다른 기계들을 움직이게 하는
기계를 말한다 : 자동차의
engine이 자동차를 움직이게
한다.

2 engine은 또한 다른 차량들
을 끌고 가는 열차의 첫번째
차량이다 : 기관사가 열차의
engine을 운전한다.

**engineer** [èndʒiníər] 몡 **기사,**
기술자, 공학자, 토목기사 ;
(철도의) **기관사**
1 engineer는 열차를 운전하는
사람이다. engineer는 열차 앞
쪽에 있는 기관차를 움직인다.
2 engineer는 또한 엔진이나
기계 혹은 건물을 짓는 법을
가르쳐 주는 사람이다.

**English** [íŋgliʃ] 몡 **영어**
English는 미국과 다른 많은
나라에서 사용하는 언어의 명

칭이다.

**enjoy** [indʒɔ́i] 탄 **즐기다,** 향락
하다, 기뻐하다
enjoy는 마음에 든다는 의미
다 : 우리는 모두 올해 휴가를
**즐겁게 보냈다.** 우리는 특히
시골에서 휴가 보내기를 **좋아
한다.**

**enough** [ináf] 1형 **충분한,** …
할 만큼의 2 부 **충분히,** (…하
기에 족할) 만큼
enough는 어떤 것이 필요한
만큼 있다는 의미다 : 소풍에
온 사람 모두가 먹을 만큼 **충
분한** 음식이 있었다. 나는 새
배트를 살 수 있는 **충분한** 돈
을 모았다.

**enter** [éntər] 탄 자 **···에 들어
가다,** ···에 입학〔가입〕하다
enter는 어떤 곳으로 들어간다
는 의미다. 문을 통해 방에 **들
어간다** : 우리는 대문을 지나서
정원에 **들어섰다.**

**envelope** [énvəlòup] 명 **봉투,**
주머니 모양의 것
envelope는 물건을 담을 수
있도록 접은 종이다. 사람들은
편지와 카드들을 envelope에

넣어 우편으로 보낸다 : 나는
envelope에 주소를 썼다.

**environment** [inváiərənmənt]
명 **주위를 에워싸는 것**〔사정,
정황〕 ; 환경
environment는 우리 주위에
있는 공기, 물, 흙과 그 외의
모든 사물을 말한다.

**equal** [í:kwəl] 형 **같은,** 동등
한 ; 평등한
equal은 양이나 크기가 같다
는 의미다 : 1 다임은 10페니와
**같다.**

**erase** [iréis|iréiz] 탄 **지우다,**
닦아내다 ; 삭제하다
erase는 연필이나 분필로 생
긴 흔적을 닦아낸다는 의미
다 : 마크가 칠판에 쓰여있는
것을 모두 **지워버렸다.**

**eraser** [iréisər|-zə] 명 **지우
개** ; 지우는 사람〔물건〕
eraser는 흔적을 없애는 데 사
용하는 것이다 : 나는 끝에
eraser가 달린 연필 몇 자루가
필요하다. eraser로 칠판의 분

필 자국을 없앨 수 있다.

**escalator** [éskəlèitər] 몡 에스
컬레이터, 자동(식) 계단
escalator는 위나 아래로 움직
이는 일련의 계단이다 : 톰과
그의 어머니는 escalator를 타
고 상점 3층으로 올라갔다.

**escape** [iskéip, es-] 재타 달아
나다, 탈출〔도망〕하다 ; 모면하
다
escape는 어떤 것에서 도망친
다는 의미다 : 앵무새가 새장에
서 **날아가 버렸다.** 사람들은
태풍이 몰려오고 있다는 사실
을 알았기 때문에, 피해를 입
지 않고 (태풍을) **모면할 수**
있었다.

**especially** [ispéʃəli, es-] 閏 특
히, 유별나게, 각별히
especially는 다른 어느 것보
다도 더 많은 의미를 부여한다
는 의미다 : 사라는 많은 것들
을 해보기를 좋아한다. 그녀는
**특히** 연기하기를 좋아한다.

**even** [íːvən] 혱 ① (표면이) **평**
**평한, 평탄한 ; 고른, 한결같은**
② (…와) **같은 높이의,** 동일

선상의 ③ **짝수의**
1 even은 평평하거나 고르다
는 의미다 : 방바닥은 **평평하**
**다.** 스커트 둘레가 전부 **고르**
**게** 되어 있는지 보여 주시오.
2 even은 또한 높이가 같다는
의미다 : 눈이 높이 쌓여 자동
차 지붕과 **높이가 같을** 정도
다.

3 even은 2로 나누어지는 수
다 : 숫자 2, 4, 6, 8과 10은 **짝**
**수다.**

**evening** [íːvniŋ] 몡 **저녁, 해질**
**무렵, 밤**
evening은 하루 중 어두워지
기 시작하는 때로, 오후와 밤
사이를 말한다 : 우리는 eve-
ning 여섯 시에 저녁을 먹는
다.

**ever** [évər] 閏 ① 일찍이 ; 이
제까지, 지금까지 ② 언제나,
**언젠가**
ever는 「언젠가」라는 의미다 :
코끼리를 본 **적이** 있니 ?

**every** [évri] 혱 **모든,** 하나도
남김없는, 어떤 …도 다 ; 매
…, …마다

every는 무리의 전부 혹은 각각의 개체를 의미한다 : **모든** 염소가 풀을 먹고 있었다. 우리반 사람 **모두**가 여행을 갔다.

**everybody** [évribàdi | -bɔ̀di] 때 각자 **모두**, 누구나, 모두
everybody는 모든 사람을 뜻한다 : 우리 가족은 **모두** 낚시질 하기를 좋아한다.

**everyone** [évriwʌ̀n] 때 **모든 사람**, 누구나
everyone은 everybody의 의미다 : 파티에 온 **사람**은 **누구나** 즐거운 시간을 보냈다.

**everything** [évriθìŋ] 때 **모든 것**, 무엇이든 다, 만사
everything은 모든 것을 뜻한다 : 거센 눈보라가 몰아친 후에, **모든 것이** 눈으로 뒤덮여 버렸다.

**everywhere** [évrihwɛ̀ər] 부 **어디든지**, 도처에, 곳곳에 ; 어디에〔로〕…하든지
everywhere는 모든 장소를 뜻한다 : 엘리자베스는 신발을 찾으려고 집안 **구석구석**을 살펴

보았다.

**evil** [íːvəl] 형 **나쁜**, 사악한
evil은 사람들을 해치려고 한다는 뜻이다 : 이야기 속의 **사악한** 마법사는 마술을 써서 왕자와 공주를 당나귀로 변하게 했다.

**excellent** [éksələnt] 형 **우수한**, 뛰어난, 탁월한
excellent는 아주 훌륭하다는 뜻이다 : 빌리는 **기발한** 생각을 했다.

**except** [iksépt] 전 **…을 제외하고**, …외에는
except는 사물이나 사람이 제외되었다는 뜻이다 : 조 **이외의** 모든 사람이 그 영화를 좋아했다. 나는 점심값과 열쇠**만** 빼고 모든 것을 배낭에 집어 넣었다.

**excited** [iksáitid] 형 **흥분한**,

활발한, 활기 띤
excited는 어떤 일에 몹시 즐거워한다는 뜻이다. **흥분을 하면** 그 밖의 다른 것을 생각하기가 어렵다 : 수는 갓 태어난 새끼 고양이를 보자 **흥분했다**. 빌리는 크리스마스 때문에 너무 **흥분해서** 잠을 잘 수가 없었다.

**exciting** [iksáitiŋ] 형 **흥분시키는**, 아슬아슬한, 조마조마하게 하는
exciting은 사람에게 엄청난 기운을 느끼게 하는 것이다 : 우리는 **손에 땀을 쥐게 하는** 이야기책을 읽었다. 피터는 불꽃놀이가 좀 무섭다는 느낌이 들었지만 **흥분을 자아내는** 놀이라는 생각도 했다.

**excuse** [ikskjúːz] 타 …을 면제하다 ; 용서하다 ; 변명하다 2 명 용서 ; 변명, 구실, 핑계 ; 사과
1 excuse는 사람에게 어떤 것을 시키지 않는다는 뜻이다 : 선생님은 질이 양호선생님에게 진찰을 받을 수 있도록 수업을 **면제해 주셨다**. 나는 무릎을 다쳐서 체육 수업을 **면제받았**

다.
2 excuse는 또한 용서한다는 뜻이다 : 일찍 떠나게 되어서 **죄송합니다**.
3 excuse는 누가 어떤 일을 왜 했는지, 아니면 왜 하지 않았는지를 밝힌다는 뜻이다 : 앨버트는 감기에 걸려 목이 아팠기 때문에 월요일에 결석했다고 excuse를 했다.

**exercise** [éksərsàiz] 1 명 ① 운동 ② 연습, 실습, 훈련 ③ 연습 문제, 과제 2 타 자 ① 운동시키다 ; 훈련시키다 ② 작용시키다 ; 발휘하다 ; 이행하다
1 exercise는 몸이 건강하고 튼튼하게 되도록 하는 것이다 : 수영은 좋은 exercise다.

2 운동을 할 때는 근육을 사용한다.

**exit** [égzit, éksit] 명 출구
exit는 방이나 건물을 나가는 통로다 : 우리 교실에는 두 개의 exit가 있다.

**expand** [ikspǽnd] 타 자 펴다, 펼치다 ; **팽창시키다** ; 부풀게 하다

expand는 더 커진다는 뜻이
다 : 풍선에 공기를 불어 넣으
면 **팽창한다**.

**expect** [ikspékt] 団 **기대하다,**
예상하다, 예측하다 ; (…이라
고) 생각하다
expect는 어떤 일을 기대하거
나 무언가가 일어날 것으로 생
각한다는 의미다 : 우리는 일요
일 가족 소풍에 50명이 갈 것
으로 **예상하고** 있다.

**expensive** [ikspénsiv] 團 **값**
**비싼** ; 비용이 드는
expensive는 어떤 것에 많은
돈이 든다는 의미다 : 나는 빨
간색 펜보다 **값이 비싸지** 않아
서 푸른색 펜을 샀다.

**explain** [ikspléin] 団困 **설명하**
**다, 분명〔명백〕하게 하다**
explain은 다른 사람들이 이해
할 수 있도록 어떤 것에 대해
서 말해 준다는 의미다 : 폴은
우리 모두가 그 경기를 할 수
있도록 경기 규칙들을 **설명해**
**주었다.**

**explode** [iksplóud] 団困 **폭발**
**하다**

explode는 갑자기 큰 소리를
내며 터진다는 의미다 : 불꽃이
**폭발하자** 하늘이 밝고 아름답
게 빛났다.

**explore** [ikspló:r] 団困 **탐험하**
**다, 답사하다** ; 탐구하다
explore는 전에 가 본 적이 없
는 곳에 가서 그 곳이 어떤 곳
인지를 알아본다는 의미다 : 동
굴이나 밀림을 **탐험하기**를 좋
아하는 사람도 있다. 사람들은
또한 물 속이나 그 밖의 다른
곳을 **탐험한다.**

**explorer** [ikspló:rər] 團 **탐험**
**가**
explorer는 새로운 것을 발견
하기 위해 멀리 떨어진 곳까지
여행하는 사람이다 : explorer
는 육지와 물 속 그리고 우주
를 조사한다.

**explosion** [iksplóuʒən] 團 **폭**
**발**, 폭파
무엇인가가 폭발을 할 때,
explosion이라고 한다 : 가스
explosion으로 건물 유리창들
이 깨졌다.

**extra** [ékstrə] 형 여분의, 임시의 ; 별도의 ; 특별한

extra는 필요 이상으로 많다는 의미다 : 나는 라디오에 쓸 여분의 건전지를 가지고 있다.

**eye** [ái] 명 눈 ; 시각, 시력 ; 관찰력

eye는 사물을 볼 수 있는 몸의 한 기관이다. 사람에게는 두 개의 eye가 있다. 대부분의 동물도 eye가 두 개다 : 그 갓난아기는 eye를 감고 잠들었다.

E

**face** [féis] 1 **명** 얼굴 ; 얼굴 표정 2 **타 자** …을 향하다, …에 면하다

1 face는 머리의 앞부분이다. face에는 눈, 코, 입이 있다.

2 face는 또한 어떤 것을 향해 얼굴을 돌린다는 뜻이다. 네가 오늘 아침 일찍 태양을 **마주 보고** 있었다면, 동쪽을 **향해 있었다.**

**fact** [fǽkt] **명** 사실, 진상
fact는 사실과 다르지 않은 것이다. 미국에 50 개 주가 있다는 것은 fact다.

**factory** [fǽktəri] **명** 공장

factory는 물건을 만들기 위해 많은 사람들이 함께 일하는 건물이다. 자동차는 factory에서 만든다.

**fair¹** [fέər] **형** ① 공평한, **공정한, 정당한** ② (여성이) 아름다운, 예쁜 ③ (날씨가) 좋은, 맑게 갠
fair는 모든 사람을 똑같이 대한다는 뜻이다 : 규칙 위반은 **정당하지 못한** 일이다.

**fair²** [fέər] **명** (정기적으로 열리는) 장 ; **박람회, 품평회** ; 유원지
fair는 사람들이 재미있게 놀려고 가는 곳이다. 자기가 키우거나 만든 것을 fair에 출품하는 사람들도 있다. 대부분의 fair에는 타고 노는 기계와 게임 놀이들이 있다.

**fairy** [fέəri] 명 요정
fairy는 요술을 부릴 수 있는 아주 작은 가공의 인물이다. fairy들은 날아 다닐 수 있다 : 카르멘은 fairy들에 관한 이야기책을 즐겨 읽는다.

**fall** [fɔ́:l] 1 자 떨어지다, (비·눈 등이) 내리다 ; 넘어지다 2 명 ① 떨어짐, 낙하 ② 가을
1 fall은 어떤 곳에서 내려온다는 뜻이다 : 하늘에서 눈이 **내리고 있었다.**

2 물건이나 사람이 갑자기 바닥이나 땅에 떨어질 때 fall이라고 한다 : 헨리는 자전거를 타다 심하게 **넘어졌다.**
3 fall은 또한 한 해의 계절을 뜻한다. fall은 여름이 가고 겨울이 되기 전에 온다. 많은 사람들이 이 계절을 fall이라고 부르는 까닭은 이 시기에 나무에서 잎들이 **떨어지기** 때문이다. fall을 나타내는 다른 말은 autumn이다.

**fallen** [fɔ́:lən] 동 fall (떨어지다)의 과거분사형
fallen은 fall의 한 형태다 : 온도가 **내려갔다.**

**false** [fɔ́:ls] 형 잘못된, 틀린 ; 거짓의, 허위의 ; 부정한
false는 사실이 아니거나 옳지 않다는 뜻이다 : 식물에게 빛이 필요하지 않다는 생각은 **잘못된 것이다.**

**family** [fǽməli] 명 ① 가족, 식구 ② 같은 혈통의 것
1 family는 보통 어머니, 아버지 그리고 그들의 자식들을 말한다. 자식과 한 쪽 부모만으로 구성된 family도 있다. 할아버지, 할머니, 이모, 삼촌과 사촌들도 family의 일원이다.

2 어떤 점에서 닮은 데가 있는 동물이나 식물 혹은 집단도 family에 속한다.

**famous** [féiməs] 형 유명한
famous는 많은 사람들이 사람이나 사물에 관해 안다는 뜻이다 : 토머스 에디슨은 전등을 발명해서 **유명해졌다.** 뉴욕시는 마천루로 **유명하다.** 자유의 여신상은 **유명한** 조각상이다.

**fancy** [fǽnsi] 1 명 공상, 환상 2 형 공상의, 상상의 ; 화려한, 장식적인

fancy는 평소보다 더 예쁘거
나 좋다는 뜻이다 : 클레어는
파티에 **화려한** 새 드레스를 입
었다.

**fantasy, phan-** [fǽntəsi, -zi]
명 **공상**, 상상, 환상 ; **공상적
인 작품**, 공상의 산물
fantasy는 실재하지 않는 것이
다. 다른 행성에 사는 사람들
에 관한 책도 fantasy다.
fantasy는 reality(현실)의 반
대말이다.

**far** [fáːr] 1 부 ① [장소·거리·시
간] **멀리**(에), 아득히 ② [정
도] 훨씬, 매우 2 형 **먼**, 멀리
로의
far는 얼마쯤 떨어져 있다는
뜻이다. 달은 여기에서 아주
멀리 **떨어져** 있다. 달에 가려
면 오랜 시간이 걸린다.

**farm** [fáːrm] 명 **농장**, 농원, 농
지
farm은 사람들이 동물이나 식
물을 기르는 곳이다. 우리가
먹는 식품 중에는 farm에서
나는 것이 많다.

**farmer** [fáːrmər] 명 **농부**, 농

장주인
farmer는 농장에서 일하는 사
람이다 : farmer들은 아침 일찍
일을 시작한다.

**farther** [fáːrðər] [far의 비교
급] 1 부 **더 멀리**, 더 앞으로 2
형 **더 먼**, 더 앞의
farther는 단어 far에서 생긴
말이다 : 레이의 종이 비행기가
테리 것보다 **더 멀리** 날아 갔
다.

**fast** [fǽst | fáːst] 1 형 **빠른**, 급속
한, 민첩한 2 부 **빠르게**, 급속
히, 서둘러서
fast는 빨리 간다는 뜻이다 :
아이들은 토끼가 그들보다 더
**빨리** 달려서 잡을 수가 없었
다.

**fat** [fǽt] 형 **살찐**, 뚱뚱한 ; 지방
이 많은
fat은 크고 둥글다는 의미다 :
돼지와 하마는 **뚱뚱하다**.

**father** [fáːðər] 명 **아버지**, 부친
father는 적어도 자식이 한 명
은 있는 남자다. father와 어
머니는 자기 자식들을 보살핀
다.

**faucet** [fɔ́ːsit] 명 (수도·통 등
의) **꼭지**, 수도 꼭지, 주둥이,
마개
faucet은 물을 틀거나 잠그기

위해 사용하는 것이다. 세면대
와 욕조에는 모두 faucet이 있
다.

에 드는 모자를 쓴다.

**fault** [fɔːlt] 명 잘못, 실수 ; 결
점, 단점, 흠
무언가를 잘못했을 때 fault라
는 말을 쓴다 : 야구공에 유리
창이 깨진 것은 내가 공을 던
졌기 때문에 내 fault다.

**favor | favour** [féivər] 명 호
의, 친절(한 행위) ; 부탁, 청
원 ; (호의 · 애정을 나타내는)
선물, 기념품
1 favor는 누군가 딴 사람을
위해서 하는 좋은 일이다 : 나
는 제인에게 그녀의 책을 도서
관에 반납해 주는 favor를 베
풀었다.
2 favor는 또한 파티에 온 사
람 누구에게나 주는 것이다 :
리언의 파티에 온 아이들은 모
두 풍선을 favor로 받았다.

**favorite** [féivərit] 1 형 마음에
드는, 아주 좋아하는 2 명 마
음에 듦, 특히 좋아하는 것[사
람]
favorite은 가장 좋아한다는 뜻
이다 : 토니는 항상 자기 **마음**

**fear** [fíər] 1 명 두려움, 무서움,
공포 ; 근심, 걱정 2 타 두려워
하다, 무서워하다 ; 걱정하다
1 fear는 두려울 때 느끼는 감
정이다. 많은 사람들이 물이나
높은 곳 혹은 아주 좁은 공간
에 fear를 느낀다.
2 fear는 무서워한다는 뜻이
다 : 찰리는 아직 수영하는 법
을 모르기 때문에 물을 **무서워
한다.**

**feast** [fíːst] 명 향연, 잔치, 연
회 ; (종교적인) 축제
feast는 보통 많은 손님을 대
접하려고 마련한 많은 양의 특
별한 식사를 말한다 : 식탁에는
휴일 feast용 음식이 많이 쌓
여 있었다.

**feather** [féðər] 명 깃털, 깃
feather는 새의 피부에 나는 것

이다. 대부분의 새는 feather
로 덮여 있다. feather는 가볍
고 부드럽다.

**February** [fébruèri | -ruəri]
명 2월
February는 일년 중 두번째 달
이다. February는 28일이나
29일이며, 1월이 가고 3월이
되기 전에 온다.

**fed** [féd] 동 feed(먹을 것을 주
다)의 과거·과거분사형
fed는 feed의 한 형태다 : 다이
애나는 오늘 아침 토끼에게 상
추를 **먹이로 주었다.**

**feed** [fíːd] 타 ① (어린애·동물
에게) **먹을 것을 주다,** (음식
을) 먹이다 ② (가축에게) 사
료〔풀〕를 주다
feed는 동물이나 사람에게 음
식을 준다는 뜻이다 : 토드는
자기의 애완동물인 토끼에게
당근을 **먹인다.** 한나는 그녀의
어린 남동생에게 **음식을 먹였
다.** 먹이를 주는데 사용하는
그릇을 feeder라고 한다. 우리
는 겨울에 새들을 위해 feeder
에 씨앗을 넣어 둔다.

**feel** [fíːəl] 1 타 자 ① **만지다,** 만
져보다 ; **느끼다,** …라고 생각
하다 ② (…한) 느낌을 주다,
**감촉이 …하다** 2 명 **감촉, 촉
감 ; 느낌,** 분위기
1 feel은 무언가를 만지거나
접촉을 통해 알게 된다는 뜻이
다 : 나는 얼굴에 빗방울이 떨
어지는 것을 **느낄 수 있다.** 나
는 새끼 고양이의 부드러운 털
을 **만졌다.**

2 feel은 또한 기분이 어떠한
지를 안다는 뜻이다 : 기분이
**언짢니?** 지미는 오늘 서커스
구경을 갈 예정이어서 **기분이
좋다.**
3 feel은 또한 무언가를 만질
때 느끼는 점을 말한다 : 앨버
트는 면의 **감촉을** 좋아한다.

**feeling** [fíːliŋ] 명 ① **감정,** 심
정, 기분 ② **촉감,** 감촉 ③ **감
각,** 지각
feeling은 기분을 알 수 있는
상태를 말한다. 무섭거나, 행
복하거나, 흥분하거나, 슬프거
나, 피곤하거나, 화가 날 때면
feeling이 나타난다 : 나는 누
군가 내게 소리를 지르면, 간
혹 feeling이 상할 때가 있다.

F

**feet** [fíːt] 명 foot 의 복수형
feet는 두 개 이상의 발을 나타낸다. 사람은 foot가 두 개고, 개와 고양이는 foot가 네 개다 : 아서는 키가 4 feet가 넘는다.

**fell** [félə l] 동 fall (떨어지다)의 과거형
fell은 단어 fall에서 생긴 말이다 : 어젯밤 많은 비가 내려서 거리가 온통 젖어 있다.

**felt** [félt] 동 feel (느끼다)의 과거 · 과거분사형
felt는 feel의 한 형태다 : 어제 베리는 너무 아파서 외출하지 못했다. 고양이 털을 만졌을 때, 부드럽다는 느낌이 들었다.

**female** [fíːmeiə l] 1 명 여성, 부인 ; (동물의) 암컷 2 형 (아이 · 새끼를 낳는) 여자의, 여성의 ; 암컷의
female은 여자 아이나 성인 여자를 말한다. 엄마와 이모는 female이다. 동물도 female일 수 있다 : 우리집 고양이 마틸다는 female이다.

**fence** [féns] 명 울타리, 담, 담장, 펜스 ; 징애물
fence는 두 곳으로 갈라놓기 위해 만든다. fence는 나무나 금속 혹은 돌로 만들 수 있다.

**fern** [fə́ːrn] 명 고사리
fern은 가는 잎이 많고 꽃이 피지 않는 식물이다. fern은 숲에서 자란다.

**ferry** [féri] 명 나룻배, 연락선 ; 나루터, 도선장
ferry는 강 건너편으로 사람이나 자동차를 실어 나르는 배다 : 우리는 ferry를 타고 그 섬에 갔다.

**festival** [féstivə l] 명 축제 ; 축제일
festival은 특별한 경축 기간을 말한다. 대부분의 festival은 일년에 한 번 치르지만, 그 기간은 하루나 그 이상 계속될 수도 있다. festival에는 흔히 연회와 댄스, 그리고 퍼레이드가 따른다.

**fever** [fíːvə r] 명 (병으로 인한) 열, 발열 ; 열병

fever가 있을 때는 체온이 높고 몸이 뜨겁다. fever가 있으면 아프다.

**few** [fjú:] 형 ① [a few로] 조금은 있는, 약간의 ; 소수의 ② [few로] **거의 없는**, 아주 조금뿐인
few는 무언가가 많지 않다는 의미다 : 나는 읽어야 할 페이지가 **조금** 남아 있다. 우리는 **며칠** 동안 여행을 떠났다.

**fiction** [fíkʃən] 명 **소설, 지어낸 이야기**, 꾸며낸 일, 허구
fiction은 실제로 존재하지 않는 사람과 사실에 관해 쓴 이야기다. fiction의 등장인물들은 가상의 인물로 작가의 상상에 따라 그려진다.

**field** [fí:əld] 명 ① 들, **들판**, 벌판, **밭** ② **경기장**, 필드 ③ (활동의) 분야
1 field는 나무가 없는 지역이다. field는 풀이나 식량을 재배하기 위해 이용된다 : 우리는 이 field에 옥수수를 심었다.
2 field는 또한 몇몇 경기가 치루어 지는 장소를 말한다 : (미식) 축구는 football field (축구장)에서 한다.

**fierce** [fíərs] 형 **사나운** ; 격렬한, 맹렬한
fierce는 거칠고 위험하다는 의미다 : 굶주린 사자는 **사납다**. 이번 폭풍은 이제까지 내가 겪은 것 중 **가장 거센** 폭풍이다.

**fight** [fáit] 1 자타 **싸우다**, 다투다 ; 전투하다 2 명 **싸움**, 격투, 전투
1 fight는 의견이 맞지 않는 사람에게 화를 낸다는 의미다. **싸우는** 사람들은 서로 고함을 지르거나 간혹 서로 치기도 한다 : 엘리자베스는 학교에서 다른 아이들과 **싸워서** 벌을 받았다.
2 fight는 사람들이 화가 나서, 서로 고함을 지를 때를 말한다 : 나는 오늘 언니와 **싸웠다**.

**fill** [fíl] 타자 **채우다**, …에 (가득) 채워 넣다 ; 가득차다, 충만하다
fill은 어떤 것을 가득 채운다는 의미다 : 블레이크는 양동이에 모래를 **가득 채웠다**.

**fin** [fín] 명 지느러미
fin은 물고기의 가늘고 평평한 기관의 하나다. 물고기는 몸 양쪽에 fin이 있다. 물고기는 fin을 이용해 헤엄을 치고 물 속에서 몸의 균형을 잡는다.

**finally** [fáinəli] 부 마침내, 드디어, 결국 ; 최후로
finally는 「마침내」라는 뜻이다 : 버스를 3시간이나 타고 온 후에야, 우리는 **마침내** 산 속 야영장에 도착했다.

**find** [fáind] 타 찾아내다, 발견하다 ; 알다, 깨닫다
find는 어디에 있는지 살펴본다는 뜻이다 : 보브는 신발을 찾으려고 방을 둘러보다가, 침대 밑에서 **찾아낸다.** 어제도 그는 침대 밑에서 양말을 3켤레 **찾아냈다.**

**fine** [fáin] 형 ① 멋진 ; (하늘이) 맑은 ② 건강한 ; 기분좋은
fine은 아주 좋다는 뜻이다 : 오늘은 산책하기에 **좋은** 날씨다. 지난 주에 헬렌은 아팠지만, 지금은 **좋아졌다.**

**finger** [fíŋgər] 명 손가락
finger는 손의 한 부위다. 양 손에는 각각 5개의 finger가 있다. 이 finger 가운데 하나가 엄지 손가락이다. 손톱은 각 finger 끝에 있는 딱딱한 부분을 말한다.

**finish** [fíniʃ] 타 끝내다, 마치다 ; 마무리하다, 완성하다
finish는 무언가의 끝에 이르렀다는 뜻이다 : 쓰고 있는 편지를 거의 다 **끝냈다.**

**fire** [fáiər] 명 불, 화재
fire는 불타고 있는 것에서 나는 불꽃과 열 그리고 빛이다 : fire로 낡은 공장이 전소했다.

**fire engine** [fáiər èndʒin] 명 소방차
fire engine은 소방수들이 불을 끌 수 있도록 사닥다리와 그밖의 장비를 갖추고 있는 트럭이다. 소방수들은 fire engine을 타고 화재 현장에 간다.

**firefighter** [fáiərfàitər] 명 소방수, 소방대원
firefighter는 불을 끄는 것이 직업인 사람이다. firefighter들은 사람들이 화염에 휩싸인 건

물에서 탈출할 수 있도록 돕는
다. firefighter들은 아주 긴 사
닥다리를 이용해 고층 건물에
난 불을 끈다.

**firefly** [fáiərflài] 명 개똥벌레,
빛을 내며 나는 곤충
firefly는 빛을 내는 작은 곤충
이다. 밤에는 firefly가 마치
아주 작은 불빛이 켜졌다 꺼졌
다하는 것처럼 보인다.

**fireplace** [fáiərplèis] 명 벽난
로, 난로
fireplace는 실내에서 불을 피
우기 위해 트여있는 곳이다.
fireplace에는 연기를 내보내는
굴뚝이 있다 : 스키를 타고 집
으로 돌아오면, 내 가족과 나
는 몸을 따뜻하게 하려고
fireplace에 불을 피우는 것을
좋아한다.

**fireworks** [fáiərwə̀:rks] 명 폭
죽, 불꽃놀이
fireworks는 요란한 소리를 내
며 멋진 불꽃 쇼를 생기게 한
다. fireworks는 특별한 때에
사용한다. 우리 마을은 (미국)
독립 기념일을 경축하기 위해
밤에 fireworks를 터뜨렸다.

**first** [fə́:rst] 1 형 첫째의, 첫
번째의, 최초의 2 부 첫 번째
로, 최초로, 맨 먼저, 처음으
로 3 명 첫째, 최초 ; 첫날 ; 1
위, 일등
first는 다른 모든 것에 앞선다
는 뜻이다 : 글자 A는 알파벳
의 **첫 번째** 글자다.

**first aid** [fə́:rst éid] 명 응급처
치, 구조요법
간혹 사람은 사고를 당하거나
갑자기 아플 때가 있다. first
aid는 의사가 오기 전에 이런
사람들에게 주는 도움이다.

**fish** [fíʃ] 1 명 물고기, 어류 ; 생
선 2 타 자 물고기를 잡다, 낚
시질하다
1 fish는 물에서 사는 동물이
다.

2 fish는 물고기를 잡는다는
뜻도 있다 : 아이들은 바닷가
근처에서 **낚시질하는** 것을 좋
아한다. **물고기를 잡는** 사람을
fisherman (어부 · 낚시꾼) 이라
고 한다. 물고기를 잡아서 파
는 fisherman들도 있다.

**fist** [físt] 명 주먹

fist는 꽉 오므려 쥔 손이다 :
톰과 빌리는 fist로 문을 두드
렸다.

**fit** [fít] 1 [타][자] ① ···에 맞다, 적
합하다 ; 어울리다 ② 꼭 끼워
넣다, 짜맞추다 2 [형] (꼭) **맞
는, 알맞은, 적당한** ; 어울리는
1 fit은 사이즈가 맞는다는 뜻
이다 : 카르멘이 즐겨 입는 셔
츠가 작년에 그에게 꼭 **맞았는
데**, 지금은 그가 너무 커서 맞
지 않는다.
2 fit은 무언가를 작은 공간에
넣는다는 뜻이다 : 찰리는 상자
하나에 장난감을 전부 **담을 수
가** 없었다.

**five** [fáiv] 1 [명] **다섯,** 5 2 [형] **다
섯의,** 5의
five는 4보다 하나 큰 수다.
five는 **5** 라고 쓴다. 4+1=**5.**

**fix** [fíks] [타] ① **고정〔고착〕시키
다,** 붙이다 ; (날짜・장소 등
을) 정하다 ② **고치다,** 수리
〔수선〕하다
fix는 고장이 났을 때, 다시
작동하게 만든다는 뜻이다 : 폴
의 자전거 바퀴가 휘어졌지만,

그는 새 것처럼 바퀴를 **고쳤
다.**

**flag** [flǽg] [명] **기, 깃발 ; 기 모
양의 것**
flag는 여러가지 색깔이 있는
천 조각이다. 그림이 그려진
flag도 있다. 모든 나라는 자
국의 flag가 있다 : 미국의 flag
는 빨간색과 흰색 그리고 파란
색으로 되어 있다.

**flame** [fléim] [명] **불길, 불꽃,
화염**
flame은 타오르는 불에서 빛
을 내며 움직이는 부분이다.
flame은 아주 뜨겁다.

**flash** [flǽʃ] 1 [자][타] **번쩍이다, 번
득이다** 2 [명] **섬광, 번득임, 플
래시**
flash는 짧은 순간에 밝은 빛
을 낸다는 뜻이다 : 등대는 밤
이나 안개 속에서도 선원들이
뱃길을 찾아갈 수 있도록, **번
쩍번쩍 빛을 낸다.**

**flashlight** [flǽʃlàit] 명 손전등, 회중전등, 플래시 ; 섬광등
flashlight는 손에 가지고 다닐 수 있는 작은 등불이다. 사람들은 밤에 외출할 때, flashlight를 휴대한다.

**flat** [flǽt] 형 ① 평평한, 납작한, 평탄한, 울퉁불퉁하지 않은 ② 단호한, 솔직한
flat은 튀어나오거나 움푹 패인 곳이 없다는 뜻이다 : 벽과 마루는 **평평하다.**

**flavor|-vour** [fléivər] 명 (독특한) 맛, 풍미, 향미
flavor는 음식이나 음료의 맛이다 : 이 디저트는 오렌지 flavor가 난다.

**flew** [flú:] 동 fly²(날다)의 과거형
flew는 단어 fly²에서 생긴 말이다 : 새들은 개가 짖어대자 **날아가 버렸다.**

**float** [flóut] 자 타 뜨다, 띄우다, 표류하다 ; 공중에 뜨다, 공중에 떠다니다
1 float는 물위에 머무른다는 뜻이다 : 레이는 **물에 뜨는** 장난감 배가 있다. 우리는 돛배를 **띄우려고** 호수에 갔다.
2 float는 또한 공중에서 천천히 움직인다는 뜻이다 : 아기가 풍선을 놓자, 풍선이 집 위로 높이 **떠올랐다.**

**flock** [flák | flɔ́k] 명 (양·작은 새 등의) **무리,** 떼
flock은 양 떼를 말한다 : flock을 한데 모을 줄 아는 개들도 있다.

**flood** [flʌ́d] 명 홍수, 범람
flood는 물이 강 언저리 위로 넘쳐 흐를 때 일어나는 것이다. flood는 보통 비가 많이 온 후에 나지만, 간혹 눈이 녹는 봄에도 일어난다.

**floor** [flɔ́:r] 명 ① 마룻바닥, 플로어 ② (건물의) **층**
1 floor는 방에서 걷거나 서 있을 수 있는 부분이다 : 우리집 침실 floor에는 푸른색 양탄자가 깔려 있다.
2 floor는 또한 건물의 일부다. 고층 건물에는 floor가 많다 : 엄마 사무실은 second floor(2층)에 있다.

**flour** [fláuər] 명 밀가루, 분말 ; 고운 가루
flour는 밀에서 얻는다. flour는 빵과 케이크같은 식품을 구워 만드는 데 사용한다 : 우리

는 슈퍼마켓에서 우유와 달걀,
미기린과 flour를 샀다.

**flower** [fláuə*r*] 명 꽃
flower는 씨가 생기는 식물 부
위다. flower는 여러가지 다양
한 색깔을 띠고 자란다. 대부
분의 flower는 날씨가 따뜻할
때 피며, 향기가 좋은 flower
도 있다.

**flown** [flóun]  동  fly² (날다)의
과거분사형
flown은 단어 fly²에서 생긴 말
이다 : 앵무새가 새장에서 **날아
가** 버렸다.

**flu** [flú:] 명 유행성 감기, 독감
《influenza의 단축형》
flu에 걸리면, 열이 나고 아프
다 : 찰리는 flu에 걸렸을 때,
머리와 배가 아프고 온 몸이
쑤셨다.

**fly**¹ [flái] 명 파리
fly는 두 개의 아주 얇은 날개

가 있는 곤충이다. 우리가 흔
히 보는 fly를 housefly(집파
리)라고 한다.

**fly**² [flái]  자 타 (새·비행기가)
**날다, 비행기로 가다** ; (연 등
을) **날리다, 띄우다**
1 fly는 날개로 **하늘을 난다**는
뜻이다 : 데일은 할머니를 방문
하려고 비행기를 **타고 갔다.**
나비들이 꽃 주위를 **날고 있었
다.**
2 fly는 또한 공중에 띄운다는
뜻이다 : 우리는 바람부는 날,
공원에서 연을 **날리는** 것을 좋
아한다.

**fog** [fág, fɔ́:g|fɔ́g] 명 안개
fog는 지면에 가까이 낀 구름
이다 : 우리는 fog 때문에 길을
찾을 수 없었다.

**fold** [fóuəld] 타 **접다**, 접어 포
개다 ; (다리 등을) 구부리다
fold는 접는다는 뜻이다 : 데이
비드는 텐트를 **접어서** 가방에
넣는 법을 나에게 가르쳐 주었
다. 제프리와 로버트는 담요를
**개서** 벽장에 넣었다.

**follow** [fálou|fɔ́l-]  타 자  ···을

쫓다, …을 따라가다 ; …의 다음에 오다, …의 뒤를 잇다
1 follow는 뒤에 간다는 뜻이다 : 제인은 그녀의 오빠를 **쫓아다니기를** 좋아한다. 그녀는 오빠가 가는 곳이면 어디든 **따라간다.**
2 follow는 또한 뒤에 온다는 뜻이다 : 해마다 3월은 2월 **다음에** 온다.

**food** [fúːd] 명 **식품, 음식**
food는 우리가 먹는 것이다 : 살아 있는 것은 모두 성장하고 생명을 유지하기 위해 food가 필요하다. 빵, 우유 그리고 야채는 중요한 food다.

**foot** [fút]   명   **발 ; 피트《길이의 단위, 약 30.48 cm》**
foot는 다리 끝에 있는 신체부위다 : 조지는 feet에 특수한 신발(축구화)을 신고 축구를 한다.

**football** [fútbɔ̀ːəl] 명 **미식축구, 축구 ; 축구공**
1 football은 큰 경기장에서 두 팀이 하는 경기다. 각 팀 선수는 11명이다. 한 팀의 선수들이 공을 던지며 상대 팀 골을 향

해 공을 갖고 달리면, 상대 팀은 이들을 저지하려고 한다.
2 football은 또한 이 경기에 사용되는 공의 이름이다.

**footprint** [fútprìnt] 명 **발자국**
footprint는 발이나 신발로 낸 자국이다 : 더러운 장화를 신은 아이들이 마루에 footprint를 냈다. 눈 속에 난 사슴의 footprint를 보았니 ?

**for** [《약》 fər, 《강》 fɔ́ːr] 전 ① [목적·대상·의향·기대·소망] **…을 위해서** ② [방향·행선지] **…을 향하여,** …**방향으로** ③ [시간·공간] **…동안**
1 for는 어떤 것이 있어야하는 이유를 나타낸다 : 목수에게는 공구를 넣어두는 상자가 있다. 나는 너에게 **주려고** 이 책을 샀다.
2 for는 무엇을 향한다는 뜻도 있다 : 사람들은 하늘을 **향해** 손을 뻗을 수는 있지만 닿을 수는 없다.
3 for는 무언가가 얼마동안 계속되고 있음을 나타낸다 : 우리는 두 시간 **동안** 야구를 했다. 나는 매일 1시간**씩** 영어를 공

부한다.

**forest** [fɔ́:rəst, fár-|fɔ́r-]　명
숲, 삼림
forest는 나무들이 많이 있는
곳이다. 많은 종류의 동물들이
forest에 살지만, forest에 사
는 사람은 거의 없다.

**forever** [fərévər]　부　영원히,
영구히 ; 끊임없이, 항상
forever는 결코 끝이 없을 것
이라는 뜻이다 : 그 동화 속에
나오는 소년 소녀는 **영원히** 늙
지 않기를 원했다.

**forgave** [fərgéiv]　동　forgive
(용서하다)의 과거형
forgave는 단어 forgive에서
생긴 말이다 : 헨리는 물어보지
도 않고 자기 자전거를 탄 동
생을 **용서해 주었다.**

**forget** [fərgét]　타　잊어버리다,
생각이 안나다 ; (소지품 등을)
놓아두고 잊다
forget은 무언가를 기억하지
못한다는 뜻이다 : 제인은 내
주소를 **잊어 버릴까봐** 적어 두
었다.

**forgive** [fərgív]　타　용서하다,
니그리이 봐주다
forgive는 누군가에게 화를 그
만낸다는 뜻이다 : 앤은 동생
잭이 그녀의 스웨터를 찢어 놓
고 **용서해** 달라고 하자, 그를
**용서해 주었다.**

**forgot** [fərgát|-gɔ́t]　동　forget
(잊다)의 과거·과거분사형
forgot은 forget의 한 형태다 :
마거릿은 차고에 자전거를 **잊
어버리고** 넣지 않아 자전거가
비에 젖어 버렸다.

**forgotten** [fərgátən|-gɔ́t-]　동
forget (잊다)의 과거분사형
forgotten은 forget의 한 형태
다 : 조는 간혹 학교에 도시락
을 가져오는 것을 잊어버린다.
그는 이번 주에 두 번이나 도
시락을 **잊어버리고** 안가져 왔
다.

**fork** [fɔ́:rk]　명　(식탁용의) **포크**
fork는 음식을 먹는 데 사용하
는 도구다. fork는 한 쪽은 손
잡이고 다른 쪽은 끝이 뾰족한
것이 두 개 이상 있다 : 나는
fork로 고기와 야채를 먹는
다.

**form** [fɔ́ːrm] 1 **명** 모양, 형태 ; 방식, 종류 2 **타****자** 형태를 이루다, (어떤) 모양이 되다
1 form은 어떤 것의 형태나 닮은 모양을 말한다. 구름은 다양한 여러 form을 띠고 있다.
2 form은 모양을 갖추게 한다는 뜻이다 : 마리아는 찰흙 한 덩어리를 빚어 개를 **만든다**. 그녀는 또 다른 찰흙을 빚어서 기린을 **만들었다**.
3 form은 또한 어떤 것의 한 종류를 뜻한다. 얼음은 물의 또 다른 form이다.

**forward** [fɔ́ːrwərd] **부** 앞으로, 전방으로, 앞쪽의, 앞부분의
forward는 앞쪽을 향한다는 뜻이다 : 스튜어트는 자기 이름이 불리워지자 **앞으로** 나갔다.

**fossil** [fásəl | fɔ́s-] **명** 화석
fossil은 오래 전에 살았던 동식물이 남아 있는 것이다. fossil은 바위나 흙 혹은 진흙 속에서 발견된다. 공룡의 **뼈**와 발자국은 fossil이다.

**fought** [fɔ́ːt] **동** fight (싸우다) 의 과거 · 과거분사형
fought는 단어 fight 에서 생긴 말이다 : 아버지는 내가 여동생과 **싸우지** 말았어야 했다고 말씀하셨다.

**found** [fáund] **동** find (찾아내다) 의 과거 · 과거분사형
found는 find의 한 형태다 : 딕은 항상 자기 침대 밑에서 무언가를 찾아낸다. 어젯밤 그는 거기에서 야구 배트를 **찾아냈다**.

**fountain** [fáuntən] **명** ① 분수, 분수탑 ② 원천, 근원 ③ 샘, 수원
fountain은 공중으로 치솟아 오르는 물줄기다. 보기에 멋있는 fountain도 있고, 식수로 쓰이는 fountain도 있다.

**four** [fɔ́ːr] 1 **명** 넷, 4, 네 개, 네 사람 2 **형** 4 의, 네 개의, 네 사람의
four는 3 보다 하나 더 큰 수다. four는 4 라고 쓴다. 3+1=4.

**Fòurth of Julý** **명** 미국 독립 기념일《1776 년 7 월 4 일에 독립을 선언한 기념일》
Fourth of July는 미국의 탄생을 경축하는 미국의 휴일이다. 이 날을 Independence Day라

고도 한다.

**fox** [fáks|fɔ́ks] 명 여우
fox는 야생 동물이다. 대부분의 fox는 작고 야윈 개처럼 보이지만, 털이 많고 꼬리가 크다. fox는 또한 뾰족한 큰 귀와 긴 코가 있다.

**free** [fríː] 형 ① 자유로운, 속박 없는 ; 한가한 ② 마음대로 … 할 수 있는 ③ 무료의
1 free는 무언가를 대가로 돈을 지불할 필요가 없다는 뜻이다 : 공원에서 하는 마술쇼는 **무료다.**
2 free는 또한 방해를 받지 않거나 갇혀있지 않다는 뜻이다 : 그 고양이는 **자유롭게** 돌아 다녔다.

**freeze** [fríːz] 자타 얼다, 얼어 붙게 하다

freeze는 날씨가 몹시 차거워지면 고체가 된다는 뜻이다. 물이 **얼면** 얼음으로 변한다 : 우리는 연못이 **얼자** 스케이트를 탔다.

**fresh** [fréʃ] 형 ① (음식이) **싱싱한**, 신선한 ② (물이) **소금기가 없는** ③ (공기가) 맑은
1 fresh는 방금 만들었거나, 방금 일을 끝냈다거나 혹은 막 수확했다는 뜻이다 : 우리는 조니의 정원에서 딴 **싱싱한** 토마토를 먹었다. 우리 슈퍼마켓은 **싱싱한** 생선을 판다. 이 빵은 오늘 아침에 구워서 아주 **신선하다.**
2 fresh는 또한 소금기가 없다는 뜻이다. 강과 호수 그리고 연못의 물은 **소금기가 없는** 물 (담수)이다. 바닷물은 소금물이다.

**Friday** [fráidei, -di] 명 금요일
Friday는 1주일 가운데 하루다. Friday는 목요일이 지나고 토요일이 되기 전에 온다.

**fried** [fráid] 1 동 fry (튀기다)의 과거・과거분사형 2 형 기름에 튀긴, 프라이 요리의
fried는 fry의 한 형태다 : 튀긴 닭고기를 즐겨 먹는 사람들이 많다.

**friend** [frénd] 명 친구 ; 동조자
friend는 굉장히 좋아해서 같이 있는 게 즐거운 사람을 말

한다 : 조이스와 켄드류는 친한 friend 사이여서 같이 노는 경우가 많다. 나는 새로 이사온 이웃 사람들과 friend가 되었다(친해졌다).

**friendly** [fréndli] 혱 **친한,** 우호적인, **친절한** ; 지지하는
friendly는 사람이나 동물이 우호적이라는 뜻이다 : 여행을 갔을 때, 나는 가는 곳마다 **친절한** 사람들을 만났다. 리언의 개는 내 개보다 더 **붙임성이 있다.**

**frighten** [fráitən] 태 **깜짝 놀라게 하다, 두려워하게 하다**
frighten은 사람이나 동물을 두려워하게 한다는 뜻이다 : 나는 다른 아이들이 나의 만성절 전야제 의상을 보고 **깜짝 놀라기**를 바란다. 고양이에게 **놀라** 새들이 날아가 버렸다.

**frog** [frág, frɔ́:g | frɔ́g] 몡 **개구리**
frog는 작은 동물이다. frog는 매끄러운 살가죽과 커다란 눈 그리고 튼튼한 뒷다리가 있다. frog는 물가에 살며 파리를 잡아 먹는다.

**from** [《약》 frəm, 《강》 frʌ́m, frám | 《약》 frəm, 《강》 frɔ́m] 젠 ① [분리·이탈·출발점·기점] ⋯에서, ⋯으로부터 ② [출처·유래] ⋯에서 ③ [원인·동기·이유] ⋯이기 때문에 ④ [간격·부재] ⋯에서 (떨어져)
**1** from은 무언가가 시작된 곳이나 때를 뜻한다 : 우리 가족은 도시**에서** 시골로 이사했다. 루이스는 8 시**부터** 3 시까지 학교에 있다.
**2** from은 또한 발단이 되는 사람이나 장소 혹은 사물이 있다는 뜻이다 : 나는 캠프장에서 친구가 **보낸** 편지를 받았다.
**3** from은 또한 거리가 떨어져 있다는 뜻이다 : 마리의 학교는 그녀의 집**에서** 2 마일 **떨어져** 있다.

**front** [frʌ́nt] 몡 **앞, 앞쪽, 앞부분, 정면**
front는 앞을 향해 있거나 맨 먼저 다가오는 부분이다. 가슴은 몸 front에 있다 : 마크의 집 front에 사과나무 한 그루가 있다.

**frost** [frɔ́ːst | frɔ́st] 명 서리 ; 결
빙, 동결
frost는 얼어서 얼음이 된 지
면의 물이다. 추운 날에는 유
리창에 낀 frost를 볼 수 있
다.

**frown** [fráun] 1 명 눈살을 찌푸
리기, 찡그린 얼굴 2 자 타 눈
살을 찌푸리다, 못마땅한〔싫
은〕 얼굴을 하다, (생각에 잠
겨) 심각한 표정을 짓다
1 frown은 smile(미소)의 반대
말이다. 기분이 나쁘다거나 생
각에 잠겨 있다는 것을 frown
으로 알 수 있다.
2 frown은 얼굴을 찡그린다는
뜻이다 : 마이크는 어떻게 해야
할지 몰라서 얼굴을 찡그렸다.

**froze** [fróuz] 동 freeze (얼다)의
과거형
froze는 freeze의 한 형태다 :
어젯밤 날씨가 너무 추워서 호
수가 꽁꽁 얼었다.

**frozen** [fróuzən] 1 동 freeze
(얼다)의 과거분사형 2 형
언, 결빙한
frozen은 freeze의 한 형태다.
얼음은 물이 얼어붙은 것이다.

**fruit** [frúːt] 명 과일 ; 열매
fruit는 씨가 있는 식물 부위
다. 사과, 복숭아, 오렌지들은
fruit의 일종이다 : 우리는 fruit
를 썰어서 샐러드를 만들었다.

**fry** [frái] 타 자 기름으로 튀기
다, 프라이로 하다
fry는 아주 뜨거운 기름에 요
리를 한다는 뜻이다 : 목요일마
다 짐의 아버지는 가족이 저녁
식사로 먹을 닭고기를 튀긴다.

**full** [fúəl] 형 가득한, 충만한
full은 더 이상 담을 수 없다는
뜻이다 : 톰은 컵에 주스를 따
르다 가득차자 그만 따랐다.

**fun** [fʌ́n] 명 재미있는 일 ; 재
미, 장난
fun은 즐겨하는 일이다 : 폴의
생일 파티에서 폴과 그의 친구
들은 노래를 부르며 오락을 했
다. 모두 아주 재미나게 놀았
다.

**funeral** [fjúːnərəl] 몡 **장례식,**
**장례 행렬**
funeral은 누군가가 죽어서 사
람들이 모이는 때다. funeral
은 사람들에게 자신들이 얼마
나 슬퍼하는 지를 보여 주고,
자신들의 슬픈 감정을 친구나
가족들과 나눌 수 있는 기회를
준다.

**funny** [fʌni] 혱 **익살맞은, 우스**
**운, 재미있는 ; 별난, 기묘한**
1 funny는 사람들을 웃게 한다
는 뜻이다 : 조의 삼촌은 **익살**
**맞은** 농담을 한다.
2 funny는 또한 이상하다는
뜻이다 : 메리는 뒷마당에서 **이**
**상한** 냄새를 맡았다.

**fur** [fəːr] 몡 **털 ; 모피, 털가죽**
fur는 부드럽고 숱이 많은 털
이다. 고양이, 개, 다람쥐, 곰
그리고 그 밖의 동물들은 fur
로 덮여 있다. fur는 추운 날
씨에도 이들 동물들을 따뜻하
게 해준다.

**furnace** [fəːrnəs] 몡 **화로, 아**

궁이 ; 용광로
furnace는 큰 스토브와 비슷하
다. furnace는 집과 건물을 따
뜻하게 하는 데 사용된다 : 우
리집 furnace는 겨울에 우리를
따뜻하게 해준다.

**furniture** [fəːrnitʃər] 몡 **가구,**
**세간, 비품**
탁자, 의자 그리고 침대는 각
기 다른 종류의 furniture다 :
우리는 이사할 때, 우리집
furniture를 전부 트럭 한 대에
실었다.

**future** [fjúːtʃər] 1 몡 **미래,** 장
래 2 혱 **미래의, 장래의**
1 future는 앞으로 다가 올 시
간을 뜻한다 : 박람회에서 우리
는 future의 자동차 모델을 보
았다.
2 future는 또한 앞으로 다가
올 시간에 일어날 일을 뜻한
다 : 작가가 되는 것이 내
future의 계획이다.

**gallon** [gǽlən] 명 갤런《용량의 단위》
gallon은 액체의 양이다. 1 gallon은 4쿼트(quart)와 같다 : 우유와 휘발유는 gallon으로 판다.

**gallop** [gǽləp] 1 자 (말을 타고) 전속력으로 달리다, 질주하다 2 명 갤럽《말의 가장 빠른 발놀림》
gallop은 빠르게 달린다는 뜻이다. 말들이 전력을 다해서 빨리 달리는 것이 galloping 이다.

**game** [géim] 명 놀이, 오락 ; 경기, 시합, 게임
game은 놀거나 재미있게 지내는 방법이다 : 카드로 하는 game도 있고 공으로 하는 game도 있다. 모든 game에는 규칙이나 주의 요강이 있다.

**garage** [gərá:ʒ, -dʒ|gǽra:ʒ, -ridʒ] 명 차고, 주차장 ; 자동차 정비소 ; (비행기) 격납고
garage는 자동차나 트럭을 세워 두는 건물이다 : 많은 집들이 garage를 갖고 있다. 도시의 대형 garage는 수백대의 차를 수용할 수 있다.

**garbage** [gá:rbidʒ] 명 (부엌의) 쓰레기 ; 음식 찌꺼기
버려지는 음식이나 그 밖의 다른 것들을 garbage라고 한다 : 소풍이 끝난 후, 우리는 garbage를 garbage can(쓰레기통)에 버렸다.

**garden** [gá:rdən] 명 뜰, 정원, 화원, 과수원

garden은 꽃이나 야채를 기르
는 곳이다 : 사촌들이 찾아오
면, 그들은 항상 자신들의
garden에서 재배한 신선한 토
마토를 가지고 온다.

**gas** [gǽs] 명 기체, 가스
 1 gas는 고체도 액체도 아니
 며, 용기에 가득히 채워서 팽
 창시킬 수 있는 것이다 : 공기
 와 증기는 gas다.
 2 gas는 또한 요리나 집 난방
 에 사용하기 위해 한데 섞은
 혼합 기체를 뜻한다 : 우리 집
 에는 gas 스토브가 있고, gas
 난방을 한다.
 3 gas는 또한 gasoline을 간
 단하게 말하는 방법이다.

**gasoline, -lene** [gǽsəliːn,
 二-二] 명 가솔린, 휘발유
 gasoline은 불에 타는 액체의
 일종이다 : 자동차나 트럭을 가
 게 하려면 gasoline을 연소시
 켜야 한다.

**gate** [géit] 명 문, 성문, 관문
 gate는 담에 나있는 문이다.
 안으로 열리는 gate가 있는가
 하면, 밖으로 열리는 gate도
 있다 : 학교는 정문으로만 들어

가거라.

**gather** [gǽðər] 자타 모으다,
 그러모으다, 모이다 ; 따서 모
 으다, 채집하다
 gather는 모여들다 또는 한데
 모아 놓다라는 뜻이다 : 사람들
 은 종종 **모여서** 음악을 듣는
 다. 피터는 장난감을 다 **그러
 모아서** 한 상자에 넣었다.

**gave** [géiv] 동  give (주다)의
 과거형
 gave는 단어 give에서 생긴
 말이다 : 클레어는 할아버지를
 **꼭 껴안았다.** 어머니는 점심으
 로 올리버에게 야채 수프와 땅
 콩 버터 샌드위치를 **주었다.**

**geese** [gíːs] 명 goose 의 복수형
 geese는 두마리 이상의 기러기
 를 나타낸다 : 가을에는 겨울을

나기 위해 남쪽으로 날아가는 geese를 볼 수 있다.

**genius** [dʒíːnjəs] 몡 천재, 귀재
genius는 지능이 매우 뛰어난 사람이다 : 저 과학자는 genius 였다.

**gentle** [dʒéntl] 혱 상냥한, 온순한, 예의바른 ; **부드러운**
gentle은 사람이나 사물이 다치지 않도록 매우 주의한다는 의미다.

**geography** [dʒiágrəfi | -ɔ́g-] 몡
**지리학** ; 지리 ; 지리(학)서
geography를 공부하면, 지구의 여러 지역에 대해 알게 된다. geography는 지역의 위치와 그 곳의 특징을 알려준다.

**germ** [dʒə́ːrm] 몡 **세균**, 병균
germ은 병에 걸리게 할 수 있는 아주 작은 생명체다. germ은 너무 작아서 현미경 없이는 볼 수 없다 : 재채기를 할 때, 나는 germ이 다른 사람에게 옮지 않도록 입과 코를 가린다.

**get** [gét] 팀짜 ① **얻다** ; 사다, **타다**, 잡다, **받다** ② (병에) 걸리다 ; (손해를) 입다 ; …하게 하다 ; 가지고 있다 ③ 이르다, 도착하다 ④ **가서 가지고 오다** ; …이 되다
1 get은 주어진 것을 갖는다는 뜻이다 : 다이애나는 매년 할머니에게서 양말 한 켤레를 선물 **받는다.**
2 get은 또한 가서 가지고 온다는 뜻이다 : 헬렌은 배가 고파서 냉장고에 가서 사과를 **꺼내왔다.**
3 get은 「…이 되다」라는 뜻일 수 있다 : 테리는 집까지 줄곧 뛰어오느라고 **지쳤다.**
4 get은 도착한다는 뜻이다 : 버스가 고장난 날, 모두가 학교에 **지각했다.**
5 get up은 일어난다는 뜻이다 : 간혹 토드는 넘어질 때도 있지만, 항상 다시 **일어난다.**

**ghost** [góust] 몡 유령, 망령
ghost는 일종의 가공 인물이다. 죽은 사람이 ghost로 다시 살아난다고 믿는 사람도 있다 : 아이들은 만성절 전날밤에 ghost로 분장했다.

**giant** [dʒáiənt] 1 휑 **거대한, 위대한** 2 몡 **거인 ; 거대한 동〔식〕물**
1 giant는 보통 것보다 훨씬 더 크다는 뜻이다 : 말처럼 큰 생쥐라면 **거대한** 생쥐일 것이다.
2 giant는 굉장히 키가 큰 사람이다 : 동화속에는 giant 이야기가 많이 나온다.

**gift** [gíft] 몡 **선물 ; (타고난) 재능, 자질**
gift는 다른 사람에게 주는 특별한 물건이다 : 이 책들은 사촌들로부터 받은 생일 gift다. gift의 다른 말은 present 다.

**gigantic** [dʒaigǽntik] 휑 **거인 같은, 거대한, 방대한**
gigantic은 거인 처럼 크다는 뜻이다 : 산꼭대기에 올라가서, 우리는 **엄청나게 큰** 바위들을 보았다.

**giggle** [gígl] 1 団 囘 **킥킥 웃다** 2 몡 **킥킥거리는 웃음**
1 giggle은 바보같이 웃는다는 뜻이다 : 내 어린 동생이 귀에 양말을 끼었을 때, 우리는 **킥킥거리며 웃었다.**

2 giggle은 또한 잠시 짓는 바보 같은 웃음을 뜻한다 : 어릿광대가 미끄러져 넘어지자, 관중속에서 아이들이 **킥킥 소리를 내며 웃어댔다.**

**ginger** [dʒíndʒər] 몡 **생강**
ginger는 식물의 뿌리다. ginger를 가루로 만들어 음식에 넣는다. ginger로 또한 캔디와 생강이 든 빵을 만든다.

**gingerbread** [dʒíndʒərbrèd] 몡 **생강을 넣은 케이크, 생강이 든 빵**
gingerbread는 케이크의 일종이다. gingerbread의 독특한 맛의 일부는 생강에서 나는 것이다.

**giraffe** [dʒirǽf|-rɑ́ːf] 몡 **기린**
giraffe는 큰 동물로, 긴 다리와 아주 긴 목을 갖고 있다. giraffe의 몸은 갈색의 반점으로 뒤덮여 있다. giraffe의 목은 나무 꼭대기의 잎을 따 먹을 수 있을 정도로 길다.

**girl** [gə́ːrəl] 몡 **여자 아이, 소녀**
girl은 여자 아이다. girl이 자라서 성숙한 여성이 된다.

**give** [gív] 団 **주다, 공급하다 ; 치르다, 지불하다**
give는 다른 사람에게 어떤 것을 가지게 한다는 뜻이다 : 앨버트는 매년 누이 생일에 선물을 **준다**.

**given** [gívən] 동  give(주다)의 과거분사형
given은 give 의 한 형태다 : 톰은 장난감 몇 개를 **줘 버렸다**.

**glad** [glǽd] 형 **기쁜**, 반가운 ; 기꺼이 (…하는)
glad는 즐겁다는 뜻이다 : 우리는 어제 야구 시합을 보러 갔는데, 날씨가 좋아서 **기분이 좋았다**.

**glass** [glǽs | glɑ́ːs] 명 ① 유리 ; (유리)컵 ; 술잔 ② [복수로]안경
1 glass는 (투명해서) 속을 들여다 볼 수 있는 단단한 물질이다. 창문은 glass로 되어 있다. glass는 주의하지 않으면 깨지기 쉽다.
2 glass는 마시는 데 이용하는 그릇이다. glass 는 대개 유리나 플라스틱으로 되어 있다 : 아기는 glass로 마시는 법을 배우고 있다. 식탁 위에 glass 와 접시가 각각 여섯 개씩 놓

여 있다.
3 더 잘 보이도록 눈에 glasses를 쓰는 사람도 있다 : 아버지는 glasses를 쓰고 신문을 보신다.

**globe** [glóub] 명 1 공, 구체 ; 지구 ; 천체 2 **지구의**, 천체의
globe는 세계 지도가 그려진 공이다 : 우리는 지리수업을 대비해서 globe에 미국과 그 밖의 다른 나라들이 어디에 있는지 공부해 두었다.

**glove** [glʌ́v] 명 **장갑** ; (야구·권투용) 글러브
1 glove는 손을 보호하기 위해 손에 낀다. glove는 천이나 모직물 혹은 가죽이나 플라스틱으로 만든다. 사람들은 대개 추운 날씨에 손을 따뜻하게 하려고 glove를 낀다.
2 야구 선수들은 공을 잡기 위해 특별한 종류의 glove를 낀다. 야구 glove 는 종류가 많다.

**glue** [glú:] 명 아교 ; 풀
glue는 끈끈한 액체다. glue는 마르면, 물건들이 따로 떨어지지 않도록 붙어 있게 한다.

**go** [góu] 자 ① **가다**, 떠나다, 나아가다 ② 없어지다 ; 죽다 ③ **…으로 되다, 진행되다 ; 작동하다** ④ 이르다, 미치다, 통하다
1 go는 한 곳에서 다른 곳으로 이동한다는 뜻이다 : 톰은 아침에 학교에 **간다**. 그는 어제 날씨가 좋지 않아서 학교에 **지각했다.**

2 go는 또한 어떤 곳을 떠난다는 뜻이다 : 너무 늦어서, **가야만** 한다.
3 go는 어딘가로 통한다는 뜻이다 : 그 길은 숲을 **지나,** 곧장 도시까지 **뻗어있다.**
4 go to sleep는 잠들다는 뜻이다 : 해리는 두눈을 감았지만 **잘 수가** 없었다.

**goal** [góuəl] 명 ① 골, (골에 넣어 얻은) **득점** ; 결승점 ② 목적지 ; (노력·야심의) 목적, **목표**

1 goal은 사람이 갖고 싶어 하거나 되려고 하는 것이다 : 토니의 goal 은 가게를 소유하는 것이다. 내 goal은 배우가 되는 것이다.
2 goal은 몇몇 경기에서 선수들이 공을 넣으려고 하는 곳이다.

**goat** [góut] 명 염소
goat는 동물이다. 대부분의 goat는 뿔이 있고, 수염이 있는 goat도 많다. 젖을 얻기 위해서 농장에서 사육하는 goat가 있는가 하면, 야생 동물로 산에서 사는 goat도 있다. goat 는 온순한 동물이다.

**goggles** [gáglz│gɔ́glz] 명 고글, **먼지〔바람〕를 막는 안경, 수중 안경,** 선글라스
goggles는 눈을 보호하기 위해서 쓰는 안경의 일종이다. 작업 중에 먼지나 날아다니는 흙으로부터 눈을 보호하기 위해서 goggles 를 쓰는 사람이

있는가 하면, 물 속에서 물고기나 임초를 보기 위해서 goggles를 쓰는 사람도 있다.

**gold** [góuəld] 몡 ① 금 ; 황금 ; 금제품 ; **금화** ② **금빛, 황금색**
1 gold는 땅이나 개울에서 발견되는 노란 금속이다. 사람들은 gold로 보석이나 주화를 만든다 : 그는 **금시계**를 찼다.
2 gold는 또 그 금속의 빛깔을 말한다 : 가을에 나뭇잎들은 붉은색과 **황금색**으로 변한다.

**goldfish** [góuəldfiʃ] 몡 금붕어
goldfish는 물고기의 일종이다. goldfish는 대개 작고 오렌지색이다. 집에서 어항에 goldfish를 기르는 사람들이 많다.

**gone** [gɔ́ːn, gán|gɔ́n] 동 go(가다)의 과거분사형
gone은 단어 go에서 생긴 말이다 : 스튜어트는 운동장에 너무 늦게 도착해서 친구들이 벌써 모두 집에 **가고** 없었다.

**good** [gúd] 혱 ① 좋은, 유익한, 훌륭한 ② 친절한 ; 선량한 ③ 행복한, 기분 좋은 ④ 유능한 ; 충분한
good은 자기나 다른 사람들의 마음에 든다는 의미다 : 이 복숭아는 맛이 **좋다.** 리처드는 고래에 관한 **유익한** 책을 읽고 있다. 내 개는 **착해서** 가구 위를 넘어다니지 않는다.

**good-bye** [gùdbái] 캄 안녕, 안녕히 가〔계〕십시오
good-bye는 떠날 때 하는 말이다 : 방과 후, 나는 선생님께 good-bye라고 말했다.

**gooey** [gúːi] 혱 끈적끈적한, 들러붙는
gooey는 무엇에나 달라붙는다는 의미다 : 꿀은 땅콩 버터 샌드위치에 바르면 떨어지지 않는다. 꿀은 단지에서 꿀을 떠내는 숟가락에도 들러붙는다. 꿀은 몹시 **끈적끈적하다.**

**goose** [gúːs] 몡 기러기(의 암컷) ; 기러기 고기
goose는 날 수 있고, 헤엄도 칠 수 있는 새다. goose는 오

리와 비슷하지만, 훨씬 더 크다.

**gorilla** [gərílə] 명 **고릴라**

gorilla는 크고 대단히 힘이 센 동물이다. gorilla는 다리가 짧고 팔이 긴 원숭이의 일종이다. gorilla는 열매와 야채를 먹고 사는 겁많은 동물이다.

**got** [gát|gɔ́t] 동 get (얻다, 도착하다)의 과거・과거분사형

got은 단어 get에서 생긴 말이다 : 악단에 새 드럼 연주자가 **들어왔다.** 나의 어머니는 6시에 **퇴근하셨다.**

**gotten** [gátən|gɔ́t-] 동 get (얻다, 사다, …이 되다)의 과거분사형

gotten은 get의 한 형태다 : 엘리자베스는 양말을 너무 많이 **사서** 어떻게 처리해야 할지를 몰랐다. 내가 언니에게 바나나를 사주려고 했으나, 그녀가 벌써 **사버렸다.** 앨버트는 놀지 못할 정도로 **지쳐본** 적이 없다. 배리는 7시 쯤에 벌써 **일어나** 있었다.

**government** [gʌ́vərnmənt] 명 ① 행정부, 내각 ② 지배, 통치 ; 행정권

government는 국가, 주 또는 도시를 통치하는 사람들의 무리다. government는 법을 제정하고 모든 사람들이 그 법을 지키는지 확인한다. 미국에서는 government의 수반을 대통령이라고 한다.

**grab** [grǽb] 타 자 **움켜쥐다, (붙)잡다** ; 낚아채다, 가로채다

grab은 갑자기 붙잡는다는 뜻이다 : 아기가 내 머리칼을 **움켜쥐었다.**

**grade** [gréid] 명 **학년 ; 성적, 평점 ; 등급,** 계급

1 grade는 학교에서의 일년간의 학업 과정이다. 같은 grade에 있는 아이들은 대부분 나이가 거의 같다 : 너 몇 **학년**이니 ?
2 grade는 또한 학생이 성취한 학업의 질을 나타내는 점수다 : 아서는 시험에서 90**점**을 받았다.

**grain** [gréin] 명 **곡물, 곡류, 곡식 ; 낟알,** (모래・소금・포

도 등의) 한 알
1 grain 은 밀, 벼 또는 옥수수
의 씨다 : 밀가루와 시리얼은
여러가지 종류의 grain으로 만
든다.

2 grain은 또한 아주 작은 알
갱이다 : 모래의 grain은 대단
히 작다.

**gram, gramme** [grǽm] 명 그
램《무게 단위》
gram은 작은 양의 무게다. 1
페니는 무게가 대략 3 gram이
다.

**grandchild** [grǽndtʃàiəld] 명
손자, 손녀
grandchild는 아들이나 딸의
자식이다. grandchild는 손녀
나 손자를 말한다.

**grandfather** [grǽndfɑ̀:ðər] 명
할아버지, 조부
grandfather는 아버지의 아버
지나 어머니의 아버지다. 간혹
grandfather를 grandpa라고도
한다.

**grandmother** [grǽndmʌ̀ðər]
명 할머니, 조모
grandmother는 아버지의 어머

니나 어머니의 어머니다. 간혹
grandmother를 grandma 나
nana 라고도 한다 : grand-
mother께서는 털실로 내 스웨
터를 뜨고 계셨다.

**grandparent** [grǽndpɛ̀ərənt]
명 조부모
grandparents는 어머니의 부
모와 아버지의 부모다. grand-
parents는 할아버지와 할머니
를 말한다.

**grape** [gréip] 명 포도 ; 포도나
무
grape는 과일의 일종으로, 작
고 둥글다. grape는 대개 딸
기류보다 크다. grape는 자주
색이나 초록색을 띠고 있다.

**grapefruit** [gréipfrù:t] 명 그레
이프프루트
grapefruit는 노란색의 둥근 과
일로, 오렌지보다 크다. 속이

연분홍색인 grapefruit 도 있다.

**grass** [grǽs | gráːs] 명 풀, 초원, 목초지 ; **잔디**(밭)
grass는 잔디밭이나 들판에서 자라는 녹색 식물이다. 많은 동물들이 grass를 먹는다.

**grasshopper** [grǽshɑ̀pər | gráːshɔ̀pə] 명 **메뚜기**, 풀무치, 여치
grasshopper 는 곤충이다. grasshopper는 뛰어 오를 때 긴 뒷다리를 사용한다. grasshopper는 또한 날개가 있지만, 대부분 날지 못한다.

**gray | grey** [gréi] 1 형 ① **회색의**, 잿빛의 ② 백발이 성성한, 희끗희끗한 ③ 창백한, 음침한
2 명 **회색**, 잿빛
gray는 검정색과 흰색을 섞으면 얻을 수 있는 색이다 : 눈동자가 **창백하거나** 머리가 **희끗희끗한** 사람도 있다. 폭풍을 몰고 오는 구름은 대개 **잿빛이**다. 그녀는 큰 **회색** 고양이를 보았다.

**great** [gréit] 형 ① **큰** ; (수·양 등이) 많은 ; 두드러진 ; 중요한 ② **위대한** ; 장엄한 ; 고귀한 ; 멋진
1 great는 크거나 많다는 뜻이다 : **많은** 사람들이 선거에 투표를 했다. 그는 **큰** 집을 샀다.

2 great는 또한 훌륭하거나 아주 중요하다는 뜻이다 : 내 여동생은 커서 **위대한** 가수가 되고 싶어한다.

**green** [gríːn] 1 명 **녹색** ; 풀밭, 잔디밭 2 형 **녹색의**, 풀빛의
green은 봄과 여름에 자라는 풀과 나뭇잎들의 색깔이다 : **푸른** 야채는 먹을 수 있다. 파란색과 노란색을 섞으면 **녹색**이 된다. 소나무는 일년내내 green을 띠고 있다.

**greenhouse** [gríːnhàus] 명 **온실**
greenhouse는 식물을 재배하는 특별한 건물이다. greenhouse는 대개 지붕이 유리로 되어 있고, 내부 공기는 항상 따뜻하다.

**grew** [grúː] 동 grow (성장하다)의 과거형
grew는 단어 grow 에서 생긴 말이다 : 그 작은 식물을 햇볕이 드는 곳에 두자, 빨리 **자랐다.**

G

**grin** [grín] 1 자 이를 드러내고 웃다, 싱글거리다 2 명 싱글싱글 웃음 ; 이를 드러냄
grin은 크게 짓는 미소다 : 보브는 만성절 전야에 쓰려고 호박에 **방긋 웃는 모양**을 새겼다. 그는 익살맞게 보이려고 비뚤어지게 **웃는 모습**으로 새기는 것을 좋아한다.

**grocery** [gróusəri] 명 ① 식료잡화 판매업 ② [복수로] 식료잡화류 ; 식(료)품점
1 grocery는 식품과 그 밖의 다른 물건을 파는 가게다 : 우리는 grocery store(식품점)에서 달걀, 우유, 빵, 그리고 비누를 샀다.

2 groceries는 식품점에서 살 수 있는 식품과 그 밖의 물건이다 : 우리는 토요일 아침에 groceries를 세 봉지 샀다.

**ground** [gráund] 명 ① 흙, 토지 ; 지면, 땅 ② 운동장, 그라운드
ground 는 땅이다 : 존은 ground에 넘어져서 무릎을 다쳤다. 식물은 ground에서 자란다.

**group** [grú:p] 명 그룹, 떼, 집단, 무리
group은 한 데 모인 셋 이상의 사람이나 물건이다 : 한 group의 아이들이 토요일에 공원에서 공놀이를 했다.

**grow** [gróu] 자타 ① 성장하다, 자라다 ; 점점 …이 되다 ② 키우다, 재배하다
1 grow는 점점 커진다는 뜻이다. 동식물은 나이를 먹을수록 **성장한다.**
2 grow up은 성인 남녀가 된다는 뜻이다 : 어른이 되면, 너는 아버지보다 키가 더 클지도 모른다.

**growl** [gráuəl] 자 (개 등이 성내어) **으르렁거리다** ; (사람이) 투덜거리다 ; (천둥이) 울리다
growl은 목구멍으로 굵직하면서도 낮게, 성난 소리를 낸다는 뜻이다 : 누군가가 문을 두드리자 개들이 **으르렁거렸다.**

**grown** [gróun] 동 grow(성장하다)의 과거분사형
grown은 grow 의 한 형태다 : 저 나무는 집을 덮을 정도로 크게 **자랐다.**

**grown-up** [gròunʌ́p] 몡 성인,
어른
grown-up은 다 자란 사람이다.
부모는 grown-ups다. grown-
up의 다른 말은 adult다.

**guard** [gáːrd] 1 目 **지키다, 보
호하다 ; 경계하다** ; 조심하다
2 몡 ① 망보기, **감시,** 경계
② **호위자 ; 수위,** 감시자
1 guard는 위험으로부터 안전
하게 하거나 어떤 것을 감시한
다는 뜻이다 : 우리가 휴가로
여행을 떠나면, 우리 개가 집
을 **지킨다.**
2 guard는 또한 어떤 사람이
나 물건을 지키는 사람이다 :
박물관의 guard는 우리에게
그림에 손대지 말라고 했다.

**guess** [gés] 目困 **추측하다, 알
아 맞히다** ; (…라고) 생각하다
guess는 답을 생각해 내려고
애쓴다는 뜻이다 : 엘렌은 자기
뒤에 누가 있는지 **맞혀보려고**
했다.

**guest** [gést] 몡 (초대받은) **손
님** ; (하숙·여관의) 숙박인
guest는 방문하러 온 사람이
다 : 어머니의 친구이신 롱 부
인은 어제 저녁 식사 때까지
계셨다. 롱 부인은 우리집의
guest 였다.

**guitar** [gitáːr] 몡 **기타**
guitar는 여섯 개 혹은 그 이
상의 줄이 있는 악기다 : 사람
들은 줄을 치거나 뜯어서
guitar를 연주한다.

**gun** [gʌ́n] 몡 **총,** 권총
gun은 무언가를 쏘는 데 쓰는
무기다 : 나는 집으로 뛰어 들
어가서 gun을 꺼냈다.

**gym** [dʒím] 몡 **체육관** ; 체육,
체조
gym은 사람들이 경기나 운동
을 하는 큰 방이나 건물이다 :
우리는 gym에서 농구를 한다.

G

**habit** [hǽbit] 명 습관, 버릇
habit 은 자주 하게 되는 것을 말한다 : 조지는 매일밤 자기 전에 물을 한 잔 마시는 habit 이 있다. 사람들은 좋은 habit 을 가질 수도 있고, 나쁜 habit 을 가질 수도 있다.

**habitat** [hǽbitæt] 명 (특히 동식물의) **서식지**, 번식지 ; 산지 ; (생물의) 환경, 주거환경
habitat 는 동물이나 식물이 살면서 성장하는 곳이다 : 사막은 낙타의 habitat 다.

**had** [hǽd] 동 have (가지고 있다)의 과거 · 과거분사형
had 는 단어 have 에서 생긴 말이다. 이미 일어난 일이나 소유하고 있는 것에 대해 이야기할 때 had 를 쓴다 : 헬렌은 어제 체조 수업이 **있었다.**

**hadn't** [hǽdnt] had not 의 단축형
hadn't 는 had not 을 줄여서 말한 것이다 : 제임스는 텔레비전을 보고 싶었지만, 아직 숙제를 **다하지 않았었다.**

**hair** [hɛ́ər] 명 **머리카락**, 머리털 ; **털**
hair 는 머리에서 자라는 것이다. 팔과 다리에도 잔 hair 가 있다 : 마크는 처음으로 hair 를 자르고〔이발을 하고〕 있다.

**haircut** [hɛ́ərkʌ̀t] 명 **이발** ; 헤어 스타일

haircut 은 머리털을 깎을 때나 깎는 법을 말한다 : 메리는 매달 haircut 을 한다.

**half** [hǽf|hɑ́:f] 명 반, 2 분의 1 ; 30 분 ; (시합의) 전반(후반)
half 는 크기가 같은 두 개 가운데 하나를 말한다 : 앨은 샌드위치를 half 로 잘랐다. half 로 자른 두 개는 크기가 똑같았다.

**hall** [hɔ́:əl] 명 홀, 집회장 ; 강당 ; (집의) 현관 ; 복도
hall 은 건물 안의 한 장소다. hall 은 한 방에서 다른 방으로 혹은 여러 방으로 통하게 되어 있다. 짧은 hall 도 있고, 길고 좁은 hall 도 있다.

**Halloween** [hæ̀louíːn] 명 핼로윈, 만성절(萬聖節)의 전날밤
Halloween 은 축제일로, 10 월의 마지막 날이다. Halloween 에는 사람들이 독특한 의상을 입고, 이웃 사람들에게 사탕을 얻으러 갈 수 있다.

**halves** [hǽvz|hɑ́:vz] 명 half 의 복수형
halves 는 half 의 복수다 : 데이비드는 감자 **반쪽**을 두 개 다 먹으려고 한다. 농구 경기는 전·후반으로 나누어져 있다.

**ham** [hǽm] 명 햄
ham 은 고기의 일종이다. ham 은 돼지고기로 만들며, 슈퍼마켓에서 살 수 있다.

**hamburger** [hǽmbə̀ːrɡər] 명
햄버그 스테이크《쇠고기 다진 것을 프라이팬에 구운 것》; (햄버그 스테이크용의) 다진 쇠고기 ; **햄버거**《햄버그 스테이크가 든 샌드위치》
1 hamburger 는 쇠고기의 일종이다. hamburger 는 여러 가지 모양으로 만들 수 있게 아주 잘게 썰어져 있다.
2 hamburger 는 샌드위치다. hamburger 는 햄버그 스테이크로 만들며, 납작하고 둥글다 : 앨버트는 롤빵에 양파와 케첩을 친 hamburger 를 즐겨 먹는다.

**hammer** [hǽmər] 1 명 해머, (쇠)망치 2 타자 망치로 치

다, 망치로 두드리다
1 hammer 는 못을 치는 데 사
용하는 도구다. hammer는 긴
손잡이 위쪽에 무거운 금속이
있다. hammer 는 물체에 박힌
못을 뽑는 데도 사용한다 :
hammer 를 다 쓰고 나면 연장
통에 도로 갖다 넣어주십시오.
2 hammer 는 또한 망치로 무
언가를 친다는 의미다 : 목수는
판자 두 개를 서로 짜 맞춘 후
모서리마다 못을 **박았다.**

**hamster** [hǽmstər] 몡 **햄스터**
hamster 는 생쥐를 닮은 동물
이다. hamster 는 몸이 통통하
고 꼬리가 짧다. 사람들은
hamster 를 애완동물로 기른
다 : 우리집은 새장에 hamster
를 기른다.

**hand** [hǽnd] 1 몡 **손**, 손 모양
을 한 것 ; (시계 등의) **바늘**
2 태 **넘겨 주다** ; 집어 주다
1 hand 는 팔의 손목 아랫부분
을 말한다. hand 로 물건을
집거나 잡는다 : hand에 무엇
을 쥐고 있니 ?
2 hand 는 시계나 계량기 혹
은 다이얼의 숫자를 가리키는
화살 모양의 것을 말하기도 한

다 : 시계 hand 가 한 시를 가
리켰디.
3 hand 는 누군가에게 무엇을
준다는 의미다 : 마가린 좀 **건**
**네 주십시오.**

**handkerchief** [hǽŋkərtʃif,
-tʃiːf] 몡 **손수건**
handkerchief 는 천조각이다.
재채기가 나면 코를 handker-
chief 로 가린다. handker-
chief 는 흰색이 많다.

**handle** [hǽndl] 몡 **손잡이**
handle 은 물건을 집어 올릴
때 잡는 부위를 말한다 : 조지
는 여행 가방을 handle 을 잡
고 집어 들었다.

**hang** [hǽŋ] 태 자 **걸다**〔걸리다〕,
매달다〔매달려 있다〕
hang 은 위에서부터 드리워져
있다는 의미다 : 마틴은 벽에
새 달력을 **걸었다.**

**hanger** [hǽŋər] 명 매다는〔거는〕 사람〔것〕; 옷걸이
옷은 hanger 에 걸어 둔다. hanger 는 보통 플라스틱이나 나무로 만든다 : 내 벽장에는 빈 hanger 가 몇 개 있다.

**Hanukkah** [hɑ́:nəkə, -nukɑ́:, xɑ́:-] 명 하누카
Hanukkah 는 12 월에 거행되는 유태인 축제다. Hanukkah 는 8 일 동안 계속되는 데, 사람들은 Hanukkah 기간 동안 8 개의 촛불을 모두 밝힐 때까지 매일 밤 촛불을 하나씩 늘려가며 켠다. Hanukkah 는 철자를 간혹 Chanukah 라고 쓰기도 한다.

**happen** [hǽpən] 자 (무슨 일이) 일어나다, 생기다; 우연히 …하다
happen은 (사건이) 발생한다는 의미다 : 그 이야기에 귀를 기울이면 다음에 무슨 일이 일어날지 듣게 될 것이다. 오늘 학교에서 무슨 일이 있었니? 어제 우리 집 앞에서 자동차 사고가 났다.

**happy** [hǽpi] 형 행복한, 즐거운, 기쁜
happy 는 기분이 좋다는 의미다 : 수잔은 즐거워서 파티에서 미소지으며 웃었다.

**harbor | harbour** [hɑ́:rbər] 명 항구
harbor는 배의 해안 접근이 안전한 곳이다. harbor는 호수나 강 혹은 바닷가에 있다 : 우리는 고기잡이 배들이 harbor로 들어오는 것을 바라보았다.

**hard** [hɑ́:rd] 형 ① 굳은, 단단한, 딱딱한 ② 튼튼한; 어려운, 곤란한 ③ 열심히 일하는, 근면한
1 hard 는 부드럽지 않다는 의미다 : 바위는 단단하고 베개는 푹신하다.
2 hard 는 많은 노력이 필요하다는 의미다 : 이 수수께끼는 풀기가 아주 어렵다.

**hardly** [hɑ́:rdli] 부 거의 …않다〔아니다〕; 간신히, 가까스로
hardly 는 「거의 …않다」는 의미다 : 구름이 너무 많이 끼어 우리는 거의 하루 종일 태양을 볼 수 없었다.

**harvest** [hɑ́:rvəst] 1 명 수확, 추수; 수확기, 추수기 2 타 자 수확하다; 거두어 들이다
1 옥수수, 밀, 과일 그리고 그 밖의 식물들을 따고 거두어 들이는 한 해의 시기를 harvest

H

라고 한다 : harvest 동안에는 많은 사람들이 일을 한다.
2 harvest는 옥수수, 밀, 과일 그리고 그 밖의 식물들을 따고 거두어 들인다는 의미다 : 농부들은 옥수수를 **수확하기** 위해 특수한 기계를 이용했다.

**has** [《약》həz, əz, z, s, 《강》hǽz] 동 조 have 의 3인칭 단수 현재형
has 는 have 의 한 형태다 : 폴은 2달러가 **있다**. 빌리 또한 2달러가 **있다**. 그들은 합쳐서 4달러를 가지고 있다.

**hat** [hǽt] 명 **모자**
hat 는 머리에 쓰는 것이다. hat 는 모양과 크기가 다양하다.

**hatch** [hǽtʃ] 타 자 (알을) 까다, **부화하다**
hatch 는 알에서 나온다는 의미다 : 암탉은 병아리를 **깐다**.

**hate** [héit] 타 **미워하다**, 증오하다, (몹시) **싫어하다**
hate 는 사람이나 사물에 대해 아주 강한 거부감을 갖고 있다는 의미다 : 해리는 공포 영화를 **몹시 싫어한다**.

**have** [hǽv] 1 타 **가지고 있다**, 소유하다, …이 있다 2 조 [have+과거분사] …하였다, …해 버렸다, 방금 막 …한 참이다 ; …해 왔다
have 는 무언가를 가지고 있다는 의미다 : 톰은 손에 책 한 권을 **갖고 있다**. 고양이에게는 부드러운 털이 **있다**.

**haven't** [hǽvnt] have not 의 단축형
haven't 는 have not 을 줄여서 말한 것이다 : 마거릿과 엘리자베스는 갓 태어난 젖먹이 남동생을 아직 보지 **못했다**.

**hawk** [hɔ́ːk] 명 **매**
hawk 는 새다. hawk 는 짧고 굽은 부리와 강한 발톱이 있다. hawk 는 하늘 높이 날며 땅 위의 작은 동물들을 낚아챈다.

**hay** [héi] 명 **건초**, 말린 풀
hay 는 베어서 말린 키가 큰 풀이다 : 말과 젖소는 hay를 먹는다.

**he** [《약》 hi, i, 《강》 hí:] 때 [인
칭 대명사 : 3인칭 단수 남성
주격] 그는, 그가, 그사람은
1 he 는 남자 아이나 성인 남
자 혹은 동물의 수컷을 나타내
는 말이다 : **토머스는** 드라이브
하러 나가고 싶다고 말했다.
2 he'd 는 he had나 he would
의 의미다 : **그는** 전에 서커스
구경을 가 본 적이 없다. **그가**
할 수 있으면 할 텐데.
3 he'll 은 he will 의 의미다 :
**리처드가** 소풍에 따라 오겠다
고 한다.
4 he's 는 he is나 he has 의
의미다 : 블레이크는 내집 근처
에 산다. **그는** 내 이웃이다.
그와 나는 친구가 된 지 2 달
이 된다.

**head** [héd] 명 **머리** ; 우두머리 ;
선두 ; 두뇌
1 head 는 목 위에 있는 신체
부위다. 눈, 귀, 코 그리고 입
은 모두 head 에 있다. head
속에 뇌가 있다 : 리처드는 키
가 빌리 보다 head 하나가 더
크다.
2 head 는 또한 어떤 것의 앞
부분을 의미한다 : 마거릿은 그
줄 head(맨 앞)에 있다.

**heal** [hí:əl] 타 자 (상처·마음의
고통 등을) **고치다** ; 낫다
heal 은 다시 건강해진다는 의
미다. 벤 상처나 부러진 뼈가
회복되었다면 그것은 **나은 것**

이다 : 팔의 벤 상처가 빨리 나
았다.

**healthy** [hélθi] 형 **건강한**, 건
강하게 보이는 ; 건강에 좋은
healthy 는 아프지 않다는 의
미다 : 수는 **건강하게** 지낼 수
있도록 몸에 좋은 음식을 먹는
다.

**hear** [híər] 타 자 **듣다**, …이
들리다 ; 들을 수 있다
hear 는 두 귀로 소리를 이해
한다는 의미다 : 토끼는 귀가
크기 때문에 잘 **들을 수 있다.**

**heard** [hə́:rd] 동 hear (듣다)의
과거·과거분사형
heard 는 hear 의 한 형태다 :
딕은 다른 방에서 시끄럽게 떠
드는 소리를 **들었다.**

**hearing aid** [híəriŋ èid] 명 **보
청기**
hearing aid 는 더 잘 들을 수

있도록 귀에 끼는 것이다 : 나는 내 hearing aid에 전지를 새 것으로 갈아 줄 필요가 있다고 생각한다.

**heart** [háːrt] 명 ① **심장, 가슴, 흉부 ; 마음 ; 중심, 핵심,** 급소, 본질 ② 감정, 애정, 동정심 ③ **하트 모양의 물건 ;** 하트(의 패)
1 heart 는 신체의 한 기관이다. heart 는 가슴 안쪽에 있으며 신체의 모든 기관에 피를 공급한다.
2 heart는 또한 ♥ 와 같은 모양이다. heart 는 보통 붉은 색이며, "나는 당신을 사랑합니다."라는 의미를 나타내기도 한다.

**heat** [híːt] 1 명 **열, 뜨거움,** 더위, 더움 ; 열기 ; 따뜻한 기간〔기후〕; 온도 ; 열렬함 2 타자 **가열하다, 데우다,** 뜨거워지다 ; 따뜻이 하다
1 heat 는 따뜻해지거나 뜨거워지는 것을 의미한다 : 오븐의 heat 로 빵이 구워진다.
2 heat 는 따뜻하게 하거나 뜨겁게 한다는 의미다 : 메리는 우유를 **데워서** 아기에게 주었다.

**heavy** [hévi] 형 **무거운 ; 대량의,** 다량의 ; **두꺼운 ;** 격렬한, 힘든
1 heavy 는 무언가를 들어올리기가 힘들다는 의미다 : 보브가

들기에는 식료품 자루가 너무 **무거웠다.** 이 큰 여행 가방은 저 작은 여행 가방보다 **무겁다.**
2 heavy 는 또한 두껍다는 의미다 : 아이들은 **두꺼운** 종이를 이용해 책 표지를 만들었다.

**heel** [híːəl] 명 **뒤꿈치 ;** (양말·구두의) **뒤축, 힐 ;** 뒤꿈치 모양의 것
1 heel 은 신체의 일부다. heel 은 발의 뒷부분인데, 구두를 신을 때 heel 이 맨 나중에 들어 간다.

2 heel 은 구두의 한 부분이다. heel 은 발 뒷부분을 받쳐 준다. heel이 높은 구두도 있다.

**height** [háit] 명 **키, 신장 ; 높이 ;** 고도
height 는 땅에서 떨어져 있는 정도를 말한다 : 톰의 height 는 3 피트다.

**held** [héəld] 동 hold (잡다)의 과거·과거분사형
held 는 단어 hold 에서 생긴 말이다 : 아빠는 쌍둥이가 잠들 때까지 **안고 계셨다.**

**helicopter** [hélikὰptər | -kɔ̀p-]
몡 헬리콥터
helicopter 는 공중을 날 수 있
는 기계다. helicopter 는 수직
으로 오르내리며 날 수 있고,
아주 좁은 장소에도 착륙할 수
있다.

**hello** [həlóu, he-] 깝 이봐, 야
아 ; [전화] 여보세요 ; [가벼운
인사] 안녕하세요
우리는 아는 사람을 만나거나
전화를 받을 때 hello 라고 말
한다.

**helmet** [héəlmət] 몡 헬멧, 철
모 ; 투구
helmet 은 머리를 보호하기 위
해 쓰는 단단한 모자다. 군인,
우주 비행사 그리고 미식 축구
선수들은 helmet을 쓴다.

**help** [héəlp] 타자 돕다, 구하
다 ; 거들다, 도움이 되다 ; 거
들어 …시키다
help 는 누군가 딴 사람을 위
해 무언가를 한다는 의미다 :
우리는 아버지께서 차고를 청

소하시는 걸 **도왔다**. 누군가
딴 사람을 위해 무언가를 하는
사람이나 물건을 helper (도와
주는 사람[것])라고 한다 : 나
의 선생님께서는 자기가 주스
를 따르는 동안 컵을 잡아 달
라고 helper 에게 부탁하셨다.

**hen** [hén] 몡 암탉
hen 은 암탉이다. hen 은 알을
낳을 수 있다.

**her** [《약》 hər, əːr, ər, 《강》
hə́ːr] 댸 ① [she 의 소유격]
**그녀의** ② [she 의 목적격] **그
녀를**, 그녀에게
her 는 여자 아이나 성인 여성
을 나타내는 말이다 : 수의 친
구가 **그녀를** 방문하려고 왔다.
her 는 또한 여자 아이나 성인
여성의 소유물이라는 의미다 :
수는 **그녀의** 우산을 홀에 두고
왔다.

**herd** [hə́ːrd] 몡 짐승의 떼 ; (특
히 소[돼지]) 떼
herd 는 함께 살거나 이동하는
동물의 무리를 말한다 : 소
herd가 땅이 거의 드러날 때
까지 풀을 뜯어먹었다.

**here** [híər] 부 여기에, 여기서,
**여기로**, 이쪽으로
here 는 바로 지금 있는 곳을
의미한다 : 컵을 **이쪽으로** 가지
고 오시오. 나는 지금 **이 곳**
부엌에 있다.

**hero** [híːrou|híər-] 몡 영웅 ; (소설·극 등의 남자) **주인공**
hero는 선행이나 용감한 일을 해서 우리가 특별한 사람으로 생각하는 사람을 말한다.

**heroine** [hérouin] 몡 여걸, 여장부 ; (소설·극 등의) 여주인공
heroine은 선행이나 용감한 일을 해서 우리가 특별한 사람으로 생각하는 성인 여성이나 여자 아이를 말한다.

**hers** [hə́ːrz] 때 [she의 소유 대명사] **그녀의 것**
hers 는 그녀의 소유물이란 의미다 : 빌리에게는 자기 방이 있고, 그의 여동생도 **자기 방**이 있다. 그녀의 방에 있는 것은 모두 **그녀의 것**이다.

**herself** [《약》 hərséəlf, ər-, ər-, 《강》 həːr-] 때 [she의 재귀 대명사] **그녀 자신 ; 그녀 자신을〔에게〕**
herself 는 누군가 딴 사람이 아닌 바로 그녀 자신이라는 의미다 : 헬렌은 거울에 **자기의 모습**을 비춰 본 다음 구두를 신었다. 아무도 그녀를 도와주지 않아서, **그녀 혼자서** 구두를 신었다.

**hid** [híd] 图 hide (숨다)의 과거·과거분사형
hid 는 hide 의 한 형태다 : 보브는 그의 누이동생에게 자기가 그녀를 찾을 수 있게 숨으라고 말하자, 그녀는 집 뒤에 **숨었다.**

**hidden** [hídən] 1 图 hide (숨다)의 과거분사형 2 혱 **숨은, 숨겨진** ; 비밀의
hidden 은 hide 의 한 형태다 : 나는 내 신발 한 짝이 침대 뒤에 **숨겨진** 것을 알았다.

**hide** [háid] 타자 **숨기다, 감추다, 가리다** ; 비밀로 하다
hide 는 아무도 볼 수 없는 곳에 무언가를 둔다는 의미다 : 딕은 간혹 몸을 **숨겼다가** 갑자기 뛰어 나와, 사람들을 깜짝 놀라게 하는 장난을 좋아한다.

**high** [hái] 1 혱 **높은, 높이가 …인** ; 물건 **값이 비싼** 2 튀 **높이, 높게** ; 비싼 값으로
1 high 는 지면으로부터 상당히 높이 떨어져 있다는 의미다 : 저 물고기는 물 밖으로 **높이** 뛰어오를 수 있다. 독수리는 하늘로 **점점 더 높이** 날아 구름속으로 사라졌다. 저 산은 미국에서 **가장 높은** 산 중의 하나다.

2 high 는 또한 많은 액수를 의미한다 : 나는 그렇게 **비싼** 값을 지불하면서까지 새 자동차를 사고 싶지 않다.

**hill** [híəl] 몡 **언덕**, 작은 산 ; 고개, 고갯길
hill 은 지대가 높은 곳을 말한다. hill 은 산 만큼 높지 않다 : 우리는 자전거를 끌고 hill 을 걸어 올라갔다.

**him** [《약》 him, im, 《강》 hím] 때 [he 의 목적격] **그를〔에게〕**
him 은 남자 아이나 성인 남성을 나타내는 말이다 : 존씨는 나에게 **자기가** 개를 훈련시키는 것을 도와 달라고 부탁했다.

**himself** [《약》 imséəlf, 《강》 him-] 때 [he 의 재귀 대명사] **그 자신(이)** ; **그 자신을〔에게〕**
himself 는 누군가 딴 사람이 아닌 바로 그 남자 자신이라는 의미다 : 마크는 얼굴에 가면을 쓰고, 거울에 **자기 모습을** 비춰 보고는 깜짝 놀랐다.

**hippopotamus** [hìpəpátəməs| -pɔ́t-] 몡 **하마**

hippopotamus 는 입이 아주 큰 거대한 동물이다. hippopotamus 는 다리가 짧고 가죽이 털이 없고 두꺼우며, 물에서 많은 시간을 보낸다. hippopotamus 를 줄여서 hippo 라고 한다.

**his** [《약》 hiz, iz, 《강》 híz] 때 [he 의 소유격] **그의** ; [he 의 소유 대명사] **그의 것**
his 는 남자 아이나 성인 남성의 소유물이라는 의미다 : 이것은 내 피자고 저것은 **그의** 피자다. 나는 **그의** 아버지를 잘 알고 있다. 잭의 야구 글러브에는 **그의** 이름이 쓰여 있다.

**history** [hístəri] 몡 **역사** ; 경력, 유래, 연혁
history 는 과거에 일어났던 일에 대한 이야기다 : 올해 우리는 학교에서 우리 도시의 history 를 배우고 있다. 저 낡은 집에는 재미있는 history 가 있다.

**hit** [hít] 타자 **때리다, 치다** ; 쳐서 맞히다 ; …에 부딪치다
hit 는 무언가에 아주 세게 닿는다는 의미다 : 야구 선수들은

배트로 공을 **치려고** 한다. 사과 하나가 나무에서 떨어져 땅에 **부딪쳤다.** 나는 문에 머리를 **부딪쳤다.**

**hive** [háiv] 명 꿀벌의 벌집
hive 는 꿀벌이 들어가 사는 통이나 집을 말한다.

**hobby** [hábi | hɔ́bi] 명 취미
hobby 는 사람들이 정말 좋아서 하는 일이다 : 스미스 집안 사람들의 hobby 는 우표 수집과 낚시, 그리고 수영이다. 피터의 hobby 는 퍼즐을 푸는 것이다.

**hockey** [háki | hɔ́ki] 명 하키
1 hockey 는 얼음 위에서 하는 경기다. 두 팀이 있어야 하며, 각 팀은 6 명의 선수로 구성된다. 선수들은 스케이트화를 신고 긴 스틱을 사용해 상대팀 골에 작은 고무 퍽을 넣으려고 한다.

2 또 다른 종류의 hockey 는 큰 경기장에서 한다. 이 경기에서, 각 팀은 11 명의 선수로 구성된다. 선수들은 고무 퍽 대신에 좀더 짧은 스틱과 공을 사용한다.

**hog** [hɔ́:g | hɔ́g] 명 돼지
hog 는 다 자란 돼지를 말한다. hog 는 고기를 얻으려고 사육한다. hog는 다리가 짧지만 대다수 사람들만큼 빨리 달릴 수 있다.

**hold** [hóuəld] 타 자 ① 쥐다, 들다, 잡다 ② 유지하다 ; 소유〔보유〕하다, 보관하다 ③ (건물 · 방 등이) **수용하다** ; (모임 등을) **열다,** 개최하다
1 hold 는 손이나 팔에 무언가를 쥐고〔안고〕 있다는 의미다 : 스콧은 문을 열 동안 마이크에게 자기 짐을 **들어 달라고** 부탁했다. 수는 차도를 건널 때 어머니 손을 **잡았다.**
2 hold 는 또한 무언가가 들어갈 공간이 있다는 의미다 : 통학 버스에는 50 명이 **탈 수 있다.** 이 여행 가방은 너무 작아서 네 장난감과 옷을 다 **넣을 수** 없다.

**hole** [hóuəl] 명 **구멍, 구덩이** ; (짐승의) **굴** ; (의류 등의) 찢어진 곳
hole 은 어떤 것의 일부가 비어 있거나 훤히 트인 것을 말한다 : 작년 가을 다람쥐들이 땅에 hole 을 파서 나무 열매를 넣어 두었다.

**holiday** [hálidèi, -di|hɔ́l-] 명 **휴일** ; **축제일** ; **휴가**
holiday 는 중요한 일이나 유명한 사람을 상기하는 특별한 날이다 : 추수 감사절, 크리스마스, 하누카는 holiday 다.

**hollow** [hálou|hɔ́l-] 형 **속이 빈** ; **우묵한, 움푹 들어간**
hollow 는 안쪽에 빈 공간이 있다는 의미다 : 농구공들은 **속이 비어** 있다. **속이 빈** 나무 속에서 사는 동물들도 있다.

**home** [hóum] 명 **집** ; **가정** (생활) ; **고향** ; **본국, 고국**
home 은 사람이나 동물들이 사는 곳이다 : 대부분의 사람들은 집이나 아파트에 home 을

꾸민다.

**homework** [hóumwə̀ːrk] 명 **숙제** ; **집에서 하는 일**
homework 는 선생님이 학생들에게 집에서 하라고 시키는 공부다 : 선생님은 homework 로 우리에게 이야기를 지어 오라고 하셨다.

**honest** [ánəst|ɔ́n-] 형 **정직한**
honest 는 진실을 이야기한다는 의미다 : **정직한** 사람들은 거짓말을 하지 않거나 자기 것이 아닌 물건을 갖지 않는다.

**honey** [hʌ́ni] 명 **벌꿀, 꿀**
honey 는 꿀벌이 만드는 단맛이 나는 액체다. honey 는 노랗고 끈끈하다 : 조는 토스트에 honey를 발라 먹는 것을 좋아한다.

**hook** [húk] 명 **갈고리, 훅** ; **걸쇠** ; **낚싯바늘**
hook 은 꼬부라진 쇠붙이를 말한다. 끝이 뾰족하여 물고기를 잡는 데 사용하는 hook 도

있고, 옷을 걸기 위해 사용하는 hook 도 있다.

**hop** [háp│hɔ́p] 타자 (도랑 등을) **뛰어넘다** ; **뛰다**, 한 발로 뛰다 ; (새 등이 한 번에 두 다리로) **깡충 뛰다**
hop 은 한 발로 짧게 뛰어 오른다는 의미다 : 두 발로도 **깡충깡충 뛰어 다닐 수 있다**. 엘리자베스는 오랫동안 **깡충깡충 뛰어 다닐 수 있다**.

**hope** [hóup] 1 자타 **바라다**, 희망을 갖다 ; 기대하다 2 명 **희망**, 소망 ; 기대
hope 는 무언가를 몹시 원한다는 의미다 : 우리는 내일 바닷가에 갈 수 있을 정도로 날씨가 화창하기를 **바라고 있다**.

**horn** [hɔ́ːrn] 명 **뿔** ; 뿔나팔 ; 호른《악기》 ; (자동차의) **경적**
1 horn 은 동물 몸의 한 부분이다 : 황소와 염소는 머리에

두 개의 horn 이 있다.

2 horn 은 또한 악기를 말한다 : 앨리스는 horn 을 불어 음악을 연주한다.
3 horn 은 공중에 큰 소리를 내는 것이다 : 우리는 그 트럭이 horn 을 두 번 울리는 소리를 들었다.

**horse** [hɔ́ːrs] 명 **말**
horse 는 다리가 4 개고 꼬리가 긴 커다란 동물이다. 자동차가 있기 전에는 사람들이 한 곳에서 다른 곳으로 가려면 horse 를 탔지만, 요즈음 사람들은 재미로 horse 를 탄다.

**horseshoe** [hɔ́ːrsʃùː] 명 **편자**
horseshoe 는 U자 처럼 생긴 쇳조각이다. 말들은 발을 보호하기 위해 horseshoe 를 단다.

**hose** [hóuz] 명 긴 양말, 여성용 스타킹 ; 호스
hose 는 고무나 천으로 만든 관을 말한다 : 소방수들은 hose 를 사용해 불에 물을 끼얹는다.

**hospital** [háspitəl|hɔ́s-] 명 병원
hospital 은 아프거나 다친 사람들이 낫기 위해 찾아 가는 곳이다 : 의사와 간호사들은 hospital 에서 일한다. 많은 갓 난 아이들이 hospital 에서 태어난다.

**hot** [hát|hɔ́t] 형 뜨거운, 더운
hot 은 아주 따뜻하다는 의미다. 무언가가 뜨거울 때 만지거나 맛을 보면 데일 수가 있다 : 딕은 뜨거운 난로를 만져서 손에 화상을 입었다.

**hot dog** [hát dɔ̀ːg] 명 핫도그
hot dog 는 길고 가느다란 모양으로 말아서 요리한 고기다 : 야구 경기할 때 팔 hot dog 가 있었다.

**hotel** [houtél] 명 호텔, 여관
hotel 은 방이 많이 있는 큰 건물이다. 집을 떠난 사람들은 hotel 에 머문다. 대도시에 hotel 이 많은 이유는 많은 사람들이 도시를 방문하기 때문이다.

**hour** [áuər] 명 한 시간, 시각
hour 는 시간의 양을 나타내는 말이다. 하루는 24 hours (시간)이고, 1 hour (시간)는 60분이다.

**house** [háus] 명 집, 주택 ; 가정, 가족
house 는 사람들이 사는 건물이다. 대개 한 house 에 한 두 가구가 산다. 거리에는 많은 house 가 있다.

**how** [háu] 부 ① 어떻게, 어떤 방법으로 ② 어떤 상태로 ; 어찌하여, 얼마만큼, 얼마나
1 how 는 질문을 할 때 사용하는 말이다 : 바깥 날씨가 얼마나 춥니 ?
2 how 는 무언가를 하는 방법에 대해 말할 때도 사용한다 : 나는 자동차를 어떻게 운전하는지 모른다.

**huddle** [hʌdl] 타 자 아무렇게나 (포개어) 쌓다, **뒤죽박죽 모으 다**; 붐비다, (떼지어) **몰리다**
huddle 은 빽빽이 모여서 작은 무리를 이룬다는 의미다 : 병아리들이 어미닭의 날개 밑으로 떼지어 몰려들었다.

**hug** [hʌg] 타 꼭 **껴안다**; 끌어안다; (편견 등을) 갖다
hug 는 두 팔로 무언가를 감싼 다음 바짝 조여서 끌어당긴다는 의미다. 많은 사람들은 만나서 반갑다는 감정을 나타내기 위해 서로 **꼭 껴안는다**.

**huge** [hjúːdʒ] 형 **거대한**
huge 는 엄청나게 크다는 의미다 : 코끼리는 **거대한** 동물이다.

**hum** [hʌm] 자 타 (벌·기계 등이) 윙윙거리다, (주저·불만·난처함 등으로) 우물우물 말하다; (콧노래를) **부르다**
hum 은 입을 다문 채로 소리는 내지만, 말은 하지 않는다는 의미다 : 가사를 모를 때, 나는 모르는 부분을 **콧노래로 부른다**.

**human** [hjúːmən] 1 형 **사람의**, 인간의   2 명 **인간**; 인류
human 은 사람이라는 의미다. human body(인체)는 사람의 몸이다. 소녀, 소년, 성인 남녀 모두 human 이다.

**hump** [hʌmp] 명 (등의) 혹; (낙타의) **등의 혹**; 둥근 언덕
hump 는 둥근 혹을 말한다. 등에 hump 가 두 개 있는 낙타도 있고, 하나 밖에 없는 낙타도 있다.

**hundred** [hʌndrəd] 1 명 **100**, 100 개, 100 명   2 형 **100 의**, 100 개의, 100 명의
hundred 는 숫자다. hundred 는 **100** 으로 쓴다. hundred 가 되려면 10이 열 개 있어야 한다. 다시 말해서 hundred 는 10×10 이다.

**hung** [hʌŋ] 동 hang (걸다)의

과거·과거분사형
hung 은 단어 hang 에서 생긴
말이다 : 원숭이는 꼬리로 공중
에 **매달려 있었다.**

**hungry** [hʌ́ŋgri] 형 배고픈, 굶
주린
hungry 는 음식을 먹고 싶다는
의미다 : 마리는 아직까지 먹은
게 없어서 위가 텅 비어 있다.
마리는 몹시 **배가 고프다.**

**hunt** [hʌ́nt] 타 자  사냥하다 ; 추
적하다 ; 찾다
hunt 는 무언가를 쫓아가 잡으
려고 한다는 의미다 : 많은 동
물들이 밤에 먹이를 **사냥한다.**
사람들도 **사냥을 하는** 데, **사
냥을 하는** 사람을 hunter 라고
한다.

**hurricane** [hə́ːrikèin|hʌ́rikən]
명 폭풍, 태풍, **허리케인**
hurricane 은 아주 강한 바람과
많은 양의 비를 동반한 폭풍이
다. hurricane 은 바다에 엄청
난 파도를 일으켜 육지를 물에
잠기게 할 수 있다. 나무를 쓰

러뜨릴만큼 강력한 hurricane
도 있다.

**hurry** [hə́ːri|hʌ́ri] 자 타  서두르
다, 급히 가다 ; 서두르게 하다
hurry 는 급히 가려고 한다는
의미다 : 늦었을 때는 **서둘러야
만 한다.**

**hurt** [hə́ːrt] 타 자  상처내다, …
을 다치게 하다 ; 고통을 주다,
**아프다**
hurt 는 통증을 느낀다는 의미
다 : 나는 배가 **아프다.** 앤드루
는 마루에 넘어져 팔을 **다쳤
다.**

**husband** [hʌ́zbənd] 명 남편
husband 는 결혼한 남자를 말
한다. 즉 그는 자기와 결혼한
여자의 husband 가 된다.
husband 와 아내는 서로 결혼
한 사이다.

**hut** [hʌ́t] 명 오두막
hut 는 아주 단순한 작은 집이
다. 보통 날씨가 따뜻한 지방
에서 hut 를 짓는다. 풀로 지
은 hut 도 있다.

H

**I** [ái] 때 [인칭 대명사 : 1인칭 단
수 주격] **나는, 내가**
I 는 자신에 관하여 말할 때 사
용하는 말이다 : 이 외투는 **내**
것이다. **나는** 겨울에 몸을 따
뜻하게 하려고 외투를 입는다.

**ice** [áis] 명 **얼음, 빙판** ; 얼음처
럼 찬 것
ice는 물이 언 것으로, 단단하
고 차갑다 : 마거릿은 연못을
덮은 ice 위에서 스케이트를
탄다. 빌은 음료수를 차게 하
려고 ice를 넣었다.

**iceberg** [áisbə̀ːrg] 명 **빙산**
iceberg는 바다에 떠있는 거대
한 얼음 덩어리다.

**ice cream** [áis kríːm] 명 아이

스 크림
ice cream은 얼린 달콤한 식
품이다. ice cream은 크림과
설탕으로 만든다.

**ice skate** [áis skèit] 1명 (빙
상) **스케이트화** 2자 [ice-
skate로] **스케이트를 타다**
1 ice skate는 밑바닥에 길고
날카로운 금속 조각이 붙어 있
는 장화의 일종이다.
2 ice-skate는 스케이트화를
신고 얼음 위를 지친다는 의미
다 : 앨은 뒤로 **스케이트를 탄
다.**

**idea** [aidíːə|-díə] 명 **생각, 관
념 ; 의견,** 견해 ; 개념
idea는 생각해 낸 것이다 : 우

리집 애완 동물인 바다거북의 이름을 뭐라고 지을 것인가를 놓고, 우리 모두는 제각기 다른 idea를 갖고 있었다.

**if** [íf] 웹 (만일) …이라면 ; 비록 …이라 할지라도 ; …인지 어떤지
if는 무슨 일이 생길지 물어보는 말이다 : 잭은 가게에 가기로 결정할 수도, 가지 않기로 결정할 수도 있다. **만약** 간다면, 그는 빵을 몇 개 살 것이다. **만약** 오늘 비가 오면, 우리는 우산을 써야 할 것이다.

**igloo, iglu** [íglu:] 명 이글루, 에스키모의 집
igloo는 집의 일종으로, 눈 덩어리로 만든다. 나무가 없는 추운 지방에 사는 사람들이 간혹 igloo를 짓는다.

**ill** [íəl] 형 병든 ; 기분이 상한 ; 나쁜, 부덕한
ill은 아프다는 의미다 : 리처드는 오늘 너무 **아파서** 밖에 나갈 수가 없다.

**I'll** [áiəl] I will, I shall의 단축형

I'll은 I will을 줄여서 말한 것이다 : 내가 이 책을 다 읽으면 기꺼이 너에게 **빌려주겠다**.

**I'm** [áim] I am의 단축형
I'm은 I am을 줄여서 말한 것이다 : **나는 거의 형만큼 키가 크다.**

**imagine** [imǽdʒin] 타 자 **상상하다**, 생각하다 ; 짐작하다, 추측하다
imagine은 마음 속에 무언가를 그려본다는 의미다 : 창밖에 눈이 내리면, 사라는 여름 정경을 **상상해 보는 것**을 좋아한다. 그녀는 따스한 햇살이 내리쬐는 해변에 있는 자신의 모습을 **상상한다.**

**imitate** [ímitèit] 타 **흉내내다**, 모방하다 ; 본받다
imitate는 다른 사람이 하는 것과 똑같이 한다는 의미다 : 앨버트가 코를 만지자, 그의 어린 여동생 앤도 자기 코를 만지며 그를 **흉내냈다.**

**immediately** [imí:diitli] 부 바로, 즉시, 곧
immediately는 「지금 곧」이란 의미다 : 우리가 **지금 당장** 출발한다면, 비행기가 뜨기 전에 공항에 도착할 수 있다.

**important** [impɔ́:rtənt] 형 중

요한, 중대한, 소중한
important는 무언가에 주의를
기울여야만 한다는 의미다 : 도
로를 건너기 전에 길 양쪽을
살펴보는 것이 **중요하다.**

**impossible** [impásəbl | -pɔ́s-] 형
**불가능한,** 있을 수 없는
impossible은 무언가가 도저히
이루어질 수 없다는 의미다 :
태양이 서쪽에서 뜬다는 것은
**불가능하다.**

**in** [ín] 전 ① [장소·위치] …의
안에, …에서 ② [이동] …속
으로 ; …쪽에,   …쪽으로   ③
[시간] …동안에, …중에
1 in은 「안쪽으로」라는 의미
다 : 나는 새장 안에 새를 넣었
다. 하마가 물 속에 서 있다.

2 in은 또한 「기간[시간] 중
에」라는 의미다 : 가을에는 나
뭇잎 색이 변한다. 나는 한 시
간 안에 숙제를 끝내겠다.

**inch** [íntʃ] 명 **인치**
inch는 길이의 양이다. 1 피트
는 12 inch 다 : 그는 키가 5 피
트 4 inch 다.

**incubator** [íŋkjubèitər] 명 (조

산아의) **보육기 ; 부화기 ;** 세균
배양기
incubator는 특별한 종류의 상
자다.  incubator 에는 신생아
를 따뜻하게 해 주는 열과 공
기가 있다 : 우리는 농장에서
병아리들이 incubator 속에서
부화되는 것을 보았다.

**independence** [ìndipéndəns]
명 **독립,** 자립, 자주 ; 독립심,
자립정신
independence는 다른 나라의
지배를 받지 않는다는 의미
다 : 미국은 독립 기념일 [7월 4
일]에 자국의 independence
를 경축한다.

**indoor** [índɔ̀:r] 형 **실내의**
indoor는 건물 내부를 의미한
다 : 우리 학교에는 **실내** 수영
장이 있다. 탁구는 **실내** 경기
다.

**indoors** [ìndɔ́:rz] 부 **실내에 [에
서, 로]**
indoors는 건물 안으로 들어간
다는 의미다 : 비가 오기 시작
하자 아이들은 **집안으로** 들

어갔다.

**information** [ìnfərméiʃən] 명
**정보**, 보고, 통지 ; **지식**, 견
문 ; **안내소**
information은 무언가를 배우
는 데 도움이 되는 일단의 사
실들을 말한다. 사전은 단어의
철자를 어떻게 쓰며, 그 의미
가 무엇인지에 대한 informa-
tion을 제공해 준다.

**injure** [índʒər] 타 **상처를 입히
다**, 다치게 하다 ; (감정을) 해
치다
injure는 다치게 한다는 의미
다 : 두 사람이 그 사고로 **다쳤
다**.

**ink** [íŋk] 명 **잉크**
ink는 글씨를 쓰는 데 사용하
는 액체다. 펜으로 글씨를 쓰
면, ink가 종이 위에 묻어 나
온다. 파란색이나 검은 색 ink
가 들어있는 펜이 많지만, 다
른 색깔의 ink도 있다.

**insect** [ínsekt] 명 **곤충**, 벌레
insect는 다리가 6개인 아주
작은 동물이다. 대부분의

insect 는 날개가 있다. 파리,
메뚜기, 개미는 insect 다.

**inside** [ìnsáid, ⸗⸗] 1명 **내부**,
안쪽 2부 **내부에**, 내부로, 안
쪽으로 3형 **안쪽의**, 내부의 4
전 **…의 안쪽에**
1 inside는 어떤 것의 안쪽을
의미한다 : 우리 자동차의
inside는 초록색이다.
2 inside는 또한 「안에 혹은
실내에」의 의미다 : 안에 아무
것도 없다.

**instant** [ínstənt] 명 **순간**, 순식
간, 찰나
instant는 아주 짧은 시간이
다. instant는 너무 짧아서 거
의 알아채지 못할 정도다 : 번
개는 **순식간**에 번쩍인다.

**instead** [instéd] 부 **그 대신에**
instead는 무언가를 어떤 다른
것으로 대신한다는 의미다 : 나
는 오늘 갈색 구두 **대신** 빨간
운동화를 신으려고 한다.

**instrument** [ínstrumənt] 명 ①
**기구**, 도구 ; 계기 ② **악기**
1 instrument는 무언가를 하는

데 도움이 되는 도구다. 펜은 글씨를 쓰는 instrument다. 포크는 음식을 먹는 데 사용하는 instrument다.

2 또 다른 종류의 instrument 는 음악을 만들어 낸다. 피아노와 바이올린은 musical instrument(악기)다.

**interest** [íntrəst, -tərèst] 1 명 흥미, 관심 ; 관심사 2 타 ···에 흥미를 일으키게 하다
interest는 보다 많이 알고 싶은 것이다 : 앤은 그림에 대단한 interest를 가지고 있다. 그녀는 그 밖의 것에도 interest 가 많다.

**interested** [íntrəstid, -tərèst-] 형 흥미를 가진
interested는 무언가에 호기심이 있다는 의미다 : 배리는 음악에 상당한 흥미를 가지고 있다.

**interesting** [íntrəstiŋ, -tərèst-] 형 재미있는, 흥미있는
interesting은 무언가를 즐거워하거나 그것에 관심을 기울인

다는 의미다 : 우리는 과학 박물관이 아주 **흥미있는** 곳이라고 생각했다.

**into** [《약》 (자음 앞) íntə, (모음 앞) íntu, 《강》 íntu:] 전 ① [내부로의 운동·동작·방향] ···**안으로**[에] ② [상태의 변화·추이·결과] (···이) ···**으로** (되다)
1 into는 무언가가 가는 장소를 나타낸다 : 아버지께서는 차를 몰아 차고에 넣으셨다.
2 into는 또한 변해서 무엇이 된다는 의미다 : 애벌레가 변해서 나방이나 나비로 된다.

**invent** [invént] 타 **발명하다**, 고안하다
invent는 아무도 전에 만든 적이 없는 것을 만든다는 의미다 : 나의 아저씨는 편리한 기계를 많이 **발명하셨다**.

**invention** [invénʃən] 명 발명, 창안 ; 발명품
invention은 처음으로 만들어 냈거나 생각해 낸 것이다 : 최초의 invention 가운데 하나가 바퀴였다.

**invisible** [invízəbl] 형 눈에 보이지 않는
invisible은 볼 수 없다는 의미다 : 이야기책 속에 나오는 착한 요정은 **눈에 보이지 않기** 때문에 아무도 그녀를 볼 수

없었다.

**invitation** [ìnvitéiʃən] 명 초대 ; 권유 ; **초대장**, 안내장
사람들에게 어떤 곳으로 와달라고 할 때, 그들에게 invitation을 준다.    invitation은 보통 카드에 쓴다.

**invite** [inváit] 타 **초대하다**, 초청하다 ; 권유하다
invite는 누군가에게 방문을 요청한다는 의미다 : 메리는 저녁 식사에 친구 세 명을 **초대했다.**

**iron** [áiərn] 명 **철, 쇠 ; 다리미**
1 iron은 단단하고 강한 금속이다 : 울타리의 빗장들은 iron으로 되어 있었다.
2 iron은 옷의 주름을 펴는 데 사용하는 것이다. iron은 밑바닥이 평평하며 뜨거워진다.

**is** [《약》 z, s, 《강》 íz] 동 be의 3인칭 단수 직설법 현재형
is는 단어 be에서 생긴 말이다 : 빌의 외투는 푸른색**이고** 수잔의 외투는 빨간색**이다.** 비

가 올 것 **같니** ?

**island** [áilənd] 명 **섬**
island는 사방이 물로 둘러싸인 육지다. 작은 island도 있고, 사람들이 살 수 있을 만큼 큰 island도 있다 : 하와이 주는 island들로 이루어져 있다.

**isn't** [íznt] is not의 단축형
isn't는 is not을 줄여서 말한 것이다 : "집에 헬렌 있습니까 ?" "아니오, **없습니다.**"

**it** [ít] 대 **그것은**, 그것이, **그것을**, 그것에
it은 언급 중인 것을 대신 나타내 주는 말이다 : 내 친구가 공을 던지고 내가 **그것을** 잡았다.

**itch** [ítʃ] 1 자 **가렵다**, 근질거리다 2 명 **가려움**
itch는 피부가 간지럽거나 쏘여서 긁고 싶다는 의미다 : 모기에 물린 팔이 몹시 **가렵다.**

**its** [íts] 대 [it의 소유격] **그것의, 그…**

its는 언급 중인 동물이나 사물에 속한 것을 나타낸다 : 고양이는 **자기의** 발을 핥았다.

**it's** [íts] it is, it has의 단축형
1 It's는 it is 의 의미다 : 이곳은 상당히 **덥다.**
2 It's는 또한 it has의 의미다 : 갓난 여동생이 집에 온지 3일이 **되었다.**

**itself** [itsélf] 대 [it의 재귀 대명사] **그 자체,** 바로 그것
itself는 다른 어떤 것도 아닌 바로 그것 자체라는 의미다 :

그 이야기 **자체**가 전혀 재미가 없다.

**I've** [áiv] I have 의 단축형
I've는 I have를 줄여서 말한 것이다 : 나는 서커스 구경을 가고 싶다. **나는** 전에 한 번도 서커스 구경을 가본 **적이 없다.**

# J

**jacket** [dʒǽkit] 명 (소매가 달린 짧은) 웃옷, 재킷
jacket 은 짧고 가벼운 상의다. jacket 은 날씨가 싸늘한 봄과 가을에 입기에 적합하다.

**jail, gaol** [dʒéiəl] 1 명 구치소, 교도소, 감옥 2 타 투옥하다
jail 은 법을 지키지 않은 사람들이 있어야 하는 곳이다 : 경찰관이 강도를 jail 에 넣었다 (투옥했다).

**jam** [dʒæm] 명 잼
jam 은 음식의 일종이다. jam 은 과일과 설탕을 함께 끓여서 만든다. jam 은 걸쭉하고 맛이 달다.

**January** [dʒǽnjuèri | -əri] 명 1 월

January 는 한 해의 첫번째 달이다. January 는 31 일이며, 12월이 끝나고 2월이 시작되기 전에 온다.

**jar** [dʒɑ́ːr] 명 병, 항아리, 단지
jar 는 물건을 담아 두는 데 사용한다. jar 는 흔히 유리로 만들며, 딱 맞는 뚜껑이 있다 : 선생님은 우리의 그림 물감을 jar 에 담아 두신다.

**jaw** [dʒɔ́ː] 명 턱
jaw 는 신체의 일부로, 얼굴 아래쪽에 있는 뼈를 말한다. 말을 하면 jaw 가 움직인다.

**jealous** [dʒéləs] 형 질투심이 많은, 시샘하는, 부러워하는
jealous 는 누군가가 자신에게

없는 것을 가지고 있어서 기분이 좋지 않다는 의미다 : 레이는 친구 찰리가 새 야구 글러브를 가지고 있어서 **시샘이 났다.**

**jeans** [dʒíːnz] 명 진으로 만든 의복, **진바지**
jeans 는 질긴 무명천으로 만든 바지를 말한다 : 아이들이 페인트칠을 하거나 찰흙을 가지고 놀 때, 낡은 jeans 를 입는다.

**jelly** [dʒéli] 명 **젤리**
jelly 는 식품의 일종으로, 과일즙과 설탕을 함께 끓여서 만든다. jelly 는 여러 가지 종류의 과일로 만들 수 있다.

**jellyfish** [dʒélifiʃ] 명 **해파리**
jellyfish 는 동물이다. jellyfish 는 몸체가 부드러우며 바다에 떠다닌다. jellyfish 가 몸에 닿으면 상처를 입을 수도 있다.

**jet** [dʒét] 명 **제트(항공)기, 제트 엔진**
jet 는 비행기의 일종이다. jet 엔진은 프로펠러를 사용하지 않는다. jet 는 다른 비행기보다 더 빨리 난다.

**jewel** [dʒúːəl] 명 **보석** ; (보석을 박은) 장신구
jewel 은 일종의 돌로, 빛이 통과할 수 있다. 다이아몬드, 에메랄드, 루비는 jewel 이다 : 사람들은 종종 많은 돈을 주고 jewel 을 산다.

**jewelry | -ellery** [dʒúːəlri] 명 **보석류** ; (보석을 박은) 장신구류
반지, 팔찌, 목걸이는 jewelry 의 일종이다.

**job** [dʒáb | dʒɔ́b] 명 ① **일** ; 볼일, 직무 ② **직업,** 일자리, 지위
1 job 은 해야 할 필요가 있는 일이다 : 개를 씻기는 일이 피터가 해야 할 job 이다. 톰은 만찬용 식탁을 차리는 job 을 한다.
2 job 은 사람이 돈을 벌기 위해 하는 일이기도 하다 : 어머니의 job 은 선생님이다.

**jog** [dʒág | dʒɔ́g] 타 자 (운동하기 위해) **천천히 뛰다, 조깅하다** ; 터벅터벅(터덜터덜) 걷다

〔타고 가다〕
jog 는 달린다는 뜻이지만, **조 깅하는** 사람들은 빨리 뛰려고 는 하지 않는다. 사람들은 건강해지려고 운동으로 **조깅을 한다.**

**join** [dʒɔ́in] 〔타〕〔자〕 결합하다, **연 결하다** ; …와 합류하다 ; 참가 하다, **…에 가입하다**
1 join 은 물건을 조립한다는 뜻이다 : 나는 장난감 철도 차 량들을 **연결하여** 열차를 만들 었다.
2 join 은 또한 어떤 것의 일부 가 된다는 뜻이다 : 다이애나는 수영 클럽에 **가입하고** 싶어 한 다.

**joke** [dʒóuk] 〔명〕 **농담**, 익살, 희 롱, **장난**
1 joke 는 사람들을 웃기는 이 야기다 : 내 여동생의 다리가 부러졌을 때, 나는 joke 로 그 녀의 기분을 한층 쾌활하게 해 주었다.
2 joke 는 또한 누군가에게 하 는 장난이다 : 우리는 joke 로 아버지의 슬리퍼를 숨겼다.

**jolly** [dʒáli | dʒɔ́li] 〔형〕 **즐거운,** 유쾌한, 흥거운, 명랑한
jolly 는 활짝 미소 지어 웃는 다는 뜻이다 : 헬렌의 아버지는 그의 생일 파티에 몹시 **즐거워** 하셨다.

**journal** [dʒə́:rnəl] 〔명〕 ① **일지,** 일기 ② 신문, **일간 신문** ; 정 기 간행물
journal 은 한 일이나 생각을 글로 써 놓은 책이다.

**journey** [dʒə́:rni] 1 〔명〕 **여행** ; 여정 2 〔자〕 여행하다
journey 는 긴 여행이다 : 카를 로스는 대양을 횡단하는 jour-ney 로 몹시 흥분했다.

**joy** [dʒɔ́i] 〔명〕 **즐거움, 기쁨,** 환 회 ; 기쁨을 주는 것
joy 는 몹시 행복할 때 느끼는 감정이다 : 메리는 애완 동물

가게에서 새로 산 강아지를 집으로 데려가면시 joy 를 느꼈다(기뻐했다).

**judge** [dʒʌdʒ] 1 명 재판관, 판사 ; (경기·토론 등의) **심판,** **심사원** 2 타 자 **재판하다, 판단하다,** 판정하다
1 judge 는 사건을 판결하는 사람이다 : 사람들은 서로 의견이 맞지 않을 때, 누가 옳은지를 판결해 주는 judge 에게 가기도 한다.
2 judge 는 결정한다는 뜻이다 : 베티와 레이는 누가 그림을 더 잘그렸는지 **판단해** 달라고 아버지에게 부탁했다.

**juggle** [dʒʌɡl] 자 타 ① 요술을 부리다 ; 속이다 ② **떨어뜨릴 뻔하다 다시 잡다,** (공을) **저글하다**
juggle 은 두 개 이상의 물건을 공중에 차례로 던졌다가 재빨리 다시 잡는다는 뜻이다. **저글을 할** 때는 물건을 던지고 잡는 행위가 동시에 이루어진다 : 나는 하나도 떨어뜨리지 않고 세 개의 공을 동시에 **저글할 수 있다.**

**juice** [dʒúːs] 명 **주스,** 즙, 액
juice 는 과일이나 야채에서 얻는 액체다 : 클레어는 토마토 juice 를 좋아한다. 마이크가 제일 좋아하는 과일 juice 는

사과 juice 다.

**July** [dʒuːlái] 명 **7 월**
July 는 한 해 가운데 한 달이다. July 는 31 일이며, 6 월이 끝나고 8 월이 시작되기 전에 온다.

**jump** [dʒʌmp] 자 타 깡충 뛰다, **뛰어오르다 ; 뛰어넘다**
jump 는 발과 다리 근육을 이용해 공중으로 솟구쳐 오른다는 뜻이다 : 스콧은 공을 잡기 위해 **깡충 뛰어야만** 했다. 사슴이 울타리를 **뛰어넘어** 숲속으로 달아났다. 다른 아이들이 줄을 돌리는 사이에 빌리는 그 줄을 **뛰어넘었다.**

**June** [dʒúːn] 명 **6 월**
June 은 한 해 가운데 한 달이다. June 은 30 일이며, 5 월이 끝나고 7 월이 시작되기 전에 온다.

**jungle** [dʒʌ́ŋgl] 명 밀림 (지대), 정글
jungle 은 수많은 나무와 식물들이 자라는 곳이다. jungle 은 무덥고 비가 많이 온다. 원숭이, 뱀, 앵무새, 모기들이 jungle 에 산다.

**junk** [dʒʌ́ŋk] 명 쓰레기, 못쓸 것, 폐물, 잡동사니 ; 고철
junk 는 사람들이 원하지 않는 것이다. 낡은 자동차와 부서진 가구는 junk 다.

**just** [《약》 dʒəst, 《강》 dʒʌ́st] 1 부 ① 정확히, 틀림없이, 바로 ② 다만, 단지, 오로지 ③ [완료형과 함께] 이제 방금, 막…했다 2 형 ① [사람・행위 등이] 올바른, 공정한 ② [가격・보수 등이] 적정한, 정당한 ③ [저울・숫자 등이] 정확한

1 just 는 「다만」이란 뜻이다 : 웬디는 창 밖에서 괴상한 동물 소리를 들었다고 생각했지만, 그것은 단지 다람쥐 소리였다.
2 just 는 또한 조금 전이라는 뜻이다 : 월터의 생일은 어제였다. 그는 막 7 살이 지났다.
3 just 는 정확한 액수〔양〕를 뜻하기도 한다 : 조지가 갖고 싶은 연은 2 달러였는 데, 그의 호주머니에는 2 달러가 있었다. 조지는 그 연을 살 만한 돈이 있었다.

J

**kangaroo** [kæ̀ŋgərúː] 명 캥거루

kangaroo 는 큰 동물이다. kangaroo 는 힘센 뒷다리로 껑충 뛰며 매우 빠르게 움직인다. 어미 kangaroo들은 배 앞쪽에 있는 주머니에 새끼들을 넣고 다닌다.

**keep** [kíːp] 타 자 ① 계속〔유지〕하다 ; 간직〔간수〕하다, **가지고 있다** ② (동물을) **기르다** ③ (법률·규칙을) 지키다 ; 관리하다 ④ …한 상태에 있다

1 keep 은 무언가를 가지고 있다는 의미다 : 윌버의 어머니는 그가 얻은 강아지를 **기르게** 했다.

2 keep 은 또한 같은 상태를 유지한다는 의미다 : 테리씨는 아이들에게 영화를 보는 동안 조용히 **하라고** 일렀다.

**kept** [képt] 동 keep (간직하다) 의 과거·과거분사형

kept 는 keep 의 한 형태다 : 앨은 3주 동안 그 책을 **갖고 있었다.**

**ketchup** [kétʃəp] 명 케첩

ketchup 은 식품의 일종이다. ketchup 은 토마토로 만드는 걸쭉하고 붉은 색을 띤 액체다.

**kettle** [kétl] 명 주전자 ; 솥, 탕관 ; (스튜를 요리하는) 냄비

kettle 은 물을 끓이는 금속제의 원통형 그릇이다. 뚜껑을 열지 않고도 kettle 에서 물을 따를 수 있다 : 우리집 kettle 은 물이 끓기 시작하면 삐하고 소리를 낸다.

**key** [kíː] 몡 ① 열쇠 ② (피아
노·타이프라이터 등의) 키,
건 ③ (문제·사건 등의) 해
답, 해결의 실마리
1 key는 자물쇠를 열거나 잠
그는 데 쓰는 것이다. 자물쇠
에는 저마다 그것에 꼭 맞는
전용 key가 있다 : 이 key로
현관문을 연다.
2 key는 또한 눌러야 작동이
되는 기계나 악기의 한 부분이
다. 컴퓨터에는 글자와 숫자를
나타내주는 key가 있다. 피아
노에는 검은 key와 흰 key가
있다.

**keyboard** [kíːbɔ̀ːrd] 몡 건반 ;
(컴퓨터의) 자판 ; 키보드
keyboard는 키가 연속해서 짜
여져 있거나 한 줄로 늘어선
것을 말한다 : 피아노와 컴퓨터
에는 keyboard가 있다.

**keyhole** [kíːhòuəl] 몡 열쇠 구
멍 ; 마개 구멍
keyhole은 자물쇠에 난 구멍
이다. 열쇠를 keyhole에 꽂고
돌려서 자물쇠를 연다.

**kick** [kík] 타자 차다, 걷어 차다
kick은 발로 무언가를 찬다는
뜻이다 : 마이크는 깡통을 걷어

찼다.

**kid** [kíd] 몡 새끼 염소(고기) ;
아이 ; 젊은이
1 kid는 새끼 염소를 말한다.
2 kid는 또한 어린 아이를 말
한다 : "너희 녀석들 야구를 하
고 싶지?"하고 켈리 아저씨가
물으셨다.

**kill** [kíl] 타자 죽이다, 살해하
다 ; (시간을) 보내다
kill은 무언가를 죽인다는 뜻
이다 : 고양이가 생쥐를 죽였
다.

**kilometer│-tre** [kilámətər,
kíləmìːtər│kíləmìːtə,
kilɔ́mətə] 몡 킬로미터
kilometer는 길이의 양이다. 1
kilometer는 1000 미터다. 1
kilometer는 반 마일이 조금
넘는다.

**kind**¹ [káind] 몡 종류
kind는 어떤 것의 종류를 뜻
한다 : 상추는 야채의 한 kind

다. 당근과 감자는 kind 가 다
르다.

**kind²** [káind] 톙 **친절한,** 상냥
한 ; 인정있는, 동정심 많은
kind 는 남을 도우려고 한다는
뜻이다 : 사라는 집이 없는 사
람들에게 **친절하게** 대하려고
한다.

**kindergarten** [kíndərgàːrtən]
톙 **유치원**
kindergarten 은 학교에 준하
며, 이곳을 거쳐서 초등학교 1
학년이 된다 : kindergarten 에
서 우리는 게임도 하고, 블록
도 쌓고, 찰흙과 그림 물감도
사용하고, 이야기도 듣는다.
우리는 또한 노래도 부르고,
악기도 연주하고, 애완 동물도
돌보고, 그림책도 보며, 우리
들 자신만의 책을 만들기도 한
다.

**king** [kíŋ] 톙 **왕**
king 은 나라를 다스리는 남자
를 말한다 : 나는 성에 사는
king 과 여왕에 관한 이야기를
좋아한다.

**kingdom** [kíŋdəm] 톙 **왕국**

kingdom 은 왕이나 여왕이 다
스리는 나라를 말한다 : 브라운
부인은 마법의 kingdom 에 관
한 동화책을 반 학생들에게 읽
어주었다.

**kiss** [kís] 1 타재 **키스하다,** 입
맞추다 2 톙 **키스, 입맞춤**
kiss 는 입술을 댄다는 뜻이
다. 우리는 사랑한다는 표시로
사람들에게 **키스를 한다** : 클레
어와 토니는 밤마다 자기 전에
부모님에게 항상 **키스를 한다.**

**kit** [kít] 톙 ① **연장통 ; 도구** 한
벌 ② 다 갖춰진 여행〔운동〕
용구 ③ (조립) **재료**〔부품〕일
습
kit 는 조립을 해야만 하는 한
세트의 재료를 말한다 : 모형
자동차와 모형 비행기는 보통
kit (조립식 부품 세트)로 되어
있다.

**kitchen** [kítʃən] 톙 **부엌**
kitchen 은 사람들이 음식을
요리하며 식사를 하는 방이
다 : 우리집 kitchen 에는 스토
브, 냉장고, 싱크대, 그리고
식탁과 의자가 있다 : 베티와
마틴 가족은 kitchen 에서 식

사를 한다.

**kite** [káit] 몡 연 ; 솔개
kite 는 긴 실 끝에 매달아 하늘에 날리는 장난감이다. kite 는 나무 막대에 종이나 플라스틱 혹은 천을 씌워 만든다. 간혹 그림이 그려진 kite 도 있다.

**kitten** [kítən] 몡 새끼 고양이
kitten 은 새끼 고양이를 말한다. 대부분의 사람들은 kitten 을 좋아한다.

**knee** [ní:] 몡 무릎, 무릎 관절
knee 는 다리가 굽혀지는 신체 부위다. knee 는 다리 중간에 있다.

**kneel** [ní:əl] 쟈 무릎을 꿇다, 무릎을 굽히다
kneel 은 무릎을 꿇는다는 뜻이다. 한쪽 무릎으로만 무릎을 꿇을 수도 있다 : 맥밀런씨는 정원에서 일할 때 무릎을 꿇고 한다.

**knew** [njú:] 됭 know (알다)의

과거형
knew 는 know 의 한 형태다 : 앤은 4 살 때 자기 이름을 쓸 줄 알았다.

**knife** [náif] 몡 나이프, 창칼 ; 식칼
knife 는 도구의 일종이다. knife 에는 손잡이와 날카로운 날이 있는 금속 조각이 있다 : 폴은 knife 로 사과를 잘랐다.

**knight** [náit] 몡 기사
knight 는 옛날에 왕이나 여왕을 위해 싸우던 병사였다. knight 들은 용감하고 정직했으며 도움이 필요한 사람들을 보호했다. knight들은 갑옷과 투구를 착용하고 말을 탔다.

**knit** [nít] 탸쟈 뜨다, 짜다 ; 뜨개질하다
knit 는 긴 바늘과 털실을 이용해 스카프, 스웨터, 그 밖의 의류나 천을 만든다는 뜻이다 : 마리아는 인형에게 입힐 빨간 모직 스웨터를 짰다.

**knives** [náivz] 몡 knife 의 복수형
knives 는 두 개 이상의 나이

K

프를 나타낸다. knife 들은 크
기와 모양이 다양하다.

**knob** [náb|nɔ́b] 명 혹, 마디 ;
둥근 덩이 ; (문·서랍·전기 기
구 등의) **손잡이**, 쥐는 곳
knob은 문이나 서랍을 여는
둥근 손잡이다 : 수는 서랍을
열려고 했으나 손에서 knob
이 빠져 버렸다. knob 은 또
한 라디오나 텔레비전 혹은 그
밖의 기계에 쓰인다. 그 knob
을 오른쪽으로 돌리면 라디오
소리가 더 커진다.

**knock** [nák|nɔ́k] 타자 ① (문
을) **두드리다**, **치다**, 때리다
② 부딪치다, **충돌하다** ; …을
두드려서 떨다, 털어내다
1 knock 은 무언가를 친다는
뜻이다. 문을 두드릴 때, 주먹
으로 문을 쳐서 소리를 낸다 :
만성절 전날 밤 우리는 과자를
달라고 이웃집 문을 **두드렸다.**
폭풍이 치는 동안 내내 나뭇가
지가 창문을 **두드려댔다.**

2 knock 은 또한 무언가를 밀

어서 떨어지게 한다는 뜻이
다 : 강아지가 램프를 **쳐서** 탁
자에서 **떨어뜨렸다.**

**knot** [nát|nɔ́t] 1 명 매듭 2 타
자 (끈 등을) 매다, 매듭짓다
knot 은 두 개의 물건을 한 데
맨 자리를 말한다. 사람들은
실이나 로프 혹은 리본으로
knot 을 짓는다.

**know** [nóu] 타자 ① 알다, 잘
**알고 있다** ② **정통하다** ③ 체
험하다 ; 식별하다
know 는 매우 확신한다는 뜻
이다 : 딕은 큰 길가에 사는 사
람들을 모두 **알고 있다.** 여름
이 끝날 때쯤, 캠프촌에 있는
아이들은 모두 다 수영하는 법
을 **알게 되었다.**

**known** [nóun] 동 know (알다)
의 과거분사형
known 은 know 의 한 형태
다 : 앨과 웬디는 서로 **알고 지**
**낸** 지 2 년이 된다.

**ladder** [lǽdər] 명 **사다리**
ladder는 올라가거나 내려가는
데 사용한다. ladder는 나무로
된 것도 있고 금속이나 밧줄로
된 것도 있다. 소방수들은 높
은 건물에서 작업을 하는데
ladder 를 사용한다.

**lady** [léidi] 명 **부인, 여자 ; 숙녀**
lady 는 성인 여자다 : 어떤
lady 에게서 엄마한테 전화가
왔다.

**laid** [léid] 동 lay¹ (눕히다, 낳
다)의 과거 · 과거분사형
laid는 단어 lay¹ 에서 생긴 말
이다 : 바다거북은 모래 속에
알을 **낳았다**.

**lain** [léin] 동 lie² (눕다)의 과거

분사형
lain은 lie²의 한 형태다 : 올리
버는 침대에 눕는 것을 좋아한
다. 그는 보통 **누우면** 몇 분
안되어 잠이 든다.

**lake** [léik] 명 **호수**
lake는 사방이 육지로 둘러싸
인 물이다. 대부분의 lake의
물은 소금기가 없다 : 우리는
여름에 lake에서 수영을 한다.

**lamb** [lǽm] 명 **새끼양, 어린
양 (고기)**
lamb은 어린 양이다. lamb에
서 얻는 모직물은 대단히 부드
럽다.

**lamp** [lǽmp] 명 **램프 ; 등불**

lamp는 어두운 곳을 밝히는 데 사용한다. 내부분의 lamp는 빛을 내는 데 전기를 이용한다.

**land** [lǽnd] 1 명 땅, 육지 ; 토지 ; 나라 ; 국토 2 자 상륙〔착륙〕하다 ; 내리다

1 land는 지구에서 물로 덮여 있지 않은 곳이다. 사람들은 land에서 산다.

2 land는 나라다 : 여러 다른 land에서 발행한 우표를 수집할 수 있다.

3 land는 사람들이 이용하는 흙이나 땅이다 : 농부들은 자신들의 land에 감자를 심었다.

4 land는 땅으로 내려온다는 뜻이다 : 블레이크는 들판에 **착륙한** 비행기를 보았다.

**language** [lǽŋgwidʒ] 명 언어, 말 ; 국어

language는 사람들이 서로에게 말을 하거나 글을 쓸 때 사용하는 것이다. 몇 개의 language를 말할 줄 아는 사람들도 있다.

**lap** [lǽp] 명 무릎

lap은 앉아 있을 때 다리의 윗부분을 말한다. 일어서면 lap은 없어진다 : 우리 고양이는 내 lap에 앉는 것을 좋아한다.

**large** [lάːrdʒ] 형 큰 ; 넓은 ; (수나 양이) 많은

large는 크다는 뜻이다. **큰** 것은 많은 공간을 차지한다 : 코끼리와 고래는 **큰** 동물이다.

**last¹** [lǽst | lάːst] [late의 최상급] 형 ① 최후의, 마지막의 ② 바로 앞의 ; 지난 …, 요전 … ③ 최근의

1 last는 마지막에 있다는 뜻이다 : 이 사전의 **마지막** 단어는 무엇이니 ? 토요일은 한 주의 **마지막** 날이다.

2 last는 또한 지난 시간을 뜻한다 : 나는 **지난** 겨울에 스키를 배웠다. **어젯**밤 빌리는 영화를 보았다.

**last²** [lǽst | lάːst] 자 계속〔지속, 존속〕하다 ; 손상되지 않다 ; 오래 가다

last는 원상태를 유지한다는 뜻이다 : 냉장고 속의 우유는 며칠 동안은 **상하지 않을 것이다**. 봄이 올 때까지 산에 눈이 **녹지 않았다**.

**late** [léit] 1 ⃞형 늦은,  지각한 ; 최근의 ; 앞서의, 이전의 2 ⃞부 늦게,  뒤늦게

late는 오기로 되어 있는 시간을 지나서 온다는 뜻이다 : 앨버트는 오늘 학교에 **늦었다**. 보브는 앨버트보다 **더 늦었다**. 카를로스가 제일 나중에 왔다. 세 사람 중에서 카를로스가 **가장 늦었다**.

**later** [léitər] [late 의  비교급] 1 ⃞형 더 늦은 2 ⃞부 후에,  나중에

later는 「시간이 더 지난 후에」라는 뜻이다 : 우리가 지금은 갈 수 없지만, **나중에** 만나게 될 것이다.

**laugh** [læf|láːf] 1 ⃞자 웃다,  웃음을 짓다 2 ⃞명 웃음 ; 웃음소리

laugh는 재미있다는 사실을 나타내려고 소리를 낸다는 뜻이다 : 배리는 재미있는 농담을 들으면 항상 **웃는다**.

**launch** [lɔ́ːntʃ, láːntʃ|lɔ́ːntʃ] ⃞타 진수시키다 ; 발사하다,  발진시키다

launch는 어떤 것을 움직여서 앞으로 내보낸다는 뜻이다.

**laundry** [lɔ́ːndri, láːn-|lɔ́ːn-] ⃞명 세탁물 ; 세탁소 ; 세탁실

laundry는 빨래하려고 하는 더러운 옷이다. laundry는 또한 방금 빨래한 깨끗한 옷이다.

**law** [lɔ́ː] ⃞명 법,  법률 ; 법규

law는 시나 주 혹은 국가의 행정부가 만든 규칙이다. law는 사람들을 안전하게 지켜준다.

**lawn** [lɔ́ːn] ⃞명 잔디 (밭)

lawn은 집이나 건물 주변의 풀밭이다 : 찰리는 격주로 토요일마다 lawn을 깎는다.

**L**

**lay**¹ [léi] 타 ① 놓다, 눕히다 ② 낳다

1 lay는 어떤 것을 내려놓는다는 뜻이다 : 그 책을 탁자 위에 **놓아 주십시오.**

2 lay는 또한 알을 낳는다는 뜻이다 : 암탉이 달걀을 두 개 **낳았다.**

**lay**² [léi] 동 lie² (눕다)의 과거형

lay는 단어 lie²에서 생긴 말이다 : 우리는 구름을 바라보며 풀밭에 **누워 있었다.**

**lazy** [léizi] 형 게으른, 나태한 ; **나른한**

lazy는 아무것도 하고 싶지 않다는 뜻이다 : 어제 날씨가 너무 좋아서 잭은 잔디를 깎고 싶지 않았다. 그는 너무 **나른해서** 일을 할 수 없었다.

**lead**¹ [líːd] 타 자 ① 인도하다, 안내하다, 데리고 가다 ② 이끌다, 지도하다, 지휘하다, …의 선두에 서다 ③ 이르다, 통하다

lead가 seed와 같은 발음이 나면, 길을 안내하거나 맨 앞에서 간다는 뜻이다 : 조는 경주에서 **선두로** 달리고 있다. 악단이 퍼레이드를 **맨 앞에서 이끌었다.**

**lead**² [léd] 명 연필의 심 ; 납

lead가 bed와 같은 발음이 나면, 자국을 내는 연필의 검은 부분을 뜻한다.

**leader** [líːdər] 명 인도자, 지도자, 리더, 수령 ; 지휘관

leader는 사람들에게 길을 안내하거나 맨 앞에 나선다 : 미국의 leader를 대통령이라고 부른다.

**leaf** [líːf] 명 잎, 나뭇잎, 풀잎 ; 꽃잎

leaf는 식물의 한 부분이다. leaves가 녹색인 나무와 꽃들이 많다. 가을에 여러 가지 색으로 변하는 leaves도 있다.

**leak** [líːk] 자 타 새다, 새어 나오다 ; 새게 하다

leak는 안에 있는 것이 작은 구멍이나 깨진 틈을 통해 천천히 밖으로 나온다는 뜻이다 : 타이어에서 바람이 **새고 있었다.**

**learn** [ləːrn] 타 자 배우다, 익히다 ; 공부하다 ; **알다** ; 듣다

learn은 어떤 것을 알게 된다는 뜻이다 : 젊은 사람이나 늙은 사람이나 언제나 새로운 것을 **배울 수 있다.**

**leash** [líːʃ] 명 (개 등을 매는) 가죽끈, 쇠사슬

leash는 개의 목걸이에 매단 로프나 체인의 일종이다 : 토니는 개가 도망치지 못하도록 나무에 leash를 묶었다.

**least** [líːst] [little의 최상급] 1 형 가장 적은〔작은〕; (중요성·가치가) 가장 낮은 2 부 가장 적게〔작게〕

least는 다른 어떤 것 보다도 더 적다는 뜻이다 : 자동차는 소음이 상당히 난다. 자전거는 소음이 덜 난다. 걷는 것은 셋 중에서 소음이 **가장 적게** 난다.

**leather** [léðər] 명 가죽, 무두질한 가죽 ; 가죽 제품

leather는 동물의 가죽으로 만든 소재로 신발, 장갑, 그 밖의 다른 물건을 만드는 데 쓰인다 : 레이의 운동화는 leather로 만든 것이다.

**leave** [líːv] 타 자 ① 떠나다, 나가다, 출발하다 ② 놓고 가다, 두고 가다 ③ 내버려 두다 ; 남기다 ; 맡기다

1 leave는 떠난다는 뜻이다 : 우리는 다섯 시에 **떠나야** 한다.

2 leave는 또한 어떤 곳에 무언가를 놓아두고 간다는 뜻이다 : 저녁 식사가 끝난 뒤에도 책을 의자에 **놓아 두어도** 좋다.

**leaves** [líːvz] 명 leaf의 복수형

leaves는 단어 leaf에서 생긴 말이다 : 가을에 나무 leaves가 선홍색으로 변했다(단풍이 들었다).

**led** [léd] 동 lead¹ (이끌다)의 과거·과거분사형

led는 lead¹의 한 형태다 : 앤은 여동생의 손을 잡아 **이끌었다.**

**left**¹ [léft] 1 형 왼편의 ; 왼쪽의 2 명 왼쪽, 왼편, 좌측

신체는 **왼편**과 오른편이 있다. 시계의 앞면을 볼 때, 9 자는 **왼편**에 있다. 책을 볼 때, 페이지의 **왼쪽**부터 읽기 시작한

다 : 내 여동생은 **왼손**으로 글
씨를 쓴다.

**left²** [léft] 통 leave (떠나다, 맡
기다)의 과거 · 과거분사형
left는 단어 leave에서 생긴 말
이다 : 우리 가족은 고양이를
친구에게 **맡겨두고** 휴가를 갔
다.

**leg** [lég] 명 **다리**, (의자 · 책상
의) **다리** ; 받침(대)
1 leg는 신체의 한 부위다. 동
물과 사람들은 leg로 걷는다.
2 leg는 또한 어떤 것을 받쳐
주는 부분이다. 대부분의 가구
에는 leg가 있다.

**lemon** [lémən] 명 **레몬** ; 레몬
나무
lemon은 과일의 일종이다.
lemon은 노랗고 신맛이 난다.

**length** [léŋkθ] 명 **길이**

length는 한쪽 끝에서 다른 쪽
끝까지의 긴 정도를 나타낸
다 : 그 수영장의 length는 50
피트다. 내 침대의 length는 6
피트다.

**leopard** [lépərd] 명 **표범**
leopard는 큰 야생 동물이다.
leopard는 고양이과에 속하며,
진노랑색의 털과 검은 반점이
있다.

**less** [lés] [little의 비교급] 1 형
**…보다 적은** 2 부 **…보다 적
게**
less는 다른 어떤 것만큼 없다
는 뜻이다 : 너에게는 7센트가
있고, 나에게는 9센트가 있
다. 너는 나보다 돈을 더 **적게**
갖고 있다. 버스를 타면, 걷는
것보다 시간이 **더 적게** 걸린
다. 이 셔츠는 저 셔츠보다 **덜
비싸다**(더 싸다).

**lesson** [lésən] 명 **학과** ; (교과서
의) **과** ; **수업** (시간), **레슨**
lesson은 배우기로 되어 있는
것이다 : 수는 무용 lesson을
받는다.

**let** [lét] 〔타〕 …하게 하다, …을
허락하다 ; 가게〔오게〕 하다
let은 어떤 것을 해도 좋다는
뜻이다 : 아버지께서는 어젯밤
우리가 늦게까지 자지 않아도
**내버려 두셨다.**

**let's** [léts] let us의 단축형
let's는 let us의 뜻이다. 누군
가와 함께 어떤 일을 하고 싶
을 때 let's를 쓴다 : 내일 동물
원에 **가자.**

**letter** [létər] 〔명〕 글자,　문자 ;
편지
1 letter는 사람들이 말을 적을
때 사용하는 부호의 하나다.
영어 알파벳의 letter는 A, B,
C, D, E, F, G, H, I, J, K, L, M,
N, O, P, Q, R, S, T, U, V, W,
X, Y 그리고 Z 다.
2 letter 는 또한 종이에 적는
메시지다 : 딕은 친구들 모두에
게 letter를 쓴다.

**lettuce** [létəs] 〔명〕 상추, 양상추
lettuce는 큰 녹색잎의　채소
로, 샐러드나 샌드위치에 넣는
다.

**liar** [láiər] 〔명〕 거짓말쟁이
liar는 진실을 말하지 않는 사
람이다.

**librarian** [laibrέəriən] 〔명〕 사
서 ; 도서관 직원
librarian은 도서관에서 일하는
사람이다 : 우리 학교의 librar-
ian 은 우리가 필요한 책을 찾
을 수 있게 도와준다.

**library** [láibrèri, -brəri|-brəri]
〔명〕 도서관,　도서실 ; (개인의)
문고
library는 많은 책이 보관되어
있는 곳이다. 사람들은 library
에서 책을 빌려 집에 가져 가
서 읽는다.

**lick** [lík] 〔타〕 핥다
lick은 어떤 것에 혀를 댄다는
뜻이다 : 고양이가　자기　몸을
**핥았다.** 엘리자베스는 아이스
크림 콘을 핥아 먹었다.

**lie**[1] [lái] 1 〔명〕　거짓말 ; 허위 2
〔자〕 거짓말을 하다
1 lie는 어떤 것을 사실과 다르
게 말한다는 뜻이다 : 마리아는
창문을 깼을 때 야단 맞고 싶
지 않았다. 그래서 그녀는 자

기가 깨지 않았다고 **거짓말을 했다.**

2 lie는 사실과 다르게 말하는 것이다 : 카를로스는 어머니에게 **거짓말을** 했지만, 나중에는 진실을 말하기로 했다.

**lie²** [lái] 째 눕다, 드러[가로]눕다 ; (어떤 상태에) 놓여 있다, 있다

lie는 수평으로 (몸을) 쭉 뻗는다는 뜻이다. **누워있다**는 것은 앉아있는 것도 아니고 서있는 것도 아니다 : 그 개는 새끼가 뜰에서 노는 동안 문 옆에 **엎드려 있는** 것을 좋아한다.

**life** [láif] 명 ① 생명 ; 생존 ; 수명 ; 일생 ② 생활, 삶 ; 인생, 인생사

1 life는 동식물이 살아있다는 것이다.
2 life는 살아있는 기간이다. 곤충의 life는 짧다. life가 아주 긴 나무도 있다.

**lift** [líft] 1 타째 들어올리다, 들다 ; 오르다, 높아지다 2 명 들어올리기 ; 승강기, 엘리베이터

lift는 어떤 깃을 집어올린다는 뜻이다 : 무거운 가방을 **든다는** 게 마이크에게는 힘든 일이었다. 제인은 팔을 **들어** 흔들며 작별 인사를 했다.

**light¹** [láit] 1 명 ① 빛 ; 밝음 ② 등불, 등, 불빛 ; 발광체 2 형 밝은 ; (색깔이) 연한, 엷은 3 타째 ① 불을 **붙이다**[켜다] ; 밝게 하다, 비추다 ② 불이 붙다 ; 켜지다 ; 밝아지다, **빛나다**

1 light는 태양에서 나오는 에너지다. light가 있을 때, 우리는 사물을 볼 수 있다.
2 빛을 내는 것을 light라고 부른다. 램프와 양초는 light다 : 마거릿은 책을 읽으려고 침실에 light를 켰다.
3 light는 무언가를 태우거나 빛을 내게 한다는 뜻이다 : 촛불을 **켤** 때 조심해라. 우리는 오늘밤 크리스마스 트리에 **불을 밝히려고** 한다.
4 light는 또한 색깔을 표현하는 방법이다. 분홍은 **엷은** 색이다.

**light**² [láit] 형 가벼운 ; 날씬한 ; 경쾌한
light는 무겁지 않다는 뜻이다 : 빈 여행 가방은 **가볍다**.

**lighthouse** [láithàus] 명 등대
lighthouse는 꼭대기에 환한 등불을 켜놓은 탑이다. lighthouse는 배가 안전하게 지나갈 수 있도록 물 속의 위험한 곳 근처에 세운다 : 우리는 배에서 lighthouse를 보고 암초를 무사히 통과했다.

**lightning** [láitniŋ] 명 번갯(불)
lightning은 하늘에서 크게 번쩍이는 빛이다. lightning은 전기의 형태를 띠고 있다. 폭풍우가 칠 때, lightning은 하늘에서 땅까지 치는 수도 있다 : 나는 어두운 하늘에서 번쩍이는 lightning을 보았다.

**like**¹ [láik] 타 자 좋아하다, 마음에 들다 ; 바라다 ; …하고 싶다
like는 어떤 것때문에 기분이 좋아진다는 뜻이다 : 잭과 그의 친구들은 피자를 **좋아한다**.

**like**² [láik] 형 같은, …와 비슷한, 닮은
like는 같다는 뜻이다 : 톰과 토니는 쌍둥이 형제다. 그들은 서로 무척 **닮았다**.

**lime** [láim] 명 라임 열매
lime은 과일의 일종으로, 초록색이며 작은 레몬처럼 생겼다. lime은 신맛이 난다.

**line** [láin] 명 ① 선, 금 ② 행, 한 줄 ③ 노선, 진로, 길 ; 줄, 열, 행렬 ④ 밧줄, 끈
1 line은 길고 가는 자국이다 : 수잔은 연필로 종이에 가로로 line을 그었다.
2 line은 또한 한 줄로 늘어선 것이다 : 우리는 버스를 타기 위해 line을 섰다.

**lion** [láiən] 명 사자
lion은 큰 야생 동물로, 큰 고양이와 비슷하다. lion은 먹이로 다른 동물들을 사냥한다. 수사자는 머리 주변에 길고 숱이 많은 털(갈기)이 있다.

**lioness** [láiənəs|-nès, -nəs] 명 암사자

lioness는 암사자다. lioness
는 수사자보다 작고, 머리 주
변에 긴 털(갈기)이 없다.

**lip** [líp] 몡 입술
lip은 얼굴에서 입을 둘러싸고
있는 부분이다. 사람들은 lip
이 두 개다.

**liquid** [líkwid] 몡 액체
liquid는 만지면 젖게 되는 것
이다. liquid는 따를 수 있다.
물과 우유는 liquid다.

**list** [líst] 몡 표, 일람표, 목록,
명부
list는 많은 것들을 기록해 놓
은 것이다 : 한나는 파티에 초
대할 사람들의 list를 작성했
다.

**listen** [lísən] 쟈 ① 듣다, 경청
하다, **귀를 기울이다** ② 들어
주다, 따르다
listen은 주의깊게 들으려고 한
다는 뜻이다 : 아이들은 이야기
에 **귀를 기울였다**. 조지는 음
악을 즐겨 **듣는다**. 나는 지붕
에 떨어지는 빗소리를 **듣는** 것
을 좋아한다.

**lit** [lít] 몽 light¹ (불을 붙이다)
의 과거 · 과거분시형
lit은 단어 light¹ 에서 생긴 말
이다 : 우리는 어두운 홀로 내
려가는 길을 찾기 위해 촛불을
**켰다**. 데이비드 아저씨는 벽난
로 안의 통나무에 **불을 붙였
다**.

**liter** | **-tre** [líːtər] 몡 리터
liter는 액체의 양이다. 1 liter
는 1 쿼트 보다 용량이 조금
더 크다.

**little** [lítl] 1 혱 ① 작은, 어린
② [a little로] **조금** ③ [little
로] **거의 없는** 2 뷔 ① [a
little로] **조금은** ② [little로]
**거의〔전혀〕 …않다**
1 little은 작다는 뜻이다 : 내
어린 여동생은 아직 걷지 못한
다. 개미는 **작다**. 그것은 내가
지금까지 본 것 중에 가장 **작
은** 강아지다.

2 little은 그다지 많지 않다는
뜻이다 : 잭은 목이 마르지 않
아서 주스를 **조금**만 마셨다.
메리는 그림에 빨간색을 **조금**
썼다. 비가 오기 시작해서 우
리는 사과를 딸 시간이 **조금**

밖에 없었다.

**live** [lív] 자 살다 ; 생존하다 ; 생활하다 ; 존속하다

1 live는 살아 있다는 뜻이다 : 현재 지구상에 **살아 있는** 공룡은 한 마리도 없다.

2 live 는 또한 집이 있다는 뜻이다 : 빌리와 조니는 우리 옆집에 **산다.**

**lives** [láivz] 명 life의 복수형

lives는 단어 life에서 생긴 말이다 : 초기 탐험가들의 lives는 위험으로 가득 차 있었다. 리언은 영웅과 여걸들의 lives에 관한 이야기를 즐겨 읽는다.

**lizard** [lízərd] 명 도마뱀

lizard는 네 개의 다리와 긴 꼬리가 있는 동물이다. 대부분의 lizard 는 곤충을 즐겨 잡아 먹는다. lizard, 뱀, 바다거북 그리고 악어는 모두 파충류다.

**load** [lóud] 1 명 짐 ; 적재량 2 타 …에 짐을 싣다

1 load는 운반하는 물건이다 : 마크는 집 안으로 나무 두 load (짐)를 가지고 들어왔다.

2 load는 운반해 갈 수 있는 곳에 물건을 놓는다는 뜻이다 : 리즈와 그녀의 남동생은 트럭에 상자들을 **실었다.** 그들은 배에 석탄을 **실었다.**

**loaf** [lóuf] 명 **한 덩어리의 구운 빵, 빵 한 덩어리** ; 로프 《구이 요리》

1 loaf는 길게 한 덩어리로 구운 빵이다 : 우리는 제과점에서 빵 두 loaf(덩어리)를 샀다.

2 loaf는 또한 빵처럼 생긴 또 다른 종류의 음식이다 : 조가 가장 좋아하는 저녁 식사는 meat loaf (빵 모양의 다진 양념 구이 고기)와 샐러드다.

**loan** [lóun] 1 명 대부, **빌려주기** 2 타 자 대부하다 ; **빌려주다** ; 돈을 빌려주다

loan 은 빌려 가도록 한다는 뜻이다 : 피터가 연필을 잊고 안가져 와서, 헬렌이 자기 연필 한 자루를 그에게 **빌려주었다.**

**loaves** [lóuvz] 명 loaf의 복수형

loaves는 두 개 이상의 빵 덩어리를 나타낸다. 가게에 있는 빵 loaves(덩어리들)는 미리 여러 조각으로 잘라 놓는 경우가 많다.

**lobster** [lábstər | lɔ́b-] 명 **바닷가재** ; 대하

L

lobster는 동물이다. lobster는 바다 밑바닥에 산다. lobster 는 단단한 껍질과 커다란 집게 발과 꼬리가 있다.

**lock** [lák | lɔ́k] 1 명 **자물쇠** 2 타자 …에 자물쇠를 채우다, **잠그다 ; 잠기다 ;** 닫히다
1 lock는 어떤 것을 잠그는데 쓰는 물건이다. 열쇠가 있어야 만 lock를 열 수 있다.
2 lock는 열쇠를 자물쇠에 꽂 아서 돌린다는 뜻이다 : 문은 모두 밖에서 **잠겨 있다.**

**log** [lɔ́:g | lɔ́g] 명 **통나무,** (제재 용의) **원목**
log는 크고 둥근 나무 토막이 다. log는 나무를 자른 것이 다. 벽난로에 쓰는 log가 있는 가 하면, 잘라서 판자로 쓰는 log도 있다.

**lonely** [lóunli] 형 **외로운 ;** 허전 한 **;** 외진
lonely는 혼자 있는 것을 불행 해 한다는 뜻이다 : 머리는 친

구들이 모두 여름을 보내려고 떠나버려 **쓸쓸하다.**

**long** [lɔ́:ŋ | lɔ́ŋ] 형 **긴 ;** 키가 **큰 ;** 오랜, 지루한 **;** …**이상 ;** 길 이가 …**인**
1 long은 어떤 것의 한쪽 끝에 서 다른 쪽 끝까지의 거리가 멀다는 뜻이다 : 1 학년 교실과 2 학년 교실 사이에 **긴** 복도가 있다.
2 long은 또한 시간이 많이 걸린다는 뜻이다 : 마이크는 피 곤해서 점심을 먹고난 뒤 **오랫 동안** 낮잠을 잤다. 1 시간은 1 분보다 **길다.** 내가 사는 곳에 서 바다까지는 차로 **한참** 가야 한다.

**look** [lúk] 자 ① **보다, 바라보 다 ;** 주시하다 ; 찾다 **;** 눈여겨보 다 ② (…로) **보이다,** (…)**인 듯싶다**
1 look은 눈으로 본다는 뜻이 다 : 해리는 나에게 자기의 새 책을 **보게** 했다. 우리는 창문 밖에 있는 사슴을 **내다 보았 다.** 테리와 스튜어트는 주의깊 게 **살펴본** 다음에 도로를 건넜 다.
2 look은 또한 사람들의 눈에

어떻게 비치는 가를 말한다 :
수는 잃어버린 개를 찾아서 기
뻐하는 것 **같았다.**

**loose** [lúːs] 혱 ① 풀린, 자유로
운 ; 떨어져 있는 ② **헐거운,**
느슨한
loose는 tight (꼭 끼는)의 반
대말이다 : 메리는 엄마 신발을
신고 걸으려고 했지만 너무 커
서 발에서 벗겨져 버렸다. 그
신발은 그녀에게 너무 **헐거웠
다.**

**lose** [lúːz] 탄 ① 잃다 ; 두고 잊
어버리다 ; (길을) **잃다** ② 놓
치다 ③ **지다** ; (시계가) **늦다**
1 lose는 어떤 것을 찾을 수
없다는 뜻이다 : 새 장갑을 **잃
어 버리지** 마라. 제니는 운동
장에서 연필을 **잃어 버렸다.**
2 lose는 또한 어떤 것을 유지
할 수 없다는 뜻이다 : 폭풍이
불어서 나무의 가지들이 많이
**떨어져 나갔다.** 엘리자베스는
균형을 **잃고** 빙판에 미끄러졌

다.
3 lose는 또한 이기지 못했다
는 뜻이다 : 조가 경주에 **졌
니 ?**

**loss** [lɔ́ːs | lɔ́s] 몡 **상실, 분실 ;
손실, 손해 ; 실패, 패배**
1 loss는 어떤 것을 잃어버린
행위나 사실이다 : 그 사고 피
해자는 기억 loss(상실)에 걸
렸다. 그 팀은 2번 이기고 3
번 loss〔2승 3패〕를 했다.
2 loss는 물건이나 사람을 잃
어버려서 생기는 고통이나 역
경이다 : 우리 모두는 개를 **잃
어버렸다고** 생각했다.

**lost** [lɔ́ːst | lɔ́st] 1 됨 lose (잃다)
의 과거 • 과거분사형 2 혱 **잃
어버린 ; 진 ; 길을 잃은**
lost 는 찾기가 힘들다는 뜻이
다 : 우리는 화장대 뒤에서 **잃
어버린** 양말을 찾아냈다.

**lot** [lát | lɔ́t] 몡 ① **많음** ② **제비**
(뽑기), 추첨 ③ **운, 운명**
lot은 어떤 것을 세거나 재는
데 오랜 시간이 걸린다는 뜻이
다 : 여름에는 할 일이 **많다.**
하마는 먹이를 **많이** 먹는다.

**loud** [láud] 혱 **목소리가 큰, 큰**

L

소리의 ; 시끄러운

loud는 소리를 많이 낸다는 뜻이다 : 폭풍우가 칠 때의 천둥소리는 수마일이나 떨어진 곳까지 들린다. 천둥은 **요란한** 소리를 낸다.

**loudspeaker** [làudspíːkər, <sup>ᐟ</sup>ᐟ--] 명 확성기

loudspeaker는 소리를 더 크게 나게 하는 것이다. 라디오에는 loudspeaker가 있다. 또한 loudspeaker가 있는 전화기도 있다.

**love** [lʌv] 타 **사랑하다, 귀여워하다 ; …을 매우 좋아하다**

love 는 어떤 것을 매우 좋아한다는 뜻이다 : 린다는 수영하는 것을 **좋아한다**. 헨리는 샌드위치를 **즐겨** 먹는다.

**low** [lóu] 1 형 **낮은 ; 값이 싼** 2 부 **낮게 ; 값싸게**

low는 바닥이나 지면에 가깝다는 뜻이다 : 담장은 손을 짚지 않고도 뛰어넘을 수 있을 정도로 **낮았다**.

**luck** [lʌk] 명 **운, 운수 ; 행운, 요행**

luck은 뜻하지 않게 우연히 일어나는 일이다. luck이 좋으면 땅에서 25센트 짜리 은화를 발견할 수도 있고, luck이 나쁘면 자전거의 타이어가 터질 수도 있다.

**lucky** [lʌ́ki] 형 **운이 좋은, 행운의, 재수 좋은**

lucky는 좋은 일이 일어난다는 뜻이다 : 마크는 **운좋게도** 보도 한가운데 떨어진 25센트 은화 두 개와 5센트 백동화 한 개를 발견했다.

**lullaby** [lʌ́ləbài] 명 **자장가**

lullaby는 아기를 재우기 위해 아기에게 불러주는 노래다.

**lumber** [lʌ́mbər] 명 (통나무 · 판자 등의 톱질해 놓은) **재목, 제재목**

lumber는 통나무를 자른 판자다 : 아버지는 내게 새 책상을 만들어 주기 위해 lumber 몇 개를 집으로 가져오셨다.

**lunch** [lʌntʃ] 명 **점심**, 런치 ;
도시락
lunch는 한 낮에 먹는 식사
다 : 타일러는 매일 학교에서
lunch를 먹는다.

**lunch box** [lʌntʃ bὰks | ˈ bɔ́ks]
명 **도시락 (상자)**
lunch box는 손잡이가 달린
금속이나 플라스틱 용기다.

lunch box에 점심을 담아서
학교나 직장으로 가지고 가는
사람들도 있다.

**lung** [lʌŋ] 명 **폐**, 허파
lung은 신체의 일부다. 가슴
안쪽에 두 개의 lung이 있다.
숨을 쉬면 공기가 lung으로 들
어갔다 나갔다한다.

L

## macaroni, macca-róuni [mǽkə-róuni] 명 마카로니

macaroni는 음식의 일종이다. macaroni는 밀가루로 만들며, 작고 속이 빈 관 모양으로 되어 있다.

## machine [məʃíːn] 명 기계, 기계 장치

machine은 인간을 위해서 일하는 물건이다. machine은 크거나 작을 수도 있고, 많은 부품으로 이루어진 것도 있다. 비행기, 컴퓨터, 풍차는 모두 machine이다.

## mad [mǽd] 형 성난 ; 미친, 실성한 ; 열광적인, 열중한

mad는 사람이 어떤 일에 화를 낸다는 의미다 : 질은 그녀가 이기고 있는 경기를 우리가 중단시키자 화를 냈다.

## made [méid] 동 make(만들다)의 과거·과거분사형

made는 단어 make에서 생긴 말이다 : 광대가 우리를 웃겼다. 그 담은 돌로 만들었다. 어머니는 내게 인형을 만들어 주셨다.

## magazine [mǽgəzìːn, ﹣﹣ﹶ] 명 잡지

magazine에는 읽을 기사와 볼 그림이 실려 있으며, 종이 표지로 되어 있다. 매주 발행되는 magazine도 있고, 한달에 한 번 발행되는 magazine도 있다 : 레이는 재담과 낱말 맞추기가 실려 있는 magazine을 좋아한다.

## magic [mǽdʒik] 1 명 마법, 마술, 요술 2 형 마법의, 신기한

magic은 신기한 일을 일어나게 하는 특별한 힘을 말한다. magic은 사실인 것 같지만, 사실이 아니다 : 앨버트가 파티에서 보여준 묘기는 magic으로 한 것 같았다. 우리는 그가 보여 주는 magic에 감탄했다.

**magician** [mədʒíʃən] 몡 **마법사, 마술사, 요술쟁이**
magician은 마술을 써서 묘기를 부리는 사람이다 : magician이 모자에서 토끼를 꺼냈다.

**magnet** [mǽgnət] 몡 **자석**
magnet은 다른 금속에 달라붙는 금속을 말한다 : 올리버는 magnet을 사용해 흩어진 못을 주웠다.

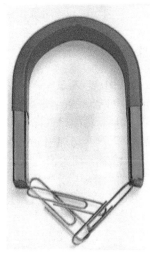

**magnifying glass** [mǽgni-faiiŋ glǽs] 몡 **확대경, 돋보기**
magnifying glass는 물체를 실제보다 더 크게 보이게 하는 유리다 : magnifying glass로 조개 껍질을 보자, 줄무늬가 있는 것을 알 수 있었다.

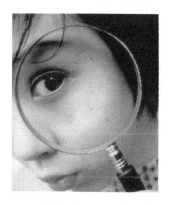

**mail** [méiəl] 1 몡 **우편, 우편제도, 우편물** 2 탐 **우편으로 보내다, 우송하다**
1 mail은 편지나 소포를 한 곳에서 다른 곳으로 보내는 방식을 말한다.
2 mail은 우편으로 무언가를 보낸다는 의미다 : 블레이크의 부모님은 지난주 캠프장에 있는 그에게 소포를 **부치셨다.**

**main** [méin] 혱 **주요한, 주된**
main은 가장 중요하다는 의미다 : 은행은 시내 **중심**가에 있다. 만찬은 우리집에서 하루 중 **가장 중요한** 식사다.

**make** [méik] 탐 ① **만들다, 제작〔제조〕하다 ; …이 되다** ② **…하게 하다** ③ (행동·동작을) **하다, 행하다**
1 make는 무언가를 조립한다

M

는 의미다 : 우리는 아버지께서 개집을 **만드시는** 것을 도왔다. 2 make는 또한 어떤 일을 일어나게 한다는 의미다 : 네가 하는 익살맞은 이야기가 항상 나를 **웃게 한다.**

**make-believe** [méikbilìːv] 1 형 **거짓의, 가공의, 상상의** 2 명 **가장, 거짓**
make-believe는 현실에 존재하지 않는다는 의미다 : 요정은 **가공의** 인물이다.

**male** [méiəl] 1 명 **남성 ; 수컷** 2 형 **남성의 ; 수컷의**
male은 남자 아이나 성인 남자를 말한다. 아버지와 아저씨는 male이다.

**man** [mǽn] 명 **남자 ; 사람**
man은 성인 남자를 말한다 : 나의 아저씨는 키가 큰 man이다.

**manners** [mǽnərz] 명 ① **예절, 예의 ; 풍습, 관습** ② [manner로] **방법, 방식 ; 태도, 거동**
manners가 바르면, 사람들에게 공손하게 대한다. "…좀 해 주십시오"나 "감사합니다"라고 말하면 manners가 바른 것이고, 입을 벌리고 음식을 씹으면 manners가 없는 것이다.

**mansion** [mǽnʃən] 명 **대저택**
mansion은 방이 많이 있는 아주 큰 집이다.

**many** [méni] 1 형 **많은, 다수의** 2 명대 **많은 사람들 ; 많은 일〔것〕**
many는 수가 많은 것을 의미한다 : 바닷가에는 아주 **많은** 모래알들이 있다.

**map** [mǽp] 명 **지도**
map은 서로 다른 장소의 위치를 나타낸 그림이다. map은 종류가 많이 있다. map으로 국가, 날씨, 대양, 강, 산 그리고 그 밖의 것들을 나타낼 수 있다 : map으로 너의 마을을 찾을 수 있느냐? 우리는 지리를 공부할 때, map을 본다.

**maple** [méipl] 명 **단풍나무**
maple은 나무의 일종이다 :

maple은 가을에 아름답게 단풍이 든다.

**marble** [máːrbl] 명 대리석 ; 공깃돌《아이들의 장난감》; [복수로] 공기놀이, 구슬치기

1 marble은 단단하고 매끄러운 돌의 일종이다 : 조각가들은 marble을 깎아서 조각상을 만든다. marble은 벽이나 건물 바닥에 사용되는 경우가 많다.
2 marble은 놀이에 쓰이는 작고 단단한 유리구슬을 말한다 : 보브는 marble 놀이를 하려고 땅에 큰 원을 그렸다.

**march** [máːrtʃ] 자 타 행진하다 ; 진군[행군]하다

march는 누군가와 동시에 같은 크기의 보폭을 취한다는 의미다 : 우리 악대는 열을 지어 **행진했다.** 군인들이 거리를 **행진했다.**

**March** [máːrtʃ] 명 3월

March는 한 해의 세 번째 달이다. March는 31 일이며, 2 월이 가고 4월이 되기 전에 온다.

**margarine** [máːrdʒərin|màː-

dʒəríːn] 명 마가린

margarine은 보통 식물성 유지로 만든 연하고 색이 노란 식품이다. 버터 대신 margarine을 이용하는 사람들이 많다.

**mark** [máːrk] 1 명 ① 표, 자국, 얼룩 ; 기호, 부호 ② 점수, 성적 2 타 ① ⋯에 표를 하다, 기호[부호]를 붙이다 ② ⋯에 오점[흔적]을 남기다 ③ (답안을) 채점하다

1 mark는 무언가에 줄이나 얼룩을 지게 한다는 의미다 : 너의 더러운 신발때문에 깨끗한 마루에 **얼룩이** 생겼다.
2 mark는 또한 표면의 긁힌 자국이나 얼룩을 말한다 : 아기가 크레용으로 벽에 mark(낙서)를 했다.
3 mark는 사람이 공부를 얼마나 잘 하는 가를 나타내는 문자나 숫자를 말하기도 한다 : 로베르토는 과학보다 미술에서 더 좋은 mark(점수)를 받았다.

**M**

**marry** [mǽri] 자 결혼하다

marry는 남편이나 아내로 누군가와 결합한다는 의미다 : 나

의 아주머니와 아저씨는 **결혼**한지 5년이 되었다.

**marsh** [máːrʃ] 명 습지, 늪
marsh는 땅이 무르고 물이 있는 지대를 말한다 : 개구리, 물새, 모기들은 marsh에서 산다.

**marshmallow** [máːrʃmèlou, -mæl- | mà:ʃmǽlou] 명 마시멜로
marshmallow는 일종의 사탕으로, 말랑말랑하고 희다.

**mask** [mǽsk | máːsk] 명 탈, 가면, **방독면**, 마스크
mask는 얼굴을 가리거나 보호하기 위해 쓰는 것이다 : 소방수들은 연기로부터 자신들을 보호하기 위해 mask를 쓴다.

**match**¹ [mǽtʃ] 타 자 …에 어울리다, 걸맞다 ; …에 필적하다 ; 조화시키다, 어울리게 하다, …와 걸맞게 하다
match는 동일하다는 의미다 : 수잔의 셔츠와 구두는 색깔이 같다. 그녀는 구두가 셔츠 색깔에 **어울려서** 샀다.

**match**² [mǽtʃ] 명 성냥, 성냥 한개비
match는 짧고 가는 나뭇조각이나 종잇조각으로, 그 끝부분을 무언가에 마찰시키면 불꽃이 생긴다. match는 불을 붙이는 데 사용한다.

**material** [mətíəriəl] 명 원료, 재료 ; 자료 ; 옷감
material은 물건을 만드는 데 쓰이는 것을 말한다 : 앨리스의 겨울 외투는 모직 material로 만들어진다. 나무, 돌, 유리는 집을 짓는 데 쓰이는 material이다.

**mathematics** [mæ̀θəmǽtiks] 명 수학
mathematics를 공부하면, 수와 양, 모양과 도량법에 관해 배운다. 더하기를 하거나 빼기를 할 때, mathematics를 이용한다.

**mattress** [mǽtrəs] 명 매트리스, 침대요
mattress는 침대의 두껍고 푹

신한 부분을 말한다 : 클레어는 mattress에 새 덮개를 깔았다.

**may** [méi] 조 ① [허가] …해도 좋다, …해도 괜찮다 ② [추측] …인지도 모른다 ③ [기원] 바라건대 …하기를, …하여 주시옵소서

1 무언가를 달라고 부탁할 때 may라고 말한다 : 주스 좀 **마실 수 있을까요**?

2 무슨 일이 일어난다고 확신하지는 않지만 그럴 가능성이 있다면, may라고 말할 수 있다 : 하늘에 먹구름이 끼어 있어서, 오늘 오후에 비가 **올지도 모른다**.

**May** [méi] 명 **5월**

May는 한 해 가운데 한 달이다. May는 31일이며, 4월이 지나고 6월이 되기 전에 온다.

**maybe** [méibi] 부 어쩌면, 아마

maybe는 무엇일지도 모른다 〔무엇일 수도 있다〕는 의미다 : 나는 누가 문을 두드리는지 알 수 없다. **어쩌면 존일지도 모른다**.

**maze** [méiz] 명 미로, 미궁

maze에는 똑같은 좁은 길이 많이 나있다. maze속에서 길을 찾아간다는 것은 힘든 일이다 : 토니는 새 학교의 maze 같은 복도에서 길을 잃어 버렸다.

**me** [《약》 mi, 《강》 mí] 대 [I 의 목적격] 나를, 나에게

me는 자기 자신에 관해서 이야기할 때 쓰는 말이다 : 나는 버스를 타고 학교에 간다.

**meadow** [médou] 명 풀밭, 목초지

meadow는 땅이 길쭉한 풀로 뒤덮인 지역을 말한다. 생쥐, 토끼, 나비들은 meadow에서 산다.

**meal** [míːəl] 명 식사

M

meal은 일정한 때에 먹는 음식을 말한다. 우리는 아침, 점심, 저녁이라고 하는 세번의 meal을 매일 먹는다.

**mean¹** [míːn] 타 **의미하다, 뜻하다 ; …할 작정이다 ; …의 뜻으로 말하다**
1 mean은 두개의 말이 같다는 것을 나타내는 데 사용하는 말이다.「거대한」은「아주 큰」이란 **뜻이다.**
2 mean은 또한 생각하고 있는 것을 나타내기 위해 사용하는 말이다 : 다이애나가 "일찍이"라고 말했을 때, 그녀는 "아침 식사전"이란 **뜻으로 말했던 것이다.**

**mean²** [míːn] 형 **비열한, 치사한 ; 천한, 초라한**
mean은 누군가에게 친절하거나 우호적이지 않다는 의미다 : 아이들이 그 신입생의 책을 벽장에 숨긴 것은 **비열한** 짓이었다.

**meant** [mént] 동 mean¹(의미하다)의 과거 · 과거분사형
meant는 mean¹의 한 형태다 : 내 **말의 뜻을** 이해했니? 영화를 보러 가는 일이 앨에게는

많은 **의미가** 있었다.

**measure** [méʒər] 타 자 **재다, 계량〔측정, 측량〕하다**
measure는 어떤 것의 크기나 양을 알아낸다는 의미다 : 마리아는 아버지가 새 울타리의 길이를 **재는** 것을 도왔다.

**measurement** [méʒərmənt] 명 ① **측량, 도량법** ② **치수, 크기, 넓이, 길이**
무언가를 측정해서 알아 낸 크기나 양을 measurement라고 한다 : 그 목수는 자를 사용해서 선반의 measurement를 알았다.

**meat** [míːt] 명 **고기, 육류**
meat는 식품의 일종으로, 동물에게서 얻는다. 닭고기, 쇠고기, 햄은 모두 meat다.

**medal** [médəl] 명 **메달, 상패, 기념패, 훈장**
medal은 동전 모양으로 생긴 금속 조각이다. medal은 흔히 리본이나 쇠사슬에 달려 있다. 간혹 medal이 용감한 일이나

**M**

중요한 일을 한 사람에게 상으로 주어지기도 한다 : 데일은 물에 빠진 소년을 구하는 걸 도왔다고 medal을 받았다.

**medicine** [médisin, médsin] 명
약, 내복약
medicine은 우리가 아플 때, 나아지려고 먹는 것이다 : 제인이 독감에 걸렸을 때, 그녀의 어머니는 하루에 두 번 그녀에게 medicine을 주셨다.

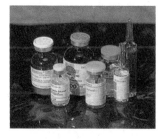

**meet** [míːt] 타자 만나다, 마중하다, 마주치다 ; …와 아는 사이가 되다
1 meet는 누군가를 알게 된다는 의미다 : 너는 학교 생활을 시작하는 첫 날에 새로운 사람들을 많이 **만날 것이다.**
2 meet는 또한 동시에 같은 장소에 있다는 의미다 : 톰과 빌은 3시에 길모퉁이에서 **마주쳤다.**

**melt** [méəlt] 자타 녹다, 녹이다 ; (감정을) 누그러지게 하다
melt는 고체에서 액체로 변한다는 의미다 : 날씨가 따뜻해지면, 얼음이 **녹아** 물이 된다.

**memory** [méməri] 명 기억, 기억력 ; 추억, 회상
1 memory는 사물을 기억할 수 있음을 의미한다 : 미미 아주머니는 날짜를 잘 memory하고 있어서, 누구의 생일이든 결코 잊어 버리지 않는다.
2 memory는 또한 기억하고 있는 사람이나 사건을 말한다 : 캠프장에서 보낸 여름이 내가 가장 행복했던 memory 중의 하나다.

**men** [mén] 명 man의 복수형
men은 2명 이상의 남자를 의미한다 : 사내아이들이 자라서 men이 된다.

**mess** [més] 명 혼란 (상태), 난잡, 어수선함, 불결(한 것), 쓰레기 더미
mess는 많은 물건들이 있어야 할 곳에 놓여져 있지 않을 때를 말한다 : 케이크를 만든 후라서 부엌이 **엉망**이었다.

**message** [mésidʒ] 명 전갈, 전언, 통신(문), 서신, 전보
message는 어떤 사람이 다른 사람에게 적어 보내는 말이다. 많은 사람들이 우편으로 message를 보낸다.

**met** [mét] 동 meet(만나다)의 과거・과거분사형
met는 meet의 한 형태다 : 데이비드는 학교 소풍에서 6명

M

의 새 친구들을 **알게 되었다.**
해리와 리처드는 음식점에서
점심을 같이 먹으려고 **만났다.**

**metal** [métəl] 명 금속
metal은 땅속에서 발견되는
빛이 나는 물질이다. 금은 일
종의 **metal**이다. 10센트 은
화, 반지, 자동차는 모두
metal로 만든다.

**meter | metre** [míːtər] 명 미
터 ; 계량기
meter는 길이의 양을 말한다.
1 meter는 1 야드가 조금 넘는
다. 1 킬로미터는 1,000 meter
다.

**mice** [máis] 명 mouse 의 복수
형
mice는 2 마리 이상의 생쥐를
나타낸다 : mice가 치즈를 전
부 먹어버렸다. 켄드류와 앨버
트, 그리고 조지는 만성절 전
야 파티에 3마리의 mice로 분
장을 했다.

**microscope** [máikrəskòup] 명
현미경

microscope는 너무 작아서 눈
으로만 볼 수 없는 물체를 관
찰하는 데 사용한다. **micro-**
**scope**는 아주 작은 물체를 크
게 보이게 할 수 있다.

**middle** [mídl] 1 명 중앙, 중간,
한가운데 2 형 중앙의, 중간
의, 한가운데의
middle은 두 끝 사이의 중심
부분을 말한다. 정오는 하루중
middle이 되는 때다 : 우리는
호수 middle(중앙)에 있는 뗏
목까지 헤엄쳐 갔다.

**midnight** [mídnàit] 명 한밤중,
자정
midnight는 밤 12시다 : 우리집
식구들은 모두 midnight에는
자고 있다.

**might** [máit] 조 may(…인지도
모르다)의 과거형
might는 단어 may에서 생긴
말이다 : 블레이크는 우리가 서
두르지 않으면 **늦을지도 모른**
**다**고 말했다.

**mile** [máiəl] 명 마일
mile은 거리의 양이다. 1 mile

은 5,280피트다 : 성인 남녀가 1 mile을 걷는 데 약 20분이 소요된다.

**milk** [mílk] 몡 **우유, 젖, 밀크**
milk는 우리가 마시는 흰 액체로, 젖소나 염소에서 얻는다 : 나는 시리얼을 milk에 넣어서 먹는 걸 좋아한다. 치즈는 milk로 만든다.

**million** [míljən] 1 몡 ① **100만, 100만개** ② [복수로] **수백만, 다수** 2 혱 **100만의, 100만개의 ; 무수한**
million은 숫자로, 1,000,000이라고 쓴다. million은 1,000이 1,000개 있다는 말이다 : 태양은 지구에서 수 million 마일 떨어져 있다.

**mind** [máind] 몡 ① **마음, 정신** ② **지성, 생각,** 의견 ③ **기억, 기억력**
mind는 생각하고, 느끼고, 배우고, 기억하고, 바라고, 상상하는 인간의 중요한 일면이다 : mind가 없다면 인간이 아닐 것이다.

**mine** [máin] 때 [I의 소유 대명사] **나의 것 ;** 나의 소유물
mine은 내 소유물을 뜻한다 : 내가 그 책을 샀으므로, 그 책은 **내것이다.**

**minus** [máinəs] 1 혱 **마이너스의, 마이너스를 나타내는** 2 젠 **마이너스의, …을 뺀**
minus는 뺀다는 의미다 : 6에서 2를 제하면 4가 된다. 즉 6 **빼기** 2는 4다. 6 **빼기** 2를 6−2로 쓸 수도 있다.

**minute** [mínət] 몡 **분**(分)
minute는 시간의 양이다. 1 minute(분)는 60초고, 1시간은 60 minute(분)다.

**mirror** [mírər] 몡 **거울**
mirror는 우리의 모습을 비춰볼 수 있는 매끄러운 유리 조각이다. 벽에 거는 mirror도 있고, 손에 가지고 다닐 수 있는 mirror도 있다 : 치과의사는 아주 작은 mirror로 내 입 안쪽을 살펴 보았다.

**M**

**miss** [mís] 타 ① 못 맞히다 ; 놓치다 ; 타지 못하다　②빼먹다 ③ …이 없어서 서운하게〔적적하게〕여기다

1 miss는 마음먹고 하려고 했던 것을 못한다는 의미다 : 서두르지 않으면, 우리는 영화의 앞부분을 **보지 못할 것이다**. 잭은 공을 치려고 배트를 휘둘러 보았지만, **헛 치고 말았다**.

2 miss는 또한 무언가를 못가져서 혹은 좋아하는 사람과 같이 있지 못해서 애석하다는 의미다 : 나는 내 여동생이 여름 캠프를 떠나고 **없어서 허전하다**.

3 miss는 또한 무언가가 없다는 의미다 : 내 낡은 재킷에는 단추 하나가 **떨어져 나가고 없다**. 네 푸른색 크레용과 초록색 크레용이 **어디가고 없다**.

**Miss** [mís] 명 …양,　선생님《미혼의 여선생님》

Miss는 결혼하지 않은 여자의 이름에 붙여서 쓰는 말이다 : 우리 음악 선생님의 이름은 Miss 브라운이다.

**mistake** [mistéik] 명 잘못,　과실, 틀림, 착오

mistake 는 틀린 것〔잘못된 것〕을 말한다 : 나는 철자법 시험에서 mistake를 하나 밖에 하지 않았다. 그런 따뜻한 날에 두꺼운 스웨터를 입은 것은 mistake였다.

**mitten** [mítən] 명 벙어리 장갑 ; (야구용)　미트 ; (여성용의) 긴 장갑

mitten은 손을 따뜻하게 하려고 끼는 것이다. 글로브는 손가락 마다 들어가는 부분이 있지만, mitten은 그런 부분이 없다 : 나는 학교에서 mitten을 잃어 버렸다.

**mix** [míks] 타자 섞다〔이다〕, 혼합하다〔되다〕 ; 섞어 만들다

mix는 서로 다른 것들을 한데 모은다는 의미다 : 내 친구들과 나는 레몬 주스와 물, 그리고 설탕을 **섞어서** 레모네이드를 만들려고 한다. 우리는 빨간색과 흰색 그림물감을 **섞어서** 연분홍색을 만들었다.

**model** [mádəl|mɔ́d-] 명 모형, 모델 ; 모범, 본보기

model은 무언가를 작게 복제한 것을 말한다 : 폴은 목제 model 비행기를 금속처럼 보

M

이게 하려고 페인트 칠을 하고
있다.

**mom** [mám|mɔ́m] 명 (구어)
**엄마**
mom은 엄마를 나타내는 호칭
이다. 또한 자기 엄마를
mommy라고 부르는 아이들도
있다.

**moment** [móumənt] 명 **순간,
찰나 ; (어느 특정한) 때**
moment는 아주 짧은 시간이
다 : 잠깐만 기다려 준다면, 가
능한한 빨리 너를 돕도록 하겠
다.

**Monday** [mʌ́ndei, -di] 명 **월요
일**
Monday는 일주일 가운데 하
루를 말한다. Monday는 일요
일이 지나고 화요일이 되기 전
에 온다.

**money** [mʌ́ni] 명 **돈, 화폐, 금
전 ; 통화**
money는 사람들이 물건을 사
기 위하여 사용하는 것이다.
사람들이 일을 하면, 일한 대
가로 money를 받는다. 페니,
5센트 백동화, 10센트 은화,
25센트 은화, 달러는 모두

money의 종류다.

**monkey** [mʌ́ŋki] 명 **원숭이**
monkey는 팔과 다리가 길고,
온 몸에 털이 있으며, 꼬리가
긴 동물이다. 나무에서 사는
monkey도 있고, 땅에서 사는
monkey도 있다.

**monster** [mánstər|mɔ́n-] 명 **괴
물, 도깨비**
monster는 세상에 존재하지
않는 크고 무시무시한 동물이
다 : 나는 머리가 2개고 다리가
6개인 붉은 monster에 관한
이야기책을 읽었다.

**month** [mʌ́nθ] 명 **(한) 달, 월**
month는 한 해의 한 부분을
말한다. 1년은 1월, 2월, 3
월, 4월, 5월, 6월, 7월, 8월,
9월, 10월, 11월 그리고 12월
의 12 month 로 되어 있다.

**M**

**mood** [múːd] 명 **(일시적인) 기
분, 감정, 심사, 마음가짐**
mood는 느끼는 점을 말한
다 : 날씨가 궂으면 잭은

mood가 나쁘다.

**moon** [múːn] 명 (천체의) 달
moon은 지구 주위를 돈다.
moon은 밤에 하늘에서 밝은
빛을 낸다. moon 전체를 볼
수 있을 때도 있고, 그 일부만
을 볼 수 있을 때도 있다.
moon이 지구 주위를 도는 데
한 달이 걸린다.

**more** [mɔ́ːr] 1 형 [many, much
의 비교급] 더 많은, 더 큰 2
부 [much의 비교급] 보다 많
이 ; 게다가, 더욱 3 명대 보
다 많은 수〔양·정도〕
more는 더 큰 수나 더 많은
양을 의미한다 : 4 는 3보다 **더
크다**. 내 컵에 있는 주스가 네
컵의 주스보다 **더 많다**.

**morning** [mɔ́ːrniŋ] 명 아침,
오전
morning은 하루 중 정오 이전
을 말한다 : 나는 햇살이 내
창문을 환하게 비치는 이른
morning에 일어나는 것을 좋
아한다.

**mosquito** [məskíːtou] 명 모기

mosquito는 날아다니는 작은
곤충이다 : 니 는 mosquito에
물리면, 가려워서 긁고 싶다.

**most** [móust] 1 형 [many, much
의 최상급] 가장 큰, 가장 많
은 ; 대개의, 대부분의 2 부
[much 의 최상급] 가장 많이
3 명대 최대량〔수〕, 대부분
most는 가장 큰 수나 가장 많
은 부분을 의미한다 : **대부분의**
아이들은 시간에 맞추어 학교
에 도착했다. 루이스는 단어
철자를 **대부분** 정확하게 썼다.

**moth** [mɔ́ːθ | mɔ́θ] 명 나방
moth는 곤충의 일종이다.
moth는 나비와 모습이 거의
비슷하다. 고치 속의 애벌레가
변해서 moth가 된다.

**mother** [mʌ́ðər] 명 어머니
mother는 아이를 1 명 이상 키
우는 여자를 말한다. 부모는
mother와 아버지를 말한다.

**motor** [móutər] 명 모터, 발동
기, 내연기관 ; 자동차
motor는 다른 기계를 움직이
게 하는 기계다 : 이 시계는 전
기 motor로 시계 바늘이 움직

M

인다. 자동차 motor가 자동차를 가게 한다. 전기 motor가 세탁기를 돌린다.

**motorcycle** [móutərsàikl] 명
모터사이클
motorcycle은 기계로, 엔진이 달린 크고 무거운 자전거와 같다. 자동차 만큼 빨리 달릴 수 있는 motorcycle도 있다.

**mountain** [máuntən] 명 산
mountain은 땅이 아주 높이 솟은 지역을 말한다. mountain은 언덕보다 훨씬 높다 : 휴가 동안에 mountain으로 스키타러 가는 사람들도 있다.

**mouse** [máus] 명 생쥐
mouse는 아주 작은 동물인데, 긴 꼬리와 짧은 털 그리고 날카로운 이빨이 있다. mice는 들판이나 숲 혹은 집에서 산다.

**mouth** [máuθ] 명 입
mouth로 말을 하고 음식을 먹

는다. 또한 mouth를 이용해 미소를 짓거나 불쾌한 표정을 짓는다. 이와 혀는 mouth 안에 있다 : 아이들은 음식을 다 먹고 나서 냅킨으로 mouth를 닦았다. 치과 의사가 "mouth를 크게 벌려요"라고 말했다.

**move** [múːv] 타 자 움직이다, 이동시키다, **옮기다** ; 이사하다
move는 한 곳에서 다른 곳으로 간다는 의미다 : 빌리는 상자를 마루에서 식탁으로 **옮겼다.** 헬렌과 그녀의 가족은 작년에 시골로 **이사했다.**

**movie** [múːvi] 명 영화 ; 영화관
movie는 움직이는 사진으로 만든 이야기다. 사람들은 극장에서 혹은 텔레비전으로 movie를 본다.

**Mr., Mr** [místər] 명 [Mister의 약어] …씨, …선생, …님, …군, …귀하
Mr.는 남자 이름 앞에 쓴다 : Mr. 워커가 올해 나의 선생님이시다.

**Mrs., Mrs** [mísiz, míz-] 명 [Mistress의 약어] …부인

M

Mrs. 는 흔히 결혼한 여자 이름 앞에 쓰인다 : Mrs. 켈리가 리처드의 어머니시다.

**Ms., Ms** [míz] 명 미혼, 기혼의 구별을 하지 않는 여성의 경칭 《Miss, Mrs 대신에 씀》
Ms. 는 흔히 여자 이름 앞에 쓰인다 : Ms. 마리, 당신이 내 형과 누이를 만나 주었으면 합니다.

**much** [mʌ́tʃ] 1 형 많은, 다량의 2 부 매우, 훨씬 3 명대 많음, 다량
much는 많은 것을 의미한다 : 아버지는 일이 너무 **많아**서 사무실에 늦게까지 남아 계셔야만 했다.

**mud** [mʌ́d] 명 진흙, 진창
mud는 축축한 흙을 말한다 : mud속에서 뒹구는 것을 좋아하는 동물들이 많다.

**muffin** [mʌ́fin] 명 머핀
muffin은 컵 모양으로 생긴 빵 같은 음식이다 : 친구들이 아침을 먹으러 우리집에 왔을 때, 우리는 muffin과 과일 그리고 우유를 마셨다.

**mug** [mʌ́g] 명 원통형 찻잔, 손잡이 있는 컵
mug는 손잡이가 달린 큰 잔이다. mug로 우유를 마시거나 수프를 먹을 수 있다 : 내 친구는 그녀가 미술 수업 시간에 찰흙으로 만든 mug를 내게 주었다.

**multiply** [mʌ́ltiplài] 1 타자 늘리다, 증가시키다 ; 곱하다 2 명 곱셈
multiply는 어떤 수에 그와 동일한 수를 여러번 더한다는 의미다. multiply를 나타내는 기호는 ×다 : 2×4는 2+2+2+2와 같다.

**muscle** [mʌ́sl] 명 근육, 힘줄
muscle은 물건을 옮기고, 들어 올릴 수 있는 힘을 제공해 주는 신체의 부위다 : 무용수는 다리 muscle이 강하다.

**museum** [mjuzí:əm, mju:-] 명 박물관
museum은 사람들이 보고 배울 수 있게 물건들을 수집해 보존하는 곳이다. 미술 작품을 전시하는 museum도 있고, 오래 전에 쓰던 물건들을 전시하

M

는 museum도 있다 : 우리 반은 공룡뼈와 오래된 암석들이 전시된 과학 museum을 방문했다.

**mushroom** [mʌ́ʃruːm, -rum] 몡
버섯 ; 버섯 모양의 것
mushroom은 작은 우산 모양을 한 균류다. mushroom은 꽃이나 잎이 없으며, 매우 빨리 자란다. 먹어도 되는 mushroom도 있지만, 먹으면 위험한 것도 많다.

**music** [mjúːzik] 몡 음악
music은 사람이 악기와 목소리로 내는 소리를 말한다 : 전 세계에는 많은 종류의 music이 있다.

**musician** [mjuːzíʃən, mjuː-] 몡
음악가
musician은 악기를 연주하거나 노래를 부르는 사람이다 : 일단의 musician들이 피터 아저씨의 결혼식에서 음악을 연주했다.

**must** [《약》məst, 《강》mʌ́st]
조 ① [절박한 필요] ···해야 한다 ② [부정문에서 금지]

···해서는 안된다 ③ [당연한 필연성·추정] ···임〔함〕에 틀림없다
1 must는 무언가를 해야만 한다는 의미다 : 너는 연에 실을 매달아야만 한다. 그렇지 않으면 연이 멀리 날아가 버릴 것이다.
2 must는 또한 「십중팔구는 〔아마도〕」의 의미다 : 그 책은 틀림없이 이곳 어딘가에 있다.

**mustache, mous-** [mʌ́stæʃ| məstɑ́ːʃ] 몡 콧수염
mustache는 남자의 입술 위쪽에 자라는 털이다 : 아버지에게 입을 맞출 때면, 아버지의 mustache 때문에 간지럽다.

**mustard** [mʌ́stərd] 몡 겨자
mustard는 맛을 첨가하려고 음식에 넣는 걸쭉한 노란 액체를 말한다. mustard는 식물의 씨앗으로 만든다 : 엄마는 햄버거에 mustard를 쳐서 먹는 것을 좋아하지만, 내 동생과 나는 케첩을 쳐서 먹는 것을 더 좋아한다.

**my** [mái] 때 [I의 소유격] 나의
my는 내 소유물을 의미한다 : 이것은 내 책이다.

**myself** [maisélf] 대 [I의 재귀대명사] **나 자신이, 나 자신을** myself는 누군가 딴 사람이 아닌 바로 나 자신을 의미한다 : 내가 거울속을 들여다 보면, **내 자신을 보게 된다. 나는 서둘러 옷을 입었다.**

**mysterious** [mistíəriəs] 형 **신비적인, 불가사의한 ; 이상한** mysterious는 무언가를 설명하거나 이해하기가 아주 어렵다는 의미다 : 우리는 빈 집에서 나는 **이상한** 소리를 들었다.

**mystery** [místəri] 명 **신비,** 불가사의 ; 괴기〔탐정·추리〕소설 mystery는 이해할 수 없는 어떤 것이다 : 마거릿은 식물이 자라는 이유를 이해하지 못하는 데, 이것이 바로 그녀에게는 mystery다. 자연은 온통 mystery로 가득하다.

M

N

**nail** [néiəl] 1 명 손톱, 발톱 ; 못, 징 2 타 못〔징〕을 박다, 못박아 붙이다, 못〔핀〕으로 고정시키다
1 nail은 손가락과 발가락 끝의 딱딱한 부분이다.

2 nail은 또한 한쪽 끝이 뾰족하고 다른 쪽 끝은 납작한 가는 금속이다. 두 물건을 한 데 고정시키기 위해서 nail을 박는다.
3 nail은 못으로 무언가를 붙인다는 뜻이다 : 우리는 벽에 **못을 박아** 그림을 **걸었다.**

**name** [néim] 명 이름, 명칭
name은 사람들이 무언가를 부를 때 사용하는 말이다. 모든 것에는 다 name이 있다. 사람들 또한 name이 있다.

**nap** [nǽp] 1 명 선잠, 낮잠, 졸기 2 자 졸다, 낮잠을 자다
take a nap은 잠시 동안 잠을 잔다는 뜻이다 : 우리는 매일 점심을 먹고 나서 nap을 잔다. 우리집 갓난아기는 nap을 많이 잔다.

**napkin** [nǽpkin] 명 (식탁용) 냅킨 ; 작은 수건
napkin은 음식을 먹을 때 무릎을 덮는 데 사용하는 천이나 종이다. 또한 napkin은 입과 손을 닦는 데 사용한다 : 우리는 소풍갈 때 종이 napkin을 가지고 갔다. 나는 napkin을

접시 옆에 놓았다.

**narrow** [nǽrou] 형 폭이 좁은,
가는
narrow는 폭이 넓지 않다는
뜻이다 : 사슴이 **좁은** 개울을
뛰어넘었다. 우리는 **좁은** 길을
한줄로 걸었다. 이 도시에는
**좁은** 길이 많이 있다.

**nature** [néitʃər] 명 자연 ; 본질,
천성, 성질
nature는 인간이 만들지 않은
모든 것을 말한다. 산, 나무,
강, 별은 모두 nature의 일부
다. 사람과 동물 또한 nature
의 일부다. 건물과 전화는
nature의 일부가 아니다.

**near** [níər] 1 부 가까이, 이웃
에, 인접하여 2 형 가까운 3
전 …의 가까이에, …의 곁에
near는 사람이나 사물에 인접
해 있거나 멀리 떨어져 있지
않다는 뜻이다 : **가장 가까운**
식품점은 여기에서 4블록 떨어
진 곳에 있다.

**neat** [níːt] 형 산뜻한, 단정한,
정돈된, 깔끔한
neat는 깨끗해 보이고 모든

것이 있어야 할 제자리에 있다
는 뜻이다 : 내 동생 방은 잘
**정돈되어** 있지만, 내 방은 엉
망이다.

**neck** [nék] 명 목 ; 옷깃 ; 목 모
양의 부분 ; (바이올린 등의)
**잘록한 부분**, 목
1 neck은 머리 바로 밑에 있
는 신체 부위다 : 나는 바깥 날
씨가 추울 때면, 재킷 지퍼를
neck까지 끌어 올린다. 기린
의 neck은 길고 가늘다. 수는
neck에 스카프를 두른다.

2 neck은 또한 생김새가 목처
럼 좁은 부분을 말한다. 바이
올린의 neck은 특수한 종류의
나무로 만든다.

**necklace** [nékləs] 명 목걸이
necklace는 목에 거는 장신구
를 말한다 : 우리는 엄마에게
생일 선물로 은 necklace를
해드렸다.

**need** [níːd] 1 타 자 …을 필요로
하다, …할 필요가 있다 2 조

…할 필요가 있다 3 **명** ① 필요, 소용 ② [보통 복수로] 필요한 물건

need는 무언가가 꼭 있어야만 한다는 뜻이다 : 식물은 물없이 살 수 없다. 식물은 사는 데 물이 **필요하다**.

**needle** [níːdl] **명** 바늘 ; 바느질 바늘 ; 뜨개질 바늘 ; (침엽수의) 잎 ; (주사 · 축음기 등의) 바늘

1 needle은 바느질을 하거나 뜨개질을 할 때 사용하는 가는 금속이다. 바느질 needle의 한쪽 끝에는 실을 꿰는 구멍이 있으며 다른 쪽 끝은 뾰족하다. 몇몇 식물들의 잎은 그 생김새 때문에 needle이라고 불린다.

2 또 다른 종류의 needle에는 의사나 간호사가 투여하는 약이 들어 있다 : 블레이크 의사는 needle로 내게 감기약을 투여했다.

**neighbo(u)r** [néibər] **명** 이웃 사람, 옆자리의 사람 ; 이웃 나라 (사람)

neighbor는 이웃에 사는 사람을 말한다 : 우리 neighbor는 우리가 휴가를 떠났을 때, 우리집 개 신바드를 봐주었다.

**neighbo(u)rhood** [néibərhùd] **명** 이웃, 근처 ; 주위 ; 이웃 사람들

neighborhood는 사람들이 사는 도시나 마을의 지역이다 : 내 neighborhood에 사는 아이들은 대부분 같은 학교에 다닌다.

**neither** [níːðər, nái-] 1 **부** ① [neither .. nor ...로] …도 아니고 …도 아니다〔않다〕 ② [부정문] …도 또한 …아니다〔않다〕 2 **형** (둘 중에서) 어느 쪽의 …도 …아닌 3 **대** 어느 쪽도 …아니다〔않다〕

neither는 (둘 중에서) 한쪽도 아니고 다른 쪽도 아니다라는 의미다 : 두 아이 중 **어느 누구도** 물에 들어가려고 하지 **않았다**. 조지도 데이비드도 그 경주에서 우승하지 **못했다**. 오늘은 **두 팀 모두가** 썩 좋은 경기를 펼치지 **못했다**.

**nest** [nést] **명** 보금자리, 둥지

nest는 새집이다. 새들은 나뭇잎, 나뭇가지, 진흙 그리고 그밖의 것들로 자신들의 nest를 짓는다. 대부분의 새들은 nest에 알을 낳는다.

**net** [nét] **명** 그물, 어망, 네트 ; 그물 모양의 것

net는 구멍이 나있는 일종의 용구로 보통 끈이나 밧줄로 만든다 : 지금 우리가 쓰고 있는 농구 net는 4군데가 찢어져서 새것이 필요하다. 곡예사 한명이 그네에서 떨어졌지만, 밑에 있는 net에 떨어졌다. 물고기를 잡으려고 바다에 나가 대형 net를 치는 어부들도 있다.

**never** [névər] 宇 **결코 …하지 않다** ; 일찍이 …(한 적이) 없다, 한 번도 …하지 않다
「이제〔지금〕까지 …않다」라는 뜻을 나타낼 때 never라고 말한다 : 우리는 마이크가 서커스 구경을 **한번도** 가본 적이 **없다**는 얘기를 듣고 깜짝 놀랐다. 나는 **이제까지** 이처럼 아름다운 꽃을 본 **적이 없다**.

**new** [njú:] 형 **새로운,** 아직 쓰지 않은, 새것의
1 new는 전에 사용해 본 적이 없다는 뜻이다 : 우리는 오래된 텔레비전이 고장이 나서 **새** 텔레비전을 샀다. 테리의 스케이트보드는 내 것**보다** 새것이지만, 해리의 스케이트보드는 우리 모두의 것 중에서 **가장 새**것이다.

2 new는 또한 이제 막 출발하거나 시작한다는 뜻이다 : 우리는 **새로운** 놀이를 하기 시작했다.

**news** [njú:z] 명 **뉴스,** 보도 ; **기사** ; **소식,** 새로운 사실
news는 방금 일어난 일에 관한 이야기다. 우리는 라디오와 텔레비전으로 news를 듣는다. 우리는 신문과 잡지에 실린 news를 읽기도 한다 : 공장 화재에 관한 news를 읽었니 ?

**newspaper** [njú:zpèipər, njú:s-] 명 **신문** ; 신문지
newspaper는 이웃이나 다른 곳에서 일어난 소식을 알려준다. newspaper는 종이에 인쇄된다. newspaper에서 스포츠와 서적에 관한 정보를 읽을 수 있다. 많은 newspaper가 광고를 실으며, 연재 만화를 싣는 newspaper도 있다.

**next** [nékst] 1 형 ① [시간·순서] **다음의,** 이번의, 오는…

② 〔공간〕 **가장 가까운, 이웃의** 2 **부** **다음에** 3 **전** …의 다음에, …의 옆에
1 next는 어떤 사람이나 물건 다음에 온다는 뜻이다 : 다음번에 식료품값을 내리려고 줄을 서 있는 사람이 빌이다.
2 next는 또한 무언가의 옆이나 가까이에 있다는 뜻이다 : 아기 사슴은 어미 사슴 옆에 있었다.

**nice** [náis] **형** 좋은, 훌륭한, 멋있는 ; 기분 좋은, 마음에 드는 ; 친절한, 다정한 ; 맛있는
nice는 사람들을 기분좋게 해준다는 뜻이다 : 어제 날씨가 너무 좋아서 데이너는 밖에 나가서 놀았다. 우리 이웃들은 친절하고 상냥한 사람들이다.

**nickel** [níkəl] **명** 5센트 백동화 ; 니켈《금속 원소》
nickel은 주화의 일종이다. 1 nickel은 5페니와 같고, 5 nickel은 1쿼터와 같다.

**nickname** [níknèim] **명** 별명, 애칭
nickname은 본명 대신에 사용하는 이름이다 : 보브는 로버트의 nickname이다. 로브의

nickname이 레드(Red)인 것은 그의 머리카락 색깔 때문이다.

**night** [náit] **명** 밤, 야간
night는 하루 중 밖이 어두울 때를 말한다. night는 해질녘에 시작된다. night에 달과 별들을 볼 수 있다. night에 사냥을 하는 동물들도 있다 : 그는 낮에는 일하고 night에는 책을 읽는다.

**nightmare** [náitmɛ̀ər] **명** 악몽, 가위눌림
nightmare는 아주 나쁜 꿈을 말한다. nightmare를 꾼 사람은 놀랄 수 있다 : 나는 지난밤 어두운 숲속에서 길을 잃어버리는 nightmare를 꾸었다.

**nine** [náin] 1 **명** 9, 9살, 9명 2 **형** 9의, 9살의, 9명의
nine은 숫자다. nine은 9라고 쓴다. 8+1 = 9.

**no** [nóu] 1 **부** ① 아니(오) ② 〔비교급 앞에서〕 조금도 …아니다〔않다〕 2 **형** 조금도〔전혀〕 …없는〔아닌〕
1 no는 동의하지 않는다는 뜻이다 : 마거릿이 디저트를 하나 더 먹어도 되느냐고 물어보았지만, 그녀의 엄마는 "안된다"고 말했다.
2 no는 또한 「조금도 …아니다〔않다〕」의 뜻이다 : 여름에는

N

눈이 **안온다.** 피터는 어제 아팠는데, 오늘도 여전히 아프다. 오늘 그의 몸은 어제와 마찬가지로 좋지 **않다.**

**nobody** [nóubədi, -bàdi | -bədi, -bɔ́di] 때 **아무도 …않다**
nobody는 한 사람도 없다는 뜻이다 : 새처럼 날 수 있는 사람은 **아무도 없다.**

**nod** [nád | nɔ́d] 1 재타 **.끄덕이다** ; 인사〔절〕하다 ; 끄덕거려 승낙〔명령〕하다 ; 꾸벅꾸벅 졸다 2 명 **끄덕임** ; 묵례 ; 졸기
nod는 머리를 위아래로 움직인다는 뜻이다. 사람들은 흔히 동의한다는 표시로 **머리를 끄덕인다.**

**noise** [nɔ́iz] 명 **소리, 소음, 잡음, 소란**
noise는 소리인 데, 시끄러운 소리를 말한다 : 공항에는 항상 noise가 많다.

**none** [nʌ́n] 때 **아무도〔아무것도〕**

**…않다〔없다〕; 조금도〔전혀〕 …않다〔없다〕**
none은 「아무도 …이 아니다」거나 「조금도 …않다」는 뜻이다 : 데이비드는 사과를 먹고 싶었지만, 바구니에는 **아무것도** 남아있지 **않았다.** 우리들 중에 빌처럼 높이 뛰어오를 수 있는 사람은 **아무도 없다.**

**nonfiction** [nànfíkʃən | nɔ̀n-] 명 **논픽션**《소설이 아닌 산문 문학 : 전기, 역사 등》
nonfiction은 실재 인물이나 실제 사건에 대해 쓴 것이다. nonfiction은 fiction(허구)의 반대말이다. 신문에 나는 기사도 일종의 nonfiction이다. 한 인간의 생애에 관한 이야기도 또한 nonfiction이다.

**noodle** [núːdl] 명 **누들, 국수**
noodle은 길고, 납작하고 가느다란 모양의 음식이다. noodle은 밀가루, 물, 달걀로 만든다 : noodle과 햄버거는 내가 가장 좋아하는 음식이다. 피터는 밥대신 수프에 noodle을 넣어서 먹고 싶었다.

**noon** [núːn] 몡 정오, 대낮
noon은 낮 12시를 말한다 :
우리는 noon에 점심을 먹는
다.

**nor** [《약》 nər, 《강》 nɔ́ːr] 졉
[neither 또는 not 과 상관적으
로] …도 또한 …않다 ; …도
…하지 않다
nor는 neither와 함께 쓰는 말
이다 : 사라도 폴도 축구하고
노는 것을 좋아하지 **않는다**.

**north** [nɔ́ːrθ] 1 몡 북, 북쪽 2
혱 북의, 북쪽에 있는 3 븟
북으로, **북쪽에**
지도를 볼 때, 위쪽 방향이
north다. 아침에 태양이 뜰
때, 태양쪽을 바라보고 있다면
north는 왼쪽이다. north의 반
대말은 south(남쪽)다.

**nose** [nóuz] 몡 코
nose는 얼굴 중앙에 있다.
nose로 숨을 쉬고 냄새를 맡
는다.

**not** [nát|nɔ́t] 븟 …이 아니다,
…않다
말이나 문장을 부정으로 만들
려고 not을 사용한다 : 마리는
집에 **없다**.

**note** [nóut] 몡 ① 메모, 짧은
편지 ; 주석 ; **주의** ② (악기의)
**소리**, 가락 ; 음표, **악보**
1 note는 음악의 한 음으로,
음악은 많은 note로 되어 있
다. 다른 사람들이 note를 읽
고서 같은 음악을 연주할 수
있도록 note를 적어 둘 수 있
다.
2 note는 또한 글로 쓴 간단
한 메시지를 말한다.

**nothing** [nʌ́θiŋ] 때 아무것도
〔아무일도〕 …아니다〔하지 않
다〕
nothing은 아무것도 없다는 뜻
이다 : 저녁 식사가 너무 맛있
어서, 접시에 음식을 남긴 사
람이 **아무도 없었다**. nothing
의 반대말은 something(어떤
것)이다.

**notice** [nóutis] 탸 쟈 알아차리
다 ; …에 주의하다
notice는 무언가를 보거나 들
어서 안다는 뜻이다 : 빌은 자
기 동생이 짝짝이 양말을 신고
있다는 것을 **알아차렸다**. 그는
나를 **알아보고** 손을 흔들기 시
작했다.

**November** [nouvémbər] 몡

N

11월
November는 한 해 가운데 한
달이다. November는 30 일이
며, 10월이 끝나고 12월이 시
작되기 전에 온다.

**now** [náu] 〔부〕 **지금**, 현재 ; 방
금 ; **지금 곧**, 바로
now는 「(바로)지금」이라는 뜻
이다 : 정말로 **지금** 가야만 하
니 ? **지금** 눈이 내리고 있는
데.

**number** [nΛmbər] 〔명〕 **수**, **숫
자** ; 번호
1 number는 무언가가 얼마나
있는 지를 알려준다 : 2 와 50
둘다 number다.
2 number는 또한 서로 별개의
것임을 구별하는 데 사용한
다 : 너의 집 전화 number를

알고 있니 ?

**nurse** [nə́ːrs] 〔명〕 **간호사** ; 유모,
보모
nurse는 아픈 사람들을 돌보
아주는 사람이다. 병원에 근무
하는 nurse도 있고, 집에 있
는 사람을 방문하는 nurse도
있다.

**nut** [nΛt] 〔명〕 **나무 열매**, **견과**
《호두·밤 등》
nut는 나무에서 자란다. nut는
대개 껍질이 단단하며, 대부분
의 nut는 먹을 수 있다.

**oak** [óuk] 명 오크 나무 ; 오크 재목의 제품
oak는 도토리가 열리는 나무다. oak 목재는 아주 견고하여 가구나 보트를 만드는 데 쓴다 : 부모님은 oak제 부엌 식탁을 사셨다.

**obey** [oubéi, ə-] 타 …에 복종하다, 따르다 ; 준수하다 ; 순응하다
obey는 어떤 사람이 시킨대로 한다는 뜻이다 : 엘리자베스는 부모님의 말씀에 순종해서 학교에서 4시까지는 귀가한다. 앤디가 개에게 앉으라고 말하자, 개는 즉시 그의 말에 복종했다.

**object** [ábdʒikt | ɔ́b-] 명 ① 물건, 물체 ; 대상 ② 목적, 목표
object는 사람들이 보거나 만질 수 있는 무생물체를 말한다. 건물, 탁자, 의자, 책, 가위, 펜 그리고 연필은 모두 object다.

**ocean** [óuʃən] 명 대양, 해양, 바다
ocean은 짠물이며, 지구의 넓은 지역을 차지한다. 물고기와 고래는 ocean에서 산다. 배는 ocean을 항해한다.

**o'clock** [əklák | əklɔ́k] 명 …시
우리는 몇 시인가를 말할 때 o'clock이라는 말을 쓴다 : 우리는 아침 8 o'clock에 학교에 간다.

**October** [ɑktóubər | ɔk-] 명 10월
October는 1년중 한 달이다. October는 31일이며, 9월이

가고 11월이 되기 전에 온다.

**octopus** [άktəpəs|ɔ́k-] 〔명〕 낙
지, 문어
octopus는 바다에 사는 동물
로, 유연한 몸체와 여덟 개의
발이 있다. octopus는 움직이
거나 먹이를 잡는 데 발을 사
용한다.

**odd** [ád|ɔ́d] 〔형〕 ① 나머지의,
남은, 우수리의 ; 한 쪽의, 짝
이 맞지 않는 ② **홀수의 ; 이상
한**, 색다른
1 odd는 이상하거나 색다르다
는 뜻이다 : 우리 차는 **이상한**
소리가 나서 수리해야 한다.
2 수에는 odd number(홀수)
도 있고, 짝수도 있다. 숫자
1, 3, 5, 7, 9는 odd number(홀
수)고, 숫자 2, 4, 6, 8, 10은 짝
수다.

**of** [《약》 əv, 《강》 ʌ́v, άv|ɔ́v] 〔전〕
① [소속・소유] …의, …에
속하는 ② [재료] …으로 (만
든) ③ [거리・위치・출처] …
에서 ; **…출신의** ④ [그릇・분
량] …이 들어 있는 ⑤ [시
간] (…분) 전
1 of는 「…으로 (만든)」이란

뜻이다 : 대부분의 탁자는 나무
로 만들어진다.

2 of는 또한 속의 내용물을 나
타낸다 : 폴은 물 한동이를 나
르고 있었다.
3 시간을 말할 때 of는 「(…
분) 전」이란 뜻이다 : 4 시 10분
전이다.

**off** [ɔ́ːf|ɔ́f] 1 〔전〕 ① …에서 떨어
져, 벗어나 ② (일 등을) 쉬고
2 〔부〕 ① [위치] 저쪽으로, 떨
어져, 떠나서 ② [분리・이탈]
벗어 ; 떼어내어 ③ (수도・가
스 등이) **꺼져**, 잠겨
1 off는 on(전기 등이 켜져 있
는)의 반대말이다 : 전등이 **꺼
지면** 집이 어두워진다.
2 off는 또한 (…에서) 떨어져
있다는 뜻이다 : 저녁 식사 전
에 식탁에서 책을 좀 **치워라**.

**offer** [ɔ́ːfər|ɔ́fə] 〔타〕〔자〕 제공하
다, 권하다 ; 제의〔제안〕하다 ;
(…하겠다고) **말하다**
offer는 어떤 것을 주거나 하
겠다는 의사를 밝힌다는 뜻이
다 : 마리아는 아버지가 갈퀴로
가랑잎을 긁어모으는 일을 돕
겠다고 **했다**.

**office** [áfis, ɔ́:f-|ɔ́f-] 명 ① 관청, 관공서 ② **사무실**, 영업소 ③ 직무, 임무
office는 일하는 곳이다. office가 많이 있는 건물도 있다 : 교장실은 복도 맨 끝에 있다.

**officer** [áfisər, ɔ́:f-|ɔ́f-] 명 ① 장교, 사관 ② 관리, **공무원** ③ **경찰**, 순경
1 officer는 군대에서 다른 사람들을 지휘해서 그들에게 해야 할 일을 일러주는 사람이다.
2 officer는 또한 경찰에서 일하는 남자나 여자다 : 그 police officer(경찰관)는 길 잃은 아이가 부모를 찾도록 도와주었다.

**often** [ɔ́:fən|ɔ́f-] 부 흔히, **자주**, 종종
often은 여러 번이라는 뜻이다 : 4월에는 비가 **자주** 온다.

**oil** [ɔ́iəl] 명 기름 ; 석유
1 oil은 채소나 동물로부터 얻는 액체로, 요리에 쓰인다 : 우리는 팝콘을 만들려고 팬과 옥수수 oil을 꺼냈다.
2 또 다른 종류의 oil은 땅 속에서 나온다. 이 oil을 때서 난방을 하고 기계를 움직인다 : 지난 주에는 밖이 워낙 추워서 난로에 oil을 많이 땠다.

**okay, okey** [òukéi] 1 형 **좋은**, 괜찮은 ; 틀림없는 2 부 좋아
okay는 좋다는 뜻이다 : 메리는 라디오가 고장났다고 생각했지만, **멀쩡했다**. 이 말은 또한 OK라고도 쓴다 : 네 스케이트보드를 빌려 타도 **괜찮겠지**?

**old** [óuəld] 형 늙은, 나이든 ; (만) …살의 ; 낡은, 헌
1 old는 오랜 세월을 살아왔다는 뜻이다 : 할아버지는 **늙었지만**, 토니는 젊다.

2 old는 물건을 오랫동안 사용했다는 뜻이다 : 우리는 우리의 **헌** 옷을 필요한 사람들에게 주었다.
3 또한 나이에 대해 말할 때 old란 말을 쓴다 : 나는 일곱 **살**이다. 너는 나보다 **나이가** 더 **많니**?

**on** [án, ɔ́:n|ɔ́n] 1 전 ① [위치]

…의 위에 ② [방향·대상] …을 향하여 ③ [관계] …에 관한 ④ [날·때] …에 2 부 ① 위에, (탈 것을) 타고 ② (옷 등을) 몸에 걸치고 ③ (전기·수도 등이) **켜져**

1 on은 off(전기 등이 꺼져 있는)의 반대말이다 : 전등이 **켜지면** 방이 환하다.

2 on은 어떤 것의 위치를 나타낸다 : 식탁 **위에** 접시가 있다.

3 on은 「…에 관한」이란 뜻이다 : 리처드는 공룡에 **관한** 책을 한 권 갖고 있다.

4 on은 또한 어떤 일이 일어나는 날을 나타낸다 : 우리는 일요일**에는** 언제나 야구를 한다.

**once** [wʌ́ns] 1 부 **한 번** ; 한번이라도, 일단 ; **예전에, 일찍이** 2 접 **…하자마자** ; …한 순간부터, 일단 …하면

1 once는 단지 한 번만 한다는 뜻이다 : 우리는 일주일에 **한 번** 식료품을 산다.

2 once는 또한 「…하자마자」란 뜻이다 : 비가 그치는 **대로** 곧 외출할 수 있다.

**one** [wʌ́n] 1 형 **한…**, 하나의 ; 어느 ; (…와) **같은** 2 명 **하나, 한 사람** ; 1 3 대 ① [일반적 용법] **사람**, 누구나 ② [명사의 반복을 피해] **같은 사람**〔물건〕, 그것《같은 종류의 것》

1 one은 숫자로, 1이라고 쓴다. 수를 셀 때, 제일 먼저 세는 수가 one이다.

2 one은 이미 말한 것을 나타낼 때 쓴다 : 사라는 청포도는 좋아하지만, 적**포도는** 싫어한다.

**onion** [ʌ́njən] 명 **양파**

onion은 채소의 일종으로, 둥글며 강한 냄새와 맛이 난다. onion은 땅 속에서 자란다.

**only** [óunli] 1 형 **단 하나의, …만**〔뿐〕**의, 유일한** 2 부 **단지, 오직** ; 다만 …뿐

only는 오직 하나 밖에 없다는 뜻이다 : 하늘에는 **오직** 하나의 달이 있을 **뿐**이다.

**open** [óupən] 1 형 **열린, 열려 있는 ; 비어있는 ; 공개된** 2 타자 **열다 ; 공개하다 ; 개업[개시]하다 ; 펼치다 ; 시작되다**

1 open은 닫거나 폐쇄하지 않았다는 뜻이다 : 항아리가 **열려** 있다면, 뚜껑이 덮여 있지 않다는 것이다. 문이 **열려** 있어서 나는 걸어 들어 갔다.

2 open은 또한 어떤 것을 열게 한다는 뜻이다 : 창문 좀 **열어 주세요.**

3 open은 또한 시작한다는 뜻이다 : 새 연극이 지난 토요일 밤부터 **시작되었다.**

**opening** [óupəniŋ] 명 ① **개방** ② **개시, 개장, 개회, 개통** ③ **(뚫린) 구멍, 틈 ; 빈터**

opening은 트인 곳이다 : 토끼가 울타리의 opening으로 빠져 나갔다.

**opossum** [əpásəm│əpɔ́s-] 명 **주머니쥐**

opossum은 털이 잿빛인 작은 동물이다. opossum은 캥거루처럼 배에 있는 주머니에 새끼들을 넣어 가지고 다닌다.

**opposite** [ápəzit│ɔ́p-] 1 형 **맞은 편의 ; 정반대의** 2 명 **정반대 사물[사람], 반대말**

1 opposite는 모든 면에서 다르다는 뜻이다 : up(위로)은 down(아래로)의 opposite다.

2 opposite는 또한 일직선상의

양끝에 있다는 뜻이다 : 동쪽과 서쪽은 **정반대** 방향이다.

**or** [《약》 ər, 《강》 ɔ́:r] 접 ① **또는, 혹은** ② [보통 콤마 뒤] **즉, 바꾸어 말하면** ③ [either ... or ...로] **…이든가 또는[혹은]** ④ [명령문 뒤] **그렇지 않으면**

단어 or는 다른 두 사물이나 두 사람에 관해 말할 때 도움을 준다 : 사과나 배 중에서 어느 것을 더 좋아하니 ? 나는 학교에서 집으로 돌아가면, 야구를 **하든가 아니면** 책을 읽을 것이다.

**orange** [ɔ́:rindʒ, ár-│ɔ́r-] 1 명 **오렌지** 2 형 **오렌지의, 오렌지색의**

1 orange는 작고 둥근 과일이다 : 아침 식사와 함께 orange를 드시겠습니까 ?

2 orange는 또한 색깔이다 : 호박은 **오렌지색**이다. 내게는 오렌지색 스카프가 있다.

**orchestra** [ɔ́:rkistrə] 명 **오케스트라, 관현악단**

orchestra는 함께 악기를 연주하는 규모가 큰 단체다. 백 명

이 넘는 사람들로 구성된 orchestra도 있다.

**order** [ɔ́ːrdər] 1 뗑 순서, 차례
정돈, 정렬 2 喬 정돈하다 ;
정리〔배열〕하다
order는 물건들이 제자리에 놓
여 있다는 뜻이다 : 빌리는 알
파벳 글자를 A부터 Z까지 **차
례대로** 말할 수 있다. 아서는
숫자를 1부터 25까지 **순서대로**
알고 있다.

**ostrich** [ástritʃ, ɔ́ːs-|ɔ́s-] 뗑 타
조
ostrich는 굉장히 큰 새로, 다
리가 길고 목도 길다. ostrich
는 날 수 없다.

**other** [ʌ́ðər] 1 뛩 다른, 그 밖
의 ; 상이한 ; (둘 중의) **또 하
나의** 2 뗴 **다른 것〔사람〕**
1 other는 둘 중의 하나라는
뜻이다 : 데일의 양말 한 짝에
는 구멍이 나 있는 데, **다른**
한 짝에는 구멍이 없다.
2 other는 또한 「다른」이라는
뜻이다 : 수잔은 오늘 놀 시간

이 없다. 언젠가 다른 때 놀
시간이 있을 것이다.

**ounce** [áuns] 뗑 온스
ounce는 무게의 양이다. 1 파
운드는 16 ounce다.

**our** [áuər, áːr] 뗴 우리 (들) 의
our는 우리의 소유물을 뜻한
다 : **우리**집은 학교 근처에 있
다.

**ours** [áuərz, áːrz] 뗴 **우리 (들)
의 것**
ours는 우리의 소유물을 뜻한
다 : 저것들은 너희들 책이고,
이것들은 **우리들** 책이다.

**ourselves** [auərséəlvz, aːr-]
뗴 우리 스스로 ; **우리들 자신
에게〔을〕**
ourselves는 누군가 딴 사람이
아닌 바로 우리 자신을 뜻한
다 : 마크와 내가 거울을 보자,
거울에 비친 **우리들의 모습**이
보였다.

**out** [áut] 1 뮈 ① 밖에, 밖으
로 ; 외출하여 ② (불 등이) 꺼
져 ③ 끝까지, 완전히 2 쩐
…을 통하여 밖으로, …으로부
터
1 out은 안에서 밖으로 나간다
는 뜻이다 : 톰은 상자에서 장
난감 기차를 **꺼냈다**.
2 out은 또한 집밖을 뜻한다 :

나가서 뒤뜰에서 놀자.

3 out은 또한 「…을 통하여」라는 뜻이다 : 우리는 비가 오고 있는지 보려고 창밖을 **내다** 보았다.

**outdoor** [áutdɔ̀:r] 형 집밖의, 야외의
outdoor는 건물 안이 아닌 건물 밖이란 뜻이다 : 우리는 **야외** 음악회에 갔다.

**outdoors** [àutdɔ́:rz] 부 집밖에서, 야외에서
outdoors는 야외에 나와 있다는 뜻이다 : 날씨가 따뜻한 저녁이면, 우리는 **집밖에서** 저녁을 먹는 것을 좋아한다.

**outer space** [àutər spéis] 명 (지구의 대기권 밖의) 우주
outer space는 지구에서 멀리 떨어져 있다. 달과 행성 그리고 별들은 outer space에 있

다 : 우주 비행사들은 우주선을 타고 outer space를 탐험한다.

**outgrow** [àutgróu] 타 몸이 커져서 (옷을) 입지 못하게 되다 ; 자라서 (습관·취미 등을) 버리다
outgrow는 몸이 너무 커져서 어떤 것이 맞지 않는다는 뜻이다 : 아기는 몇 달마다 **자라서** 옷이 **맞지 않는다.** 앤은 발이 **커져서** 운동화를 **못** 신게 되어, 새 것을 사야 했다.

**outside** [àutsáid, ⁻⁻] 1 명 외부, 바깥쪽 ; 표면, 겉모습, 생김새  2 형 바깥쪽의 ; 외부의  3 부 바깥쪽에 ; 집밖으로
1 outside는 바깥 부분이다 : 우리집 outside는 하얀 페인트로 칠해져 있다.
2 outside는 또한 안이 아니라 밖이라는 뜻이다 : 나는 학교 **밖에서** 종소리를 들었다. 사내 아이들은 뜰에서 놀려고 **밖으로** 나갔다.

**oval** [óuvəl] 1 형 달걀 모양의 ; 타원형의 2 명 달걀 모양의 것 ; 타원형

oval은 달걀처럼 생긴 모양이다 : 칠면조 고기가 큰 **타원형** 접시 위에 놓여 있다.

**oven** [ʌ́vən] 명 **오븐, 화덕 ; 솥, 가마**
oven은 음식물을 데우거나 요리하는 스토브의 내부를 말한다 : 클레어와 그녀의 언니는 oven에 빵을 구웠다. 우리는 그 남자가 우리가 주문한 피자를 구우려고 oven에 넣는 것을 지켜보았다. microwave oven(전자 레인지)은 음식을 아주 빨리 요리할 수 있는 특별한 종류의 oven이다.

**over** [óuvər] 1 전 ① **…의 위에** ② **…을 넘어, …저편의, …건너의** ③ **…을 넘는, …이상** 2 부 ① **위에 ; 온통** ② **건너서, 넘어서** ③ **위에서 아래로, 넘어져** ④ **되풀이 하여** ⑤ **끝나서, 지나서**
1 over는 「…의 위에」라는 뜻이다 : 헬리콥터가 우리 집 **위로** 날아갔다.

2 over는 또한 「…에 더하여, …위에」라는 뜻이다 : 헬렌은 셔츠 위에 스웨터를 입었다.
3 over는 또한 「…이상, …을 넘는」이라는 뜻이다 : 앤드루의 아버지는 키가 6 피트가 **넘으신다.**
4 over는 또한 「위에서 아래쪽으로」란 뜻이다 : 앨버트는 우유 한 컵을 쳐서 **쓰러뜨렸다.**
5 over는 또한 되풀이한다는 뜻이다 : 악단이 노래를 연주했는 데, 모든 사람들이 좋아해서 그것을 **되풀이해** 연주했다.
6 over는 끝났다는 뜻이다 : 영화가 **끝나자** 우리는 집으로 갔다.

**owe** [óu] 타 **…을 지불할 의무가 있다, …에게 빚이 있다 ; (…의) 은혜를 입다**
owe는 어떤 사람에게 무언가를 주어야만 한다는 뜻이다 : 토드는 그 가게에 사과 값으로 25센트를 **빚지고** 있다.

**owl** [áuəl] 명 **올빼미**
owl은 머리가 크고 눈이 둥글고 큰 새다. owl은 보통 밤에 먹이를 사냥한다.

**own** [óun] 1 형 **자기 자신의 ; 독특한** 2 타 **소유하다**
own은 어떤 것을 갖고 보관한다는 뜻이다 : 제인은 책과 장난감을 많이 **가지고** 있다.

**pack** [pǽk] 타 자 싸다, **짐을 꾸리다**

pack 은 무언가를 가져 가기 위해 여행 가방이나 상자에 넣는다는 의미다 : 월터는 휴가를 떠나려고 옷과 책 몇 권을 **꾸렸다.**

**package** [pǽkidʒ] 명 꾸러미, **소포, 짐 ; 포장한 상품**

package 는 묶어서 우송하는 물건이다. 사람들은 package 를 부치려고 우체국으로 가져온다.

**pad** [pǽd] 명 (충격·마찰·손상을 막는) **덧대는 물건**, 깔개 ; **메워 넣는 것** ; (상처에 대는) 거즈, 탈지면 ; (한 장씩 떼어 쓰게 된) **종이철**

pad 는 한쪽 가장자리를 하나로 붙인 종잇장들로 되어 있다. pad 의 지면들은 글씨를 쓰거나 그림을 그릴 수 있도록 백지로 되어 있다. 우리는 메시지를 적기 위해 전화기 가까이에 pad 와 연필을 놓아둔다 : 사라는 자기의 pad 에다 그림을 그렸다.

**page** [péidʒ] 명 페이지, 쪽, 책의 면

page 는 책, 잡지 혹은 신문의 한쪽 면이다 : 웬디는 책의 첫 page 에 자기 이름을 썼다. 그 잡지의 어느 한 page 도 찢어서는 안됩니다.

**paid** [péid] 통 pay (지불하다)의 과거·과거분사형

paid 는 pay 의 한 형태다 : 빌은 4달러를 **내고** 영화표를 샀다.

**pail** [péiəl] 명 들통, 양동이

pail 은 물건을 담는 데 쓴다. pail 은 금속이나 플라스틱으로 만들며, 밑바닥이 평평하고 둥글다. pail 은 버킷과 같은 (종류의) 물건이다.

**pain** [péin] 명 아픔, **고통**

pain 은 다쳤을 때 느끼는 감각이다. 음식을 너무 급하게 먹

으면 배가 **아플** 수도 있다.

**paint** [péint] 1 명 페인트, 그림 물감 2 타자 ···에 페인트를 칠하다, (그림 물감으로) **그리다**

1 paint 는 색이 있는 액체를 말한다. 사람들은 보기 좋게 하려고 물건에 paint 를 칠한다. 화가는 paint 로 그림을 그린다.

2 paint 는 페인트로 칠한다는 의미다 : 베티와 그녀의 엄마는 한 방은 노란색 **페인트**로, 다른 방은 파란색 **페인트**로 **칠했다.**

**painting** [péintiŋ] 명 **그림**, 회화 ; 그림 그리기

painting 은 그림 물감으로 그린 그림이다 : 내가 그린 공룡 painting 은 미술 전시회에 출품되어 있다.

**pair** [péər] 명 **한 쌍**, 한 벌, 한 켤레 ; 한 짝 ; 한쌍의 남녀, 부부

pair 는 서로 짝을 이루는 두 개의 물건이다. 구두, 양말, 장갑은 pair 로 되어 있다.

**pajamas | pyjamas** [pədʒá:-məz, -dʒǽməz | dʒá:-] 명 파자마《잠옷》

pajamas 는 잠잘 때 입는 옷이다. 대부분의 pajamas 는 따뜻하고 부드럽다.

**palace** [pǽləs] 명 **궁전** ; 훌륭한 저택 ; 호화로운 건물

palace 는 왕이나 여왕 혹은 그 밖의 다른 통치자가 사는 아주 크고 아름다운 집이다. palace 는 주위에 많은 정원이 있다 : 마리아와 데일은 방이 50 개나 있고 바닥이 대리석으로 된 palace 를 방문했다.

**palm** [pá:m] 명 **손바닥**

palm 은 손의 안쪽을 말한다. 우리 손의 palm에는 많은 금들이 있다.

**pan** [pǽn] 명 **납작한 냄비** ; 접시 모양의 그릇

pan 은 요리할 때 쓰는 평평한 금속제 그릇을 말한다. 대부분의 pan에는 긴 손잡이가 달려 있다 : 우리는 큰 pan 에다 생선을 요리했다.

**pancake** [pǽnkèik] 명 **팬케이크**

pancake 는 음식의 일종으로, 얇고 판판한 케이크를 말한다. pancake 는 밀가루와 달걀 그리고 우유를 한데 섞은 다음 달궈진 팬에 굽는다.

**pants** [pǽnts] 명 바지
pants 는 옷의 일종이다. 사람들은 다리에 pants 를 입는다. 대부분의 pants 에는 양옆에 호주머니가 있다.

**paper** [péipər] 명 종이 ; 종이와 같은 것
paper 는 글씨를 쓰는 데 사용하는 것이다. paper 는 나무로 만들고, 책과 신문은 paper 로 만든다.

**parachute** [pǽrəʃùːt] 명 낙하산
parachute 는 비행기에서 사람이나 물건을 천천히 그리고 안전하게 떨어뜨리는 데 사용한다. parachute 는 커다란 우산처럼 보인다.

**parade** [pəréid] 명 행렬, 행진, 퍼레이드 ; 열병(식)
parade 는 거리를 따라 함께 행진하는 사람들의 무리다. 대부분의 parade 에는 행진할 때 음악을 연주하는 악대가 따른다. parade 는 축제에 하는 경우가 많다.

**parakeet** [pǽrəkìːt] 명 (작은) 잉꼬
parakeet 는 길고 뾰족한 꼬리가 있는 작은 새다. parakeet 는 청색, 녹색, 그리고 노란색의 깃털이 있다.

**parent** [pɛ́ərənt] 명 ① 부모, 어버이《아버지 또는 어머니 중 한 분》 ② [복수로] 양친
parent 는 어머니거나 아버지다 : 제인의 parents 는 우리를 데리고 스케이트를 타러 갔다.

**park** [páːrk] 1 명 공원 2 타 (놓아) 두다 ; (자동차를) 주차시키다
1 park 는 사람들이 놀거나 휴식을 취할 수 있는 장소다. 대부분의 park 에는 나무와 잔디 그리고 벤치들이 있다.
2 park 는 또한 무언가를 잠시 동안 한 곳에 세워 둔다는 의미다 : 보브는 자동차를 차고에 **주차시켰다.**

**parking lot** [pá:rkiŋ làt] 명
주차장
　parking lot은 사람들이 잠시
동안 자기 차를 세워 둘 수 있
는 곳이다 : 우리는 쇼핑하러
갔을 때 parking lot에 차를
세워 두었다.

**parrot** [pǽrət] 명 앵무새
　parrot은 새의 한 종류다.
parrot은 부리가 크고 깃털은
색깔이 선명하다. 몇 마디 말
을 배울 수 있는 parrot도 있
다.

**part** [pá:rt] 명 ① **부분**, 일
부 ; 요소 ② [복수로] (기계
의) **부품**
　part는 어떤 것의 일부다. 머
리는 몸의 part다. 텔레비전은
많은 parts로 되어 있다.

**party** [pá:rti] 명 **모임, 파티**
　party는 사람들이 모여서 즐
겁게 지내는 시간이다 : 생일에
party를 여는 사람들이 많다.

**pass** [pǽs|pá:s] 자 타 ① **지나
다, 통과하다** ② **넘겨 주다,
건네 주다** ③ (시험·검사에)
**합격하다**
　1 pass는 지나간다는 의미
다 : 우리는 학교 가는 길에 너
의 집을 **지나간다.**

　2 pass는 또한 물건이 한 사
람에게서 다른 사람에게로 옮
겨 간다는 의미다 : 시리얼 좀
**건네 주십시오.**
　3 pass는 또한 어떤 것을 다
시 배울 필요가 없을 만큼 충
분히 알고 있다는 의미다 : 나
는 내일 철자법 시험에 **합격하
기를** 바란다.

**Passover** [pǽsòuvər|pá:s-] 명
**유월절**《유태력 1월 14일에 행
하는 유태인의 축제》
　Passover는 봄에 거행하는 유
태인의 축제다. 가족과 친구들
은 Passover 날 함께 모여 특
별한 음식을 먹으며, 그 축제
일에 얽힌 이야기를 나눈다.

**past** [pǽst|pá:st] 1 형 **지나간,**
과거의, 이제 까지의 ; 끝난 2
명 **과거** 3 전 [시간·장소]
**…을 지나서** 4 부 **지나쳐서,
지나서**

1 past 는 이미 지나가 버린 시간의 일부다. 어제는 past 다.

2 go past 는 지나쳐서 간다는 의미다 : 큰 강은 많은 마을과 도시를 **지나쳐** 흐른다.

**paste** [péist] 1 타 **풀로 붙이다** 〔바르다〕 2 명 **풀** ; 반죽, 가루 반죽

1 paste 는 물건을 한 데 붙이는 데 사용하는 것이다 : 잊지 말고 paste통 뚜껑을 닫아라, 그렇지 않으면 paste 가 굳어버린다.

2 paste 는 또한 풀로 물건을 붙인다는 의미다 : 찰리는 책장마다 사진을 모두 **붙였다.**

**pat** [pǽt] 타자 **가볍게 두드리다**, 가볍게 치다, 쓰다듬다
pat 는 손으로 부드럽게 만진다는 의미다 : 내 말은 머리를 **가볍게 다독거려주**면 좋아한다.

**patch** [pǽtʃ] 명 (덧대어 깁는) **천조각** ; (경작한) 좁은 땅, 밭, 한 구획
1 patch 는 작은 천조각이다.

사람들은 찢어진 데를 가리려고 옷에 patch 를 덧대어 꿰맨다.

2 patch 는 또한 땅의 한 구역을 의미한다 : 그 농부는 자신의 호박 patch 에 호박을 재배했다.

**path** [pǽθ|pɑ́:θ] 명 **좁은 길**, 오솔길 ; 통로
path 는 들판이나 숲을 걸어서 지나갈 수 있는 곳이다 : 데이비드와 그의 친구들은 path 를 따라 호수까지 갔다.

**pattern** [pǽtərn] 명 **모범** ; 원형 ; (행동 등의) 유형, 양식 ; 도안, **무늬**
pattern 은 물건의 표면에 색상이나 선 혹은 기호가 배치된 방식과 모양을 말한다 : 앨리스의 셔츠에는 연분홍색 꽃 pattern 이 있다. 이 나비의 날개에는 초록색과 검은색 점으로 된 pattern 이 있다.

**paw** [pɔ́:] 명 (개 · 고양이 등의 갈고리 모양의 발톱이 있는) **발**
paw 는 몇몇 동물의 발이다. 개, 고양이, 곰, 토끼는 모두

paw 가 4 개다.

**pay** [péi] 타 자 **지불하다,** 대금
을 치르다
pay 는 어떤 것의 대가로 돈을
지불한다는 의미다 : 내가 팝콘
**값을 내겠다.** 아버지께서 우리
차를 수리해준 사람에게 **수리**
**비를 지불하셨다.**

**pea** [píː] 명 **완두(콩)**
pea 는 작고 둥근 초록색 야채
다 : 아버지께서 지난밤 pea
수프를 만드셨다.

**peace** [píːs] 명 **평화**
peace 는 전쟁이 없는 시기를
말한다. 세상이 peace 로울
때는 전쟁이 없다 : 우리 나라
는 peace 롭다.

**peach** [píːtʃ] 명 **복숭아**
peach 는 둥글고 단맛이 나는
과일이다. peach 의 껍질은
노란색과 빨간색을 띠고 있
다 : 우리는 디저트로 peach
를 먹었다.

**peak** [píːk] 명 **뾰족한 끝 ; 산꼭**
대기 ; 절정, 최고점

peak 는 산의 맨 꼭대기 지점
을 말한다 : 우리는 눈으로 덮
인 peak 사진을 찍었다.

**peanut** [píːnʌt] 명 **땅콩**
peanut 은 먹는 것이다. pea-
nut 의 껍질은 갈색이며 땅속
에서 자란다 : 우리는 항상
peanut 한 봉지를 사서 야구
경기를 본다.

**peanut butter** [píːnʌt bʌ̀tər]
명 **땅콩 버터**
peanut butter 는 땅콩으로 만
든 부드러운 식품이다 : 마이클
은 크래커에 peanut butter 를
발라서 먹는 것을 좋아한다.

**pear** [pέər] 명 **서양배 ; 서양배**
나무
pear 는 단맛이 나는 과일로,
껍질은 노란색이나 갈색 혹은
붉은 색을 띠고 있다. pear 는
윗 부분보다 아랫 부분이 더
크다 : 우리는 디저트로 pear
와 치즈를 먹었다.

**pebble** [pébl] 명 **조약돌,** 자갈
pebble 은 작은 돌이다 : 그 바
닷가에는 모래는 별로 없고
pebble이 많이 있었다. 내 신

발 속에 들어간 pebble 하나
를 찾아냈다.

**peek** [píːk] 区 살짝 들여다보
다, **몰래 엿보다**
peek 는 재빨리 혹은 아무도
모르게 무언가를 본다는 의미
다 : 다람쥐가 나무 뒤에서 **살
짝 모습을 드러냈다.**

**peel** [píːəl] 匝 **껍질을 벗기다**
peel 은 몇몇 과일과 야채의
껍질이나 외피를 벗긴다는 의
미다 : 제인은 여동생에게 주려
고 오렌지 **껍질을 벗겼다.**

**pen**¹ [pén] 몡 **펜촉 ; 펜 ; 깃펜**
pen 은 글씨를 쓰는 도구다.
pen 은 대개 플라스틱이나 금
속으로 만든다 : 그는 파란색
pen 으로 자기 이름을 썼다.

**pen**² [pén] 몡 **우리, 축사**
pen 은 동물을 기르려고 울타
리를 친 지역을 말한다 : 돼지
들은 pen 에서 산다.

**pencil** [pénsəl] 몡 **연필**
pencil 은 글씨를 쓰는 도구
다. pencil 은 보통 속에 흑연

이 들어 있는 긴 나무 막대기
를 말한다. 대부분의 pencil
에는 한쪽 끝에 지우개가 달려
있다 : 수는 뾰족한 pencil 심
을 부러뜨렸다.

**penguin** [péŋgwin] 몡 **펭귄**
penguin 은 새의 일종이다.
penguin 은 아주 추운 지방의
바닷가에 산다. penguin 은 날
수 없지만, 날개를 이용해 물
속에서 헤엄을 칠 수 있다.

**penny** [péni] 몡 **페니**
penny 는 주화인 데, 가장 적
은 금액이다. 1 penny는 1 센
트다. 1 쿼터는 25 penny 고,
1 달러는 100 penny 다.

**people** [píːpl] 몡 (세상) **사람
들 ; 국민, 민족**
people 은 두 명 이상의 사람
을 나타낸다 : 세상에 똑같은
people 은 없다.

**pepper** [pépər] 몡 **후추 ; 고추**
1 pepper 는 톡 쏘는 맛을 내
기 위해 음식에 치는 것이다.
pepper 는 대개 검은색이지만,

간혹 붉은색이나 흰색도 있다.
2 pepper 는 노한 야채나.
pepper 는 붉은색이나 초록색
혹은 노란색을 띠며, 날로 먹
거나 요리해서 먹는다.

**perfect** [pə́ːrfikt] 형 결점이 없
는, **완전한** ; 정확한
perfect 는 잘못된 게 하나도
없다는 의미다 : 제인은 수학
시험을 **완벽하게** 봤다. 그녀는
틀린 게 하나도 없었다.

**perhaps** [pərhǽps, pərǽps] 부
**어쩌면, 아마**
perhaps 는 어떤 일이 일어날
지도 모른다는 의미다 : 오늘
오후에는 비가 올 것으로 예상
되지만, **어쩌면** 비대신 햇빛이
날 수도 있다.

**period** [píəriəd] 명 **기간** ; 시기,
**시대** ; **마침표,** 피리어드
1 period 는 문장 끝에 있는 작
은 점이다. 문장은 period 로
끝난다.
2 period 는 또한 시간의 양을
말한다 : 그들은 6**주간** 휴가
중이었다.

**permit** [pərmít] 타 자 **허락하
다,** 허가하다 ; ⋯하게 내버려
두다
permit 는 누군가에게 무언가
를 하도록 허가한다는 의미
다 : 나의 부모님은 날이 어두
워진 후에는, 언니와 내가 밖
에서 노는 것을 **허락하지** 않을
것이다.

**person** [pə́ːrsən] 명 **사람**
person 은 한 명의 남자나 여
자 혹은 어린아이를 말한다 :
50 명이 그 버스에 탈 수 있지
만, 단지 한 person만이 버스
를 운전할 수 있다.

**pet** [pét] 명 **애완 동물,** 페트
pet 는 사람들이 집에서 돌보
는 동물이다. 개와 고양이는
pet 다 : 헬렌은 pet 로 작은 잉
꼬 두 마리를 기른다.

**petal** [pétəl] 명 **꽃잎**
petal 은 꽃의 일부다 : 데이지
petal 은 가늘고 흰색이나 노
란색을 띤다.

**pharmacy** [fáːrməsi] 명 **조제
(법)** ; 약학 ; 제약업 ; **약국**

pharmacy 는 약을 파는 상점이다. pharmacy 의 다른 명칭은 drugstore 다.

**phone** [fóun] 1 몡 전화, 전화기 2 ᄍ 탄 전화를 걸다 ; 전화로 이야기하다
1 phone 은 telephone 의 줄인 말이다 : 켈리 씨네 집에는 세 대의 phone 이 있다.
2 phone 은 전화를 사용한다는 의미다 : 우리는 오늘밤 아주머니에게 **전화를 걸어** 그녀에게 "생일 축가"를 불러 드렸다.

**photograph** [fóutəgræf | -grὰːf] 몡 사진
photograph 는 카메라로 찍는 사진이다 : 엘리자베스는 우리 반 photograph 를 찍었다.

**piano** [piǽnou, pjǽn-, pjάːn-] 몡 피아노
piano 는 악기다. piano 에는 흰색과 검은색 키가 88 개 있다. 손가락으로 키를 눌러 음악을 연주한다.

**pick** [pík] 탄 (과일 · 꽃 등을) 따다, 꺾다, 뜯다 ; 골라잡다, 고르다
1 pick 은 무언가를 손에 쥔다는 의미다 : 우리는 아버지의 생신을 축하드리기 위해 꽃을 **꺾으려고 한다.** 아이들은 자기 장난감을 **주워서** 치웠다.
2 pick 은 또한 무언가를 고른다는 의미다 : 어머니께서 내가 파티에 입을 드레스를 **고르는 것을** 도와 주셨다.

**picnic** [píknik] 몡 피크닉, 소풍
picnic 을 갈 때면 야외에서 먹을 음식을 가져간다 : 우리는 picnic 가서 먹을 샌드위치와 과일을 가져왔다.

**picture** [píktʃər] 몡 그림, 회화 ; 사진
picture는 선을 긋거나 그림 물감으로 그린 것을 말한다. 카메라로 picture 를 찍을 수도 있다 : 내 방 벽에는 배 한 척이 그려진 picture가 걸려 있다.

**pie** [pái] 명 파이

pie 는 먹는 것으로, 모양은 대개 둥글다. pie 속에는 과일, 고기, 달걀 혹은 그 밖의 것들을 넣을 수 있다. 너는 사과 pie를 먹어 본 적이 있니?

**piece** [píːs] 명 조각 ; (기계 등의) 부품, 부분 ; 한 조각, **한 부분**

1 piece 는 전체 가운데 한 부분을 말한다 : 우리는 제각기 점심 식사후 호박 파이 한 piece 씩을 먹었다.

2 piece 는 또한 많은 것들 가운데 하나를 말한다 : 퍼즐 piece 들을 모두 이 상자에 넣어 주세요.

**pig** [píg] 명 돼지

pig 는 통통한 몸과 짧은 다리, 짧고 똘똘 말린 꼬리가 있는 동물이다.

**pile** [páil] 1 명 쌓아올린 것, 더미 2 타자 쌓아올리다, 겹쳐쌓다

1 pile 은 서로의 위에 놓여 있는 많은 물건을 말한다 : 우리는 오래된 신문지들을 모두 문 옆에 **쌓아** 놓았다.

2 pile 은 무언가를 서로의 위에 놓는다는 의미다 : 아버지는 통나무를 차고 옆에 **쌓아 올리셨다.**

**pill** [píl] 명 **알약**, 환약 ; (흔히) 캡슐[교갑]에 든 약

pill 은 아플 때 먹는 작고 딱딱한 종류의 약이다 : 간호사는 물 한 잔과 함께 먹으라고 pill 하나를 내게 주었다.

**pillow** [pílou] 명 베개

휴식을 취하거나 잠을 잘 때 pillow 를 머리밑에 댄다. pillow 는 대개 푹신하며, 대부분의 pillow 는 깃털이나 고무 종류로 만든다.

**pilot** [páilət] 명 (비행기·우주선 등의) **조종사** ; 수로 안내인

pilot 은 비행기를 조종하는 사람이다 : pilot 은 우리에게 안전띠를 매라고 말했다.

**pin** [pín] 명 핀 ; 장식핀

pin 은 끝이 뾰족한 짧고 가느다란 금속이다. 옷을 꿰매는 동안 옷을 한 데 고정시키는 데 pin 을 사용한다.

**pine** [páin] 명 솔, 소나무
pine 은 바늘 같은 잎이 일년 내내 달려 있는 나무다. pine 목재는 가구를 만드는 데 쓰인다.

**pink** [píŋk] 1 명 연분홍색 2 형 연분홍색의
pink 는 엷은 빨간색을 말한다. 흰색과 빨간색을 섞으면 pink가 된다 : 추운 날씨에 밖에 나가 있어서 우리의 뺨이 **연분홍빛**을 띠었다(불그스름해졌다).

**pint** [páint] 명 파인트 ; 1 파인트들이 용기
pint 는 액체의 양이다. 2 pint 는 1 쿼트와 같다.

**pipe** [páip] 명 관, 파이프, 도관 ; (담배) 파이프
pipe 는 액체나 가스가 통과할 수 있는 기다란 금속이나 플라스틱이다. 집이나 아파트의 물은 pipe 를 통해 개수대까지 온다.

**pirate** [páiərit] 명 해적 ; 해적선 ; 훔치는 사람, 약탈자
pirate 은 해상에서 다른 배의 물건을 강탈하는 뱃사람이다 : pirate 들은 섬에 보물을 파묻었다.

**pitch** [pítʃ] 타 자 던지다 ; 시합에서 투수를 맡다
pitch 는 경기에서 배트로 공을 치려는 선수에게 공을 던진다는 의미다 : 보브가 우리 야구팀의 **투수를 맡았다. 공을 던지는** 사람을 pitcher (투수)라고 한다 : 상대팀 pitcher 는 게일이었다.

**pizza** [píːtsə] 명 피자
pizza 는 대개 납작하고 둥근 음식이다. pizza의 밑부분은 빵 종류로 되어 있고, 그 위에 치즈와 토마토가 얹혀 있다. 간혹 위에 야채나 고기가 얹혀 있는 pizza 도 있다.

**place** [pléis] 명 장소, 곳 ; 좌석, 자리 ; 지위 ; 일자리
1 place 는 무언가가 있는 장소다. place 는 또한 무슨 일

이 일어나는 장소를 말한다 : 우리는 외투를 걸어 둘 place 를 찾아야만 했다. 우리 마을 은 살기 좋은 place 다.

2 place 는 또한 사람을 위한 자리나 좌석을 말한다 : 모든 사람이 다 식탁에 앉을 만한 충분한 place 가 없었다.

**plaid** [plǽd] 몡 바둑판 무늬
plaid 는 색이 다른 줄무늬를 서로 교차시킨 무늬의 일종이 다 : 헬렌은 빨간 스웨터에 plaid 스커트를 입었다.

**plain** [pléin] 혱 평탄한 ; 분명 한, 똑똑히 보이는(들리는) ; 알기 쉬운, 간단한
plain 은 무언가를 보거나 듣거 나 혹은 이해하기가 쉽다는 의 미다 : 비행기가 착륙하기 시작 하자, 지상의 사람과 집들이 똑똑히 보였다. 내 친구들은 나와 의견이 다르다는 사실을 명백하게 밝혔다.

**plan** [plǽn] 1 몡 계획, 생각, 방식 2 탄 잔 계획하다, 궁리 하다, 계획을 세우다
1 plan 은 어떤 일을 하기 전 에 일할 방법을 생각해 본다는 의미다 : 그 팀은 경기에 이길 수 있는 방법을 궁리했다.
2 plan 은 일을 어떻게 할 것 인가에 대한 생각이다 : 우리는 여름 휴가 plan 을 세우고 있 다.

**plane** [pléin] 몡 비행기
plane 은 airplane 의 줄인 말 이다 : 마리아는 모형 plane 을 만드는 것을 좋아한다.

**planet** [plǽnət] 몡 행성
planet 은 태양 주위를 돈다. 9 개의 planet 이 태양 주위를 도는 데, 그 planet 중 하나가 지구다.

**plant** [plǽnt|plάːnt] 1 몡 식물, 초목 2 탄 심다 ; (씨를) 뿌리 다
1 plant 는 사람이나 동물이 아 닌 생명체다. 대부분의 plant 는 땅에서 자란다. 꽃, 나무, 야채는 모두 plant 다.

2 plant 는 땅에 씨앗이나 작은 식물을 심는다는 의미다 : 제인이 봄에 **심은** 씨앗이 자라 가을에 큰 호박이 되었다.

**plastic** [plǽstik] 명 (재료로서의) 플라스틱 ; 플라스틱 제품
plastic 은 여러 가지 물건을 만드는 재료다. plastic 은 딱딱할 수도 있고 유연할 수도 있다. plastic 으로 만든 병들도 있다.

**plate** [pléit] 명 접시
plate 는 접시로, 대개 둥글고 납작하며, 음식을 담을 수 있다 : 조니는 저녁 식사를 차리려고 식탁에 plate 를 놓았다.

**play** [pléi] 1 자 타 ① **놀다** ; (경기·운동 등을) 하다 ② 연주하다 ; 상연〔연기〕하다 ③ 배역을 맡다 2 명 **놀이** ; 연극 ; 시합, 경기
1 play 는 재미로 무언가를 한다는 의미다 : 우리는 야구 경기를 **하려고** 한다.
2 play 는 또한 음악을 연주한다는 의미다 : 조는 어제 학교에서 피아노를 **연주했다.**
3 play 는 또한 연극이나 영화 혹은 그 밖의 연애 프로그램에 출연한다는 의미다 : 해적 **역을 맡았던** 배우는 익살맞았다.
4 play 는 실제로 연기해 보이는 이야기다 : 우리반이 play 를 하고 있다.

**player** [pléiər] 명 **선수** ; 연주자 ; 배우
player 는 운동이나 경기를 하는 사람, 혹은 음악을 연주하거나 그 밖의 일을 하는 사람을 말한다 : 마리는 우리 하키팀 player 다.

**playground** [pléigràund] 명 **운동장, 놀이터**
playground 는 옥외에서 뛰어 놀 수 있는 장소를 말한다.

**please** [plí:z] 타 자 ① **기쁘게 하다,** 만족시키다 ② [부탁의

말에 곁들여] **부디, 아무쪼록**
please 는 무언가를 정중하게
부탁할 때 쓰는 말이다 : 땅콩
좀 건네주십시오.

**plenty** [plénti] 몡 **많음, 풍부**
**함, 다량 ; 충분**
plenty 는 어떤 것이 아주 충
분히 있다는 의미다 : 소풍 온
사람들이 모두 먹을 만큼 옥수
수가 **많이** 있었다.

**plow | plough** [pláu] 몡 **쟁기 ;**
쟁기 모양의 기구
plow 는 농부가 땅을 파서 일
구는 데 사용하는 큰 연장을
말한다. 대개 트랙터나 동물이
plow 를 끈다.

**plural** [plúərəl] 1 몡 **복수 ; 복수**
**형**(의 낱말) 2 혱 **복수의, 두**
**개 이상의**
plural 은 둘 이상을 의미한다.
둘 이상의 사람이나 물건을 말
하고 싶을 때 plural 을 쓴다 :
child 의 plural 은 children 이
고, book 의 plural 은 books
다.

**plus** [plʌ́s] 1 젠 **…을 더하여 ;**
**…을 (덧)붙인** 2 혱 **더하기**
**의, 플러스의, 양수의** 3 몡
**플러스 부호, 양수**
plus 는 더한다는 의미다 : 2 와
3 을 더하면 5 다. 2 **플러스** 3
은 5 다. 2 **플러스** 3 은 2+3
이라고도 쓴다.

**pocket** [pákit | pɔ́k-] 1 몡 **호주**
**머니, 포켓** 2 혱 **포켓용의,**
**소형의**
pocket 은 물건을 넣어두는 곳
이다 : 수는 한 쪽 pocket 에는
장갑을, 다른 쪽 pocket 에는
열쇠를 넣었다. 그는 양손을
pocket 에 넣고 걷고 있었다.

**poem** [póuəm] 몡 **(한 편의) 시**
poem 은 특별한 종류의 글이
다. 운이 맞는 말로 쓰여진
poem 도 있다. poem 을 다른
말로 poetry 라고 한다.

**poet** [póuət] 몡 **시인**
poet 은 시를 쓰는 사람이다.

**point** [pɔ́int] 1 몡 **뾰족한 끝 ;**
**지점, 장소 ; 점수, 득점** 2 탄
자 **뾰족하게 하다, 날카롭게**
**하다 ; 가리키다**
1 point 는 뾰족한 끝이다 : 핀,
바늘 그리고 화살에는 point
가 있다.
2 point 는 어떤 것의 위치를
가리켜 준다는 의미다 : 마크는

동생이 달이 어디 있냐고 묻
자, 손가락으로 하늘에 있는
달을 **가리켰다.**

**pole** [póuəl] 명 **막대기, 장대,
기둥**; **전주**; **극, 극지**
pole 은 기다란 나무나 금속
이다 : 전화선 pole 이 공중에
서 전선을 떠받치고 있다.

**police** [pəlíːs] 명 **경찰**; 경찰관
police 는 다른 사람을 보호하
는 것이 직업인 사람들이다.
그러나 사람들이 법을 위반하
면, police는 그들을 투옥할
수 있다.

**polite** [pəláit] 형 **공손한**; 예의
바른
polite 는 친절하며 남을 배려
해 준다는 의미다 : **공손한** 사
람은 예절이 바르다.

**polka dot** [póuəlkə dàt] 명 **물
방울 무늬**(의 직물)
polka dot 는 천이나 그 밖의
소재에 무늬가 되는 동그란 많
은 점들 가운데 하나다 : 조니
의 할머니는 조니에게 붉은
polka dot 들이 있는 스카프를

사주셨다.

**pollute** [pəlúːt] 타 **더럽히다,
오염시키다**
pollute 는 자연계의 무언가를
더럽힌다는 의미다.

**pollution** [pəlúːʃən] 명 **불결,
오염**; 환경 파괴; **공해**
pollution 은 자연계의 무언가
가 더럽혀졌다는 의미다. 수질
pollution 으로 물고기가 죽어
가고 있다. 대기 pollution 은
호흡 곤란을 초래할 수 있다.

**pond** [pánd|pɔ́nd] 명 **못**; 연
못; 늪
pond 는 한 곳에 모두 괴어
있는 많은 양의 물이다. 수영
을 할 수 있을 정도로 큰
pond 도 있다. pond 는 호수
보다 작다.

**pony** [póuni] 명 **조랑말**; 작은
말
pony 는 몸집이 작은 종자의
말이다 : 나는 박람회에서
pony 를 탔다.

**pool** [púːəl] 명 **물웅덩이**; (액체

가) 괸 곳 ; (수영) 풀
pool 에는 수영을 한 수 있도
록 물이 채워져 있다 : 우리 학
교에는 실내 pool 이 있다. 우
리는 여름에 공원에 있는 pool
로 수영하러 간다.

**poor** [púər, pɔ́ːr] 형 가난한 ;
불쌍한 ; 초라한 ; 서투른
poor 는 돈이 거의 없다는 의
미다 : 음악회 수익금은 **가난한**
사람들을 돕는 데 쓰여질 것이
다.

**pop** [páp|pɔ́p] 자 펑 소리가 나
다 ; 펑 터지다 ; 펑하고 폭발하
다 ; 펑하고 튀다
pop 은 짧게 큰소리를 낸다는
의미다. 풍선이 터질 때, **펑**
**소리가 난다**고 말한다 : 레이는
풍선이 펑하고 **터져버려서** 슬
프다.

**popcorn** [pápkɔ̀ːrn|pɔ́p-] 명
옥수수 튀긴 것 ; 팝콘
popcorn 은 식품이다. pop-
corn 알갱이들은 튀기면 크고
부드러워진다. popcorn 알갱
이들은 튀겨질 때 큰 소리가
난다.

**porch** [pɔ́ːrtʃ] 명 포치 ; 현관,
입구 ; 베란다
porch 는 집의 바깥 부분을 말
한다. 간혹 porch 에 지붕이
있기도 하다 : 우리가 여름철에
porch 에 앉아 있는 것은 거기
가 시원하기 때문이다.

**possible** [pásəbl|pɔ́s-] 형 가능
한 ; 있음직한, 일어날 수 있는
possible 은 무슨 일이 일어날
수 있다는 의미다 : 몇몇 새에
게는 말하는 법을 가르치는 것
이 **가능하다**. 물고기에게 글쓰
는 법을 가르치는 것은 불**가능**
**한** 일이다. 영어를 마스터하는
것은 누구나 **가능하다**.

**post office** [póust àfis] 명 우체
국
post office 는 편지나 소포를
부치는 곳이다. 거기에서 우표
도 산다. post office 로 자기
우편물을 가지러 가는 사람들
도 있다.

**pot** [pát|pɔ́t] 명 원통형의 그
릇, 단지 ; 병, 항아리 ; (운두
가 높은) 냄비
pot 는 요리용의 깊게 패인 둥
근 그릇을 말한다 : 우리는 큰
pot 에 스튜를 만든다.

**potato** [pətéitou] 명 감자
  potato 는 땅 속에서 자라는 야채다 : 우리는 저녁 식사로 먹을 potato 를 구웠다.

**pound** [páund] 명 파운드
  pound 는 무게의 양이다. 1 pound 는 16 온스다.

**pour** [pɔ́:r] 타 자 따르다, 쏟다, 붓다, 흘리다 ; 흘러나오다, 넘쳐흐르다
  pour 는 액체를 한 곳에서 다른 곳으로 흘러 가게 한다는 의미다 : 다이애나는 병에 든 주스를 자기 컵에 **따랐다.**

**powder** [páudər] 명 가루, 분말 ; 분말 제품 ; **가루약**
  powder 는 수없이 많은 아주 작고 바싹 마른 알갱이들로 이루어진 것이다 : 발이 가려웠을 때, 엄마가 발에 powder 를 발라 주셨다.

**power** [páuər] 명 힘, 능력 ; 권력, 세력, 지배력 ; 동력, (특히) 전력
  1 power 는 일을 할 수 있는 능력을 말한다 : 불도저는 큰 흙더미를 옮길 만한 power 가 있다.

  2 power 가 있다는 말은 중요한 일을 결정할 수 있다는 의미다 : 과거에는 왕과 여왕에게 많은 power 가 있었다.
  3 power 는 전기를 의미한다 : 큰 폭풍우가 친 후 우리 이웃에 power 가 끊겼다.

**practice, -tise** [prǽktis] 1 타 자 실행하다 ; 연습하다, 실습하다 2 명 연습 ; 실행, 실시
  practice 는 잘할 수 있도록 여러번 반복해서 무슨 일을 한다는 의미다 : 음악을 연주하는 사람들은 **연습하는** 시간을 많이 가져야 한다.

**pray** [préi] 자타 **간청하다**, 빌다 ; (…에게) **기원하다**, 기도하다
pray 는 신에게 이야기한다는 의미다.

**prepare** [pripέər] 타자 **준비하다**, 채비하다, 마련하다
prepare 는 준비한다는 의미다 : 빌은 여행 가방에 옷을 챙겨 야영갈 **준비를 했다.**

**present¹** [prézənt] 명 **선물**
present 는 특별한 이유로 주는 것이다 : 아이들은 각자 파티에 present 를 가져 왔다. present 의 또다른 말은 gift 다.

**present²** [prézənt] 1 명 **지금, 현재** 2 형 **있는 ; 출석한 ; 현재의**
present 는 지금 존재하고 있는 시점을 말한다. 지금 이 순간도 present 의 일부다.

**president** [prézidənt] 명 **대통령 ; 의장, 회장, 총재 ; 총장 ; 사장**
president 는 한 집단의 사람들을 이끌어 가는 사람이다 : 미국의 president 를 뽑는 선거는 4 년마다 11 월에 있다. 조지 워싱턴과 에이브러햄 링컨은 유명한 president 였다. 다음주에 우리반 president 를 뽑는

선거가 있을 예정이다.

**press** [prés] 타자 **누르다, 밀어 붙이다 ; …을 눌러 펴다**
1 press 는 무언가를 민다는 의미다 : 머리가 버튼을 **누르자,** 엘리베이터가 (그가 있는 층으로) 왔다.
2 press 는 또한 다리미를 사용한다는 의미다 : 나는 파티에 입을 수 있도록 내가 가장 좋아하는 셔츠를 **다렸다.**

**pretend** [priténd] 타자 **거짓으로 …이라고 하다, …인 체하다 ; …인 것처럼 행동하다, 가장하다**
pretend 는 가장한다는 의미다 : 제임스와 마리는 로봇 흉내를 냈다. 데이비드는 잠든 체해서 나를 속였다.

**pretty** [príti] 형 **예쁜, 귀여운 ; 좋은, 멋있는, 훌륭한**
pretty 는 보기에 좋다는 의미다 : 누구나 **예쁜** 꽃을 좋아한다.

**pretzel** [prétsəl] 명 **프레첼《꽈배기 모양의 짭짤한 비스킷》**
pretzel 은 매듭 모양이나 막대

기 모양으로 구운 식품으로, 겉에 소금이 뿌려져 있다 : 조와 웬디는 방과 후 pretzel 을 한 봉지 사서 나눠 먹는 것을 좋아한다.

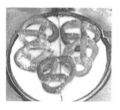

**price** [práis] 명 **가격**, 값 ; 대가 ; 시세
price 는 무언가를 얻기 위해 지불해야만 하는 금액을 말한다 : 영화표 한 장의 price 는 6달러다.

**prince** [príns] 명 **왕자**, 황태자
prince 는 왕이나 여왕의 아들이다.

**princess** [prínsəs, -ses | prinsés, prínses] 명 **공주**, 황녀
princess 는 왕이나 여왕의 딸이다.

**principal** [prínsipəl] 1 명 **우두머리** ; 장, **교장** 2 형 **주요한**, 주된
principal 은 학교의 지도자를 말한다 : 우리 학교 principal 은 브라운 여사다.

**print** [prínt] 1 타 자 **인쇄**〔출판, 간행〕하다 ; (사진을) 인화하다 ; 활자체로 똑똑히 쓰다 2 명 인쇄(물), 활자체
1 print 는 책에 있는 글자와 같은 서체로 글씨를 쓴다는 의미다 : 선생님은 칠판에 선생님 이름을 **활자체로 똑똑히 쓰셨다.**
2 print 는 또한 기계를 이용해 종이 위에 글자나 그림을 찍는다는 의미다 : 수학 여행 때에 우리는 기계가 책을 **인쇄하는** 걸 보았다.

**printer** [príntər] 명 **인쇄업자**, 인쇄공 ; **인쇄기** ; (컴퓨터의) **프린터**
printer 는 컴퓨터와 함께 사용하는 기계다. printer 는 컴퓨터에 저장된 단어들을 받아서 종이에 인쇄한다.

**prison** [prízən] 명 **교도소**, 감옥 ; 구치소
prison 은 법을 어긴 사람이 있어야 할 곳이다. prison은 jail 의 또 다른 말이다.

**privacy** [práivəsi|prív-, práiv-] 명 **사적〔개인적〕자유 ; 사생활**, 프라이버시 ; 은둔, 은퇴 생활

사람들은 혼자 있고 싶을 때, privacy 를 원한다고 말한다 : 조니는 혼자 생각할 **시간을 갖고** 싶어서 자기 방으로 갔다.

**prize** [práiz] 명 상, **상품**, 상금, 경품

prize 는 이기면 받는 것이다. prize 는 컵이나 리본, 돈이나 그 밖의 여러가지 것들이 될 수 있다.

**probably** [prábəbli|prɔ́b-] 부 **아마도**

probably 는 무언가가 사실과 다르지 않다고 거의 확신한다는 의미다 : 스티븐스는 토요일마다 우리 집에 온다. 그는 **아마도** 이번 주 토요일에도 역시 올 것이다.

**problem** [prábləm|prɔ́b-] 명 **문제**, 의문 ; 귀찮은 일〔사람〕

1 problem 은 해답을 요하는 문제를 말한다 : 오늘 우리가 볼 수학 시험엔 10 개의 problem 이 출제된다.

2 problem 은 또한 곰곰이 생각해야 할 일을 말한다 : 우리는 앤터니의 집주소를 잃어버려 그의 집을 찾는 데 problem 이 있었다(고생했다).

**program | -gramme** [próu-grǽm] 명 **프로그램**, 프로그램〔차례·순서〕을 적은 것 ; 예정, 예정표

program 은 텔레비전으로 보거나 라디오로 듣는 방송 프로그램을 말한다 : 내가 가장 좋아하는 program 은 6 시에 한다.

**promise** [prámis|prɔ́m-]  1 타 자 **약속하다** ; 가능성이 있다  2 명 **약속** ; 가능성, 유망

1 promise 는 무언가를 하겠다고 말한다는 의미다 : 레이는 그 다음날 돌려주기로 **약속하고**, 제인의 야구 글러브를 빌렸다.

2 promise 는 하겠다고 단언하는 것을 말한다 : 사람은 항상 자기가 한 promise 를 지켜야 한다.

**propeller** [prəpélər] 명 **프로펠러**, 추진기 ; 추진하는 사람

propeller 는 기계 장치의 일부로, 나무나 금속으로 만든다. propeller 는 공기나 물을 뒤로 밀어내어 비행기와 배를 움직이게 한다.

**protect** [prətékt] 타 **보호하다,** 지키다, 막다

protect 는 위험으로부터 지킨다는 의미다 : 어미 곰은 다른 동물로부터 자기 새끼들을 **지켰다.** 안전띠는 자동차 사고 때 사람을 **보호하는 데** 도움이 된다.

**proud** [práud] 형 **자랑으로 여기는,** 자랑할만한 ; 거만한, 뽐내는

proud 는 자신의 소유물이나 자신이 한 일을 사람들에게 기꺼이 내보인다는 의미다 : 베티는 자기가 만든 케이크를 **자랑했다.**

**prove** [prú:v] 타 자 **증명하다,** 입증하다 ; …임을 알다, (…이) 되다

prove 는 무언가가 사실임을 밝힌다는 의미다 : 책에 내 이름이 있기 때문에 이 책이 내 것이라는 사실을 **입증할 수 있다.**

**public** [pʌ́blik] 형 **공공의 ;** 공립의 ; 공적인 ; **공공연한,** 공개의

public은 모든 사람들을 위한

다는 의미다 : 우리 마을 아이들 대부분이 **공립** 학교에 다닌다. 우리 **공립** 도서관은 일요일만 빼고 매일 개방한다.

**publish** [pʌ́bliʃ] 타 **발표〔공표〕하다 ;** (서적·잡지 등을) **출판하다,** 발행하다

publish 는 신문, 잡지, 책 혹은 그 밖의 문자로 된 것을 인쇄하여 팔려고 한다는 의미다 : 나의 할머니께서는 오래전에 시집을 한 권 쓰셔서 **출판한** 적이 있었다. 마거릿의 아저씨는 말에 관한 잡지를 **발행하신다.**

**pudding** [púdiŋ] 명 **푸딩**《밀가루에 과일·우유·계란 등을 넣고 단맛이 나게 구운 디저트용 과자》

pudding 은 부드럽고 달콤한 디저트다 : 수가 가장 좋아하는 디저트는 초콜릿 pudding 이다.

**puddle** [pʌ́dl] 명 **물웅덩이**

puddle 은 비가 오거나 눈이 녹을 때 생기는 작은 물웅덩이

를 말한다 : 나는 puddle 을 밟아 물을 튀기는 것을 좋아한다. 비가 온 뒤 길에 puddle 들이 생겼다.

**pull** [púəl] 타자 **끌다**, 끌어당기다 ; (이·마개 등을) **뽑다**, **빼다** ; 움직이다

pull 은 무언가를 뒤따라 오게 만든다는 의미다 : 찰리는 차고에서 큰 상자를 끌어 내어 안에 든 것을 전부 꺼냈다.

**pumpkin** [pʌ́mpkin] 명 (서양) **호박**

pumpkin 은 땅 위에서 자라는 크고 둥근 오렌지색 열매다 : 우리는 만성절 전날밤에 쓰려고 pumpkin 에 얼굴 모양을 새겼다.

**punch** [pʌ́ntʃ] 1 타 **주먹으로 치다** ; …에 **구멍을 뚫다** 2 명 주먹으로 치기 ; 구멍 뚫는 기구 ; 펀치

punch 는 주먹으로 어떤 것을 세게 친다는 의미다 : 앨과 보브가 싸울 때 앨이 보브의 팔을 **주먹으로 쳤다**.

**punish** [pʌ́niʃ] 타 **벌하다**, 징계하다 ; (상대방을) 혼내주다

punish 는 누군가를 범죄나 잘못 혹은 비행의 대가로 고통을 겪게 한다는 의미다 : 나에 대한 **벌로**, 부모님께서 내 용돈을 빼앗으셨다.

**pupil** [pjúːpəl] 명 (흔히 초등학교·중학교) **학생**

pupil 은 학교에 다니는 사람이다 : 우리 반에는 25 명의 pupil 이 있다. pupil 의 또 다른 말은 student 다.

**puppet** [pʌ́pit] 명 (인형극에 쓰이는) **인형** ; 꼭두각시

puppet 은 손에 끼고 손가락으로 움직이는 인형이다. 줄을 당겨 움직이게 하는 puppet 종류도 있다 : 우리는 학교에서 puppet 극을 공연했다.

**puppy** [pʌ́pi] 명 **강아지**

puppy 는 새끼 개를 말한다 : puppy 들은 어미 곁에서 잠을 잤다.

**purchase** [pə́ːrtʃəs] 1 타 **사다**, 구입〔구매〕하다 ; 얻다 2 명 **구입**, 구매, 구입〔구매〕품

purchase 는 돈을 지불하고 무언가를 산다는 의미다 : 우리는

철도역에서 열차표를 **구입했다**. 그는 새 자동차를 **샀다**.

**pure** [pjúər] 휑 순수한, 불순물이 없는 ; 깨끗한, 순결한
pure 는 다른 것이 섞이지 않았다는 의미다 : 내 스카프는 순모로 되어 있다. 우리는 **맑은 공기를** 원한다.

**purple** [pə́:rpl] 1 명 자줏빛 2 휑 자줏빛의
purple 은 색이다. 빨강과 파랑을 섞으면 purple 이 된다.

**purpose** [pə́:rpəs] 명 목적, 의도, 취지
purpose 는 무언가를 하는 행위에 이유가 있다는 의미다 : 마거릿은 큰소리를 내어 우리를 놀라게 할 purpose 로 책을 떨어뜨렸다.

**purr** [pə́:r] 자 타 (고양이가) 그르렁거리다, 목구멍을 울리(며 소리내)다
purr 는 낮고 조용하게 소리를 낸다는 의미다 : 고양이들은 기분이 좋으면 **가르랑거린다**. 우리 고양이는 등을 긁어 주면 항상 **가르랑거린다.**

**purse** [pə́:rs] 명 돈지갑, 돈주머니 ; 지갑
purse 는 돈과 그 밖의 작은 물건들을 휴대하기 위한 백이다. purse 는 천이나 플라스틱 혹은 그 밖의 부드러운 소재로 만든다 : 엘리자베스는 그녀의 purse 에 열쇠를 넣었다.

**push** [púʃ] 타 자 밀다, 밀고 나아가다
push 는 어떤 것을 앞으로 나아가게 한다는 의미다 : 조지는 엄마 대신 쇼핑용 손수레를 **밀었다.**

**put** [pút] 타 놓다, 두다, **넣다**
put 은 무언가를 둘 장소를 찾아내, 그 곳에 놓아 둔다는 의미다 : 다이애나는 학교에 가져가려고 도시락에 샌드위치를 **넣었다.**

**puzzle** [pʌ́zl] 명 수수께끼, 알아맞히기, 퍼즐 ; 난제 ; 당황
1 puzzle 은 놀이 도구다. 그림이 되도록 한데 짜맞추어야 하는 종이나 나뭇조각으로 된 puzzle 도 있고, 머리나 혹은 연필과 종이를 써서 풀어야 하는 어려운 문제로 된 puzzle 도 있다.
2 puzzle 은 또한 이해하기 힘든 것이다 : 제인은 언니가 어떻게 자기보다 먼저 집에 왔는지 **납득이 가지 않았다.**

**quart** [kwɔ́:rt] 뗑 **쿼트**
quart 는 액체의 양이다. 1 갤
런은 4 quart 다. 1 quart 는 1
리터보다 조금 적은 양이다.

**quarter** [kwɔ́:rtər] 뗑 ① **4 분
의 1**；15 분；**25 센트** 은화；4
등분한 한 부분 ② **방면**, 지
역；(도시의) **지구**, …거리
1 quarter 는 주화의 일종이다.
1 quarter는 5 센트 백동화 5
개와 같고, 4 quarter는 1 달러
와 같다.
2 quarter 는 크기가 똑같은 4
조각 가운데 1개를 말한다.
너는 파이를 quarters 로 자를
수 있다.

**queen** [kwí:n] 뗑 **여왕**, 왕비
queen 은 나라를 통치하는 여
자다 : queen 은 마차를 타면
서 사람들에게 손을 흔들었다.

**question** [kwéstʃən] 뗑 **질문**,
물음；**의문문**；의심；(해결할)
문제
question 은 알고 싶은 것을
묻는 말이다 : 간혹 선생님께서
는 아무도 대답할 수 없는
question 들을 하신다.

**question mark** [kwéstʃən
mɑ̀:rk] 뗑 의문 부호, **물음표**
question mark 는 의문문 끝에
온다 : 이 문장은 question
mark 로 끝나니, 아니면 마침
표로 끝나니 ?

**quick** [kwík] 뤵 **급속한**, 신속
한 ; **재빠른**, 민첩한 ; 영리한,
이해가 빠른
quick 은 무언가가 빠르게 움
직이거나 짧은 시간 안에 일어
난다는 의미다 : 우리는 **재빨리**
점심을 먹었다.

**quickly** [kwíkli] 뿐 **빠르게**, 급
히, 곧

quickly 는 무언가를 빨리 한다는 의미다 : 교통 신호등이 녹색으로 바뀌자, 어빙은 **재빨리** 도로를 건넜다.

**quiet** [kwáiət] 형 **조용한**, 평온한, 소리를 내지 않는
quiet 는 소리를 거의 내지 않는다는 의미다 : 우리 이웃들은 밤에 아주 **조용하게** 지낸다.

**quilt** [kwíəlt] 명 **누비 이불**, 누비 침대 커버
quilt 는 담요와 같은 것이다. quilt 는 두 천조각 사이에 부드러운 소재를 채워서 만든다 : 나는 겨울에 부드럽고 따뜻한 quilt 를 덮고 잔다.

**quite** [kwáit] 부 **아주**, 완전히, 꽤, **상당히**
quite 는 「매우」 혹은 「많은」이란 의미다 : 오늘은 날씨가 **꽤** 따뜻하다. 새 가게가 문을 열자 **아주** 많은 사람들이 몰려들었다.

**quiz** [kwíz] 명 (구두 또는 필기에 의한 간단한) **질문**, **시험** ; (라디오·텔레비전의) **퀴즈**
quiz 는 간단한 시험이다 : 오늘 우리는 어제 배운 새 단어의 철자법 quiz 를 보았다.

Q

**rabbit** [rǽbit] 명 집토끼 ; [일반적으로] 토끼

rabbit 은 귀가 길고, 털이 부드러우며, 꼬리가 짧은 작은 동물이다. rabbit 은 튼튼한 뒷다리로 아주 빨리 깡충깡충 뛰어 다닐 수 있다.

**raccoon** [rækúːn | rə-] 명 미국너구리

raccoon 은 몸이 작고, 부드러운 털이 있는 동물이다. raccoon은 얼굴에 가면처럼 생긴 검은 점이 있으며, 꼬리에도 고리 모양의 검은 테가 있다 : 우리는 어제 숲에서 두 마리의 raccoon 을 보았다.

**race** [réis] 명 경주

race 는 누가 가장 빠른가를 알아내는 경기다. 사람들은 도보, 자동차, 말 그리고 그 밖의 여러가지 방법으로 race 를 펼친다.

**radar** [réidɑːr] 명 레이더, 전파 탐지기

radar 는 비행기, 자동차, 폭풍 같은 것을 찾아내서 추적하는데 쓰는 기구다. 조종사는 radar 의 도움을 받아 비행기를 안전하게 착륙시킨다.

**radio** [réidiòu] 명 라디오, 라디오 방송

radio 는 음악이나 뉴스 혹은 그 밖의 프로그램을 들으려고 작동시키는 기계다 : 우리는 저녁에 radio 로 음악을 듣는 날도 있다. radio 를 꺼 주십시오.

**raft** [ræft | rɑ́ːft] 명 뗏목 ; (고무로 만든) 구명 뗏목

raft 는 통나무나 판자를 하나로 이어서 만든 평평한 배의 일종이다. 고무나 플라스틱으로 만들어 공기를 채운 raft 도

있다 : 호수 한가운데에 raft를
띄우고 있는 것이 무더운 오후
를 보내는 최상의 방법이다.

**rag** [ræg] **명** 넝마 ; 걸레 ; 누더
기 옷
rag는 작은 천조각으로, 대개
헤진 헝겊으로 만든다 : 아서와
빌리는 rag를 사용하여 세차
를 했다.

**railing** [réiliŋ] **명** 난간, 울타
리, 담
railing은 떨어지거나 빠지지
않도록 해주는 울타리다 : 우리
는 수영장 주위에 railing을
설치했다.

**railroad** [réiəlròud] **명** 철도,
선로
railroad는 열차가 달리는 철
길이다. railroad로 다리를 건
너고, 터널을 통과하고, 산 너
머로 갈 수 있다.

**rain** [réin] 1 **명** 비 ; 빗발치듯
하는 것 2 **자** 비가 내리다〔오
다〕
1 rain은 구름에서 방울져 떨
어지는 물이다. 식물이 성장하
려면 rain이 필요하다.
2 rain은 물방울들이 떨어진

다는 뜻이다. 비가 오면 모든
것이 젖는다.

**rainbow** [réinbòu] **명** 무지개 ;
무지개 모양의 것
rainbow는 비가 그친 후 간혹
하늘에서 보게 되는 빛깔을 말
한다. rainbow는 곡선 모양이
고, 햇빛이 대기 중의 아주 작
은 물방울들을 통해서 비칠 때
생긴다.

**raincoat** [réinkòut] **명** 레인코
트, 비옷
raincoat는 비에 젖지 않도록
입는 외투다 : 우리는 비가 올
때, 외출하려고 raincoat와 장
화 그리고 모자를 썼다.

**raise** [réiz] **타** ① (위로) 올리
다 ; 높이 게양하다 ② (가축·
작물을) 기르다, 재배하다 ③
(집을) 세우다, 짓다 ④ (돈
등을) 모금하다, 마련하다
1 raise는 무언가를 올린다는
뜻이다 : 잭과 앨리스는 선생님
께서 기를 깃대 꼭대기에 게양
하시는 것을 도왔다. 메리는
선생님께서 하신 질문의 답을
알았기 때문에 손을 들었다.

2 raise 는 또한 어떤 것의 성장을 돕는다는 뜻이다 : 우리 마을의 한 농부는 옥수수를 **재배하고**, 또 다른 농부는 닭을 **키우고** 있다.

**rake** [réik] 1 명 갈퀴, 써레 2 타 자 (갈퀴로) **긁어 모으다**
1 rake 는 나뭇잎이나 그 밖의 것들을 한 데 긁어 모으는 도구다. rake 는 빗처럼 살이 있고 손잡이가 길다.
2 rake 는 또한 갈퀴로 물건을 한 데 모은다는 뜻이다 : 리처드와 짐은 나뭇잎을 모두 **긁어 모아** 수북이 쌓아 놓았다.

**ramp** [rǽmp] 명 경사로
ramp 는 한 곳에서 다른 곳으로 올라가게 만든 길이나 보도의 일종이다. ramp 에는 계단이 없다 : 우리 학교에는 계단을 이용할 수 없는 사람들을 위한 ramp 가 있다.

**ran** [rǽn] 동 run (달리다) 의 과거형

ran 은 단어 run 에서 생긴 말이다 : 그 여우는 우리가 자기에게 다가가는 것을 보고는 숲속으로 다시 **뛰어 들어 갔다.**

**ranch** [rǽntʃ | rɑ́ːntʃ] 명 목장
ranch 는 소나 양 혹은 말을 기르는 일종의 농장이다 : 나의 아주머니와 아저씨는 ranch 에 살면서 소를 기른다.

**rang** [rǽŋ] 동 ring² (울리다) 의 과거형
rang 은 단어 ring² 에서 생긴 말이다 : 찰리가 초인종을 **울리자** 브라운 씨가 문을 열었다. 화재 경보기가 **울려서** 우리는 건물 밖으로 뛰쳐 나갔다.

**ranger** [réindʒər] 명 산림 경비대원 ; 배회자, 방랑자
ranger 는 산림과 공원 그리고 그 밖의 지역을 보호하는 일을 하는 사람이다 : ranger 가 우리에게 소풍 장소를 가르쳐 주었다.

**rat** [rǽt] 명 쥐
rat 은 동물인 데, 꼬리는 길고 털은 짧으며 이빨은 날카롭다. rat 은 생쥐보다 크다.

**raw** [rɔː] 형 생것의, 날것의, 가공하지 않은
raw 는 요리하지 않았다는 뜻이다 : 마크는 익히지 않은 당근과, 토마토 그리고 상추로 만든 샐러드를 즐겨 먹는다.

**reach** [ríːtʃ] 타 자 (…을 잡으려고) 손을 뻗치다 ; …에 닿다, …에 도착하다
1 reach 는 무언가를 만지려고 손을 내민다는 뜻이다 : 조는 발끝으로 서지 않으면, 맨 윗 선반에 손이 닿지 않는다.
2 reach 는 또한 어떤 장소에 도착한다는 뜻이다 : 버스가 우리가 사는 거리에 도착하자, 우리는 운전 기사에게 세워달라고 부탁했다.

**read** [ríːd] 타 자 읽다, 독서하다 ; 낭독하다
read 는 글을 보고 그 의미를 안다는 뜻이다 : 레이는 글 읽는 법을 배우고 있다. 그는 엄마나 아버지와 함께 자주 이야기 책을 읽는다.

**ready** [rédi] 형 준비된, 채비를 갖춘

ready 는 해야 할 일이 생겼을 때, 곧바로 할 수 있다는 뜻이다 : 일단 옷을 챙겨서 여행갈 준비를 해 놓겠다. 모두 경주를 시작할 준비가 되어 있다.

**real** [ríːəl, ríəl | ríəl, ríːəl] 형 현실의, 실제의, 진짜의
real 은 무언가가 사실임을 안다는 뜻이다 : 그것은 진짜 곤충이냐, 아니면 플라스틱으로 만든 것이냐? 동화속의 거인은 실재 인물이 아니라 가공 인물이었다.

**reality** [riǽliti] 명 현실, 실제, 사실, 진실
reality 는 사실적인 것을 뜻한다. 매일 일어나는 일들이 reality 다. 자신이 하는 일에 관해 글을 쓸 때는 reality 를 쓰는 것이다. reality 의 반대말은 fantasy (환상)다.

**really** [ríːəli | ríəli] 부 실제로, 정말로, 참으로
1 really 는 단어 real 에서 생긴 말이다. 어떤 일을 아주 확신할 때 really 라는 말을 쓴다 : 나는 정말로 의사가 되고 싶다.

2 really 는 또한 「아주, 매우」라는 뜻이다 : 우리는 축제를 아주 재미있게 보냈다.

**reason** [ríːzən] 몡 이유, 까닭 ; 변몡 : 이성
reason 은 어떤 일이 생긴 이유를 나타낸다 : 앤은 음악회에 늦은 reason 이 교통체증 때문이라고 했다.

**recess** [ríːses, risés] 몡 쉼, 휴식 ; (학교의) **휴식시간**
recess 는 일[공부]을 중단하는 짧은 시간을 말한다 : 우리는 recess 동안 학교 밖에서 놀았다.

**recipe** [résipi] 몡 (요리의) **조리법** ; (음료의) **제조법**
recipe 는 음식 만드는 방법을 가르쳐 준다 : 수프를 만들기 전에 recipe 를 읽어라.

**record** [rékərd|-kɔːd] 몡 ① 기록, 등록 ② 성적 ; 경기 기록 ③ 음반, 레코드
record 는 플라스틱으로 만든 둥글고 납작한 디스크다. record 에는 음악이나 그 밖의 소리가 실려 있다 : 우리는 파티에서 record 를 들으며, 다 같이 노래를 따라 불렀다.

**rectangle** [réktæŋgl] 몡 **직사각형**
rectangle 은 네 변과 네 각으로 된 모양을 말한다 : 이 책의 표지 모양은 rectangle이다.

**recycle** [risáikl] 퇌 **재활용하다** ; 재순환시키다
recycle 은 무언가를 다시 사용할 수 있도록 만든다는 뜻이다 : 우리 마을은 깡통, 병, 신문지들을 **재활용한다.**

**red** [réd] 1 혱 **빨간**, 적색의 2 몡 **빨강**, 적색
red 는 핏빛을 말한다 : 대부분의 소방차는 **빨간** 페인트로 칠해져 있다.

**reflection** [riflékʃən] 몡 **반사** ; 반영 ; 영상 ; (물에 비친) **그림자**
reflection 은 거울이나 잔잔한 수면을 바라볼 때 비치는 것을

말한다 : 나는 연못에 비친 내 reflection 을 본다.

**refrigerator** [rifrídʒərèitər]
명 냉장고
refrigerator 는 음식을 차게 보관하는 큰 기계다 : 우리는 우유를 신선하게 보관하려고 refrigerator 에 넣었다.

**relative** [rélətiv] 명 친척, 인척, 친족
relative 는 가족의 일원인 사람이다. 부모님, 누이, 형제 그리고 할아버지, 할머니는 relative 다. 작은 엄마, 작은 아버지, 사촌들도 relative 가 된다.

**relax** [rilǽks] 자 타 ① 피로를 풀다, 쉬다 ; 긴장을 풀다 ② 늦추다 ; 느슨해지다
relax 는 쉬면서 마음을 편안하게 갖는다는 뜻이다. **피로를 푸는** 몇가지 방법으로는 독서나 텔레비전 시청 혹은 산책이 있다 : 한나는 추리 소설을 읽으며 **쉬는** 것을 좋아한다.

**remember** [rimémbər]   타 자
기억하다, 잊지 않고 ⋯하다 ; 생각해 내다, 상기하다
remember 는 무언가를 다시 생각해 내거나 잊지 않고 있다는 뜻이다 : 조는 외출할 때 **잊지 않고** 문을 닫았다.

**remind** [rimáind] 타  생각나게 하다, 상기시키다
remind 는 누군가에게 (⋯하는 것을) 생각나게 해준다는 뜻이다 : 언니는 내게 잊지 말고 학교 가기 전에 고양이에게 먹이를 주라고 **일러 주었다.**

**rent** [rént] 명 집세, 방세 ; 임대료, 사용료
rent 는 무언가를 이용하기 위해 지불하는 돈이다 : 부모님께서 매달 아파트 rent 를 내신다.

**repeat** [ripíːt] 1 타  되풀이하다, 반복하다 2 명 반복
repeat 는 어떤 것을 다시 하거나 말한다는 뜻이다 : 선생님께서는 내가 한 말을 듣지 못하셔서, 대답을 **다시 하라고** 하셨다.

R

**reptile** [réptəl|-taiəl] 명 파충류의 동물

reptile 은 배로 기거나 아주 짧은 다리로 걷는 동물의 일종이다. 뱀, 바다거북, 도마뱀은 모두 reptile 이다. 대부분의 reptile 은 알을 낳으며, 악어도 reptile 의 일종이다.

**responsibility** [rispὰnsəbíliti|-spɔ̀n-] 명 책임, 의무

responsibility 가 있다는 것은 하기로 되어 있는 일이 있다는 말이다 : 제인은 자기의 애완 동물을 보살펴야 할 responsibility 가 있다.

**rest¹** [rést] 1 자 쉬다, 휴식하다 2 명 휴식 ; 안정

1 rest 는 피곤해서 하던 것을 잠깐 멈춘다는 뜻이다 : 아이들은 점심식사 후, 다시 나가 놀기 전에 **쉬어야** 한다.
2 rest 는 쉬는 시간이다 : 장시간 도보여행을 한 뒤여서, 우리는 모두 rest 를 취했다.

**rest²** [rést] 명 나머지, 잔여

rest 는 남아 있는 것을 말한다 : 톰은 점심 때 샌드위치를 절반 먹고, rest는 수업이 끝난 뒤에 먹으려고 남겨 두었다.

**restaurant** [réstərənt|réstərɔ̀nt] 명 음식점, 레스토랑

restaurant 은 사람들이 식사를 하러 가는 곳이다. 대부분의 restaurant 들은 여러가지 다양한 종류의 음식을 만든다 : 우리는 restaurant 에서 저녁을 먹었다.

**return** [ritə́ːrn] 자타 돌아오다, 돌아가다 ; **돌려주다**, 반환하다

1 return 은 돌아온다는 뜻이다 : 겨울에 남쪽으로 갔던 새들이 매년 봄 **되돌아 온다**. 그는 막 집에 **돌아왔다**.
2 return 은 또한 돌려준다는 뜻이다 : 피터는 책들을 읽고 나서 도서관에 **반납했다**.

**reward** [riwɔ́:rd] 명 보수, 보상, 보답 ; 보상금, **사례금**
중요한 물건을 잃어 버리면, 그것을 찾아준 사람에게 reward 를 줄 수 있다 : 브라운 부인은 그녀의 잃어버린 개를 찾아준 reward 로 보브에게 5달러를 주었다.

**rhinoceros** [rainɑ́sərəs|-nɔ́s-] 명 코뿔소, 무소
rhinoceros 는 코에 한 개 내지 두 개의 큰 뿔이 있는 동물이다. rhinoceros 는 가죽이 매우 두껍고 굵으며, 다리는 짧다.

**rhyme, rime** [ráim] 1 자 시를 짓다 ; 운이 맞다 2 명 운
rhyme 은 같은 음으로 끝난다는 뜻이다. cook 은 book 과 **운이 맞고**, group 은 soup 와, tall 은 small 과 **운이 맞는다.** 운이 맞는 단어들을 사용해 쓴 시들이 많다.

**ribbon** [ríbən] 명 리본, 띠, 장식끈
ribbon 은 길고 가는 천이나 종이를 말한다. ribbon 은 여러가지 색으로 되어 있다. 흔히 선물은 종이로 포장해서 ribbon 으로 묶는다.

**rice** [ráis] 명 벼 ; 쌀 ; 밥
rice 는 식품의 일종이다. rice 의 낟알들을 요리하면 부드러워진다. rice 는 따뜻한 지방에서 자라는 풀의 씨앗이다.

**rich** [rítʃ] 형 부자의, 부유한 ; (…이) 많은, 풍부한
rich 는 돈이 많다는 뜻이다. **부유한** 사람들은 큰 집에서 살면서, 아주 비싼 자동차와 그 밖의 물건들을 소유하는 경우가 많다.

**ridden** [rídən] 동 ride (타다)의 과거분사형
ridden 은 ride 의 한 형태다 : 마거릿은 자전거 타는 걸 좋아한다. 그녀는 이번 주에 매일 자전거를 **탔다.** 말을 **타본** 적이 있니 ?

**riddle** [rídl] 명 **수수께끼**
riddle 은 대답하거나 이해하기 어려운 질문이나 문제다 : 두 손은 있지만 손가락이 없는 것은 무엇입니까 ? 라는 riddle 이 있는 데, 답은 시계다.

R

**ride** [ráid] 1 [타][자] **타다,** 타고 가다 ; **승마하다** ; 말을 부리다 2 [명] **탐,** 타고 감 ; **타는 시간** ; 승마 여행 ; (유원지 등의) **탈 것**

1 ride 는 움직이는 것 안에 앉아 있거나, 위에 걸터 앉아 있다는 뜻이다 : 목동들은 말을 **탄다.** 아이들은 버스를 **타고** 학교에 간다.

2 ride 는 무언가를 타는 때다 : 일요일마다 우리 가족은 시골로 **드라이브하러** 나간다.

**right** [ráit] 1 [형] **오른쪽의** ; 옳은, 정확한 2 [부] 오른쪽에 ; 옳게, 정확히 ; 바로 3 [명] 오른쪽, 우측 ; 정의, 정도 ; **권리**

1 right 는 left (왼쪽의)의 반대말이다 : 미국에서는 사람들이 도로 **오른쪽으로** 차를 몬다.

2 right 는 또한 틀린 것이 없다는 뜻이다 : 낸시는 시험 문제의 **정답을** 모두 알았다.

3 right 는 또한 「즉시」란 뜻이다 : 점심을 먹고 **곧장** 떠나자.

**ring**¹ [ríŋ] [명] **반지,** 고리, 바퀴 ; 고리 모양의 것

ring 은 가운데가 빈 고리다. 손가락에 금이나 은으로 된 ring 을 끼는 사람들도 있다.

**ring**² [ríŋ] [타][자] (종·벨·전화 등을) **울리다,** 울려서 알리다 ; 울려 퍼지다, (종·벨 등이) **울리다**

ring 은 종으로 소리를 낸다는 뜻이다 : 야영장에서는 식사가 준비되면 **종을 울린다.**

**rink** [ríŋk] [명] (실내) **스케이트장** ; 롤러 스케이트장 ; 아이스 하키장

rink 는 스케이트나 롤러 스케이트를 타는 곳이다.

**rip** [ríp] [타] **찢다** ; 찢어〔벗겨, 베어〕내다

rip 은 종이나 천같은 것을 찢는다는 뜻이다 : 아기가 책장을 **찢지** 못하게 해라.

**ripe** [ráip] [형] (과일·곡물이) **익은,** 여문 ; (기회가) 무르익은

ripe 는 무언가가 다 자라서 먹어도 된다는 뜻이다 : 바나나가 노랗게 되면 **익은** 것이다.

R

**rise** [ráiz] 자 **오르다**, 떠오르
다 ; **일어나다**, 일어서다 ; **상승
하다**
rise 는 올라간다는 뜻이다 : 태
양은 매일 아침 동쪽에서 **떠오
른다.** 무더운 날에는 바깥 기
온이 **올라간다.**

**risen** [rízən] 동 rise (오르다) 의
과거분사형
risen 은 rise 의 한 형태다 : 마
이크는 해돋이를 보고 싶었지
만 늦잠을 자서, 깨어났을 때
는 이미 태양이 **떠올라 있었
다.**

**river** [rívər] 명 **강**
river 는 양 측면이 육지인 넓
은 물길을 말한다. 길이가 수
백 마일 되는 river 도 있다.

**road** [róud] 명 **길, 도로**
road 는 자동차가 다니는 넓은
길이다. 자동차가 있기 전에는
말과 짐마차들이 road를 지나
다녔다 : 우리는 어제 인부들이
road 의 패인 곳을 메우는 것
을 구경했다.

**roar** [rɔ́ːr] 자 (짐승이) **으르렁**
거리다, 포효하다 ; 울려 퍼지
다 ; 고함치다
roar 는 크고 저음의 굵직한
소리를 낸다는 뜻이다. 곰, 사
자, 호랑이들은 **포효할 수 있**
다 : 비행기가 착륙할 때, 우리
는 **굉음을 내는** 엔진 소리를
들을 수 있었다.

**roast** [róust] 타 (고기를) **굽
다** ; 오븐[뜨거운 재]에 익히
다 ; 불에 쬐다
roast 는 오븐이나 불에 요리
한다는 뜻이다 : 할머니께서 오
늘밤 저녁 식사로 닭고기를 **구
우셨다.**

**R**

**rob** [ráb|rɔ́b] 타 **강탈하다**, 약
탈하다, 빼앗다
rob 은 사람에게서 물건을 빼
앗는다는 뜻이다 : 화요일에 3
인조 강도가 은행을 **털어서,**
돈을 몽땅 가져 갔다.

**robin** [rábin|rɔ́b-] 명 (유럽)
**울새, 로빈**
robin 은 새의 일종으로, 앞
부분이 빨갛다.

**robot** [róubɑt|-bɔt] 명 로봇 ; 인
조 인간, 기계 인간
robot 은 기계로, 사람이 하는
일을 똑같이 할 수 있다. 사람
이 하기에는 위험한 일을 하는
robot 들도 있다.

**rock¹** [rák|rɔ́k] 명 바위, 암석,
암반, 암벽
rock 은 큰 돌을 말한다 : 빌과
켄드류는 공원에 있는 rock 에
올라갔다.

**rock²** [rák|rɔ́k] 타 자 흔들다,
흔들어 움직이다 ; 흔들리다,
진동하다
rock 은 전후 좌우로 부드럽게
움직인다는 뜻이다 : 나는 아기
를 안아서 흔들었다.

**rocket** [rákit|rɔ́k-] 명 로켓
rocket 은 하늘로 아주 빠르게
날아 오를 수 있는 기계다 : 사
람들은 아주 큰 rocket 을 타
고 우주를 여행한다.

**rocking chair** [rákiŋ tʃɛ̀ər]
명 흔들의자
rocking chair 는 곡선 모양의
두 개의 긴 나무 위에 얹혀 있
는 의자다 : rocking chair 에
앉아서 몸을 앞뒤로 숙이면 의
자가 흔들린다.

**rode** [róud] 동 ride (타다)의
과거형
rode 는 단어 ride 에서 생긴
말이다 : 우리는 바닷가에서 말
을 **탔다**.

**rodeo** [roudéiou, róudiòu] 명
로데오
rodeo 는 남녀 목동들이 말을
타고 묘기를 부리는 대회가 펼
쳐지는 구경거리를 말한다.

**roll** [róuəl] 타 자 **굴리다, 굴러
가다** ; 감다, 말다 ; 구르다 ;
(차에) **타고 가다,** (탈 것이)
**달리다**
1 roll 은 계속 반복해 돌면서
나아간다는 뜻이다 : 공을 내게
**굴려라**. 그러면 내가 다시 너
에게 차 주겠다.
2 roll 은 또한 바퀴 달린 것을
탄다는 뜻이다 : 다이애나와 그
녀의 친구들은 스케이트보드를
타고 거리를 **달려 내려갔다**.

**roller skate** [róulər skèit] 1
명 롤러스케이트(화)
2 [roller-skate로] 자 **롤러스
케이트를 타다**
1 roller skate 는 바닥에 바퀴

R

가 달린 스케이트다.
2 roller-skate 는 롤러스케이트를 탄다는 뜻이다 : 우리는 토요일 아침에 **롤러스케이트를 타러** 공원에 갔다.

**roof** [rú:f] 명 **지붕**
roof 는 건물의 맨 윗부분이다. 도시에는 roof 가 평평한 집이 많다 : 우리집 roof 꼭대기에는 굴뚝이 있다. roof 에 올라가지 말아라.

**room** [rú:m, rúm] 명 ① **방** ② **장소, 공간,** 자리 ③ **여지, 여유** ; 기회
1 room 은 집이나 다른 건물의 한 부분을 말한다. 잠을 자는 room 은 침실이다 : 이것은 누구의 room 이니 ?
2 room 은 또한 공간을 뜻한다 : 그 차에는 여섯 사람이 탈 충분한 room 이 있다. 나는 저녁을 너무 많이 먹어서 디저트를 먹을 room 이 없다.

**rooster** [rú:stər] 명 **수탉**
rooster 는 수탉이다. rooster 는 해가 뜨는 이른 아침이면 큰 소리로 운다.

**root** [rú:t] 명 **뿌리** ; 근원, 근본
root 는 식물의 일부로, 대개 땅속에서 자란다. 식물은 root 로 땅에서 양분을 얻는다.

**rope** [róup] 명 새끼, 끈, **밧줄**
rope 는 사물을 끌어 당기거나, 들어 올리거나 매다는 데 쓰는 아주 질기고 굵은 끈이다. rope 는 또한 무언가를 한 곳에 고정시키는 데 사용된다 : 우리는 rope 를 사용해 상자를 모두 한 데 묶었다.

**rose**¹ [róuz] 명 **장미,** 장미꽃
rose 는 관목에서 자라는 꽃이다. rose 는 빨간색, 흰색, 노란색, 혹은 그 밖의 여러가지 색깔이 있다 : 메리의 집에는 rose 정원이 있다.

**rose**² [róuz] 동 rise (떠오르다) 의 과거형
rose 는 rise 의 한 형태다 : 오늘 아침 6 시에 해가 **떴다.**

R

**rough** [rʌf] 형 울퉁불퉁한, 우툴두툴한 ; **거친**, 난폭한
1 rough 는 돌기가 잔뜩 있다는 뜻이다 : 나무 껍질은 **우툴두툴하다.**
2 rough 는 또한 온순하지 않다는 뜻이다 : 아이들이 너무 **거칠게** (미식) 축구를 해서, 루이스가 손을 다쳤다.

**round** [ráund] 1 형 둥근, 원통형의 ; 한 바퀴 도는 2 부 돌아서, 빙 돌아 ; 사방에
round 는 무언가가 공이나 천체 모양을 하고 있다는 뜻이다 : 원은 **둥글다.** 지구는 **둥글다.**

**row** [róu] 명 열, 줄 ; (극장 등의) **좌석줄**
row 는 사람이나 물건이 늘어선 줄을 말한다 : 내 책상은 교실 맨 뒷 **줄**에 있다. 수잔은 담을 따라 한 **줄**로 꽃을 심었다.

**rub** [rʌb] 타 **문지르다**, 문질러 닦다, 비비다
rub 는 어떤 것을 눌러서 앞뒤로 나아가게 한다는 뜻이다 : 제프리는 먼지를 닦으려고 헝겊으로 창문을 **문질렀다.**

**rubber** [rʌ́bər] 명 고무, 고무세품
rubber 는 잡아 당겨도 끊어지지 않는 물질이다. 타이어는 rubber 로 만든다. rubber 는 또한 물을 차단하는 성질이 있어서, rubber 로 만든 장화도 있다 : 해리는 비가 오면 rubber 장화를 신는다.

**ruby** [rú:bi] 명 루비 ; 홍옥
ruby 는 보석의 일종으로, 빨간색이다.

**rude** [rú:d] 형 **버릇없는**, 무례한
rude 는 사람에게 공손하게 대하지 않는다는 뜻이다 : 톰이 엘리자베스에게 책을 빌려달라고 부탁했을 때, 엘리자베스가 톰에게 버럭 소리를 지른 것은 **예의없는** 짓이었다.

**rug** [rʌg] 명 깔개, 양탄자
rug 는 아주 질긴 천으로 되어 있어 바닥에 까는 데 이용된다 : 내 침실에는 rug 가 깔려 있다.

**rule** [rúːl] 1 **명** 규칙, 규정 ; 지배, 통치 2 **타 자** 다스리다, 지배하다, 통치하다

1 rule 은 해도 되는 것과 해서는 안되는 것을 가르쳐 준다 : 학교에서 지켜야 할 rule 가운데 하나는 복도에서 뛰어서는 안된다는 것이다.

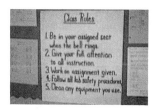

2 rule 은 또한 이끌어 간다는 뜻이다 : 그 여왕은 나라를 잘 **다스렸다.**

**ruler** [rúːlər] **명** 통치자, 지배자 ; 자

1 ruler 는 길이가 얼마인지를 재는 도구로, 길고 곧다. 또한 ruler 를 이용해 직선을 그을 수도 있다 : 나는 ruler 로 내가 그린 그림의 치수를 쟀다.

2 ruler 는 또한 한 나라의 지도자인 사람이다 : 그 왕과 여왕은 공정한 ruler 였다.

**rumble** [rʌ́mbl] **자** (천둥이) 우르르 울리다 ; (수레 등이) 덜커덕거리며 가다〔지나다〕

rumble 은 낮고 굵직한 소리를 낸다는 뜻이다 : 데이비드는 번갯불을 본 바로 직후에, 천둥이 우르르 울리는 소리를 들었다. 낡은 트럭이 울퉁불퉁한 도로를 덜커덕거리며 지나갔다.

**run** [rʌ́n] **자 타** ① 달리다, 뛰다, 달려가다 ② (기계가) 돌아가다, 작동하다 ③ 경영하다, 관리하다

1 run 은 다리로 가능한한 빨리 나아간다는 뜻이다 : 토니는 버스를 타기 위해 **뛰어야** 했다. 나의 부모님은 매일 **달리기**로 운동을 하신다.

2 run 은 또한 아무런 문제없이 작동한다는 뜻이다 : 우리 차는 고장이 나자 **움직이질** 않았다. 차를 고치고 난 후에야 다시 **움직였다.**

**rung** [rʌ́ŋ] **동** ring² (울리다)의 과거분사형

rung 은 단어 ring² 에서 생긴 말이다 : 종이 **울리면**, 우리는 운동장에 나가서 쉴 수 있다.

**rush** [rʌ́ʃ] **자 타** 돌진하다 ; 달려들다 ; 서둘러 하다 ; 부랴부랴 보내다〔데리고 가다〕

rush 는 재빨리 이동하거나, 급히 가거나 온다는 뜻이다 : **빨리 뛰어가야**만 한다, 그렇지 않으면 우리는 학교에 지각할 것이다. 경찰은 환자를 병원으로 **급히 옮겼다.**

R

**sad** [sǽd] 휑 슬픈, 슬픔에 잠
긴 ; 슬픈듯한, 애처로운
sad는 몹시 불행하다고 느낀
다는 의미다. 슬플 때면 울기
도 한다 : 그녀는 그 소식을 듣
고 **슬픔에 잠겼다.**

**safe** [séif] 휑 안전한, 위험이
없는, 무사한
safe는 위험에 처해 있지 않다
는 의미다 : 밖에서는 폭풍이
심하게 치고 있었지만, 집안에
있는 사람은 모두 **안전했다.**

**said** [séd] 됭 say(말하다)의 과
거·과거분사형
said는 단어 say에서 생긴 말
이다 : 그는 내 야구 글러브가
어디 있는지 알고 있다고 **말했
다.**

**sail** [séil] 1 圀 돛 2 困타 항해

하다, 배로 가다 ; 출범하다 ;
(장난감 배를) 띄우다
1 sail은 배에 달려 있는 커다
란 천 조각이다. sail이 바람
을 받으면, 배가 앞으로 나아
간다.

2 sail은 또한 (배가) 물 위를
다닌다는 의미다 : 아이들은 연
못에 장난감 배를 **띄웠다.**

**sailboat** [séiəlbòut] 圀 돛단배,
범선
sailboat는 돛을 사용해서 물
위를 다니는 배다.

**sailor** [séilər] 圀 선원, 뱃사람
sailor는 배를 조종하는 사람이
다. sailor는 바람과 물에 관해
서 많이 알고 있다.

**salad** [sǽləd] 圀 샐러드
salad는 여러 가지 야채나 과

일 혹은 고기로 만든 찬 음식
이다. 상추와 토마토로 만든
salad도 있고, 닭고기나 생선
혹은 국수가 들어간 salad도
있다.

**sale** [séiəl] 몡 판매, 팔기 ; **특
매, 염가매출,** 재고 정리 판매
sale은 물건을 보통 때 가격보
다 싸게 판다는 뜻이다 : 그 가
게는 진바지를 sale하고 있다.

**salt** [sɔ́ːlt] 몡 소금
salt는 바다나 땅에 있다. 맛
을 더 좋게 하려고 음식에
salt를 넣는 사람도 있다. salt
는 희다.

**same** [séim] 톙 [the same 으
로] **같은,** 동일한
same은 모든 점에서 일치한다
는 뜻이다 : 베티와 사라 두 사
람 모두 눈이 파랗다. 두 사람
의 눈동자 색깔은 **같다.**

**sand** [sǽnd] 몡 모래 ; 모래밭
sand는 아주 작은 돌 부스러
기로 된 흙의 일종이다. 바닷
가와 사막에 sand가 있다.

**sandwich** [sǽndwitʃ|sǽnwidʒ,
-witʃ] 몡 샌드위치
sandwich는 음식의 일종으로,
두 쪽의 빵 사이에 고기, 치즈,
땅콩 버터 혹은 그밖의 것들을
넣어 만든다 : 점심으로 sand-
wich를 먹는 사람들이 많다.

**sang** [sǽŋ] 통 sing(노래하다)
의 과거형
sang은 sing의 한 형태다 : 다
이애나는 어제 새 노래를 배워
서, 온종일 그 노래만 **불렀다.**

**sank** [sǽŋk] 통 sink(가라앉다)
의 과거형
sank는 단어 sink에서 생긴
말이다 : 내 발이 모래에 **빠졌
다.**

**sat** [sǽt] 통 sit(앉다)의 과거 ·
과거분사형
sat은 단어 sit에서 생긴 말이
다 : 새가 울타리에 **앉았다.**

**Saturday** [sǽtərdèi, -di] 몡
토요일
Saturday는 한 주 가운데 하
루다. Saturday는 금요일이
지나고 일요일이 되기 전에 온
다.

S

**saucer** [sɔ́:sər] 명 받침 접시

saucer는 그다지 깊게 패이지 않은 작은 접시다. saucer는 보통 컵밑에 둔다. 사람들은 간혹 고양이가 마실 수 있도록 saucer에 우유를 부어 둔다.

**save** [séiv] 타 자 ① **구출하다**, 구조하다 ② **저축하다**, 비축하다, **남겨두다** ③ **절약하다**

1 save는 사람이나 물건을 안전하게 한다는 의미다 : 소방수들이 불길에 휩싸인 건물에서 그 가족을 **구조했다.**

2 save는 또한 나중에 간직하거나 사용하려고 무언가를 따로 떼어놓아 둔다는 의미다 : 부모님이 내 젖먹이 적 사진들을 모두 **소중히 간직하고 계셨다.** 나는 돈을 **모아서** 게임용품을 사려고 한다.

**saw**¹ [sɔ́:] 명 **톱**

saw는 날에 날카로운 금속 '이'가 있는 도구다. saw는 나무, 금속, 플라스틱을 자르는 데 쓴다.

**saw**² [sɔ́:] 동 see (보다)의 과거형

saw는 단어 see에서 생긴 말이다 : 우리는 동물원에서 코끼리를 **보았다.**

**say** [séi] 타 자 **말하다**, 이야기하다

say는 말한다는 의미다. 딕은 전화를 받으면, "여보세요!"라고 **말한다.**

**scale** [skéiəl] 명 ① **저울** : 저울눈, **눈금** ② **규모** ③ **비늘**

1 scale은 물건의 무게의 정도를 나타내는 기계다. 사람, 야채, 트럭의 무게를 다는 여러 가지 종류의 scale이 있다 : 우리는 scale에 토마토를 두 개 더 올려놓았다.

2 scale은 또한 물고기, 뱀, 그밖의 다른 몇몇 동물의 몸을 덮고 있는 단단하고 작은 표피다.

**scare** [skέər] 타 자 …에게 겁을 주다, **놀라게 하다**

scare는 두려운 생각이 들게 한다는 의미다 : 강아지는 항상

큰소리에 **겁을 먹는다.**

**scarecrow** [skέərkròu] 명 **허
수아비**
scarecrow는 새들의 접근을
막기 위해 들판에 설치한다.
scarecrow는 낡은 옷을 입고
있는 사람과 모습이 비슷하다.

**scarf** [skάːrf] 명 **스카프**
scarf는 머리나 목에 두르는
천 조각이다.

**school** [skúːəl] 명 **학교**
school은 배우려고 가는 곳이
다. school에서는 선생님이
읽고, 쓰고, 셈하는 방법같은
중요한 것들을 가르쳐 준다.

**science** [sáiəns] 명 **과학** ; 학문
science는 학교에서 공부하는
것이다. science는 동식물에
관한 것을 가르쳐 줄 수 있다.
또한 science를 통해 지구와
별들에 관한 것도 배울 수 있
다.

**scientist** [sáiəntist] 명 **과학자**
scientist는 과학의 한 특정 분
야에 종사하는 사람이다. 날씨
를 연구하는 scientist도 있다.

**scissors** [sízərz] 명 **가위**
scissors는 두 개의 날카로운
날이 있는 도구다. 물건을 자
르는 데 scissors를 사용한다.

**scratch** [skrǽtʃ] 타 자 **할퀴다** ;
(가려운 데를) **긁다**
scratch는 물건에 자국을 낸다
는 뜻이다 : 유리는 돌에 **긁힌
다.** 고양이는 발톱으로 **할퀼
수 있다.**

**scream** [skríːm] 자 타 **비명을
지르다, 소리치다**
scream은 큰 목소리로 외치거
나 부르짖는다는 뜻이다. 사람
들은 놀라거나 화가 나거나 흥
분할 때면 **비명을 지른다.**

**screen** [skríːn] 명 ① **방충망**
② **칸막이** ③ **스크린**, 영사막
screen은 곤충은 들어오지 못
하게 하고 공기는 통하도록 창
문 위에 설치한다.

**scrub** [skrʌb] 탄 짠 비벼 씻다
〔빨다〕, 북북 문시르나〔닦나〕
scrub은 비벼 씻거나 문질러
서 닦는다는 의미다 : 찰흙을
갖고 놀아서 우리는 흙을 닦아
내려고 손을 **문질러 씻어야만
했다.**

**sea** [síː] 명 바다
sea는 ocean의 또 다른 말이
다 : 오래전에 해적들은 보물을
찾아 sea를 항해했다.

**seal**[1] [síːəl] 명 바다표범, 물개
seal은 대부분의 시간을 바다
에서 살며, 헤엄을 잘 치는 동
물이다. seal은 털이 많고 매
끄러우며, 몸은 길다. seal은
개가 짖는 듯한 소리를 낸다.

**seal**[2] [síːəl] 탄 ① 날인하다, 조
인하다 ② 봉하다, 밀폐하다
seal은 열리지 않게 봉한다는
의미다 : 우리는 발렌타인 카드
를 부치기 전에, 봉투를 모두
**봉했는지** 확인하려고 점검했
다.

**season** [síːzən] 명 계절
season은 한 해 가운데 한 시

기로, 1년은 4 season 으로
되어 있다. season이란 봄,
여름, 가을 그리고 겨울을 말
한다 : 너는 어느 season을 가
장 좋아하느냐 ?

**seat** [síːt] 명 자리, **좌석**
seat는 앉을 수 있는 곳이다 :
보브는 방 뒤쪽에 앉았다. 당
신 seat로 돌아가십시오.

**seatbelt** [síːtbèəlt] 명 안전띠
seatbelt는 자동차나 비행기를
탈 때 둘러매는 띠의 일종이
다. seatbelt는 충돌이나 사고
가 났을 때 좌석에서 떨어져
나가지 않게 해준다.

**second**[1] [sékənd] 형 두 번째
의, 제 2 의
second는 첫 번째 바로 다음
이라는 의미다 : 알파벳의 **두
번째** 글자는 B 다.

**second**[2] [sékənd] 명 초 ; 매우
짧은 시간
second는 분의 일부다. 1분
은 60 second (초)다.

**secret** [síːkrət] 1 명 비밀 2 형

비밀의, 은밀한
secret는 많은 사람들이 모르고 있는 것이다. 간혹 한 사람만이 secret를 알고 있을 수도 있다 : 어머니께 드리는 생일 선물은 나만의 secret다.

**secretary** [sékrətèri|-təri] 명
비서, 서기 ; (협회의) **간사**
secretary는 다른 사람이나 특정 집단을 위해서 서류를 작성하고 업무를 봐주는 사람이다 : 조는 우표 수집 동호회의 secretary로 선출되었다.

**see** [síː] 타 자 ① **보다**, 보이다
② **만나다** ③ 알다 ④ **구경하다** ; **살펴보다**, 조사하다
1 see는 눈으로 사물을 본다는 뜻이다 : 나는 피터의 연이 하늘 높이 올라가는 것을 **볼** 수 있었다.
2 see는 또한 찾아낸다는 뜻이다 : 주스가 더 있는지 **알아보자.**

**seed** [síːd] 명 씨, 씨앗, 종자
seed는 식물의 일부로, 그것에서 새 식물이 자란다 : 우리 집 채소밭에 심은 seed가 자라서 토마토와 피망이 되었다. 우리는 또한 호박 seed도 심었다.

**seem** [síːm] 자 …으로 보이다, …인 것 같다
seem은 무엇처럼 보인다는 뜻이다 : 이 곳은 소풍을 가기에 좋은 장소인 **것 같다.**

**seen** [síːn] 통 see(보다)의 과거분사형
seen은 단어 see에서 생긴 말이다 : 코끼리를 **본** 적이 있습니까 ?

**seesaw** [síːsɔ̀ː] 명 시소, 널뛰기
seesaw는 두 사람이 앉아서 오르락내리락 하도록 만든 긴 널판자다. seesaw의 한쪽 끝이 내려가면 다른 쪽 끝은 올라간다.

**select** [səlékt] 타 고르다, 선택하다, 선발하다
select는 골라낸다는 뜻이다 : 엄마는 오늘밤 우리 가족이 볼 비디오 테이프를 우리가 **골라**

도 된다고 말씀하셨다. 마음에
느는 야구 배트를 **골랐니 ?**

**selfish** [sélfiʃ] 형 **이기적인,** 이
기주의의, 자기 본위의
selfish 는 남과 물건을 공유하
기를 싫어한다는 의미다 : 스미
스가 사촌 조에게 자기 장난감
을 가지고 놀지 못하게 한 것
은 **이기적인** 행동이었다.

**sell** [sél] 타 자 **팔다,** 매각하다
sell은 물건의 대가로 돈을 낸
사람에게 물건을 준다는 의미
다 : 가구점은 탁자와 의자 그
리고 침대를 **판다.** 나는 내 헌
자전거를 **팔고** 새 자전거를 샀
다.

**send** [sénd] 타 자 **보내다**
send는 사람이나 물건을 어딘
가로 가게 한다는 의미다 : 수
잔은 친구들에게 편지를 **보내**
는 것을 좋아 한다. 프랭크의
어머니는 빵을 좀 사오라고 그
를 가게로 **보냈다.**

**sent** [sént] 동 send (보내다) 의
과거 · 과거분사형
sent는 send의 한 형태다 : 다
이애나의 할아버지께서 그녀의

생일에 선물을 **보내주셨다.**

**sentence** [séntəns] 명 **문장**
sentence는 단어들이 모여서
하나의 완전한 생각을 만드는
것이다. sentence의 첫 글자
는 대문자로 시작한다 : 이것은
대단히 긴 sentence다.

**September** [septémbər] 명 **9
월**
September는 1년중 한 달이
다. September는 30일이며,
8월이 가고 10월이 되기 전에
온다.

**serious** [síəriəs] 형 **진지한,** 엄
숙한, **심각한** ; 중대한
serious는 우습지 않다는 의미
다 : 바트는 **심각한** 기분이어
서, 농담을 들어도 웃고 싶지
않다.

**serve** [sə́:rv] 타 자 ① …에게
**시중 들다,** 섬기다, …에 봉사
**하다** ② (음식을) **차리다**
serve는 먹으려고 하는 곳으로
음식을 내온다는 의미다 : 우리
는 부엌에 점심을 **차렸다.**

**set** [sét] 1 **타** ① **두다**, 놓다 ② (때·장소를) 정하다 ③ **준비하다**, 차리다 2 **자** (해·달이) **지다** 3 **명** 한 세트, **한 벌**

1 set는 어떤 물건을 다른 물건 위에 놓는다는 뜻이다 : 앤은 책을 탁자 위에 **놓았다**. 나는 식탁에 저녁을 **차려 놓았다**.

2 set는 함께 어우러져 한 무리를 이룬 물건들을 말한다.

**seven** [sévən] 1 **명** **7**, 일곱 살, 일곱 시, 일곱 개 2 **형** **7의**, 일곱 살의, 일곱 개의

seven은 6 보다 하나 더 크다. seven은 **7** 이라고 쓴다 : 6＋1＝**7**.

**several** [sévərəl] 1 **형** **몇몇의**, 몇 개의, 몇 사람의 2 **대** **몇몇**, 몇 개, 몇 사람

several은 서넛보다 많다는 뜻이다 : 마리아는 신간 서적을 **몇** 권 가지고 있다. **몇** 사람이 방을 나갔다.

**sew** [sóu] **타** **자** **꿰매다**, 집다, 바느질하다

sew는 실 꿴 바늘로 한데 붙인다는 뜻이다 : 나는 셔츠에 단추를 꿰매 **달았다**. 엄마는 내 진바지의 찢어진 곳에 헝겊 조각을 대고 **깁고** 있다.

**shade** [ʃéid] 1 **명** **그늘**, 응달 ; **차양**, (램프 등의) **갓** 2 **타** **그늘지게 하다**, 가리다

1 shade는 햇볕이 가려진 곳이다 : 날씨가 너무 더워서, 우리는 shade에 앉았다. 몇몇 아이들은 나무 shade에서 놀고 있다.

2 shade는 또한 빛을 못들어오게 하거나 빛을 덜 밝게 해주는 것이다 : 내 침실 창문에는 shade가 처져있다.

**shadow** [ʃǽdou] **명** **그림자**

shadow는 빛이 사람이나 사물에 비칠 때 간혹 생기는 어두운 부분이다. shadow는 사람이나 사물과 같은 모양이다 : 엄마는 양손으로 토끼가 말하는 것처럼 보이는 shadow

를 만들 수 있다.

**shake** [ʃéik] 탄 자 흔들다, 뒤흔
들다 ; 흔들리다, 떨다
shake는 상하 혹은 좌우로 움
직인다는 의미다 : 따기 전에
주스 병을 흔들어라. 우리집
개는 몸을 흔들어 털에 묻은
물을 털어냈다.

**shaken** [ʃéikən] 동 shake (흔들
다)의 과거분사형
shaken은 shake의 한 형태
다 : 우리는 개가 물에 젖으면,
집에 들어오기 전에 물을 털어
냈는지 꼭 확인한다.

**shall** [《약》 ʃəl, 《강》 ʃǽl] 조 ①
[I〔we〕 shall …의 단순 미래
로] …일 것이다, …이 되다
② [shall I〔we〕 … ? 로] …
할까요, …하면 좋을까요
shall은 「…일 것이다」의 의미
다 : 개학을 했으면 좋겠다.

**shape** [ʃéip] 1 명 모양 ; 형체 ;
모습 2 탄 자 모양을 짓다, 만
들다 ; 모양을 갖추다
1 shape는 물체의 외형이나
형태를 말한다 : 야구공과 농구

공의 shape는 둥글다. 상자는
정사각형의 shape다.

2 shape는 무언가에 형태를
부여한다는 의미다 : 데일의 아
저씨는 진흙 덩어리로 공을 만
들었다.

**share** [ʃέər] 탄 자 공유하다, 분
담하다 ; 나누다, 분배하다
1 share는 가진 것의 일부를
누군가에게 준다는 의미다 : 리
처드는 우리에게 자기 쿠키를
나누어 주겠다고 말했다.
2 share는 또한 함께 사용한
다는 의미다 : 나는 내 장난감
들을 언니와 오빠와 같이 가지
고 논다.

**shark** [ʃáːrk] 명 상어
shark는 바다에 사는 물고기
로, 날카로운 이빨이 있는 큰
입이 있다. shark는 다른 물
고기를 잡아 먹는다.

**sharp** [ʃáːrp] 형 날카로운, 예
리한, (날이) 잘 드는, 뾰족한
sharp는 물건을 자를 수 있는

뾰족한 끝이나 얇은 날이 있다는 의미다 : **예리한** 날이 있는 칼들도 있다.

**she** [《약》 ʃi, 《강》 ʃíː] **대** ［인칭 대명사 : 3인칭 단수 여성 주격］ **그녀는, 그녀가**

1 she는 소녀나 성인 여자 혹은 동물의 암컷을 나타내는 말이다 : **어머니**께서는 내게 곧 돌아오겠다고 말씀하셨다.
2 she'd는 she had나 she would의 뜻이다 : **그녀는** 항상 헬리콥터를 타고 싶어했다.
3 she'll은 she will의 뜻이다 : 서두르지 않으면 **그녀는** 지각할 것이다.
4 she's는 she is의 뜻이다 : **그녀는** 나와 함께 도서관에 가려고 한다.

**sheep** [ʃíːp] **명** **양**

sheep는 곱슬곱슬한 털이 있는 동물이다. 양모는 sheep의 털로 만든다. 어린 sheep를 lamb이라고 한다.

**shelf** [ʃélf] **명** **선반**

shelf는 물건을 올려놓는 곳이다. shelf는 나무나 금속 혹은 플라스틱으로 만든다 : 내 방에는 벽에 내 책과 장난감들을 두는 shelf가 있다.

**shell** [ʃél] **명** (달걀 · 조개 등의) **껍질** ; (거북의) 등딱지

shell은 무언가를 덮고 있는 단단한 부분이다. 달걀과 견과는 shell이 있다. 바다거북처럼 shell이 있는 동물들도 있다. 바닷가에서 볼 수 있는 shell에는 원래 그 안에 동물이 살았었다.

**shine** [ʃáin] **자** **타** **빛나다**, 번쩍이다, 비치다 ; (구두 등을) **닦다**, 광택을 내다

1 shine은 빛을 내거나 광채가 난다는 뜻이다 : 낮에는 태양이 **빛난다.**
2 shine은 또한 무언가를 빛나게 한다는 뜻이다 : 마크 아저씨는 오늘 아침 출근하기 전에 자기 구두를 **닦았다.**

**ship** [ʃíp] 1 **명** **배**, 선박 2 **타** **배**에 **싣다**, **배로 보내다** ; (기차 · 트럭 등으로) **수송하다**

1 ship은 바다나 큰 호수 혹은 강을 다니는 큰 배다. ship은

사람과 물건을 물 위로 실어 나른다. ship은 돛이나 엔진을 이용해서 움직인다. 항구에 ship이 있다.

2 ship은 또한 다른 장소로 무언가를 보낸다는 뜻이다 : 새로운 마을로 이사하게 되면, 우리는 트럭으로 가구를 거기까지 **수송할 것이다.**

**shirt** [ʃə́ːrt] 몡 셔츠, 와이셔츠
shirt는 옷의 일종으로, 사람들은 상체에 shirt를 입는다. 단추가 있는 shirt가 많다.

**shoe** [ʃúː] 몡 신, 구두
shoe는 발을 감싸는 것이다. shoe는 가죽이나 천 혹은 플라스틱으로 만들어진다. 사람들은 보통 양말을 신고 shoe를 신는다.

**shoelace** [ʃúːlèis] 몡 구두 끈
shoelace는 신발이 발에 붙어 있게 하는 끈이다 : 마이크는 shoelace를 매는 법을 알고 있다.

**shone** [ʃóun | ʃɔ́n] 통 shine (빛

나다)의 과거·과거분사형
shone은 단어 shine에서 생긴 말이다 : 달빛이 창문에 **비쳤다.**

**shook** [ʃúk] 통 shake (흔들다)의 과거형
shook는 shake의 한 형태다 : 빌은 주스가 다 섞일 때까지 병을 **흔들었다.** 그가 수에게 더 마시겠느냐고 묻자, 그녀는 싫다는 뜻으로 머리를 흔들었다.

**shoot** [ʃúːt] 타 자 ① (총·화살을) **쏘다,** 발사하다 ; 사격하다 ② (골을 향해 공을) **차다, 던지다**
1 shoot은 빠르게 치솟거나 나간다는 의미다 : 로켓들이 하늘 높이 **치솟아 올랐다.**

2 shoot은 또한 어떤 쪽으로 가게 한다는 의미다 : 토니는 골을 향해 농구공을 **던진다.**

**shop** [ʃáp | ʃɔ́p] 1 몡 가게, 상점

2 [자][타] 물건을 사다, 쇼핑하
러 가다
1 shop은 물건을 살 수 있는
곳이다 : 앨리스는 물고기 먹이
를 사려고 애완 동물 shop에
갔다. 앤은 저 shop에서 사과
를 세 개 샀다.
2 shop은 또한 물건을 산다는
뜻이다 : 우리는 토요일 아침에
식료품을 **사러 갔다**.

**shore** [ʃɔ́ːr] [명] **바닷가**, 해변 ;
(바다·호수·강의) 기슭
shore는 바다, 호수 혹은 강
가의 땅이다 : 우리는 shore를
따라 걸으면서 예쁜 조개 껍질
을 찾았다. shore를 깨끗이
보존하는 것이 중요하다.

**short** [ʃɔ́ːrt] [형] **짧은**, 키가 작
은 ; 간결한, 간단한
short는 한쪽 끝에서 다른쪽
끝까지의 거리가 멀지 않다는
뜻이다. short는 또한 길거나
키가 크지 않다는 뜻이다 : 내
개는 다리가 **짧다**. 마리아는
머리카락이 **짧고** 빨갛다. 테리
는 점심을 먹고 나서 **잠깐** 낮
잠을 잤다.

**shot** [ʃát|ʃɔ́t] [동] shoot (쏘다)의

과거·과거분사형
shot은 shoot의 한 형태다 : 그
들은 우주로 로켓을 **발사했다**.

**should** [《약》 ʃəd ; 무성음 앞에
서 ʃt, 《강》 ʃúd] [조] ① shall
(…일 것이다)의 과거형 ②
[의무·당연함을 나타내어] **…
하여야 한다〔할 것이다〕** ; …하
는 것이 당연하다〔좋다〕
should는 어떤 일을 하는 게
중요하다는 뜻이다 : 너는 아침
을 **먹어야만 한다**.

**shoulder** [ʃóuəldər] [명] **어깨**
shoulder는 몸의 한 부분으로,
목과 팔 사이에 있다.

**shouldn't** [ʃúdnt] should not 의
단축형
shouldn't는 should not의 뜻
이다 : 너는 차도로 뛰어 들면
**안된다**.

**shout** [ʃáut] [자][타] **외치다** ; 고함
지르다
shout 는 아주 큰 목소리로 말
한다는 뜻이다 : 우리는 흥분을
하거나 화가 나면 간혹 **고함을
지른다**.

**shovel** [ʃʌ́vəl] 1 명 삽 2 타 삽으로 뜨다, (길 등을) 삽질하여 만들다
1 shovel은 긴 자루가 달린 도구로, 땅을 파는 데 사용한다.
2 shovel은 또한 삽을 이용한다는 의미다 : 삽으로 눈을 **치우자.**

**show** [ʃóu] 1 타 ① 보이다, 내놓다 ② 전시하다 ; 상영하다 ③ **가르치다,** 설명하다 2 명 ① 보이기 ; 전시회, 전람회 ② **구경거리, 연극, 쇼** ; (방송의) 프로그램
1 show는 무언가를 보여 주거나 설명한다는 의미다 : 나는 내 친구에게 새로 산 자전거를 **보여 주고** 싶다. 사라는 내게 새 컴퓨터 프로그램의 사용법을 **가르쳐 주었다.** 역으로 가는 길을 **가리켜 주시겠어요?**
2 show는 또한 텔레비전이나 극장에서 보는 것이다 : 우리는 오늘 puppet show (인형극)를 구경가려고 한다.

**shower** [ʃáuər] 1 자 타 **소나기가 오다, 샤워를 하다** ; 흠뻑 적시다 2 명 **소나기, 샤워**
1 shower한다는 것은 떨어지는 물로 몸을 씻는다는 의미다 : 마리는 목욕 대신에 shower를 했다.
2 shower는 또한 잠깐동안 내리는 비를 말한다 : 우리는 오늘 shower가 올 것으로 예상하고 우산을 가지고 왔다.

**shut** [ʃʌ́t] 타 자 (문을) **닫다, 닫히다,** 잠기다 ; (입·눈을) 다물다, 감다
shut은 닫는다는 의미다 : 창문 좀 **닫아** 주십시오. 배리가 눈을 **감자,** 그의 친구들은 뛰어가 숨었다.

**shy** [ʃái] 형 소심한, **수줍어하는,** 부끄러움을 잘 타는 ; 조심성 많은
shy는 주위에 사람이 있으면 약간 겁을 먹는다는 의미다 : **부끄러움을 잘 타는** 어린 소년은 손님들이 오자 엄마 뒤로 숨었다.

**sick** [sík] 형 **병에 걸린,** 아픈, 몸이 불편한
sick는 몸이 좋지 않다는 의미다. 간혹 **병에 걸리면,** 머리나 배가 아프다. 의사와 간호사는 **아픈** 사람들을 돌본다.

**side** [sáid] 명 ① 편, 쪽 ; 측면 ② 면, 변 ③ 옆, 곁 ; 옆구리 ④ 가, 가장자리
side는 물건 바깥쪽의 평평한 부분이다. 한 장의 종이에는 두 side가 있다. 정사각형은

네 side가 있다.

**sidewalk** [sáidwɔ̀:k] 명 (포장된) **보도**, 인도
sidewalk는 차도 옆의 걸어다닐 수 있는 곳이다 : 나는 우리 집 앞 sidewalk에서 롤러 스케이트를 타는 것을 좋아한다.

**sight** [sáit] 명 ① **시력 ; 시야 ;** 봄, 보임 ② 광경, 경치
1 sight는 눈으로 보는 능력이다 : 조지의 sight는 안경을 쓰기 시작하면서 좋아졌다.
2 sight는 또한 눈으로 볼 수 있는 거리를 말한다 : 비행기가 멀리 날아가 **시야**에서 사라졌다.

**sign** [sáin] 명 ① **기호, 부호** ② **신호 ; 손짓, 몸짓** ③ **표지, 간판** ④ **기색 ; 징조**
1 sign은 기호를 말한다 : 플러스와 마이너스의 sign은 + 와 − 다.
2 sign은 또한 메시지가 인쇄되어 있는 평평한 금속판이나 나무판을 말한다 : road sign (도로 표지)은 사람들에게 방향을 가리켜 준다. 그 방은 「금연」 sign이 되어 있다.

**signal** [sígnəl] 명 **신호 ;** 신호기
signal은 사람들에게 어떻게 하라고 가르쳐 주는 방법이다. signal은 말 대신에 사용한다. signal이 불빛, 기호, 깃발, 손놀림 혹은 소리가 될 수도 있다. 빨간 신호등은 열차가 곧 온다는 signal이다 : 그는 signal로 한 손을 들었다.

**silence** [sáiləns] 명 **침묵,** 무언 ; **고요함,** 정적
silence는 아무 소리도 없다는 뜻이다. silence가 흐를 때는 아주 조용하다 : 우리 선생님께

서 철자법 시험을 보는 동안 **조용히** 하라고 하셨다.

**silent** [sáilənt] 혭 **침묵하는, 말 없는** ; 고요한, 소리 없는
silent는 전혀 소리를 내지 않는다는 뜻이다 : 딕이 **소리를 내지 않아서** 그의 누나는 문 뒤에 숨은 그를 찾지 못했다.

**silly** [síli] 혭 **어리석은, 바보 같은**, 분별없는
silly는 우스운 행동을 한다는 뜻이다 : 스콧과 그의 친구들은 킥킥거리며 방안을 이리저리 뛰어다녔다. 그들은 **바보 같은** 짓을 하고 있었다.

**silver** [sílvər] 1 몡 **은** ; 은제품 2 혭 **은의** ; 은제품의
silver는 여러가지 모양으로 만들 수 있는 광택이 나는 흰 금속이다. silver는 주화, 장신구, 사발, 포크 그리고 그 밖의 물건들을 만드는 데 쓴다.

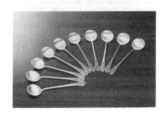

**simple** [símpl] 혭 **단순한, 간단한** ; 순진한 ; 소박한 ; 검소한
simple은 화려하지 않다는 뜻이다 : 헬렌은 4개의 선과 1개의 원만으로 **간단한** 사람 그림을 그릴 수 있다.

**since** [síns] 1 혩 **…이후, …로부터** (지금까지) 2 혪 **그 후** (지금까지) 3 졥 ① **…한 이래** ② **…이므로, …까닭에**
1 since는 「그때부터 지금까지」란 뜻이다 : 빌은 월요일**부터** 아팠다. 우리는 내가 아기 **때부터** 이 집에 살고 있다.
2 since는 또한 「…때문에」란 의미다 : 일요일**이어서**, 우리는 학교에 안 가도 된다.

**sing** [síŋ] 탵 쟵 **노래하다** ; (새가) 지저귀다
sing은 목소리로 음악을 만든다는 뜻이다 : 다 함께 **노래를 부르자.** 새들이 나무에서 **지저귀다.** **노래를 부르는** 사람을 singer라고 한다.

**sink** [síŋk] 1 몡 (부엌의) **개수대, 싱크** ; 세면대 2 쟵 탵 **가라앉다〔앉히다〕, 침몰하다**
1 sink는 물건을 넣고 씻는 것이다. sink에는 물을 받고 내보내는 특별한 부분이 있다 : 우리는 부엌 sink에서 야채를

씻었다.

2 sink는 또한 물 속에 잠긴다는 의미다 : 나는 연못에 돌을 던져, 돌이 바닥에 **가라앉는** 것을 지켜 보았다. 잠수부들이 **침몰한** 배에서 보물을 찾았다.

**sip** [síp] 타 자 **조금씩 마시다**
sip은 한번에 아주 적은 양만 마신다는 의미다 : 수프가 뜨거우니, 천천히 **조금씩 마시세요.**

**sister** [sístər] 명 자매, 누이
sister는 자기와 같은 부모를 둔 여자다 : 내 sister와 나는 둘 다 눈동자가 파랗다.

**sit** [sít] 자 **앉다**, 착석하다
sit는 엉덩이를 무언가의 위에 얹는다는 뜻이다 : 해리는 아버지 무릎에 **앉았다.** 내 개와 나는 마루에 **앉겠다.**

**six** [síks] 1 명 **6**, 여섯 시, 여섯 살, 여섯 명 2 형 **6**의, 6시의, 여섯 명의
six는 5보다 하나가 크다는 의미다. six는 **6** 이라고 쓴다 : $5 + 1 = 6$.

**size** [sáiz] 명 **크기** ; 신장 ; 치수 ; 사이즈
size는 크거나 작은 정도를 말한다 : 너는 저 나무의 size를 알아맞힐 수 있니 ? 내 신발은 모두 size가 같다. 어떤 size를 원하니 ? 이 책은 저 책과 같은 size다.

**skate** [skéit] 1 명 **스케이트**(화) 2 자 **스케이트를 타다**
1 롤러 스케이트를 타거나 스케이트를 탈 때 skate를 발에 신는다. 신발 위에 착용하는 skate도 있고, 신발처럼 생긴 skate도 있다 : 아버지는 내게 skate를 한 켤레 사주셨다.
2 skate는 또한 스케이트를 탄다는 뜻이다 : 우리는 호수가 얼면 그 위에서 **스케이트를 탄다.** 그녀는 음악에 맞추어 스케이트를 잘 **탔다.** 스케이트를 타는 사람을 skater라고 한다.

**skateboard** [skéitbɔ̀ːrd] 몡 스
케이트보드
skateboard는 바닥에 바퀴가
달린 낮고 평평한 판자다.
skateboard위에 서서 한 발로
밀치며 skateboard를 탄다.

**ski** [skíː] 1 몡 스키 2 짜 태 스
키를 타다 ; 스키로 가다
1 ski 는 나무나 금속 혹은 플
라스틱으로 된 길고 가느다란
판이다 : 사람들은 눈 위를 빨
리 가기 위해 발에 ski 를 신
는다.
2 ski 는 눈 위에서 스키를 탄
다는 의미다 : 앨리스는 **스키를**
**타고** 산을 내려 왔다.

**skin** [skín] 몡 ① (사람의) 피
부, (동물의) 가죽 ② (과일
의) 껍질, (곡물의) 겉껍질
skin 은 무언가의 표면을 감싸
고 있다 : 나는 추우면 skin 전
체에 소름이 돋는다.

**skip** [skíp] 짜 태 가볍게 뛰다
skip은 먼저 한쪽 발을, 그 다
음엔 다른쪽 발을 내딛어 뛰면
서 나아간다는 의미다 : 메리는
거리를 **깡충깡충 뛰면서** 내려
갔다.

**skirt** [skáːrt] 몡 스커트
skirt 는 소녀나 성인 여성이
입는 옷으로, 허리에서 아래로
걸친다.

**skunk** [skʌ́ŋk] 몡 스컹크
skunk 는 동물로, 크기는 고
양이만 하다. skunk 는 꼬리
가 크고 등에 흰 줄무늬가 있
다. skunk 는 아주 심한 악취
를 내서 다른 동물들을 쫓아낼
수 있다.

**sky** [skái] 몡 하늘
sky 는 밖에 있을 때 머리
위로 보이는 것이다 : 밤중에
sky 에 있는 달과 별들을 볼
수 있다.

**skyscraper** [skáiskrèipər] 몡
고층 건물, 마천루
skyscraper 는 아주 높은 건물
이다 : 뉴욕시와 시카고는 sky-
scraper 로 유명하다.

**sled** [sléd] 몡 (어린이용의) 소
형 썰매
sled 는 장난감이다. 사람들은
눈 위에서 sled 를 탄다. sled
는 나무나 금속 혹은 플라스틱
으로 만든다.

**sleep** [slíːp] 재 타 잠자다
　sleep 은 눈을 감고 쉰다는 의미다 : 우리집 고양이는 양지에서 **자는** 걸 좋아한다. 나는 어젯밤 8시간 동안 **잤다.**

**slept** [slépt] 동 sleep (잠자다)의 과거・과거분사형
　slept 는 sleep 의 한 형태다 : 웬디는 어젯밤 그녀의 친구 집에서 **잤다.**

**slide** [sláid] 1 재 타 **미끄러지다**, 미끄러져 가다 2 명 미끄러짐, **미끄럼틀**
　1 slide 는 어떤 것의 위로 원활하게 움직인다는 의미다 : 그녀는 책을 탁자 위로 **밀어서** 내게 건네 **주었다.**
　2 slide 는 꼭대기로 올라가서 미끄러져 내려오며 놀 수 있는 기구다.

**slip** [slíp]　　재 타 (찍) 미끄러지다, **미끄러져 넘어지다**, 미끄러져 떨어지다 ; …에서 빠져나가다
　slip 은 미끄러져 넘어진다는 의미다 : 물기가 있는 마룻바닥에 **미끄러져 넘어지지** 않도록 조심하시오. 접시가 손에서 **미끄러져** 마룻바닥에 **떨어져** 깨지고 말았다.

**slipper** [slípər] 명 슬리퍼, 가벼운 실내화
　slipper 는 실내에서 신는 폭신하고 편안하며 넉넉한 신발이다.

**slippery** [slípəri] 형 **미끄러운**, 반들반들한
　slippery 는 미끄러져 넘어지거나 활주할 수 있다는 의미다 : 길에 물이 있거나 얼음이 얼면 **미끄럽다.**

**slow** [slóu] 형 (속도가) **느린**, 더딘 ; (시계가) 늦는
　slow 는 시간이 오래 걸린다는 의미다 : 바다거북은 아주 **느리다.**

**small** [smɔ́ːl] 형 **작은**, 소규모의 ; 얼마 안 되는, 적은
　small 은 크지 않다는 의미다 : 생쥐는 **작은** 동물이다. 생쥐는 고양이보다 훨씬 **더 작다.**

**smell** [smél] 1 자 타 냄새맡다 ;
냄새가 나다 ; 낌새가 있다 2
명 냄새, 향기 ; 낌새
1 smell 은 코로 무언가를 들
이마신다는 의미다 : 마리아는
부엌의 오븐에서 음식이 탈 때
나는 연기 **냄새를 맡았다.**
2 smell 은 냄새를 맡아서 알
아낸다는 의미다 : 부엌에서 굽
는 빵에서 좋은 **냄새가 난다.**
3 smell 은 냄새를 맡도록 풍
기는 것이다 : 스컹크는 지독한
**악취**를 낼 수 있다.

**smile** [smáiəl] 1 자 타 미소짓
다, 방긋〔생긋〕웃다 2 명 미
소, 생긋 웃기
1 smile 은 양 입가가 위로 향
한다는 의미다. 기분이 좋을
때 **미소를 짓는다** : 사진을 찍
을 때 우리는 모두 **방긋 웃었
다.**

2 smile 은 얼굴에 미소를 띠
고 있다는 의미다 : 우승팀 선
수들의 얼굴에 smile 이 가득
했다.

**smoke** [smóuk] 명 연기
smoke 는 타고 있는 것에서
나는 검은 연무다 : 우리는 굴

뚝에서 나는 smoke 를 보았
다.

**smooth** [smúːð] 형 매끄러운,
반질반질한, 평탄한
smooth 는 무언가를 만질 때
울퉁불퉁한 것이 전혀 느껴지
지 않는다는 의미다 : 사과 껍
질은 오렌지 껍질보다 더 **매끄
럽다.**

**snake** [snéik] 명 뱀
snake 는 파충류로 몸통은 길
고 가늘며 팔이나 다리는 없
다. 대부분의 snake 는 작지
만, 아주 긴 snake 도 있다.

**snap** [snǽp] 타 자 덥석 물다,
**뚝 부러뜨리다,** 찰깍〔딱〕하고
소리를 내다
snap 은 신속하면서도 갑작스
럽게 소리를 낸다는 의미다 :
우리가 마른 잔가지들을 밟자
**뚝하고 부러졌다.**

**sneak** [sníːk] 자 살금살금 들어
오다〔나가다〕, 서성거리다
sneak 는 은밀하게 움직이거
나 행동한다는 의미다 : 손님들

은 조에게 깜짝 파티를 열어
주려고 그의 집에 **몰래 들어갔
다.**

**sneaker** [sníːkər] 명 운동화
sneaker 는 바닥에 고무를 대
고 윗부분은 천이나 그 밖의
다른 소재를 댄 폭신하고 편안
한 신발이다 : 나는 나가 놀기
전에 sneakers 를 신었다.

**sneeze** [sníːz] 1 자 재채기를
하다 2 명 재채기
sneeze 는 큰소리를 내며 입
과 코로 공기를 뿜어 낸다는
뜻이다 : 나는 감기에 걸리면
항상 **재채기를** 많이 **한다.**

**snow** [snóu] 1 명 눈 2 자 눈이
내리다
1 snow 는 하늘에서 얼어 붙
은 비다 : 어젯밤에 snow가 많
이 내렸다.
2 snow 는 또한 눈이 내린다
는 뜻이다 : 우리는 **눈이 오면**
썰매를 꺼내서 타는 것을 좋아

한다. 어제 하루 종일 **눈이 왔
는데,** 오늘도 여전히 **눈이 내
리고 있다.**

**snowman** [snóumæn] 명 눈사
람
사람 모양으로 만들어진 눈을
snowman 이라고 한다 : 우리
는 세 개의 큰 눈덩이를 서로
포개 놓아 snowman 을 만들
었다.

**so** [sóu] 부 ① 그와 같이, 그렇
게 ② 매우 ③ ···도 (또한) ④
그렇고 말고 ⑤ **그래서**
1 so 는 「아주, 매우」의 뜻이
다 : 어젯밤 날씨가 **너무** 추워
서 호수가 얼었다.
2 so 는 「또한」의 뜻이다 : 나
는 (미식) 축구 경기를 구경가
려고 하는 데, 데이비드 **역시**
그렇다.

**soap** [sóup] 명 비누
soap 를 물과 섞으면 때를 없
애 준다 : 조니는 **비눗**물로 손
을 씻는다.

**soccer** [sákər|sɔ́kə] 몡 축구
soccer 는 길고 넓은 운동상에
서 두 팀이 하는 경기다. 각
팀은 11 명이고, 선수들은 손
이나 팔을 제외한 신체 부위로
둥근 공을 차거나 쳐서 골안에
넣으려고 한다.

**sock** [sák|sɔ́k] 몡 짧은 양말
sock 은 발을 감싸는 부드러운
덮개다. sock 은 신발 안에 신
는다.

**soft** [sɔ́:ft|sɔ́ft] 혱 ① 부드러
운, 폭신한 ; 보들보들한 ② 다
정한, 너그러운 ; 온화한
1 soft 는 감촉이 매끄럽다는
의미다 : 우리집 새끼 고양이는
털이 **부드럽다**.
2 soft 는 딱딱하지 않다는 의
미다 : 리처드는 **폭신한** 베개를
베고 자는 것을 좋아한다.

**soil** [sɔ́iəl] 몡 흙, 토양
soil 은 지면의 맨 윗부분이다.
대부분의 식물은 soil 에서 자
란다.

**sold** [sóuəld] 동 sell (팔다)의
과거 · 과거분사형
sold 는 sell 의 한 형태다 : 마
크의 아버지는 자동차를 판매
하시는 데, 지난 주에 4 대의
자동차를 **파셨다**.

**soldier** [sóuəldʒər] 몡 (육군)
군인 ; 병사

soldier 는 군대의 일원인 사람
이다.

**solid** [sálid|sɔ́l-] 혱 고체의, 단
단한 ; 견고한
solid 는 단단하다는 의미다 :
나무와 강철로 만든 물건은 **견
고하다**.

**some** [《약》 səm, 《강》 sʌ́m] 1
혱 ① 얼마간, 약간의 ; 대체
로, 약 ② 사람〔물건〕에 따라
…(도 있다), 그 중에는 …(도
있다) ③ 무언가의, 누군가의
2 대 다소, 얼마간 ; 어떤 사
람들, 어떤 것
some 은 물건의 일부나 무리
중의 일부를 의미한다 : 나는
저 샌드위치를 **좀** 먹고 싶다.
강아지 중에는 검은 털과 흰
털이 난 **것**도 있었고, 온통 검
은 털만 난 **것**도 있었다.

**somebody** [sʌ́mbàdi, -bədi|
-bədi, -bɔ̀di] 대 **누군가**, 어떤
사람
somebody 는 누군가를 의미한
다 : 우리는 누가 경주에서 우
승했는지 모르지만, 틀림없이
**누군가**가 우승했을 것이다.

**someone** [sʌ́mwʌ̀n] 대 **누군가,**
어떤 사람
someone 은 somebody 를 나
타내는 다른 말이다 : **누군가가**
내가 외출한 사이에 내 방에
있는 라디오를 켰다.

**somersault** [sʌ́mərsɔ̀ːlt] 명
**재주넘기,** 공중제비
somersault 는 두 발이 머리
위로 넘어가도록 몸을 굴린다
는 의미다 : 곡예사는 먼저 앞
으로 somersault 를 한 다음
다시 뒤로 somersault 를 했다.

**something** [sʌ́mθiŋ] 대 **어떤**
**일, 어떤 것,** 무엇인가
something 은 실체를 모르는
어떤 것이다 : 먹을 **것** 좀 주십
시오. 새로 산 라디오의 **어딘**
**가가** 고장나서 우리는 그것을
도로 가게로 가지고 갔다.

**sometimes** [sʌ́mtàimz] 부 **때**
**때로,** 이따금, 간혹
sometimes 는 항상은 아니고
가끔씩이라는 의미다 : 언니는

때때로 내가 자기 옷을 입어도
내버려 둔다.

**somewhere** [sʌ́mʰwɛ̀ər] 부
**어딘가에,** 어디론가 ; 언젠가
somewhere 는 위치를 모르는
어떤 장소를 의미한다 : 나는
웃옷을 학교나 그렇지 않으면
**딴 곳에** 잊고 두고 왔다.

**son** [sʌ́n] 명 **아들**
son 은 어머니와 아버지의 사
내 자식이다. son 은 소년이나
성인 남자일 수 있다 : 아버지
는 너의 조부모님의 son 이다.

**song** [sɔ́ːŋ | sɔ́ŋ] 명 **노래,** (새
등의) 지저귀는 소리
song 은 노랫말이 있는 음악이
다 : 수잔이 피아노를 치고 우
리는 song 을 불렀다.

**soon** [súːn] 부 ① **이윽고,** 머지
않아, 곧 ② **빨리,** 급히
soon 은 「아주 짧은 시간내에」
라는 의미다 : 우리는 시험의
합격 여부를 **곧** 알게 될 것이다.

**sore** [sɔ́ːr] 형 (상처가) **아픈,**
**피부가 까진,** 욱신욱신 쑤시는
sore 는 신체의 한 부분이 아
프다는 의미다 : 나는 계단에서
넘어져 등이 **쑤셨다.**

**sorry** [sɑ́ri, sɔ́ːri | sɔ́ri] 형 ① **유**
**감스러운,** 가엾은, 딱한 ② **미**
**안한,** 죄송한

sorry 는 무언가를 슬퍼한다는 의미나 : 폴은 유리를 깨서 **미안하게 여겼다**. 오늘 나를 찾아 줄 수 없다니 **섭섭하다**.

**sort** [sɔ́:rt] 1 타 **분류하다**, 가려내다 2 명 종류

sort 는 물건을 그룹별로 나누어 놓는다는 의미다 : 아서는 양말을 **분류하여** 한 쪽에는 갈색 양말을, 다른 한 쪽에는 파란 양말을 쌓아 놓았다.

**sound** [sáund] 1 명 소리, 음 2 자타 소리가 나다, 울리다

1 sound 는 들을 수 있는 것이다 : 천둥은 큰 sound 를 낸다. 나는 새들이 창 밖에서 지저귀는 sound 를 좋아한다. 피아노, 트럼펫, 북은 모두 다른 sound 를 내는 악기다.
2 sound 는 또한 말을 할 때 내는 소리다 : 단어 "bat"과 "cat"은 다른 sound 로 시작하지만, 같은 sound 로 끝난다.

**soup** [súːp] 명 수프

soup 는 숟가락으로 먹는 음식이다. soup 는 액체며 보통 뜨겁다 : 토마토 soup 와 닭고기 soup 중 어느 것을 더 좋아하느냐 ?

**sour** [sáuər] 1 형 시큼한, 신 2 명 신맛

sour 는 맛의 일종이다 : 레몬주스는 **신맛**이 난다.

**south** [sáuθ] 1 명 남쪽, 남부 2 형 남쪽의 3 부 남쪽으로, 남쪽에

south 는 방향으로, 지도를 볼 때 아랫 부분이 south 다. 저녁에 태양이 지는 쪽을 마주 바라보고 있다면, 왼쪽이 south 가 된다. south 의 반대말은 north (북쪽)다.

**space** [spéis] 명 ① 공간, 장소 ; 여백, 지면 ② 우주

1 space 는 안에 아무것도 없는 빈 곳이다 : 엄마는 자동차를 주차시킬 space 를 찾았다. 종이 위쪽 space 에 너의 이름을 써라.
2 space 는 또한 모든 행성과 별들이 있는 곳이다 : 지구, 달, 그리고 태양은 space 에 있다.

**spaceship** [spéisʃip] 명 우주선

spaceship 은 우주 비행사와 그들의 장비들을 우주로 실어나른다 : 우주 비행사들은 spaceship 을 타고 달에 갔다. spaceship 안에 있는 카메라가

우주 여행을 하는 동안 사진을 찍었다. spaceship 의 다른 말은 spacecraft 다.

**spaghetti** [spəgéti] 명 스파게티
spaghetti 는 줄처럼 생긴 길고 가는 국수다 : 나는 토마토와 치즈가 들어간 spaghetti 를 즐겨 먹는다.

**speak** [spíːk] 자 타 **이야기하다,** 말하다
speak 는 말한다는 의미다 : 제인은 낸시 아주머니와 전화로 **이야기하려고** 한다.

**special** [spéʃəl] 형 ① **특별한,** 특수한, **각별한** ② 전문의, 전공의
special 은 중요하며 딴 것과는 다르다는 의미다 : 생일은 **특별한** 날이다. 앤디는 **각별한** 내 친구다.

**spell** [spéʃl] 타 (낱말을) **철자하다,** 철자를 말하다〔쓰다〕; …의 철자다
spell 은 단어가 되도록 글자를 짜맞춘다는 의미다 : 네 이름의 **철자를 쓸 줄** 아느냐? 앤은 9

개의 단어는 **철자를** 바르게 **쓰고** 1 개는 틀리게 **썼다.**

**spelling** [spéliŋ] 명 **철자(법) ;** 철자하기
spelling 은 단어의 철자를 쓰는 방법이다 : ketchup 과 catsup 은 같은 말을 나타내는 2 개의 spelling 이다. 우리는 매일 오후 학교에서 spelling 을 배운다.

**spend** [spénd] 타 자 (돈을) **쓰다,** 소비하다 ; 낭비하다, 다 써버리다
spend 는 물건을 사려고 돈을 낸다는 의미다 : 마이크는 책을 사는데 돈을 **쓰는** 경우가 많다. 오늘 아침 그는 6 달러를 **주고** 새 책 3 권을 샀다.

**spent** [spént] 동 spend (돈을 쓰다)의 과거 · 과거분사형
spent 는 spend 의 한 형태다 : 조는 자기 돈을 대부분 장난감을 사는 데 **썼다.**

**spice** [spáis] 명 **양념**
spice 는 특정 식물의 씨앗이나 그 밖의 부분에서 얻으며 음식에 맛을 첨가하는 데 사용

한다 : 후추는 spice 다.

이다. 바다표범이 찬 바닷물 속으로 텀벙 뛰어 들었다.

**spider** [spáidər] 명 거미
spider 는 다리가 8개 있는 아주 작은 동물이다. spider 는 곤충이 아니다. 그러나 spider 는 자신이 친 거미줄로 곤충을 잡는다.

**spill** [spíl] 자 타 엎질러지다, 흘러나오다 ; 흩뜨리다
spill 은 안에 있던 것이 밖으로 나온다는 의미다 : 내가 크레용 상자를 떨어뜨려서, 마루에 온통 크레용이 흩뜨러졌다.

**spin** [spín] 타 자 ① (실을) 잣다 ② (팽이 등을) 돌리다, 회전시키다 ; (차 바퀴가) 헛돌다
spin 은 원을 그리며 돈다는 의미다 : 소년이 팽이를 돌리고 있다.

**splash** [splǽʃ] 타 자 (물 등을) 튀기다, (사람에게) 끼얹다
splash 는 물이나 어떤 다른 액체를 뿌린다는 의미다 : 뒤로 물러서라, 그렇지 않으면 자동차가 너에게 흙탕물을 튀길 것

**spoke** [spóuk] 동 speak (말하다)의 과거형
spoke 는 단어 speak 에서 생긴 말이다 : 나는 전화로 빌리와 이야기했다.

**spoken** [spóukən] 동 speak (말하다)의 과거분사형
spoken 은 단어 speak 에서 생긴 말이다 : 테리는 오늘 많은 사람들과 이야기를 나누었다.

**spoon** [spúːn] 명 숟가락, 스푼
spoon 은 음식을 먹는 도구다. spoon 은 손자루가 달린 작은 사발처럼 생겼다. 사람들은 spoon 으로 수프나 아이스크림을 먹는다.

**sport** [spɔ́ːrt] 명 스포츠, 운동
경기
sport 는 경기의 일종이다. 야
구, 미식 축구, 하키, 테니스,
농구, 축구는 모두 종목이 다
른 sport 다.

**spot** [spát|spɔ́t] 명 ① 반점,
점, 얼룩 ② 장소, 지점, 곳
1 spot 은 주위와 다른 색을
띤 작은 자국이다 : 동물 중에
는 온몸이 spot 으로 뒤덮인
것도 있다.

2 spot 은 또한 장소를 말한
다 : 헨리는 앉기에 아주 좋은
spot 을 찾아냈다.

**spring** [sprín] 명 봄
spring 은 계절이다. spring 은
겨울이 지나고 여름이 되기 전
에 온다. spring 에는 날씨가
점점 따뜻해져서 꽃이 피기 시
작한다.

**spun** [spán] 동 spin (팽이 등을
돌리다)의 과거 · 과거분사형
spun 은 단어 spin 에서 생긴
말이다 : 자동차 바퀴가 진흙탕
에 빠져 헛돌았다.

**square** [skwɛ́ər] 명 정사각형
square 는 모양이다 : square
의 4 변은 모두 길이가 같다.

**squeeze** [skwíːz] 타 자 죄다,
압착하다 ; 짓눌러 찌그러뜨리
다, 짜다
squeeze 는 어떤 것의 측면을
힘껏 밀어 붙인다는 의미다 :
메리는 오렌지즙을 짜냈다.

**squirrel** [skwə́ːrəl|skwír-] 명
다람쥐
squirrel 은 큰 꼬리가 있는 작
은 동물이다. squirrel 은 나무
에서 산다.

**stable** [stéibl] 명 마구간, 가축
우리
stable 은 말과 그 밖의 동물
들을 사육하는 농장 건물이다.

**stage** [stéidʒ] 명 무대, 스테이
지 ; 연단

stage 는 관객이 지켜보는 가운데 사람들이 연기를 하거나 춤을 추거나 노래를 부르는 곳이다 : 관현악단이 학교 stage 에서 연주회를 가졌다.

**stairs** [stέərz] 명 계단, 층계
stairs 는 연속해서 하나로 이어진 발판이다. stairs를 이용해 오르내린다 : 우리는 stairs 를 걸어 올라가 2층으로 갔다.

**stamp** [stǽmp] 명 우표 ; 스탬프, (고무) 인장
stamp 는 우편으로 보내려고 편지 위에 붙이는 작은 종잇조각이다. 우체국에서 stamp 를 산다. 사람들은 간혹 stamp 를 수집한다.

**stand** [stǽnd] 1 자 ① 서다, 서 있다, 일어서다 ② (어떤 곳에) **위치하다** 2 타 **세우다**, 세워놓다
stand 는 몸을 똑바로 해서 모든 체중을 양 발에 싣고 있다는 의미다. 물체는 다리나 바닥을 땅에 대고 **설 수 있다** : 케이트의 책상은 문 옆에 **있다.**

**star** [stɑ́ːr] 명 별 ; 별 모양의 물건
1 star 는 밤하늘에서 볼 수 있는 작고 밝은 불빛이다. star 는 아주 멀리 떨어져 있다. star 가 무리를 지어 하늘에 모양을 만드는 것도 있다.
2 star 는 또한 뽀족한 끝이 5개 또는 그 이상 있는 모양이다 : 미국 국기에는 50 개의 star 가 있다. 내 재킷은 주머니마다 작은 star 들이 그려져 있다.

**stare** [stέər] 자 타 응시하다, 노려보다, 빤히 쳐다보다
stare 는 오랫동안 매섭게 쳐다본다는 의미다 : 잭과 톰은 우스꽝스런 모자를 쓰고 있던 한 남자를 **빤히 쳐다보았다.**

**start** [stɑ́ːrt] 자 타 ① **시작하다** ; 출발하다 ② (기계가) **움직이다**
1 start 는 어떤 것을 하기 시작한다는 의미다 : 린다의 피아노 교습은 4 시에 **시작된다.**
2 start 는 또한 어떤 것을 생기게 하거나 움직이게 한다는 의미다 : 루이스는 배에 올라 엔진 시동을 **걸었다.**

**state** [stéit] 몡 **국가, 나라** ; (미국의) **주**
state 는 나라의 한 지방을 말한다 : 미국은 50 개의 state 가 있다. 미국의 state 는 대부분 다른 state 와 인접해 있지만, 알래스카와 하와이는 다른 state 와 멀리 떨어져 있는 state 다.

**station** [stéiʃən] 몡 ① **정거장, 역** ; **위치, 장소** ② **서(署), 국(局), 부(部)**
station 은 특별한 장소나 건물을 말한다. train station(기차역)은 기차가 정지하는 곳이다. gas station(주유소)은 사람들이 자동차용 휘발유를 사는 곳이다. 텔레비전 쇼는 television station(텔레비전 방송국)에서 내보낸다. 경찰관은 police station(경찰서)에 있다.

**statue** [stætʃuː] 몡 **조상, 소상, 초상**
statue 는 예술의 일종이다. statue 는 대개 사람이나 동물과 모양이 비슷하다. statue 는 돌, 점토, 나무 혹은 금속으로 만들며, 작은 것도 있고

큰 것도 있다.

**stay** [stéi] 쟈 **머무르다, 체재하다** ; **…인 채로 있다**
stay 는 한 곳에 있으며 떠나지 않는다는 의미다 : 보브와 앨버트는 오후에 학교에 남아 다른 몇 명의 아이들과 야구를 했다.

**steady** [stédi] 혭 **확고한, 고정된, 흔들리지 않는** ; **안정된**
steady 는 흔들리지 않는다는 의미다 : 데일이 나무 위의 오두막으로 올라가는 동안 레이는 사다리를 흔들리지 않게 꼭 붙잡았다.

**steak** [stéik] 몡 **스테이크**
steak 는 음식의 일종이다. 대부분의 steak 는 쇠고기로 만든다. steak 는 집 밖의 화롯불이나 오븐에 굽는다.

**steal** [stíːəl] 탸 쟈 **훔치다, 몰래 빼앗다** ; **도둑질하다**
steal 은 자신의 소유물이 아닌 것을 갖는다는 의미다 : 누군가

가 은행에서 돈을 **훔치려고** 했
다.

**steam** [stíːm] 명 증기, 수증기,
스팀
물은 끓으면 steam 으로 변한
다. steam 은 건물 난방이나
엔진을 움직이는 데 이용되는
경우가 많다 : 우리는 주전자에
서 steam 이 나자 스토브를
껐다.

**steel** [stíːəl] 명 강철, 스틸
steel은 금속으로, 철을 녹여
서 만든다. steel은 매우 단단
하고 강하다. steel은 교량과
건물 그리고 그 밖의 다른 것
들을 만드는 데 쓰여진다.

**stem** [stém] 명 (풀·나무의) 줄
기, 대
stem 은 식물에서 잎과 꽃이
달려 있는 부분이다. 양분과
수분이 땅에서 stem 을 타고
올라와 식물의 모든 부분에 전
해진다.

**step** [stép] 1 자 타 걷다, (발
을) 땅에 밟다 2 명 ① 걸음,
걸음거리 ② (계단의) 단, 발

판 ③ [복수로] 계단
1 step 은 한 곳에서 발을 들
어 딴 곳에 내려 놓는다는 의
미다 : 물웅덩이를 **밟지** 않도록
조심하시오.
2 step 은 또한 올라가거나 내
려갈 때 발을 딛는 곳을 의미
한다 : 그는 steps를 뛰어올라
갔다. 우리는 집 앞 steps 에
앉았다.

**stethoscope** [stéθəskòup] 명
청진기
stethoscope 는 의사나 간호사
가 심장 소리를 듣는 데 사용
하는 기구다.

**stew** [stjúː] 명 스튜 (요리)
stew 는 고기와 야채 혹은 생
선과 야채를 한 냄비에 같이
넣고 끓인 요리다.

**stick**[1] [stík] 명 막대기, 나무토
막 ; **지팡이**, 단장
stick 은 길고 가느다란 나뭇조
각이다 : 내가 stick 을 던지자,
개가 그것을 쫓아갔다.

**stick²** [stík] 1 [타] 찌르다 ; 붙이다 2 [자] ① 찔리다 ; 달라붙다 ② [보통 수동태로] 움직이지 못하게 하다

1 stick 은 예리한 물건으로 쑤셔 넣는다는 의미다 : 핀으로 풍선을 **찌르면**, 풍선이 펑 터질 것이다.

2 stick 은 또한 무언가의 위에 머물러 있게 한다는 의미다 : 조지는 봉투에 우표를 **붙였다.**

**still** [stíl] 1 [부] ① 아직도, **여전히** ② 그럼에도, …하지만 ③ [비교급과 함께] 더욱, 더 한층 2 [형] **조용한**, 소리없는 ; 정지한

1 still 은 어떤 것이 멈추지 않았다는 의미다 : 언니는 어제 내게 화를 냈다. 그녀는 오늘도 **여전히** 내게 화가 나 있다.

2 still 은 또한 움직이지 않는다는 의미다 : 바람 한 점 불지 않을 때는 수면이 아주 **잔잔하다.**

**sting** [stíŋ] 1 [명] **찌르기, 쏘기 ; 찔린 상처** ; (벌의) 침 2 [타] [자] **찌르다, 쏘다**

sting 은 곤충에게 물린 작은 상처다 : 벌에게 **쏘여** 발이 아프다.

**stir** [stə́ːr] [타] [자] **휘젓다, 뒤섞다** ; 움직이다

stir 는 숟가락이나 막대기로 휘저어 섞는다는 의미다 : 페인트를 사용하기 전에 잘 **섞어라.** 나는 수프에 우유를 넣고 **저었다.**

**stole** [stóuəl] [동] steal (훔치다) 의 과거형

stole 은 단어 steal 에서 생긴 말이다 : 고양이가 조리대에서 생선 한 토막을 **훔쳤다.**

**stolen** [stóulən] [동] steal (훔치다) 의 과거분사형

stolen 은 단어 steal 에서 생긴 말이다 : 작년에 도서관에서 책을 몇권 **도난당했다.**

**stomach** [stʌ́mək] [명] **위 ; 배, 복부**

stomach 는 신체의 일부다. 우리가 먹은 음식은 stomach 로 들어간다.

S

**stone** [stóun] 명 돌, 돌멩이
stone 은 작은 바윗조각이다. 반질반질한 stone 은 바닷가와 호숫가 그리고 강가에 있다.

**stood** [stúd] 동 stand (서다)의 과거·과거분사형
stood 는 단어 stand 에서 생긴 말이다 : 대통령이 방으로 걸어 들어오자 모든 사람들이 **일어섰다.**

**stool** [stú:əl] 명 (등받이가 없는) 의자
stool 은 자리의 일종이다. stool 은 등받이와 팔걸이가 없다 : 저 피아노 연주자는 긴 의자 대신 stool 에 앉아 있다.

**stop** [stáp|stɔ́p] 자 타 멈춰서다 ; 멈추다
stop 은 움직이지 않는다는 의미다 : 버스는 사람들이 타고 내릴 수 있도록 여러 장소에 **멈춰선다.**

**stoplight** [stáplàit] 명 (교통의) 정지신호, (자동차 후미의) 정지등

stoplight 는 traffic light (교통신호등)의 다른 말이다.

**store** [stɔ́:r] 1 명 가게, 상점 ; 저장, 저축 2 타 저장하다, 저축하다
1 store 는 물건을 사는 곳이다 : 우리는 신발 store 에 가서, 내 새 신발을 한 켤레 샀다.
2 store 는 또한 나중에 쓸 수 있도록 무언가를 따로 남겨둔다는 의미다 : 다람쥐들은 겨울 동안에 먹으려고 가을에 먹이를 **저장해 두었다.**

**storm** [stɔ́:rm] 명 폭풍, 폭풍우 ; 모진 비바람
storm 은 강한 바람이다. storm 이 불면 대개 비나 눈이 온다. 또한 많은 storm 이 천둥과 번개를 동반한다.

**story** [stɔ́:ri] 명 이야기
story 는 사람이나 지역에 어떤 일이 일어났는지를 알려주는 말이다. story 는 사실인 것도 있고 꾸며낸 것 일 수도 있다.

**stove** [stóuv] 명 스토브, 난로
stove 는 음식을 요리하는 데

사용하는 것이다. stove 는 가
열시키기 위해 전기나 가스 혹
은 장작을 사용한다.

**straight** [stréit] 형 ① 곧은,
똑바른, 일직선의, 수직의 ②
(머리카락이) **곱슬곱슬하지 않
은**
straight 는 한 쪽으로 휘거나
구부러지지 않았다는 의미다 :
아빠는 벽에 사진이 **똑바로** 걸
렸는지 확인했다. 책상에 **똑바
로** 좀 앉도록 해라. 이 길을
따라 **곧장** 가시오.

**strange** [stréindʒ] 형 **이상한,**
기묘한 ; 낯선, 생소한
strange 는 예상한 것과 아주
다르다는 의미다 : 부엌에서 **이
상한** 냄새가 났다. 조지프는
빨간 귀가 있는 **이상한** 동물을
그렸다.

**stranger** [stréindʒər] 명 **모르
는 사람, 낯선 사람**
stranger 는 모르는 사람이다 :
그는 전혀 **모르는** 사람이다.

**straw** [strɔ́:] 명 (음료용의) **스
트로, 빨대** ; 짚, 밀짚
1 straw 는 음료를 마시는 가
느다란 관으로, 종이나 플라스
틱으로 되어 있다 : 톰은 straw

로 우유를 마신다.
2 straw 는 또한 몇몇 식물의
마른 줄기다 : 우리집 조랑말은
헛 간 의    straw 에 서    잔다.
straw 로 만든 비도 있다.

**strawberry** [strɔ́:bèri | -bəri] 명
**딸기**
strawberry 는 작은 씨들이 붙
어 있는 작고 빨간 과일이다 :
나는 토스트에 strawberry 젤
리를 얹어 먹는 것을 좋아한
다.

**stream** [strí:m] 명 **시내**
stream 은   좁은   물길이다.
stream 은 한 방향으로 흐르
며, 강 만큼 크지 않다.

**street** [strí:t] 명 **거리,** 가로
street 는 도시나 시내에 나 있
는 길이다. 대도시에는 street
가 많다.

**stretch** [strétʃ] 자 타 **늘어나다,**
잡아 당기다 ; (손발 등을)펴
다, 내밀다
stretch 는 잡아 당겨서 모양을
변화시킨다는   의미다 : 고무와
몇몇 종류의 플라스틱은 쉽게
**늘어난다.**

**strike** [stráik] 〔타〕〔자〕 ① 치다 ;
부딪치다 ② (성냥을) 켜다
strike 는 무언가를 친다는 의
미다 : 내 장난감 비행기가 나
무 줄기에 **부딪쳤지만**, 부서지
지 않았다.

**string** [stríŋ] 〔명〕 끈, 줄, 실 ;
(악기의) 현
string 은 물건을 매는 데 사용
한다. string 은 길고 질긴 식
물이나 특수한 종류의 플라스
틱으로 만든다. string 은 크기
와 색이 다양하다. 밧줄은 많
은 string 을 한 데 꼬아서 만
든다.

**string bean** [striŋ bíːn] 〔명〕 꼬
투리째 먹는 콩
string bean 은 야채의 일종이
다 : string bean 은 길고 초록
색이며, 관목에서 자란다.

**strip** [stríp] 〔명〕 (천·판자 등의)
한 조각 ; **길고 가느다란 조각**
strip 은 길고 가느다란 조각이
다 : 그들은 종이를 여러가지
길이의 strip 으로 찢었다.

**stripe** [stráip] 〔명〕 줄무늬, 줄
stripe 는 옆의 것과 색이 다른
긴 줄무늬다 : 호랑이와 얼룩말
은 stripe 가 있다.

**strong** [strɔ́ːŋ|strɔ́ŋ] 〔형〕 **강한,**
힘센 ; (천 등이) **질긴, 견고한**
1 strong 은 힘이 세다는 의미
다 : 올리버는 짐이 가득찬 여
행 가방 두 개를 들 수 있을
정도로 **힘이 세다.**
2 strong 은 또한 부수기 어렵
다는 의미다 : 강철로 만든 물
건들은 매우 **견고하다.**

**struck** [strʌ́k] 〔동〕 strike(치다)
의 과거·과거분사형
struck 은 단어 strike 에서 생
긴 말이다 : 나무가 번개에 **맞
아** 상했다.

**stuck** [stʌ́k] 〔동〕 stick² (움직이
지 못하게 하다)의 과거·과거
분사형
stuck 은 단어 stick² 에서 생

긴 말이다 : 우리 자동차가 진
창에 빠져 **꼼짝 못했다.**

**student** [stjú:dənt] 명 학생
student 는 배우려고 학교에
다니는 사람이다 : student 는
수업시간에 선생님께 배운다.

**study** [stʌ́di] 1 타 자 **공부하다,**
배우다, 연구하다 2 명 공부,
연구
study 는 무언가를 배우려고
몹시 애쓴다는 뜻이다 : 마리아
는 발레를 **배운다.** 해리는 고
래에 관한 책을 **연구해서** 그것
들에 관한 이야기를 썼다. 우
리반은 행성을 **연구하고 있다.**

**stuff** [stʌ́f] 타 **채우다,** 채워넣다
stuff 는 물건을 꽉 채운다는
뜻이다 : 우리는 여행 가방 하
나에 우리 옷을 전부 **넣었다.**
제니는 자기 배낭에 책과 재킷
을 **채워 넣었다.**

**stung** [stʌ́ŋ] 동 sting (찌르다)
의 과거·과거분사형
stung 은 단어 sting 에서 생긴
말이다 : 벌이 내 팔을 **쏘아서**
아팠다. 조랑말이 벌에 **쏘였**
**다.**

**submarine** [sʌ́bmərìːn, ⌐⌐⌐]
명 잠수함
submarine 은 물 속으로 다닐
수 있는 배다.

**subtract** [səbtrǽkt] 타 **빼다,**
공제하다
subtract 는 어떤 수에서 다른
수를 **뺀다**는 뜻이다. 9 에서 4
를 **빼면** 5 가 된다. 「**뺀다**」는
기호는 ― 다 : 9−4＝5.

**subway** [sʌ́bwèi] 명 **지하철**
subway 는 지하로 나 있는 도
시의 철도다 : 많은 사람들이
subway 를 타고 출근한다.

**such** [《약》 sətʃ, 《강》 sʌ́tʃ] 형
① [형용사를 수반하여] 그 만
큼, 이 만큼 ; 그렇게, 이렇
게 ; 매우, 대단히 ② 그러한,
이러한
such 는 「굉장히, 매우」의 뜻
이다 : 파티는 **아주** 즐거웠어 !

**sudden** [sʌ́dən] 형 **돌연한,** 불
시의, 갑작스러운
sudden 은 아무도 예상하지
못하게 순식간에 일어난다는
뜻이다 : 우리는 **갑작스러운** 폭

풍에 놀랐다.

**suddenly** [sΛ́dənli] 부 **갑자기,** 불시에, 느닷없이
suddenly 는 아주 빠르다는 뜻이다 : 우리가 소풍에서 즐거운 시간을 보내고 있을 때, **갑자기** 비가 오기 시작했다.

**suds** [sΛ́dz] 명 **비누거품,** 비눗물
suds 는 비눗물에 생기는 수많은 작은 거품들을 말한다 : 토니는 세차할 때 suds 를 많이 내는 것을 좋아한다.

**sugar** [ʃúgər] 명 **설탕**
sugar 는 단맛을 내려고 음식에 넣는 것이다. sugar 는 흰 것도 있고 갈색인 것도 있다. 사탕에는 sugar 가 많이 있다.

**suit** [súːt|sjúːt] 명 **(의복의) 한 벌, 한 벌의 옷**
suit 는 걸맞는 한 벌의 옷을 말한다. 같은 천으로 만든 재킷과 바지 혹은 재킷과 셔츠가 suit 다 : 많은 남녀가 suit 를 입고 출근한다.

**suitcase** [súːtkèis|sjúːt-] 명 **여행 가방,** 슈트케이스
suitcase 는 여행할 때 옷을 넣어 가지고 다니는 일종의 상자다. 모든 suitcase 에는 손잡이가 있고, 작은 바퀴가 달린 것도 많다.

**sum** [sΛ́m] 명 **합계,** 총계, 총액
sum 은 두 수를 더할 때 얻게 되는 수다 : 2 와 3 의 sum 은 5 다. 이것을 다르게 쓰면 2+3=5 다.

**summer** [sΛ́mər] 명 **여름**
summer 는 계절이다. summer 는 봄이 지나고 가을이 되기 전에 온다. summer 에는 날씨가 무더운 경우가 많다 : 많은 학교가 summer 에 방학을 한다.

**sun** [sΛ́n] 명 **태양,** 해 ; 햇빛, 햇볕
sun 은 별이다. 우리는 낮에 하늘에서 sun 을 볼 수 있다. sun 은 우리에게 빛을 주며 우리를 따뜻하게 해준다.

**sunburn** [sΛ́nbə̀ːrn] 명 **햇볕에**

탐
sunburn 은 햇볕에 피부가 상
해 불그스름하게 된다는 의미
다 : 수는 **햇볕에 타지** 않으려
고 그늘에서 놀았다.

**Sunday** [sʌ́ndei, -di] 몡 **일요일**
Sunday 는 일주일 가운데 하
루다. Sunday 는 토요일이 지
나고 월요일이 되기 전에 온
다.

**sung** [sʌ́ŋ] 뙹 sing (노래부르다)
의 과거분사형
sung 은 단어 sing 에서 생긴
말이다 : 학교 합창단은 음악제
에서 여러번 **노래를 불렀다.**

**sunk** [sʌ́ŋk] 뙹 sink (가라앉았다)
의 과거·과거분사형
sunk 는 단어 sink 에서 생긴
말이다 : 그 낡은 배는 태풍으
로 **침몰했다.**

**sunlight** [sʌ́nlàit] 몡 **햇빛**
sunlight 는 태양에서 나는 빛
이다. sunlight 는 식물과 동물
에게 유익하다.

**sunrise** [sʌ́nràiz] 몡 **해돋이,
일출 ; 동틀녘**
sunrise 는 태양이 뜨는 때다.
아침마다 해가 뜨지만, 구름이
너무 많이 끼면 sunrise 를 볼
수 없다.

**sunset** [sʌ́nsèt] 몡 **일몰 ; 해질
녘, 저녁놀**
sunset 은 태양이 지는 때다 :
많은 사람들이 밖에 나가 아름
다운 sunset 을 구경하는 것을
좋아한다.

**supermarket** [súːpərmàːrkit |
sjúː-] 몡 **슈퍼마켓**
supermarket 은 식품과 그 밖
에 비누나 종이, 수건 같은 물
건들을 파는 큰 상점이다.

**supper** [sʌ́pər] 몡 **저녁식사**
supper 는 식사다. 사람들은
저녁에 supper 를 먹는다.

**suppose** [səpóuz] 탸 **추측하다,
상상하다 ; …라고 생각하다**
suppose 는 확실하게 알지 못
할 때 예상을 한다는 의미다 :
5 명의 학생이 지각을 했을
때, 우리는 통학 버스가 고장

이 났기 때문이라고 **생각했다.**

**sure** [ʃúər | ʃɔ́ː, ʃúə] 1 형 ① 틀림없는, 확실한 ; 확신하고 있는 ② 꼭〔반드시〕…하는 2 부 확실히, 꼭
sure 는 생각하고 있는 것이 사실임을 알고 있다는 의미다 : 나는 네가 우리 학교 도서관에서 파충류에 관한 자료를 얻을 수 있을 거라고 **확신한다.**

**surface** [sə́ːrfis] 명 표면, 외부 ; 외관, 겉보기
surface 는 사물의 바깥면이나 윗부분이다 : 배들은 바다의 surface 를 항해한다. 거울의 surface 는 매끄럽다.

**surprise** [sərpráiz] 1 명 놀람 ; 놀라운 일〔것〕, 뜻밖의 일〔것〕 2 타 (깜짝) **놀라게 하다**
1 surprise 는 예상하지 못했던 일이다 : 우리는 오늘 날씨가 화창할 것으로 생각했는 데,

비가 오기 시작해서 **놀랐다.**
2 surprise 는 사람들이 예상하지 못했던 일을 한다는 의미다 : 조의 친구들이 그의 생일에 파티를 열어 주어 그를 **깜짝 놀라게 했다.**

**swallow** [swálou | swɔ́l-] 타 삼키다, 들이켜다
swallow 는 음식을 입에서 위로 넘긴다는 의미다 : 바트의 어머니는 그에게 음식을 씹은 다음에 **삼키라고** 말했다.

**swam** [swǽm] 동 swim (수영하다)의 과거형
swam 은 단어 swim 에서 생긴 말이다 : 우리는 오전 내내 풀장에서 **수영을 했다.**

**swamp** [swámp, swɔ́ːmp | swɔ́mp] 명 늪, 저습 지대, 수렁
swamp 는 땅이 무르고 물이 고여 있는 지역이다. 개구리, 모기, 뱀 그리고 악어는 swamp 에서 산다.

**swan** [swán, swɔ́ːn | swɔ́n] 명 백조
swan 은 물에 사는 큰 새다.

swan 은 목이 길다. 흰 깃털
이 있는 swan 이 많다.

**sweater** [swétər] 명 스웨터
sweater 는 옷의 일종이다. 사
람들은 셔츠 위에 sweater 를
입는다. sweater 는 모직이나
면으로 만드는 경우가 많다.

**sweep** [swíːp] 타 자 청소하다,
쓸다, 털다
sweep 는 비나 솔로 깨끗이
한다는 의미다 : 브라운 부인은
매일 그녀의 가게 앞 보도를
**쓴다.**

**sweet** [swíːt] 1 형 단, 달콤한
2 명 단 맛, 단 것
sweet 는 맛의 일종이다. 설
탕, 사탕, 케이크 그리고 쿠키
는 맛이 **달다.**

**swept** [swépt] 동 sweep (청소
하다)의 과거·과거분사형
swept 는 단어 sweep 에서 생
긴 말이다 : 형이 부엌 바닥을
**청소했다.**

**swim** [swím] 1 자 수영하다, 헤

엄치다 2 명 수영, 헤엄
swim 은 물 속에서 움직인다
는 의미다. 사람들은 팔과 다
리를 써서 **수영을 한다** : 우리
는 올 여름에 호수에서 **수영을**
**하려고 한다.** 오리들이 연못에
서 **헤엄을 쳤다.**

**swing** [swíŋ] 1 타 자 흔들다 ;
빙돌리다, **휘두르다** ; 매달다
2 명 휘두르기, 진동 ; 그네
1 swing 은 어떤 것의 한 쪽
끝을 잡고, 한 쪽에서 다른 쪽
으로 돌린다는 의미다 : 티나는
공을 치려고 배트를 **휘두른다.**
2 swing 은 밧줄이나 쇠사슬에
달려 있는 좌석이다 : 아이들은
공원이나 운동장 혹은 자기집
뜰에서 swing 을 타고 **논다.**

**swum** [swʌ́m] 동 swim (수영하
다)의 과거분사형
swum 은 swim 의 한 형태다 :
피터는 오전 내내 수영을 하고
있다. 그는 약 1마일은 **수영**
**을 했을** 것임에 틀림없다.

**swung** [swʌ́ŋ] 동 swing (휘두
르다)의 과거·과거분사형
swung 은 swing 의 한 형태
다 : 리처드는 배트를 **휘둘러**

공을 쳤다.

**symbol** [símbəl] 명 상징, 심
벌 ; **기호, 부호**
symbol 은 무언가를 의미하는
표시나 기호다. 알파벳 문자는
음을 나타내는 symbol 이다.

**synagogue** [sínəgɑ̀g|-gɔ̀g] 명
(예배를 위한) 유태인 집회,
유태교 회당
synagogue 는 유대인들이 기
도와 찬송 그리고 공부를 하러
가는 건물이다.

**syrup** [sírəp, sə́ːr-|sír-] 명 시럽
syrup 은 걸쭉하고 단맛이 나
는 액체다. syrup 은 설탕이나
몇몇 식물에서 나는 즙으로 만
든다.

S

**table** [téibl] 명 테이블, 식탁, 탁자

　table 은 가구의 일종으로, 위가 평평하고 다리가 4 개다. 사람들은 table 에 앉아 음식을 먹는다.

**tadpole** [tǽdpòuəl] 명 올챙이

　tadpole 은 개구리 새끼다. tadpole 은 알에서 부화되며, 아주 작고 꼬리가 있다. 검은 tadpole도 있고, 투명한 tadpole도 있다.

**tag** [tǽg] 명 술래잡기

　tag 는 놀이를 하는 사람 가운데 한 명이 "술래"가 되는 놀이다. "술래"인 사람은 누군가를 잡을 때까지 다른 사람들을 쫓아다닌다. 그래서 잡힌 사람은 "(새) 술래"가 된다.

**tail** [téiəl] 명 (동물의) 꼬리

　tail 은 동물의 꽁무니에 내민 부분이다. 고양이, 개, 물고기는 tail 이 있다.

**take** [téik] 타 ① (손으로) 잡다, (움켜) 쥐다 ② 받다 ; 벌다 ; 사다 ③ 가지고 가다 ; 데리고 가다 ④ 타다 ; 먹다, 마시다 ⑤ …이 걸리다 ; (…이라고) 생각하다, 간주하다 ⑥ (사진을) 찍다 ; (질병에) 걸리다 ; (마음을) 끌다

1 take 는 데리고[가지고] 간다는 뜻이다 : 오늘 오후에 아빠가 우리를 영화관에 **데려갈** 것이다. 우리는 소풍에 치즈 샌드위치를 **가지고 간다.** 우산을 **가지고 가거라.**

2 take 는 또한 어떤 것을 잡는다는 뜻이다 : 책상에서 책을 **치워라.**

3 take 는 또한 어떤 것을 타

거나 이용한다는 뜻이다 : 우리
는 버스를 **타고** 학교에 간다.
4 take 는 어떤 것을 하거나
배운다는 뜻이기도 하다 : 앤은
야영장에서 친구들의 사진을
**찍어 주었다.** 마리아는 컴퓨터
수업을 **받고** 있다.

**taken** [téikən] 동 take (잡다,
(사진을) 찍다)의 과거분사형
taken 은 take 의 한 형태다 :
다이애나가 오빠의 사진을 두
장 **찍었을** 때 "한 장만 더 찍
어 줘 ! "라고 오빠가 말했다.

**tale** [téiəl] 명 **이야기**, 설화
tale 은 이야기다 : 조는 해상
생활에 관한 tale 을 듣기를 좋
아한다.

**talk** [tɔ́ːk] 타 자 **말하다 ; 이야기**
**하다**
talk는 누군가와 이야기한다는
뜻이다 : 카를로스와 톰은 소풍
에 관해서 **이야기했다.**

**tall** [tɔ́ːl] 형 **키가 큰** ; 높이 [키]
가 …인 ; 긴
tall 은 땅 위에 높이 서있다는
뜻이다 : 대도시에는 **고층** 건물
이 많다.

**tame** [téim] 형 **길든**, 길러서
길들인 ; 온순한
tame 은 사람들이 원하는 대
로 한다는 뜻이다 : **길들여진**
동물들은 좋은 애완 동물이 된
다.

**tap** [tǽp] 타 **가볍게 두드리다**
〔치다〕, 똑똑 두드리다
tap 은 가볍게 친다는 뜻이
다 : 선생님은 우리의 주의를
끌기 위해 책상을 **가볍게 두드**
**리셨다.**

**tape** [téip] 명 (납작한) **끈** ;
(접착용) **테이프 ; 녹음 테이**
**프 ; 비디오 테이프**
1 tape 는 플라스틱・천・금속
으로 된 길고 가느다란 조각이
다. 접착제가 있어서 물건을
붙이는 데 쓰는 tape 도 있
다 : 제인은 tape 로 책의 찢어
진 면을 맞추어 붙였다.
2 tape 는 또한 음악이나 화상
이 담긴 길고 가느다란 플라스
틱이다. 사람들은 기계를 이용
하여 이러한 종류의 tape를
듣거나 본다.

**taste** [téist] 1 명 **미각 ; 맛 ; 맛**
**봄 ; 기호, 취미** 2 타 자 **맛보**

다 ; 시식하다 ; 맛을 알다

1 taste 는 음식을 입에 넣었을 때 그 음식의 맛을 알려준다 : 레몬은 신 taste가 나고, 설탕은 단 taste가 난다.

2 taste 는 또한 어떤지 알아 보려고 음식을 입에 넣는다는 뜻이다 : 수프의 **맛을 봐도** 될까요 ? 수잔은 푸딩이 다 되었는지 알아 보려고 **맛을 보고** 있다. 배리는 자기가 아버지와 함께 만든 생선 요리를 **맛보았다.**

**taught**[tɔ́:t] 동 teach (가르치다)의 과거 · 과거분사형

taught 는 단어 teach 에서 생긴 말이다 : 프랭크 아저씨는 지난 여름에 내 사촌과 나에게 수영하는 법을 **가르쳐 주셨다.**

**taxi**[tǽksi] 명 택시

taxi 는 요금을 내고 타는 자동차다 : 우리는 taxi 를 타고 공항에 갔다. taxi 의 다른 말은 cab 이다.

**teach**[tí:tʃ] 타 **가르치다,** 교수하다 ; 훈련시키다 ; 길들이다

teach 는 무언가를 배울 수 있도록 도와준다는 뜻이다 : 이웃 사람이 내게 새 카메라의 사용법을 **가르쳐** 줄 것이다. 나는 우리집 개에게 새로운 재주를 **가르치고** 있다.

**teacher**[tí:tʃər] 명 가르치는 사람, **선생님,** 교사

teacher 는 배울 수 있도록 도와주는 사람이다 : 그린 양은 2학년 teacher 다.

**team**[tí:m] 명 **팀,** 조

team 은 같이 일을 하거나 경기를 하는 일단의 사람들이다. team의 인원수는 각기 다를 수 있다. 많은 스포츠가 두 team 이 서로를 상대로 하여 시합을 한다.

**tear**[1][téər] 타 자 **찢다, 찢어지다** ; 째다, 째지다

tear 는 잡아 찢는다는 뜻이다. tear 는 hair 와 같은 소리가 난다 : 미술 선생님은 우리에게 종이를 반으로 **찢으라고** 말씀하셨다. 해리는 주의를 하지 않아서 바지가 못에 걸려

T

찢어졌다.

**tear²** [tíər] 명 [보통 복수로]
눈물
tear 는 울 때 눈에서 나오는
물방울이다. tear 는 hear 와
같은 소리가 난다 : 레이는 아
기의 얼굴에 흐르는 tears 를
닦아주었다. 메리는 너무 많이
웃어서 tears 가 나왔다.

**tease** [tíːz] 타 못살게 굴다, **괴
롭히다** ; **놀리다**, 조롱하다
tease 는 사람들을 괴롭히거나
조롱한다는 뜻이다 : 클레어가
공을 놓치자 상대팀 선수들이
그녀를 **놀려댔다**. 그들이 그녀
를 **놀린** 것은 비열한 짓이었
다.

**teddy bear** [tédi bɛər] 명 장
난감 곰
teddy bear 는 장난감의 일종
으로, 촉감이 부드럽고 갈색이
다. teddy bear 는 큰 것도 있
고 작은 것도 있다

**teeth** [tíːθ] 명 tooth 의 복수형

teeth 는 단어 tooth 에서 생긴
말이다 : 아기에게 두 개의 새
teeth 가 났다. 빌리는 teeth에
치열 교정기를 씌우려고 한다.

**telephone** [téləfòun] 명 전화 ;
전화기
telephone 은 멀리 떨어져 있
는 사람과 이야기할 때 이용한
다. telephone 에는 목소리를
전달하는 전선이 있다 : 나는
친구와 telephone 으로 이야기
하는 것을 좋아한다. phone
은 telephone 을 줄인 말이다.

**telescope** [téləskòup] 명 망원
경
telescope 는 멀리 떨어져 있
는 것을 더 크고 더 가깝게 보
이게 하는 기구다 : telescope
로 보자, 우리가 이전에 보지
못했던 별과 행성들을 볼 수
있었다.

**television** [téləvìʒən] 명 텔레
비전 ; 텔레비전 수상기
television 은 소리와 함께 화
상을 보여준다. 사람들은
television 으로 뉴스나 다른
프로그램을 본다. TV 는 tele-

vision 을 줄인 말이다.

**tell** [tél] 타 자 ① **말하다, 이야기하다** ② 가르쳐주다 ③ 명령하다 ④ **알다**, 이해하다
1 tell 은 어떤 것에 관하여 이야기한다는 뜻이다 : 보브는 마술을 부린 다음, 친구들에게 어떻게 마술을 부렸는지 **가르쳐 주었다.**
2 tell 은 또한 안다는 뜻이다 : 수잔은 낮이 점점 짧아지는 것으로 겨울이 다가오고 있음을 **알 수 있다.**

**temperature** [témpərətʃər] 명 **온도 ; 기온 ; 체온**
temperature 는 덥거나 찬 정도를 알려준다 : 바깥 temperature 가 너무 차서 물웅덩이가 얼었다. 의사는 내게 열이 있는 지 알아 보려고 체온계로 내 temperature 를 쟀다.

**temple** [témpl] 명 신전, 사원, 절 ; 교회당
temple 은 사람들이 노래로 찬양을 하거나 기도를 하러 가는 건물이다.

**ten** [tén] 1 명 **10**, 10 개, 10 명 2 형 **10 의**, 10 개의
ten 은 9 보다 하나 더 큰 수다. ten 은 **10** 이라고 쓴다 : 9+1 = **10.**

**tennis** [ténis] 명 **테니스**
tennis 는 두 명이나 네 명이 하는 경기다. 사람들은 tennis 를 할 때, 네트 위로 공을 쳐서 서로 상대방에게 보낸다 : 내 여동생은 학교 tennis 팀의 선수다. 우리는 일과 후에 tennis를 쳤다.

**tent** [tént] 명 **텐트, 천막**
tent 는 야영할 때 잠을 자는 곳으로, 천으로 되어 있다 : 서커스는 대형 tent 안에서 펼쳐졌다.

**tepee, tee-** [tí:pi:] 명 **티피**
tepee 는 원뿔꼴의 텐트다. tepee 는 장대 위에 동물 가죽을 펴서 만든다 : 옛날에 아메리칸 인디언들은 tepee 에서

살았다.

**terrible** [térəbl] 형 ① 무서운, 겁나는 ; 굉장한 ② **지독한** ; 서투른 ; 심한

1 terrible 은 두려움을 느끼게 한다는 뜻이다 : 천둥 소리가 **굉장했다.**

2 terrible 은 또한 아주 나쁘다는 뜻이다 : 휴가 동안에 날씨가 **몹시 나빴다.** 매일 비가 왔다. 저 새로 생긴 레스토랑의 음식은 **맛이 형편없었다.**

**test** [tést] 명 시험, 검사, 테스트

test 는 얼마나 알고 있는 가를 보여준다. test 에는 답해야 할 질문이 있고, 풀어야 할 문제가 있다 : 나는 오늘 철자법 test 에서 두 단어의 철자를 잘못 썼다.

**than** [《약》 ðən, 《강》 ðǽn] 접 …보다 ; …할 바에는 (차라리) 사물이 서로 어떻게 다른 가를 말할 때 than 을 쓴다 : 어미 고양이는 새끼 고양이들**보다** 더 크다. 1시간은 1분**보다** 훨씬 더 길다. 나는 내 동생**보다**

2인치 더 크다.

**thank** [θǽŋk] 타 …에게 **감사하다** ; …에게 고맙다고 하다

thank 는 자신을 위해 무언가를 해주었거나 무언가를 준 사람에게 기쁜 마음을 말로 표현한다는 뜻이다 : 앨리스는 그녀의 친구들에게 생일 선물을 줘서 **고맙다고 말했다.**

**Thanksgiving** [θæ̀ŋksgíviŋ, ーー-] 명 추수감사절

Thanksgiving 은 11 월의 네번째 목요일에 거행하는 축제일이다. 많은 사람들은 Thanksgiving 에 저녁 식사로 칠면조 고기를 먹으며, 자신들의 물질적 소유에 대해 감사해 한다.

**that** [ðǽt] 1 형 그, 저, 저쪽의, 그쪽의 2 대 그것, 저것, 그 일〔사람〕 3 부 그만큼, 그렇게 4 접 [ðət] …라는 것은, …라는 것을

1 that 은 가까이 있지 않은 것을 뜻한다 : 거리에 차가 두 대 보이는 데, 가까이 있는 이 차는 파란색이고, 멀리 떨어져 있는 나머지 **저** 차는 빨간색이

다.

2 that 은 문장 속의 두 요소를 결합시킬 때 사용한다 : 마 거릿은 엄마에게 새 드레스를 사고 싶다고 말했다.

**the** [《약》 (자음 앞) ðə, (모음 앞) ði, 《강》 ðíː] 관 **그**《번역 하지 않는 경우가 많음》

어떤 특정한 사람이나 물건 혹은 집단에 관해 말할 때 the 를 쓴다 : 빨간 드레스를 입고 있는 **여자분**이 나의 어머니다. **문** 좀 닫아 주십시오. **태양**은 아주 밝게 빛난다.

**theater｜theatre** [θíːətər | θíə-] 명 **극장**

theater 는 영화나 연극을 보러 갈 수 있는 곳이다 : 우리 가족 은 theater 에서 새로 공연되는 연극을 즐겨 본다.

**their** [《약》 ðər, 《강》 ðέər] 대 [they의 소유격] **그들의, 그 것들의**

their 는 다른 사람에게 속한 것을 뜻한다 : **그들의** 개는 흰색

이고, 우리 개는 갈색이다. 우 리 차는 밖에 있고, **그들의** 차 는 차고에 있다.

**theirs** [ðέərz] 대 [they의 소유 대명사] **그들〔그것들〕의 것**

theirs 는 그들의 소유물을 뜻 한다 : 학생들은 모두 어항에 넣을 물고기를 샀다. 그 물고 기는 **그들의 것**이다.

**them** [《약》 ðəm, 《강》 ðém] 대 **그들〔그것들〕을〔에게〕**

them 은 둘 이상이라는 뜻이 다 : 낸시의 집마당에는 새가 몇 마리 있다. 그녀는 **그들**에 게 먹이로 씨앗과 빵을 준다.

**themselves** [ðəmsélvz] 대 [they의 재귀 대명사] **그들 〔그것들〕 자신(이)**

themselves 는 다른 사람이 아 닌 바로 그들 자신을 뜻한다 : 아기들은 **그들 스스로** 옷을 입 을 수 없기 때문에 입혀주어야 만 한다.

**then** [ðén] 부 **그 때(는), 그 당 시(는) ; 그리고 나서**

1 then 은 「그때에」란 뜻이 다 : 지금은 날씨가 춥지만, 지 난 여름에는 춥지 않았다. **그 때는** 날씨가 따뜻했다.

2 then 은 「다음에」란 뜻이 다 : 폴은 썰매를 끌고 언덕을 올라갔다. **그리고 나서** 다시

타고 내려왔다.

**there** [《약》ðər, 《강》ðέər] 부
저기에, 그곳에, **거기에**
1 there 는 「그곳에」란 뜻이
다 : "이 통나무들을 어디에 둘
까요 ? "라고 데일이 아버지에
게 묻자 아버지는 벽난로를 가
리키며 "저기에 내려 놓아라. "
라고 대답하셨다.
2 there is나 there are 는 무
언가가 있다는 뜻이다 : "뒤뜰
에 닭 한 마리가 **있어 ! "**라고
스티브가 외쳤다.

**thermometer** [θərmámətər |
-mɔ́m-] 명 **온도계 ; 체온계**
thermometer 는 온도를 재는
데 쓰는 도구다. 바깥 날씨의
덥고 추운 정도를 나타내주는
thermometer 도 있고, 아픈
사람들의 체온을 나타내는 데
쓰는 thermometer 도 있다.

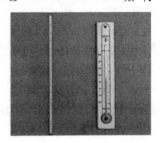

**these** [ðíːz] 1 대 **이것들** 2 형
이것들의
these 는 단어 this 에서 생긴
말이다 : **이 차들은 내 것이고,
저 차들은 네 것이다. 이 꽃들
은 예쁘다.**

**they** [ðéi] 대 **그들〔그것들〕, 그
사람들 ; 세상 사람들**
1 둘 이상의 사람이나 사물에
대해 이야기할 때 they 를 쓴
다 : **톰과 마이크는 버스를 놓
쳐서 학교에 지각했다.**
2 they'd 는 they had 나 they
would를 뜻한다 : **수와 보브는
전에 그 연극을 보았다고 말했
다. 그들이 우리와 함께 가 주
었으면 좋겠다.**
3 they'll 은 they will 을 뜻한
다 : **그들은 곧 올 것이다.**
4 they're는 they are 란 뜻이
다 : **그들은 우리가 사는 거리
에 새 집을 짓고 있다.**
5 they've 는 they have 란 뜻
이다 : **그들은 이미 파티에 가
고 없다.**

**thick** [θík] 형 **두꺼운 ; 굵은 ;
무성한 ; 진한, 짙은, 걸쭉한**
1 thick 은 한 쪽에서 다른 쪽
까지의 간격이 제법된다는 뜻
이다 : **이것은 두꺼운 책이다.**

2 thick 은 액체를 따르기가 힘들다는 뜻이다 : 토니는 병에 된 풀을 따르는 데 오랜 시간이 걸렸다.

**thief** [θíːf] 명 **도둑, 좀도둑**
thief 는 훔치는 사람이다 : thief 들이 가게에서 텔레비전을 훔쳤다.

**thin** [θín] 형 ① **얇은** ② **가는, 홀쭉한 ; 야윈** ③ (머리털이) 성긴 ; 드문드문한 ④ **묽은**
1 thin 은 한 쪽과 다른 쪽 사이의 공간이 많지 않다는 뜻이다 : 나는 샌드위치에 **얇은** 치즈 한 조각을 얹어 먹고 싶다. 종이가 너무 **얇아서** 그것으로 비춰볼 수가 있었다.
2 thin 은 또한 살찌지 않았다는 뜻이다 : 말의 얼굴은 길고 **홀쭉하다.**

**thing** [θíŋ] 명 ① **물건, 물체, 사물 ; 생물, 동물, 초목** ② **일** ③ **짓, 행위, 소행 ; 생각**

1 thing 은 물건이나 동물 혹은 식물을 말한다. 박물관에서는 흥미있는 thing 들을 많이 볼 수 있다.
2 thing 은 또한 사람의 행위를 말한다 : 한나는 자기의 점심을 루이스에게 좀 주었다. 한나가 한 일은 좋은 thing 이었다.

**think** [θíŋk] 타 자 (…라고) **생각하다, 믿다 ; 기대〔예상〕하다 ; 잘 생각하다**
1 think 는 마음속에 생각을 품어서 결정을 내린다는 뜻이다 : 데이비드는 토요일에 무엇을 할건지 **생각하고 있다.**
2 think 는 또한 믿는다는 뜻이다 : 나는 폭풍이 끝났다고 **생각한다.**

**third** [θə́ːrd] 1 형 **세번째의 ; 3분의 1의** 2 명 **세번째, 3분의 1**
third 는 두번째 것 다음이라는 뜻이다 : 내 여동생은 3학년이다. 3월은 한 해의 **세번째** 달이다.

**thirsty** [θə́ːrsti] 형 **목마른 ; 메마른, 건조한 ; 갈망하는**
thirsty 는 마실 것을 원한다는 뜻이다 : 우리는 너무나 **목이 말라서** 각자 큰 컵으로 물을 두 잔씩 마셨다.

**this** [ðís] 1 형 **이(것), 여기의,**

이 쪽의 ; **지 금 의** 2 [대] **이 것,**
이 물건[사람, 일] ; 지금, 오늘
1 다른 어떤 것보다도 더 가까
이 있는 것에 대해 이야기할
때 this 를 쓴다 : 이 코트는 내
것이고, 저 코트는 네 것이다.
2 또한 여기에 있는 것[속해
있는 시점]에 대해 이야기할
때 this 를 쓴다 : 오늘 아침은
날씨가 맑게 개었다. 이 책은
사전이다. 이 사람은 내 사촌
앤드루다.

**those** [ðóuz] 1 [대] **그것들, 그**
**사람들** 2 [형] **그것들의, 저**
those 는 단어 that 에서 생긴
말이다 : 이 글러브들은 내 것
이고, **저것들**은 앤디의 것이
다. 내가 **저** 쿠키들을 구웠다.
나는 **저** 사람들이 누군지 모른
다.

**though** [ðóu] 1 [접] ···임에도 불
**구하고, ···이지만 ; 만일 ···한**
**다 해도 ; 비록 ···이라 할지라**
**도** 2 [부] **그래도, 그렇지만**
나는 일찍 일어났음에도 불구
하고 학교에 지각했다. 영화는
재미있었**지만** 지난 주에 본 영

화만큼 재미있지는 않았다. 그
렇지만 니는 재미있게 보았다.

**thought** [θɔ́ːt] 1 [동] think (생각
하다)의 과거・과거분사형 2
[명] **생각, 사색 ; 의견 ; 사상,**
사조
1 thought 는 단어 think 에서
생긴 말이다 : 우리는 비가 올
것 같은 **생각**에 우산을 갖고
갔다.
2 thought 는 생각이다 : 헬렌
은 그녀가 읽은 책에 대해서
느낀 thought 를 적었다.

**thousand** [θáuzənd] 1 [명] **천,**
**1000개〔명〕; 다수, 무수 ; 수천**
2 [형] **1000 의, 천 개의, 1000**
**명의 ; 다수의, 무수한**
thousand 는 숫자로, **1, 000** 이
라고 쓴다. thousand 는 10 이
100 개 있다는 뜻이다 : **수 천**
**명의** 사람들이 (미식) 축구 경
기를 보러 갔다.

**thread** [θréd]　[명]　**실 ; 바느질**

실 ; 꼰 실

thread 는 아주 가는 줄로, 색
깔이 다양하다. 사람들은 바늘
에 thread 를 꿰어서 옷을 꿰
맨다.

**three** [θríː] 1 몡 **3**, 세 개, 세
명 2 혱 **3** 의, 세 개의, 세 명
의

three 는 2 보다 하나 더 큰 수
다. three 는 **3** 이라고 쓴다 :
$2 + 1 = 3.$

**threw** [θrúː] 툉 throw (던지다)
의 과거형

threw 는 단어 throw 에서 생
긴 말이다 : 로버트는 공을 잡
아서 다시 제인에게 **던졌다.**

**throat** [θróut] 몡 **목구멍**

throat 는 목 앞부분에 있는 신
체의 일부다 : 병이 났을 때 나
는 throat가 아팠다.

**through** [θrúː] 1 젠 …을 통하
여, …을 지나서 2 튄 통하
여, 꿰뚫어, 지나서 ; 처음부터
끝까지

through 는 「한 쪽에서 다른
쪽까지, 끝에서 끝까지」란 뜻
이다 : 제프리는 걸어서 들판을
지나 학교에 도착했다. 새가
열린 창문으로 우리 집에 날아
들어왔다.

**throw** [θróu] 탄자 **던지다,** 팽
개치다

1 throw 는 공중으로 어떤 것
을 보낸다는 뜻이다 : 개에게
공을 **던져라.** 그러면 네게 다
시 가져올 것이다.
2 throw away 는 어떤 것을
더 이상 원하지 않는다는 뜻이
다 : 우유에서 상한 냄새가 나
면 **버려야만** 한다. 마크는 부
서진 장난감 몇 개를 **버렸다.**

**thumb** [θʌ́m] 몡 **엄지손가락**

thumb 은 손의 가장자리에 있
는 짧고, 굵은 손가락이다.
thumb 은 물건을 쉽게 집어
올리게 해준다.

**thunder** [θʌ́ndəɾ] 몡 **천둥**

thunder 는 하늘에서 번개가
친 다음에 나는 큰 소리다 : 우
리는 폭풍우가 칠 때 thunder

소리를 들을 수 있다.

**Thursday** [θə́ːrzdei, -di] 명 목
요일
Thursday 는 일주일 가운데 하
루다. Thursday 는 수요일이
지나고 금요일이 되기 전에 온
다.

**ticket** [tíkit] 명 표, 입장권, 승
차권
ticket 은 어떤 것의 대가로 돈
을 지불한 사실을 증명해 주는
종잇장이다. 열차를 타려면
ticket 이 있어야 한다 : 우리는
극장 출입구에 있는 남자에게
ticket을 냈다.

**tickle** [tíkl] 타 간질이다 ; 근질
근질하게 하다
tickle 은 사람을 웃기려고 손
으로 살살 만진다는 뜻이다.

**tie** [tái] 1 타 붙들어 매다, 묶
다 ; (매듭을) **짓다** 2 명 맨
것, 매듭 ; 넥타이
1 tie 는 끈이나 밧줄로 한 데
결합시킨다는 뜻이다 : 조지는
보트를 선착장에 묶어 둔다.
2 tie 는 일종의 의류다. tie 는
사람들이 목둘레에 매는 가

느다란 천조각이다. tie 는 색
깔이 다양하다.

**tiger** [táigər] 명 호랑이
tiger 는 큰 야생 동물로, 상당
히 큰 고양이와 비슷해 보인
다. tiger 는 검은 줄무늬 털이
있다.

**tight** [táit] 형 단단히 맨, 단단
한 ; 빈틈이 없는, 새지 않는 ;
**팽팽한 ; 꼭 끼는**
tight 는 끄르〔벗〕거나 분리하
기 힘들다는 뜻이다 : 딕의 신
발은 그에게 너무 작아서 **꼭
끼었다.**

**time** [táim] 명 ① 때, **시각, 시
간** ② 세월 ; **기간** ③ 시절, 계
절 ; 일생 ④ 시대, 연대 ; (지
낸) **시간** ; 소요시간
1 time 은 어떤 일이 일어나는
때다. 탁상 시계나 손목 시계
는 우리에게 time을 알려준
다 : 내가 가장 좋아하는 텔레
비전 프로그램이 시작할 time
이 다 됐다.
2 time 은 또한 소요되는 시간
의 정도를 말한다 : 우리는 시
험을 마무리 할 time 이 많지

않다.

3 time은 또한 하고 지낸 일일 수도 있다 : 우리는 오늘 해변에서 즐거운 time 을 보냈다.

**times** [táimz] 명 회, (몇)번 ; 배, 곱

한 수에 어떤 수를 곱할 때, times라는 말을 쓴다 : 2 **곱하기** 2는 4다. 2 **곱하기** 2를 2×2로 쓰기도 한다.

**tin** [tín] 명 주석 ; 양철 ; 깡통, 통조림

tin 은 금속의 일종으로 깡통, 장난감, 그밖의 다른 것들을 만드는 데 이용한다.

**tiny** [táini] 형 조그마한, 아주 작은

tiny 는 아주 작다는 뜻이다 : 개미는 **아주 작은** 곤충이다.

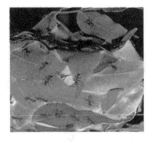

**tire** | **tyre** [táiər] 명 타이어

tire 는 바퀴 둘레에 끼는 둥근 고무다. 자동차, 버스, 자전거 그리고 트럭에는 모두 tire 가 있다. 대부분의 tire에는 공기가 채워져 있다 : 나는 tire에

구멍이 나서 교체했다.

**tired** [táiərd] 형 피로한, 지친 ; (…에) 싫증이 난

tired 는 몸이 쇠약해져 쉬어야 한다는 뜻이다. 사람들은 일을 많이 하거나 많이 놀면 **지쳐버린다** : 우리는 차고를 청소하고 나자 **피곤했다.**

**to** [《약》 tə (자음 앞), tu (모음 앞) 《강》 túː] 전 ① [방향] …쪽으로, …로 향하여 ② [시간] …까지, …전 ③ [목적] …을 위해서 ④ [상태·환경의 변화] …으로 ⑤ [대변·대립] 마주 향하여

1 to 는 가는 장소를 알려준다 : 우주 비행사들은 달을 **향해** 비행했다.

2 to 는 또한 「…까지」라는 뜻이다 : 그 가게는 아홉 시에 문을 열어서, 여섯 시에 닫는다. 그 가게는 아홉 시에서 여섯 시**까지** 영업한다.

3 to 는 또한 어떻게 변하는지를 알려준다 : 마이클은 노란 벽을 하얀색으로 칠했다. 그는 벽을 노란색에서 하얀색**으로** 바꿨다.

**toad** [tóud] 몡 **두꺼비**
load 는 개구리와 비슷한 동물
이다. toad 의 살갗은 건조하
고 우툴두툴하며, 아주 멀리
뛸 수 있다. toad 는 개구리처
럼 물에서 살지 않고, 마른 땅
에서 살기를 좋아한다.

**toast** [tóust] 몡 **토스트, 구운
빵**
toast 는 열을 가해 갈색으로
구운 빵이다. toaster 는 toast
를 만드는 기계다 : 나는 점심
으로 치즈 toast를 먹었다.

**today** [tədéi] 1 몡 **오늘** ; 현대,
현재 2 閉 **오늘, 오늘은** ; 현재
에는
today 는 오늘이다 : today 는
머리의 생일이다. **오늘** 공원에
가고 싶니 ?

**toe** [tóu] 몡 **발가락** ; **발끝** ; (구
두 등의) **앞부리**
toe 는 발의 한 부위다. 발에
는 각각 다섯 개의 toe 가 있
다 : toe 가 차서 나는 양말을
신었다.

**together** [təgéðər] 閉 ① **함
께, 같이** ; 합쳐져서, 모여져서
② 일제히, 동시에

together는 사람이나 물건들이
같은 장소에 있다는 뜻이다 :
마리아와 제인은 **함께** 버스를
타고 학교에 간다. 아빠는 우
유와 달걀을 **한데** 섞었다. 젖
소들이 모두 **모여** 들 한복판에
서 있었다.

**toilet** [tɔ́ilət] 몡 **화장실, 세면
실, 변소** ; **변기**
toilet은 몸 속의 배설물을 없
애기 위해 가는 곳이다.

**told** [tóuəld] 동 tell (말하다)의
과거 · 과거분사형
told 는 tell 의 한 형태다 : 메
리는 어제 자기의 여행담을 우
리에게 **말해 주었다.**

**tomato** [təméitou | -máː-] 몡 **토
마토**
tomato 는 열매로, 둥글고 빨
갛다. 케첩은 tomato로 만든
다.

**tomorrow** [təmɔ́ːrou, -már- |
-mɔ́r-] 몡 **내일** ; (가까운) **장
래**
tomorrow 는 오늘 바로 다음날
로, 미래에 속한다. 오늘이 월
요일이면, tomorrow 는 화요일
이 된다.

**tongue** [tʌ́ŋ] 명 혀

tongue 은 입의 한 부분으로, 길어서 입 밖으로 내밀 수 있다. tongue 은 음식을 맛보거나 삼키거나 말을 할 수 있게 도와준다.

**tonight** [tənáit] 1 명 오늘밤 2 부 오늘밤에

tonight 는 오늘과 내일 사이의 밤이다 : 우리는 오늘 아침에는 박물관에 가고, **오늘밤**에는 하키 시합을 보러 가려고 한다.

**too** [tú:] 부 ① (…도) **또한**, 게다가 ; **역시** ② [too ~ to … 로] 너무 ~하여 …할 수 없다

1 「또한」이란 뜻으로 too 를 쓴다 : 조지와 아서는 야구하는 것을 좋아하는 데, 그들의 동생 **또한** 좋아한다.

2 어떤 것이 아주 충분하다는 뜻으로도 too 를 쓴다 : 상자 안에 장난감이 **너무** 많아서 상자가 닫히지 않았다. **너무** 추워서 바다에서는 수영할 수 없다.

**took** [túk] 동 take (가지고 가다) 의 과거형

took 은 단어 take에서 생긴 말이다 : 짐은 친구들에게 보여주려고 새로 산 책을 학교에 **가져 갔다**.

**tool** [tú:əl] 명 연장, 도구, 공구 ; 공작 기계

tool 은 일할 때 사용하는 것이다. 망치, 갈퀴, 자는 종류가 다른 tool이다.

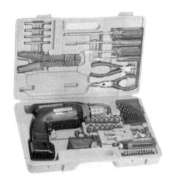

**tooth** [tú:θ] 명 이 ; 이 모양의 것

1 tooth 는 입 속에 있는 단단하고 하얀 부분 중의 하나다. teeth 는 음식을 베어 물고 씹는 데 사용한다 : 치과 의사는 나에게 하루에 두 번 teeth를 닦으라고 말했다.

2 tooth 는 또한 빗이나 갈퀴 끝에 일렬로 뾰족하게 나와 있는 것 중의 하나다 : 내 빗은 tooth 가 두 개 빠졌다.

**toothbrush** [tú:θbrʌ̀ʃ] 명 칫솔

toothbrush 는 손잡이가 긴 작은 솔로, 이를 닦는 데 쓴다.

**top**¹ [táp|tɔ́p] 명 ① 정상, 꼭

대기 ; 위쪽, **윗부분** ② 지붕,
포장 ; **뚜껑** ③ 최상위, 선두,
**톱** ; 결정, 극치
1 top 은 가장 높은 부분이
다 : 클레어는 미끄럼틀의 top
에 올라갔다.
2 top 은 또한 무언가를 덮는
부분이다 : 상자의 top 을 도로
닫아 주십시오.

**top²** [táp | tɔ́p] 몡 팽이
top 은 원뿔 모양의 장난감이
다. top은 뾰족한 끝으로 돈
다.

**tore** [tɔ́ːr] 동 tear¹ (찢다)의 과
거형
tore 는 단어 **tear¹** 에서 생긴
말이다 : 엘리자베스는 셔츠를
울타리에 **찢겼다.**

**torn** [tɔ́ːrn] 동 tear¹ (찢다)의
과거분사형
torn 은 단어 **tear¹** 에서 생긴
말이다 : 그녀의 셔츠는 두 갈
래로 **찢어졌다.**

**tornado** [tɔːrnéidou] 몡 **토네
이도** ; 회오리 바람

tornado 는 대단히 강한 바람
으로 공중에서 소용돌이치는
원뿔 모양이 된다. tornado 는
집을 무너뜨리고 땅에서 나무
를 뿌리째 뽑을 수도 있다.

**toss** [tɔ́ːs | tɔ́s] 타 (가볍게) **던지
다** ; 가볍게 던져 올리다, **토스
하다** ; (공을) 높이 쳐 올리다
toss 는 가볍게 던진다는 뜻이
다 : 양말 한 켤레만 좀 **던져
주십시오.**

**touch** [tʌ́tʃ] 타 **만지다, 대다**
touch 는 어떤 것에 손을 댄다
는 뜻이다 : 새끼 고양이의 털
을 **만져 보면** 그것이 얼마나
부드러운지 알 것이다.

**tow** [tóu] 타 **끌다, 밧줄** 〔쇠사
슬〕로 **끌다** ; 견인하다
tow 는 무언가를 끌어당기거나
끌고 간다는 뜻이다 : 우리 차
가 고장났을 때, 트럭이 우리
차를 주유소로 **끌고 갔다.** 어
제 나는 트럭이 버스를 **견인하**
는 것을 보았다.

**toward** [tɔ́ːrd, təwɔ́ːrd] 전 ①
**…쪽으로, …을 향하여** ② **…
경에, …무렵에**
무언가가 있는 방향으로 간다
고 말할 때 toward 를 쓴다 :
강아지들이 모두 어미를 **향해**
달려갔다. toward 를 **towards**
로 쓰기도 한다 : 나는 친구들
을 만나기 위해 운동장 **쪽으로**

걷기 시작했다.

**towel** [táuəl] 몡 **수건, 타월**
towel 은 어떤 것을 닦거나 말리는 데 쓰는 종이나 천 조각이다 : 톰은 샤워를 하고 나서 towel 로 몸을 감쌌다.

**tower** [táuər] 몡 **탑,** 망루
tower 는 건물 꼭대기의 높고 폭이 좁은 부분이다 : 우리 큰 길가의 교회에는 종 tower 가 있다.

**town** [táun] 몡 **읍**《village보다 크며, city의 자격이 없는 것》; 도회지 ; **도심 지구**
town 은 사람들이 생활하고 일하는 곳으로, 집과 그 밖의 건물들이 있다. town 은 city(도시)보다 작다 : 우리 town의 중심가에는 우체국, 은행, 주유소, 극장 그리고 레스토랑이 있다.

**tow truck** [tóu trʌ̀k] 몡 **구난용 트럭, 레커차**
tow truck 은 움직일 수 없는 차를 끌고 갈 수 있다. tow truck 은 고장이 났거나 진흙이나 눈에 빠져 꼼짝못하는 차를 옮기는 데 쓴다 : 사고가 나서 tow truck 이 우리 차를 정비소로 견인해 갔다.

**toy** [tɔ́i] 몡 **장난감**
toy 는 가지고 노는 물건이다. 사람과 동물들은 toy 를 가지고 논다. 인형, 연, 공은 toy 다 : 우리집 고양이는 toy 생쥐를 가지고 노는 것을 좋아한다.

**trace** [tréis] 탐 ① (…의 자국을) **따라가다, 추적하다** ② (선・윤곽・지도를) **긋다,** 그리다 ③ (위에서 따라) **베끼다,** 투사하다
trace 는 사진 위에 얇은 종이를 얹고 연필로 그 사진의 선을 따라가면, 다 그렸을 때 사진과 똑같은 그림이 종이에 생기게 된다는 뜻이다 : 토니는 공룡그림을 **베꼈다.**

**track** [trǽk] 몡 ① **지나간 자국** ; 흔적 ; **발자국** ② 밟아 다져진 길 ③ **철도 선로,** 궤도 ; **(경)주로, 트랙**
1 track 은 열차 바퀴가 지나가는 긴 쇠붙이 가운데 하나다.

2 track 은 또한 동물의 발이 남긴 자국이다 : 우리는 숲속에

서 사슴의 track을 보았다.

**tractor** [trǽktər] 명 트랙터 ; 견인 (자동) 차
tractor 는 강력한 엔진과 무거운 타이어를 갖춘 기계다. tractor 는 고르지 못한 땅에서 무거운 것을 끄는 데 사용된다.

**trade** [tréid] 자 타 장사하다 ; 매매하다 ; **거래〔무역〕하다** ; 교환하다
trade 는 어떤 것의 대가로 무언가를 준다는 뜻이다 : 내 친구들과 나는 장난감 자동차를 **바꿔서** 놀기를 좋아한다.

**traffic** [trǽfik] 명 왕래, **통행**, 교통 ; **교통량**
traffic 은 동시에 도로를 운행하는 자동차, 트럭, 버스들을 말한다 : 내가 사는 곳의 도로는 traffic 이 많지 않다.

**traffic light** [trǽfik làit] 명 교통 신호(등)
traffic light 는 길모퉁이에 있는 큰 불빛이다. traffic light 는 자동차와 사람들이 어떻게 해야 하는 지를 가르쳐 주기

위해 색깔을 바꾼다. 녹색불은 가라는 뜻이고, 노란 불은 주의하라는 뜻이고, 빨간 불은 멈추라는 뜻이다 : traffic light 가 녹색불이었지만, 우리는 소방차가 지나가도록 멈췄다.

**trail** [tréiəl] 명 지나간 자국, 흔적 ; (짐승의) 냄새 자취 ; (산속의) 오솔길
1 trail 은 사람이 살지 않는 곳에 나 있는 길이다 : 야영객들은 trail을 따라 숲속을 통과했다.
2 trail 은 또한 사람이나 동물이 남긴 흔적이나 냄새 혹은 길이다 : 토끼는 눈에 발자국 trail 을 남겼다.

**trailer** [tréilər] 명 끄는 사람〔것〕; 트레일러
trailer 는 자동차나 트럭이 끄는 것으로, 바퀴는 있지만 모터가 없다. 물건을 나르는 trailer 도 있고 사람이 살 수 있게 만든 trailer 도 있다.

**train** [tréin] 1 명 열차, 기차 ;

행렬 ; 연속 2 [타][자] 가르치다,
교육〔훈련〕하다, 길들이다 ; 훈
련을 받다

1 train 은 일렬로 연결된 철도
차량이다. train 은 사람이나
물건들을 한 곳에서 다른 곳으
로 실어 나르는 데 이용된다 :
우리는 할아버지를 방문하러
갈 때 train 을 탔다.

2 train 은 또한 사람이나 동물
에게 어떤 것을 하는 법을 가
르친다는 뜻이다 : 어머니는 사
람들에게 컴퓨터 사용법을 **가
르치신다.** 우리는 공을 던지면
다시 가져오도록 개를 **훈련시
켰다.**

**trap** [træp] 1 [명] 덫 ; 올가미 ;
함정, 계략, 책략 2 [타] **덫으
로 잡다 ; 덫을 설치하다 ;** 함정
〔계략〕에 빠뜨리다

1 trap 은 야생 동물을 잡는 방
법이다. 강철로 만든 trap 도
있고, 땅에 판 구덩이가 trap
인 경우도 있다.

2 trap 은 덫〔함정〕으로 동물
이나 사람을 잡는다는 뜻이
다 : 거미는 거미줄로 **덫을 놓
아** 곤충을 **잡는다.**

**trash** [træʃ] [명] 쓰레기, 잡동사
니, 폐물

trash 는 버리는 물건이다. 우
리가 버리는 trash 의 대부분
은 종이, 박스 그리고 오래된
음식들이다.

**travel** [trǽvəl] [자] **여행하다 ;**
(탈 것을) 타고 가다 ; 달리다,
걷다, 나아가다

travel 은 한 곳에서 다른 곳으
로 간다는 뜻이다 : 우리는 휴
가 때 자동차로 **여행했다.**

**treasure** [tréʒər] [명] 보물, 보
화 ; **귀중품 ;** 부, 재산 ; 금전

treasure 는 돈이나 보석 또는
그 밖의 중요한 물건이다 : 왕
과 왕비는 별실에 treasure 를
숨겼다.

**treat** [tríːt] [명] **특별한 즐거움,
큰 기쁨,** 경사 ; 아주 좋은
것 ; 대접

treat 는 즐겁고 특별한 것이

다 : 서커스 구경을 가는 것이
우리에게는 treat 였다.

**tree** [tríː] 몧 **나무, 수목**
tree 는 식물의 일종으로, 가
지와 잎이 있다. tree 는 대단
히 크게 자랄 수도 있다. 목재
는 tree 에서 얻는다.

**triangle** [tráiæŋgl] 몧 **삼각형 ;**
**삼각자 ; 트라이앵글**
1 triangle 은 세 변이 직선인
형태다.
2 triangle 은 또한 세 변으로
된 악기다. triangle 은 금속으
로 만들며 금속 막대로 치면
소리가 울린다.

**trick** [trík] 1 몧 **묘기 ; 요술 ;**
**곡예 ; 술책, 속임수 ; 장난, 농**
**담 2** 팀짜 **속이다,** 야바위치
**다 ; 장난치다**
1 trick 은 불가능해 보이는 것
이다 : 잭은 마술사가 토끼를
사라지게 하는 것을 보았다.
그는 그것이 trick 이란 걸 알
고 있었다. 왜냐하면 그 누구
도 무언가를 정말로 사라지게

할 수는 없기 때문이다.
2 trick 은 하고 싶지 않은 것
을 하게끔 한다는 뜻이다 : 크
리스의 개가 아팠을 때, 개가
약을 먹으려 하지 않았다. 그
래서 크리스의 엄마는 먹이에
약을 넣어 개를 **속였다.**

**tricycle** [tráisikl] 몧 **삼륜차 ;**
**세발 자전거**
tricycle 은 뒷바퀴가 둘이고
앞바퀴는 하나다. tricycle 은
자전거와 비슷하지만, 타기가
더 쉽다 : 앤은 공원 길에서
tricycle 을 타는 것을 좋아한
다.

**tried** [tráid] 통 try (시도하다)
의 과거·과거분사형
tried 는 단어 try 에서 생긴 말
이다 : 마리아는 큰 여행용 가
방을 들어 올리려고 했지만 그
녀가 들기에는 너무 무거웠다.

**trip** [tríp] 몧 **(짧은) 여행, 소**
**풍 ; (짧은) 항해**
trip 은 한 곳에서 다른 곳으로
간다는 뜻이다 : 우리는 산으로
trip 을 갔다(나들이 갔다).

**trombone** [trambóun | trɔm-]
몧 **트롬본**

trombone 은 악기로, 호른의 일종이다. trombone 은 서로 이어 맞춘 긴 금속관으로 되어 있다.

**troop** [trúːp] 명 (특히 이동 중인 사람·짐승·조류의) **무리, 떼** ; 많은 사람 ; 군대, 병력
troop 은 사람들의 집단이다 : 많은 troop의 소년·소녀들이 지난 여름에 야영을 갔다.

**trophy** [tróufi] 명 전리품 ; 전승 기념물 ; 우승 기념품, 상품, **트로피**
trophy 는 작은 조상이나 그 밖의 상이다. trophy 는 경기나 시합에서 이긴 사람이나 특별한 일을 한 사람에게 주어진다 : 나의 형은 학교 농구팀에서 가장 훌륭한 선수로 뽑혀 trophy 를 받았다.

**trouble** [trʌ́bl] 명 ① **근심**(거리), 걱정 ; 고민 ; **괴로움**, 고생 ② 재난, 불행 ③ **고생**(두통)**거리** ; **성가신 일**
1 trouble 은 어떻게 해야 할지 알기 어렵게 하는 것이다 : 딕은 더하기나 빼기를 잘 못한다. 그는 산수 때문에 trouble 한다.
2 be in trouble은 누군가가

화를 낸다는 뜻이다 : 헨리는 (미식) 축구를 하다가 새 셔츠를 찢겼다. 그는 집에 가면 **야단 맞으리라는** 것을 알았다.

**trousers** [tráuzərz] 명 (남자의) **바지**
trousers 는 옷의 일종이다. 사람들은 다리에 trousers를 입는다. 대부분의 trousers 에는 호주머니가 있다.

**truck** [trʌ́k] 명 **트럭**, 화물 자동차
truck 은 큰 자동차와 비슷하다. 사람들은 truck 을 이용해 크고, 무거운 물건을 나른다 : 우리는 truck 을 이용해 새 집으로 가구를 옮겼다.

**true** [trúː] 형 **정말의**, 진실인 ; 진정한, **진짜의** ; 틀림없는 ; 들어맞는
true는 정확하고 틀리지 않다는 뜻이다 : 내년에 조가 우리 학교에 다니게 된다는 것이 **사실이냐?** 코끼리가 다리가 4개라는 것은 **틀림없다.**

**trumpet** [trʌ́mpit] 명 트럼펫
trumpet 은 금속으로 만든 악기다. trumpet 의 한 쪽 끝을 불면, 다른 쪽 끝에서 소리가 난다.

**trunk** [trʌ́ŋk] 명 ① (나무의) 줄기 ; 몸통 ; 본체, 주요부 ② 여행용 큰 가방, 트렁크 ③ (자동차의) 트렁크 ; (코끼리의) 코
1 trunk 는 나무 중간의 굵은 부분이다. 나무 trunk 는 땅에서 자라고, 가지는 trunk 에서 싹튼다.
2 trunk 는 또한 코끼리의 한 부위로, 대단히 긴 코와 같다 : 코끼리는 trunk 로 물건을 집어 올릴 수 있다.
3 trunk 는 또한 큰 상자기도 하다. 사람들은 보통 여행할 때 trunk 에 옷과 다른 물건들을 챙겨 넣는다.

**trust** [trʌ́st] 1 명 신뢰, 신임, 신용 2 타자 신뢰〔신임·신용〕하다 ; 믿다
trust 는 어떤 사람이 정직하다고 믿는다는 뜻이다 : 나는 빌에게 나만의 비밀을 이야기했다. 왜냐하면 그를 믿을 수 있기 때문이었다.

**truth** [trúːθ] 명 진리, 진실 ; 사실 ; 성실, 정직
truth 는 사실인 것이다 : 사람들이 truth 를 말하지 않으면, 너는 그들을 믿을 수 없다.

**try** [trái] 타자 시도하다, 해보다, (…하려고) 노력하다 ; 실지로 해보다
try 는 어떤 것을 할 수 있는지 알아본다는 뜻이다 : 나는 언덕을 뛰어 올라가려고 했지만 몹시 지쳐 있었다.

**tub** [tʌ́b] 명 통, 함지 ; 목욕통, 욕조
1 tub 는 목욕할 때 쓰는 크고 덮개가 없는 용기다 : 그녀는 tub 에서 옷을 빤다. tub 를 다른 말로 bathtub 라고 한다.

2 tub 는 또한 버터나 벌꿀 혹은 다른 음식들을 담는 데 쓰는 둥근 용기다.

**tube** [tjúːb] 명 관, 통 ; 튜브, 짜내게 되어 있는 용기
tube 는 속이 빈 유리나 고무 혹은 플라스틱이나 금속으로, 때로는 파이프 형태로 되어

있다. tube 는 액체나 가스를 운반하거나 담는 데 쓴다.

**Tuesday** [tjúːzdei, -di] 몡 화요일

Tuesday 는 일주일 중의 하루다. Tuesday 는 월요일이 지나고 수요일이 되기 전에 온다.

**tug** [tʌ́g] 타 자 (세게) 당기다, 잡아끌다

tug 는 힘껏 당긴다(끈다)는 뜻이다 : 어린 아이들은 때때로 부모의 주의를 끌기 위해서 부모의 외투를 **잡아 당긴다.**

**tugboat** [tʌ́gbòut] 몡 예인선, 끌배, 터그보트

tugboat 는 매우 강력한 엔진이 달린 보트다. tugboat 는 큰 배들이 움직일 공간이 별로 없을 때, 그것들을 밀거나 잡아끈다.

**tulip** [tjúːlip] 몡 튤립

tulip 은 컵 모양의 꽃이다. tulip 은 알뿌리에서 자란다.

**tunnel** [tʌ́nəl] 몡 굴, 터널, 지

하도 ; 갱도

tunnel 은 땅 속의 긴 구멍이다. 사람들이 한 곳에서 다른 곳으로 갈 수 있도록 산을 통과하는 tunnel 도 있다.

**turkey** [tə́ːrki] 몡 칠면조 ; 칠면조 고기

1 turkey 는 새의 일종으로 목이 길다. turkey 는 고기를 얻으려고 기르며, turkey 중에는 야생인 것도 있다.

2 turkey 는 칠면조에게서 얻는 고기다.

**turn** [tə́ːrn] 타 자 ① 돌리다(돌다), 회전시키다(회전하다) ; (페이지를) 넘기다 ; (옷을) 뒤집다 ② 방향(위치)을 바꾸다 ; 마음을 바꾸게 하다

1 turn 은 원형으로 움직인다는 뜻이다 : 자전거가 움직일 때는 자전거 바퀴가 **돈다.**

2 turn 은 머리를 옆으로 움직인다는 뜻이다 : 타일러는 방에 누가 들어왔는지 보려고 머리를 **돌렸다.**

3 take turns 는 한 사람이 하고 나면 또 다른 사람이 이어

서 한다는 뜻이다 : 월터와 스
튜어트는 샌드위치 한개를 나
눠 먹었다. 먼저 월터가 한 입
베어 먹고 나면 그 다음엔 스
튜어트가 한 입 베어 먹었다.
그들은 샌드위치를 다 먹을 때
까지 **번갈아** 한입씩 먹었다.

**turquoise, -quois** [tə́:rkwɔiz]
명 터키석 ; 하늘색, 청록색
1 turquoise 는 색깔이다. 녹색
과 파란색을 섞으면 turquoise
색이 된다.
2 turquoise 는 또한 장신구를
만드는 데 쓰는 돌 이름이다.

**turtle** [tə́:rtl] 명 바다거북
turtle 은 다리가 짧고, 단단한
등딱지가 몸을 덮고 있는 동물
이다. turtle 은 육지와 물속에
서 산다. turtle은 두려움을 느
끼면, 머리와 다리를 등딱지
안으로 끌어당긴다.

**twice** [twáis] 부 두 번, 2회 ;
두 배로
twice 는 두 번(두 배)이란 뜻
이다 : 앨리스는 **두 번**을 볼 정
도로 그 영화를 굉장히 좋아했
다.

**twig** [twíg] 명 작은 가지, 잔가
지
twig 는 나무의 작은 가지다 :
우리는 숲으로 캠핑을 가면 마
른 twig로 불을 일으켰다.

**twin** [twín] 명 쌍둥이(의 한 사
람)
twin 은 같은 부모에게서 동시
에 태어난 두 아이 중의 한 명
이다. 대부분의 twins 는 비슷
하게 생겼다.

**twist** [twíst] 타 꼬다 ; 엮다 ; 꼬
아(엮어) 만들다 ; **휘감다** ; 비
**틀다,** 뒤틀다
twist 는 반복해서 회전시킨다
는 뜻이다 : 밧줄은 한데 **꼬인**
몇 가닥의 줄로 되어 있다.

**two** [túː] 1 형 둘의, **2** 의, 두
명의 2 명 둘, 2, 두 개, 두
사람 ; 두 시
two 는 1보다 하나 더 큰 수
다. 숫자 two 는 2라고 쓴다.

**tying** [táiiŋ] 통 tie 의 현재분
사ㆍ동명사형
tying 은 단어 tie 에서 생긴 말
이다 : 미첼은 끈으로 소포를
묶고 있다.

**ugly** [ʌ́gli] 휑 **추한,** 보기 싫은, 못생긴 **; 험악한**
ugly는 예쁘지 않다는 뜻이다 : 리처드는 나를 놀라게 하려고 **험악한** 표정을 지었지만, 나는 오히려 웃음이 났다.

**umbrella** [ʌmbrélə] 몡 **우산**
umbrella는 비나 햇볕으로부터 자신을 보호하는 데 사용하는 것이다. umbrella는 긴 손잡이가 있는 사발을 뒤집어 놓은 모양처럼 생겼다. umbrella의 윗부분은 천과 금속으로 되어 있다.

**umpire** [ʌ́mpaiə r] 몡 **심판(원),** 심판자, (특히 야구의) 엄파이어
umpire는 야구 경기에서 규칙을 지키는지 확인한다 : "경기 시작 !"이라고 umpire가 외쳤다.

**uncle** [ʌ́ŋkl] 몡 **아저씨, 백부, 숙부,** 외삼촌, 이모부, 고모부
uncle은 아버지의 남자 형제나 어머니의 남자 형제를 말한다. 이모의 남편 또한 uncle이다.

**under** [ʌ́ndə r] 1 휀 ① …의 아래에, …의 밑에 ② …미만의 ③ …하는 중에 2 휋 밑에, 아래에
under는 딴 것보다 더 낮은 곳을 뜻한다 : 개가 침대 **밑에** 숨어 있었다. 내가 찾지 못했던 종이가 책 **밑에** 있었다. 잭은 재킷 **밑에** 스웨터를 입고 있다.

**underground** [ʌ́ndə r gràund] 1 휑 **지하의,** 지하에 있는 ; 숨은 2 [ʌ̀ndə r gráund] 휋 **지하에서, 지하로** ; 비밀로, 몰래
underground는 땅 밑을 뜻한다 : 지렁이는 **땅 속에서** 산다.

**underline** [ʌ̀ndə r láin] 휄 **…의 밑에 선을 긋다**
underline은 어떤 것 밑에 선을 긋는다는 뜻이다 : 리언은

그 페이지에 있는 자기 이름 밑에 **줄을 친다**. 사람들은 흔히 중요한 것에 **밑줄을 친다**.

**understand** [Ʌndərstǽnd] 타 자 **이해하다, 알다**
understand는 무슨 의미인지를 알고 있다는 뜻이다 : 루이스가 **아는** 유일한 언어는 영어다. 앤디는 영어와 스페인어를 둘 다 **알아** 듣는다.

**understood** [Ʌndərstúd] 동
understand (이해하다)의 과거·과거분사형
understood는 understand의 한 형태다 : 나는 경기하는 방식을 몰랐는 데, 마크가 규칙을 설명해 주어서 **알게 되었다**. 앨버트는 선생님의 질문을 **이해했다**.

**underwater** [Ʌndərwɔ́ːtər] 1 부 **물 속에서** 2 형 **물 속의, 물 속에서 쓰는**
underwater는 수면 아래를 뜻한다 : 낸시와 조지는 **물 속에서** 수영하는 법을 알고 있다. 언젠가 그들은 **수중** 동굴을 탐험했었다.

**underwear** [Ʌndərwɛ̀ər] 명 **내의, 속옷**
underwear는 옷 밑에 입는 의류다 : 나는 세탁이 끝난 underwear를 개켜서 치웠다.

**undress** [Ʌndrés] 타 자 **…의 옷을 벗기다 ; 옷을 벗다**
undress는 옷을 벗는다는 뜻이다 : 내 남동생은 혼자 **옷 벗는** 법을 배우고 있다. 한나는 인형의 옷을 입혔다 **벗겼다** 하면서 가지고 노는 것을 좋아한다.

**uneasy** [Ʌníːzi] 형 **불안한**
uneasy는 안전한 느낌이 들지 않는다는 뜻이다 : 메리는 처음으로 비행기를 타게 되어 약간 두려웠다. 그녀는 비행기를 타는 게 **불안했다**.

**uneven** [Ʌníːvən] 형 **평탄하지 않은, 울퉁불퉁한**
uneven은 매끄럽거나 평탄하

지 않다는 뜻이다 : 우리는 들
판을 걷기가 힘들었다. 그곳
땅이 매우 **울퉁불퉁했다.**

**unhappy** [ʌnhǽpi] 형 **불행한,**
불운한, 비참한
unhappy는 행복하지 않다는
뜻이다 : 여동생이 내가 가장
아끼는 장난감 트럭을 망가뜨
렸을 때 나는 몹시 **기분이 언
짢았다.**

**unicorn** [júːnikɔ̀ːrn] 명 **일각수**
unicorn은 머리 중앙에 한 개
의 긴 뿔이 있는 흰 말 처럼
생긴 상상의 동물이다 : 나는
unicorn에 관한 동화를 즐겨
읽는다.

**uniform** [júːnifɔ̀ːrm] 명 **제복,**
군복 ; (운동 선수의) 똑같은
운동복, **유니폼**
uniform은 특별한 종류의 옷이
다. 사람들은 자신이 어떤 집
단에 속해 있는 지를 나타내기
위해 uniform을 입는다. 경찰
관, 간호사, 운동 경기 팀은
uniform을 입는다.

**United States** [junàitid stéits]
명 **미국**, 아메리카 합중국
United States 는 국가로,
United States of America라고
도 부른다. United States의
수도는 워싱턴 D.C.다.

**universe** [júːnivə̀ːrs] 명 **우주,**
만물, 삼라만상, **전세계**
universe는 우리가 사는 세상
과 우주에 모여 있는 모든 것
이다. 지구, 태양, 달 그리고
별들은 모두 universe의 일부
다.

**unless** [ənlés] 접 **만약 …하지
않으면, …하지 않는 한**
내 자전거를 조심스럽게 다루
겠다고 약속**하지 않으면** 네게
빌려 줄 수 없다. 비가 오지
**않는 한**, 오늘 오후에 야구 경
기가 열릴 것이다. 서두르지
**않으면**, 우리는 음악회에 늦을
것이다.

**unlucky** [ʌnlʌ́ki] 형 **불운한,**
불행한 ; 불길한
unlucky는 운이 나쁘다는 뜻
이다 : 제인은 지난 토요일 소
풍을 가고 싶었지만, 비가 왔
다. 그녀는 자기 생일에 파티

를 열고 싶었지만, 병이 나고
말았다. 제인은 몹시 **운이 나
쁘다.**

**untie** [ʌntái] **타** 풀다, (꾸러미
등의) 매듭을 끄르다
untie는 매듭을 없앤다는 뜻이
다 : 마이크는 혼자서 구두끈을
**끌렀다.**

**until** [əntíəl] **전 접** ① **…까지,**
…이 되기까지 ② [부정어와
함께] **…까지 …않다,** …에 이
르러 비로소 (…하다)
until은 「…할 때까지」의 뜻이
다 : 우리는 어두워질 **때까지**
밖에서 놀 수 있다.

**unusual** [ʌnjúːʒuəl] **형 이상한,
보통이 아닌,** 드문 ; 유별난
unusual은 우리가 예상하던
바가 아니라는 뜻이다 : 7월에
눈이 온다면, 아주 **보기 드문**
날씨가 될 것이다. 그녀가 화
를 내다니 **이상하다.**

**up** [ʌp] **부** ① **위로, 위에, 위쪽
으로** ② **일어나서,** 일어서서
③ …쪽으로, 접근하여
1 up은 낮은 곳에서 높은 곳으
로 간다는 뜻이다 : 클레어는

계단을 **올라가** 건물 안으로 들
어 갔다. 데이비드가 방에 들
어 오자, 수잔은 책을 읽다가
고개를 들어 **올려다** 보았다.
2 up은 또한 잠자리에서 일어
난다는 뜻이다 : 나는 오늘 아
침 9시까지 **일어나지** 못했다.
조와 빌리는 아직까지 **일어나
지** 않고 있다.

**upon** [əpán, əpɔ́ːn|əpɔ́n] **전**
**…의 위에**
upon은 「…위에」라는 뜻이
다 : 새가 나뭇가지 **위에** 앉아
있었다.

**upset** [ʌpsét] **타** ① **뒤집어 엎
다,** (계획 등을) 망쳐버리다
② (마음을) 어지럽히다, **당황
케 하다**
upset은 화가 나거나 감정이
상하거나 혹은 불행하다고 느
낀다는 뜻이다 : 앤은 가장 친
한 친구가 자기의 파티에 오지
않자 **당황했다.**

**upside-down** [ʌpsaiddáun] **부**
**거꾸로 된,** 뒤집힌 ; 엉망이 된
upside-down은 위쪽이 아래로
향하고, 아래쪽이 위로 향한다
는 뜻이다 : 마거릿이 우연히
디저트를 쳐서 식탁에서 떨어
뜨렸는 데, 디저트가 마룻바닥
에 떨어져 **엎어졌다.**

**us** [《약》 əs, 《강》 ʌ́s] **대** [we 의

목적격] **우리들을, 우리들에게**
우리들 자신에 관한 말을 할
때 us라는 말을 쓴다 : 벤 아
저씨가 어제 **우리를** 동물원에
데리고 갔다.

**use** [júːz] 〔타〕 **사용하다**, 이용하
다, 쓰다
use는 무언가를 갖고 작업을
한다는 뜻이다 : 목수는 연장과
나무 그리고 못을 **사용해** 집을
짓는다.

**useful** [júːsfəl] 〔형〕 **쓸모 있는,**
**유용한,** 유익한
useful은 무언가를 하는 데 도
움이 된다는 뜻이다 : 연장은
물건을 수리하거나 만드는 데
**유용하다.**

**usual** [júːʒuəl] 〔형〕 **보통의,** 일상
의, 평소의
usual은 예상대로라는 뜻이
다 : 7·8월에는 **흔히** 날씨가
덥다.

**usually** [júːʒuəli] 〔부〕 **보통으로,**
**평소에,** 일반적으로
usually는 「거의 언제나」의 뜻
이다 : 보브는 학교에서 집으로
**대개** 자전거를 타고 간다.

U

# V

**vacation** [veikéiʃən, və-] 명 휴
가, 방학, 휴일
vacation은 사람들이 일을 하
지 않거나 학교에 가지 않는
기간이다 : 우리 가족은 작년
여름에 바닷가로 vacation을
갔었다.

**valentine** [vǽləntàin] 명 발렌
타인 카드〔선물〕
valentine은 성 발렌타인 축제
일에 사랑하는 사람에게 보내
는 카드다. valentine에는 대
개 하트 모양의 그림이 있다.
성 발렌타인 축제일은 2월 14
일이다.

**valley** [vǽli] 명 계곡, 골짜기
valley는 언덕이나 산들 사이
에 있는 낮은 지역을 말한다.
valley에는 강이 흐르는 경우
가 많다.

**van** [vǽn] 명 밴, 유개 트럭,
운반차
van은 트럭이나 소형 버스 비
슷한 자동차다. 대형 van은
동물이나 가구 혹은 그밖의 큰
물건들을 옮기는 데 이용한다.
소형 van은 사람이나 작은 물
건들을 실어 나르는 데 이용한
다.

**vanilla** [vənílə] 명 바닐라
vanilla는 향료로, 일종의 씨앗
으로 만든다. vanilla는 아이스
크림과 그밖의 디저트에 이용
된다.

**vegetable** [védʒtəbl] 명 야채,
채소
vegetable은 먹을 수 있는 식
물이나 식물의 한 부분이다.
상추, 양파, 완두콩은 vegeta-
ble이다.

**very** [véri] 부 ① 대단히, 매우, 몹시 ② [부정문에서] 그다지 (…않다)
very는 보통 이상이라는 뜻이다 : 곰은 큰 동물이다. 코끼리는 아주 큰 동물이다.

**veterinarian** [vètərinɛ́əriən] 명 수의사
veterinarian은 동물을 보살피는 의사다 : 에디는 동물을 좋아해서 veterinarian이 되고 싶어한다. 낸시는 동물원의 veterinarian이 되어서 야생 동물을 돌보고 싶어한다.

**village** [vílidʒ] 명 마을, 촌락
village는 소규모의 가옥 집단으로, 대개 시골에 있다. village는 시내만큼 크지 않다.

**vine** [váin] 명 덩굴 ; 포도나무
vine은 길고 가느다란 줄기가 있는 식물이다. vine은 땅 바닥으로 뻗거나, 나무줄기와 벽을 타고 위로 자란다. 포도와 호박은 vine에서 자란다.

**violin** [vàiəlín] 명 바이올린

violin은 나무로 만든 네 줄짜리 악기다. violin 몸통을 턱 밑에 대고 활로 연주한다.

**visit** [vízit] 타 자 방문하다, 체재하다, …의 장소에 머물러〔놀러〕가다
visit는 잠시 어딘가에 묵거나 누군가의 집에 머문다는 뜻이다 : 우리 학급은 지난 주에 동물원을 방문했다.

**voice** [vɔ́is] 명 목소리, 음성
voice는 입으로 내는 소리다. 말을 하거나 노래를 부를 때는 voice를 사용한다.

**volcano** [vɑəlkéinou | vɔ́l-] 명 화산
volcano는 꼭대기에 큰 구멍이 나 있는 산처럼 보인다. volcano밑에 암석은 지열로 녹는 데, 간혹 그 녹은 암석〔용암〕이 volcano에서 분출할 때도 있다.

**volunteer** [vɑ̀ləntíər | vɔ̀l-] 명 지원자, 지원병

V

volunteer는 보수를 받지 않고 일하는 사람이다 : 내가 사는 마을의 소방수들은 모두 volunteer다.

**vote** [vóut] 1 타 자 **투표로 결정 하다,** 가결하다 ; 투표하다 2 명 **투표,** 표결
vote는 어떤 것에 찬성이나 반대 의사를 나타낸다는 뜻이다 : 우리 마을은 새 운동장을 건설하기로 **가결했다.**

**vowel** [váuəl] 명 **모음**
vowel은 자음이 아닌 알파벳 문자다. vowel은 a, e, i, o, u인 데, y를 vowel속에 넣을 때도 있다.

V

**wagon** [wǽgən] 명 (각종) **4 륜 차, 짐마차, 왜건**

wagon 은 사람이나 물건을 한 곳에서 다른 곳으로 실어 나르 는 데 이용한다. wagon 은 바 퀴가 4 개며 간혹 큰 wagon 은 말들이 끌기도 한다.

**wait** [wéit] 자 타 **기다리다, 대 기하다**

wait 는 사람이 오거나 어떤 일이 일어날 때까지 한 곳에 머무른다는 뜻이다 : 메리는 비 가 그칠 때까지 **기다린** 후에야 밖에 나가 놀 수 있었다. 이 방에서 **기다려** 주십시오.

**wake** [wéik] 자 타 **눈을 뜨다, 깨다, 일어나다 ; 깨우다**

wake 는 잠을 그만 잔다는 뜻 이다 : 너는 아침 몇시에 **일어** 나니? 우리가 시끄럽게 해서 아기를 **깨웠다.**

**walk** [wɔ́:k] 자 타 **걷다, 걸어가 다, 산책하다**

walk 는 한 발을 다른 발 앞에 놓으며 나아간다는 뜻이다 : 내 여동생은 이제 막 **걸음마를** 배 우려 한다.

**wall** [wɔ́:əl] 명 **벽 ; 담**

1 wall 은 방의 한쪽 면이다. 대부분의 방은 천장과 바닥 그 리고 네 면의 wall 로 되어 있 다.

2 wall 은 한 곳을 다른 곳과 분리하려고 쌓은 것이다 : 농부 는 자기 밭 주위에 돌 wall 을

쌓았다.

**want** [wánt, wɔ́:nt|wɔ́nt] 타 탐
내다, **원하다**, 갖고 싶어하다
want 는 무언가를 갖고 싶다는
뜻이다 : 피터는 그 어떤 것보
다 트럼펫을 **갖고 싶어한다.**

**war** [wɔ́:r] 명 전쟁
war 는 국가간의 싸움이다 :
war 가 끝나자 모든 사람이 기
뻐했다.

**warm** [wɔ́:rm] 형 **따뜻한**, 약
간 더운
warm 은 아주 덥지는 않다는
뜻이다 : 바깥 날씨가 추우면,
우리집 개는 **따뜻한** 집안에 있
기를 좋아한다.

**was** [《약》wəz, 《강》wʌ́z, wɑ́z|
wɔ́z] 통 be 의 1인칭 및 3인
칭 단수 과거형
was 는 단어 be 에서 생긴 말
이다 : 새가 둥지를 짓고 **있었
다.** 현관에 **있었던** 사람은 누
구지? 카르멘은 지난주에 **아
팠다.**

**wash** [wɑ́ʃ, wɔ́:ʃ|wɔ́ʃ] 타 **씻다**,
빨다, 세척하다
wash 는 비눗물로 무언가를
깨끗이 닦는다는 뜻이다 : 우리
는 저녁을 먹기 전에 손을 **씻
었다.** 우리는 루이스가 **세차하
는** 것을 도왔다. 찰리와 프레

드는 저녁을 먹고 나면 번갈아
**설거지**를 한다.

**wasn't** [wɑ́znt|wɔ́z-] was not
의 단축형
wasn't 는 was not 을 줄여서
말한 것이다 : 앨버트는 빌리를
만나러 그의 집에 갔는데 빌리
가 집에 **없었다.**

**waste** [wéist] 타자 **낭비하다**,
허비하다
waste 는 필요 이상으로 많이
쓴다는 뜻이다 : 수도 꼭지를
잠그지 않으면, 물을 **낭비하게
된다.**

**watch** [wɑ́tʃ, wɔ́:tʃ|wɔ́tʃ] 1 타자
**지켜 보다**, 주시하다 ; 구경하
다 ; 돌보다 2 명 ① 경계, 조
심, 주의 ② **손목시계**
1 watch 는 주의깊게 본다는
뜻이다 : 애를 봐주는 사람은
아이들이 노는 동안에 그들을
**지켜보았다.**
2 watch는 또한 손목에 차는
작은 시계다. watch는 몇 시
인지를 알려준다.

**water** [wɔ́:tər] 명 물
water는 액체의 일종으로, 투
명하고 맛이 없다. 사람과 동

식물들은 살아가는 데 water
가 필요하다.

**wave** [wéiv] 1 자 타 **파도치다**,
(깃발·가지 등이) **흔들리다** ;
**흔들다** 2 명 **파도, 물결**
1 wave는 위아래로 혹은 양옆
으로 흔든다는 뜻이다. 사람들
은 종종 인사말을 하거나 작별
을 고할 때 한쪽 손을 흔든
다 : 깃발이 바람에 **펄럭였다.**
2 wave는 또한 바다에서 올라
갔다 내려왔다하는 물이다 : 배
가 wave에 오르락내리락 했
다.

**wax** [wǽks] 명 **밀초**, 밀랍, 광
내는 약
wax는 양초와 크레용같은 물
건을 만드는 데 쓰는 재료다.
wax는 또한 가구나 자동차를
광내는 데도 사용한다.

**way** [wéi] 명 ① **길**, 도로, 통
로 ② **방식**, 방법 ③ 방향
1 way는 무언가를 하는 방법
이다 : 나는 이 경기를 하는 두
가지 way를 알고 있다.
2 way는 또한 한 곳에서 다른
곳으로 가기 위해 택하는 도로
나 길을 뜻한다 : 아서는 가게
로 가는 way를 알고 있다.

**we** [《약》 wi, 《강》 wíː] 대 [인칭
대명사 : 1인칭 복수 주격] **우
리는, 우리가**
1 사람들은 자기 자신들에 관
해 말할 때 we를 사용한다 :
**우리는** 좋은 친구 사이다.

2 we'd 는 we had 나 we
would 의 뜻이다 : **우리는** 날이
밝기까지 약 6시간 정도를 잤
다. **우리가** 갈 수만 있다면,
너와 같이 가겠는 데.
3 we'll 은 we will 의 뜻이다 :
나는 내일 **우리가** 경기에 이길
거라고 생각한다.
4 we're 는 we are 의 뜻이
다 : **우리는** 집에 있다.
5 we've 는 we have 의 뜻이
다 : **우리는** 그 도시를 두 번
방문했다.

**weak** [wíːk] 형 **약한**, 연약한,
허약한, 무력한
1 weak 는 부러지거나 넘어질
수 있다는 뜻이다 : 식탁 다리
가 **약하다.**
2 weak는 또한 강하지 않다
는 뜻이다 : 병에 걸린 조랑말
은 **허약했다.**

**weapon** [wépən] 명 **무기**, 병

W

기, 흉기

사람들은 싸울 때 weapon 을 사용한다. 총과 칼은 weapon 이다.

**wear** [wɛ́ər] 타 (옷을) **입고 있다**, 몸에 걸치고 있다, 신고 〔쓰고·끼고〕 있다

wear 는 몸에 옷이나 그 밖의 다른 것들을 걸친다는 뜻이다 : 마크는 비가 오면 비옷과 장화를 **신는다**. 앨리스는 새 목걸이를 **걸고 있다**.

**weather** [wéðər] 명 일기, **날씨, 기후**

비나 눈 혹은 더위나 추위가 어느 정도인져를 말할 때는 weather 에 관해 이야기하고 있는 것이다 : 오늘은 weather 가 화창하다.

**web** [wéb] 명 **거미줄**, 거미집

web 은 거미가 먹이를 잡으려고 만든다. web 은 가는 실로 만들어진다 : 곤충 한 마리가 거미의 web 에 걸려 들었다.

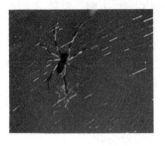

**wedding** [wédiŋ] 명 **결혼식,** 혼례

wedding 은 두 사람이 결혼을 하는 득별한 때다.

**Wednesday** [wénzdei, -di] 명 **수요일**

Wednesday 는 일주일 가운데 하루다. Wednesday 는 화요일이 지나고 목요일이 되기 전에 온다.

**week** [wíːk] 명 **주, 일주일**

week 는 7 일이다. week 란 일요일, 월요일, 화요일, 수요일, 목요일, 금요일, 그리고 토요일을 말한다.

**weigh** [wéi] 타 자 **무게를 달다,** 저울에 달다, 무게를 재다 ; 무게가 …이다

weigh 는 얼마나 무거운 지를 잰다는 뜻이다. 식품 가운데는 **무게를 달아** 보고 사는 것이 많다.

**weight** [wéit] 명 **무게,** 중량, **체중**

weight 는 물건의 무거운 정도를 말한다 : 의사는 제임스가 얼마나 자랐는지 알아 보려고 그의 몸무게를 쟀다. 그 여의

사는 제임스가 그녀를 방문할 때마다 그의 weight 를 알려준다.

**welcome** [wélkəm] 1 타 환영하다, 기꺼이 맞이하다 2 형 환영받는 3 감 어서 오십시오, 잘 오셨습니다

welcome 은 만나서 반가워하거나 기꺼이 무언가를 해준다는 뜻이다 : 우리는 새 이웃을 **따뜻이 대해 주려고** 했다. "멋진 선물을 주셔서 고맙습니다"라고 제인이 앤에게 말하자, "**천만에요**"라고 앤이 대답했다.

**well**¹ [wél] 1 부 잘, **훌륭하게**, 능숙하게 ; 충분히, 적절히 2 형 **건강한**, (형편이) 좋은

1 well 은 무언가를 잘 한다는 뜻이다 : 나의 아저씨는 피아노를 **잘** 치신다. 마거릿은 글씨를 **잘** 쓴다.

2 well 은 또한 아프지 않다는 뜻이다 : 에밀리는 지난 주에 아팠는데 지금은 다 **나았다.**

**well**² [wél] 명 우물, (유전 등의) 정 (井)

well 은 땅 속의 아주 깊은 구멍이다. 사람들은 지하에 있는 물이나 석유 혹은 그 밖의 것들을 얻기 위해 well 을 판다.

**went** [wént] 동 go (가다)의 과거형

went 는 단어 go 에서 생긴 말이다 : 언니와 나는 어제 치과에 **갔다.**

**were** [《약》 wər, 《강》 wə́:r] 동 are 의 과거형

were 는 단어 be 에서 생긴 말이다 : 우리는 공원에서 너무 재미있게 놀고 **있어서** 집에 가고 싶지가 않았다. 보브와 톰은 오후 내내 도서관에 **있었다.**

**weren't** [wə́:rnt] were not 의 단축형

weren't 는  were not 의  뜻이
다 : 우리는 학교에 징각에 도
착해서 지각하지 **않았다.**

**west** [wést] 1 명 서쪽 2 형 서
쪽의 3 부 서쪽으로
west 는    방향이다 : 태양은
west 로  진다.  west 는  east
(동쪽) 의 반대말이다.

**wet** [wét] 형  젖은,  축축한 ; 비
내리는, 비의
wet 은 물이나 다른 액체가 묻
어 있다는 뜻이다 : 한나는 물
웅덩이를 밟아서 신발이 **젖었**
**다.**

**whale** [hwéiəl] 명 고래
whale 은 바다에 사는 아주 큰
동물이다.  whale 은 헤엄을 칠
수 있지만, 물고기는 아니다.

**what** [hwát, hwʌ́t | wɔ́t] 1 대
무엇, 어떤 것 ; (…하는) 것
2 형 무슨, 어떤
what 은 사람이나 사물에 관해
서 질문을 할 때 쓴다 : **무슨**
책을 읽고 있니 ?

**whatever** [hwàtévər, hwʌ̀t-|

wɔ̀t-] 1 대 …하는 것은 무엇
이든, 무엇을 …하든지 2 형
…하는 모든, 어떤 …이라도
whatever 는 「무엇이든 다」라
는 뜻이다 : 블레이크는 아버지
가 자기를 위해 만들어 주는
음식은 **무엇이든 다** 먹는다.

**wheat** [hwíːt] 명 밀
wheat 는  풀의    일종이다.
wheat 의 씨앗은 밀가루나 그
밖의 식품을 만드는 데 이용된
다.  wheat 는 사람과 동물에
게 중요한 식품이다.

**wheel** [hwíːəl] 명    바퀴 ; (자동
차의)  핸들
wheel 은 물체가 쉽게 움직이
도록 해주는 나무나 금속 혹은
고무로 된 둥근 물건이다.  자
동차, 자전거, 짐마차, 롤러
스케이트에는 wheel 이 있다.

**wheelchair** [hwíːəltʃɛ̀ər]      명
휠체어
wheelchair 는 바퀴 달린 의자
다.  걸을 수 없는 사람들이 한
곳에서 다른 곳으로 가기 위해
wheelchair 를 사용한다 : 내가
다니는  학교에는  wheelchair
를 사용하는 아이와 선생님들

W

을 위한 전용 경사로가 있다.

**when** [*hwén*] 1 부 언제 ; …하
는〔한, 인, 할〕 때 2 접 …할
때는, …하니〔하자, 하면〕
when 은 언제 무슨 일이 일어
나는 지를 묻거나 말할 때 쓴
다 : 쇼는 **언제 시작하니 ? 언
제** 방문해도 되는지 말씀해 주
십시오.

**where** [*hwɛ́ər*] 1 부 어디에,
어디로 ; 그러자 그곳에(서),
그리고 거기서 2 접 …하는
곳에〔으로〕
where 는 장소에 대해서 묻거
나 말할 때 쓴다 : 너는 **어디에**
사니 ? 내 책을 **어디에** 두고
왔는지 기억이 나지 않는다.

**which** [*hwítʃ*] 1 대 어느 쪽
〔것〕 ; 그리고 그것은〔을〕, 그
러나 그것은 2 형 **어느**, 어떤
which 는 무리 중의 한 사람이
나 사물에 대해서 물을 때 쓴
다 : 이 외투들 중에 **어느 것이**
너의 외투냐 ? **어느** 여자 아이
가 너의 친구냐 ?

**while** [*hwáiəl*] 1 명 잠시, 동
안, 시간 2 접 …하는 동안
(에) ; 그런데, 한편으로는
1 while 은 짧은 시간을 뜻한
다 : 그만 놀고 **잠시** 쉬자.
2 while 은 또한 「무언가 다른
일이 생긴 동안」을 뜻한다 : 어
머니는 아기가 낮잠을 자는 동

안에 점심을 드셨다.

**whisper** [*hwíspər*] 자타 속삭
이다, 작은 소리로 말하다
whisper 는 조용한 목소리로
말한다는 뜻이다 : 다른 사람들
에게 폐가 되지 않도록 사람들
은 도서관에서 **작은 소리로 이
야기한다.**

**whistle** [*hwísl*] 1 자타 휘파람
을 불다, (개 등을) 휘파람으
로 부르다 2 명 휘파람, 호
각, 경적
1 whistle 은 입술이나 이를 통
해 공기를 밀어내서 소리를 낸
다는 뜻이다 : 내 개는 항상 내
가 **휘파람을 불면** 달려온다.
물이 끓자 주전자에서 **쉭쉭 소
리가 났다.**
2 whistle은 또한 바람을 불어
넣어 휘파람같은 소리를 내는
것이다 : 경찰관이 whistle 을
불자 자동차가 모두 멈췄다.

**white** [*hwáit*] 1 명 흰색, 백색
2 형 흰, 백색의
white 는 가장 밝은 색이다 :
눈과 소금은 **희다.**

**who** [《약》 *hu*, 《강》 *húː*] 대 ①
[주격] **누구**, 누가 ② [목적

격〕 **누구를**〔에게〕 ③ …하는 사람 ④ 그리고 그 사람은

1 who 는 사람에 대해서 물을 때 쓴다 : **누가** 문을 두드렸느냐 ?

2 who 는 어떤 사람을 나타낸다 : 그 가게에서 일하는 **남자**는 아주 친절하다.

**whoever** [hùːévər] 때 **누구든지, 누가** …하더라도

whoever는 「누구든지」의 뜻이다 : **누구든** 가장 빨리 달리는 사람이 경주에 이길 것이다. 부모님께서는 내가 원하는 사람은 **누구든지** 내 파티에 초대하라고 말씀하셨다.

**whole** [hóuəl] 1 형 **전부의, 전체의, 모든** 2 명 **전체, 전부**

whole 은 빠진 부분이 없다는 뜻이다 : 마이크는 혼자서 오렌지를 **전부** 먹었다. 우리는 피자 하나를 **통째로** 사서, 모두 한 쪽씩 나누어 먹었다. 스튜어트는 꼭 이틀만에 그 책을 **다** 읽었다.

**whom** [《약》 hum, 《강》 húːm] 때 [who 의 목적격] ① **누구를** ② …하는 (사람)

whom 은 who 의 한 형태다 : 피터는 공원에서 누구를 만났니 ? 피터가 만난 **사람**은 앤이라는 소녀다.

**who's** [《약》 huz, 《강》 húːz] who is, who has 의 단축형

1 who's 는 who is 를 줄여서 말한 것이다 : 부엌에 **누가** 있느냐 ?

2 who's 는 또한 who has 를 줄여서 말한 것이다 : **누가** 동물원에 가본 적이 있니 ?

**whose** [《약》 huz, 《강》 húːz] 때 [who 의 소유격] ① **누구의, 누구의 것** ② 그 사람의〔그의〕 …이〔한〕

whose 는 소유자가 누구인가를 말할 때 쓴다 : 나는 이 롤러 스케이트가 **누구의 것인지** 모른다.

**why** [ʰwái] 부 ① 왜, 어째서 ② …하는 (이유)
why 는 어떤 것에 대한 이유를 물을 때 쓴다 : 나는 마리아가 우리와 함께 소풍을 갈 수 없는 **이유**를 알고 있다. 너는 **왜** 웃고 있느냐 ?

**wide** [wáid] 1 형 폭넓은, 폭이 …인 ; 넓은 2 부 널리, 광범위하게
wide 는 한 쪽에서 다른 쪽까지의 폭이 아주 넓다는 뜻이다 : 의자의 폭이 너무 **넓어서** 문을 빠져나갈 수가 없었다. 저 다리는 강 폭이 가장 **넓은** 곳을 가로 질러 놓여 있다.

**width** [wídθ, wítθ] 명 폭
width 는 물건의 폭이 넓은 정도를 말한다 : 데일의 종이는 width가 8 인치다.

**wife** [wáif] 명 아내, **부인**, 처
wife 는 결혼한 여자다 : 그녀는 그에게 좋은 wife가 될 것이다.

**wild** [wáiəld] 형 야생의
wild 는 사람이 키우거나 돌보지 않는다는 뜻이다 : 그 영화는 **야생** 동물들에 관한 것이었다.

**will** [《약》 wəl, əl, 《강》 wíəl] 조 ① [미래] …일〔할〕 것이다 ② [의지] …할 작정이다 ③ [사물의 본질·경향] …하는 법이다 ④ [현재의 습관] 곧잘 …하곤 하다
will 은 무언가를 하려고 한다고 말할 때 쓴다 : 우리는 내일 공원에 **가려고 한다**. 피터는 곧 10 살이 **된다**.

**win** [wín] 타 자 이기다, 승리하다 ; 획득하다
win 은 시합이나 경연에서 가장 뛰어나다는 뜻이다 : 너는 딴 사람보다 빨리 달릴 수 있어서 경주에 **이길** 것이다.

**wind** [wínd] 명 바람
wind 는 움직이는 공기다 : wind 가 세차게 불어 나무가 쓰러졌다.

**windmill** [wín♂mìəl] 명 풍차
windmill 은 기계다. windmill 은 바람의 힘으로 움직인다.

W

땅에서 물을 퍼올리는 wind-
mill 도 있고, 전기를 일으키는
windmill 도 있다.

**window** [wíndou] 몡 창, 창문
　window 는 공기와 빛이 들어
　오게 벽을 터 놓은 곳이다.
　window 는 유리로 되어 있
　다 : window 를 닫으면 찬 공
　기가 들어오지 않을 것이다.

**wing** [wíŋ] 몡 날개
　wing 은 나는 데 이용되는 부
　위다. 새와 곤충은 wing 이 있
　다. 비행기도 wing 이 있다.

**winter** [wíntər] 몡 겨울
　winter 는 한 해의 계절이다.

winter 는 가을이 지나고 봄이
되기 전에 온다 : 나는 winter
에 스케이트 타러 가는 것을
좋아한다.

**wipe** [wáip] 태 닦다, 훔치다,
닦아내다
　wipe 는 문질러서 깨끗하게 하
　거나 물기를 없앤다는 뜻이
　다 : 현관 밖에 있는 깔개에 진
　흙 묻은 신발을 **닦으시오.** 아
　버지는 아기가 엎지른 우유를
　**훔쳐 냈다.**

**wire** [wáiər] 몡 철사, 전선
　wire 는 쉽게 휘는 긴 줄이나
　실 모양의 금속 조각이다 : 전
　기는 wire 를 통해 흐른다.

**wish** [wíʃ] 1 자태 ① 바라다,
원하다 ② …하고 싶다(고 생
각하다), (누구에게) …해주기
를 바라다 ③ …하면〔했으면〕
좋겠다고 여기다 2 몡 소원,
소망 ; 바라는 것, 원하는 것
　1 wish 는 몹시 원한다는 뜻이
　다 : 지금이 여름이라면 좋으련
　만. 잭은 자기 형처럼 그림을
　잘 그렸으면 **좋겠다고 생각했**
　**다.** 온 세계가 평화를 **바라고**

W

있다.

2 wish 는 몹시 원하는 것이다 : 수잔은 새 자전거를 갖게 해 달라는 **소원**을 빈 다음, 생일 케이크의 촛불을 불어서 껐다.

**witch** [wítʃ] 명 **마녀, 여자 마법사**

witch 는 마력을 가진 여자다 : 우리는 이야기책에서 착한 witch 와 나쁜 witch 에 관한 얘기를 읽었다.

**with** [wið, wiθ] 전 ① [동반·동거] **…와 함께,** …의 집에 ② [소유·소지] **…을 가진,** …이 있는 ③ [수단·도구] **…으로,** …을 사용하여 ③ [재료·내용물] **…로,** …을 ④ [원인] … 때문에, …으로 인해

1 with 는 「함께」라는 뜻이다 : 나는 언니, 오빠와 **함께** 야구 경기를 보러 갔다.

2 with 는 무언가를 이용한다는 사실을 나타낼 때 쓴다 : 앤은 삽**으로** 구덩이를 팠다.

3 with 는 또한 사람이 무언가

를 갖고 있다는 것을 나타낼 때 쓴다 : 빨간 재킷을 **입은** 남자 아이가 내 동생이고, 머리카락이 갈색인 여자 아이가 내 여동생이다.

**without** [wiðáut] 전 ① **…이 없이** ; …이 없다면 ② **…하지 않고**

without 은 무언가가 없거나 어떤 일을 하지 않는다는 뜻이다 : 나는 신발을 신지 **않고** 모래 위를 걷는 것을 좋아한다. 헬렌은 너무 급해서 우리에게 작별 인사도 **하지 않고** 떠났다. 엄마, 아빠는 형과 나를 **남겨두고** 두 분만 영화 구경을 가셨다.

**wives** [wáivz] 명 **wife 의 복수형**

wives 는 두명 이상의 아내를 나타낸다 : wives 와 남편들은 서로 결혼으로 맺어진 사이다.

**wizard** [wízərd] 명 **(남자) 마법사, 마술사**

wizard 는 마술사다 : 영화 속

의 wizard 는 길고 흰 머리카
락에 끝이 뾰족한 모자를 쓰고
있었다.

**woke** [wóuk]  동  wake (깨다)
의 과거형
woke 는 단어 wake 에서 생긴
말이다 : 나는 아래층에서 개가
짖는 소리를 듣고 **잠에서 깼
다.**

**woken** [wóukən]  동  wake (깨
다)의 과거분사형
woken 은 단어 wake 에서 생
긴 말이다 : 9 시인 데, 보브는
아직 **일어나지 않았다.**

**wolf** [wúəlf]  명  늑대, 이리
wolf 는 야생 동물로, 큰 개와
비슷하다.  wolf 는 떼를 지어
먹이를 사냥한다.

**wolves** [wúəlvz]  명  wolf 의 복
수형
wolves 는 두 마리 이상의 늑
대를 나타낸다. wolves 는 털
이 많다.

**woman** [wúmən]  명  여성, 부
인, 여자

woman 은 성숙한 여자를 말
한다.  여자 아이가 자라서
woman 이 된다.

**women** [wímin]  명  woman 의
복수형
women 은 두명 이상의 여성
을 나타낸다 : 파티에 몇 명의
women이 있었느냐 ?

**won** [wÁn]  동  win (이기다)의
과거 · 과거분사형
won 은 단어 win 에서 생긴 말
이다 : 폴은 수영 경기에서 **우
승했다.**

**wonder** [wÁndər]  1  타  …을
이상하게 여기다 ; …가 아닐까
생각하다 2  자  놀라다,  의아
하게 여기다
wonder 는 호기심을 끄는 것
에 대해 생각해 본다는 뜻이
다 : 나는 커서 어떤 사람이 되
어 **있을까.**

**wonderful** [wÁndərfəl]  형  놀
랄만한, 이상한 ; 훌륭한, 굉장
한
1 wonderful 은  놀랄만하거나
보통이 아니라는 뜻이다 : 곡마
단에서 **멋진** 묘기를 부리는 곡
예사를 우리는 모두 눈을 동그
랗게 뜨고 쳐다보았다.
2 wonderful 은 또한 아주 훌
륭하다는 뜻이다 : 우리는 지난
일요일에 **멋진** (미식) 축구 경
기를 구경했다.

**won't** [wóunt] will not 의 단축형

won't 는 will not 의 뜻이다 : 잭은 오늘 우리와 함께 놀 수 **없다**고 말했다.

**wood** [wúd] 명 **나무**, 목재, 재목 ; 장작

wood 는 나무로 만든 것이다. wood 는 집이나 그 밖의 물건을 만드는 데 쓴다 : 엄마가 난로에 wood 를 더 넣었다.

**woods** [wúdz] 명 **숲**, 수풀

woods 는 많은 나무와 그 밖의 식물이 있는 지역이다. 동물들은 woods 에서 산다 : 우리는 걸어서 woods 를 통과했다.

**wool** [wúəl] 명 **양털**, 울 ; 모직물

wool 은 양에서 자라는 털이다. wool 은 옷과 담요용의 실이나 천을 만드는 데 이용한다. wool 로 만든 스웨터가 많다.

**word** [wə́:rd] 명 (음을 가진) **말**, 언어 ; (글자로 쓴) **단어**, **낱말**

word 는 특별한 의미를 지닌 음이나 글자다. 우리는 말을 하거나 글씨를 쓸 때마다 word 를 사용한다.

**word processor** [wə́:rd prɑ̀sesər] 명 **자동 문서 작성기**, 워드 프로세서

word processor 는 글자를 쓰고, 바꾸고, 저장하고, 인쇄할 수 있는 컴퓨터의 일종이다 : 엄마는 소설을 쓸 때 word processor 를 이용한다.

**wore** [wɔ́:r] 동 wear (입고 있다)의 과거형

wore 는 단어 wear 에서 생긴 말이다 : 사라는 머리에 빨간 리본을 **달았다.**

W

**work** [wə́:rk] 1 명 일, 작업 ; 공부 : **직업** 2 자타 ① **일하다, 근무하다**, 종사하다 ; 일시키다 ② 공부하다 ③ (기계 등이) **움직이다, 작동하다**

1 work 는 사람이 하는 일이다. 사람들은 대개 돈을 벌려고 work 를 한다 : 나의 어머니는 은행에서 work 하신다.
2 work 는 또한 돈을 번다는 뜻이다 : 나의 아버지는 제과점에서 **일하신다.**
3 work 는 또한 일을 하는데 에너지를 쓴다는 뜻이다 : 소녀들은 부지런히 나뭇잎을 갈퀴로 긁어 **모았다.**
4 work 는 기계가 일을 한다는 뜻이다 : 텔레비전이 **나오지** 않는다.

**worker** [wə́:rkər] 명 일〔공부〕하는 사람 ; 근로자, 종업원
worker 는 일하는 사람이다 : 다이애나는 회사에 근무한다. 그녀는 열심히 일을 한다. 그녀는 유능한 worker 다.

**world** [wə́:rld] 명 세계, 세상 ; 지구 ; 우주, 만물
world 는 모든 세상 사람들이 살고 있는 곳이다. world 의 다른 말은 earth 다. world 에는 많은 나라들이 있다 : 미리아의 이모는 world 일주 여행을 했다.

**worm** [wə́:rm] 명 벌레, (특히) 지렁이
worm 은 길고 다리가 없는 동물이다. worm 은 땅을 기어다닌다 : 데이비드와 조지는 낚시 가서 쓰려고 worm 을 몇마리 땅 속에서 파냈다.

**worn** [wə́:rn] 동 wear (입고 있다)의 과거분사형
worn 은 단어 wear 에서 생긴 말이다 : 너는 새 모자를 벌써 **써보았니** ?

**worry** [wə́:ri | wʌ́ri] 자타 **걱정하다, 근심하다** ; 괴롭히다
worry 는 나쁜 일이 일어날지도 모른다고 생각한다는 뜻이다 : 부모님은 간혹 내가 집에 늦게 가면 **걱정하신다.**

**worse** [wə́:rs] 1 형 [bad, ill 의 비교급] **보다 나쁜**, 더욱 나쁜 2 부 [badly, ill 의 비교급] **더욱 나쁘게**

worse 는 「더욱 나쁜」의 뜻이다 : 나는 스케이트를 잘 못타지만, 내 친구는 **더 못탄다.**

**worst** [wɔ́ːrst] 1 형 [bad, ill 의 최상급] **가장 나쁜** 2 부 [badly, ill의 최상급] **가장 나쁘게**

worst 는 「가장 나쁜」의 뜻이다 : 내가 앓은 감기 중에서 이번 감기가 **가장 지독하다.**

**would** [《약》 wəd, əd, 《강》 wúd] 조 will (…할 것이다)의 과거형

would 는 단어 will 에서 생긴 말이다 : 우리는 너와 함께 가고 **싶다.** 저 책 좀 **건네 주시겠어요 ?**

**wouldn't** [wúdnt] would not 의 단축형

wouldn't 는 would not 을 줄여서 말한 것이다 : 고양이가 나무에서 **도무지** 내려 오려고 하지 **않았다.**

**wrap** [ræp] 타 **감싸다, 싸다**

wrap 은 종이나 천으로 무언가를 싼다는 뜻이다. 사람들은 대개 생일 선물을 **싼** 다음, 나비 모양의 매듭으로 묶는다 : 마이클은 강아지를 담요로 **감쌌다.**

**wren** [rén] 명 **굴뚝새**

wren 은 작은 새다. wren 은 갈색 깃털과 간혹 위로 곧게 뻗어 내미는 꼬리가 있다 : 우리는 뒤뜰에서 wren 이 지저귀는 소리를 들었다.

**wrinkle** [ríŋkl] 명 **주름, 주름살** ; (천의) **구김살**

wrinkle 은 피부의 주름살이다 : 이 개는 wrinkle 이 있다.

**wrist** [ríst] 명 **손목**

wrist 는 팔과 손 사이에 있는 신체 부위로, 구부릴 수 있다. 사람들은 wrist에 팔찌와 시계를 찬다.

**write** [ráit] 타 자 (글씨·문장·편지·원고 등을) **쓰다 ; 편지를 쓰다 ;** 저술하다

write 는 종이나 그 밖의 것에 말을 써 넣는다는 뜻이다. 연필, 펜, 크레용 혹은 분필로 글씨를 **쓸 수** 있다 : 수잔은 할아버지께 편지를 **썼다.**

W

**writer** [ráitər] 몡 **작가, 기자**
writer 는 돈을 벌기 위해 소설
이나 시 혹은 책을 쓰는 사람
이다 : 헨리의 어머니는 우리
마을 신문에 스포츠 기사를 쓰
는 writer 다.

**written** [rítən] 동 write (쓰다)
의 과거분사형
written 은 write 의 한 형태
다 : 켄드류는 그의 친구 조니
에게 많은 편지를 **써보냈다.**

**wrong** [rɔ́ːŋ|rɔ́ŋ] 1 혱 ① (도
덕적으로) **그릇된**, 나쁜 ② **잘
못된**, 틀린 ③ 상태가 나쁜,
고장난 2 봄 부정하게 ; 틀리
게 ; 나쁘게
wrong 은 정확하지 않다는 뜻
이다 : 클레어가 선생님의 질문
에 **틀린** 대답을 하자, 선생님
이 그녀에게 정답을 말해주었
다.

**wrote** [róut] 동 write (쓰다) 의
과거형
wrote 는 write 의 한 형태다 :
빌은 페이지 상단에 날짜를 **썼
다.**

**X ray** [éks rèi] 명 X 선, 뢴트
겐선 ; X 선〔뢴트겐〕 사진
X ray 는 에너지의 일종으로,
물체를 투과할 수 있다. 의사
는 신체의 내부 사진을 찍는
데 X ray 를 이용한다.

**xylophone** [záiləfòun] 명 실로
폰, 목금
xylophone 은 악기다. xylo-
phone은 나무 토막이나 금속
조각이 일렬로 배열되어 있는
데, 특수한 채로 그 토막〔조
각〕들을 쳐서 소리를 낸다.

X

**yard**¹ [jáːrd] 몡 뜰, 안마당 ;
구내 ; 교정
yard 는 집이나 그 밖의 건물
주위에 있는 땅이다 : 우리집
yard 에는 그네가 있다.

**yard**² [jáːrd] 몡 야드
yard 는 길이의 양이다. 1 yard
는 3 피트와 같다. yard 는 거
의 미터와 같은 길이다.

**yarn** [jáːrn] 몡 짜는 실, 뜨개
실, 꼰 실
yarn 은 실의 일종으로, 털실이
나 무명실 혹은 그 밖의 실을 한
데 꼬아서 만든다. 스웨터나
양말을 짜는 데 yarn 을 쓴다.

**yawn** [jɔ́ːn] 1 몜몠 하품하다 ;
하품하면서 말하다 2 몡 하품
yawn 은 입을 크게 벌리고 심
호흡을 한다는 뜻이다 : 아기는
피곤해서 **하품을 했다.**

**year** [jíər | jíə, jə́ː] 몡 ① 해,
연 ; 한 해, 1 년(간) ② 연도,
학년 ③ 연령, …살
year 는 열 두달의 긴 기간이
다 : 카르멘은 네 살이다.

**yell** [jéəl] 몜몠 외치다, 고함치
다 ; 큰소리로 말하다 ; (응원단
등이) 큰소리로 성원하다
yell 은 소리친다는 뜻이다 : 하
키 시합은 아주 재미있었고,
우리는 **소리쳐** 우리 팀을 응원
**했다.**

**yellow** [jélou] 1 몧 노란 2 몡
노랑, 노란색
yellow 는 바나나, 버터 그리
고 레몬의 색깔이다 : 나는 **노
란색** 크레용으로 태양을 그렸
다.

**yes** [jés] 1 목 네, 그렇다 2 몡

Y

「네」라는 말〔대답〕, **찬성**
yes 는 동의한다는 뜻이다 : 제
인이 수잔에게 방과 후에 자기
집에 오라고 하자 수잔은 "**그
래**, 나도 가고 싶어"라고 말했
다.

**yesterday** [jéstərdi, -dèi] 1 [부]
**어제**(는) ; 어저께 2 [명] **어제**
yesterday 는 오늘의 하루 전
날이다. 오늘이 월요일이면
yesterday 는 일요일이었다 :
메리는 **어제** 그녀의 할아버지
께 편지를 쓰기 시작해서, 오
늘에야 끝냈다.

**yet** [jét] [부] ① [부정문에서] **아
직** (…않다) ② [의문문에서]
**이미**, **벌써** ③ [긍정문에서]
아직껏, 여전히
yet 은 「지금까지」의 뜻이다 :
영화는 **아직** 시작되지 않았다.

**you** [《약》 ju, jə, 《강》 júː] 　[대]
[인칭 대명사 : 2인칭 단수·
복수의 주격 및 목적격] **당신**
(들), **너**(희들)
1 you 는 어떤 사람이 다른 사
람에게 말을 걸 때 쓰는 말이
다 : 나는 **너**를 좋아한다. **너는**
오늘 피곤해 보인다.
2 you'd 는 you had 나 you
would 의 뜻이다 : 내가 늦게
와서 보니 **너는** 이미 떠나고
없었다. **너라면** 우주비행사에
관한 프로그램을 재미있게 봤
을 것이다.

3 you'll 은 you will 의 뜻이
다 : 이 새로운 놀이를 해보자.
**너도** 좋아할 거라고 생각한다.
4 you're 는 you are 의 뜻이
다 : **너는** 수영을 잘 한다.

5 you've 는 you have 의 뜻이
다 : **너는** 흐뭇한 미소를 지었
다.

**young** [jʌ́ŋ] [형] **젊은**, **어린** ; **청
춘시대의**, 청년의
young 은 늙지 않았다는 뜻이
다 : 나의 두 누이 중에서 앤이
나이가 **더 어리고**, 내가 세 사
람 중에서 **가장 어리다**.

**your** [《약》 jər, 《강》 júər, jɔ́ːr]
[대] [you의 소유격] **당신**(들)
**의**, **너**(희들)**의**
your 는 너의 소유물을 뜻한
다 : **너의** 집에서 놀자. 네 코
트는 푸른색이고 내 코트는 붉
은색이다.

Y

**yours** [júərz, jɔ́ːrz] 때 [you의 소유대명사] 당신(들)의 것, 너(희들)의 것
yours 는 너의 소유물을 뜻한다 : 그 컵은 네 것이고, 이 컵은 내 것이다.

**yourself** [juərsélf, jɔ́ːr-, jər-] 때 [you의 재귀대명사] 당신(들) 자신, 너(희들) 자신
yourself는 다른 누구도 아닌 바로 너 자신이다 : (너는) 저 뜨거운 다리미에 데지 않도록 조심해라.

**yo-yo** [jóujou] 명 (장난감의) 요요《차바퀴 모양의 것》
yo-yo 는 한 가닥의 실에 감겨 올라갔다 내려갔다하는 장난감이다 : 헬렌은 yo-yo로 많은 묘기를 부릴 수 있다.

Y

**zebra** [zíːbrə | zé-, zíː-] 몡 **얼룩말**

zebra 는 몸에 검은색과 흰색의 줄무늬가 있는 말처럼 생긴 동물이다.

**zero** [zíərou] 몡 **0, 영 ; 영점 ; 최하점 ; 무, 제로**

zero 는 아무것도 없다는 뜻이다. 동전 **한푼없다**면, 돈이 전혀 없다는 의미다. zero 는 또한 **0** 이라고 쓴다 : 우리는 그 시합을 9 대 **0**으로 이겼다.

**zipper** [zípər] 몡 **지퍼**

zipper 는 옷이나 그 밖의 다른 물건들이 서로 붙어 있게 한다. zipper는 금속이나 플라스틱으로 만들 수 있다 : 너의 재킷은 zipper로 잠그니 아니면 단추로 잠그니 ? 클라라는 짐을 다 싼 다음 여행 가방의 zipper를 잠궜다.

**zoo** [zúː] 몡 **동물원**

zoo 는 사람들이 볼 수 있도록 동물을 사육하는 곳이다. zoo 의 동물들은 대부분 우리에 살지만, 특정 구역에서는 밖에서 사는 동물들도 있다 : 우리는 zoo 에서 원숭이와 코끼리를 보았다.

# 불규칙 동사 · 조동사 변화표

| 현　재 | 과　거 | 과거 분사 | 현　재 | 과　거 | 과거 분사 |
|---|---|---|---|---|---|
| **am** 이다 | was | been | **drive** 몰다 | drove | driven |
| **are** 이다 | were | been | **eat** 먹다 | ate | eaten |
| **awake** 깨우다, | ⎰awoke | ⎰awoke | **fall** 떨어지다 | fell | fallen |
| 깨닫다 | ⎱awaked | ⎱awaked | **feed** 먹을 것을 | fed | fed |
| | | | 주다 | | |
| **be** ⎰am ⎱are 이다 ⎱is | ⎰was ⎱were | been | **feel** 느끼다 | felt | felt |
| | | | **fight** 싸우다 | fought | fought |
| **bear** 낳다 | bore | ⎰born | **find** 발견하다 | found | found |
| | | ⎱borne | **fly** 날다 | flew | flown |
| **become** …되다 | became | become | **forget** 잊다 | forgot | ⎰forgotten |
| **begin** 시작하다 | began | begun | | | ⎱forgot |
| **bite** 물다 | bit | bitten | **get** 얻다, …시 | got | ⎰gotten |
| **blow** 불다 | blew | blown | 키다 | | ⎱got |
| **break** 깨뜨리다 | broke | broken | **give** 주다 | gave | given |
| **bring** 가져오다 | brought | brought | **go** 가다 | went | gone |
| **broadcast** 방송 | ⎰broadcast | ⎰broadcast | **grow** 자라다 | grew | grown |
| 하다 | ⎱broad- | ⎱broad- | **hang** 매달다 | hung | hung |
| | casted | casted | **has** ⎱가지고 **have**⎰있다 | had | had |
| **build** 세우다 | built | built | | | |
| **burn** 불태우다, | ⎰burned | ⎰burned | **hear** 듣다 | heard | heard |
| 불타다 | ⎱burnt | ⎱burnt | **hide** 감추다 | hid | ⎰hidden |
| **buy** 사다 | bought | bought | | | ⎱hid |
| **can** 할 수 | could | —— | **hit** 치다 | hit | hit |
| 있다 | | | **hold** 손에 들다 | held | held |
| **catch** 잡다 | caught | caught | **hurt** 상처내다 | hurt | hurt |
| **choose** 고르다, | chose | chosen | **is** 이다 | was | been |
| 선택하다 | | | **keep** 유지하다 | kept | kept |
| **come** 오다 | came | come | **knit** 짜다, | ⎰knitted | ⎰knitted |
| **cut** 자르다 | cut | cut | 뜨다 | ⎱knit | ⎱knit |
| **deal** 다루다 | dealt | dealt | **know** 알다 | knew | known |
| **dig** 파다 | dug | dug | **lay** 놓다 | laid | laid |
| **do** 하다 | did | done | **lead** 이끌다 | led | led |
| **draw** 그리다 | drew | drawn | **learn** 배우다 | ⎰learned | ⎰learned |
| **dream** 꿈꾸다 | ⎰dreamt | ⎰dreamt | | ⎱learnt | ⎱learnt |
| | ⎱dreamed | ⎱dreamed | **leave** 떠나다 | left | left |
| **drink** 마시다 | drank | drunk | **lend** 빌려주다 | lent | lent |

| 현　재 | 과　거 | 과거 분사 | 현　재 | 과　거 | 과거 분사 |
|---|---|---|---|---|---|
| let …시키다 | let | let | shut 닫다 | shut | shut |
| lie¹ 거짓말하다 | lied | lied | sing 노래하다 | ⎰sang | sung |
| lie² 가로 눕다 | lay | lain |  | ⎱sung |  |
| light 불을 | ⎰lit | ⎰lit | sink 가라앉다 | ⎰sank | ⎰sunk |
| 　붙이다 | ⎱lighted | ⎱lighted |  | ⎱sunk | ⎱sunken |
| lose 잃다 | lost | lost | sit 앉다 | sat | sat |
| make 만들다 | made | made | sleep 자다 | slept | slept |
| may …해도 | might | —— | smell 냄새를 | ⎰smelt | ⎰smelt |
| 　좋다 |  |  | 　맡다 | ⎱smelled | ⎱smelled |
| mean 의미 | meant | meant | speak 말하다 | spoke | spoken |
| 　하다 |  |  | spell 철자를 | ⎰spelt | ⎰spelt |
| meet 만나다 | met | met | 　쓰다 | ⎱spelled | ⎱spelled |
| mistake 틀리다 | mistook | mistaken | spend 소비하다 | spent | spent |
| must …해야 | must | —— | spread 펴다 | spread | spread |
| 　한다 |  |  | spring 뛰다 | ⎰sprang | sprung |
| pass 지나가다 | passed | ⎰passed |  | ⎱sprung |  |
|  |  | ⎱past | stand 일어서다 | stood | stood |
| pay 지불하다 | paid | paid | steal 훔치다 | stole | stolen |
| put 놓다 | put | put | stick 찌르다 | struck | ⎰struck |
| read 읽다 | read | read |  |  | ⎱stricken |
| ride 타다 | rode | ridden | sweep 쓸다 | swept | swept |
| ring 울리다 | rang | rung | swim 헤엄치다 | swam | swum |
| rise 일어나다 | rose | risen | take 손에 쥐다 | took | taken |
| run 달리다 | ran | run | teach 가르치다 | taught | taught |
| say 말하다 | said | said | tear 찢다 | tore | torn |
| see 보다 | saw | seen | tell 말하다 | told | told |
| sell 팔다 | sold | sold | think 생각하다 | thought | thought |
| send 보내다 | sent | sent | throw 던지다 | threw | thrown |
| set 놓다 | set | set | understand 이 | under- | under- |
| sew 꿰매다, | sewed | ⎰sewed | 　해하다 | stood | stood |
| 　바느질하다 |  | ⎱sewn | wake 깨다 | ⎰waked | ⎰waked |
| shake 흔들다 | shook | shaken |  | ⎱woke | ⎱woken |
| shall …일 것 | should | —— | wear 입고 있다 | wore | worn |
| 　이다 |  |  | weep 울다 | wept | wept |
| shine¹ 빛나다 | shone | shone | will …일 것 | would | —— |
| shine² 구두를 | shined | shined | 　이다 |  |  |
| 　닦다 |  |  | win 이기다 | won | won |
| shoot 쏘다 | shot | shot | wind 감다 | wound | wound |
| show 보이다 | showed | ⎰shown | write 쓰다 | wrote | written |
|  |  | ⎱showed |  |  |  |

## 영영한 입문 사전

1997년  2월 10일        초판 발행
2024년  1월 10일    초판 17쇄 인쇄
2024년  1월 25일    초판 17쇄 발행

엮은이    사 서 부
펴낸이    양 진 오
펴낸데    ㈜교학사

판권 본사 소유

서울특별시 금천구 가산디지털1로 42(공장)
서울특별시 마포구 마포대로14길 4(사무소)

전  화: 02) 707-5147
등  록: 1962. 6. 26(18-7)

정가 24,000원